4/03

ENCYCLOPEDIA OF JAPANESE BUSINESS AND MANAGEMENT

ENCYCLOPEDIA OF JAPANESE BUSINESS AND MANAGEMENT

Edited by Allan Bird

ROUTLEDGE
ROUTLEDGE
Taylor & Francis Group

London and New York

First published 2002
by Routledge
11 New Fetter Lane, London EC4P 4EE

Simultaneously published in the USA and Canada
by Routledge
29 West 35th Street, New York, NY 10001

Routledge is an imprint of the Taylor & Francis Group

Typeset in Baskerville by Taylor & Francis Books Ltd
Printed and bound in Great Britain by TJ International, Padstow, Cornwall

British Library Cataloguing in Publication Data
A catalogue record for this book is available from the British Library

Library of Congress Cataloging in Publication Data
Encyclopedia of Japanese business and management/edited by Allan Bird.

Includes bibliographical references and index.
1. Japan–Commerce–Encyclopedias. 2. Industrial management–Japan–
Encyclopedias. 3. Corporations, Japanese–Management–Encyclopedias.
4. Business enterprises–Japan–Encyclopedias. 5. Japan–Commerce–
Dictionaries. 6. Japanese language–Dictionaries–English. I. Title: Japanese
business and management. II. Bird, Allan.
HF1001 .E467   2001
I650′.0952–dc21   2001019952
ISBN 0–415–18945–4

Contents

List of contributors   vii

Acknowledgements   xi

Introduction   xiii

How to use this book   xv

Thematic entry list   xvi

Entries A–Z   1

Index   483

Contributors

Editorial team

Volume editor

Allan Bird
University of Missouri, St. Louis

Consultant editors

Nigel Campbell
University of Manchester

Mitsuyo Hanada
Keio University

Stephen Nicholas
University of Melbourne

Thomas Roehl
Western Washington University

Shane J. Schvaneveldt
Weber State University

Joop Stam
Erasmus University

Mark Tilton
Purdue University

Mitsuru Wakabayashi
Nagoya University

Eleanor D. Westney
Massachusetts Institute of Technology

Hideki Yoshihara
Kobe University

List of contributors

James C. Abegglen
Asia Advisory Service KK

Tetsuo Abo
Teikyo University

Raj Aggarwal
Kent State University

Nathaniel O. Agola
Nagoya University

Christine L. Ahmadjian
Columbia University

Jennifer Amyx
Research School of Pacific and Asian Studies,
Australian National University

Marie Anchordoguy
University of Washington

Fumie Ando
Nanzan University

Hirotaka Aoki
Tokyo Institute of Technology

David M. Arase
Claremont College, Pomona

William Barnes
University of Portland

Michael Beeman
US Department of Commerce

Theodore Bestor
Harvard University

Mary Yoko Brannen
San Jose State University

Robert Brown
Greenebaum, Doll & McDonald Pllc,
Louisville, KY

Ronda Roberts Callister
Utah State University

Meika Clucas
California Polytechnic State University

Alexandra Cohen
California Polytechnic State University

Richard A. Colignon
Duquesne University

Tim Craig
University of Victoria, Canada

Edwin C. Duerr
San Francisco State University

Mitsuko S. Duerr
San Francisco State University

Dayo Fawibe
University of Missouri, St. Louis

David Flath
NCSU Department of Economics

Michael Gerlach
University of California, Berkeley

Georgios Giakatis
Tokyo Institute of Technology

Susumu Hagiwara
Hosei University

Ehud Harari
Hebrew University of Jerusalem

Hitoshi Higuchi
Shinshu University

James E. Hodder
University of Wisconsin

Ippei Ichige
Aoyama Gakuin University

Ralph Inforzato
JETRO Chicago

Kenji Ishihara
Association for International Cooperation of
Agriculture

Hiroshi Itagaki
Musashi University

Tetsuya Iwasaki
Shinshu University

Megumi Katsuta
Aoyama Gakuin University

Martin Kenney
University of California, Davis

Harold Kerbo
California Polytechnic State University

Jo-Seoul Kim
Shinshu University

Hiroki Kondo
Shinshu University

Aya Kubota
Aoyama Gakuin University

Hiroshi Kumon
Hosei University

James R. Lincoln
University of California, Berkeley

Terri R. Lituchy
California Polytechnic State University

Leonard H. Lynn
Case Western Reserve University

Mark Mason
Yale University

Aki Matsunga
Aoyama Gakuin University

John A. McKinstry
California Polytechnic State University

Mari Miura
University of Tokyo

Dario Ikuo Miyake
University of São Paulo

Shintaro Mogi
Shinshu University

Sean Mooney
G2

Tetsu Morishima
Aoyama Gakuin University

Kazuharu Nagase
Shinshu University

Takeshi Nakajo
Chuo University

Jay Nelson
SS Media, New York

Stephen Nicholas
University of Melbourne

Keith A. Nitta
University of California, Berkeley

Kazahiro Okazaki
Aichi Institute of Technology

Soyeon Park
Aoyama Gakuin University

Vladimir Pucik
IMD

William Purcell
University of New South Wales

Jörg Raupach-Sumiya
German Institute for Japanese Studies

Thomas Roehl
Western Washington University

Elizabeth L. Rose
University of Auckland

Pernille Rudlin
Brighton, UK

Ulrike Schaede
University of California, San Diego

Mark J. Scher
Institute for Financial Affairs, New York

Shane J. Schvaneveldt
Weber State University

Roblyn Simeon
San Francisco State University

Ron Singleton
Western Washington University

Michael Smitka
Washington and Lee University

Lucrezia Songini
Bocconi University

Brenda Sternquist
Michigan State University

Yasuo Sugiyama
University of Tokyo

Noriya Sumihara
Tenri University

Margaret Takeda
Aoyama Gakuin University

Sumihiro Takeda
Aoyama Gakuin University

Ogiwara Takeshi
Aoyama Gakuin University

Jay Tate
University of California, Berkeley

Mark Tilton
Purdue University

De-bi Tsao
Tokyo Institute of Technology

William M. Tsutsui
University of Kansas

Tsutomu Tsuzuki
Shinshu University

Victor K. Ujimoto
University of Guelph

Robert Uriu
University of California, Irvine

Terri Ursacki
University of Calgary

Chikako Usui
University of Missouri, St. Louis

Carien Van Mourik
Eramus University, Rotterdam

Steven Vogel
University of California, Berkeley

Mitsuru Wakabayashi
Nagoya University

Eleanor D. Westney
Massachusetts Institute of Technology

Michael A. Witt
Harvard University

Bernard Wolf
York University, Canada

Heung-wah Wong
University of Hong Kong

Brian Woodall
Georgia Institute of Technology

Takehiko Yasuda
Shinshu University

Masanori Yasumoto
Shinshu University

Toru Yoshikawa
Nihon University

Patrick Ziltener
Max Planck Institute for the Study of Societies,
Germany

Acknowledgements

Over the last several years I have found myself paying closer attention to the acknowledgements that precede most books. Perhaps it is simply a sign of advancing maturity, or age, but I have become more curious about who people choose to recognize as contributing to a particular effort. After all, there are a host of people associated with any published work, and an even larger number involved in support of the research that goes into a scholarly volume. It is with that thought in mind that I sat down to pen a note of recognition for those who have contributed to this volume.

An encyclopedia is, by its very nature, the offspring of myriad parents – an insight I knew with my head at the outset of this undertaking. Now, at the conclusion, I know it with my heart as well. It is only fitting, before proceeding on to introduce the volume itself, to recognize those many individuals who have contributed to this effort. Though it is impossible to acknowledge everyone, certain people stand out for both their personal contribution, their insightful counsel or their guiding spirit.

I was aided in the difficult task of surveying an ill-defined academic field by an able group of colleagues who served as Consulting Editors. I stand in admiration of each of them individually. Collectively, they served as a brain trust in helping to identify the breadth and depth of the volume. Part of their task was to help set the markers which would define the amorphous field we chose to label "Japanese business and management." Though named elsewhere in this volume, I would be remiss not to personally acknowledge their contribution here: Nigel Campbell, Manchester University; Mitsuyo Hanada, Keio University; Stephen Nicholas, Melbourne University; Thomas Roehl, Uni-

versity of Western Washington; Joop Stam, Erasmus University; Mark Tilton, Purdue University; Mitsuru Wakabayashi, Nagoya University; Eleanor Westney, Massachusetts Institute of Technology; and Hideki Yoshihara, Kobe University.

Possibly the greatest challenge confronting the compilation of any encyclopedia is the myriad detail that must be sorted through. Once entries have been defined, authors must be identified and contacted, manuscripts for each entry must be received and reviewed, revisions requested, completed entries properly formatted, and the final product forwarded to the publishers. The task is difficult enough without the added challenge of working with academic scholars, who as a group, give added meaning to the phrase "herding cats." I was ably assisted in the process of managing all these details by three research assistants. Indeed, truth be told, I was the inept professor doing what I could to assist them. I began the project with Alexandra Cohen, who did much of the initial organizing and preparation of databases. With about year to go in completing the project Alex headed off to Germany to continue her studies there. Before leaving she selected and trained her replacement, Erin Montgomery. Several months later I moved from the California Polytechnic State University in San Luis Obispo to the University of Missouri-St. Louis. It fell upon Erin to see that all databases, files and records were organized so thoroughly that "not even Dr. Bird" can foul them up. In St. Louis, with little help from me, Dayo Fawibe picked up where Erin had left off and helped carry the project through to completion.

In addition to an excellent trio of research assistants, I have been blessed to have very solid clerical and administrative support. In San Luis

Obispo, Sharon R. Leib helped to hide my mutlitude of shortcomings while I tried to juggle my responsibilities as editor with my duties as area coordinator. In St. Louis, Kathleen Mohrmann provided a calm and cheerful personality while taking care of the details involved with setting up life at a new university, thereby allowing me to concentrate on the encyclopedia.

In addition to the many authors who contributed to this volume, I have enjoyed the support of numerous colleagues. Each in their own way offered words of encouragement and support as well as providing examples of scholarship on which I might model my own humble efforts. In particular, I would like to thank Roger Dunbar (New York University), Kiyohiko Ito (Univerity of Hawaii, Manoa), Gil Latz (Portland State University), Harold Kerbo, Colette Frayne and Lynn Metcalf (California Polytechnic State University), Tish Robinson (Univeristy of California, Berkeley), Schon Beechler (Columbia University), Martha Maznevski (IMD), Mark Mendenhall (University of Tennessee-Chattanooga) and Joyce Osland (University of Portland).

There were several other individuals who, with one exception, had little direct involvement with this volume, but who nevertheless contributed to its creation through their impact on my life as an academic. In my first years in college, Lloyd Laughlin taught me to how to think critically and respectfully. At a time when I was a simple undergraduate student Sidney Chang saw a path for me to take and pushed me in that direction. In Japan, Gregory Clark challenged my understanding of Japan and convinced me that my "future is in studying business, not history." Susumu Takamiya served as a wise and gentle mentor during my few short years at the Sanno Institute of Business Administration. Finally, James C. Abegglen provided a model of abiding interest in Japan and keen insight into Japanese business and management.

This volume would not have been possible without the strong support of a very talented staff at Routledge who provided not only counsel and direction, but also timely and much-needed encouragement along the way. In particular, Fiona Cairns was instrumental in getting this project off the ground and underway. The matching bookend to Fiona was Dominic Shryane, who was largely responsible for bringing it to a successful conclusion.

A "thank you" is also due to Kyle, Allyson, Jared and Campbell. They think what I do is okay. Lastly, I would like to thank my wife, Diane, whose constant love and support over the past twenty-three years has enabled and allowed me to do what I do. It is hard for me to envision what I have done here as worthwhile without someone to share it with.

Allan Bird
St. Louis, Missouri

Introduction

Background

From 1979 to 1989 the world witnessed the arrival of a global economic superpower. During this ten-year period Japanese foreign direct investment (FDI) totaled $67.5 billion. Of all Japanese investment overseas, nearly 50 percent occurred within the USA. On a world scale, by 1993 Japanese firms had been so successful that 281 of *Businessweek*'s Global 1,000 were Japanese firms.

In light of these developments, one would anticipate a well-developed interest in Japanese firms among business executives, government administrators and management scholars. Yet, an analysis of the leading journals in the management field (*Administrative Science Quarterly, Strategic Management Journal, Academy of Management Journal,* and *Academy of Management Review*) reveals a dramatically different story. Of the roughly two thousand articles and research notes published in these four journals from 1980 through 1994, less than 3 percent address or directly relate to either the domestic or international behaviors of Japanese firms or their employees. The situation is only slightly better when it comes to the coverage of Japanese firms in practitioner periodicals such as *Harvard Business Review* or *Sloan Management Review,* or in business periodicals such as the *Financial Times, The Economist, Businessweek* and *Fortune*.

At first blush an observer might conclude that Western management scholars are guilty of gross ethnocentrism. Although a severe case of parochialism may be part of the explanation, I believe a more benign interpretation is available. Japanese practices are fundamentally different from those found in the West, particularly the USA. Additionally, Japan is located in Asia, far away from many of the academics and journalists interested in business. Lacking fluency in Japanese, and in the absence of writings by Japanese academics and authors in English or other Western Languages, it has been more difficult for non-Japanese to gain an accurate understanding.

In the past three decades a body of work sufficient to spark further interest and desire to learn about Japanese business has developed. Unfortunately, much of it is specialized. There is no single source to which a person interested in Japanese business can turn to find out specific practices, learn about distinctive concepts or identify key personalities or institutions. The *Encyclopedia of Japanese Business* is intended to address this deficiency.

There are several general sources on Japan, among them the *Cambridge Encyclopedia of Japan* and Kodansha's *Japan: An Illustrated Encyclopedia*. However, these give short shrift to the Japanese business system or the environment in which it operates. In a similar vein, there are encyclopedias of international busines and of specific business disciplines such as marketing and finance. Unfortunately, these volumes provide, at best, limited coverage of specific Japanese business concepts, practices, individuals or entities. More recently MIT Press has published *The MIT Encyclopedia of the Japanese Economy*. As its name implies, this book focuses specifically on economics, which of course has a large overlap with business and management. However, again, it misses important areas of business and management.

Aims of the Encyclopedia

The aim of the *Encyclopedia* is to offer an accessible and readable reference source of interest to both the non-specialist and the specialist seeking information on specific aspects of Japanese business. Though focused primarily on post-Second World War developments, practices and related concepts, entries on history provide grounding in the past. An effort was made to position the writing and content of entries such that they encourage use of the volume by both non-specialists (a journalist wanting background on the Tokyo Stock Exchange or a student looking for information on Toyota) and specialists (a management scholar interested in the use of *shokutaku shain* (contract employees) in human resource staffing strategies). Additionally, entries are oriented toward more recent developments and topics. However, a strong commitment was also made toward providing appropriate historical context for understanding Japanese business culture.

Structure

The structure of the *Encyclopedia* consists of one volume divided into fourteen topical categories. Individual entries are in one of four lengths. First-level entries run about 2000 words in length, second-level entries are approximately 1000 words, third-level entries 500 words and fourth-level entries 150 words. The first paragraph of each entry follows a format in which basic information is provided upfront, followed by historical background which, in turn, is followed by a deeper discussion. Entries were prepared in this manner so that readers anxious to gain a quick overview could read the first few paragraphs, while those readers requiring more detail could proceed deeper into the longer entries.

Cross-referencing within the volume allows the reader to see and follow connections among topics. Furthermore, authors of longer entries have provided selected readings so that those readers wishing to pursue a topic further may do so.

Timeliness

Encyclopedias, representing as they do a snapshot of current knowledge about a field, suffer obsolescence almost from their moment of conception. This is even more the case when compiling knowledge and understanding about a field that is in a constant state of flux. The Japanese business system and its environment are undergoing rapid and widespread change. Mergers, acquisitions and company failures have taken place at a fast clip during the 1990's and into the new millennium. Additionally, government ministries have undergone significant restructuring as well as some mergers of their own. In many cases, both in the private and public sectors, changes have been accompanied by changes in names. For example, the Ministry of International Trade and Industry (MITI) is now operating as the Ministry of Economics, Trade and Industry (METI). No doubt further changes will take place in the next several years, generating additional shortcomings in the titles and contents of entries. Nevertheless, a concerted attempt has been made by authors and editors to see that all entries are accurate and up-to-date.

Conclusion

In commenting on the creation of this encyclopedia, contributing authors frequently voiced two observations. When asked to write on a particular topic, they would usually respond that "surely someone has already written a clear explanation" of this topic or that issue. Then, upon further reflection, occasionally accompanied by a quick search in the library, they would express surprise that no one had. "After all," as one author said about a topic he had been asked to write on, "this is widely understood by everyone doing research in the area." The second observation followed from the first, and usually came after completion of an entry: it is good to get all of this information organized and gathered into a single source. This, of course, was the purpose of publishing this volume all along. We hope you will agree – it was good to pull this information together in one place.

How to use this book

This is an easy to use book. The articles/topics have been ordered both alphabetically and categorically. Entries can be searched using either approach. The categories are namely:

- Economics
- Finance
- General Management/ Business Administration
- Government Institutions/ Business-Government
- History
- Human Resource Management
- Influential Industries
- Influential Japanese Companies
- Influential Social/ Business Entities
- Influential Social/ Business Personalities
- Industrial Relations
- Japanese Business Overseas
- Manufacturing
- Marketing and Distribution
- Research and Development

Entries for topics and terms which are commonly referred to in English using either the original Japanese or the English translation are cross-referenced with both terms. For example, the entry Keidanren can be searched using either that name or the English translation, Federation of Economic Organizations. Cross-references appear in bold type. Related entries are also noted in the *See also* section at the conclusion of each entry.

Where deemed appropriate, entries also include a *further readings* section, where authors have identified several books or articles helpful to the reader in providing further coverage of the topic.

Thematic entry list

Economics

agricultural co-operatives
appreciating yen
bad debt
Bank of Japan
Banking Act of 1982
banking crises
bubble economy
city banks
consumption tax
Development Bank of Japan
dollar shock in 1971
dual structure theory
economic growth
economic ideology
Heisei boom
income doubling plan
Izanagi boom
Japan Development Bank
liberalization of financial markets
main bank system
sarakin
unemployment

Finance

banking crises
capital markets
corporate finance
cross-shareholdings
debt/equity ratios
postal savings
promissory note
shareholder weakness
takeovers
venture capital industry

General management/business administration

accounting in Japan
bankruptcies
bottom-up decision making processes
business ethics
commercial code
competition
contracts
corporate governance
daihyoken
environmental and ecological issues
habatsu
industrial groups (keiretsu)
joint stock corporation
joint ventures
Kansai culture
kansayaku
madogiwa zoku
maruyu
mochiai
Naniwashi bushi
negotiations
nemawashi
nihonteki keiei
nikkei jin
office ladies (OL)
organizational learning
restructuring
ringi seido
salaryman
small- and medium-sized firms
stockholders general assembly
strategic partnering
supply chain management in Japan
three sacred treasures
white-collar workers

women's roles
zaibatsu

Government institutions/business–government relations

administrative guidance (gyosei shido)
agricultural policy
amakudari
cartels
dango
depressed industries
Depressed Industries Law, 1978
deregulation
environmental regulations
Fair Trade Commission
foreign aid
industrial policy
industrial regions
Japan Inc.
madoguchi shido
men in charge of MoF
Ministry of Construction
Ministry of Finance
Ministry of International Trade and Industry
Rengo
trade barriers
trade negotiations

History

American occupation
banto
Buddhism
distribution system
geography
guilds (za and kabunakama)
history of the labour movement
ie
industrial efficiency movement
Meiji restoration
Post-WWII recovery
Prince Shotoku's 17 Article Constitution
Samurai, role of
Tokugawa period
wartime legacy

Human resource management

allowances and non-salary compensation
appraisal systems
burakumin
contract employees
education system
genba-shugi
human relations management
internal labour markets
karoshi
lifetime employment
outplacement
permanent employee
seniority promotion
shukko

Industrial relations

enterprise unions
foreign workers
Japan Productivity Center for Socio-Economic
    Development
Ministry of Labour
Sohyo

Influential industries

airline industry
automotive industry
banking industry
computer industry
construction industry
electronics industry
motorcycle industry
pharmaceuticals industry
retail industry
software industry
telecommunications industry

Influential Japanese companies

Ajinomoto
Arabian Oil
Bank of Tokyo
Canon
Daiei, Inc
Daiichi Kangyo Bank
Export-Import Bank of Japan

foreign companies in Japan
Fuji Photo Film
gaishikei kigyou
Honda Motor Co. Ltd.
ITOCHU Corporation
Ito-Yokado Company, Ltd.
Japan Airlines
Japan National Railways
Kao
Kirin Brewery Company
Kyocera Corporation
Long-Term Credit Bank of Japan
Marubeni Corporation
Matsushita Electric Industrial Company Limited
    (MEI)
Mitsubishi Corporation
Mitsui & Co., Ltd.
Mitsukoshi, Ltd.
NEC
Nintendo Co. Ltd.
Nippon Telegraph and Telephone (NTT)
Nissan Motor Company
Nomura Securities
Norin Chukin Bank
Seven-Eleven Japan
Sharp Corporation
Sony
Sumitomo Corporation
Toshiba
Toyota
Yamato Transportation

Influential social/business entities

Central Union of Agricultural Cooperatives
industry and trade associations
Japan Association of Corporate Executives
Japan Automobile Manufacturers Association
Japan Chamber of Commerce and Industry
Japan External Trade Organization
Japan Federation of Economic Organizations
Japan Federation of Employers' Associations
Keio University
Liberal Democratic Party
Nihon Keizai Shimbun
sokaiya
Tokyo University

Influential social/business personalities

Abegglen, James C.
Cole, Robert
Deming, W. Edwards
Dodge, Joseph M.
Dokoh, Toshio
Dore, Ronald
Fukuzawa, Yukichi
Hayakawa, Tokuji
Hayato, Ikeda
Honda, Soichiro
Inamori, Kazuo
Ishikawa, Kaoru
Iwasaki, Yataro
Johnson, Chalmers
Juran, Joseph M.
Koike, Kazuo
Komiya, Ryutaro
Matsushita, Kounosuke
Minomura, Rizaemon
Morita, Akio
Nakauchi, Isao
Nonaka, Ikujiro
Ohmae, Kenichi
Ono (Ohno), Taichi
Shibusawa, Eiichi
Shingo, Shigeo
Taguchi, Genichi
Tanaka, Kakuei
Ueno, Yoichi

Japanese business overseas

economic crisis in Asia
general trading companies
Japanese business in Africa
Japanese business in Australia
Japanese business in Canada
Japanese business in China
Japanese business in Germany
Japanese business in Italy
Japanese business in Korea and Taiwan
Japanese business in Latin America
Japanese business in Mexico
Japanese business in Southeast Asia
Japanese business in the Middle East
Japanese business in the UK

Japanese business in the United States of America
Japanese investment patterns
Japanese MNEs
localization
New United Motor Manufacturing Inc. (NUMMI)
overseas business of small- and medium-sized
    enterprises
overseas education.
overseas production
overseas R&D
US investment in Japan

Manufacturing/production

5S campaign
ISO issues
Japanese Industrial Standards (JIS)
just-in-time
kaizen
quality control circles
quality management
standard setting
subcontracting system
suggestion systems
total productive maintenance
Toyota production system

Marketing and distribution

advertising

after-sales pricing
Akihabara
central wholesale markets
chugen
consumer movement
creative houses
Dentsu
department stores
discounters
e-commerce
konbini (convenience stores)
Large Retail Store Law, 1974
marketing in Japan
one-to-one marketing
pricing practices
social marketing
superstores
tonya
Tsukiji market

Research and development

export and import of technology
firm strategies for technology
patent system
product development
research cooperatives
science and technology policy
VLSI Research Cooperative

Abegglen, James C.

The most influential author on Japanese business and management, Abegglen's pioneering work, *The Japanese Factory*, set the focus and direction of future analyses of the Japanese management system. To date, he has authored or co-authored ten books, including two other volumes receiving significant attention: *Kaisha: The Japanese Corporation* (with George Stalk, Jr.) and *Sea Change: Pacific Asia as The New World Industrial Center*. Abegglen first came to Japan in 1945, living and working there a majority of time since then. In 1965 he was one of the founding officers of the Boston Consulting Group (BCG) and established BCG's Tokyo office. Eighteen years later he established Asia Advisory Services. Abegglen also remained active in academia through his position as a faculty member at Sophia University, where he was director of the university's Institute of Comparative Culture from 1987 to 1990. Although he did not coin the term "Japan, Inc.," he is widely associated with it because of his active commentary on Japanese business through his writings in business periodicals, both in and out of Japan.

The Japanese Factory (1958) was a detailed examination of the patterns of social life and influence relations in a Japanese factory. In his analysis, Abegglen pointed out a key difference from the American factory in that a person entering the employment of a Japanese factory was making a lifetime commitment. He argued that this extraordinary commitment helped to explain both the all-consuming demands that management exacted from workers in terms of loyalty and also the depth of concern management demonstrated for the total welfare of those employees. In addition to lifetime employment, Abegglen also identified how rewards were based on group, not individual, performance. He also drew attention to the emphasis on length of tenure over pure merit-based criteria in promotion decisions. He concluded that Japan's pattern of industrialization differed from the US and other Western countries as a consequence of the larger social and cultural context in which Japanese work organizations were embedded.

In 1985, *Kaisha: The Japanese Corporation* had an equally profound impact on a western business community trying to understand the foundation of competitiveness on which Japanese firms were achieving market share worldwide. It outlined both the strengths and weaknesses of Japanese corporations.

Further reading

Abegglen, J.C. (1958) *The Japanese Factory*, Glencoe, IL: The Free Press.

Abegglen, J.C. and Stalk, G., Jr. (1985) *Kaisha: The Japanese Corporation*, New York: Basic Books.

ALLAN BIRD

accounting in Japan

Accounting standards and financial reporting in Japan are similar in many ways to US and International Accounting Standards; however, differences exist. Differences also exist in accounting standard setting and regulations.

Accounting standard setting and regulations

Accounting standards and regulations are strongly influenced by governmental agencies and laws in Japan. Three primary sets of laws must be considered when analyzing accounting and reporting standards in Japan. The Commercial Code, administered by the Ministry of Justice, prescribes accounting standards for limited liability companies (*kabushiki kaisha*). The Commercial Code has a strong legal focus and is primarily concerned with creditor and shareholder protection. The Securities and Exchange Law, administered by the Ministry of Finance, applies to companies that list their stock on exchanges. The primary interest of the Securities Laws is to provide information for investor decision making. The final influential law affecting Japanese accounting standards is the Corporate Income Tax Law. This law basically requires that income and deductions for tax purposes also be the same as those used for financial accounting purposes. These three laws are the primary laws and regulations governing accounting and financial reporting in Japan.

Accounting rules and standards

Accounting rules and standards are concerned with how the accounts are measured and how amounts are calculated. As previously noted, the Commercial Code, Securities Laws and Corporate Income Tax Laws generally determine specific accounting rules and standards.

Accounts and notes receivable are based on amounts owed to the company. The calculation of the allowance for doubtful accounts is usually based on the amount allowed by tax law. This is in contrast to the USA, where the estimate of future bad debts is based on the amount that will prove uncollectible.

Recent changes in accounting for marketable securities now require firms to use the year-end market values of the securities for valuation purposes. This is in contrast to historical cost that was previously used. Pending changes require that changes in market values of securities classified as "trading" securities be reflected in income for the period. In contrast to trading securities, unrealized changes in the value of securities classified as "available for sale" are reflected in shareholders' equity and do not affect current period income. Accounting for investments in securities that result in over 20 percent ownership of the investee is discussed below.

Accounting for inventories in Japan is similar to most countries. The company may value inventory using either the historical cost or the lower of cost or market value. Typically, historical cost is used. The lower of cost or market method requires that the decline in value be significant (at least 50 percent) before adjustments to market are made, thus inventories may be overstated to some extent. Inventory cost may be based on specific, identifiable values if available, or cost flow assumptions, such as FIFO, LIFO or average cost, may be used. Replacement cost is not allowed. The same accounting method must be used for both financial accounting and tax purposes.

Tangible assets, such as buildings and equipment, are recorded at historical cost. Revaluation is not permitted. Thus, land accounts in the financial statements may be overstated in view of the recent decline in Japanese land values. Depreciation is based on amounts allowed for tax purposes, and typically calculated by one of the accelerated methods. Land is not depreciable. Leased tangible assets that transfer the risks and rewards of ownership to the lessee are accounted for as capitalized leases and treated in a similar manner to purchased assets. However, capitalization of leases is not a common practice in Japan.

The valuation of intangible assets depends on the nature of the asset. Internally generated goodwill is not recognized. Purchased goodwill is capitalized and amortized over five years, although there are proposals to increase the amortization period to twenty years. Goodwill generated in the acquisition of another company is measured based on the book value of the net assets acquired instead of fair market value. Research and development expenditures may be capitalized and amortized over five years, although most companies write off the expenses in the year incurred.

Accounting for longer term investments in other companies is determined by the degree of ownership. The equity method is used for investments that represent 20–50 percent ownership of the investee and for joint ventures. Investments of over 50 percent ownership in subsidiaries are consolidated and discussed below. Business combinations are accounted for as a purchase. Generally the pooling method is not allowed.

A major change in Japanese accounting has been in accounting for employer provided pensions. In the past, pension liabilities and expenses were accounted for on a "pay as you go" basis. The result was a significant understatement of pension liabilities. Recent changes now require that pension liabilities be accounted for using accrual concepts and market valuations. The funding status of the company's pension plans must also be disclosed. These adjustments and changes are expected to have significant effects on the financial statements of Japanese firms.

Deferred taxes arise when the timing of income and expenses for financial accounting purposes is different from the recognition for income tax purposes. Deferred tax accounting is common in the financial statements of many other countries; however, it is rare in Japan. Basically, recognition of deferred tax assets is not allowed and usually firms will not recognize deferred tax liabilities, even in consolidated financial statements. Typically, there is no need for deferred taxes since the tax code requires that most items of income and expenses be treated the same for both financial accounting and tax purposes.

Leased assets in Japan are usually accounted for as operating leases and charged to expense when incurred. Currently, capitalized lease accounting may apply in a few limited cases; however, the trend is toward requiring capitalized leases in the future.

The consolidation of foreign subsidiaries requires the translation of foreign currency accounts into yen equivalents. Assets and liabilities of foreign subsidiaries are translated using the exchange rate in effect at the end of the year, and income statement items are generally translated using the average exchange rate for the year. Translation adjustments are recorded as an asset or liability on the balance sheet.

An additional major difference between Japanese accounting and accounting in other countries, such as the USA, is the use of reserves. Reserves are often used in Japanese accounting, but rare in the USA. The reserves basically represent appropriations of income or retained earnings and generally do not contain a cash component. The Commercial Code requires companies to maintain legal reserves. The legal reserve represents an annual allocation or appropriation of income equal to at least 10 percent of cash dividends and bonuses to directors. The annual appropriation is required until the reserve is equal to 35 percent of capital stock. Thereafter, appropriations are voluntary. The requirement for a legal reserve is an example of the focus on creditor protection by discouraging excessive dividends and bonuses to directors. In addition, discretionary reserves are permitted and have led some analysts to conclude that managers of Japanese firms use reserves to smooth income or manage earnings.

A final noteworthy accounting practice in Japan, and one that differs from most countries, is the charging of directors' bonuses directly to retained earnings instead of an expense against income for the period. The bonuses are viewed as a distribution of corporate profits instead of an expense.

Financial reporting

Financial reporting is concerned with how accounting information is presented or reported in the basic financial statements. Both the Commercial Code and the Securities and Exchange Law require firms to file a business report, a balance sheet, income statement, proposed statement of appropriations of retained earnings and supplemental schedules. However the format, classification, extent of disclosure and type of supplemental information differs between the two agencies. Examples of supplemental information required by the Commercial Code include:

- changes in capital stock and reserves
- changes in bonds payable and other debt instruments
- changes in fixed assets and accumulated depreciation
- disclosure of debt guarantees and disclosure of collateralized assets
- extensive disclosure of related party transactions,

such as with subsidiaries, directors and controlling shareholders
- ownership of subsidiaries (and reciprocal ownership)

The Securities and Exchange Law requires similar information to be filed with the Ministry of Finance. The Ministry of Finance requires additional disclosure of information such as details of pension obligations: marketable securities, subsequent events, intangible assets and so on. A cash flow statement and six month cash flow forecast is also required, but is not audited. Additional forecasts, such as for capital expenditures and debt retirement, are required to be filed with the Ministry but are usually not disclosed in the shareholder reports.

Consolidated financial statements are also required of firms that are listed on security exchanges and subject to the Securities and Exchange Laws. The consolidated statements include the balance sheet and income statement, but are expanded to include a cash flow statement. A subsidiary's financial statements are consolidated with those of the parent company if the parent owns over 50 percent of the subsidiary company's stock. It is important to note that there are regulations that allow exclusions of some subsidiaries from the consolidated group. The requirement for consolidated financial statements has increased the transparency of the firm's activities and led to disclosure of losses by unprofitable subsidiaries.

The format of the financial statements varies depending on the filing requirements. However, the balance sheet requires that assets, liabilities and equity be classified separately and that current assets and current liabilities be distinguished from long-term items. The income statement has an additional section for special gains and losses, but the definition of special gains and losses is not as restrictive as the definition of extraordinary items required in the USA. Also, prior period adjustments are included in the special gain or loss section as opposed to a restatement of retained earnings.

The Ministry of Finance also requires footnote disclosure of the major segments of a firm's operations. The segments are classified by line of business and by geographical sector. Specifically,

each segment's turnover (sales revenue), assets and operating income must be disclosed.

Each company must have a statutory auditor who attests to the financial statements. The statutory auditor is usually not a Certified Public Accountant and often is an employee of the firm. Companies are required to have an audit by an independent Certified Public Accountant if they are listed on a stock exchange, or for unlisted companies, if their share capital is over 500 million yen or liabilities exceed 20 billion yen.

Summary

Japan's accounting standards, rules and reporting requirements are similar in many ways to those of other countries, and are becoming more harmonized in response to global economic forces. Many differences remain, however, and the rules are somewhat complicated by the multi-agency standard setting process.

Further reading

Choi, F.D.S., Frost, C.A. and Meek, G.K. (1999) *International Accounting*, 3rd edn, Englewood Cliffs, NJ: Prentice Hall.

Haskins, M.E., Ferris, K.R. and Selling, T.C. (2000) *International Financial Reporting and Analysis: A Conceptual Emphasis*, 2nd edn, Boston: Irwin McGraw Hill.

Kiyomitsu Arai (1994) *Accounting in Japan*, Tokyo: Institute for Research in Business Administration, Waseda University, Tokyo, Japan.

KPMG Peat Marwick (1993) *Comparison of Japanese and U.S. Reporting and Financial Practices*, Tokyo, Japan.

Nobes, C. and Parker, P. (1998) *Comparative International Accounting*, 5th edn, London: Prentice Hall Europe.

RON SINGLETON
KAZAHIRO OKAZAKI

administrative guidance

The term "administrative guidance" or *gyosei shido* refers to non-codified, extralegal regulation whereby a ministry attempts to induce certain behavior in a company or industry with the aim of realizing an administrative goal. The process is typically not transparent and the resulting regulation has a strong situational character, because rules may be invoked or revoked at the discretion of the ministry without cabinet or parliamentary approval. During the heyday of industrial policy in the 1950s and 1960s, administrative guidance was the predominant regulatory tool used to align business strategies and public policy goals.

There are two forms of administrative guidance: written and oral. Written guidance typically establishes industry-wide rules that are valid in the medium run and published in one volume at the end of the fiscal year. An example of written guidance would be a notification (*tsutatsu*) from the **Ministry of Finance**'s (MOF) Insurance Bureau that life insurance companies are allowed to invest a lower or higher maximum percentage of their total assets in the stock market, effective from a certain date. Oral guidance typically remains undisclosed and involves delicate conversations between ministry officials and industry representatives. For instance, when the Nikkei 225 stock index fell significantly in the early 1990s, MOF officials called up several investment banks and in the course of a jovial conversation pointed out just how detrimental they thought the depressed stock market was for the overall economy. In reaction, the banks were said to have bought large positions in Japan's flagship companies.

Enforcement is based on a *quid pro quo*, or "carrot and stick," approach. Companies know that if they follow the ministry's "advice" they may reap rewards later, whereas refusal to comply may lead the ministry to obstruct future business opportunities. "Carrots" are offered by the ministry in the form of subsidies or lenient regulation, whereas the "stick" may be a threat to withhold a business license, curb an import quota or give preferential treatment to a competitor. Because compliance is voluntary, there is effectively no legal recourse for firms subjected to administrative guidance. Neither is there a legal means for the regulating ministry to enforce its guidance.

Importantly, administrative guidance is not usually a "one-way street" with the ministry unilaterally designing all the rules. Precisely because it is extralegal, ministries have to ensure that the regulation garners sufficient industry support to be meaningful. The process of designing guidance therefore often entails sending a draft of a new rule to the trade association concerned, to be discussed and modified by the presidents of the leading companies. The association then reports the presidents' opinion to the ministry. In this sense, administrative guidance often emerges out of discussions between bureaucrats and the regulated industry.

The trade association's function in monitoring the implementation of rules is as important as their input in regulatory policy creation. After a new rule has been issued by the ministry, the regulatees themselves often assume the task of ensuring adherence. It is much easier for the firms in an industry rather than bureaucrats to observe the market behavior of their competitors. Because it is extralegal and informal, administrative guidance invites cheating, and it can only be enforced with group pressure and controls by the industry concerned. Given that administrative guidance builds on self-regulation for enforcement, it can be either extremely effective (if all companies agree to comply) or completely ineffective (if they choose to ignore the ministry's guidance).

Changes in the 1980s

Two major currents combined to diminish ministerial leverage with which to enforce administrative guidance in the 1980s. First, as companies grew and became world competitors, the "carrots" offered by their ministries, such as access to loans or foreign exchange, became less appealing. Second, deregulation and the opening of financial markets undermined the effectiveness of both "carrots" and "sticks."

The primary "carrots," or rewards, that ministries used for implementing **industrial policy** in the postwar period came in two forms: (a) access to and allocation of imported and scarce raw materials, and (b) opening of new business opportunities through such means as granting licenses, subjecting product innovation to approval, or furnishing low-interest loans through public financial institutions. The allocation of raw materials and foreign technology worked well until 1965, when a revision of the Foreign Investment Law diminished the **Ministry of International Trade and Industry**'s (MITI) control over foreign reserve allocation. The revision of the Foreign Exchange and Trade Law in 1980 further curtailed MITI's command over trade flows. No longer could the ministry reward cooperative firms through the allocation of scarce raw material imports.

Second, changes in financial markets in the 1980s seriously undercut the ministries' ability to punish manufacturing firms and banks that resisted administrative guidance. With the development of the bond and stock markets, firms became less dependent on bank financing, so banking regulation no longer translated into manufacturing guidance. As manufacturing firms became more able to raise funds abroad, the government's threat of punishing mavericks by blocking access to loans became meaningless. For the banks, deregulation meant less dependence on **Ministry of Finance** (MOF) licenses and approvals. Yet the need for constant monitoring remained greatest in the banking industry, and banks continued to stay close to their regulators by designating MOF-tan.

Thus, the liberalization of trade rules and access to financial markets in the 1980s undermined government guidance of both the manufacturing and the financial sectors. While the practice continues to be more institutionalized and extensive than moral suasion in other countries, the effectiveness of guidance depends increasingly on the willingness of industry to cooperate, with ministries having fewer means at their disposals to create such willingness.

Further reading

Johnson, C. (1982) *MITI and the Japanese Miracle: The Growth of Industrial Policy 1925–1875*, Stanford, CA: Stanford University Press.

Schaede, U. (2000) *Cooperative Capitalism: Self-Regulation, Trade Associations, and the Antimonopoly Law in Japan*, Oxford: Oxford University Press.

Upham, F. (1987) *Law and Social Change in Postwar Japan*, Cambridge, MA: Harvard University Press.

ULRIKE SCHAEDE

advertising

Advertising in Japan is typified by its lack of product focus. Many advertisements don't show the product at all. Rather than promoting product features or brand, Japanese advertising generally strives to promote a positive image of the company producing the product. This soft-sell style of advertising has long been described by Westerners as image, or mood advertising. While message content is of utmost importance in advertising in the West, in Japan, the method of conveying the message is more important.

The soft-sell approach in Japanese advertising is a direct influence of Japan's culturally ingrained avoidance of the direct approach. Japanese ads are designed to appeal to the target audience's emotions. To achieve this, advertisements tend to place heavy emphasis on visual imagery, and less on written copy. The resulting advertisements build a positive image of the corporation placing the advertisement, and thus their products, while providing very little detailed product information.

In general, Japanese advertising has traditionally focused on building a corporation's image. Vying to capture the viewers' attention in the deluge of advertising, advertisements tend to be oriented around building a positive image of a corporation. In many cases this results in advertisements where the product is not shown, let alone mentioned. Such ads tend to have a sign-off with the corporate name.

The theory behind this image advertising is that if a consumer has a good impression of a corporation, they would tend to buy that company's products. Product branding has not gained the stature in Japan that it enjoys elsewhere in the world. As a result, most television commercials end with the corporation's name and logo, which also feature prominently in print advertisements.

One reason advertisements in Japan can omit product description is the wealth of product information available in other venues. A visit to a retailer provides the consumer with a wealth of highly descriptive complimentary product catalogues. Further detailed product information can be found in the many magazines dedicated to supplying in-depth product reviews.

The one glaring exception to the soft-sell approach is in the case of products for which detailed information in the form of brochures and magazine reviews is not available. An example is advertising for products such as washing detergents which will often contain straightforward messages and demonstrations of the product's cleansing properties.

Due to the Japanese culture of group conformity, Japanese ads are targeted towards the group, rather than to the individual. Horizontal identification is important. Advertisements that are perceived as containing an authoritarian tone, such as a hard sell from an authority figure, are rejected. Similarly, ads containing a blatant message of vertical aspiration to a higher social station are also suspect. Successful advertisements in Japan aim to build empathy with the target group. A common method is featuring the product's acceptance by a peer, who is often also a celebrity.

The lack of comparison ads in Japan has also been attributed to Japan's group culture. It has been argued that advertisements that compared a firm's product to that of a competitor would be rejected by Japanese consumers. However, in the few cases where comparative ads have been run, it was found that Japanese consumers did not reject them. Most likely, the dearth of comparative advertisements in Japan is due to many ad agencies having more than one client per industry category, and to industry self-regulation.

Regardless of the many quirks of advertising in Japan, the nation is flooded with advertising, from television to cloth placards attached to telephone poles, to digital text messages broadcast to small screens inside taxis. There are two reasons for the prevalence of advertising in Japan. One is the insatiable Japanese demand for information which results in nationwide newspapers with circulation in the millions. The other is the relatively lax laws and regulations on advertising. Most industries are encouraged to conduct self-regulation regarding advertising. In addition, most media also regulate what they will, and will not, allow in an advertisement.

Acquiring mass media ad space in Japan is extremely expensive as well as highly competitive. Both newspaper and magazine ad space is limited by restrictions on the number of pages available for advertising. Television has only five nationwide terrestrial stations, although satellite and cable penetration are growing.

A major factor in acquiring space in the mass media is the fact that not every ad agency can buy space. To buy space, an agency must have an account with the media vehicle in question, and these vehicles don't give the accounts away easily. As a result, very few of Japan's ad agencies can buy ad space directly. Rather, they have the larger agencies buy the space for them. Once ad space is acquired, getting an ad noticed among the clutter of mass media advertising is a continuous challenge for advertisers and their agencies. This is especially true in the case of television, where the majority of spots are mainly of fifteen-second length.

A typical solution to the problems particular to advertising in Japan is the use of celebrities, both Japanese and foreign. Estimates put the use of celebrities in Japanese commercials at between 60 to 70 percent. These celebrities range from Japanese comedians to pop singers, and from Hollywood box office stars to foreign scientists. The use of celebrities is believed to help a commercial stand out from the competition, as well as to link a corporation's image with that of the celebrity. Generally, these celebrities do not appear as spokespersons for a product, rather, their appearance has little to do with the product.

SEAN MOONEY

after-sales pricing

After-sales pricing, or *ato-gime*, is pricing which takes place after a product has been sold and delivered. It is a reflection of weak price competition. The opposite of *ato-gime* is *jangime* (pricing at the time of sale). Such pricing, though standard in the West, is unusual enough in certain Japanese industries to require a special term.

In a market economy, buyers shop around for the best value. Shoppers look at quality, service and price, while producers compete to give shoppers the best deal. When buyers shop around, supply and demand forces determine how much they pay for the product they end up buying. If supplies are plentiful and demand is weak, shoppers can bargain for a lower price. If supplies are scarce and there is much demand, sellers will be in a strong position and able to raise prices.

However, both shopping and competing have costs. It takes time for shoppers to look around and it may be hard to find out how reliable a particular supplier is. Shoppers may prefer to stick with particular producers so that they can save shopping time and be confident in the quality of the goods they buy, even if they have to pay a bit more. Competing is also tough on sellers. Intense price **competition** brings down prices and can even drive firms out of business. Thus, both buyers and sellers have reasons to avoid constant shopping around on the basis of price. When buyers are not choosing their suppliers on the basis of price, they typically base prices on producers' costs. But if a sale is not based on price, the door is left open for negotiations over the exact price to drag out long after the sale and delivery has been made.

There are three types of after-sales pricing. First, when sellers are engaged in a cartel, it may take a while for them to decide on final prices in industries in which costs fluctuate considerably. The primary example of this is the petrochemical industry. During the 1970s and early 1980s, when petroleum prices were rising sharply, petrochemical producers tried hard to get buyers to pay the full cost of expensive petroleum feedstocks they used to make their products. Even though in principle buyers were supposed to pay the full cost of production, the petrochemical companies found that they were being forced to compete on price and were losing money. To solve this problem, the petrochemical industry adopted a price-fixing formula in 1983 to set prices for petrochemicals based on the cost of feedstocks, which has been in effect ever since. Of course each company knows how much it had spent on feedstocks by the time it delivered its chemicals, but chemical producers want to be sure that the formula is implemented uniformly and that there is no price competition. So all the chemical producers wait until the government publishes average prices for the main feedstock, naphtha. Because the industry is pricing on the basis of a cartel, and because it needs to wait for these price figures, pricing of products throughout the petrochemical industry is delayed for several months.

Second, if the cartel is waiting to decide on a price, but the cartel relies on the good will of

buyers, the cartel needs to negotiate over a final price with buyers as a group. This is in fact how industry-wide pricing in the petrochemical industry has worked. Prices in the industry have been modified by considerations of two factors. Prices may be modified to favor either sellers or buyers who are in a particularly difficult financial position. That is, prices may be modified in the opposite direction from market pressures. Or alternatively, prices may be modified *with* the market, in favor of either buyers or sellers depending on supply-demand conditions. Typically, whichever side is in a favorable position argues during negotiations that cost-based, after-sales pricing should be abandoned because it is old-fashioned and succeeds in using this rhetorical ploy to adjust prices in its favor.

Finally, after-sales pricing may take place between individual buyers and sellers based on these same considerations of fairness and market conditions. Most commonly, this kind of after-sales pricing serves as a discount on a cartel-based price.

The broad purpose of after-sales pricing is to modify prices somewhat in uncompetitive markets with high prices. However, after-sales pricing brings certain disadvantages. The lack of transparent prices makes it more difficult for a new firm to enter a market and attract customers with low prices. In a market where there are no definite prices at the time of sale, it is difficult for the new entrant to know what price it is competing against. Foreign firms trying to break into the Japanese glass market have made this complaint.

Second, when prices are undecided for as long as a year, as they are sometimes in the chemical industry, it becomes difficult for firms to carry out normal accounting procedures. How do firms know what their revenues, expenses, and profits are when prices are left dangling? However, the chief problem with after-sales pricing is that it is a symptom of weak price competition in Japanese industries such as chemicals, glass and pharmaceuticals. Weak price competition fails to give producers incentives to cut costs and become more productive.

See also: cartels; competition; pricing practices

Further reading

Tilton, M. (1996) *Restrained Trade: Cartels in Japan's*

Basic Materials Industries, Ithaca, NY: Cornell University Press.

MARK TILTON

agricultural cooperatives

Modern agricultural cooperatives began in Japan following the land reform carried out by the Occupation Forces after the Second World War. The land reform took the form of the state purchase of tenant farm land from landowners and subsequent sale thereof to tenant farmers, creating a large number of very small owner-farmers with an average of 1.1 hectares of farm land. However, because these small-scale owner-farmers could not expect to bring about agricultural development individually, an attempt was made at united efforts in improving productivity and living standards through mutual aid and cooperation among farmers. Accordingly, the Agricultural Cooperative Society Law was enacted after the land reform was started. The law was modeled after cooperative group principles of 1936 and the US law on cooperatives. Cooperative organizations had also been in existence in Japan for half a century, beginning with the Industrial Cooperative Society Law which was enacted in 1900. Agricultural cooperatives thus can be described as cooperative societies seeking to make a fresh start on the basis of industrial cooperatives (*sangyo kumiai*).

The difference between industrial and agricultural cooperatives lay in their respective membership: industrial cooperatives' membership could include not only farmers, but also fishermen, foresters, businessmen in commerce and industry as well as consumers, while the agricultural cooperative was intended to be a craft union composed of farmers as its regular members. The organizational structure, consisting of unit agricultural cooperatives at the municipal level and federations established at the prefectural and national levels according to their respective business functions, has been attributable to the tradition of industrial cooperative societies.

Agricultural cooperatives can be divided into two groups: single-purpose agricultural cooperatives organized for the purpose of marketing specific types of farm products (dairy farming, horticulture, fruit culture, stock farming, etc.) and multipurpose agricultural cooperatives engaging in activities in the field of loan and credit extension, mutual aid insurance, welfare (health and medical care), consultation and guidance, and economic (marketing and purchasing) services. Agricultural cooperatives are generally called *nokyo* in Japanese. When people refer to *nokyo*, they usually have the latter type of cooperatives in mind. These cooperatives are based on communities involved with rice culture or production of crops and other farm products. Agricultural cooperatives have a total membership of 9,128,000 (as of 1998), consisting of 5,344,000 regular members and 3,784,000 associate members (non-farmers such as consumers). The number of agricultural cooperatives stood at 1,411 in the year 2000. The government is promoting the amalgamation of agricultural cooperatives, and the number of cooperatives is expected to fall to 570 by 2010.

Observing specific fields of services provided by agricultural cooperatives as of fiscal 1997, marketing/distribution totaled ¥5.7 trillion (comprising of ¥1.6 trillion from rice, ¥1.35 trillion from vegetables and ¥3.8 billion from livestock), and purchasing amounted to a total of ¥2.9 trillion (made up of ¥478.6 billion for feedstuff, ¥611.3 billion for oil products, ¥357.2 billion for fertilizers and ¥342.4 billion for agricultural machinery). The percentage shares of the agricultural cooperatives to the total amount of sales and purchases made by the agricultural sector have been on the decline in recent years: for example, agricultural cooperatives accounted for 60 percent of vegetable sales and 60 percent of the purchase of agricultural chemicals made by member farmers. The percentage of farming households using the services of agricultural cooperatives has also been falling. Revenues from marketing and purchasing services were down 20 percent and 12 percent respectively from those in fiscal 1985.

In the area of credit activities, the balance of savings deposited with agricultural cooperatives as of the end of fiscal 1998 stood at ¥69 trillion, accounting for 7.4 percent of the entire deposits and savings in Japan. On the fund application side, the outstanding loan balance amounted to ¥22 trillion, bringing the ratio of loans to deposits to a little under 30 percent. Most funds received as deposits and savings by individual cooperatives are in turn deposited with the prefectural credit federations of agricultural cooperatives (*Shinnoren*) and the **Norin Chukin Bank**. Because agricultural cooperatives' credit services are operated in parallel with other lines of business, the amount of deposits/savings held by each operating entity is small, only about ¥34.1 billion. Cooperative deposits/savings are characterized by disproportionately high percentages of personal savings (83.5 percent) and time deposit (79.4 percent). The percentages of personal loans and long-term loans are also high at 81.5 percent and 87.3 percent, respectively, of total cooperative loans outstanding. Unlike ordinary city banks, agricultural cooperatives specialize in retail banking. With the progress of financial deregulation, cooperatives have been increasing their focus on retail banking. Against this backdrop, entities in other business categories have moved into rural areas for new opportunities, putting downward pressure on operating income. Accordingly, gross profits from agricultural cooperative business dropped to 35.4 percent from 40 percent.

The mutual aid services of cooperatives correspond to life insurance and non-life insurance business in the private sector. With a total of ¥34 trillion in outstanding plan balance, agricultural cooperatives' mutual aid plans account for 13.4 percent of the life insurance market and 15.35 percent of the non-life insurance market. Agricultural cooperatives boast the second largest assets after Nippon Life Insurance Co. in terms of their life insurance portfolio, and are the top non-life insurer in Japan in terms of the total amount of non-life insurance. The National Mutual Insurance Federation of Agricultural Cooperatives (*Zenkyoren*) has ¥34 trillion in total assets, accounting for 24.0 percent of the agricultural cooperatives' gross operating income. The mutual aid insurance business is the second largest business area after credit activities, and represents the most profitable operating area.

Advice on farming and better living are offered to member farmers as a non-profit undertaking, and are funded by revenues from the cooperatives' credit, mutual aid and economic activities. Cooperatives provide member farmers with advice on not only production but also marketing and distribution with a view to improving farming operation and management. Better living guidance is related to consumer activities and involves health/medical care services for farmers. In the area of medical care in particular, welfare federations are organized in twelve prefectures. With over 20,000 beds, they operate the largest number of hospitals after the Japanese Red Cross Society. As public medical institutions, these hospitals contribute to the development of medical services in the community.

In the past when they were part of industrial cooperative societies, Japanese agricultural cooperatives, together with other agricultural organizations, were fostered by the State as institutions for exercising agricultural policies. With the change in agricultural policies, however, agricultural cooperatives have had to face critical tests. Liberalization of agricultural trade and financial deregulation since 1990 have not allowed cooperative development of farms, but forced the realignment of the three-tiered organizational structure and rationalization of individual cooperatives. Future challenges for the agricultural cooperatives include whether these new developments can be implemented in concurrence with the primary structure of existing cooperatives which are based on the function of rural communities.

Confronted by broad changes in Japanese agriculture, the declining number of people who may in future be engaged in agriculture and the progress of urbanization in rural areas, agricultural cooperatives are uncertain about their direction. It is possible that they may develop as cooperative organizations within the community more broadly, encompassing not only farmers but also consumers and smaller businesses in commerce and industry.

KENJI ISHIHARA

agricultural policy

Agricultural policies in Japan after the Second World War started with land reform. The central policy focus was on the securing of the food supply and controlling its distribution in a time when a planned economy and food shortages continued from prewar days. With the revival of the economy in 1950, however, domestic resource development began. Development of wild land and land reclamation projects were pursued for the purpose of enlarging arable land areas. This was because during the period of so-called economic independence in the late 1950s, food accounted for as high as one-third of the total imports, which placed pressure on foreign exchange availability and imposed restrictions on the import of raw materials for use by exporting industries. The business community thus called for the attainment of self-sufficiency in food.

During the 1960s, when Japan entered into a period of high economic growth, industrial combines centering on steel production and petrochemical complexes were constructed in the Pacific belt zone in accordance with the National Income Doubling Program. Even in this period, a policy of food self-sufficiency was maintained in order to avoid consuming foreign currency reserves through food imports, reflecting constraints on the balance of payments which were serious fiscal and financial issues. The income disparity that existed between rural and urban areas was regarded as a problem, and the Agricultural Basic Law was enacted in 1961 with the intention to raise farm product prices, particularly rice prices, in order to prevent the rapid migration of the labor force from rural to urban areas. Rice prices rose 10 percent or more in the 1960s. At the same time, as a result of the introduction of farm machinery as well as progress in production technologies such as fertilizers and agricultural chemicals, food self-sufficiency was attained in the latter half of the 1960s. From the 1970s and thereafter, implementation of rice production adjustment and treatment of surplus rice surfaced as major issues. Shortly after achieving food self-sufficiency, however, the importation of farm products was called for because of the need to further promote imports as a result of high economic growth. There was no longer a balance of payments constraint. Subsequently, starting with livestock products, the importation of all kinds of farm products accelerated. Throughout the 1970s, agricultural policies focused mainly on rice. Although rice prices were kept in check, production adjustment subsidies and voluntarily marketed

rice premiums were provided to serve as additional means of income redistribution.

Japan's industrial structure underwent significant changes around 1977. Companies, having overcome the oil shock, promoted lean management. Emphasis shifted from the petrochemical/heavy industries to microelectronics (ME). Globalization progressed sharply. In the period of high economic growth, agriculture had a role in attaining food self-sufficiency because of Japan's inadequate foreign currency reserves. In subsequent years, it played a two-pronged role. One role was to provide a stable food supply at low prices, and another was to act as a regulating valve to control the labor force in keeping with the cyclical fluctuation of the economy. A stable food supply at low prices was subsequently satisfied by farm product trade liberalization, and the role of a regulating valve to control the labor force was played by workers in the tertiary industry rather than those in the primary industry. From the latter half of the 1970s, those concerned with agriculture have advocated regionalism together with the idea of settlement zones in the Third Comprehensive National Development Plan. Non-farming households have come to account for 60 percent of the agricultural community. Political and economic roles of rural areas have also undergone transformation.

Deregulation of agricultural product trade, which began with liberalization of beef and oranges, started to affect rice in the 1980s. The Second Ad Hoc Commission on Administrative Reform (Second Rincho) was established in 1981. The Commission called for the reduction of price support for rice and other agricultural products, on the assumption that trade in agricultural products would be fully deregulated. Agricultural policies would shift their emphasis from an income redistribution function to agricultural life environment enhancement projects, including farm road construction/farming village drainage projects in addition to agricultural infrastructure construction program. The Agricultural Basic Law was reorganized into the Basic Law of Food, Agriculture and Rural Areas. The new Law emphasizes the importance of food security and the multifunctional roles of agriculture in the community. This Basic Law's key points are as follows:

1   The establishment of a basic plan and setting of food self-sufficiency ratio targets. The target for the food self-sufficiency ratio is to be established with the aim of improving the food self-sufficiency ratio and to serve as a guideline for domestic agricultural production and food consumption, while identifying issues which farmers and other relevant parties should address.

2   Development of a food policy emphasizing consumers. Guidelines for a healthy dietary pattern are to be set, the public's knowledge of food consumption broadened, and relevant information provided.

3   Establishment of a desired agricultural structure and development of farm management policies. Measures are to be taken to encourage efficient and stable farm management and to construct an agricultural structure in which such management can play a major part. Measures are to be taken to revitalize family farming, and to promote the incorporation of management.

4   Measures to ensure price formation reflecting appropriate market evaluation and management stability.

5   Maintaining and improving the natural cyclical function of agriculture. Agricultural production is to be developed in harmony with the environment through the proper use of agricultural chemicals and fertilizers and by improving soil fertility.

6   Compensation for disadvantages in agricultural production in hilly and mountainous areas. Support is to be provided (in the form of direct subsidies) to help maintain adequate agricultural production activities.

KENJI ISHIHARA

airline industry

In a rapidly changing and highly competitive global business environment, Japan's airline industry has faced considerable challenges during the 1990s. The three major airlines in Japan, **Japan Airlines** (JAL), All Nippon Airways (ANA) and Japan Air System have all been affected by the prolonged recession in Japan, the steeply **appre-**

ciating yen, rising fuel prices, high airport usage and landing fees, and the deregulation of the domestic airline industry.

Deregulation

Deregulation of the Japanese aviation industry commenced in 1985 with the granting of permission to ANA and JAS to operate internationally. In March 1986, ANA began scheduled international service from Tokyo to Guam. Until then, JAL was the only Japanese carrier allowed to fly regularly scheduled international routes and the Ministry of Transport coordinated all domestic routes served by Japanese airlines. In 1986, the Japanese government relinquished its investment in JAL and JAL became a private corporation. As a part of the government administrative reform movement, the previous system of route allocation was abolished. Deregulation eventually resulted in the removal of restrictions on overlapping or multi-tracking routes and the partial liberation of air fares. A significant result of deregulation was the take off of Skymark Airlines in September 1998 and the commencement of daily service from Haneda Airport to Fukuoka at half the cost in air fares charged by other domestic carriers. Equally important was the fact that Skymark Airlines was the first new airline to be established in Japan in over thirty-five years. Another new airline that marked its inaugural flight in 1998 was Hokkaido International Airlines (Air Do) which commenced three daily round-trip flights in December between Haneda Airport and the New Chitose Airport in Sapporo, Hokkaido. The substantially lower air-fares provided by the new upstart airlines meant increased domestic competition for the other three dominant carriers.

According to Civil Aviation Bureau statistics, the Tokyo–Hokkaido and Tokyo–Fukuoka routes are the two busiest in the world, with an annual traffic of approximately 8 million and 7 million passengers respectively. Thus, in order to remain competitive, both Skymark and Air Do have instituted unique means of keeping their operational costs low. For example, Air Do flight attendants do not serve drinks or meals on their flights, however, they do have the additional task of cleaning and maintaining the cleanliness of aircraft. Skymark does not use printed tickets but makes use of thermal paper which can be inspected by staff and thus does not require expensive automated ticket readers. Not only does Skymark attempt to keep costs down, it also generates additional revenue by selling advertising space on the exterior of its aircraft fuselages.

Strategic management

The economic turbulence experienced by Japanese airlines during the 1990s was not limited to domestic routes only but extended to international routes as well. In 1994, the Transport Ministry issued a warning to JAL, ANA and JAS to reduce their labor costs in order to remain competitive with other international airlines. As a result, these three airlines postponed their plans to hire new flight attendants that year. In the meantime, JAL had already begun a program to reduce its labor costs by employing foreign flight attendants on a limited contractual basis. These foreign flight attendants were based overseas where the cost of living was substantially lower than in Japan.

Another cost-cutting measure instituted by JAL and ANA was to reduce the overall number of employees. JAL planned to reduce its personnel from 22,000 to 17,000 in the period from 1994 to 1998. Similarly, ANA planned to reduce its personnel from 15,000 to 13,500 by 1995. At ANA, this was carried out through early retirement schemes and special bonus programs for flight attendants over thirty years of age. The social impact of these reductions on employee morale was considerable as the traditional concept of **lifetime employment** at major Japanese corporations was rapidly eroded.

In keeping with the traditional employment practices of many large Japanese corporations, annual pay increases were based on one's seniority or length of service with one's company. As a result of this practice, annual labor costs increased regardless of productivity. Thus JAL, for example, has opted for expanded use of its lower cost subsidiaries such as JAL Express (JEX) on more domestic flights, JALways (formerly Japan Air Charter JAZ) for international routes, and J Air and its Okinawa-based affiliate, Japan Transocean Air for regional commuter flights.

Japan Airlines' strategy to transfer more routes to JAL subsidiaries resulted in improved productivity as determined by the International Civil Aviation Organization (ICAO) measure of cost per available ton kilometer (ATK). In 1997, JAL's cost to travel 1 kilometer carrying 1 metric ton was approximately 53 cents, compared to the world average of 47 cents. By fiscal 1998, JAL's ATK was reduced to 48 cents through efficient use of aircraft and personnel. Similar cost-cutting measures were also instituted by All Nippon Airways and Japan Air System. Both airlines restructured their workforce, froze new hiring and transferred less profitable routes to subsidiaries or to affiliated companies. For example, All Nippon Airways' subsidiaries Air Nippon (ANK) and Nippon Cargo Airlines (NCA) have lower operational costs as their employees are paid less for doing similar work

A major problem faced by both domestic and international airlines operating in and to Japan is the excessively high landing fee, which far exceeds that charged at other major airports. For example, the overall landing fee for a Boeing 747-400 at the New Tokyo International Airport, Narita, is $11,807, nearly triple the $4,361 fee for New York and nearly double the landing fee of $6,685 for Paris. Furthermore, the Japanese government has set a very high fuel tax. Ballantyne (2000: 19) reports that for JAL alone, fees and fuel tax account for some 24 percent of the domestic operating costs and 14 percent of total operating costs. There is very little likelihood of a lower landing fee or lower fuel tax as there are limited airport slots available.

Resource optimization

In addition to changes in human resources management to improve productivity, Japanese airlines have had to resort to other means to maintain global outreach and competitive advantage. The management strategies employed by each of the Japanese airlines, however, differed somewhat in addressing issues that developed from the liberalization of global aviation markets. In October 1999, All Nippon Airways joined the Star Alliance, which consists of several leading airlines such as United Airlines, Lufthansa, Air Canada, SAS, Thai, Ansett Australia and several other airlines. In contrast, as of August 2000, Japan Airlines has not joined a major alliance but has continued to establish code-shared arrangements with various airlines that belong to competing alliances. Similarly, Japan Air System has embarked on code-shared routes but not as extensively as JAL.

One major benefit of joining an alliance or code-shared arrangement with other airlines is that customers are able to take advantage of a much wider and seamless airline route network. At the same time, both customer services (such as more convenient flight schedules, joint use airport lounges, and reciprocal frequent flyer programs) and operational services (flight and briefings, maintenance, ramp facilities, and catering) are considerably enhanced.

Another major benefit accruing from an alliance partnership, from an operational perspective, is that maintenance employees and the deployment of spare parts along the route network can be reduced through the reciprocal provision of both personnel and essential parts and equipment. The avoidance of duplication results in savings that can be passed on to customers.

Kizuki system

The success of an alliance, code-sharing or related partnership arrangement ultimately depends on the firm understanding and integration of human factors throughout the system. In the case of Japan Airlines maintenance, the company has developed a system of responsibility known as the *kizuki* system which consists of a group of dedicated engineers and mechanics to maintain and monitor the performance of the aircraft to which they are assigned. The term *kizuki* is a combination of *ki*, which refers to aircraft, and *zuki*, which means "to stick to." A keen sense of responsibility and special attachment to each aircraft assigned to the maintenance personnel are developed by having the names of the team leaders and their titles – for example chief engineer or mechanic – prominently displayed on the cockpit bulkhead. Group loyalty and pride in the well-being of the crew and flight safety are thus achieved. Maintenance crew members must be well coordinated in their scheduling of tasks to cover the various shift cycles

necessary to handle various aircraft arrivals and departures.

From a productivity perspective, the *kizuki* system and **kaizen** in Japanese aviation is best illustrated by the educational and training programs provided by the major Japanese airlines. In order to develop human resources management skills in addition to various technical skills, courses on the principles of management and organizational behavior, error management, risk assessment, quality standards, problem consciousness and creativity are provided. From a *kaizen* perspective, discussions are held on how to examine and improve the organization as well as specific procedures associated with daily tasks that can be instituted.

Technological change and crew resource management

For Japan Airlines, All Nippon Airways and Japan Air System, the introduction of advanced jet aircraft and the computerization of the cockpit created an urgent requirement to integrate human knowledge into their traditional training curricula. The traditional perspective on organizational behavior in which operational directives flowed from the captain to his crew was no longer satisfactory for the highly complex computerized flight management system. Since human errors do occur when programming flight plan data, new procedures required a cross-checking of procedures and data inputs prior to executing instructions via the flight management system.

New training procedures focused initially on improving cockpit communication between the captain and his first officer. This enabled them to operate as a cohesive team in which greater situation awareness was achieved and maintained during flight. At the outset, the concept was known as Cockpit Resource Management; however, with the inclusion of extremely sophisticated flight entertainment and other medical systems on modern jumbo aircraft, it became necessary to expand the concept to Crew Resource Management (CRM) to recognize the important role provided by flight attendants.

CRM training programs at the three major Japanese airlines differ slightly in their contents as each of the airlines has different operating routes and conditions as well as different corporate cultures. However, the basic conceptual and philosophical elements are similar in that the main objective is to provide a greater appreciation and respect for what each crew member's skills and responsibilities are so that crucial decisions can be made on the basis of having full knowledge of a given situation. Situation awareness at all times during a flight is most important from a flight safety perspective.

Future outlook

The challenges resulting from the deregulation of the Japanese aviation industry are being met directly by Japanese airlines through **restructuring** of their respective organizations and by joining alliances or by entering into code-shared arrangements with other airlines. The benefits that have accrued from these strategies are at best short-term solutions. The rapidly evolving technological changes in the aviation industry have proceeded much more rapidly than the institutional changes necessary to accommodate the technology-driven economic circumstances. Japan's aviation industry must recognize the highly competitive global aviation environment as well as the domestic transportation environment. In the deregulated market, sweeping reductions in personnel and wage cuts can only be a short-term measure. The increasing surplus of airline capacity will impact on Japanese airlines through competitive airfare pricing, and thus, reduced revenue. This calls for greater rationalization of routes through either alliances, or bilateral code-sharing arrangements on international routes.

On the Japanese domestic scene, the new start-up airlines have not impacted on the major airlines to any great extent as airport slots are limited and thus competition has been controlled indirectly. The greatest competition in the nation's most heavily travelled corridor, however, comes from the *shinkansen* bullet train service. It remains to be seen whether or not the airlines will not only lower their airfares but also provide more frequent service through better scheduling and avoidance of simultaneous flight departures.

Further reading

Ballantyne, T. (2000) "Deregulation," *Orient Aviation* July: 16–19.

Saito, M. (1993) "Challenges to Human Factors Issues in JAL Maintenance," in *Human Factors in Aviation*, Montreal: International Air Transport Association, 187–195

Ujimoto, V. (1997) "Changes, Challenges, and Choices in the Japanese Aviation Industry: The Development of Crew Resource Management in Japan Airlines," in H. Millward and J. Morrison (eds), *Japan at Century's End*, Halifax: Fernwood Publishing Ltd, 150–60.

Yamamori, H. (1993) "Keeping CRM is Keeping the Flight Safe," in E.L. Weiner, B.G. Kanki and R.L. Helmreich (eds), *Cockpit Resource Management*, New York: Academic Press, 399–420.

VICTOR K. UJIMOTO

Ajinomoto

In 1908, Dr. Kikunae Ikeda discovered that glutamic acid was a source of flavoring for food and immediately patented his discovery. He named the seasoning Ajinomoto and sold his discovery to Saburonosuke Suzuki in 1917, the founder and first president of Suzuki Shoten. Suzuki subsequently changed the company name to Ajinomoto Co., Inc. due to the success of the Ajinomoto brand.

Today, Ajinomoto has four main product segments in the food business: seasoning, edible oils, processed foods, and beverages and dairy products. In the seasoning segment, the company has many products. Most Japanese housewives have used seasonings such as Cook-Do and Gohan Ga Susumu Kun seasonings designed to enhance flavor and save cooking time for busy housewives. Ajinomoto has always focused upon expanding its product line to meet the tastes of people as well as serve their need for time savings and convenience.

In the chemicals segment, there are three main product lines: amino science, feed-use amino acids and pharmaceuticals. These lines include such products as sweeteners, pharmaceutical intermediates, functional nutritional foods and ingredients for cosmetics and toiletries.

In the amino science segment, Ajinomoto uses

amino acids as raw materials in clinical nutrition products, gastrointestinal medicines and hypertension medications. Because of continuously changing eating habits and increasing health consciousness, the demand for a sweetener by amino acid has been increasing. These products are in Japan as well as in North America, Europe, Southeast Asia, and South Africa. In the feed-use amino acids segment, Ajinomoto has a 35 percent worldwide market share for feeds containing lysine. In the pharmaceuticals segment, Ajinomoto focuses research and product development on health issues such as diabetes, infusions, clinical nutrition, gastrointestinal diseases and cardiovascular diseases.

In fiscal 1999, worldwide sales topped ¥8 trillion ($800 million) of which foods accounted for 72.2 percent, fine chemicals for 16.2 percent and other products 11.6 percent. Ajinomoto is the sixth largest company in the food industry in Japan. Although its domestic market share has remained stable, recently, it has become more difficult for Ajinomoto to expand its business in Japan, due to fierce competition and changing economic factors. Thus, the company has focused efforts on building its business overseas, which still only accounts for about 15 percent of its overall sales.

Currently, the Ajinomoto seasoning is sold in more than 100 countries. Since Ajinomoto opened its first overseas office in New York in 1917, the company has internationalized its business. Today, the company's products are produced and sold all over the world. Recently Ajinomoto expanded into China, Vietnam and Myanmar. The company's strategy for globalization is to understand each country's situation and to behave like a domestic company. In spite of health warnings about the possible ill effects of monosodium glutamate, annual worldwide sales are growing at about 6 percent per year. Ajinomoto now supplies almost one-third of the global market for monosodium glutamate

MARGARET TAKEDA
AYA KUBOTA

Akihabara

Akihabara, commonly referred to as Electric Town or Electric City, is an area in downtown Tokyo famous for its concentration of shops selling electrical and electronic products. Located in the Kanda district of Tokyo, the area is crowded with large shops where electronic goods of all varieties are sold at a discount, and small stalls in the side streets and under the elevated train tracks where electronic parts are sold.

In Japan, and to a lesser extent overseas, Akihabara is famous as a showcase for Japanese electronic technology. In Akihabara, practically any electric gadget or appliance can be found, from digital audio recorders the size of a stick of gum to the latest handheld organizers that let you surf the internet, to more mundane items such as washers and refrigerators. The area is also well known for its discounted prices.

With so many stores crammed in the few blocks surrounding Akihabara station carrying electronic products, competition is fierce. Each store vies with its hundred's of competitors to carry the latest, the smallest, the most powerful versions of differing goods. Store displays change from day to day depending on what new goods have come in. Price competition is also strong, and most stores, in an effort to keep prices low, spend the bare minimum on interior design. Products are stacked on metal shelves, or from the floor to the ceiling. Price cards are usually handwritten, as are posters outside the stores announcing the day's specials. The stalls selling electronic components are tiny cubicles crammed with items in a layout only understood by the stall keeper. Above all, the noise, the crowds, and the hustle and bustle of Akihabara resemble an open-air flea market more than a clearing center of sophisticated high-tech product.

The area where Akihabara is located was originally the site of a vast clearing. This open field was created by local authorities as a firebreak after a devastating fire ravaged Tokyo in 1870. Eventually, the clearing was surrounded by trees, and became known as Akibonohara, the Field of Autumn Leaves. In 1890, the Sobu train line built a train station on Akibonohara. Yet, a misinterpretation of the three *kanji* (ideograms) forming the station name "Akibonohara" resulted in the pronunciation of the name as Akihabara.

When Tokyo's Yamanote line also reached Akihabara station with elevated train tracks in the early twentieth century, Akihabara became a major center of goods being transported through-out the capital. Yet the impetus for Akihabara's rise as a commercial district was the elevated train tracks themselves. During Japan's immediate post-war period, hundreds of black-marketers set up stalls beneath the tracks in Akihabara. At the time, the majority sold hard to get radio and electrical parts. As Japan's economy entered its high growth period in the 1960s, Akihabara's stall-keepers began expanding their wares to include household appliances such as refrigerators, televisions and washing machines, as post-war demand for these items surged.

Over the years, Akihabara's storekeepers be-came respectable merchants, and their presence attracted established electronic retailers. Yet the influence of Akihabara's black market days lives on in its free-wheeling style and its hodgepodge of shops and stalls. It is estimated that within the multiple square blocks occupied by Akihabara, there are now over 600 stores selling electric and electronic equipment and parts.

The main street running through the heart of Akihabara, Chuo-dori, is lined with stores that sell the latest electronic gadgets and appliances. Many stores specialize in particular goods, such as household appliances, computers, or audio equip-ment. However, most carry a wide variety of goods like phones, fax machines, computers, heaters, air conditioners, televisions, VCRs, video games and so on. The majority of these shops have a small floor space, but are several stories high and covered with neon signs. Many of the larger stores segregate their products by floor, with washers and dryers on one floor, fax machines and telephones on another, and cellular phones on yet another.

Specialty stores, such as those that concentrate only on audio-visual equipment, or on digital cameras and camcorders, abound. There are also many duty-free shops crammed with electronic goods for export, catering to the many tourists who visit Akihabara. In addition, there are discount stores carrying huge arrays of electronic gadgets at discounted prices, and also stores that exclusively carry used electronic products.

As well as the specialty stores lining the main street, a few hundred stalls filled with hundreds of products are still located beneath the train tracks. These stalls have only enough room for the vendor,

and are stocked with thousands of electronic components, such as capacitors, vacuum tubes, adapters, transistors, circuit boards, etc. The do-it-yourself fanatic can find any part needed, regard-less of how obscure it may be.

With the rise of the computer generation, in the latter 1990s a large number of shops have emerged in Akihabara that exclusively carry computers, peripherals and software. Many Japanese high-tech companies use Akihabara either to test new products' acceptance, or to conduct consumer surveys. With its concentration of well over 600 stores dealing exclusively with electrical and electronic goods, Akihabara draws crowds of consumers daily. Japanese electronic firms con-tinuously make use of this fact to test new products' marketability. The lifespan of some of these products in Akihabara is less than one month. Those that prove successful are taken to full production and released nationwide, and even-tually to overseas markets. Consumer surveys are also carried out so often in Akihabara that shoppers have been known to complain that filling out survey forms takes more time than shopping.

SEAN MOONEY

allowances and non-salary compensation

Allowances and other non-salary benefits comprise an important portion of an average Japanese employee's overall compensation package. Though the actual percentage amount of an employee's total compensation package tied up in allowances and non-salary benefits may vary significantly based on several key factors, estimates generally set it at somewhere between 25 and 35 percent. The specific types of allowances remain fairly stable across industries and across firms within an industry. However, the size of specific allowances is often closely aligned with a company's relative ranking within the industry and the industry's relative position within the private sector. In the latter part of the twentieth century, adjustments in allowances and non-salary compensation often occupied a more central position during the spring labor offensive (*shunto*), than did hourly wage and semi-annual bonuses.

Allowances and non-compensation benefits reflect both the historical roots of Japanese organizations and a pragmatic approach to addressing the current economic and sociocultural constraints of modern Japan. The practice of providing allowances and benefits, over and above wages and salary, can be traced back to the ***ie*** of pre-Meiji Japan. For example, loyal ***banto*** and *tedai* (clerks) in the merchant houses could expect some assistance from the *ie* in buying their own house or in renting living quarters. In the immediate postwar period, at a time when many firms were confronted with liquidity problems, allowances represented one way of attracting and retaining employees without having to significantly increase cash outlays for wages and salaries. During extended periods of economic growth in the 1960s and 1970s, and into the 1980s when Japanese economic prosperity was at its height, allowances remained a critical component of the average employee's compensation package because the benefits had come to be seen as an integral part of the overall package, and because the value of some allowances represented a significant value not available outside the firm. For example, newly hired single salarymen (see **salaryman**) are often housed in company dorms where the monthly rent may be less than one-third the cost of comparable housing on the open market.

The effect of having such a large number of allowances and having them constitute such a large percentage of an employee's total compensation package is not inconsequential in its impact on intra-firm and inter-firm wage differentials. In the case of inter-firm differentials, employees of two firms may start out with monthly salaries that differ by only five or six thousand yen. However, once differences in allowances are factored in the final amount of difference can be in excess of ¥30,000 or more. Calculated over a full year, such a difference becomes substantial.

A second effect of allowances is to dilute the impact of merit-based increases in salary. Allowances are provided on a non-merit basis to all employees. For example, an outstanding single employee living in a company apartment receives the same housing allowance as does an average

single employee in the same apartment. Similarly, allowances can also reduce the differential effect of tenure. A thirty-year-old married employee with two pre-school children will receive the same family allowance as a married middle manager with two high school-age children.

A typical package of allowances and non-compensation benefits would include the following: family allowance (covering both spouse and children); housing allowance; transportation allowance; paid holidays; paid annual vacation; leaves of absence; company-sponsored health insurance; company-subsidized home loans at favorable terms; and access to special consideration and discount packages through company-arranged consumer goods and services purchasing programs. The relative size of these benefits has, over time, come to be fairly standard among firms. Nevertheless, there are important differences from industry to industry and from firm to firm. These differences reflect variances in working conditions, geographical factors and a firm's relative position within the industry and corporate culture and personnel practices. Top-ranked firms tend to offer more generous allowances than lower ranked firms. With regard to differences in corporate culture and personnel practices, many corporations have developed distinctive orientations reflecting underlying corporate values which then become codified in personnel practices that become institutionalized over time. In the case of the corporate values, Pioneer, for example, has always tended to provide more generous family allowances than other firms in the electronics industry.

Family allowance

Family allowance refers to a monthly allowance that is paid to employees to cover the additional cost of supporting dependents. It assumes that employees (who are overwhelmingly male) are the sole income-earner in the household and therefore require additional support to fulfill this role. Indeed, married employees are referred to as "income earners." Although there is some variation in how the allowance is calculated, in most firms the allowance for the first dependent – which is assumed to be the spouse – will be significant. The incremental increase in allowance for a second dependent and any others thereafter will be significantly lower. For example, in 1991 **Toyota** paid a monthly family allowance of ¥19,500 for the first dependent and ¥3,500 for a second dependent. Variations on this allowance tend to occur in two areas. Although rare, some firms make no distinction between the first dependent and subsequent dependents. In firms where this is the case, the first dependence allowance is usually lower than industry average, but the subsequent dependent allowance is two to three times higher. The second area where firms may vary their practice is whether the size of allowance for subsequent dependents will vary based on number; that is, the allowance is larger for the second dependent than it is for the third or fourth. Again, in some firms the allowance per dependent remains constant regardless the number of dependents, in others it will decrease. Returning to the Toyota example, the allowance for dependents two and three would have been ¥3,500 each, but the allowance for a third or more dependents would have dropped to ¥2,000 each. By comparison, in that same year, Daihatsu Motors paid a first dependent allowance of ¥13,000 and a second dependent (and all subsequent dependents) allowance of ¥3,500. Differences between Toyota and Daihatsu in first dependent allowance reflect their relative positions within the automotive industry, whereas differences in second and subsequent dependent allowances reflect differences in corporate culture and personnel practice. This type of difference persists across all allowances.

Housing allowance

Of all the allowances that companies provide, the greatest variation can be found in the housing allowance. Differences in the geographic location of employment create the need for most companies to develop contingencies. For example, the cost of housing for a single employee working at a corporate headquarters in Osaka may be significantly higher than the cost a single-family dwelling for a married employee working at a manufacturing facility in Matsue. Marital status and whether an employee has an apartment or a single-family dwelling are two other factors influencing housing allowance policy. Finally, many companies place an age cap on the housing allowance, usually 40 years old. Employees are expected to have purchased their own home (possibly by means of a company-subsidized low-interest rate mortgage) by that age.

To understand variations in housing allowances, compare two companies: Fujitsu and Toshiba in the mid-1990s. At Fujitsu, a housing allowance is available to single employees over twenty-two years old until they reach thirty. Income earners (married employees) will receive an allowance for thirteen years or age forty, which ever comes first. For both singles and income earners, this salary varies by geographic location and is lower for singles. For income earners, Tokyo and Kanagawa employees the most, followed by those in Osaka, Hyogo, Chiba and Tokyo satellites receiving less and employees anywhere else in Japan receiving the least. For singles, the first two classifications remain, however, single employees outside of the Tokyo and Osaka metropolitan areas receive no housing allowance. Toshiba divides housing along geographic lines as well, with those in Tokyo receiving more than those outside metropolitan areas. Also, singles receive a lower allowance than income earners. Lastly, Toshiba provides a supplement to those employees not in company housing, but renting on their own.

Transportation allowance

Many companies provide transportation allowance to employees working in metropolitan areas or in areas where it is expensive or unrealistic for employees to use their own transportation to get to and from work. The typical allowance covers the cost of train and bus passes from the residence to work.

Non-salary benefits

Non-salary benefits include such items as holidays, paid vacations and leaves of absence. There are twelve national holidays, although the norm in most companies is to have all twelve days off, there is widespread variation among those companies that do observe all twelve, ranging from eleven days all the way down to four. Additional holidays may include the company's founding day, and personal memorial days (involving familial responsibilities relating to religious observances).

Paid vacation days vary by tenure. Most companies offer 14–15 paid vacation days after the first year, up to a maximum of twenty days after ten years of service. Given the tendency of most employees not to take their full allotment of paid vacation days, companies also have policies pertaining to the transfer of vacation days from one year to the next. In a few firms, employees can transfer vacation days over a two-year period, but for the vast majority the limit on transfers is no more than one year.

Companies grant leaves of absence for marriage, funeral services and childbirth. As with the family allowance, there is widespread variation across firms, most often reflecting firm-specific choices. The longest leaves are granted for mourning. For a spouse, parent or child, the average leave granted is seven days. For one's own grandparents or brothers and sisters, the average is five days. Leaves for other relations tend be shorter: a spouse's parents (five days), grandchildren (three days), children's spouses (two days) and aunts and uncles (one day). Leave for what are classified as happy events – marriage, spouse's childbirth and children's marriage – average five days, three days and three days respectively.

Changes over time

The variety and size of allowances companies offer has evolved over time in response to economic pressures and to changing mores regarding what companies should and should not do for their employees. More recently, particularly in the 1990s, the trend has been to reduce the size of allowances and increase the size of the base salary component in the overall compensation calculation. A change has been the lowering impact of company rank within industry on allowances. In response to an aging workforce, a labor shortage among new recruits, increased competition and the presence of non-Japanese firms offering a variety of, for Japanese, non-typical incentives such as stock options, Japanese firms have been experimenting. As with other elements of the Japanese management system, this is an area where further

changes will occur, though their direction is difficult to predict.

See also: lifetime employment; seniority promotion

Further reading

Brown, C., Nakata, Y., Reich, M. and Ulman, L. (1997) *Work and Pay in the United States and Japan*, New York: Oxford University Press.

Japan Council of Metalworkers' Union (Annual) *Wages and Working Conditions*, Tokyo.

Tachibanaki, T. (1996) *Wage Determination and Distribution in Japan*, New York: Oxford University Press.

ALLAN BIRD

amakudari

Amakudari (descent from heaven) refers to the re-employment of high-ranking civil servants to key positions in diverse sectors of Japanese society upon their retirement from the central bureaucracy. The literal translation as "descent from heaven" invokes the cultural symbolism of working in the bureaucracy and implies a distinction between the life of the sacred and the profane. Before the Second World War, civil servants worked directly for the emperor who was considered sacred, a god, and the embodiment of the Japanese nation. Bureaucrats were seen as in heaven by their noble and sacred work for the god and the nation. Upon retirement, bureaucrats were viewed as descending in status by re-employment in the profane world of material self-interest.

The pressures arising out of the seniority system within ministries feed *amakudari*. Entering civil servants, upon passing the civil servant exam (type 1) and being selected to the ministry, receive extensive training and advance together as a cohort. As they reach their forties, their career mobility options begin to narrow. There are few section chief positions, fewer bureau chief positions, and only one vice-ministership for each ministry. The final weeding out process comes when a new vice-minister is chosen and all the new vice-minister's classmates and earlier cohorts resign to insure that the new vice-minister has absolute seniority within the ministry. Ultimately, everyone must "descend" because of the unremitting pressure from new entering classes advancing from below. The usual retirement age for the vice-minister is slightly over fifty, but retirement age varies across ministries. The new vice-minister and the chief of the Secretariat are responsible for finding the retiring officials good positions in the private or public sectors.

Discussion of *amakudari* has increasingly penetrated the western literature on Japanese social structure, especially within the topics of the Japanese "power structure," "Iron Triangle" or "**Japan Inc.**" *Amakudari* is viewed as a key institutional arrangement fusing relationships among the political, economic and bureaucratic operations. This imagery of *amakudari* as power structure is partially the result of perceived differences between the USA and Japan. The USA tends to separate the executive bureaucracy from the economic market and legislative political processes with the conviction that separate spheres produce the best results for everyone. This separation is celebrated in principles of checks and balances, the *laissez-faire* tradition, an open market economy, and a weak state bureaucracy with strict limits on government regulation. Japan, by contrast, is characterized as fusing these linkages through extensive formal and informal relationships in the belief that these ties induce cooperation and produce the best outcome for all.

Definitions

Conventional usage of *amakudari* is generic. It simply means the different ways in which civil servants exploit their positions for post-retirement careers. Analytic usage differentiates the major paths of *amakudari* by destinations. The most widely known definition of *amakudari* is a movement to profit-making enterprises and is subject to legal restrictions. The second form of *amakudari* is a movement to public corporations that are established by law and financed in part from public funds. It is sometimes called "sideslip" (*yokosuberi*) and is not subject to legal restrictions. The third form of *amakudari* is a movement into the political world, by becoming a candidate for election to the Diet. It is sometimes called "position exploitation" (*chii riyo*) and is usually open to those who served in choice national or regional posts suitable for building political support. Another, though less well-known, form of *amakudari* is a movement from central government to local government or industrial associations. Finally, *amakudari* may involve a sequence of retirement positions in the career of an ex-civil servant. This multi-step retirement process is called "migratory bird" (*wataridori*). *Wataridori* among some public corporations is regulated by the Diet, but it is a prevalent, institutionalized pattern of re-employment among top level ex-civil servants. These five forms of *amakudari* are interrelated. Discussion of all the paths provides a more holistic appreciation of why *amakudari* constitutes a key element of the Japanese power structure.

History of *amakudari*

There is no consensus on the origin of *amakudari*. In part, this ambiguity results from different interpretations of what constitutes *amakudari*. It began as a diffuse movement of individuals between ministries and the private sector or public offices reaching back to at least the beginning of the Meiji period (1868–1912). However, after the Second World War these diffuse flows became controlled and routinized within the administrative apparatus of each ministry and agency.

There are scattered references to the movement of government officials into the business sector that occurred during the early Meiji period. A popular novelist and social critic, Uchida Roan (1868–1929) used the term *amakudaru* (noun form of *amakudari*) in his social criticism, entitled *Shakai hyakumenso* (Society of Kaleidoscope) published in 1902. Uchida may be the one who coined the term *amakudari*. Later scholars wrote of an emerging distinction in forms of retirement (*amakudari* and *chii riyo*) between 'economic' and 'social' ministries. Kubota (1969) and Garon (1987) suggest that after the First World War those retiring from 'economic' ministries, such as the Ministry of Finance and the Ministry of Agriculture and Commerce, drew on "contacts with business clientele" to take top positions in private corporations (*amakudari*). Retiring bureaucrats from "social" bureaucracies, such as Home Ministry tended to remain within government or joined political parties, often with cabinet appointments (*chii riyo*).

The pivotal distinction for identifying the origin of *amakudari* is whether one defines it as a routinized personnel movement orchestrated by the ministries, or a movement based exclusively on individual initiative. *Amakudari* before the Second World War was individually negotiated and primarily restricted to retired army and navy personnel. After the war the number of *yokosuberi* expanded as the number of public corporations rose and ministries assumed more responsibility for placing their retirees. A recent survey of high-ranking ex-officials by Cho (1995) found that three times as many *amakudari* officials attributed their retirement positions to ministry placements instead of individual contacts.

Different views of amakudari

There is general agreement among scholars on the existence of *amakudari* but there are disagreements over its interpretation. Chalmers Johnson (1974, 1978) popularized the concept of *amakudari* in his discussion of the Japanese developmental state. He suggested *amakudari* as "maintaining coordination and cooperative interactions among the iron triangle of Japanese power elites – an aspect of what the Japanese call *nemawashi* ('preparing the groundwork') and what foreigners describe as consensual decision making among the bureaucracy, the conservative party, and the business community." According to Johnson, the cooperation and avoidance of conflict attributed to "national character" is really the outgrowth of institutions like *amakudari* facilitating common orientations and cooperative ties between the government, private sector, and the political world.

Daniel Okimoto (1989) built on Johnson's work by discussing *amakudari* in the context of numerous relationships that make Japan's industrial policy effective. He called the public-private relationships "the network of ad hoc, informal ties that give industrial policy and government-business interactions the resilience and adaptability for which Japan is renowned." For Okimoto, *amakudari* is the best unobtrusive indicator of relative bureaucratic power *vis-à-vis* other ministries.

Other scholars, such as Peter Evans (1995) and T.J. Pempel (1998), see *amakudari* as ties binding the bureaucracy and private corporations and representing the basis of "state embeddedness" resulting in policy effectiveness. Like Johnson and Okimoto, these authors treat *amakudari* as a flexible and principal empirical illustration, not of elite cohesion *per se*, but of the embeddedness of the developmental state (using Japan as the archetypal developmental state). Evans views *amakudari* as providing institutionalized channels for the continual negotiation and re-negotiation of goals and policy. Similarly, Pempel (1998) sees *amakudari* as the "blurring of the line between elected officials and career civil servants" and the development and maintenance of ties between private interests and particular ministries of the central government. To Pempel, *amakudari* is the stuff of inter-elite cooperation and alliances, fusing of the state with the public and private sectors, providing the basis for stability and development. Pempel, however, sees the bases of this fusion as undergoing substantial changes in the 1990s.

In contrast, some authors challenge the notion of *amakudari* representing elite cohesion and policy effectiveness. Calder (1989) questions the utility of *amakudari* as a mechanism of elite cohesion much less bureaucratic dominance. Instead, *amakudari* simply "broadens the access of less economically powerful firms." The bureaucracy exercises a limited influence through *amakudari* since it is mostly concentrated in second tier, weak private corporations, not in top corporations and banks. Other authors, following Calder, maintain *amakudari* is not sufficient to affect industrial direction since it involves a small number of firms (less than 10 percent of the listed firms in any one year) and takes place mostly in small, not large firms. In addition, they point to a weakening significance of former officials in political office since the 1990s as the number of former civil servants in political office declines.

In summary, various scholars agree on a high level of interaction, communication and cooperation among politicians, career bureaucrats and business people throughout the postwar era, but they disagree on the interpretation of *amakudari* as important inter-institutional relations. To some authors, *amakudari* represents elite cohesion providing the stability, flexibility, and effectiveness of state policy. Others question the effectiveness of this type of elite cohesion. Further, some authors distinguish different forms of *amakudari* (for example, *amakudari*, *yokosuberi*, *chii riyo*, and *wataridori*) that represent distinct analytic and empirical phenomena. Finally, scholars are in agreement that inter-institutional (inter-elite) relations began changing in the 1990s, though they differ on the degree of change, its interpretation, and direction. International markets, a new electoral system, a realignment of voters, weakening linkages of the major *keiretsu*, and a reduction in the policy tools of the bureaucrats are seen as causes of changing relations among the bureaucracy, private sector and the legislature.

Limitations

There is substantial recognition that Japan is a network society and the Japanese state is a network state embedded in Japanese society. *Amakudari* is but one type of network between the state and Japanese society among a myriad of crisscrossing, overlapping, and multiplex relationships. However, *amakudari* is the apex of networks. *Amakudari* and *amakudari*-like processes operate everywhere in Japan, including the personnel movements from large to medium and medium to small affiliated companies. Similar personnel movements take place from the central bureaucracy to local governments and from local governments to private and public sectors and local political offices. Thus, any analysis of *amakudari* is at best a "biopsy" of the networking. In this sense, we only scratch the surface of a fundamental socioeconomic Japanese institution.

See also: nemawashi

Further reading

Blumenthal, T. (1985) "The Practice of *Amakudari* within the Japanese Employment System," *Asian Survey* 25(3): 310–21.

Calder, K. (1989) "Elites in an Equalizing Role: Ex-bureaucrats as Coordinators and Intermediaries in the Japanese Government-Business Relationship," *Comparative Politics* 21(4): 379–404.

Cho, K.C. (1995) "Nihon no Seifu & Kigyo kankei

to Seifu Shigen Douin no Osmotic Networker to shite no Amakudari," Ph.D. dissertation, Tsukuba University, Japan.

Evans, P. (1995) *Embedded Autonomy: States and Industrial Transformation*, Princeton, NJ: Princeton University Press.

Garon, S. (1987) *The State and Labor in Modern Japan*, Berkeley, CA: University of California Press.

Inoki, T. (1995) "Japanese Bureaucrats at Retirement: the Mobility of Human Resources from Central Government to Pubic Corporations," in H. Kim *et al.* (eds), *The Japanese Civil Service and Economic Development*, Oxford: Clarendon Press, 213–34.

Johnson, C. (1974) "The Reemployment of Retired Government Bureaucrats in Japanese Big Business," *Asian Survey* 14: 953–65.

—— (1978) *Japan's Public Policy Companies*, Washington, DC: American Enterprise Institute for Public Policy Research.

Koh, B.C. (1991) *Japan's Administrative Elite*, Berkeley, CA: University of California Press.

Kubota, A. (1969) *Higher Civil Servants in Postwar Japan: Their Social Origins, Educational Backgrounds, and Career Patterns*, Princeton, NJ: Princeton University Press.

Okimoto, D. (1989) *Between MITI and the Market: Japanese Industrial Policy for High Technology*, Stanford, CA: Stanford University Press.

Pempel, T.J. (1998) *Regime Shifts: Comparative Dynamics of the Japanese Economy*, Ithaca, NY: Cornell University Press.

Schaede, U. (1995) "The 'Old Boy' Network and Government-Business Relationships in Japan," *Journal of Japanese Studies* 21(2): 293–317.

Usui, C. and Colignon, R. (1995) "Government Elites and Amakudari in Japan, 1963–1992," *Asian Survey* 35(7): 682–98.

RICHARD COLIGNON

American occupation

By August of 1945 Japan lay utterly defeated, completely at the mercy of the victors. Fortunately for Japan, what the USA wished was to transform Japan from an authoritarian, militaristic, elitist and internally exploitative society into a society more like its own, which the Americans saw as more pluralistic, democratic, egalitarian, and without the influence of a virtually uncontrolled military which had caused so much suffering throughout Asia (see **wartime legacy**), and indeed within Japan itself. The United States virtually ruled Japan for over six years, instituting many changes and reforms. All in all, observers both American and Japanese evaluate the American occupation of Japan as highly successful.

By 1944, although it was not clear how long the war would last, everyone on the American side knew that the end was near in terms of Japan's ability to sustain military conflict. There was considerable debate within the War Department and in congress over such issues as what should happen to the Japanese emperor. It was decided that when the war ended a large contingent of administrators would go to Japan and force major changes in Japanese institutions. Above the administrators in authority would be the United States Army; President Roosevelt chose General Douglas MacArthur to be supreme commander of the occupation administration, even though the President did not personally like the general and considered him a likely future presidential candidate for the Republican party.

Initial stages

The first Occupation officials arrived on Japanese soil August 30, 1945, fifteen days after Japanese representatives signed the formal surrender. The situation did not bode well for implementing an ambitious plan for virtually remaking a modern society. The first problem envisioned by the victors was getting the Japanese to go along with reforms dictated by its former enemy. The war had seen some of the most bitter and desperate fighting in history; physical destruction of Japanese cities was on a scale never experienced before in any country. Originally planned as a joint effort between the allied nations most directly involved in fighting against Japan: the USA, Britain, the Soviet Union, and China. It was difficult to see how any kind of successful policy making could take place among nations who were suspicious of and at times even hostile toward one another. The American who was to preside over the mix was characterized by

some as a right-wing ideologue with a mountainous ego.

In spite of all this, the six years and eight months of the formal Occupation of Japan was in the judgment of most observers a surprisingly positive and liberating force for Japan, as well as an advertisement of some of the best qualities of American culture. The fear of a resentful and hostile Japanese populace was instantly wiped away by the courtesy and cooperation of people at all levels, from ordinary citizens to high-ranking officials in the government from the very beginning. Japan had lost the war, the Emperor had declared so; there was a new ultimate authority in the nation, and almost all Japanese as a matter of course directed the same sincere respect toward it as they had to the old authority.

The problem of the multinational character of the Occupation turned out to be partially solved by the image of General MacArthur as an egomaniac. It had been agreed upon among the USA and its allies that Japan would be administered by the Allied Council for Japan (ACJ) with representation from all four nations mentioned above. Legally, General MacArthur, as Supreme Commander of the Allied Powers (SCAP), was nothing more than chairman of that body. However, MacArthur simply refused to share power with any non-American. He and his subordinates completely ignored ACJ, never once acting on any of its suggestions, and taking no note at all of its many complaints. It was in every respect an American occupation.

Although MacArthur was always firmly in command, the Occupation was not in the strictest sense a military government. He was very serious about carrying out this historically important mission successfully. Later in his memoirs he explained that what he wanted to accomplish was first to end the military power of Japan and punish war criminals, then to build sound representative government, enfranchise women, liberate farmers and workers, liberalize education, decentralize economic power, establish a free and responsible press, and finally to separate church and state. In a few cases the plan could not be completely realized, but it is remarkable how close SCAP came to fulfillment of those goals.

Before Occupation administrators could get started, three important tasks were given to the

US military: demilitarization of the country, identification and punishment of people Americans considered to be war criminals, and untangling the human mess of Japanese abroad and non-Japanese in Japan, the result of invasion, colonization and forced labor. The two million soldiers and sailors of the Imperial Army who were still in Japan, for the most part simply went home, demilitarizing themselves. Six million Japanese, about half military personnel and half civilians, were returned from territory Japan no longer controlled. Three million Taiwanese and Korean laborers, many brought to Japan by force, were brought back to their homelands by the US Navy.

A series of war crimes trials, begun prior to the end of the war in the Philippines, continued on in Japan for two years. This was the only aspect of the Occupation that was truly international: the trials were conducted by judges from eleven nations including Australia, Canada, France, India, the Netherlands, New Zealand, and the Philippines together with the four nations of the ACJ. In all, about 6,000 people were indicted as war criminals. Seven men were convicted as Class A war criminals and were hanged in September 1948, including General Tojo Hideki, Prime Minister and war minister from 1941–1944. Sixteen other Class A criminals were sentenced to life imprisonment by the international tribunal, and two others given shorter prison terms. Interestingly, far more Class C (lower level personnel charged with minor atrocities) criminals were actually put to death in trials conducted in Yokohama by the US Eighth Army, over 700 in total.

There was considerable support in Washington and elsewhere for putting the Emperor on trial for war crimes. However, General MacArthur staunchly opposed the idea, arguing that if the Emperor were humiliated in such a way it would turn many Japanese against the aims of the Occupation, and make the task of reform far more difficult, perhaps even dangerous. As with most matters in the early days of the Occupation, he got his way.

Reforming Japan

The actual administration of the conquered nation was given over to various SCAP administrative sections, or missions as they were called, roughly equivalent to the branches of the Japanese bureaucracy. Personnel were selected from the appropriate sector of US society related to its mission. Businessmen and a few professors of business for the economics mission which worked mainly with the Finance Ministry and the Ministry of International Trade and Industry; labor leaders for the mission related to labor relations which worked mainly with the Labor Ministry, and so on. They were defined as "advisors," and stayed behind the scenes, issuing SCAP "administrative guidance," a concept the Japanese were completely familiar with from the role customarily played by their own bureaucracies. It was Japanese government bureaucrats who actually carried out the policies, with SCAP personnel having little direct contact with the local population.

A new constitution was drawn up by MacArthur's staff and virtually forced on the Japanese. It was the most significant factor in the democratization of Japan, establishing sovereignty with the people through two popularly elected houses of the Diet, giving women the right to vote, clarifying the status of the Emperor as a mere figurehead, limiting the power of the police, denouncing war for all time, and providing for a host of further democratic guarantees. It was first presented to the Japanese public on March 7, 1946 as a product of the Japanese government, but obvious direct translations from English in the document suggested otherwise.

Initially SCAP planned to completely dismantle the Japanese economic system by shipping industrial equipment to the countries most damaged by Japan in the war. MacArthur eventually decided on a more moderate policy of dissolving the *zaibatsu* and establishing anti-monopoly laws. Originally established with government sponsorship, the *zaibatsu* system was closed in the sense that once it was put into place, no new large industrial competition was permitted. Suppression of the *zaibatsu* ushered in a new wave of entrepreneurial energy. Enterprises with fresh ideas joined the older established order, some enjoying great success, companies such as Honda Motors and Sony Electronics, companies which were to contribute significantly to Japan's version of the postwar "economic miracle." This window of opportunity for new industrial organizations to reach the top tier of Japan's economy began to close somewhat in the 1960s, but it never returned to totally exclusive *zaibatsu* levels. The most enduring Occupation reforms put in place by the SCAP sections related to land reforms, labor reforms and education reforms.

At war's end, about 70 percent of Japanese farmers were tenants. Under SCAP guidance, the Diet outlawed absentee landlordism, forced land-owners to sell their land to the government at very low prices, and sold it to the farmers for nominal sums, effectively transferring land to the people who actually worked it. Rent for the small percentage of land that remained under tenancy was fixed by government regulation. Today, farms remain small by the standards of industrial nations, but are highly productive per acre. This reform changed most farmers from tenant peasants to small businessmen; their standard of living in-creased dramatically during the years following land reform, and today they are among the most prosperous small farmers in the world.

A labor movement had begun in Japan in the 1920s, but by the 1930s the government had completely quashed it; work stoppage was treated as an act of treason. With the full compliance of the Supreme Commander, considered a conservative Republican, SCAP officials, some labor leaders themselves, pushed through the Diet a trade union law which guaranteed workers, including public service employees and teachers, the right to organize, engage in collective bargaining, and strike. A labor standards law was designed by SCAP setting maximum working hours, vacation, safety and sanitation safeguards, sick leaves, accident compensation, and restrictions on the hours and conditions under which women and children could work. Some of the provisions of the labor laws were later modified by the Japanese, and in some cases standards have been ignored, but the overall impact of SCAP labor reforms was extremely favorable for the working public, creat-ing conditions comparable with other industrial democracies.

Touching by far the most people were SCAP education reforms. Pre-war education in Japan was modeled somewhat on a European elitist system, completely controlled by the national government,

and considered by SCAP an instrument of ultra-nationalist and racist propaganda. The entire system was completely redesigned in both structure and philosophy to conform to American ideas; a new 6-3-3-4 structure of elementary education through college was set up under the direction of local school boards, including the Parent Teacher Association (PTA) which still plays a powerful role in Japanese education. Higher education was greatly popularized, with over 170 new universities and about 200 new junior colleges coming into existence.

Further reading

Cohen, T. (1987) *Remaking Japan: The American Occupation as a New Deal*, New York: The Free Press.

Hane, M. (1996) *Eastern Phoenix: Japan Since 1945*, Boulder, CO: Westview Press.

James, D.C. (1975) *The Years of MacArthur*, Boston: Houghton-Mifflin.

Kawai, K. (1960) *Japan's American Interlude*, Chicago: University of Chicago Press.

Reischauer, E.O. (1950) "Broken Dialogue with Japan," *Foreign Affairs*, October.

JOHN A. McKINSTRY

appraisal systems

The appraisal system in a typical large or medium-size Japanese firm follows the policies and principles gradually elaborated in the "boom years" of Japanese management during the 1980s. Although always a core part of the Japanese employment practices, it has not received as much research attention as some other features of Japanese management. However, the evolution of "Japanese" performance appraisal illustrates well the challenges and dilemmas facing Japanese companies today in the field of human resource management.

Appraisal process

How does the Japanese appraisal mechanism work? Typically, periodic appraisals of employee performance are conducted three or four times a year. Performance evaluations usually precede salary increase decisions due in April of each year, the summer and winter bonus determination, and the annual career development review, with timing dependent on the employee's status or position. In some firms, the evaluation for the annual salary increase and the career development review may be combined to reduce the number of evaluations; in others, yet another set of evaluations takes place every time an employee becomes eligible for a promotion.

During the appraisal, employees are compared to other members of their peer group and ranked accordingly. Who is in the peer group? At the start of one's career, the core peer group is the cohort of entry: employees of equal educational level (e.g. college graduates) who joined the firm during the same year. After the first promotion, the comparisons are more complex. Managers can be ranked within the original cohort, or against all others with similar tenure in the same grade, or two rankings can be combined. In this case, the rating score reflects not only employee performance relative to their peers, but also their years of tenure in particular positions.

As in many Western firms, the evaluation criteria depend on the position class. For example, one set of criteria is used up to the level of a supervisor, another for those in higher positions. Typically, the evaluations for professional employees and managers have four major components: (1) scores measuring job-related abilities such as human relations skills, business judgment, coordination, and planning; (2) scores measuring job-related attributes such as creativity, leadership, and reliability; (3) scores measuring personality-related attributes such as sociability, flexibility, confidence; and finally (4) a single achievement score. The idea behind the multiple scores is to create an environment where the employee is not made to feel that the "bottom line" – which may sometimes be beyond his control – is the only dimension of the evaluation.

There are some conceptual similarities between categories of job-related abilities and attributes and "competency models" increasingly popular in Western organizations. However, while the competency model is usually a cornerstone for an in-

depth developmental discussion with the employee, direct feedback on appraisal results is still rather rare in most Japanese firms. Only a few firms have a formal policy requiring performance feedback. In most cases, feedback is recommended, but the form of feedback is left to the discretion of individual managers. Starting the appraisal process with a self-evaluation by the employee is now an increasingly popular practice, a major change from the times when even blank appraisal forms were considered confidential.

With respect to performance feedback, there is still a widespread belief among many personnel executives that the ability to solicit information about one's standing in the organization through "back channels" is a legitimate part of the appraisal process itself, a mark of how well the employee mastered informal communication. In other words, "If you have to ask, you can't be that good."

Even if individual supervisors are willing to provide performance rating feedback to subordinates, they often cannot do more than inform an employee about what ratings were suggested. Appraisal items are marked first by the direct supervisor, then the scores are reviewed by at least two other higher level managers or executives, with an emphasis on the harmonization of standards across departments and divisions, and at each level the initial scores are subject to modification. Finally, as most companies use some version of the forced distribution approach, ratings are also adjusted at the corporate level so the final results fit the corporate guidelines. The results of these adjustments are not always transmitted back to the first-level evaluator.

However, from the first year on the job, salary increases each year contain some variance for merit, which, although very small in absolute amounts, may convey appropriate messages to employees and impart status differences within the cohort. As the information on the average increase for a given cohort is usually distributed through the company union, employees can have a reasonably good idea where they stand. Ranking results can be inferred by comparing one's paycheck with those of the peer group or with announced average salary increases. Obviously, those who received higher than the average increase encourage informal comparisons to make their success known. Those receiving less than the average would rather avoid it.

Coexistence of competition and cooperation

Intensive appraisals occur regularly from the very first year a new employee enters the firm. These evaluations clearly discriminate among employees. They have a major impact on employees' future careers, but they are a closely held secret. Therefore, the competitive nature of the appraisal and the resulting intra-cohort rankings are not very visible during the first ten–twelve years of tenure in the organization. This led many observers of Japanese companies to observe that performance evaluation in large Japanese firms is long term, based on years of careful judgments and comparisons and that **competition** for promotion does not start until later in one's career. While the first observation is correct, the second is not. In fact, when the consequences of ranking within the cohort become visible, it is usually too late to do anything about it. In most firms, the chances for recovery from low ratings are slim (see **seniority promotion**).

The fierce internal competition could create a hostile, individualistic work environment were it not for two characteristics of the Japanese work system: group-based organizations and vague job descriptions. Usually performance is evaluated relative to similar groups in the company and, therefore, each employee must cooperate with colleagues to achieve the best results. Even the best individual performers will not succeed if their unit does not perform well. What is rewarded most is credibility and ability to get things done in cooperation with others. The competition with peers is keen, but its focal point is building cooperative networks with the same people who are rivals for future promotions. This emphasis on cooperation serves as a powerful check on a divisive competitiveness.

The invisible race creates constant fears of lagging behind and being outperformed. At the same time, even those who are left behind do not have to fear losing their jobs; the system encourages internal competition while maintaining social harmony inside the organization. For an extended period of time, the vast majority of employees are treated as potential "winners," with only small differences between the top and the middle of the cohort, as opposed to a typical Anglo-Saxon system focused on early identification of high-potential "winners" with corresponding salary differentiations. The effect is to elicit full dedication and loyalty from the employees, engaging them in unending competition for as long as possible. When the cumulative impact of less than perfect rankings becomes visible in salary or promotions late in an employee career, there is always a socially acceptable way out – after all, one works hard for the company, not for money or promotions – one explanation of why work commitment of male employees in large Japanese firms tends to increase with age.

Problems with Japanese-style appraisals

The objective of the traditional Japanese appraisal system is to induce employees to work hard on behalf of the firm. Over the years it was remarkably effective, but its fundamental contradictions are now quite apparent. One major problem with the system is that in the long run, it inevitably leads to risk-avoidance. Because the chances for recovery from a low ranking are slim, employees may focus on not making any mistakes, rather than on taking the initiative. With high job security for anyone with at least close to average performance, and no incentives for bold actions, there is no surprise that the culture in many Japanese firms today resembles more a mediocre and complacent planned economy bureaucracy than the fearless global competitor of the 1980s.

The inability to manage performance is the core of the problem. The system was created in a period of rapid growth where dealing with low performance was not much of an issue – an occasional *kata-tataki* (tap on the shoulder – selective dismissal) was a sufficient deterrent and reminder to everyone to play by the rules. But what to do about a committed '**salaryman**' who works hard for long hours, yet the added value from all this effort is poor?

In the past, there were enough positions to 'park' such an employee as *madogiwazoku* (group by the window) until retirement, or in an affiliate firm, without hurting the overall results of the firm.

However, two trends made such arrangements increasingly problematic. Lower growth rates and bulging cohorts of middle management – the results of hiring sprees of more than two decades ago – clogged the hierarchy. With estimates of up to 40–60 percent of middle managers in some firms being placed in phantom jobs, the formerly virtuous cycle of competition and cooperation has degenerated into a vicious cycle of ballooning cost and paralyzed decision making.

In addition, the odds have changed. While in the past employees had a reasonable chance to be promoted at least to middle-management position, it is now all too visible that most will not make it; there is simply no more room at the top. Therefore, there is not much incentive to compete, and without internal competition, the much praised work ethic has declined very quickly. With most white-collar jobs still secure, the low output does not have any consequences, and the annual appraisal becomes an empty ritual.

A related problem with Japanese appraisal is that it is very difficult to implement in a global context, making it virtually impossible for a Japanese multinational to unify its organization in one global structure. Foreign employees generally resent the lack of direct feedback, but the lack of experience with face-to-face performance review dialogue is a serious handicap facing Japanese managers working overseas. An even more fundamental flaw is the simple fact that the labor market structures overseas are different, and the incentives embedded in the traditional Japanese appraisal – a slow but sure rise to the top – do not have much meaning.

Current changes

When the performance of a firm declines, recalibrating the appraisal process is the usual first response. Japan is no exception. Influenced by appraisal innovations introduced by foreign-owned companies, many firms are modifying evaluation criteria, or adjusting the appraisal cycle to incorporate 360-degree feedback. However, the major impact, some of it unintended, comes from changes in two areas: communication with the employee during and after the appraisal, and early and visible identification of high-potential employees.

An increasing number of firms now require managers to conduct an appraisal interview with the employee and also to inform the employee about the appraisal results. An unintended but predictable consequence is that the distribution of ratings become slanted with a vast majority of employees ranked as average or better, making it even more difficult to address the performance problems.

Early identification of high potentials is meant to stem the outflow of talent to foreign-owned firms. What it does is making obvious what was hidden before, namely that long-term decisions regarding an employee's career are made rather early. However, while the chosen few may appreciate the early recognition, for the majority of employees this is not good news. The combination of "early identification–no reselection" is just another factor lowering employee commitment.

In summary, marginal adjustments will not be of much help. The fundamental roadblock in reforming the Japanese appraisal system is the unwillingness to deal with the consequences.

VLADIMIR PUCIK

appreciating yen

Appreciating yen (AY), often called "high yen" is not simply a phrase meaning the strong value of the Japanese currency. It refers more broadly to a ceaseless upward trend, with sharp fluctuations, in the currency value of yen. This trend has had distinctive impacts on the Japanese economy and its international relations in the post-Bretton Woods era after the "Nixon shock" of 1971.

What is AY? Following the breakdown in 1973 of the multilateral pegged exchange rate system, a floating exchange rate regime was established. As part of the original system established at Bretton Woods, the yen was set at $1: ¥360. Under the floating exchange rate system, the value of the yen increased nearly fourfold. In spring of 1995 the rate stood at about $1: ¥80. In spring of 2001 it had retreated to $1: ¥108. This increase in currency value has had a direct impact on the continuous huge foreign trade and current account surpluses sustained by Japan over a nearly thirty year period. The strength of the currency has been based mainly on the strong competitive power and the tremendous export potential of Japanese manufacturing industries such as electronics, automobile, and machine industries. AY has appeared most obvious when seen in light of the performance of the US dollar, which has depreciated over the long-term trend. The depreciation of the US dollar is ascribed to the declining competitive power of American industries in the 1970s and 1980s, a period during which the US also accumulated large foreign trade deficits. The US foreign trade deficit stems mainly from purchase of Japanese imports and, since the 1980s, also purchases from many East Asian countries.

Another important feature of AY is the heavy and steep up and down movements of the exchange rate of yen that have pressured Japanese industries and firms to adapt to such urgent changes in every half a decade. The 36 percent AY from ¥360 in July 1971 to ¥264 in July 1973 was the first such movement. The second occurred between December 1975 and October 1978 when there was a 66 percent AY from ¥306 to ¥184 in October 1978. There was a third significant movement resulting beginning with a rate of ¥260 in May of 1985. The economic expansion and high interest rate policies of the Reagan administration, followed by the Plaza Agreement in September 1985 led to a 109 percent appreciation to ¥124 in May 1988. There was another appreciation, this one of 88 percent, between April 1990 (¥158) and April 1995 (¥84). The first four months of 1995 were witness to one of the more cataclysmic shifts. In early January the rate stood at $1: ¥100. By mid April of 1995, it had appreciated to $1: ¥79, as much as 20 percent AY in three months (around 70 percent annual rate of change) from ¥100 in the early January, decisively smashing any possible chance of economic recovery in Japan since the breakdown of the **bubble economy** in the early 1990s.

What are the mechanism and effects of AY? There is a "general theory" on the mechanism of a floating exchange rate system. This theory states that the floating system can adjust automatically to recover the balance of a foreign trade surplus or deficit between two countries as a result of the nominal increase (decrease) in foreign currency prices of export (import) goods in the trade surplus country (vice versa). However, the historical experiences since 1973 of Japan and US have proven that this mechanism does not necessarily work in such a symmetrical way, depending on the managerial constitution of companies in both countries. It is important to note that especially in Japan there has been a unique mechanism for firms to accelerate successively the processes of AY. In many cases, until the 1980s in particular, Japanese companies did not raise the US dollar prices of their export goods by the same degree as yen was appreciating, which means that they preferred to keep their market shares of exports in lieu of maintaining their profit margins. This is very much a Japanese orientation to competition, and stands in contrast to the typical response of US companies in international markets. In addition, "J-Curve" effects (time lag effects due to export prices determined at contract) and the increase of "follow on" exports of parts and components and equipment to subsidiary plants abroad caused Japan's foreign trade surplus to continue to increase. A vicious cycle seemed to ensue in which the yen appreciated, resulting in a larger trade surplus and leading Japanese firms to accept lower profit margins, leading to an appreciation of the yen, and so on.

The AY cycle, along with the "trade friction" between Japan and the USA, has propelled Japanese foreign direct investment (FDI) since the early 1980s. Because an AY implies and reflects high expressed price values for domestic human resources and materials it is more advantageous for **Japanese multinational enterprises** to implement local manufacturing abroad. In this context, it is especially noteworthy that AY after the 1980s has played a critical role particularly in supporting the "miracle of economic growth" in the larger East Asian region. Here, AY was not only an important factor in determining the location of Japanese FDI, it was a significant factor in the promotion of technology transfer. It was also a factor in Asian countries realizing a more competitive edge in international markets as their own currencies depreciated *vis-à-vis* the yen.

What are the main problems of AY? From a macroeconomic perspective, the cyclical and unstable nature deeply affects Japanese firms and the economy. The large scale ups and downs in exchange rates affect basic price levels in Japan and its international economic relations. From a microeconomic perspective, firms and individuals must implement 'risk management' plans to deal with the irregularly fluctuating foreign exchange. Particularly for export-oriented firms such as **Toyota** and **Sony** a single AY movement against the US dollar can result directly in the loss of several billion yen in their financial accounts. Another serious problem is foreign exchange losses for investors in foreign portfolio assets. In Japan such huge losses occurred in the third AY period, 1985–8, when many of Japanese institutional investors such as life insurance companies were heavily damaged. Notwithstanding such experience, Japanese private portfolio investors as well as public institutions such as the **Bank of Japan** have again built up enormous portfolio assets abroad. At the start of the twenty-first century, overseas portfolio assets were more than $1 trillion, mostly in the USA.

This situation is also reflected on the US approach to foreign exchange known as "high dollar policy". The main purpose of this policy has been to prevent the US economy from getting caught up in a "vicious circle" – i.e. sharp depreciation of the dollar followed by a rise of prices in import goods and then a rise in the domestic price level, a rise in interest rates and a collapse of stock markets.

Further reading

Abo, T. (ed.) (1994) *Hybrid Factory: The Japanese Production System in the United States*, Oxford: Oxford University Press.

Kawai, M. (1996) "The Japanese Yen as an International Currency: Performance and Prospects," in R. Sato, R.V. Ramachandran and H. Hori (eds), *Organization, Performance and Equity: Perspectives on the Japanese Economy*, Dordrecht: Kluwer Academic Publishers.

TETSUO ABO

Arabian Oil

Founded in 1958, with annual sales of approximately $1.8 billion in 1999, Arabian Oil is Japan's largest oil producer. The Tokyo-based firm used to operate the Khafji oilfield, a large offshore oilfield in the former neutral zone on the Saudi Arabia–Kuwait border. As a result, the Saudi Arabian and Kuwaiti government owned 11 percent of its publicly traded stock and 60 percent of its disposition rights on crude oil production.

Japan imports 99.7 percent of its oil supply, of only which 15 percent is produced by Japanese companies. In 1998, Arabian Oil produced 280,000 barrels per day, 150,000 barrels of which were exported to Japan and accounted for 4 percent of Japan's total oil imports from oilfields mined by Japanese companies. However, in February 2000 it lost an important forty-year-old concession in the Saudi Arabian section of the neutral zone due to its unwillingness to meet Saudi Arabia's demands for a mine railway infrastructure investment. Japanese officials argued that a study showed the proposed mine railway would be certain to run at a loss for a long time. However, the company still continues to drill from the portion of the oilfield controlled by the Kuwaiti government.

In November 2000, Japan and Iran reached an agreement that gives Japanese oil companies negotiating rights to a portion of the Azadegan oilfield in Iran, the world's largest underdeveloped oilfield. This field has a potential to produce 400,000 barrels a day. This new source of oil is expected to help the Ministry of Economics, Trade and Industry (METI) plan to raise the ratio of oil produced by Japanese companies.

To combat the loss of rights to drill in the Saudi Arabia section of the Khafji field, Arabian Oil hopes to begin producing in Vietnam, while continuing oil and gas production in offshore China and the Gulf of Mexico. Crude oil represents most of Arabian Oil's sales; the remainder comes from petroleum products. It has four consolidated subsidiaries located in Japan, the Cayman islands, the United States and Norway.

See also: Japanese business in the Middle East

DAYO FAWIBE

ASIAN ECONOMIC CRISIS *see* economic crisis in Asia

ATO-GIME *see* after-sales pricing

automotive industry

From 1980 through 1993 Japan was the world's largest automobile producer, turning out a peak of 13.5 million units in 1990. Today output is stalled at 10 million units, though another 5.5 million were produced overseas, including 3.1 million in NAFTA. In addition, consolidation in 1999 and 2000 left **Toyota** and **Honda** the only two independent firms, with **Nissan**, Mazda, Isuzu and **Mitsubishi** under foreign control. Still, the majority of domestic employment is with suppliers, not assemblers, and with 880,000 employees the auto industry is the second largest manufacturing sector (after electronics). Once dealerships, gas stations and so on are included, the sector accounts for about 5 percent of the economy, and vehicles alone for 15 percent of Japan's total exports.

Japan's history shaped the industry. Motorization began with Model T buses imported after the 1923 earthquake destroyed Tokyo's trolley system. Ford and General Motors soon set up assembly plants, and in 1936 Ford was preparing to build an integrated facility as its vanguard plant in Asia. But war closed these firms and led to import restrictions that lasted from 1936 through the 1970s. Instead of having efficient (albeit foreign-owned) producers, trade barriers encouraged entry, and in the early 1950s Japan was burdened with a large number of inefficient, poor-quality makers. Three-wheel vehicles comprised the largest segment until 1962, and sales of passenger cars only surpassed those of trucks in 1968. New entry ceased in 1964, when Honda began regular production, while several early entrants exited, including Prince in 1966. Nine producers of cars and light trucks survived until 2000, with another two firms producing primarily heavy trucks.

From the 1940s, output remained divided among multiple firms in a variety of product segments. Costs remained high; total production was under 2 million units in 1965 and just over 5 million in 1970, including exports. Management faced many challenges. One was simply to increase capacity, given the rapidly growing domestic market. But firms were also aware of their high costs and poor quality, and the crowded domestic market generated strong rivalry. Capital market liberalization and lower trade barriers, targeted for 1971, added the threat of future foreign competition. A positive dynamic developed: costs could clearly be lowered each year, and quality improved; firms thus actively sought out new ideas both at home and abroad. By the late 1960s they were competitive in the small car market in the USA, where their major rival was not the American Big Three but rather Volkswagen. By the late 1970s the Japanese firms had established a reputation for high quality.

This rapid improvement reflected the introduction of the set of management techniques known as "lean" production. Supporting implementation was senior management, who with few exceptions came from careers based in factory management and engineering; noticeably absent were people from finance and marketing. Firms were thus highly receptive to the best in industrial engineering techniques, including statistical process control (SPC), continuous improvement (*kaizen*) and total quality management (TQM), as well as flow-dominated factory layout, rapid tooling changes and "**just-in-time**" (JIT) production scheduling, implemented at Toyota through the use of *kanban* cards. These techniques, developed during the 1950s and early 1960s, were widely publicized at the time in the business press and engineering journals. Implementation, however, was achieved in stages, with assemblers putting them in place in the latter 1960s and suppliers in the 1970s. This helped bring about large gains in quality and productivity following the first oil crisis of 1973.

Suppliers were critical because they are more important than assembly both in terms of employment (77 percent of the industry total) and costs. After the Second World War, existing assemblers spun off most internal parts manufacturing, while new entrants used outside suppliers from the start, thereby lessening their capital requirements. Another impetus was a strong labor movement that won employment guarantees at the firm level. By turning to suppliers, assemblers were able to raise output without expanding their own employment until well into the 1960s.

Coordinating the supply chain was a challenge. By the 1960s direct suppliers were organized into *kyoryoku-kai*, formal supplier associations. Purchasing departments oversaw the interaction of suppliers with engineering at the development end and with the factory once vehicles entered production, and also organized consulting efforts that diffused the latest in manufacturing and management techniques to them. With interfirm organization built up over decades – most ties date back to 1960 or earlier – the cumulative benefits of ongoing relationships improved the capabilities of the supply base as a whole, raising the quality and lowering the cost of the finished vehicle.

Supporting this relationship were clear pricing rules, using standard cost models as a starting point, that made setting the terms of transactions less fractious. In turn, assemblers typically contracted the full production run of four or more years to a single supplier, and (conditional on quality and delivery, and general cost competitiveness), suppliers could generally count on customers trying to give sufficient orders for keeping their capacity utilized. Within this ongoing relationship, rules of thumb for sharing the gains from engineering improvements gave suppliers the incentive to develop and implement new designs and manufacturing methods, and share new ideas with their customers. With assemblers marketing several separate product lines, they could have two–three firms supplying brakes, seats or other components; suppliers could and did periodically lose business to rivals, keeping them honest. On the flip side, most large parts firms sold to several different assemblers, though there was less overlap among suppliers to Nissan and Toyota due to capacity and geographic considerations. Together, these two features speeded the diffusion of best practice throughout the industry.

Suppliers also became integral to vehicle engineering and development. Within the auto companies, stylists, and product and process engineers were organized in platform teams. This facilitated overlapping different elements of the overall process, and such simultaneous engineering speeded product development, cutting costs and improving market fit. Supplier input was crucial.

They contributed about half of total engineering hours, coordinated in part through "design-in" (the co-location of supplier staff at their customers). In general, Japanese suppliers tended to do more "black box" work, developing parts to performance specifications, while US suppliers worked to blueprints supplied by their customers. (In the latter 1990s the USA and the EU industries converged rapidly towards the Japanese model.)

On the opposite end of the industry is vehicle distribution and repair. As in most other markets, users in Japan buy from franchised dealers, not from the assemblers themselves. Dealers in Japan are typically large, multi-store operations with an exclusive prefectural-level sales territory, a legacy of the 1950s, when few dealerships were needed while registration procedures made it difficult to sell across prefectural boundaries. At the same time, the initially limited but geographically dispersed customer base – plus expensive real estate in major urban markets – meant that salesmen visited likely customers, rather than waiting for potential buyers at dealership sites. As the market expanded, dealers set up new sales branches within their existing sales territory; until recently, they were prohibited by their franchise contracts from "dualing," selling the cars of more than one maker. But with selling labor intensive, even in good times new cars were relatively unprofitable.

Instead, dealers' profits relied upon a local monopoly on vehicle repairs and on *shaken*, the mandatory inspection of cars required every two–three years by the Ministry of Transport. High fees from inspections (at one time $1,500 or more) and fat margins on repairs more than compensated for the low profitability of vehicle sales. Because inspections became annual after the tenth year, few cars were kept after that point. The market for used cars thus remained thin, and (again unlike in the USA) was not a significant source of profits. Without "dualing" imports were unimportant; the few firms that specialized in foreign cars (such as Yanase Motors) were low-volume operations with few sales points, focusing on high-margin models, and handling many makes in parallel. This, together with the cost of setting up an independent distribution system, kept foreign penetration low. However, firms that made the requisite investments, such as BMW after 1982, increased their sales volume and earned high profits.

The distribution system is now in flux. The prefectural scope of the typical franchise meant that from the assembler's perspective a dealer was too big to fail. Toyota did well after 1982, and its dealers thus had the resources to expand into the newly prosperous suburbs. In contrast, Nissan's sales stagnated, and it had to bail out several major dealers, but managers from corporate headquarters proved no more adept at running dealerships than the unlucky entrepreneurs whom they replaced, and had no resources to expand to the suburbs. This vicious circle made it even more difficult to maintain sales volume.

The incipient weakness of this structure hit home with the 25 percent drop in sales after 1990. Of course, some dealers overextended themselves during the "bubble" (as Mazda did at the corporate level, trying to match Toyota's five sales channels despite its much smaller size). In addition, deregulation of the *shaken* in 1996 led to both fewer inspections and lower prices. Combined with the market downturn following the consumption tax hike in April 1997, the majority of dealerships operated in the red during 1998–2000, and required subsidies from car makers to stay in business. This is surely a source of unease in the entire industry, even at Toyota, Honda and Suzuki, whose domestic sales have held up best.

International sales began with truck exports to developing country markets in the 1950s. Passenger car exports came later, when the success of the Volkswagen Beetle in the late 1960s expanded the market for compact cars in the USA. New US emissions regulations in 1970 and the oil crises of 1973 and 1979 further boosted the small car segment to a peak of one-third of all sales. Rather than developing their own small cars, the Big Three turned to Japanese makers as a source of captive imports, with General Motors taking equity stakes in Isuzu and Suzuki, Ford in Mazda, and Chrysler in Mitsubishi Motors. Helped by good quality and a favorable exchange rate, Japanese producers captured the majority of this new segment, some 2 million vehicles in 1980, or about 20 percent of the US market. (In contrast, Japanese firms fared poorly in Europe, with its many

producers of small cars, and significant import barriers.)

In the USA, seven Japanese firms vied for share, keeping profits modest. They likely would have exited the market when the small car segment faded in the mid-1980s, as happened with European imports in both the 1950s and 1960s. But in the spring of 1981 the Reagan administration asked the Japanese government to impose a VER ("voluntary" export restraint) of 1.68 million units. Despite public handwringing (and genuine confusion among executives), Japanese firms soon realized the benefits of a formal cartel, and raised prices for popular models by as much as 25 percent. Since only a limited number of cars could be sold, firms also had an incentive to move upscale and the VER provided the profits needed to develop bigger vehicles. Finally, the VER encouraged local "transplant" assembly, since parts were not subject to import restrictions. Honda opened the first such plant in 1982, and by the end of the 1980s eight producers had operations in either the USA or Canada. This process accelerated after the Plaza Accord of 1986, when the steep appreciation of the yen made parts imports from Japan unattractive.

These ventures proved surprisingly successful. There are now twenty assembly, engine and transmission plants in the USA and Canada run by Japanese car makers, and at least 300 plants run by "transplant" suppliers. In 1999 they accounted for 3 million units, 18 percent of NAFTA output. The transplants initially focused on small vehicles, with low profit margins, but Honda and Toyota now produce more cars than Chrysler, and all are rushing to launch products in the minivan, SUV and pickup truck segments. Drawing upon their experience in the US, Japanese firms then expanded into the EU. Most chose Britain as their base, but the strong pound later hurt sales elsewhere in Europe. Japanese firms, however, dominate Asian markets, lagging only in China and Korea, and are expanding in Latin America.

What of the future? The industry built 1.5 million units of new plants inside Japan at the start of the 1990s, leaving it with roughly 15 million units capacity. But between the collapse of the "bubble" and the strong yen, domestic output appears likely to remain closer to 10 million units.

While Honda and Toyota have done well in the USA, and minicar demand has expanded inside Japan, profits have otherwise proved elusive, both at home and abroad. Adjustment to this unpleasant reality has been slow. During the 1990s several temporary upturns lulled the industry with hopes that plant closures could be forestalled. The steep recession that began with the consumption tax increase of April 1997 dashed these hopes, and a wholesale restructuring of the industry is underway. Ford took control of Mazda in 1996, and General Motors has 49 percent of Isuzu, giving it *de facto* control. In 1999 Nissan was taken over by Renault, and in 2000 DaimlerChrysler took a potentially controlling stake in Mitsubishi. General Motors has increased its positions at Suzuki and Fuji Heavy Industries (Subaru), and Toyota absorbed Daihatsu and Hino. (The fate of Nissan Diesel is still unclear). Toyota and Honda thus remain the only independent producers. A similar process of realignment will follow in the parts sector: Bosch (Germany) and Delphi (USA), for example, have already taken over suppliers historically associated with Nissan. In addition, while imports might appear to comprise a trivial 6 percent share of the market, they are concentrated in the high-margin luxury segment, and foreign firms now have potential additional sales channels through their new Japanese subsidiaries.

The future entails many management challenges. New owners must restructure and absorb their purchases, despite little or no experience operating in Japan. Meanwhile, Toyota and Honda – and many suppliers – are only now grappling with overseas operations that will end up more important than their domestic ones. Finally, an aging labor force and overall high wages make it likely that much parts production will move offshore, making factory management more complex. Japan will remain a major producer, with domestic output of 10–11 million units and strengths in engineering small vehicles, but it is almost certainly past its heyday.

MICHAEL SMITKA

B

bad debt

Bad debt, more commonly referred to as "non-performing" or "bad loans," are amounts loaned by banks but which fail to generate returns. Precise definitions vary from country to country but, however defined, regulatory authorities generally require banks to set aside capital to cover potential losses arising from bad debt becoming unrecoverable debt.

In Japan, the definition of non-performing loans was more restrictive than generally accepted standards in other advanced industrial countries until the latter 1990s. Before fiscal year 1994, for example, loans to borrowers in legal bankruptcy or considerably past due were classified as non-performing but restructured loans were not. From fiscal year 1995 on, however, regulatory authorities progressively widened the definition. Today, definitions of bad debt in Japan fall in line with globally accepted standards.

Repercussions of bad debt

Bad debt has a number of repercussions. The presence of large amounts of non-performing loans impairs the capital ratios of banks, thereby shrinking the amount of capital banks have available to lend to other borrowers. In this way, large amounts of non-performing loans may induce credit crunches where potentially productive ventures are unable to obtain sufficient capital because capital is tied up in unproductive investments.

Since deposit-taking financial institutions serve essentially as an intermediary, lending deposits to third parties, a rise in amounts of debt not repaid also means that the chances of a bank not having the money needed to return a depositor's money rises. If a bank then becomes insolvent and fails, confidence in other banks also drops and depositors may rush to withdraw deposits. Such a run on the banks can, in turn, lead to a liquidity crunch. At any given time, most banks will not have the cash on hand to pay out every depositor, since a significant portion of deposits will be tied up in loans extended to customers. Thus, even solvent banks have the potential to collapse when another bank fails due to excessive bad debt. A rapid increase in amounts of bad debt in any nation's financial system should thus be a phenomenon of concern to policy makers and regulatory authorities.

Sources of bad debt

Bad debt arises for a number of reasons. Excessive risk-taking by management is often a primary cause. This was the case in the latter 1980s when banks loaned funds for speculative purposes. Bad debt may also arise from an economic downturn. When the economy enters a recession, as Japan's did twice in the 1990s, company profits tend to fall, making it more difficult for borrowers to repay debt. Because of this correlation between economic performance and bad debt levels, banks and their regulators often initially delay in aggressively addressing non-performing loan problems, hoping that bad debt will simply shrink to an acceptable level with an economic recovery.

Bad debt is also commonly spurred by exogenous shocks. For example, the Great Hanshin

Earthquake that struck the Kobe area in Japan in 1995 destroyed the business foundations of many companies, and therefore led to a surge in bad debt for banks with heavy lending in this region. Likewise, dramatic shifts in exchange rates or in oil prices may affect the profit bases of particular sectors of the economy with a high dependence on imported materials or export markets, suddenly making them unable to repay debts.

Procedures for dealing with bad debt and the financial crisis of the 1990s

Prior to the collapse of Japan's asset bubble in 1991, financial institutions infrequently encountered distress due to high levels of non-performing loans. If a bank did face insolvency as a result of high levels of bad debt, the **Ministry of Finance** (MOF) arranged a "rescue merger" behind the scenes, relying on a stronger bank to absorb the weaker. In an era of heavy regulation, stronger banks had incentives to participate in such rescue procedures, for doing so meant gaining valuable retail branches. With the 1991 bursting of the nation's asset bubble, however, all Japanese banks became burdened with large amounts of non-performing loans and limited deregulation meant that the relatively stronger banks had fewer incentives to assist in "rescue mergers."

The magnitude of nonperforming loans in the Japanese banking sector only began to be revealed to the public in 1995, when a Finance Ministry official testified in the Diet concerning the grave condition of the housing and loan corporations called *jusen*. Even then, only estimates of aggregate totals for the banking sector as a whole were revealed. Aggressive measures to deal with the high levels of bad debt in the banking system were postponed by authorities until the eruption of acute financial crisis in 1997–8. By this time, the magnitude of non-performing loans in the Japanese banking system was estimated at close to one trillion dollars.

In 1998 and 1999, the government injected public funds into a number of Japan's large commercial banks in an attempt to boost their capital bases and aid them in the disposal of their bad debt. With the use of public funds, banks were required for the first time to disclose amounts of non-performing loans to the public. Although

banks carried out record write-offs and recorded record losses in 1999 and 2000, the continued economic downturn and decline in asset prices led the number of corporate bankruptcies to continue to climb and additional bad debt to emerge. Japanese banks therefore remained burdened with large amounts of non-performing loans as they entered the twenty-first century.

Further reading

Amyx, J. (2000) "Political Implications to Far-reaching Banking Reforms in Japan: Implications for Asia," in G. Noble and J. Ravenhill (eds), *The Asian Financial Crisis and the Architecture of Global Finance*, New York: Cambridge University Press, 132–51.

JENNIFER AMYX

Bank of Japan

The Bank of Japan (BOJ), the nation's central bank, was established in 1882 by the Finance Minister as a joint undertaking of government and business. The BOJ's mission is to lay the foundation for sound economic development through the maintenance of price stability and ensuring the stability of the financial system. To fulfill this mission, it issues and manages banknotes, implements monetary policy, provides financial settlement services, manages the business of Japanese government securities, acts as a representative of the **Ministry of Finance** (MOF) in the foreign exchange markets, compiles data, and carries out economic analysis and research. The BOJ's Policy Board serves as the highest decision-making body of the bank.

Monetary policy

The BOJ implements monetary policy through setting the official discount rate and through market operations. Both activities influence interest rates and interest rates, in turn, affect various price levels. The discount rate is the standard rate of interest on loans made by the central bank to private financial institutions. Loose monetary policy (low rates) makes it easier for banks to attract loan customers because it enables them to make loans at lower interest rates. In general, the central bank raises the rate when the economy becomes overheated and lowers the rate when there are deflationary trends.

Through market operations, the Bank guides the key unsecured overnight call money rate. From 1950–91, the BOJ also influenced the availability of credit through the exercise of "window guidance" or **madoguchi shido**. Through "window guidance," the BOJ indicated to commercial banks the amount of lending it deemed proper.

In the late 1980s, prolonged expansionary monetary policy by the BOJ fueled a speculative asset "bubble" of unprecedented magnitude. In February 1987, the BOJ dropped the discount rate to a (then) postwar historic low of 2.5 percent and held this rate until May 1989. With an abundance of "cheap" money available, many companies and individuals borrowed for the purposes of speculative investment and from 1987 to 1989, the Tokyo Stock Exchange Nikkei 225 Average nearly doubled in value. The eventual tightening of monetary policy, however, led to a bursting of this bubble.

In attempting to shore up banks burdened with massive amounts of non-performing loans or dead debts that emerged from the bubble's collapse, the central bank again loosened monetary policy. In April 1995, the discount rate was lowered to a new historic low of 1 percent and then further lowered to 0.5 percent in September 1995. In an emergency measure extending from February 1999 through August 2000, the BOJ also set the target overnight call rate at zero percent following a series of financial institution bankruptcies.

Ensuring stability of the financial system

The BOJ provides and maintains a settlement system for financial transactions between financial institutions. Funds are transferred across the current account held by each financial institution at the central bank. The BOJ also serves as the lender of last resort to financial institutions facing liquidity problems, extending uncollateralized loans to financial institutions if the stability of the financial system is perceived to be in danger. To prevent financial institutions from falling prey to

the "moral hazard" of regarding infusions of capital from the BOJ as a form of insurance, the BOJ conducts regular on-site examinations of those financial institutions with accounts at the central bank.

The rescue operations of the BOJ saved large banks from failure in the Banking Crisis of 1927. The BOJ also came to the aid of Yamaichi Securities and other brokerages in 1965. More recently, the BOJ provided funds in 1994 and the years thereafter to execute schemes for facilitating the rescue of credit unions and banks burdened with massive amounts of nonperforming loans.

International activities

The BOJ's international activities are threefold. First, the Bank engages in international transactions by providing yen accounts to central banks and government institutions overseas. Second, the Bank plays a central role in monitoring and intervening, when necessary, in currency markets. For example, in the 1990s, the BOJ's massive interventions in the form of dollar buying were key to suppressing the strength of the yen and making up for the shortfall between Japan's current and capital accounts. Finally, the BOJ's international activities also involve participation in international forums such as the meetings of the Bank for International Settlements (BIS), G7, and the International Monetary Fund.

The new Bank of Japan Law

For most of the postwar period, the BOJ lacked independence. Monetary policy strongly reflected the influence of the MOF and the Bank's decision-making autonomy was also compromised by the conduct of its personnel and budget matters. The MOF appointed the BOJ's executive auditors and comptroller and had the power to dismiss Bank officials, including the governor. The BOJ budget also required approval by the Finance Minister.

With the 1997 passage of the New Bank of Japan Law and the enactment of this law in April 1998, however, the central bank gained greater independence in the conduct of monetary policy and more autonomy in personnel matters. The new law also introduced greater transparency into decision-making processes within the BOJ. The central bank's budget remains subject to MOF approval.

The impetus for the new BOJ Law was the recognition of the MOF's undue influence over the BOJ in its conduct of monetary policy in the bubble period and the linkage of this policy breakdown to the nation's prolonged recession and financial crisis in the 1990s. Reorganization of the central bank under the new law was also accelerated by the emergence of scandals in the latter 1990s. These scandals centered on dubious interactions between BOJ officials and private financial institutions.

Further reading

Bank of Japan Annual Review (annual) Tokyo: Bank of Japan.

Cargill, T., Hutchison, M. and Ito, T. (1997) *The Political Economy of Japanese Monetary Policy*, Cambridge, MA: MIT Press.

Yamawaki, T. (1998) *Nihon Ginko no Shinjitsu* (The Truth of the Bank of Japan), Tokyo: Diamond-sha.

JENNIFER AMYX

Bank of Tokyo

The Bank of Tokyo (BOT) was founded in 1880 as the Yokohama Specie Bank, which contributed to the internationalization of domestic industries through international finance operations. After the Second World War, in 1946, the bank was reorganized as a commercial bank, and the Bank of Tokyo was established. In 1952, the BOT opened its first foreign branches in New York and London, and in 1954 the BOT became Japan's only specialized foreign exchange bank. In 1962 the BOT was authorized to issue debentures (a type of bond) to support its yen funding. The debentures issued by BOT were abbreviated as Wari-To (discounted-Tokyo), and represented a service where the bank offered individual investors the ability to purchase bonds. In Japan a limited number of financial institutions were authorized to issue debentures (authorized banks are long term

credit banks, the **Norin Chukin Bank**, Shyoko Chukin Bank, Shinkin Central Bank and BOT, with BOT being the only commercial bank to be authorized with such powers). This privileged position helped the BOT to develop a reputation as a professional bank of international finance, in turn helping it to dominate the Japanese inter-bank foreign exchange markets.

In 1996, the BOT merged with Mitsubishi Bank, to become Tokyo-Mitsubishi Bank. This new colossal bank, with combined assets of ¥72.8 trillion, 36 percent larger than the title-holder Sumitomo Bank and more than five times bigger than America's Citibank, became the world's largest bank. It is still one of the largest banks in the world with subsidiaries and associated banks on five continents.

In its domestic business, the bank provides a full array of commercial banking services. Its international banking services include investment financing. The Tokyo-Mitsubishi Bank has most recently assisted the **Export-Import Bank of Japan** and the Overseas Economic Co-operation Fund in extending credit. It is a major commissioned bank for foreign bonds issued in yen denominations.

Further reading

Blanden, M. (1995) "Japan," *The Banker*, 145(836): 26.

Cashmore, N., Ramillano, M., Playfair, A., Shimomura, K. and Horsburgh, K. (1996) "The Best Banks in Foreign Exchange," *Asiamoney* 7(3): 21.

Shale, T. (1995) "Or the World's Greatest Bank?" *Euromoney* 31, May.

"Bank of Tokyo Wins U.S. Clients Through Credit System," (1994) *Nihon Keizai Shimbun*, October 16.

SUMIHIRO TAKEDA

Banking Act of 1982

The Banking Act of 1982 represented the first comprehensive revision of the Banking Law of 1927. The Act governed the behavior of all "ordinary" banks in Japan and served as the legal basis for the on-site inspections carried out periodically by the Inspections Bureau in the **Ministry of Finance** (MOF). The Act's purpose was to maintain the smooth flow of credit and financing while at the same time protecting depositors by ensuring prudent management of the banking business (Article 1). Its passage in the Diet on May 25, 1981 and enactment on April 1, 1982 followed decades of debate and numerous unsuccessful attempts by the Ministry of Finance (MOF) to draft a banking law revision.

The beginning of securitization of the banking sector

The Banking Act of 1982 was most notable for its provisions widening the scope of business for banks. More specifically, the Act marked the beginning of the securitization of the Japanese banking sector.

The issuance of large amounts of government debt in the 1970s affected the profit margins of banks because banks comprised the government bond syndicate, absorbing government bonds at below market and holding them until the **Bank of Japan** (BOJ) reabsorbed them. With a surge in debt issues, however, banks began to show significant losses from their government bond holdings. As a result, they demanded the right to retail government bonds. Although MOF made adjustments at the margins in response to these profit concerns of banks – including altering accounting methods for government bonds – the banks remained dissatisfied. In 1978, the banks boycotted the issue of long-term government bonds. This action spurred the government to seek alternative measures to resolve the problem.

The provisions eventually contained in the Banking Act of 1982 permitted banks to enter the part of the securities business involving the sale of government bonds to the public. This outcome, however, was the product of a fierce battle between the banking and securities industries. Brokerages naturally opposed entry by banks into any aspect of the securities industry, seeing it as an encroachment on their turf. The MOF therefore was forced to broker a compromise that enabled banks to avoid losses on government bonds but at the same time compensated the brokerages for the limited entry by banks into their business territory.

In the Act's final provisions, banks were permitted to invest in equities and bonds on their own behalf, underwrite and offer for sale govern-

ment and other public bonds, act as securities agents, and loan securities as ancillary businesses. With this newly granted permission, major Japanese banks were able to turn to bond dealing and investment as a new source of profits. Receiving permission to enter the government bond business was especially important for the **city banks**, whose major borrowers and depositors were corporations making the shift away from capital-intensive undertakings at this time. As a concession to brokerages, securities companies were permitted to start lending money secured by government bonds.

Notably, the Banking Act of 1982 did not entirely settle the debate over banks entering the securities business, however. Many other areas of the securities business remained closed to the banking sector and plans for major changes thereafter became replaced by a step by step liberalization process. Brokerages continued to fiercely resist the encroachment upon their territory by banks, thereby impeding efforts to do away more quickly with compartmentalization of the financial industry

Supporting the status quo with disclosure requirements

A significant feature of the Banking Act of 1982 (as well as of its predecessor, the Banking Act of 1927) was its lack of explicit details regarding banking regulations, leaving these instead to **administrative guidance**. Thus, MOF officials continued to enjoy a large degree of discretion in carrying out banking regulation. In the past, the ministry had preferred this approach to formally legislating changes, as the strategy of obtaining cooperation enabled the ministry to maintain a great deal of flexibility in response while also enjoying discretionary authority. In the years leading up to the passage of the Banking Act of 1982, however, the ministry found reliance on extralegal administrative guidance to be a double-edged sword. Instances of bank defiance of MOF guidance were on the rise. In the lead up to the passage of the Banking Act, therefore, the ministry in fact sought to formalize some of its guidance, drafting proposals for stricter disclosure requirements to be included as part of the Banking Act legislation.

MOF officials believed that consolidation of the sector was needed to make the banking industry more efficient. Since the deposit insurance scheme was not credibly funded, the ministry hoped to eliminate the weakest banks through mergers rather than inducing failures. The weaker banks had little incentive to cooperate in such mergers, however, since the ministry's implicit guarantee against failure remained in place. Thus, MOF officials sought tougher disclosure requirements as a means of facilitating the needed consolidation.

The All Japan Bankers' Federation, *Zenginkyo*, opposed the MOF's proposal, however, and fiercely lobbied Liberal Democratic Party (LDP) officials to veto the proposal on their behalf. The banking industry's critical role as a provider of large amounts of political funds helped it gain the LDP's sympathy. In the end, the banking industry was able to foil the MOF's attempt to introduce more market discipline and the status quo *vis-à-vis* disclosure was upheld. The MOF's failure on the disclosure issue was compounded as well by its failure to obtain legal authority to dispose of bad bank management.

Other provisions

The Banking Act of 1982 also incorporated for the first time an upper lending limit on the sum that could be loaned to a single party, thereby reducing the risk of excessively concentrated borrowing. Loans to a single customer could not exceed 20 percent of capital and surplus funds (Supplementary Provisions, Article 4). This upper limit on lending had previously been specified through MOF circulars rather than by law but was made into law at the behest of the Financial System Research Council.

Further reading

Rosenbluth, F. (1989) *Financial Politics in Contemporary Japan*, Ithaca, NY: Cornell University Press.

JENNIFER AMYX

banking crises

The decade of the 1990s was characterized by a series of banking crises in Japan. In this period,

major banks and securities firms in Japan were allowed to fail for the first time in the post-Second World War era. In the 1990s Japanese banks and securities firms failed primarily due to large proportions of non-performing loans. The proximate cause of these banking problems seems to be the 1990 bursting of the asset price bubble of the late 1980s. By the end of the 1990s, many large and small Japanese banks were insolvent and non-performing loans were estimated to be over $1 trillion and, on average, over 20 percent of Japanese bank assets. Non-performing assets were undoubtedly much higher than 20 percent at many banks.

It has been contended that only liberal accounting procedures permitted most banks to satisfy the Basel capital standards, while implicit government guarantees prevented depositor runs. In spite of these guarantees and accounting treatments, Japanese banks continued to face severe liquidity problems in financial markets and several Japanese banks have had to be rescued or closed in the later half of the 1990s. The origin of this recent banking crisis in Japan can be traced to the poor state of the Japanese economy and the collapse of asset prices in the beginning of the 1990s. While there have been a number of banking crises in Japan, especially in the 1920s, the 1990s crisis was the first major crisis in the post-Second World War era.

On August 30, 1995, Hyogo Bank, a mid-sized regional bank with about $37 billion in total assets, became the first commercial bank in Japan to fail since the end of the Second World War. While all depositors were paid, in a departure from the traditional 'convoy system' shareholders and non-depositor creditors of Hyogo Bank suffered losses. As in the past, the business of Hyogo bank was re-organized with funds from its major owners, other large banks, and taken over by a new entity. Payments associated with this resolution depleted all deposit insurance funds and the government announced that it would not allow any of the country's twenty largest banks to fail before the year 2000.

Nevertheless, three major institutions failed in 1997, Sanyo Securities on November 4, Hokkaido Takushoku Bank on November 17, and Yamaichi Securities on November 24. Similarly, two major institutions also failed in 1998, **Long-Term**

Credit Bank of Japan on October 23 and Nippon Credit Bank on December 13. Other Japanese financial institutions continued to fail intermittently in 1999 and 2000. Why has the banking crisis in Japan lasted for all of the 1990s and is still continuing in early 2001?

Until recently, the Japanese banking system was heavily regulated and segmented. Different types of banks were permitted to serve only a certain type of customer. For example, city banks specialized in short-term loans, long-term credit banks specialized in long-term developmental loans, and trust banks specialized in the money management business. In addition to banks, Japan also has numerous financial institutions and cooperatives that specialize in lending to small businesses, agriculture, forestry and fisheries, securities finance companies, insurance companies, and government financial institutions. The largest holder of savings in Japan, the Postal Savings System, is part of the last category.

Like other central banks, the **Bank of Japan** must balance the conflicting objectives of providing confidence in the system for financial intermediation to take place while limiting the moral hazard costs of rescuing banks in trouble. With an emphasis on stability in bank regulation, all bank deposits in Japan are insured by the government and, from the Second World War until the mid-1990s, no Japanese bank had been allowed to fail. Typically a merger partner would be found for an ailing bank and in the so-called "convoy escort system," major competitor banks were expected to contribute funds for such rescues. In this system, bank relationships with commercial customers were long-term in nature, there was little competition, innovation, or push for efficiency among banks, and any change was slow and limited by the slowest bank in a group. Public disclosure of loan quality, capital ratios, and other data by banks in Japan has generally been of relatively low quality. For example, Japanese banks were not required to report non-performing loans until 1993 and were not required to use US and international standards for such reports until 1998.

In recent years, driven by technology and globalization, the Japanese financial system is being gradually deregulated. Trading in new financial instruments was progressively permitted all through the 1980s, derivatives markets were allowed by the late 1980s, and interest rates were deregulated in the early 1990s. The 1993 Financial System Reform Act dismantled barriers between banking and securities businesses and the implementation of the 'Big Bang' set of financial deregulations was started in 1998.

Based on this brief review, we can now begin to answer why have Japanese banks been in crisis since the beginning of the 1990s and continued to fail in the second half of the 1990s? One reason seems to be the sudden collapse of asset prices in the first part of the 1990s. But why has the crisis lasted so long? One reason may be that Japanese regulators initially may have hoped to grow out of the crisis as bank profits rose with economic recovery. However, economic recoveries in Japan in the 1990s have been weak and short-lived. In addition, there has been little political will to inject the money needed to rescue Japanese banks, especially since the government in Tokyo is a coalition government and the **banking industry** and its regulators have been tainted by corruption scandals. Another explanation notes that Japanese banks have not developed credit analysis capabilities having depended on government directed and collateralized lending and, given the generally poor levels of disclosure, nor have they been subject to market discipline. Under the prevailing *amakudari* practice where retiring senior regulators were virtually guaranteed senior positions with the institutions they regulated, it is contended that bank regulation in Japan has been less than fully effective. However, bank regulation may also have lost its effectiveness as Japan gradually moved to a more market-oriented economy and financial system.

While there are many causes of this continuing banking crisis in Japan, Japanese banks must be restructured to reduce or eliminate non-performing loans from their balance sheets so that they can restart lending. This will require government funds and decisive action by the government. It would also be useful if Japanese banks develop better credit assessment skills, improve disclosure, and become more subject to market discipline.

Further reading

Aggarwal, R. (ed.) (1999) *Restructuring Japanese*

Business for Growth, Boston, MA: Kluwer Academic Publishers.

Genay, H. (1998) "Assessing the Condition of Japanese Banks: How Informative are Accounting Earnings?" *FRB Chicago Economic Perspectives* 4: 12–34.

Hanazaki, M. and Horiuchi, A. (2000) "Is Japan's Financial System Efficient?" *Oxford Review of Economic Policy* 16(2): 61–73.

Hoshi, T. (2000) "What Happened to Japanese Banks?" Bank of Japan, IMES Discussion Paper Series, 2000-E-7, March.

Hoshi, T. and Kashyap, A. (1999) "The Japanese Banking Crisis: Where Did It Come From and How Will It End?" *NBER Macroeconomics Annual* 129–201.

Motonishi, T. and Yashikawa, H. (1999) "Causes of the Long Stagnation of Japan During the 1990s: Financial or Real?" *Journal of Japanese and International Economies* 12(2): 181–200.

RAJ AGGARWAL

banking industry

Japan's banking industry began in the early **Tokugawa period** with the development of exchange houses and money lending stores within the family of enterprises of the great merchant houses or *ie*. These merchant banking operations were to become the banks of the *zaibatsu* family groups, as they were known starting in the early modern period through the prewar period. These groups are still in operation today, including Mitsui group (Sakura Bank), Sumitomo group and bank, Konoike household (Sanwa Bank). Most merchant banking operations were not granted commercial banking licenses until the 1890 Banking Act.

The Meiji leadership of Japan's early modern period, seeking to promote economic development through modernization of its financial system, first adopted the US banking model. The National Bank Act of 1872 created a system of national chartered banks with the authority to issue bank notes. By 1879, 153 banks had been chartered, but their demise was equally rapid. Over-issuance of notes by the banks led to inflation, and limited capitalization led to quick bank failures, largely due to inexperience with lending risk on the part of the former *samurai* owners, who used their government retirement bonds as capital.

The failure of the National Bank model and the pressing need to stabilize the economy next led the Meiji *genro* (oligarchic leadership) of the "elder statesman period" to the adoption of a European model based upon the establishment of a central bank. On the initiative of Meiji Finance Minister Matsukata, the charters of more than thirty central banks were examined, after which a decision was made in favor of the German model. In 1882 the **Bank of Japan** (BOJ) was created. The Reichsbank model was chosen (notwithstanding apocryphal stories of the selection of the Belgium model) and was reaffirmed at the BOJ's rechartering in 1942 because it gave the maximum amount of power to the **Ministry of Finance** (MOF) to the exclusion of any parliamentary authority.

Chief among the reasons for the founding of the Bank of Japan was the need to regulate and control Japan's currency. The BOJ was given the sole right to issue currency. It took the government four years, until 1886, however, to accumulate enough gold to redeem the still outstanding private bank notes. This action initiated what proved to be the beginning of a long history of government bailouts of the commercial banking sector. Another decade was required to accumulate an adequate gold reserve before the Bank of Japan could achieve its ultimate goal in 1897 of placing Japan on the gold standard.

From the late nineteenth century to the present, the Ministry of Finance, which wields active control over the banking sector, has managed Japan's economic development policies. Matsukata, who was noted for his predilection for autocratic control, ruled the MOF for twenty years and was responsible for initiating the practice of using of the banking system for policy-based finance, which characteristic has identified Japan's banking system for most of the past 120 years.

First enunciated by Matsukata, government banking policy aimed to create a system that was non-competitive and highly segmented. This system was designed to meet the specific needs of business for short-term financing, long-term commercial goals, foreign exchange and commerce requirements, and the establishment of savings banks. Specialized public sector policy-based financial institutions were established to promote economic development, industrial, regional, export and import trade, colonial development and, until the end of the Second World War, to finance Japan's military economy. It was Matsukata's expectation that the Ministry of Finance would control the activities of all of these institutions. This segmented system lasted until the liberalization of the financial sector took place a century later in the 1990s.

The only notable exception to the tight control wielded by the central bank occurred during the post-First World War decade when the government's *laissez-faire* policies let loose a period of freewheeling financial markets. This period came to an abrupt end with the 1927 banking crisis, which followed the Bank of Japan's dubious discounting of bills as a relief measure after the Great Kanto Earthquake (1923). Eventually a panic run ensued on a number of banks, which were thought to be holding the worthless paper. The subsequent collapse of many banks led the Ministry of Finance to take a direct hand in the failing banking industry. The government took over ownership of a number of the failing banks, reorganizing and consolidating them. The newly organized banks were soon pressed into the service of the emerging military economy of the 1930s.

The bank-centered financing regime gave the Ministry of Finance a considerable amount of power in directing economic development policy, particularly in comparison to its inability to direct the equity-capital markets. In the tight credit conditions of the postwar period, the **main bank system**, in which banks were the chief suppliers of **corporate finance**, became the MoF's principal mechanism of rationing funds.

In the 1980s the rapid expansion of credit provided by banks for speculative investment in real estate and construction was one of the main sources fueling what later became known as the "bubble economy." The collapse of the bubble led to the most profound recession since the end of the Second World War. Today, non-performing loans still carried by the banks are estimated to range from upwards of ¥63.3 trillion to twice that amount, and have led to consolidations and mergers within the commercial banking sector as

well as the bankruptcy of two of Japan's three long-term credit banks. This in turn has resulted in the creation (to date) of four giant holding companies which encompass all of Japan's remaining city banks together with trust banks.

After the revaluation of the yen following the 1985 Plaza Accord agreement, Japanese banks took a proactive role in financing the expansion of Japanese direct investment overseas, most conspicuously, the development by companies and industries of subsidiary operations overseas, the acquisition of existing companies, and the building of new production facilities. In North America in the 1980s, every Japanese city bank and long-term credit bank, followed by more than 65 regional banks, all opened branch offices in New York as well as another 120 branches in other US cities. Their lending to construction and the real estate market in the USA led to a collapse in the US real estate bubble in the early 1990s, as it had earlier in Japan.

This pattern was repeated in the mid-1990s by Japanese banks which engaged in similar lending for speculative investment in Asia. Their extensive lending to companies in the region led to speculation in real estate and local equities markets. The number of Japanese bank branches in Hong Kong exceeded their number in New York. The collapse of the resulting speculative bubble, which had been financed by Japanese bank lending, helped precipitate the Asian financial crisis of 1997.

Throughout the postwar period, until financial liberalization policies were instituted in the 1990s, the financial sector was strictly segmented into the following categories of short-term lending institutions: city banks, regional banks, and *sogo* (mutual) banks. The city banks were large-scale commercial banks with nationwide franchises that served primarily as chief main banks to major commercial clients, such as the large-cap firms listed in the First Section of the Tokyo Stock Exchange (TSE). Among this group of banks were the then so-called Big Six, which were the main banks for the giant *kigyo shudan* (corporate enterprise groups) of the same names: Mitsui (later re-named Sakura), Sumitomo, and Mitsubishi Banks, all former *zaibatsu* banks, and for the so-called bank-centered groups: Daiichi Kangyo (DKB), Sanwa, and Fuji

Banks. Another half-dozen city banks had largely regional client bases. The **Bank of Tokyo** was also a city bank. Formerly government owned, it was a specialized foreign exchange bank with a large clientele among Japanese corporations doing business overseas.

The second category of commercial banks was the more than sixty-five regional banks. Their commercial base as main banks was among medium-sized businesses (typically Second Section firms listed on the TSE) and large privately held firms. They also enjoyed the patronage of large corporations in their regions but not usually with main bank status.

The third category of short-term lending institutions were the *sogo* (mutual) banks which were re-chartered as second-tier regional banks in the late 1980s. These banks catered primarily to small-scale corporations and privately held businesses within their regions. The legal distinctions between the city banks, the regional banks, and the second-tier regional banks were erased in the 1990s when they were all reclassified as commercial banks, but they still have retained their characteristic markets.

The long-term credit banks were organized to provide long-term financing, principally through the sale of long-term debentures. The Hypothec Bank of Japan, organized by the government in 1896, was the first bank of its type in Japan and was modeled after the Credit Foncier of France. As its name implies, this land-collateral based bank made loans secured by agricultural properties. The purpose of the bank was to provide long-term credits for agricultural and enterprise development. In addition, local banks known as Agricultural and Industrial Banks were established in each prefecture between 1897 and 1900. The capital of these banks was held by individuals and the prefectural governments. Similar to the Hypothec Bank in function, they raised funds by issuing debentures. In 1921 they were amalgamated to become the Hypothec Bank's regional branches.

In 1900 the Industrial Bank of Japan (IBJ), patterned after France's Credit Mobilier, was established. Its purpose was to provide long-term developmental loans for vital industries, such as shipping, iron and steel, and chemicals, usually for a term of at least five years. Local government

bonds as well as debentures, shares of companies, mortgages of land and buildings, factories, ships, and railways could be used as loan collateral. The IBJ's operations were supervised by the government, and it also raised funds through the sale of debentures. A large share of its capital stock, some 43 percent, was raised in the London market and held by foreigners. In the 1930s the bank was reorganized to provide long-term credits for industries supporting the military economy.

In the postwar period three long-term credit banks registered under the Long-Term Credit Act (1952) for the purpose of providing long-term loans to industry: a newly organized **Long-Term Credit Bank of Japan**, the Industrial Bank of Japan, and later the Nippon Credit Bank, successor to the Hypothec Bank. Up until the 1980s their distinctive ability to offer long-term credit became blurred as city banks also began extending long-term loans on a *de facto* basis by the rollover of short-term credits. Seeking to regain profits from the loss of their market share to the city banks, the Long-Term Credit Bank and Nippon Credit Bank ultimately became casualties of the non-performing high-risk loans they had made for construction and real estate and would declare bankruptcy. The Industrial Bank of Japan, the strongest of the three, merged with **Daiichi Kangyo Bank** and Fuji Bank to form the Mizuho Financial Holding Group.

The Yokohama Specie Bank (YSB) was created by the government with the mandate of financing foreign trade. Until 1880 almost all foreign exchange in Japan had been conducted by foreign-owned banks. When currency depreciations led to extreme fluctuations in exchange rates making foreign commerce difficult, the government created the Yokohama Specie Bank in order to bring this problem under control. The YSB held the exclusive franchise to deal in foreign exchange until the end of the First World War when commercial banks were allowed to enter the foreign exchange market. Following the Second World War the bank was reorganized as the Bank of Tokyo and once again held until the 1970s the exclusive authority to deal in foreign exchange. In the 1990s the bank merged with Mitsubishi Bank.

The Savings Bank Act of 1890 was passed to protect depositors, who were mostly peasants. By

1901 there were 2,355 independent savings and deposit banks. Although the government earlier sought to consolidate them, it was not until 1943 that the Ministry of Finance ordered them closed and the personal savings they held transferred into commercial banks to strengthen financing for the war effort. At this point individual and household savings became a large component of main bank system profits. Today, the only remaining savings deposit takers are the *shinkin* (non-profit financial cooperatives) and the **postal savings** system. The commercial banking system for many years has called for the breakup and privatization or the outright abolishment of the postal savings system, which comes under the supervision of the Ministry of Posts and Telecommunications rather than the Ministry of Finance.

Since the late 1990s and up to the present, many changes have taken place in the consolidation of Japan's banking industry. The number of bank failures continues apace as a result of the ongoing non-performing loan crisis, which are chiefly loans to real estate and construction interests. This problem continues to plague the financial sector since the collapse of the bubble economy of the late 1980s and has driven the trend to takeovers and mergers among financial institutions.

The recent enactment of the Financial Holding Company Act has made it possible for commercial banks to merge without reducing their **cross-shareholdings** in client firms. The Act also permits different categories of banks – commercial, long-term, and trust banks – as well as securities firms and insurance companies to join together, in essence, granting them universal banking capabilities. This liberalization overturns existing financial segmentation policies first laid down by the Ministry of Finance in the nineteenth century and reinforced in the postwar **American occupation** period by the incorporation of the principles of United States' Glass-Steagall Act within Article 65 of Japan's Banking Law. As of today, all of Japan's top city banks, remaining long-term credit bank (IBJ), and most of its trust banks, together with several insurance companies have been merged into four megabanks.

As mentioned earlier, one of the paramount difficulties facing the banking industry today is the continuing non-performing loans problem, which

has withstood both the creation and demise of the unsuccessful Financial Reconstruction Commission (1997–2001). Other problems confronting the banking industry include the still growing non-performing loan portfolio of the regional banks, the entry of foreign financial competitors into Japan's formerly closed financial markets, as well as new domestic competitors, such as retailers and manufacturers which have set up new institutions offering financial services. Despite the injection of public funds to recapitalize the banks and the near-zero interest-rate policy of the Bank of Japan, banks have refused to issue new loans due to the continuing declining value of bank-held shares in their client firms which severely lowers their capital/asset ratio requirements.

Further reading

Scher, M.J. (1996) *Japanese Interfirm Networks and Their Main Banks*, London: Macmillan and New York: St. Martin's Press.

Scher, M.J. and Beechler, S.L. (1994) "Japanese Banking in the U.S. – From Transient Advantage to Strategic Failure," Working Paper Series, Center on Japanese Economy and Business, New York: Columbia University.

MARK J. SCHER

bankruptcies

Bankruptcy involves an individual or corporation seeking legal protection from creditors because of insolvency. Comparatively speaking, the incidence of corporate bankruptcy in postwar Japan has been extremely high. In 1977, for example, more than 18,000 firms went bankrupt in Japan, while in the same year fewer than 800 firms went bankrupt in the United States.

Firms may go bankrupt for a number of reasons. In general, however, the number of bankruptcies tends to rise substantially when an economy enters recession, experiences a shock in the presence of latent business weakness, or undergoes structural changes. Until the latter 1970s, most companies that went bankrupt in Japan did so as a result of temporary critical conditions. From the latter

1970s through the 1980s, however, structural causes were more often the reason. In the 1990s, unsound investments made during Japan's "bubble" period of the latter 1980s were a primary cause of failure, as asset prices declined continuously over the course of the decade.

The "dual-structure economy" and bankruptcy patterns

A distinctive feature of corporate bankruptcy patterns in Japan until the latter 1990s was the concentration of these failures almost exclusively in **small and medium-sized firms**. The failure of large corporations was extremely rare. In 1993, for example, of the total number of bankruptcies leaving debts of ten million yen or more, over 99 percent were accounted for by small and medium enterprises with a capitalization of less than 100 million yen.

The heavy concentration of bankruptcies among smaller firms reflected the dual structure of the Japanese economy. Extensive subcontracting by large corporations to smaller firms meant that the smaller firms played the role of shock absorber in periods of economic downturn. Smaller firms typically engaged in work for a single larger firm but the larger firms retained numerous subcontractors. When economic shocks hit, then, subcontractors – financially dependent on the larger firms – tended to bear the brunt of the pain and go under in high numbers.

In contrast to the vulnerability of small and medium-sized firms, the safety net for large corporations was distinctively strong in Japan. Although large Japanese corporations maintained a high degree of dependence on bank-centered financing, most companies developed a long-term relationship with a so-called main bank, through which the corporation procured the majority of its funds and all of its financial services. Close monitoring by the main bank meant that problems were often caught before they led a firm to reach the point at which liquidation was the only option. And, if a corporate borrower did become financially distressed, debt claims were often renegotiated. The main bank's role in the shadow of bankruptcy also might include the supply of emergency funds or the arrangement of financing

for the distressed firm through cooperation with other banks. This means of addressing problems was seen as less costly than liquidation. **Lifetime employment** practices in large firms meant the underdevelopment of a labor market for mid-career employees. Therefore, employees left jobless due to bankruptcy were likely to find reemployment difficult. In smaller firms, in contrast, the expectation of lifetime employment was not as firmly entrenched, the labor market was more mobile, and re-employment was easier to find.

Occasionally, the monitoring mechanisms of the **main bank system** fell short, however. This was the case with Sanko Kisen, a Japanese shipping company with the largest tanker fleet in the world that filed for protection from creditors in 1985 after many years of over-expansion. Such high-profile bankruptcies were extremely rare through the mid-1990s, however.

The extraordinary commitment of banks to large corporate borrowers was supplemented by government support both in the prevention of bankruptcy and in support of rescues in cases when large corporations approached the brink of insolvency. In the financial sector, for example, the fear of bankruptcy was never real until the mid-1990s. Under the so-called convoy approach to regulating financial institutions, failure was not an option. **Competition** was suppressed by the **Ministry of Finance** (MOF) so that no firm moved forward so fast as to leave any others behind. If a financial institution nonetheless came under financial distress, the Finance Ministry arranged for a stronger bank to absorb the ailing one. When necessary, as in the case of Yamaichi Securities in 1965, the **Bank of Japan** stepped in to supply funds to prevent failure, in the interests of financial system stability. Avoiding bankruptcy meant protecting depositors and helped maintain confidence in the financial system.

Heavy regulation in many other sectors of the Japanese economy also guarded against "excessive competition" that might otherwise have led to bankruptcy and protected companies from being exposed fully to market forces. These regulations typically included strict entry and exit requirements, price controls and other means to induce companies to cooperate even as they competed.

Surge in bankruptcies in the latter 1990s

After Japan's asset bubble burst in 1991, many companies struggled under the weight of high interest payments on large debts and sluggish revenues. Massive amounts of fiscal stimulus, government efforts to prop up the stock market, and low interest rates initially staved off large-scale bankruptcies. Lax accounting and disclosure standards by banks and their borrowers also helped postpone bankruptcy for many ailing firms and their financiers. Companies often transferred debts to subsidiaries or paper companies. Because consolidated accounting practices were not in place, this enabled parent companies to erase the debt from their books and thereby mask their financial distress. Banks also developed practices to avoid the classification of loans as non-performing. One commonly used means involved banks issuing new loans to companies to enable them to pay the interest on existing loans.

These efforts at hiding problems and postponing reckoning with financial distress became increasingly inadequate, however, as the nation moved into the second half of the 1990s decade. In the fiscal year 1996, the level of debt left by corporate bankruptcies reached the highest in history to that point, spurred by an increase in large-scale bankruptcies of bubble-floated finance companies. The high amounts of debt left by bankruptcies in the four years thereafter reflected the emergence of a number of large-scale bankruptcies such as department store operator Sogo, listed on the First Section of the Tokyo Stock Exchange, and major financial institutions.

The rise in large-scale bankruptcies from 1999 on also was a byproduct of a new system of financial regulation put in place in October 1998. Regulatory authorities tightened disclosure requirements and asset classification standards for banks, moves that translated into increased pressure on borrowers to restructure. At the same time, an infrastructure for dealing with insolvent banks was established, meaning that problems with delinquent loans could be dealt with more aggressively. While **restructuring**, mergers and acquisitions, and tie-ups with foreign firms were able to stave off bankruptcy for some firms as the economy continued to flounder, others succumbed. The number of bankruptcies resulting from falling sales and the inability to collect account receivables soared in 2000 on the backdrop of slowed growth, weak consumer spending, and the reluctance of banks to extend new credit or roll over loans to troubled firms. The retail and construction sectors were hit particularly hard in this period.

Small and medium-sized companies also found conditions to be harsh in the latter 1990s. In 1998, amid a sharp credit crunch and financial system instability, the government adopted a special thirty trillion yen loan guarantee program for small and medium-sized enterprises. Despite these efforts to prop up weak companies, however, thousands of firms taking out loans ended up insolvent. The number of failures of semipublic companies (ventures between the public and private sectors) also increased in the second half of the 1990s and accelerated further in 1998 and 1999, damaging the financial health of local governments.

Developments in bankruptcy legislation

Japanese bankruptcy laws were relatively strong and included the removal of top management. Yet, they were rarely used in the case of large corporations over the postwar period. Until 2000, bankruptcy procedures were undertaken in accordance with the Composition Law. The introduction of the Civil Rehabilitation Law on April 1 of this year, however, made it easier for small and midsize companies to declare bankruptcy and began to speed up the corporate rehabilitation process. The new law has led to a surge in bankruptcy applications.

Under the law, companies may apply for court protection and dispose of debt even before their liabilities exceed their assets. As a result, the new law has given rise to some distrust between banks and their borrowers, as banks now have incentives to try to collect as many loans as possible before borrowers go bankrupt. This changed bank behavior contrasts sharply with that behavior observed when the main bank system functioned effectively in earlier periods.

The new law also permits debtors to initiate bankruptcy proceedings and allows managers to stay in their positions. The Ministry of Justice furthermore revised bankruptcy-related laws in

2000 so that the overseas assets of failed firms operating across national borders would fall within the scope of Japanese bankruptcy proceedings. This change enabled the recovery of loans from such assets by creditors in a more orderly fashion than in the past. The absence of such a provision had impeded plans by Yamaichi Securities Co. to restructure its operations prior to its voluntary closure in November 1997.

Rise in personal bankruptcies following the bursting of the bubble

The 1990s saw many changes in the level of personal bankruptcies as well. In this decade, the number of cases of personal bankruptcy rose tenfold. In 1991, cases of personal bankruptcy doubled on the year with the bursting of the speculative asset bubble to number approximately 23,000. Although the incidence of personal bankruptcy rose somewhat in the years thereafter, numbers surged significantly in 1996. And, in fiscal year 1998, the number of cases exceeded 100,000 for the first time.

The record high numbers of personal bankruptcies reflected the strain placed on household finances by rising **unemployment** levels and the growth in the consumer loan industry. Consumer debt doubled in the 1990s decade and non-bank consumer loan companies – not subject to the Interest Rate Restriction Law – were able to charge exorbitant interest rates on loans. Many individuals were also driven into bankruptcy after serving as guarantors for collateral-free loans extended by non-banks to small enterprises.

The surge in personal bankruptcies had a significant impact on Japanese society, perhaps most notably in the incidence of suicide. Nearly 3,000 individuals were reported to have committed suicide in fiscal year 1998, due to excessive personal debts.

Further reading

Pascale, E. and Rohlen, T. (1983) "The Mazda Turnaround," *Journal of Japanese Studies* 9(2): 219–63.

Saxonhouse, G. (1979) "Industrial Restructuring in Japan," *Journal of Japanese Studies* 5(2): 289–320.

JENNIFER AMYX

banto

Banto was the highest position of authority within a traditional merchant house, equivalent to head clerk. Within smaller merchant houses, the *banto* often held near absolute authority in business decisions. In larger houses, there might be several *banto*, in which case one would be designated *shihainin*, chief manager. *Banto* could use their own savings to set business on the side. They were also permitted to have a separate household and commute to work. If his business were successful he might be given permission to set up his own, separate house, *bekke*. In such instances, he still had an obligation of loyalty to his former house. He would demonstrate that loyalty by regularly paying his respects to the house and by assisting it as called upon. Failure to honor his obligations could result in recision of the *bekke* and a return to his former House.

One enduring and popular type of tale is of the loyal *banto* who, through daring, cleverness or great courage rescues the house from financial distress or ruin. Typical of this type of tale is the example of **Minomura** Rizaemon, who saved **Mitsui** from bankruptcy and guided it onto greatness.

The characteristics and role of the *banto* foreshadow several distinctive aspects of what has come to be known as the Japanese management system. *Banto* worked their way up to the position through a process of apprenticeship and demonstration of skill. Young men would enter the house at the age of twelve or thirteen and be assigned the rank of *detchi*. For a period of five to six years the *detchi* would learn to read and write, to do math, and how to handle many of the small tasks and routines of the house. At seventeen or eighteen the *detchi* would be promoted to the rank of *tedai* and be given a set salary. After ten to twelve years, usually around age thirty, a *tedai* who had demonstrated superior skill and business acumen would be promoted to *banto*. This practice of entering the house at an early age and then working one's way to the top is a type of internal labor market comparable to what is found in present day Japanese firms (see **internal labor markets**).

In a similar vein, the opportunity given *banto* to branch out and start one's own business draws a close parallel to the modern day practice of corporate spin-offs whereby successful units within the company are allowed, even encouraged, to separate from the parent organizations and achieve their own measure of independence. Such spin-offs continue to maintain close ties to their parents and, in some instances, rescue them from financial difficulties.

Further reading

Hirschmeier, J. and Yui, T. (1981) *The Development of Japanese Business*, 2nd edn, London: Allen & Unwin.

ALLAN BIRD

bottom-up decision-making processes

The Japanese, so-called "bottom-up" decision-making process has launched many an organizational change effort seeking to uphold consensus in hopes of delivering smooth and efficient implementation marked by strong employee ownership. While it is true that implementation of organizational decisions tends to proceed more smoothly in Japanese organizations, this is not because the outcomes come about by consensus, nor because they are bottom instigated. Rather, the key to Japanese decision-making is its distinctive emphasis on information gathering.

After an idea is formulated in a Japanese company it is explained, discussed, and confirmed by all those who might have input into or be affected by the decision. This procedure called **ringi seido** is most accurately understood as a political confirmation-authorization process. First, the initiator writes a proposal in the form of a *ringi-sho*. The proposal is then circulated to all who might be able to input critical information into the decision and to all who will be affected by it. The initiator (or an emissary) will then meet with each

decision-making contributor one or more times to discuss at length the various elements of the proposal. This critical aspect of the process is called **nemawashi**, preparing the ground for optimal germination.

Once all aspects of the decision have been analyzed and confirmed, each contributor affixes his/her seal (*hanko*) to the *ringi-sho* document and it is then sent to top management for final approval – or disapproval. Given the extremely competitive nature of Japanese firms both within and without Japan, it would be naive to perpetuate an understanding of "bottom-up" as delegation of strategic decision-making to middle managers and line workers. On the contrary, an important decision cannot be confirmed without ultimate approval by top management. Furthermore, it is more the norm that the initial idea is passed down from top-level executives.

The *ringi-sho* itself can be seen as an instrument that gives opportunity to participate in the decision-making process, documents the record of approval, and transmits a decision to organizational units affected by it. Finally, it is used as a corporate record that serves to protect the continuity of corporate policies.

The net used to gather pertinent information for decision making is therefore rather large and widely cast. In addition, most of the information-gathering discussions are conducted one-on-one and face-to-face bases to promote trust, avoid public confrontation and encourage complete and open sharing of ideas. Decision making in the Japanese style is consequently time-consuming.

Advances in communication technology such as the facsimile (fax) of the 1990s and electronic mail (e-mail) in the latter part of the decade, have increased the speed of some aspects of the decision-making process. For instance, some of the information gathering is currently done through these communication media. However, *nemawashi* continues to be done one-on-one, and face-to-face thereby preserving the value of frankness while minimizing conflict.

Viewing decision making as a process rather than an event is key to understanding the time factor in the Japanese system. Gathering information and confirmation from a wide array of organizational actors one-on-one takes time. Even more time is required if several iterations of *nemawashi* with the same individuals is necessary. Once the decision has been made, however, very little time is required to take action, last-minute surprises are extremely rare, and very little resistance to implementation is encountered.

An important ramification of the Japanese-style decision-making process is that since decisions are a collective effort, a conscious mutual dependence of seniors and juniors in a company is nurtured. Responsibility in the Japanese context means a symbolic assumption of guilt. The rules of this sort of responsibility revolve around the tenets of a vertically integrated society: when something goes wrong, the most senior person presiding over the error takes the "blame." This means that those above must rely on their subordinates not to make errors that will lead to their having to take the necessary consequences associated with symbolic responsibility such as resignation, or transfer.

Further reading

Smith, L. (1985) "Japan's Autocratic Managers," *Fortune*, 7 January.

Whitehill, A.M. (1991) *Japanese Management: Tradition and Transition*, New York: Routledge.

MARY YOKO BRANNEN

bubble economy

The Japanese economy in the late 1980s was characterized by what seems to be an asset price bubble. Land and stock prices reflected much speculative activity and rose to record levels that were unusually high multiples of the present value of future cash flows. Unfortunately, land and stock prices collapsed in 1990 and were still less than 40 percent of their peak levels a decade later. The Nikkei 225 stock index peaked on the last trading day of 1989 (29 December) at just below 40,000 and at that time the land below the Imperial Palace in Tokyo was reputedly worth more than all of the land and real estate in California. The Japanese economy has suffered from highly anemic growth (of around 1 percent) for the decade of the 1990s. How did Japan, an **economic growth** miracle of

the post-Second World War period, develop this bubble and why is it suffering from its after-effects a decade later?

After Second World War much of the Japanese economy lay in ruins and Japanese industry and economy, as well as its political and financial systems were restructured by the occupying forces led by General Douglas McArthur and his staff. Fortunately, Japan enjoyed a period of rapid economic growth in the forty-year period, 1950–90, rebuilt its economy to prewar levels by the early 1960s, and had become the second largest economy in the world by the 1970s. Unfortunately, economic growth in Japan virtually stopped at the beginning of the 1990s with the collapse of the asset price bubble. How did this asset price bubble arise?

While there may be little agreement on details such as the technical definition of a bubble and the exact starting and ending dates for the bubble, there is little disagreement on the broad features of the late 1980s and 1990s episode of the speculative rise in asset prices and then their sudden decline with adverse consequences for the Japanese economy. The following is a brief outline of this bubble episode, its possible causes, and a review of efforts to mitigate its negative economic consequences.

The late 1980s bubble in Japan seemed to have started as a consequence of the efforts to fight off the 1986 recession caused by the sudden jump in the value of the yen associated with the international Plaza Accord in 1985. In the late 1980s the government continued efforts to balance its budget even in the face of a recession using monetary policy as the primary means of economic stimulus. Consequently, there was an unprecedented lowering of interest rates (from 5 percent in January 1986 to 2.5 percent in February 1987) and an expansionary monetary policy starting in 1986 (in response to the recession resulting from the 1995 *endaka* rise in the Yen engineered by the Plaza Accord). This extraordinary episode of monetary expansion seemed to have started an asset price bubble that then characterized the late 1980s Japanese economy.

Contributing to this bubble in Japan were a number of institutional practices that accelerated the bubble with positive feedbacks. For example, as most lending in Japan tends to be based on collateral value, asset price increases led to higher collateral values and higher levels of lending which then led to higher asset prices and so forth in an ever accelerating set of self reinforcing cycles. Unfortunately, there were few if any mechanisms in Japan at that time to discipline or stop the bubble in asset prices.

Between the start and end of the second half of the 1980s, stock prices rose 3.1 times (to a Nikkei Index of 38,915) and land prices rose four times. In relative terms, for the last half of the 1980s, the ratio to GDP for land prices increased 3.67 times and for stock prices by 1.51 times with the combined ratio increasing by 4.52 times. By any measure these were extraordinary increases in asset prices unprecedented in recent Japanese history. Price earnings ratios and other valuation measures for Japanese equities were in a much higher zone than similar ratios elsewhere in the world. With these highly valued assets, Japanese companies went on a spending spree buying up prime real estate and other assets in many foreign countries at what later turned out to be highly inflated values. The easy availability of money in the second half of the 1980s also led to poor investment decisions domestically.

As this late 1980s asset price bubble led to increasing inequality and other social problems including a potential breakdown of the social compact, the Japanese government and the **Bank of Japan** started to take steps to deflate the bubble, raising interest rates from 2.5 percent in May 1989 to 6 percent in August 1990 and curtailing monetary growth severely also during this period. However, instead of a soft landing, the bubble collapsed in 1990. The value of the collateral underlying most bank loans collapsed along with the asset price bubble. Consequently, since the bursting of the bubble, bank lending has been restricted by the continuing high levels of non-performing bank loans (Japanese banks had yet to be restructured a decade later). It seems that the same positive feedback cycles that accelerated Japanese economic growth were now working in reverse accelerating the decline in Japanese economic growth. Since the bursting of this bubble in 1990, the Japanese economy has suffered a

number of recessions and a very low overall rate of growth in the 1990s.

In spite of fiscal stimuli in the form of numerous government spending packages, an expansionary monetary policy, and other efforts by the government, the Japanese economy has been in a state of recession or very anemic growth since the early 1990s bursting of the bubble. The government launched nine major deficit spending packages totaling about $1.2 trillion between 1992 and 1999. The Bank of Japan steadily lowered interest rates to virtually zero by the end of the 1990s. The ineffectiveness of Japanese monetary policy to stimulate the economy has led many to contend that Japan is in a liquidity trap. Given the high savings rate in Japan and its low, demographically limited long-term economic growth prospects, the savings-investment equilibrium real interest rate is estimated to be negative. Thus, given a nominal interest rate floor of zero, a positive expected rate of inflation is necessary for equilibrium. Indeed, since the mid-1990s there seems to be considerable evidence of money hoarding in Japan with significant growth of the money supply but zero or negative growth in bank lending.

However, an alternative explanation of the ineffectiveness of monetary and fiscal policies in Japan in the 1990s may be the credit crunch associated with the high levels of non-performing loans among Japanese banks. Tankan, the Bank of Japan survey of business conditions, provides some evidence supporting the credit crunch explanation. It seems that the financial system needs to be restructured so it can contribute to economic growth with non-performing loans written off, sold, or otherwise taken off the books.

Others have contended that the failure of the Japanese economy to respond to fiscal and monetary stimulus since 1990 can only be ended with massive structural reform and deregulation of Japanese business and industry. Deregulation can be accomplished either in one or a few major episodes, or can be undertaken slowly allowing time for the affected firms to adjust. As may be expected, deregulation changes the competitive structure in an industry and many inefficient firms are forced out of business. Business failures create economic discomfort (for example, higher unemployment rates) and declines in consumer confidence. While there has been slow and steady deregulation of Japanese business and industry, there have been no major changes or deregulatory moves. It is clear that Japan has chosen to deregulate only at a slow and steady pace.

Another factor constraining the economic recovery in Japan has been the bubble-related changes in political governance in Japan. The **Liberal Democratic Party** (LDP) that had governed Japan for most of the post-Second World War period lost its majority in the Diet, the Japanese Parliament, soon after the collapse of the asset price bubble and Japan has been governed by a coalition of political parties since the early 1990s. Public confidence in the government and other large institutions has also been sapped by many corruption scandals involving elite officials. In this situation, political power has been dispersed and it seems that there has been little political will for strong and decisive action to restore economic growth.

Regardless of the reasons for the failures of policies for economic recovery, the Japanese economy faced a critical impasse by the end of the 1990s in terms of policies to restore economic growth. Fiscal policy options were constrained by the rapid growth of Japanese government debt in the 1990s (to $6 trillion, about 1.3 times GNP) and at the same time, monetary policy options were also limited as interest rates had already been dropped to near zero.

Before the last decade of the twentieth century, Japan's bank-centered system of capitalism was considered perhaps the best alternative for developing countries, especially in Asia. The US system with its more unfettered capitalism was considered suitable only for a highly developed and powerful country such as the USA. Indeed, many in the USA also believed that the Japanese version of industrial policy was more humane and a better alternative, even for the USA. While the dismal performance of the Japanese economy since 1990 has been a major cause for reassessing these views, the failure of the banking system in Japan also calls into question the nature and effectiveness of the Japanese bank-centered system of corporate governance where main banks closely monitored their commercial clients so that other stakeholders did not have to engage in wasteful duplicate monitor-

ing. After all, efficient monitoring is incompatible with the emergence of massive levels of non-performing loans and bad debts that have characterized the Japanese economy in the last decade of the twentieth century.

One explanation of this failure notes that Japanese banks have not developed credit analysis capabilities, having depended on government directed and collateralized lending and, given the generally poor levels of disclosure, nor have they been subject to market discipline. Under the prevailing *amakudari* practice where retiring senior regulators were virtually guaranteed senior positions with the institutions they regulated, it is contended that bank regulation in Japan has been less than fully effective. However, bank regulation may also have lost its effectiveness as Japan gradually moved to a more market-oriented economy and financial system. Regardless, the traditional (prior to the 1990s) Japanese system of bank-centered capitalism is now being widely questioned, even in many Asian developing countries though, this bank-centered financial system was associated with high rates of growth in the post-Second World War period until the late 1980s. Indeed, while there is widespread agreement in Japan that this old economic and financial system must be changed, there is less agreement on the form of the new system, and very little agreement on how to (and how fast to) move to a new economic and financial system.

Further reading

Aggarwal, R. (1996) "The Shape of Post-Bubble Japanese Business: Preparing for Growth in the New Millennium," *International Executive* 38(1): 9–32.

—— (ed.) (1999) *Restructuring Japanese Business for Growth*, Boston, MA: Kluwer Academic Publishers.

—— (1999) "Assessing the Asian Economic Crises: The Role of Virtuous and Vicious Cycles," *Journal of World Business* 34(4): 392–408.

Mori, N., Shiratsuka, S. and Taguchi, H. (2000) "Policy Responses to the Post-Bubble Adjustments in Japan: A Tentative Review," Bank of Japan, IMES Discussion Paper Series, 2000-E-13, May.

Motonishi, T. and Yashikawa, H. (1999) "Causes of the Long Stagnation of Japan During the 1990s: Financial or Real?" *Journal of Japanese and International Economies* 12(2): 181–200.

Okina, K., Shirakawa, M. and Shiratsuka, S. (2000) "The Asset Price Bubble and Monetary Policy: Japan's Experience in the Late 1980s and the Lessons," Bank of Japan, IMES Discussion Paper Series, 2000-E-12, May.

Olson, M. (1982) *Rise and Decline of Nations*, New Haven, CT: Yale University Press.

RAJ AGGARWAL

Buddhism

The majority of Japanese are nominally followers of various sects of the Buddhist religion; but they also practice observances of Shinto, a nature-oriented series of religious beliefs and practices unique to Japan. Buddhism was brought both to Japan from China, and brought into Japan from China by native Japanese beginning in the sixth century AD. Buddhism and Shintoism have remained co-religions since that time. Eventually purely Japanese versions of Buddhism were developed, and in the nineteenth and twentieth centuries several new religions based loosely on Buddhist teachings have emerged. Japan is unique in the modern world in that, while having two major religions, it is not, as is usually the case, divided by religion. Over 90 percent of the more than one hundred twenty million Japanese subscribe at least passively to both Shinto, the native religion, and Buddhism.

Toward the end of the sixth century, a newly united China began to spread its cultural brilliance outward toward its periphery, first to Korea, and eventually reaching Japan. Some leaders of an emerging Japanese government were greatly attracted to many aspects of Chinese civilization, its literacy, sophisticated architecture, advanced metallurgy, forms of urban life, and rational forms of governmental structure. Buddhism, of course, was part of it all, and Koreans who visited Japan with Buddhist artifacts and scriptures were eagerly accepted by Japanese as teachers. For the first and only time in Japanese history, an open rivalry was evidenced between Shinto, championed by a conservative element at the center of power, and a more progressive body of aristocrats who saw Buddhism as a hallmark of modernization and progress. Early in the seventh century the prince regent, Prince Shotoku, was eventually successful in establishing a form of Chinese Buddhism as a kind of semi-official court religion. Beyond the immediate community of the ruling elite, Shinto in its many manifestations remained the religious orientation of the masses.

For the first five hundred years of Japanese Buddhism it remained closely tied to the ruling nobility. Buddhist temples were sponsored by various noble families, and were more like centers of political organization and intrigue than as places to practice a religion. Buddhist scripture and rituals were generally accepted as a type of applied magic for most people who had access to them, although a few scholar/monks as early as the seventh century came to understand quite clearly the philosophical nature of Indian and Chinese Buddhism, and their teachings had some influence over the ruling elite.

It was not until the turmoil of the early twelfth century that Buddhism actually began to function as popular religion in Japan. It was a time of uncertainty and change; civil war broke out in various places, accompanied by a shift in political power from the nobility in Kyoto to a new warrior class more closely attached to common people. Four new and purely Japanese versions of the religion appeared: Jodo (Pure Land), Jodo Shinshu or True Jodo, Hokke or Lotus (often called Nichiren Buddhism, named after its founder the monk Nichiren), and Zen Buddhism. All four of these new versions of the religion featured heroic leaders and simple methods of devotion which could be utilized regardless of level of intelligence or learning, occupation, sex or class. While the warrior class itself leaned strongly toward the more contemplative Zen version of Buddhism, the other three swept across the land and are still the most prominent versions of Buddhism followed in Japan.

As ordinary people embraced popular Buddhism, they did not turn away from the native Shinto. The two religions were given their own areas of special emphasis and have continued on until the present with a peaceful accommodation.

Shinto has come to be associated with such tasks as marriage, christening, blessing of buildings, and thousands of local rituals involving the agricultural cycle. Buddhism deals with death and the departed: funerals, memorials at intervals after death, and to a somewhat more modest degree than in Christian and Moslem societies, serves as a guide to thinking and behavior.

In response to the growing popularity and power of the new versions of Buddhism, older sects headquartered at Kyoto and Nara eventually modified the way people related to religious practices. This was done to the extent that the great bulk of Japanese Buddhist observance has been for centuries either carried out entirely by professional clergy, or given over to extremely simple acts such as repeating phrases over and over. There is much depth to the purely intellectual part of Buddhism both inside and outside of Japan; writers inspired by aspects of Japanese Buddhist thinking now and in the past have had a respected and international audience. It is also true that Buddhism has had a significant impact on Japanese culture in an indirect way through its influence on the *samurai* class, and the subsequent influence that class had on modern Japan during the **Meiji restoration**. It must be noted, however, that except for a small segment of intellectuals and members of minority religions, the Japanese are very casual about matters relating to religion, viewing religion as not much more than a series of rituals. "Faith," in the Christian or Islamic sense, is a concept not intricately woven into Japanese culture.

In the nineteenth and twentieth centuries, several new religions emerged in Japan. Spka Gakkai, purported to be a reinterpretation of Buddhism, is the largest of these, and has grown to have considerable resources and influence in Japanese society.

See also: Prince Shotoku's Seventeen-Article Constitution

Further reading

Hori, I. (ed.) (1989) *Japanese Religion*, Tokyo: Kodansha International.

Kodo, M. (1982) *Introducing Buddhism*, Rutland, VT: Tuttle.

Prebish, C.S. (1975) *Buddhism: A Modern Perspective*, University Park, PA: Penn State University Press.

JOHN A. McKINSTRY

burakumin

Origins of burakumin

The term *burakumin* literally means "people of the hamlet," with earlier terms *eta* (polluted) and *hinin* (non-human), also used to label extremely low status people in Japan. The origins of *burakumin* people are not exactly clear and in dispute, but there are historical records going back to 600 AD of a low-status people similar to *burakumin*. Much like the untouchables or outcastes of ancient India, it is believed that *burakumin* originally had occupations that were seen as unclean or polluted in the eyes of Buddhists and Hindus, occupations such as dealing with dead animals (skinning and tanning of hides for example). However, new historical works suggest that having such occupations were not so much the cause of *burakumin* status but rather reinforced the status. There were several reasons a person could fall to a low position (such as being charged with criminal activity or falling into debt) and it was the limitations on what activities and occupations these people could have once in this lowly position that helped legitimize and perpetuate their status. It is also known that there were levels or degrees of this low outcaste status, with *eta* (polluted) being higher than *hinin* (non-human).

The Tokugawa stratification system

Much more is known about the status of *burakumin* from around the beginning of the fifteenth century. When the Tokugawa or Edo period began in Japan (early 1600s), the Tokugawa Shogun imposed more rigid controls upon the population and regional opponents to consolidate and maintain power in a country that had seen nothing but regional warfare for hundreds of years. One means of control imposed by the Tokugawa Shogun was the institutionalization of a system of social stratification, called *shi noo koo shoo* (literally meaning warriors, peasants, artisans, and merchants), with rigid and mostly hereditary ranks much like the caste system of ancient India. There were four primary status positions under the emperor and ruling shogun military clan; the samurai, peasants, craftsmen and artisans, with merchants on the bottom. Following the logic of the Indian caste system, of course, there was a status grouping, since called *burakumin*, who were even further down the ranks of the stratification system, and were so "unclean" or "polluted" as to have no real position at all; that is, they were "outcastes." Unlike the Indian caste system which used the Hindu concept of reincarnation and "bad karma" (sins in a previous life) to explain a person's position in the caste system, the *shi noo koo shoo* stratification in Japan did not specifically invoke religion as a legitimating force. It is estimated that there were about half a million people in this outcaste position during the Tokugawa period of Japanese history.

Burakumin in modern Japanese history

With the fall of the Tokugawa Shogun by 1868 and the beginning of the Meiji Period, the rigid Tokugawa stratification system was eliminated. The new political elite of Japan formally eliminated the position of *burakumin* in 1871 and made discrimination against former *burakumin* people illegal. As has happened many times in India since the formal elimination of the old caste system, however, people considering themselves above outcastes or *burakumin* rioted in response to government attempts to attain more opportunity for these people. Crowds as large as 26,000 at any one time were reportedly involved in these anti-*burakumin* riots, with more than 2,200 *burakumin* homes burned in Fukuoka during 1871.

Burakumin today

There are estimated to be about 2–3 million people of *burakumin* heritage in Japan today, but unlike people of Korean or Chinese descent, there are no cultural, much less biological or racial, distinctions between people of *burakumin* heritage and all other Japanese. As recently as 1965, however, opinion polls showed that some 70 percent of Japanese

people still believed people of *burakumin* descent were of a different race.

The negative status has remained alive, therefore, and Japanese people have gone to great lengths to determine if a person has *burakumin* ancestry. Before parents will approve a marriage or employers will hire new employees for important positions, for example, there is often a search of past records to make sure the prospective marriage partner or employee is "clean" of *burakumin* ancestry. There are hundreds of detective agencies that specialize in tracking down information on *burakumin* ancestry, contributing to a somewhat significant percent of the Japanese economy.

One of the typical methods of detecting *burakumin* lineage is through old village family records. All Japanese citizens have their name listed in an official family registry. Most often this family registry is located in a small village because of the recent agricultural history of Japan with the majority of population in farming occupations until well into the twentieth century. Because of strict discrimination, most *burakumin* lived in separate villages (or hamlets) from other Japanese and thus it was not difficult to track down a person's *burakumin* heritage through examination of these village records. During the 1970s, in an attempt to further reduce discrimination against *burakumin*, the Japanese government required that family registries in former *burakumin* villages be kept from the general public.

However, in the last three decades, Japanese government has become involved in *doowa*, the official term for conditions and issues related to *burakumin*. Programs to reduce discrimination against *burakumin* (much like affirmative action programs in the United States) have shown considerable success since the late 1960s and early 1970s. It is estimated that about $30 billion was spent on these programs between the 1960s and 1993. Poverty rates are lower and educational attainment is higher. And whereas 90 percent of *burakumin* married other *burakumin* as recently as 1960, it is now estimated that about three in four marriages by people of *burakumin* lineage are with people of non-*burakumin* ancestry.

Further reading

Buraku Mondai Kenkyujo (ed.) (1997) *Buraku no*

Rekishi to Kaihoo Undoo. Gendai Hen (Buraku History and Liberalization Movement), Kyoto.

Hane, M. (1982) *Peasants, Rebels, and Outcastes: The Underside of Modern Japan*, New York: Pantheon.

Kerbo, H. and McKinstry, J. (1998) *Modern Japan: A Volume in the Comparative Societies Series*, New York: McGraw-Hill.

Komori, T. (1990) *Doowa Mondai no Kiso Chishiki* (Fundamental Knowledge of Doowa Problems), Tokyo: Akashi Shoten.

Noguchi, M. (2000) *Buraku Mondai no Paradaimu Tenkan* (Paradigm Shift for the Buraku Problems), Tokyo: Akashi Shoten.

MEIKA CLUCAS
HAROLD KERBO

business ethics

Business ethics has become an established discipline in Japan in the 1990s. However, there is no clear-cut definition of the term. In Japanese, *keizai* (economy) is a compound word consisting of *kei* and *zai*, which means governing the world in harmony and bringing about the well-being of people. Therefore both *keizai* and *keiei* (business) include a component of ethics. In the past, however, the Japanese did not define or use the term in a similar fashion to the Western view of ethics. However, in the early 1990s, the public was presented with scandal after scandal of governmental officials being paid huge bribes. Most officials resigned their positions, although a few were prosecuted and convicted. Because of this, business ethics has grown to become important within the Japanese business community.

During the Meiji period (1868–1912), **Shibusawa** Eiichi, a business leader, called for the unity of morality and economy. He cautioned against unethical business practices. He also argued that Confucian values provided the correct path to doing business in an ethical manner. Prior to the mid-1960s, the priority of Japanese business was on economic growth. Companies were unlikely to address ethical, social or environmental issues. Even when a corporation had caused serious damage to its neighbors or consumers, unless coerced by governments, consumer groups or local communities, disputes were settled by paying a small sum of money known as *mimaikin* or sympathy payment.

Victims of air pollution and toxic substance poisoning in the 1950–60s became dissatisfied with *mimaikin* and with informal dispute resolution methods and filed lawsuits against the polluting companies. Pollution in Minamata, a small city in Kumamoto Prefecture on Kyushu, Japan's southern island, was the first of several pollution cases. Minamata, which was mostly a fishing and agriculture society, was also home to Chisso Corporation, a large factory that produced nitrogen-based chemical fertilizers and plastics. Fish, birds and cats became sick. When this spread to humans, the companied denied that they were the cause, but paid *mimaikin*. The cause was later shown to be mercury poisoning from the factory's wastewater.

A second strange disease, similar to the outbreak in Minamata, was found in Niigata Prefecture. The victims' diets consisted mostly of fish from the Agano River. The cause was mercury poisoning from a Showa Denko factory. Victims filed lawsuits against the company in 1967. This was the first pollution suit against a major company in Japan.

Three months later, a lawsuit was filed in Yokkaichi in central Japan. A company was sued for air pollution. The Yokkaichi's court opinion criticized the government for lack of environmental planning. In 1968, a third case involved cadmium poisoning in Toyama. Finally, in 1969, a case was brought against Chisso Corporation by some of the victims in Minamata. Together, these cases came to be known as the "Big Four." These changed the field of business ethics in Japan. All four cases were decided in favor of the plaintiffs. The companies held to have legal responsibility due to the harm caused by their business operations. Changes in regulation administrative procedures, the growth of the consumer movement were a few of the changes.

The Japanese government passed a series of statutes and established a scheme to compensate pollution victims. Polluting firms were required to pay for this scheme. The Basic Law for Environmental Pollution Control and the Environmental Agency were established. Japanese firms began to take social responsibilities more seriously. The "Big

Four Pollution Suits" also gave rise to a social movement in Japan known as *shimin undo* (citizens' movements). Citizens' movements formed around local or regional environmental issues and focused on local governments for response and relief. Only rare cases, like the Big Four, were of national scale.

A second ethical issue, the contribution of corporations to society, first became an issue in Japan during the 1970s oil crisis. People resented corporations cornering the oil supply and their subsequent reluctance to sell oil. Firms were seen as anti-social, so public opinion turned against the companies. In the 1980s as corporations attempted to change from heavy industry to more sophisticated products, there was also a shift towards a greater concern for corporate social responsibility. During the **bubble economy** of the 1980s, the Japanese public seemed to think that since Japanese business was efficient it must also be ethical. Many business people also believed that their success was proof of excellent business practices.

Since the late 1980s, a series of business scandals have surfaced. They include illicit political donations, *dango* practices; loss compensation for favored clients in securities industries; bad loans and mismanagement of financial institutions; and the sale of HIV-tainted blood. These scandals were often industry-wide and appeared to be rooted in the Japanese way of doing business. The result was a passive trend in business ethics.

Social changes also contributed to a passive trend of business ethics by Japanese firms in the 1990s. These included public interest in the environment; international pressures to open Japanese markets; passage of product liability laws; revision of the commerce law to dilute **corporate governance**; and lack of empowerment of the Japan **Fair Trade Commission** (FTC). The Japanese law on product liability makes it the plaintiff's responsibility to prove design or manufacturing negligence, which is virtually impossible, especially given the complex, high-technology used in most products today. While the FTC is supposed to enforce antitrust laws, it has been called a "toothless tiger" because it is essentially powerless against the **Ministry of Finance** and **Ministry of International Trade and Industry**, both of which have vested interests in protecting Japanese

businesses. When the FTC has investigated powerful industries such as automotives and automotive parts, construction, glass, and paper industries, it has punished them with "recommendations."

In the late 1990s, many cases of Japanese corporations violating business ethics continued to be reported by the Japanese media. These include payoffs to corporate racketeers, loans without collateral by banks, and disclosure of unfair trade practices. Unlike in the USA where many firms have codes of ethics and systems in place to monitor compliance, most Japanese firms do not have explicit corporate codes of conduct or business ethics. A 1996 survey by the Japanese Business Ethics Society found that 35 percent of Japanese corporations have ethics checks by in-company committees; 25 percent of managers stress the importance of business ethics; 23 percent of firms have a code of ethics in place; and only 5 percent have introduced business ethics education into their corporations. Of the companies with ethics systems in place, 11 percent have a company ethics committee or department; 8 percent have a full-time officer in charge of ethics; 5 percent have a system for handling in-company suggestions on or complaints about company ethics; and only 3 percent have voluntary reporting of activities which run counter to the company's ethics policy. Companies with mission statements that include statements on ethics usually have such vague or abstract statements that they are of little help to company employees. In an influential article on business ethics in *Look Japan*, Koyama Hiroyuki argued that Japanese corporations must do three things in order to establish strong business ethics: (1) create a clear code of ethical business conduct showing what actions are expected in concrete terms; (2) establish a system for ensuring that the code of ethics is followed such as having an ethics officer or survey of employees; and (3) ensure everyday compliance of business ethics.

These issues continue to be prominent within the Japanese business community: corruption, industrial espionage and violation of intellectual property rights (IPR). A 1992 agreement between the USA and Japan led to a revision of Japan's Copyright Law. The revisions give copyright protection to foreign sound recordings before 1978; give foreign producers the right to authorize the rental of their recordings; and extend the protection period for records from 20–30 years. Intellectual property rights continued to be an issue in the Japan-US Economic Framework Talks in 1994. The Japanese government agreed that the Japanese Patent Office (JPO) would permit foreign nationals to file patent applications in English (with Japanese translations to follow) and, prior to the grant of a patent, the JPO would permit correction of translation errors. The US government agreed that the US Patent and Trademark Office (USPTO) would introduce legislation to amend US patent law to change the term of patents from seventeen years from date of grant to patent to twenty years from date of filing an application.

Industrial espionage has become more and more common in the 1990s. Japanese companies have been caught using a spy technique called "tunneling" in which they set up a fake subsidiary and hire away the foreign, competitor company's knowledgeable employees. In a survey on theft of intellectual property of American firms, the Japanese ranked fifth after China, Canada, France, and India. Moles planted as employees in competitors firms are another espionage technique. Foreign businesspersons have also complained about their rooms being bugged in Japanese hotels. Japanese businesses were widely accused of violating Intellectual Property Right laws during their earlier stages of economic development. More recently however, Japanese firms have become strong supporters of laws to protect IPR laws.

The roots of good corporate citizenship in Japan are different from the West. Japanese corporations' views of citizenship consists of donations to local festivals. From the early 1990s, executives started to consider adopting a western style of corporate citizenship. This includes social contributions by firms to environmental groups rather than just contributions to, or sponsorships, of cultural events and the arts, *mecenat*. Companies are trying to protect the environment and are giving scholarships to students from less developed countries. As part of the Agreements in the Japan-US Economic

Framework Talks, the US and Japan set a common agenda for cooperation in global perspective that includes twenty working groups. Seven working groups have to do with environmental issues: environmental policy dialogue; forests; oceans; Global Observation Information Network; environmentally friendly and energy-efficient technologies; conservation; and development assistance for the environment.

According to a Mecenat Association survey, 180 companies gave ¥23.6 billion in assistance to support arts and culture in 1993. In 1994, this total decreased by 13 percent; however, 190 companies provided assistance. Many companies believe that activities related to their main line of business such as research and development of pollution prevention technology constitute a social contribution. Social contributions outside of the main line of business include: *mecenat*, support for guide dogs for the blind, support of children whose parents have died in traffic accidents, and forest conservation. Social contributions of Japanese corporations are becoming necessary during the economic slump. Companies have come to believe that they cannot survive without consumer support and that being good corporate citizens will give them a competitive advantage. Japanese companies are also engaging in good corporate citizenship behaviors in the USA and Europe, but appear less likely to do so in Asia and other parts of the world.

See also: environmental regulations; overseas research and development; Japanese business in the USA

Further reading

Koyama, H. (1997) "What Happened to Japanese Business Ethics?" *Look Japan* 43(497): 14–16.
Taka, I. (1997) "Business Ethics in Japan," *Journal of Business Ethics* 16: 1499–1508.

TERRI R. LITUCHY

C

Canon

Canon, headquartered in Tokyo and originally best known for its cameras, competes today globally with a full range of consumer and professional imaging and information products. These include not only cameras, copiers and computer peripherals familiar to consumers around the world, but also fax machines, video and broadcasting equipment, and optical products for semiconductor manufacturing and medical fields. The company has manufacturing and marketing subsidiaries in all continents, and the global Canon Group is made up of more than 100 companies with over 80,000 employees and sales of $25 billion.

Canon's roots date back to 1933 with the founding of Precision Optical Instruments Laboratory. The laboratory was created with the aim of producing high-quality cameras capable of competing with the best in the world, such as Leica of Germany. Within a year, the prototype of Kwanon, Japan's first 35mm focal-plane-shutter camera, was produced, and in 1937 the orginal laboratory was reorganized as a joint-stock company under the name of Precision Optical Industry Co., Ltd. Ten years later, under the leadership of Dr. Takeshi Mitarai, the company was renamed Canon Camera Co., Inc.

Through successive model improvements and the introduction of new cameras, Canon Camera's reputation for quality and value soon began to gain attention outside of Japan. The company launched its international marketing efforts in 1951, and in 1955 took the first major step toward internationalization with the opening of the New York branch. Two years later the company made first inroads into Europe with the establishment of Canon Europa.

Since the 1950s Canon pursued an aggressive strategy to evolve from a specialized camera manufacturer into a versatile producer of business machines. In 1962 the company adopted its first five-year plan to diversify its product offerings. The first non-camera product was an electronic calculator, but the real breakthrough came when Canon entered the copy machine business. It was the first company able to challenge the dominant leader with products based on its own technology. These successful diversification efforts led the company to change its name in 1969 to Canon, Inc.

Entering new markets through unique technology has always been a foundation of the Canon business strategy. It is a company strongly focused on research and development and the creation of breakthrough products, and for that purpose maintains an extensive R&D network worldwide. Its dedication to innovation produced results: the company is consistently among the top patent recipients in the USA and ranks second in terms of patents registered in the USA in the 1990s. Canon's current strategic objective is to secure a global leadership position in the field of digital imaging equipment and network-based application services.

Canon's corporate philosophy of *kyosei* (first articulated by the former chairman Ryuzaburo Kaku) – living and working together for the common good – is the guiding principle for Canon companies around the globe and for long-term collaborative relationships with other companies.

Within the Canon organization, the principles of *kyosei* are complemented by the "three-self" concept: self-motivation, self-awareness, and self-management, reflecting Canon's management culture of independence, innovation, and entrepreneurship.

Further reading

Sandoz, P. (1997) *Canon*, London: Penguin Books.

VLADIMIR PUCIK

capital markets

Japan is the second largest economy in the world and the Japanese capital markets are some of the largest in the world. As in other countries, capital markets in Japan consist of the equity markets, government and corporate bond markets, and markets for longer term swaps, futures, options, and other derivatives.

The financial system in Japan is still mainly bank-centered with securities markets playing a relatively smaller role. Banks and internal financing are the main sources of funds for most companies in Japan. Companies in Japan generally have larger levels of debt in their capital structure than in the USA, with a great deal of debt in the form of short term loans that are routinely rolled over and are treated like long-term debt. Perhaps reflecting the higher savings rate in Japan, the real cost of capital in Japan has often been lower in these than in the USA.

Although it is changing and becoming more liquid, the Japanese market for corporate control is somewhat limited as companies are often closely held and hostile offers are generally not viewed favorably. Japanese accounting and reporting standards (see **accounting in Japan**) reflect the culture and are generally not as stringent as in the USA. While Japan has well-developed money markets with trading in short-term government, financial institution, and corporate securities, this note will focus on capital markets, the financial markets for longer-term securities.

The first issues of equities by a Japanese company took place in 1878. The first stock exchanges in Japan were set up in 1878, with the number of stock exchanges peaking at 123 in 1895. In these early days, trading on Japanese securities exchanges was limited mainly to bonds and futures on shares. Spot trades in shares remained very thin until the modern (post-Second World War) era as the *zaibatsu* business groups and other major companies were held privately in a pattern of cross-holdings.

Currently, there are eight stock exchanges and a fledgling JASDAQ over-the-counter market set up in collaboration with the US-based NASDAQ. The Tokyo Stock Exchange (TSE) is the largest stock exchange, accounting for over 85 percent of all Japanese equity market valuation and trading volume. In size, the TSE is followed by the Osaka Stock Exchange (also a major center for trading in derivatives), and by exchanges in Nagoya, Kyoto, Hiroshima, Fukuoka, Niigata, and Sapporo. Each of the three largest exchanges, Tokyo, Osaka, and Nagoya, also has second sections for smaller companies. The two major stock indexes for Japanese equities are the price-weighted Nikkei 225 and the value-weighted Tokyo Stock Exchange Index, Topix. Equities in Japan are traded in lots of 1,000 and each exchange-traded share has limits on daily price changes depending on share price category. New issues of equity in Japan are regulated by the **Ministry of Finance**. Preferential allocation of under-priced new issues is used to supplement the low (3.5 percent) underwriting expense.

Most fixed income securities are traded over the counter in Japan. Japanese bonds generally have a denomination of ¥100,000 and pay interest twice a year. The market for Japanese government bonds is now one of the largest in the world. In this market, certain bonds are identified as "benchmark bonds" and traded heavily while the prices of other bonds are based on market prices of these highly liquid bonds. The corporate bond market is less well-developed and fairly small in comparison. A large proportion of this corporate bond market consists of equity-linked bonds of financial institutions and utilities. Most corporate bonds are secured with access to the bond market limited mainly to the top corporations.

The Japanese economy in the late 1980s was characterized by what seems to be an asset price bubble (see **bubble economy**). Between the start and end of the second half of the 1980s, stock prices rose 3.1 times (to a Nikkei Index of 38,915) and land prices rose four times. In relative terms, for the last half of the 1980s, the ratio to GDP for land prices increased 3.67 times and for stock prices by 1.51 times with the combined ratio increasing by 4.52 times. By any measure these were extraordinary increases in asset prices, unprecedented in recent Japanese history. These land and stock prices reflected much speculative activity and rose to record levels that were unusually high multiples of the present value of future cash flows. The Nikkei 225 stock index peaked on the last trading day of 1989 (December 29) at just below 40,000, and at that time the land beneath the Imperial Palace in Tokyo was reputedly worth more than all of the real estate in California.

Unfortunately, land and stock prices collapsed in 1990 and were still less than 40 percent of their peak levels a decade later. In spite of fiscal stimuli in the form of numerous government spending packages, an expansionary monetary policy, and other efforts by the government, the Japanese economy has been in a state of recession or very anemic growth since the early 1990s bursting of the bubble. Compared to the second half of the 1980s, capital market activity has similarly been much lower in the 1990s. The 1990s saw the failure of many banks, securities firms, and investment banks.

In recent years, driven by technology and globalization, the Japanese financial system is being gradually deregulated. Trading in new financial instruments was progressively permitted all through the 1980s, derivatives markets were allowed by the late 1980s, and interest rates were deregulated in the early 1990s. The 1993 Financial System Reform Act dismantled barriers between banking and securities businesses and the implementation of the "Big Bang" set of financial deregulations was started in 1998. The Japanese financial system is changing and is gradually moving away from an over-reliance on banks to a more market-oriented system.

Further reading

Aggarwal, R. (1994) "Characteristics of Japanese Finance," *Global Finance Journal* 5(2): 141–68.

—— (1996) "The Shape of Post-Bubble Japanese Business: Preparing for Growth in the New Millennium," *International Executive* 38(1): 9–32.

—— (1999) *Restructuring Japanese Business for Growth*, Boston, MA: Kluwer Academic Publishers.

Mori, N., Shiratsuka, S. and Taguchi, H. (2000) "Policy Responses to the Post-Bubble Adjustments in Japan: A Tentative Review," Bank of Japan, IMES Discussion Paper Series, 2000-E-13, May.

Motonishi, T. and Yashikawa, H. (1999) "Causes of the Long Stagnation of Japan During the 1990s: Financial or Real?" *Journal of Japanese and International Economies* 12(2): 181–200.

Takagi, S. (1993) *Japanese Capital Markets*, Cambridge, MA: Blackwell Publishers.

RAJ AGGARWAL

cartels

A cartel is an agreement among independent firms to regulate prices by restricting production and competition. Restricting production makes a good or service scarce, and allows producers to be less likely to cave in to pressure from buyers to sell at lower prices. The Japanese government has encouraged cartels in order to keep prices high and help industry grow. During the late 1980s the government discontinued most legal cartels, but cartels continue unofficially, sometimes with informal government blessing and support, in important industries.

The USA was the first nation to adopt strong anti-cartel legislation, in the form of the Sherman Anti-trust Act of 1890. The primary goal of the Sherman Anti-trust Act was to protect small farmers and business from price gouging by big business, though many economists also thought that the economy would work more efficiently if there was free competition instead of control by cartels. Neither European nations nor Japan took a strong stand against cartels in the late nineteenth and early twentieth centuries. At that time, Japan had not yet developed true cartels with formal price or production agreements in its major industries, though **zaibatsu** in many industries informally coordinated prices. The absence of formal cartel agreements was in contrast to Europe, and especially Germany, where cartels were powerful. The Japanese government developed cartel legislation in 1925, but the legislation was pro-cartel. The Important Industries Law of 1925 allowed the government to supervise cartels and gave industry associations the right to set prices and production quotas and to force companies to join cartels. As the effects of the Great Depression hit Japan in 1930, the government mandated cartels in some industries and supervised their implementation. By 1932, virtually all heavy industry was organized into cartels.

Although the goal of American antitrust legislation had been to protect small farmers and businesses from price gouging by big business, the goal of Japan's pro-cartel legislation was to strengthen the nation's industries by helping them support prices. Cartels played a central role in Japan's **industrial policy** both before and after the Second World War. Although neoclassical economic theory holds that cartels make an economy less efficient by distorting prices, Japanese developmentalist thinking has held that in a late-industrializing country the state can use price distortions to promote industries that would not develop through the market. Cartels are meant to raise and stabilize prices for goods, thus encouraging investment and helping firms survive depressions.

When the Second World War ended in 1945, the victorious Allied powers occupied Japan for seven years. The occupation, which was dominated by the USA, tried to reshape Japanese institutions in order to turn Japan into a democracy which would not engage in military aggression. As part of this process, the American authorities wrote a law banning cartels, the Anti-monopoly Law. The Americans saw the great monopoly power of big business as responsible to a great extent for Japan's military expansion in the 1930s and 1940s.

Most Japanese leaders saw the attempt to suppress cartels as an American plot to weaken Japan's manufacturing industries. When the occupation ended, the Japanese government watered down the Anti-monopoly Law, opening the door to extensive cartel activity. From the 1950s through the 1980s the **Ministry of International Trade and Industry** (MITI) used official cartels as a core element of its industrial policy. It actively encouraged the use of cartels, helped organize them, and sometimes pressured firms to participate in them through the use of **administrative guidance**. Cartels were used in a wide variety of industries, from concentrated industries with just a few very large firms, like steel and chemicals, to industries, like textiles, with many firms. Various kinds of cartels were used, most of which restricted production in some way. Cartels were relied on especially during times of recession, but also during times of expansion. For instance, in industries such as cement and chemicals, firms agreed to take turns building new production facilities to limit the volume of new products coming onto the market at any one time. These cartels did not always work, and even when they did MITI would often monitor them informally to make sure they did not raise prices so high as to create large profits.

The peak period for legal cartels in Japan was from 1965 to 1972. During the 1950s many industries saw the **Japan Fair Trade Commission** (JFTC) as so weak that they did not need to bother to get permission for their cartels. Until the early 1970s, political leaders and the public were largely supportive of cartels because they thought them necessary to support weak industries. In 1973, however, the public became enraged when it learned that oil refiners had used their cartel to boost profits during the crisis when the Organization of Petroleum Exporting Countries (OPEC) withheld oil supplies. This outrage gave the JFTC the political support it needed to crack down on a number of illegal cartels. In 1973 it recommended that sixty-seven industries involving thirty-three trade associations desist from monopolistic activities. In addition, for the first time the commission filed criminal charges. The oil companies that were charged did not dispute that they had conspired to fix prices and restrict output, but they argued that they were following MITI's administrative guidance and therefore were not guilty of violating the law. The Tokyo High Court ruled against the oil companies in 1980, arguing that MITI did not have explicit authority to direct a cartel and that therefore the cartel was illegal.

Somewhat fewer cartels were used in the 1970s and 1980s, but nevertheless between 1978 and 1987 a number of declining industries used cartels to cut capacity and support prices under MITI guidance. In the mid-1980s another source of political opposition to cartels arose, this time from the USA. Japan's trade surpluses with the USA grew large at that time, and Americans argued that Japan was using cartels to block access to its markets. In response to American criticism, Japan largely abandoned officially sanctioned cartels.

Japan's cartels become somewhat more difficult to understand at this point. It is significant that Japan no longer sponsors large numbers of legal cartels. Yet there is considerable evidence that at least some of the cartels have simply gone underground.

The steel cartel

The steel industry is a good illustration of the ways in which Japan's government supports cartels. In order to work efficiently, the integrated steel plants that make steel from iron ore and form it into products such as sheets and beams must be very large. Steel firms are therefore also large and there are few of them. It is easier to make agreements to limit competition in a concentrated industry, that is one with few firms, because there is less chance that firms will cheat on the agreement. In all countries, steel is a relatively easy industry in which to form a cartel. European steel cartels were important through much of the twentieth century, and American steel companies were good at informally coordinating prices until the early 1960s. But in recent decades the Japanese steel industry has been much more successful at maintaining a cartel than the steel industries of Europe and the USA, and the reason has largely to do with support from MITI and the weakness of the JFTC.

There are five major integrated steel makers in Japan, which produce about two-thirds of Japan's steel. Minimills, which operate cheaply by melting down scrap steel to make new steel products, compete with the integrated steel makers, but there are many products the minimills cannot make and which the integrated makers have a monopoly over. Japan's integrated steel producers have been successful at keeping prices high and they have done so by maintaining a remarkably successful production cartel.

Demand for steel is quite sensitive to the business cycle and steel sales expand and contract by wide margins. Steel companies agree to support prices by restraining production amounts, especially when demand is weak. To spread the pain of production cuts evenly, the steel companies make sure that each company always produces the exact same share of the total volume of steel coming out of Japan's integrated steel plants. For example, Nippon Steel's share of total integrated steel production ranged between 40.8 percent and 41.5 percent. Variation in the other four companies' volumes of production is similarly slight. It would be impossible for the industry to keep market shares so stable for so long in such a volatile market without a cartel agreement. Without this careful dividing up of market shares, each steel firm would be tempted to try to produce more during business downturns and prices would fall further than they otherwise would. By maintaining their production cartel steel companies keep their prices far higher than prices in the USA and other countries.

The steel industry and MITI deny that there is a cartel. An agreement to limit production is illegal under the Anti-Monopoly Law. How does the steel industry manage to maintain the cartel even if it is illegal?

First, MITI helps out. The Ministry of International Trade and Industry (MITI) asks firms once a quarter to submit projections of production and guides them as to how much steel they should produce. Second, the JFTC allows the firms to continue the cartel. The JFTC has issued reports on the industry and has stated that there are worrisome signs of restraints on competition that bear watching. The JFTC has investigated and fined smaller industries. But it lacks the political support and resources to go after big industries like steel that flagrantly violate the Anti-Monopoly Law.

Despite Japan's high prices for steel, few imports make it into the market. Why do buyers not simply avoid the cartel by buying cheaper imports? In part this is because major users actually support the cartel. Big users like auto and electronics firms say they buy domestic steel in order to help assure that Japan maintains a strong steel industry, and because the Japanese steel industry provides high levels of quality and service that they value (see **competition**). This support from users also helps explain why the steel cartel enjoys diffuse political support and why the JFTC does not crack down on it. Yet while principal industrial users may pay the cartel's high prices voluntarily, the steel cartel reportedly threatens less committed buyers that it will cut off future supplies of Japanese steel if they buy imports. Middleman companies, including trading companies and the processing firms that cut and distribute steel, also reportedly hesitate to buy imports because of fear of retaliation from steel manufacturers. By keeping imports out, steel makers ensure that imports do not put too much downward pressure on domestic prices. This is in contrast to the USA and Europe, where large volumes of steel imports have pushed prices down.

Similar cartels operate in other concentrated industries, including chemicals, glass and cement. Cartels do not always work, and the possibility of JFTC enforcement against them is one of the factors that prevents them from raising prices high enough to produce large profits. However, the fact that such a blatant cartel as steel has operated for so long in Japan suggests that Japan's government is more tolerant and supportive of cartels than the governments of other industrialized countries.

Further reading

Freeman, L. (2000) *Closing the Shop: Information Cartels and Japan's Mass Media*, Princeton, NJ: Princeton University Press.

Johnson, C. (1982) *MITI and the Japanese Miracle: The Growth of Industrial Policy, 1925–1975*, Stanford, CA: Stanford University Press.

Kikkawa, T. (1997) "Functions of Japanese Trade Associations before World War II: The Case of Cartel Organizations," in H. Yamazaki and M. Miyamoto (eds), *Trade Associations in Business History*, International Conference on Business History, Vol. 14, Proceedings of the Fuji Conference.

Noble, G. (1998) *Collective Action in East Asia: How Ruling Parties Shape Industrial Policy*, Ithaca, NY: Cornell University Press.

Tilton, M. (1996) *Restrained Trade: Cartels in Japan's Basic Materials Industries*, Ithaca, NY: Cornell University Press.

Yamamura, K. (1982) "Success That Soured: Administrative Guidance and Cartels in Japan," in K. Yamamura (ed.), *Policy and Trade Issues of the Japanese Economy: American and Japanese Perspectives*, Seattle, WA: University of Washington Press.

MARK TILTON

Central Union of Agricultural Cooperatives

The Central Union of Agricultural Cooperatives (*Zenchu*) is a central organization of **agricultural cooperatives** (*Nokyo*) established by the 1954 amendment to the Agricultural Cooperative Society Law. The amendment called for the setting up of a prefectural union of agricultural cooperatives in each prefecture, and the Central Union of Agricultural Cooperatives at the national level. The Central Union was created for the purpose of strengthening organizational structures within the agricultural cooperative mvement, and in concrete terms, for the purpose of improving the cooperatives functions in terms of providing farm guidance, better living guidance, and audits of agricultural cooperatives' new undertakings.

Zenchu's purpose, therefore, were described as auditing, farm guidance, better living guidance, management guidance and agricultural administration activities. Auditing and management guidance involved the provision of services directly to agricultural cooperatives. Farm guidance was originally started as production guidance aimed at achieving increased food production and self-sufficiency of rice. Its purpose shifted in the 1960s to provide guidance on diversificattion from rice culture to stock raising, fruit growing and horticulture, and to turn respective areas into main production centers of the relevant crops. Excess rice production became an issue in the 1970s. Major challenges at the time were the implementation of rice production adjustment and crop diversification.

In addition to these problems, increasing attention was given to the perspectives of international competition from the beginning of the 1990s. Opportunities to pursue expansion of the farm-operating scale through coordination of agricultural land use, and to nurture a new generation that would be the support and driving force of future agriculture were explored. In the area of better living guidance, *Zenchu*'s efforts initially centered on the modernization of kitchens and toilets in farmers' households, and provision of community-based assistance such as establishment of day nurseries and lunch delivery service during the busiest farming season. Subsequently, in the 1960s the focus of *Zenchu*'s efforts shifted to consumer activities for food safety, and health management and group health checkup associated with the use of agricultural chemicals. *Zenchu* has recently taken part in activities relating to health care for elderly in the community.

The Central Union of Agricultural Cooperatives' rice price struggle in the 1960s, its movements against farm product trade liberalization, and fierce protest against the government and foreign countries concerning the issue of taxation and agricultural land in urban areas in the 1970s and 1980s all helped to make its name widely known in Japan and abroad. After farm product trade liberalization, however, these activities have lost some of their former momentum. *Zenchu* has shifted its focus to the issue of management conditions of individual cooperatives and the problem of organizing members. Improvement of the management of agricultural cooperatives is considered by *Zenchu* as its most important task. To cope with financial deregulation, and maintain or improve soundness of management, agricultural cooperatives are urgently enhancing their auditing capabilities. *Zenchu* in the meantime is required to promote the qualitative transformation of these agricultural cooperatives as quickly as possible.

KENJI ISHIHARA

central wholesale markets

The distribution of many perishable foodstuffs in Japan is organized through a national system of central wholesale markets (*chuo oroshiuri shijou*) and regional wholesale markets (*chihou oroshiuri shijou*). Altogether, slightly more than 1,500 wholesale markets throughout Japan trade in seafood, fresh fruits and vegetables, fresh meat, eggs and poultry, and cut flowers. Seafood and produce are the major commodities that pass through these market systems; many markets handle only one or two commodities although a few deal in all types. The structures of production and distribution for various commodities differ widely and so the market channels for each are quite distinct, although seafood and produce often converge in major urban markets.

The national market system is organized around two interlocking dimensions of vertical integration. One is the functional classification of markets at different scales and levels: central vs. regional wholesale markets, the latter further divided between production or consumption areas. This hierarchy is paralleled by and maintained through a complex system of licensing for markets and traders, which defines the scope of activity at each market level and structures the chains of transactions that link them.

Market levels

In 1998, the most recent year for which figures are available, there were 87 central wholesale markets and 1,447 regional wholesale markets in Japan. Of the central wholesale markets, 72 handled produce with a total sales value of ¥2.7 trillion; 53 handled seafood (¥2.9 trillion); 23 dealt in flowers (¥160 billion); and 10 dealt in meat products (¥240 billion). The total sales volume of regional wholesale markets, across all commodity categories and including both production and consumption regions, was ¥4.8 trillion.

Foodstuffs enter and circulate through the market system in many ways. At "upstream" markets – that is, production region markets – some of the products may go for local consumption, but producers and producer co-operatives primarily sell to brokers, processors, and agents of higher-level urban markets. These traders, in turn, bulk or consolidate catches into larger shipments for sale or consignment in other markets "downstream," closer to urban consumers, including central wholesale markets in large cities as well as consumption region markets. These markets break or disassemble commodity flows into lots small enough to be of use to a retailer or restaurateur. Production region markets and higher-level regional markets depend exclusively on domestic production. Central wholesale markets receive products from lower level regional and local markets, as well as directly from individual producers, and imported foodstuffs often enter the market system at this level, from trading companies and foreign producers. Consumption region markets generally depend on central wholesale markets for their supplies.

The Ministry of Agriculture, Forestry, and Fisheries (*Nourinsuisanshou*, also known by the acronym MAFF) charters central wholesale markets in cities with populations greater than 200,000. MAFF sets national standards, enforces policies to ensure fair trading practice, and grants licenses to the auction houses or primary wholesalers that supply these markets. Local authorities (municipal or prefectural governments), on the other hand, oversee the day-to-day operations of these markets, issue licenses for local wholesalers, and enforce local regulations governing market operations, such as setting hours of operations, allocating space, and determining specific categories of goods to be traded.

Regional wholesale markets are chartered by prefectural governments and are operated as municipal, co-operative, or private ventures (which make up roughly 85 per cent of the total). These markets are divided into those that serve "production regions" (*sanchi*) and those for "consumption regions" (*shouhichi*), generally in regional cities and suburbs. Markets in production regions are often closely linked to local branches of the national system of **agricultural cooperatives** (*nougyou kyoudou kumiai* or *noukyou*) and fisheries cooperatives (*gyogyou kyoudou kumiai* or *gyokou*), which in some cases operate the local markets. Consumption region markets are mostly owned and operated by private corporations.

Production markets funnel foodstuffs from local farmers and fishers into national distribution channels in various ways: regional brokers may purchase local products for shipment and resale to urban markets; cooperativess themselves may create a local brand for products that they sell on consignment either through the regional market or directly through urban central wholesale markets; and individual producers may bypass regional markets and consign their products directly to a central wholesale market.

The entire system operates under the Central Wholesale Market Law (*Chuo Oroshi Shijou Hou*),

which was originally passed in 1923 in response to the so-called "Rice Riots" of 1918. In protest against speculative trading in foodstuffs and consequent severe shortages, residents violently stormed rice and other food dealers and markets in over 100 cities and towns, until the Japanese army quelled the riots. The law, which has been revised and updated several times since then, established publicly regulated markets to prevent price-fixing, collusion, and other anti-competitive practices.

Licensing and regulation

Competitive auctions are the core mechanism of central wholesale markets to ensure that transactions are "impartial and equitable" (*kouhei to kousei*). The rules and regulations under which auctions must take place are spelled out in general terms by national regulations and in minute detail by local ordinances as well as in the customary understandings that surround trade in a particular marketplace.

Primary wholesalers or auction houses, known officially as *oroshiuri gyousha* (wholesale dealers) or *niuke gaisha* (freight receivers, i.e. consignees) are licensed directly by MAFF to operate in a specific marketplace. Their licenses give them exclusive rights to make markets for products and also require them to attract a steady supply for that market's demand. There are about 260 auction houses nationwide. (Auction houses in regional markets are licensed by prefectural authorities; there are roughly 1,700 such regional auction houses.) Many auction houses are affiliated with national chains, or *keiretsu*, that have similar auction houses in other major markets. In seafood markets, for example, the Maruha Corporation (formerly known as Taiyou Gyogyou KK) controls a dozen subsidiary firms that operate auction houses in major central wholesale markets, and Maruha also has close ties with many other auction houses in regional markets.

Auction houses obtain products on consignment (*itaku hanbai*) or on their own account (*kaitsuke*). Domestically, consignments come directly from producers, from producer cooperatives, and from brokers operating in regional markets. Imported products, unlike domestic ones, are more likely to enter the **distribution system** at the level of central wholesale markets rather than through regional markets. Imported products are purchased outright from foreign producers by the auction houses and their overseas affiliates, or arrive on consignment from major trading companies, **joint ventures** between foreign producers and Japanese food companies, and directly from foreign producers.

Auction houses sell through various forms of auctions (known collectively as *seri* or *seri-uri*, but more precisely classified as open bidding auctions (*seri*) or sealed bid auctions (*nyousatsu* or *nyousatsu-seri*)). In addition, auction houses may sell products to licensed wholesalers through negotiated sales (*aitai-uri*). Auction houses receive commissions that are set by local regulations. The precise methods of auction and rules surrounding negotiated sales vary from marketplace to marketplace and from commodity to commodity. Auctioneers (*serinin*) are salaried employees of the auction houses and are individually licensed by the local authorities responsible for administering marketplaces.

Auction houses in turn sell to intermediate wholesalers (*nakaoroshi gyousha* or *nakagainin*) who are licensed by the local authorities who administer each market. Nationally, there are about 6,000 intermediate wholesalers, each licensed – just like the auction houses – to operate only in a single marketplace. Many of the intermediate wholesaling firms are small family-owned businesses, some of which can trace their histories in the trade back many generations, in some cases to the markets of the feudal Tokugawa period (1600–1868). Contemporary wholesale markets, therefore, tend to be close-knit, insular, and imbued with a strong ethos of tradition, both in terms of commercial practice and in relation to Japanese food culture as an important cultural legacy.

In larger markets, intermediate wholesalers are highly specialized; at Tokyo's enormous **Tsukiji market** (where there are, respectively, for seafood and produce seven and four auction houses, 953 and 126 intermediate wholesalers, and 388 and 1,018 authorized buyers) individual firms specialize in particular varieties of produce (onions or citrus fruits) or species of seafood (tuna or shrimp or octopus). In smaller markets, intermediate wholesalers may handle almost the full range of products found in the market as a whole. Intermediate

wholesalers are authorized to operate their own shops within a marketplace to resell products. In addition, some marketplaces license "authorized buyers" (generally retailers or secondary distributors) to participate in auctions, but they are not allowed to resell in the marketplace. Nationally, there are approximately 48,000 "authorized buyers." At regional markets of all kinds, there are a total of approximately 185,000 licensed buyers.

Recent trends

Despite the enormous volume of foodstuffs that continues to pass through the national system of wholesale markets, since the 1980s its overall significance has declined, because of changes both in the structure of distribution and in consumer behavior.

People in the food and distribution industries use the term *jounai ryuutsuu* (distribution within the market system) to describe transactions and channels that make use of the national system of wholesale markets, auctions, and licensed dealers. This is in contrast to *jougai ryuutsuu* (distribution outside the market system) which refers to the non-regulated free trade in food products. As the Japanese domestic economy has changed over the past generation, *jougai ryuutsuu* has become much more important than it was in the past, in part because advances in communications and transportation make the shipment of perishable foodstuffs very easy nationwide, thus reducing some of the function of the nodal distribution system organized around central markets.

In addition, large-scale retailers such as supermarket chains have developed their own independent distribution channels directly linking them both to domestic producers and importers. Large trading companies, many of which have major investments in supermarket and restaurant chains, have also become much more active in importing foodstuffs, some of which is sold through central wholesale markets, but much of which goes directly to large-scale retail chains.

Paralleling these trends are changes in Japanese consumer behavior. Traditional small-scale retailers have steadily lost sales over the past fifteen years to supermarkets and convenience stores (**konbini**), which handle increasingly large arrays of prepackaged and processed products. Distinct changes in the average diet and consumption patterns of average Japanese consumers have had direct impact on the sales of many of the kinds of fresh foodstuffs that the market system has traditionally handled. Wholesale markets handle less and less of the high volume sales of the most basic foodstuffs that supermarkets and restaurant chains can arrange through their own distribution networks.

Markets therefore have become more specialized at the top end of the spectrum: high quality and high value products that are in demand for premier restaurants and for discriminating consumers who continue to shop in specialty retail shops. During the boom years of the so-called **bubble economy**, the market system prospered on this sector, characterized as "*gaishoku* [eating out] and gourmet." However, specialization in the highest quality and highest priced spectrums of products, including many pricey imported foodstuffs, has left the wholesale market system vulnerable throughout the economic recession of the 1990s, when they have been particularly hard hit by the decline in business entertainment, more frugal consumers, and intensified competition with supermarkets and other alternative distribution systems.

Further reading

Bestor, T.C. (2002) *Tokyo's Marketplace*, Berkeley, CA: University of California Press.

THEODORE BESTOR

Chugen

Chugen refers to the Japanese midyear gift-giving season. This traditional summer exchange of gifts occurs during the first two weeks of July, before the Obon holiday. The giving of summer gifts originated as an offering to families that had experienced a death during the first half of the year. To this day, Chugen takes place during the two weeks before the obon (the Buddhist holiday for honoring dead ancestors).

The gifts, commonly referred to as *ochugen*, are given as an expression of gratitude to either private individuals or work related individuals to whom the gift giver has been obliged to during the year. Many individuals send *ochugen* to their boss and their customers in the hopes of retaining their continued support and business. The sending of *ochugen* to valued customers is obligatory in Japanese corporate culture. All Japanese companies maintain a Chugen budget, for giving gifts to important customers as a means of showing the company's appreciation of their business.

The giving of *ochugen* to superiors, clients, and others as an expression of gratitude for their guidance, patronage, or kindness is a well-established social and corporate custom in Japan. While the amount spent on *ochugen* varies, it is generally agreed that the average price is ¥5,000 each. As a result of this obligatory summer gift giving, a vast market has been created.

As the Chugen season coincides with the Japanese summer bonus season, it is a busy time of year for many Japanese retailers. **Department stores**, with the largest share of Chugen sales, set up special areas dedicated to *ochugen*, displaying a variety of specially packaged gifts at a range of prices. Gift-wrapping and delivery services are also provided. Supermarkets and convenience stores also sell *ochugen*, and provide delivery service.

Competition among retailers for chugen business is fierce. Some offer free delivery for a limited range of items within a delineated delivery area, while others counter with offers of a flat delivery rate to any domestic location. Discounts are also offered on selected goods, as are monetary incentives in the form of gift certificates with purchases over a certain amount.

During the Chugen season, large retailers such as department stores and supermarkets devote entire sections exclusively to such gifts. Although gifts usually belong to high-end product categories, they tend to be practical items that can be used, or consumed, at the recipient's home. Common gifts include boxes of soap, cooking oil, cookies, liquor, canned food, instant coffee, and beer, in addition to traditional gifts such as *nori* (dried seaweed), *katsuobushi* (dried fish), and *oshinko* (pickled vegetables).

Japan's other major gift-giving season is the year-end, between December 10 and the New Year holidays. Gifts exchanged at this time are referred to as *oseibo*. In general, *oseibo* are given to the same individuals to whom an *ochugen* was given.

SEAN MOONEY

city banks

City banks are major commercial banks with headquarters in a large metropolitan area and nationwide branch networks. The eight city banks rank among the world's largest banks. Controlled, regulated and protected by the **Ministry of Finance**, they played a major role in bankrolling major corporations in the wartime economy and during the period of high **economic growth**. Ill-executed **deregulation** of this system commencing in the 1970s culminated in the banking mess of the 1990s, as it created a situation of moral hazard in which banks had no incentive to develop business expertise and felt free to take risky positions in the mistaken belief that the ministry would bail them out if necessary. While the banking crisis seems to be under control for now, city banks still face serious challenges in the form of impending mergers, technical deficiencies, and internationalization.

Overview of the individual city banks

As of September 2000, there are eight city banks. In alphabetical order, these are:

- Asahi Bank. Tracing its history back to 1945, Asahi Bank is the product of the 1991 merger of two city banks, Kyowa Bank and Saitama Bank, and adopted its present name in 1992. Asahi Bank maintains its headquarters in Tokyo, employs 10,448 staff, and possesses a branch network of 365 offices. Its total assets (consolidated) amount to about ¥28.8 trillion, which makes Asahi Bank the seventh largest city bank in Japan and the thirty-fifth largest bank in the world.
- Bank of Tokyo-Mitsubishi. Its history reaching back to 1919, the Bank of Tokyo-Mitsubishi is the result of the 1996 merger between Mitsubishi Bank and the **Bank of Tokyo**. Headquartered in Tokyo, it employs 17,412 staff and runs 375 branch offices. With total assets (consolidated) of about ¥74.8 trillion, it is the second largest bank in Japan and the fourth largest bank in the world

by assets. The Bank of Tokyo-Mitsubishi is the main bank of the Mitsubishi *keiretsu* (see **main bank system**; *zaibatsu*) and plans to merge with Mitsubishi Trust & Banking, Japan's premier trust bank, in April 2001 to form the Mitsubishi Tokyo Financial Group.

- Daiwa Bank. Founded in 1918, Daiwa Bank grew out of the old Osaka Nomura Bank when its securities division separated and became **Nomura Securities**. Headquartered in Osaka, the Daiwa Bank has 7,315 employees and a branch network of 191 offices. Its total assets (consolidated) of about ¥15.4 trillion make it Japan's smallest city bank and earn it a rank of seventy-one worldwide by assets. Daiwa Bank gained international notoriety in 1995 in a scandal involving unreported bond-trading losses of $1.1 billion in the USA, as a consequence of which the bank saw itself stripped of its US banking license.
- Mizuho Financial Group. Mizuho Financial Group is the result of the September 2000 merger of **Daiichi Kangyo Bank** – itself the outcome of the 1971 merger of two city banks, Daiichi Bank and Nippon Kangyo Bank – Fuji Bank, and the Industrial Bank of Japan. Headquartered in Tokyo, the group's firms combined employ 33,914 staff and run 747 branch offices. With total assets (consolidated) of ¥157.2 trillion, the Mizuho Group is the world's largest bank. Given its constituent banks, the Mizuho Financial Group will probably serve as the main bank of the Ikkan and the Fuyo *keiretsu*.
- Sakura Bank. Tracing its history back to 1876, Sakura Bank is the result of the 1990 merger of Mitsui Bank and Taiyo-Kobe Bank, with the latter having itself grown out of a merger between Taiyo Bank and Kobe Bank in 1973; it assumed its present name in 1992. With headquarters in Tokyo, Sakura Bank has 14,930 employees and the largest branch network of all city banks with 438 offices. Its total assets (consolidated) are worth about ¥48.5 trillion, which makes it Japan's fourth-largest city bank and the world's fifteenth largest bank by assets. Sakura Bank is the main bank of the Mitsui *keiretsu* and is scheduled to merge with Sumitomo Bank into the Sumitomo Mitsui Banking Corporation in April 2001.
- Sanwa Bank. Sanwa Bank was founded in 1933.

It has its headquarters in Tokyo, employs 12,997 staff, and possesses 331 branch offices. It has total assets (consolidated) of about ¥46.9 trillion and is thus Japan's fifth-largest city bank and the world's seventeenth largest bank by assets. Sanwa Bank is the main bank of the Sanwa *keiretsu* and plans to set up a joint holding company with Tokai Bank and Toyo Trust in April 2001.

- Sumitomo Bank. Tracing its history back to 1912, Sumitomo Bank strengthened its Tokyo business by acquiring Heiwa Sogo Bank, a regional bank, in 1986. With its headquarters in Osaka, it maintains a staff of 14,394 and possesses 353 branch offices. Total assets (consolidated) of about ¥53.8 trillion make it Japan's third largest and the world's ninth largest bank by assets. Sumitomo Bank is the main bank of the Sumitomo *keiretsu* and will merge with Sakura Bank to form the Sumitomo Mitsui Banking Corporation in April 2001.

- Tokai Bank. Tokai Bank was founded in 1941. The only city bank headquartered in Nagoya, it employs 9,675 staff and runs a branch network of 280 offices. Its total assets (consolidated) amount to about ¥30.5 trillion, which makes it Japan's sixth largest city bank and the world's thirty-second largest bank ranked by assets. Tokai Bank acts as the main bank of the Tokai *keiretsu* and plans to create a joint holding company with Sanwa Bank and Toyo Trust in April 2001.

Noteworthy also is the Hokkaido Takushoku Bank, the only city bank to have failed. Headquartered in Sapporo, Hokkaido Takushoku Bank was the smallest of all city banks when it collapsed under the burden of massive bad loans on November 17, 1997. Its demise and the subsequent bankruptcy of Japan's fourth-largest securities firm, Yamaichi Securities, on November 24, 1997 greatly exacerbated the Japanese financial crisis of the 1990s and served to focus the attention of the government authorities on the weakness of the Japanese financial system (see **banking crises**).

History and status quo

Most, though not all, of today's city banks developed out of the "big banks" of the prewar era. In the early days of industrialization, Japan featured several thousand banks. Size varied enormously, from numerous tiny banks to the "Big Five": Mitsui Bank (now Sakura Bank), Daiichi Bank (later Daiichi Kangyo Bank), Mitsubishi Bank (now Bank of Tokyo-Mitsubishi), Sumitomo Bank, and Yasuda Bank (now Fuji Bank). These big banks played an important role for their respective *zaibatsu*, but overall their role in the economy was limited by strong competition with other banks and flourishing financial markets: the Big Five provided only about twenty percent of total bank loans, which in turn accounted for only about 20 percent of total assets in the economy until the 1930s.

Several factors strengthened the hand of the big banks from the late 1920s onward. First, a number of banking crises led to increased concentration in the banking sector. Second, and more importantly, as the country prepared for war, banks assumed a central role in the bureaucracy's efforts to bring the economy under control. In order to channel funds to industries central to the war effort, the state promoted further banking concentration, specialization, and a system of "indirect finance," in which firms received their capital through banks rather than directly from the capital markets.

Like so many aspects of the Japanese wartime economy, the highly controlled and regulated system of indirect finance survived both defeat and Allied occupation and became a cornerstone of the high-growth era. As during the war, city banks were instrumental in funneling scarce capital to major corporations (see also industrial policy). Several phenomena were characteristic of this role: "overloan," that is, the over-extension of commercial loans sustained by lending from the Bank of Japan (see **madoguchi shido**); "overborrowing," that is, the extreme dependence of corporations on bank lending; and the imbalance of bank liquidity (*shikin henzai*) between city banks and the smaller, local banks resulting from the inability of city banks to raise enough deposits through their relatively small branch networks to cover their large lending volumes.

Throughout this period of high economic growth, the city banks enjoyed a symbiotic relationship with the **Ministry of Finance** (MOF). MOF used **administrative guidance**, price setting, protection, and restriction of competition to keep the banking system stable. Interest rates were set with spreads wide enough to keep all banks profitable, and the "convoy" (*goso sendan*) system ensured that the assets of all banks grew at about the same rate, their relative ranking remained unchanged, and no bank failed. Success under these conditions was arguably more dependent on good relations with the ministry than on business acumen.

This system contained the seeds of the banking mess of the 1990s. As the economy matured in the early 1970s, the combination of slower growth, high government debt, internationalization, a shift of **corporate finance** away from bank lending, and increasingly diversified demand for financial services gave the impetus for slow but steady deregulation. However, MOF failed to create a system of prudential regulation as deregulation proceeded and stuck to the old convoy system. This created a situation of moral hazard in which the city banks had no incentive to develop business expertise and felt free to take risky positions within Japan (especially during the **bubble economy**) and overseas (especially in Asia) in the conviction that MOF would bail them out if necessary. However, when many of these loans went bad following the bursting of the bubble as well as the **economic crisis in Asia**, the resulting banking crisis turned out to be too large for MOF to handle. Hokkaido Takushoku Bank went under, other city banks presumably came close.

While a ¥7.45 trillion public aid package for the big banks and massive write-offs appear to have stabilized the city banks for now, they still face considerable challenges. First, it is not clear that the proposed banking mergers will show any benefits beyond making city banks bigger. Second, city banks have proved incapable of incorporating technological change. Their expertise in important areas such as risk management and sophisticated financial products remains low, as they lack the necessary specialists and have been spending too little on information technology. Third, city banks face increasing internationalization, which impacts them not least through competition from sophisticated foreign competitors such as Citigroup entering the Japanese market.

Further reading

Field, G. (1997) *Japan's Financial System: Restoration and Reform*, London: Euromoney Publications.

Japanese Bankers Association (2000) *Japanese Banks*, Tokyo: Japanese Bankers Association.

Johnson, C. (1982) *MITI and the Japanese Miracle: The Growth of Industrial Policy, 1925–1975*, Stanford, CA: Stanford University Press.

Kitagawa, H. and Kurosawa, Y. (1994) "Japan: Development and Structural Change of the Banking System," in H.T. Patrick and Y.C. Park (eds), *The Financial Development of Japan, Korea, and Taiwan*, Oxford: Oxford University Press, 18–128.

Patrick, H.T. (1999) "The Causes of Japan's Financial Crisis," *Pacific Economic Paper No. 288*, Canberra: Australia-Japan Research Centre, 1.1–1.19.

Tsutsui, W.M. (ed.) (1999) *Banking in Japan*, 3 vols, London: Routledge.

Top 1000 World Banks (2000) *The Banker*, July: 78–110.

Toyo Keizai Shinposha (2000) *Japan Company Handbook: First Section Firms, Fall 2000*, Tokyo: Toyo Keizai Shinposha.

MICHAEL A. WITT

Cole, Robert

Educator and writer on Japanese organizational behavior. Building on the earlier work of James Abegglen's *The Japanese Factory* (1958), which focused on the factory as a key to understanding Japanese industrialization, Cole studied the workers within the factories. Cole described how the Japanese focus on scarcity is reflected in its economy.

Cole developed a theory of functional alternatives in which he looked at industrial relation systems by viewing their features not as unique but as functional equivalents, variations and exaggerations of tendencies common to all industrial societies (Cole 1971). Under this theory, he attempted to bridge the gap between convergence theory (under which all economies would develop similar characteristics) and historical uniqueness (under which there would be no convergence since each nation is unique).

In his comparison of work practices in Detroit and Yokohama (Cole 1979), Cole found that while convergence did exist, there were also continuing differences as the Japanese adapted Western ideas and practices to their own needs. He described the greater worker participation among Japanese in shop floor management. While he found a distinctive Japanese work ethic, the differences tended to lie along very specific dimensions. First, the social organization of a Japanese firm is characterized by a lack of sharp job definition. This results in a low concern with promotion to particular jobs, job performance less important to promotion, extensive job rotation, tasks perceived as group projects and low commitment of employees to particular jobs. Second, the social organization of a Japanese firm has a strong internal labor market with employees having greater career commitments to the company, including low quit rate, stronger company training, employees have less job security concern, selective new employee recruitment, and low union involvement in job assignments. These differences, according to Cole, even if unique, were solutions to common problems.

Further reading

Abegglen, J.C. (1958) *The Japanese Factory: Aspects of its Social Organization*, Glencoe, IL: The Free Press.

Cole, R.E. (1971) *Japanese Blue Collar: The Changing Tradition*, Berkeley, CA: University of California Press.

—— (1979) *Work, Mobility, and Participation: A Comparative Study of American and Japanese Industry*, Berkeley, CA: University of California Press.

ROBERT BROWN

Commercial Code

History

The Commercial Code is part of a series of laws that also includes the Constitution, the Civil Code, and the Criminal Code. These laws were intended to make Japan a modern state equal to western states. At the time when Japan was forced to open up its borders by the "black ships" of US Commodore Perry, Japan had been forced into unequal treaties with Western states such as the USA, the UK, and the Netherlands. Meiji-era leaders were determined to prevent Japan from being colonized. In order to be internationally recognized as an equal power, modernization of the Japanese society and economic development became important goals for the Meiji government. The government sent out many scholars to Germany, France, and the USA to study industrialization, banking systems, and Western law. In the meantime, the Japanese government embarked on the modernization of the financial system by establishing the **Ministry of Finance** in 1869, promulgating a National Bank Act in 1872, and establishing the Tokyo Stock Exchange in 1878.

The Japanese Commercial Code was based on the German Commercial Code. Like the Constitution, the old Commercial Code was drafted by Karl Friedrich Hermann Roesler in 1890. The parts concerning companies, bills and bankruptcies were implemented in 1893, the other parts following in 1898, to be replaced by the new Commercial Code in 1899. The old Commercial Code had been considered too foreign, and was said to disregard customary business practices.

Development

Prewar amendments took place in 1911 and 1938. They consisted of changes in valuation standards from market value, to lower-of-cost-and-market (1911), to historical cost (1938). In 1950, amendments included the introduction of the authorized capital system and the non-par value stock system in order to facilitate the introduction of foreign capital. The revisions that took place in 1962 established the supremacy of accounting rules (concerning measurement, valuation and recognition) in the Commercial Code over the regulations of the Securities and Exchange Law and the Statement of Business Accounting Principles. The Commercial Code falls under the administration of the Ministry of Justice, whereas the latter two are under the jurisdiction of the Ministry of Finance. The 1974 revision to the Commercial Code made the audit system compatible with the audit system under the Securities and Exchange Law, and thus contributed to the unification of the Japanese accounting system.

Later amendments occurred in 1981, 1990, 1994, and 1997, and included rules that accompanied the deregulation of Japanese financial markets and the internationalization of business in general. Examples of the first include issuance and administration of corporate bonds and derivatives. Examples of the latter include foreign investments or mergers and acquisitions. The latest revisions are a consequence of the financial and accounting Big Bangs. In 1998 the Commercial Code was amended to relax the purchase of treasury stock. From 1999 the Commercial Code permits the establishment of holding companies again. When the **zaibatsu** were dismantled, holding companies had been prohibited. Furthermore, since 1999, new rules include fair value for financial products. Revisions in 2000 lay down the rules for company splits. Within the framework of the accounting Big Bang, more revisions are likely to follow.

Character

The Commercial Code applies to all companies. However, for certain regulations there are exceptions based on size. For example, external audits are not required for small and medium-sized companies. For companies with a capital stock of over ¥500 million or liabilities totalling more than ¥20 billion, under the "Law concerning the exceptions to the Commercial Code regarding the audit of *kabushiki kaisha*," Art. 16 stipulates that in case the external auditor concludes in its report that, as a result of the audit of the accounts, they have not found any improper items, approval by the general shareholders meeting is not necessary. A mere presentation of the contents of the financial statements is enough.

It is generally acknowledged that the Commercial Code is primarily concerned with the protection of creditors rather than shareholders. One important aspect of Roesler's draft that remains a characteristic of the Japanese accountability system until today is the relationship between the board of directors, the statutory auditors and the general shareholders meeting. Both the statutory auditors and the board of directors are appointed by the general shareholders' meeting. In some cases, this would be the shareholders' only direct means of control.

Outline

Book One of the Commercial Code is concerned with general principles, and contains chapters on regulations for carrying out the law, merchants, business registration, firm names, business account books, business users, and agents. Book Two consists of a chapter on general principles which mainly deals with definitions, and another chapter which is concerned with stock companies, their establishment, stock, institutions, general shareholders meeting, auditing, company accounts, bonds, amendment of the articles of incorporation, increase or decrease of capital stock, liquidation, and penal regulations.

See also: joint stock corporation; *zaibatsu*

CARIEN VAN MOURIK

competition

Competition in Japan has certain unique features. The fact that prices have been persistently higher than in other nations suggests that price competition is relatively weak. And while Japan has ended most of its legal **cartels**, informal restraints on competition appear more widespread than in many other industrialized countries. Yet competition over quality and service is intense. Japanese firms in many industries compete hard to create innovative, well-crafted goods that enjoy great success in world markets.

The question of just how competitive Japan's markets are is hotly debated for several reasons. The first has to do with explaining economic growth. Neoclassical economic theory holds that competitive markets promote growth, while restraints on competition take away incentives to innovate and cut costs. The Japanese economy has grown quickly during most of the post-Second World War period. During much of this time of rapid growth, the Japanese government encouraged cartels and protected domestic industries from imports. Was there intense competition anyway? If not, how did the economy grow so fast? Is neoclassical economic theory wrong about the importance of competition for economic growth? Some scholars argue deductively from neoclassical economic theory that since Japan had high rates of economic growth from 1952–91, and since markets must be competitive to generate rapid growth, that Japan must therefore have had an intensely competitive market. Others argue that neoclassical economic theory is wrong, and that certain restraints on competition can promote growth in late-developing economies that are struggling to accumulate capital and catch up with more advanced nations (see **industrial policy**).

Another reason scholars and policy makers debate the nature of competition in Japan is because of its significance for Japan's international trade relations. Critics of Japan argue that private firms collude to keep prices high and to use their market power to keep new firms from undercutting these prices, while the government fails to enforce the nation's Anti-Monopoly Law and uses informal regulation to help stifle competition. They hold that anti-competitive activities unfairly enable Japanese firms to keep prices high, keep imports out, and then sell cheaply overseas.

Opponents of this view argue that Japanese markets are in fact very competitive and that the difficulty foreign firms have in making sales in Japan is because Japanese firms compete so intensely to provide excellent goods and services. They argue that Japan's high prices reflect the high quality of goods that consumers demand as well as high production and distribution costs and that, while there are some illegal cartels, these do not last long nor have great overall effect on prices.

As with many debates, there is truth to both positions. Japanese markets are less competitive than the markets of other industrialized nations in certain respects, but very competitive in others. Compared to the USA or the European Union, competition policy is lax, and the Japan Fair Trade Commission is more tolerant of cartels. Japan's high prices suggest that price competition is weak. Japanese prices are much higher than in the USA and Western Europe. The explanation for these high prices might be partly that high distribution costs force prices up and that the yen has been overvalued. But the high distribution costs themselves appear to be due to restraints on competition

in industries such as trucking or retail sales. And the yen has been high since 1985. One would think that the high prices in Japan would attract cheap imports that would put downward pressure on Japanese prices. The fact that the expected cheap imports have not succeeded in driving down Japanese prices suggests there are barriers to new entrants in Japan's markets.

Yet while competition over prices is weak on average, competition over quality and service is intense. What causes this difference in competition, and how does an emphasis on competition over quality and service instead of price affect the economy?

Competition can be shaped both by vertical and horizontal relations among firms. First, vertical relations between buyers and sellers in Japan are more often long-term and stable than in such countries as the USA or the UK. Buyers make a long-term commitment to buy from a particular supplier and sellers make a long-term commitment to make a particular good to the buyer's precise specifications. Buyers and sellers do not constantly shop around for a better price, but that does not mean there is no competition. Instead, buyers use "controlled competition" to get better prices, quality and service from sellers. Under controlled competition, buyers have long-term relations with several suppliers. They limit their purchases to these designated suppliers, and negotiate prices with them that cover production costs. The various designated suppliers cooperate to some degree to produce the goods the buyer wants, but the buyer also pressures these suppliers to compete to provide good quality and service, and to gradually improve productivity and bring down costs. This kind of competition is common among providers of intermediate industrial goods, such as telecommunications equipment or automotive parts.

Horizontal ties among competitors producing the same good or service also can lead to an emphasis on competition over quality and service instead of price. An example of an industry in which firms compete intensely over quality and service is the petrochemical industry. Japanese petrochemical companies produce ten times as many different grades of chemicals as in other countries and they are willing to make deliveries of much smaller quantities. Firms provide these fine gradations in quality and excellent service because they are competing to gain or keep customers. At the same time, the Japanese chemical industry charges very high prices for its goods. What explains this pattern of intense competition over quality and service and weak competition over prices? The reason Japanese companies compete intensely to produce so many fine grades of chemicals is that they have agreements not to compete over price (see **after-sales pricing**). The **Ministry of International Trade and Industry** has encouraged the petrochemical industry to come to an agreement not to make so many grades, but as long as firms are prevented from competing over price, they have an incentive to compete over non-price differentiations between products.

One could argue that customers really want a large variety of grades of chemicals and deliveries of tiny quantities, and that this is the main reason that Japanese chemical companies compete in this specific way. One could also argue that Japan's extraordinary levels of quality and service shows that it is one of the most competitive chemical markets in the world. However, given that we know that chemical companies have price-fixing agreements, we must conclude that it is the lack of price competition that is pushing chemical companies to instead compete over service and quality. Is this wasteful? Thinking in terms of *static* economic efficiency, that is, the efficiency of distributing resources that are available right now, the answer is yes. The result of such arrangements is that Japanese consumers pay high prices and have a lower level of consumption. On the other hand, a widespread emphasis on quality rather than price competition is one of the factors that has enabled Japanese manufacturers to be leaders in the production of high quality goods. Car companies say that they value the ability to get precisely the kind of chemical products they want and on very convenient delivery schedules. This orientation to quality over price may produce *dynamic* efficiencies. That is, it may increase the amount of resources available in the future by stimulating innovation.

People understand competition in Japan somewhat differently than in Britain or the USA. A key concept for discussing competition in Japan is "excessive competition" (*kato kyoso*). Excessive competition means that supplies greatly exceed demand, prices are below costs, and producers are in danger of being pushed out of business. Proponents of this concept argue that excess competition develops when firms have high sunk costs. That is, firms have invested in production facilities, such as factories and equipment, which they cannot easily sell off or use for some other productive purpose. Firms that are stuck with big interest payments on a factory are forced to keep producing goods even if they're not making enough money to cover the full costs of production in order to stay in business. Americans and Britons tend to see business failure as a normal part of a market economy, but the use of the term "excessive competition" suggests many Japanese observers see it as abnormal. The term is important because it has often been used to justify government intervention to reduce competition and protect the beleaguered firms. It is this thinking which provides the political support for the restrictions on competition that the petrochemical industry uses to maintain a system of competition that emphasizes quality and service instead of price.

Perhaps the best way to understand competition in Japan is to say that it operates somewhat differently from economies such as the USA where price competition is more intense and where market relationships are more fluid. Higher prices cause some losses in efficiency, but high levels of quality can also provide some advantages. Joseph Schumpeter, an Austrian economist writing in the middle of the twentieth century, disagreed with neoclassical economic theory and argued that the most important kind of competition in a market economy is not over price, but over innovation. His way of thinking may explain why Japan has managed to achieve remarkable long-term economic growth even with many official cartels and high prices. Yet the long recession that began in 1991 has caused many observers both within and outside Japan to wonder whether the old formula can still work and whether Japan may need stronger price competition in order to push inefficient companies out of business and create space for new industries. Observers concerned with international trade equity argue that Japan needs more competition in its domestic markets in order to ensure that foreign firms have the same access to

Japanese markets that Japanese firms enjoy overseas.

Further reading

Flamm, K. (1996) *Mismanaged Trade? Strategic Policy and the Semiconductor Industry*, Washington, DC: The Brookings Institution.

Fransman, M. (1995) *Japan's Computer and Communications Industry*, Oxford: Oxford University Press.

Lincoln, E. (1999). *Troubled Times: U.S.-Japan Trade Relations in the 1990s*, Washington, DC: Brookings Institution Press.

Lynn, L.H. and McKeown, T.J. (1998) *Organizing Business: Trade Associations in America and Japan*, Washington, DC: American Enterprise Institute for Public Policy Research.

Odagiri, H. (1994) *Growth through Competition, Competition through Growth: Strategic Management and the Economy in Japan*, Oxford: Oxford University Press.

Schumpeter, J. (1976) *Capitalism, Socialism and Democracy*, New York: Harper Torchbooks.

Tilton, M. (1998) "Regulatory Reform and Market Opening in Japan," in M. Tilton and L. Carlile (eds), *Is Japan Really Changing Its Ways? Regulatory Reform and the Japanese Economy*, Washington, DC: Brookings Institution Press.

MARK TILTON

computer industry

Introduction

Japan is the only nation other than the USA to develop a competitive computer industry. With heavy state support in the 1960s and 1970s, Japanese firms were able to become world leaders in computer hardware. Their weakness has been in software, and like IBM, they missed the trend toward downsizing to smaller computers in the late 1980s. Japanese firms took over or formed key partnerships with Europe's top computer makers in the 1980s and 1990s and today supply the world with advanced computer hardware and components.

The 1960s and 1970s

The Japanese computer industry started to develop in the 1960s, largely as a result of government initiative. To help nurture a domestic industry to catch up with IBM, the state used four primary policies: protectionism, a quasi-public computer rental company called the Japan Electronic Computer Company (JECC), financial assistance, and a variety of state-sponsored cooperative research and development projects. These policies were critical in helping the industry create a competitive hardware industry by the late 1970s.

Protectionism included conventional tariffs and quotas, but also a variety of limitations on foreign investment, which influenced the type and quantity of machines IBM could produce in Japan, how much it had to export, how many parts it could import, and how much profit it could repatriate. IBM only got permission to produce in Japan when it agreed to license its patents at reasonable royalty fees to local firms. Similar restrictions constrained the activities of Sperry Rand (UNIVAC computers), which was forced into a joint venture with Oki Electric, as well as other US players such as Hewlett-Packard. While protectionism usually leads to sluggishness and inefficiency, domestic competition was encouraged, requiring that firms make increasingly better machines in order to stay in business. The result was increased demand for domestic machines, which stimulated supply.

The JECC was set up in 1961, and about 50 percent of its financing came from government low-interest loans. It worked in the following way: when a user decided which specific machine it wanted to rent, it told JECC, which bought the machine from the designated maker and rented it to the user for a reasonable monthly fee. The user had to keep the computer for at least 15 months or pay a penalty. When a machine was returned, the computer maker was forced to repurchase it at book value from JECC. The effect was to give Japanese domestic computer firms an immediate return on their investment. If the firms had had to finance their own rentals, they would have received returns in small monthly payments over a 4 year period. Since JECC only purchased machines users specifically asked to rent, there was a direct link to the market. If no one asked for your machine,

JECC did not buy it. Thus, the firms making the best machines got the most benefit from JECC. From 1961 to 1981 the government funneled some $2 billion in loans into JECC to finance computer rentals. JECC still exists today but rents only a small percentage of the total number of rented machines.

State financial aid to the computer industry came in various forms. The absolute amount of subsidies, tax benefits, and low-interest loans has been quite small compared to the huge sums the USA funneled into Pentagon projects. But the amounts were very large compared to what the firms were investing themselves. For example, a conservative estimate suggests that from 1961–9 subsidies and tax benefits ($132 million) were equivalent to 46 percent of what the computer firms themselves were investing in R&D and plant and equipment. If we include government low interest loans, total aid ($542.8 million) was equal to 188 percent of what the firms were investing. Indeed, the state was also providing funds for working capital. From 1970 to 1975, subsidies and tax benefits ($636.55 million) were equivalent to 57 percent of what the firms were investing, 169 percent ($1.88 billion) if we include government loans. Software and hardware were formally liberalized in the mid-1970s yet from 1976 through 1981 subsidies and tax benefits ($1.03 billion) were still 25.2 percent of what the firms were investing; including state loans, total aid ($3.74 billion) was still equal to 91.6 percent of what the firms were investing.

Various cooperative R&D projects, mainly focused on catching up with IBM, were conducted in the 1960s and 1970s. Their overall effect was to reduce the costs and risks of doing R&D by pooling resources and sharing R&D results. The VLSI Project (1976–79) and the New Series Project (1972–76) were key projects that helped Japanese firms, especially the three dominant companies – Fujitsu, Hitachi, and **NEC** – catch up with IBM in hardware by the late 1970s.

Success in hardware was contingent on nurturing a competitive semiconductor industry. The R&D cooperative computer projects all involved making advances in semiconductor technology. Other policies also helped nurture the world's most advanced memory makers, including heavy-

handed state intervention to handicap foreign semiconductor makers, such as Texas Instruments, Motorola, and Fairchild in the 1960s and 1970s. With US makers focusing on bipolar semiconductors in the early 1970s, Japanese firms and MITI decided to focus on a specific niche market: memory semiconductors or DRAMS, which were in great demand for use in calculators and watches. The technological trajectory was stable for these chips, they were highly sensitive to production economies of scale, and success depended on high-quality process technology and attention to manufacturing detail, areas where Japanese firms have traditionally excelled. Japanese firms did not get heavily involved in developing microprocessors, so-called systems on a chip. Microprocessors have a very heavy software component, an area where Japan continues to lag.

The success of policies toward hardware in the 1960s and 1970s was undoubtedly dependent on several conditions. Most important was that while the firms were protected from international competition, domestic competition was strongly encouraged. Even though cooperation was substantial on products, investment, and R&D, market forces were kept intact enough to force the firms to advance technologically and cut costs in order to survive over the long term. A broad societal consensus to allow the bureaucracy to decide what industries to target was also critical. So was a stable institution – the **Ministry of International Trade and Industry** (MITI) – which had consistent policies that did not change with each new administration. A relatively large domestic market in which to gain economies of scale was important as was access to foreign markets for technology and to sell products. Overall macropolicies that encouraged savings and investment and discouraged consumption enabled Japan to remain independent of foreign loans while still investing heavily in strategic industries.

Software was not subsidized much in the 1960s and 1970s and the aid it received was generally not very effective. The real focus was on hardware not software. The firms essentially used modified versions of foreign software. Hitachi and Fujitsu, for example, decided in the early 1970s to make IBM clones, but they modified the IBM hardware and software enough to lock customers into their

closed, incompatible standards. NEC had technological ties with Honeywell, but also created its own
closed standard.

The 1980s

Fujitsu and Hitachi's strategy of "borrowing"
IBM's software backfired in summer 1982 when
they were caught stealing IBM technology in an
FBI sting case. This meant the free ride on IBM
was no longer free. The firms now had to pay huge
annual licensing fees to IBM. From then on, the
firms tried to diversify their reliance on IBM's
mainframe standard. In the 1980s, there was a
strong move toward UNIX-based systems and an
attempt to create a unique Japanese operating
system standard called TRON. This latter pursuit,
overly ambitious, was not successful though it still
exists today.

It was also in the early 1980s that Japan's three
top makers moved into supercomputers, initiated
by the government in a fully-funded R&D
cooperative project. By the early 1990s, they were
very competitive in traditional vector supercomputers for certain types of applications. They have
been less successful at making massive parallel
processing machines, but are aggressively research-
ing this area.

The 1990s

By the 1990s, Japan's mainframe makers, like IBM,
were caught with big machines when demand
soared for smaller computers. They were slow to
downsize and restructure their operations, but were
kept afloat by their telecommunications, semiconductor, and consumer electronics divisions. At this
same time the firms' strategy of using closed
standards to lock users into their respective brands
began to haunt them. The market's dependence on
fragmented, non-compatible standards denied
users the positive network externalities that come
with using common, compatible standards.

Concern over their growing lag in computer
software reached crisis proportions in the 1990s,
especially as the Internet and other software-
related industries emerged. The software industry
was at a crossroads: it could continue offering
closed, modified versions of foreign standards or

unbundle (sell hardware and software separately)
and embrace open, internationally-accepted standards. The firms, users, and the government,
realizing they were falling further behind in
software, chose the latter path.

The 2000s

In 2000, Japanese firms are still hoping for open
source solutions to prevent the total dominance of
operating systems by Western firms. The computer
firms are offering machines with the free-of-charge
Linux operating system on them, though most
experts believe Linux is too user-unfriendly to
become prevalent. The government is much less
involved in the industry than in the past but Japan's
lag in software, massive parallel processing, and the
Internet has led to an explosion of state-sponsored
projects in these and other related areas.

Many argue that Japan's efforts to support the
computer industry have not been successful
because Japanese firms do not currently dominate
the world computer market. It is true that Japanese
firms have not taken over these markets. But their
success in semiconductors, supercomputers, and
the overall components of most computers is
providing the nation with billions of dollars in
revenues and positions them well for success in the
future. Computer knowledge has also been key to
their success in related areas such as computer-
operated numerically-controlled machine tools and
telecommunications equipment. Indeed, other
than the USA, Japan is the only nation competitive
in a wide array of high-tech computer-related
products.

It is clear, however, that other late developing
nations such as South Korea and Taiwan have
assiduously studied Japan's industrial and corporate strategies. With significantly lower wages, they
are beginning to take market share from Japan in
key components such as memory chips. To make
the jump from success in hardware to software,
telecommunications, and internet technologies,
Japan needs to make a transition from a manufacturing superpower to a more invention-oriented
nation. Making this leap involves dismantling some
of the institutional arrangements that helped Japan
catch up with the West but which now hinder its
transition to a more inventor and entrepreneur-

friendly system. These arrangements include the bank-centered financial system, the **main bank system** of **corporate governance**, the *keiretsu* industrial groups, and various employment practices such as **lifetime employment** and seniority wages. Unfortunately, Japan needs to make this change at a time when it is experiencing its deepest and longest postwar recession. There is an acute awareness of the need to change but vested interests and a weak financial system mean change will be slow.

See also: software industry; telecommunications industry

Further reading

Anchordoguy, M. (1989) *Computers, Inc.: Japan's Challenge to IBM*, Cambridge, MA: Harvard University Press.

—— (1994) "Japanese-American Trade Conflict and Supercomputers," *Political Science Quarterly* 109(1): 35–80.

—— (1997) "Japan at a Technological Crossroads: Does Change Support Convergence Theory?" *Journal of Japanese Studies* 23: 363–97.

—— (2000) Japan's Software Industry: A Failure of Institutions?" *Research Policy* 29: 391–408.

MARIE ANCHORDOGUY

construction industry

Construction is Japan's largest industry, accounting for approximately 15 percent of GDP at the close of the twentieth century and equivalent in absolute size to the US and Western European construction industries together. With over 10 percent of the nation's labor force, it is the country's largest employer, with more than twice as many workers as the auto and electronics industries combined. In contrast to those highly competitive industries, however, the construction industry has, since the late 1980s, been portrayed in Japan and abroad as the epitome of the worst features of the Japanese business system: protected, overmanned, costly, and corrupt. And yet, the leading construction firms also exhibit some of the strengths associated

with the best of Japanese industry: quality control, technical innovation, and reliability.

Japan's construction industry is conventionally divided into two sectors: *kenchiku* (building, which is the larger sector and includes office buildings, factories, schools, and housing) and *doboku* (civil engineering, which includes dams, bridges, roads, and other infrastructure projects). The distinction is long-standing: statistics on the construction industry and individual company revenues are both presented in terms of the two categories. The market is also divided into two categories: public (national, prefectural, and local governments) and private (corporations and individuals). The public sector is the primary market for civil engineering projects, although private firms such as railway companies and real estate development firms also fund major infrastructure projects. Public expenditure on construction has long been one of the main tools of economic policy in Japan: government spending on construction rises in economic downturns, with the goal of stabilizing employment and stimulating related industries such as steel, cement, and transport. In the 1980s and the 1990s, the public sector accounted for just over one-third of construction spending (with the notable exception of the construction boom of the **bubble economy**; in 1990, at its peak, private sector construction accounted for nearly 80 percent of the total).

The structure of the industry is complex: there are almost as many establishments engaged in construction (over 650,000 in the late 1990s) as there are in manufacturing (770,000). These range in scale from the top general contractors, with thousands of highly qualified engineers and architects, to one-man subcontracting operations engaged in traditional carpentry. Many accounts of the industry call it a "two-tier" industry, divided into modern, technologically and managerially sophisticated general contractors on the one hand and small-scale traditional subcontractors on the other. But the industry structure is far more complex than this suggests. The principal industry association for construction, the Japan Federation of Construction Contractors (*Nihon Kensetsu-gyoo Dantai Rengookai*), has a membership of ten further specialized associations (including associations for civil engineering, building, electrical power construction, railway construction, and so on) and seventy individual companies, the largest firms in the industry. At the top of the industry status hierarchy are the top twenty-three firms, identified in the many industry guides published in Japan in terms of three categories: the Big Five (*oode* – Kajima, Ohbayashi, Shimizu, Taisei, and Takenaka), which for a decade from the mid-1980s to the mid-1990s became the Big Six (with Kumagai temporarily rising from the next category); nine (or ten) "Quasi-Big" (*jun-oode*) firms, and nine or ten medium-ranking (*chuuken*) firms.

All of the top twenty-three firms trace their origins to the Meiji period (1868–1912) or earlier (Shimizu began in 1804, and Kajima in 1840). When Western construction technology was introduced to Japan in the 1860s and 1870s, local construction houses served as subcontractors on projects such as railways, factories, and new government buildings. They were able to draw on capabilities accumulated on construction projects in the previous era, including castles, road-building, temples, and land reclamation, which involved both relatively advanced construction techniques and complex social organization, including subcontracting. Well before the Second World War, the largest of the construction houses moved from the traditional household-based enterprise to more modern forms of the incorporated enterprise, including the publicly-listed joint stock company, although the founding families continued to own most of the company. Indeed, to this day, a distinctively large number of construction companies are *dozoku-gaisha* – family-linked companies – where the founding family members own significant blocks of shares and have preferential access to top management positions.

Most of the leading construction firms expanded their activities into Japan's growing Asian colonial possessions before or during the Pacific War. Defeat, however, focused their activities on rebuilding Japan's infrastructure. The high-growth era was a golden age for the construction industry, and even after the first oil shock in 1973 construction spending remained at a high level. The second oil shock in 1979, however, ushered in what industry leaders called the "winter era," when profits fell, competition intensified, and the outlook for the industry appeared gloomy. Japan's leading firms

began to adopt strategies of aggressive and proactive growth, which included engaging in project development (such as resort development, partnering with real estate firms in speculative building, and project financing), property management (especially through build-and-lease projects), and international expansion (Hasegawa 1988). The bubble economy, in which Japanese private investment in construction boomed, reinforced these aggressive strategies, and when the bubble burst in the early 1990s, most construction firms were carrying large amounts of debt and were committed to projects whose economic value had suddenly plummeted.

In the 1980s, however, the top general contractors seemed well positioned to become more global players, like their manufacturing counterparts, and for some of the same reasons. Japanese general contractors had followed their manufacturing clients in adopting quality control programs (in 1979, Takenaka was the first of several contractors to win the Deming Prize for quality). They invested more in technology development than most of their foreign counterparts: the top 20–30 general contractors maintained substantial R&D centers, and although construction accounted for only about 2 percent of the country's total R&D expenditures, this was significantly higher than in any other nation. Research areas in which Japanese general contractors made impressive contributions included tunneling, construction robotics, building materials, and earthquake protection. In 1986, 15 percent of the country's engineering graduates went into the construction industry. Their investments in construction technology were a major asset in winning public works contracts internationally in the 1980s. But they also were often able to draw on low-cost financing from Japanese banks and trading companies, a more controversial source of competitive advantage.

The leading general contractors also had an advantage in internationalization because of their close relationships with their Japanese clients. As Japan's manufacturing firms expanded their production facilities abroad, they turned to the general contractors with whom they worked in Japan to build their plants abroad. Japanese large-scale building projects have followed a "design-and-build" model, in which a contractor's internal staff of highly trained architects and designers develop the design and its managers then supervise the construction process. This has several advantages over the "design-bid-build" model prevailing in the USA and elsewhere, in which one firm produces the design and the client then solicits bids from other companies for the actual construction. "Design-and-build" fosters the integration of building design and the construction process, in ways comparable to the "design for manufacturability" characteristic of Japanese product design, and it enables a contractor to keep within the agreed parameters of cost and schedule. Foreign companies contracting with Japanese general contractors for buildings in Japan have been pleasantly surprised by the absence of construction delays and cost overruns. Critics of the model suggest, however, that it has produced unimaginative buildings and that clients have paid more than they would under a more competitive system. But Japanese firms accustomed to the "design-and-build" system often preferred to work with Japanese contractors when they planned production facilities abroad (Ohbayashi, for example, was the designer and contractor for Toyota's Kentucky plant).

As Japanese construction firms became more active abroad in the mid-1980s, and even began to win public works contracts in the USA (such as the mid-1980s subway contracts in Los Angeles and Washington, DC), US firms sought to counter by competing in the Japanese market. But they faced formidable obstacles. Japanese public works contracts worked on a system of designated bidders, in which firms had to gain prior approval to submit bids, based on a complex array of criteria that included past project performance on Japanese projects and R&D expenditures. Newcomers could rarely qualify. Moreover, the *dango* system, in which companies agreed in advance on which company would submit the low bid, constituted a corrupt practice under American law. So did the system whereby winning contractors on public works were expected to make political contributions at the local or the national level that were roughly proportionate to the size of the contract. On the grounds that such practices constituted unfair trade barriers, American engineering firms and US politicians made the opening of Japan's construction market a major issue in trade negotiations, and in 1987 Congress voted to exclude Japanese firms from bidding on federally funded construction projects. Japan moved slowly to address these concerns, and construction remained a major issue for negotiations through the mid-1990s, when domestic reform pressures on the inflated costs of public works and **Liberal Democratic Party** (LDP) corruption became the main force for change in public works contracts. Prosecutions of the leading general contractors for bid-rigging became more aggressive in the late 1990s, and in September 2000 a major **Fair Trade Commission** inquiry targeted thirty major construction firms, including the top three general contractors.

The pressures on profit margins in public works, the slow but steady contraction of expenditures during the long economic slowdown of the 1990s, and the huge debt overhang from the aggressive investments of the bubble years have all combined to make construction one of Japan's most troubled sectors. The Big Five have been quicker to restructure and rationalize than some of the companies immediately below them in the industry hierarchy, and they are likely to survive and even flourish. But bankruptcies have been increasing among construction firms, and may become the dominant vehicle for the badly needed **restructuring** of the industry.

No discussion of construction in Japan would be complete without some mention of housing. Because about 15 percent of housing construction is of prefabricated units, and because even conventional housing construction often uses manufactured sub-assemblies like unit baths, housing in Japan straddles construction and manufacturing. Japan leads the world in manufactured housing (that is, modules and subassemblies built in factories and shipped to and assembled on site). Sekisui House, for example, produces 50–60,000 units per year at five factories located throughout Japan. Homebuyers can customize their house by choosing various frames, floor plans, colors, and so on. Prefab housing in Japan is not the low-end sector that it is in most countries; prefab housing companies cater to middle and upper-middle income customers. In contrast to the century-old general contractors, Japan's leading housing companies were established in the 1960s and 1970s. Prefab housing in Japan has the advantage of speedy construction, important in a country where many customers are rebuilding on the site of the old homes. It does not, however, have a significant price advantage over a house custom-built by a local contractor, although many argue that it has a quality advantage. Prefab housing firms also differ from the general contractors in having significantly higher profit levels.

See also: Ministry of Construction

Further reading

Coaldrake, W. (1990) *The Way of the Carpenter: Tools and Japanese Architecture*, Tokyo: Weatherhill.

Hasegawa, S. and the Shimizu Group FS (1988) *Built by Japan: Competitive Strategies of the Japanese Construction Industry*, New York: Wiley.

Levy, S.M. (1990) *Japanese Construction: An American Perspective*, New York: Van Nostrand Reinhold.

—— (1993) *Japan's Big Six: Inside Japan's Construction Industry*, New York: McGraw-Hill.

Woodall, B. (1996) *Japan Under Construction: Corruption, Politics, and Public Works*, Berkeley, CA: University of California Press.

ELEANOR D. WESTNEY

consumer movement

Japan's postwar economic system has often been referred to as a "producer" system, yet Japan has a large and well-organized consumer sector as well. Consumer groups have successfully lobbied for stronger health and safety regulation, especially with respect to food. More surprisingly, however, Japanese consumers have crusaded against trade liberalization and economic deregulation, policies which economists would expect to improve consumer welfare substantially. Only in recent years have consumer groups become somewhat more favorable toward economic liberalization (Vogel 1999).

Japan's postwar system favored producers over consumers in many ways: financial regulation kept deposit interest rates below market levels, trade barriers allowed domestic producers to charge higher prices, weak antitrust policy allowed price cartels, and a wide range of economic regulations impeded competition, bolstered corporate profits, and increased price levels in sectors as diverse as retail and construction. Yet Japanese consumer groups did not oppose most of these policies, and actively supported many of them.

Postwar history

The postwar consumer movement grew out of groups of housewives joining together, often for the practical purpose of collective purchases rather than for any larger political goal. Consumer groups focused on lifestyle issues, and channeled their energy more at the local level than the national. The most prominent consumer group, the Housewives' Federation (known as *Shufuren*), started in 1948 by protesting faulty matches. *Shufuren* then developed its own laboratory to test products for quality, safety, and truth in labeling. It launched campaigns to ban additives from pickled radish (*takuan*), to strengthen labeling requirements for juice packages, and to crack down on companies marketing whale and horse meat as beef. *Shufuren* and other groups consolidated their gains with a new law on labeling and marketing standards (*futokeihinrui oyobi futohyoji boshiho*) in 1962. Consumer groups were not always successful in specific cases, but by mobilizing public opinion and establishing consumer protest as a credible threat they fostered a phenomenal increase in the scope and stringency of health and safety regulation.

By the 1960s, consumer groups had not only achieved some notable breakthroughs, but had gained an institutionalized role within the policy process. In 1968, the government passed the Consumer Protection Law (*shohisha hogo kihonho*), setting forth government and corporate responsibilities in responding to consumer concerns and creating a cabinet-level Consumer Protection Council (*shohisha hogo kaigi*). The government also cultivated a national network of semi-public consumer information centers (*kokumin seikatsu sentaa*).

Consumer groups became even more aggressive in the late 1960s and 1970s, challenging corporations directly through public denunciation, product boycotts, and law suits. In 1969, a disgruntled former Agriculture Ministry official by the name of Takeuchi Naokazu joined others to found Japan's most outspoken consumer group, the Consumers Union of Japan (*Nisshoren*). *Nisshoren* insisted on political neutrality, refused government financial support, only enlisted private individuals as members, and brought denunciation into the strategic arsenal of the consumer movement. In 1969, for example, it launched a campaign against cola – which it felt was unhealthy and perhaps even dangerous – by publicly accusing Coca-Cola Japan of violating Japanese laws regarding foreign firms' activities in Japan. In 1970, consumer groups boycotted color televisions in protest of manufacturers' dual-pricing schemes. The groups argued that manufacturers published official prices far above the actual prices charged by most retailers, and that manufacturers and retailers used this system to get less savvy customers to pay the higher prices. The boycott resulted in a sharp decline in sales, and the government eventually convinced manufacturers to lower their prices. Although consumer groups were generally less successful in court, they used lawsuits to publicize their concerns and thereby alter corporate behavior.

Consumers vs. liberalization

When the Japanese government announced an "Action Program" to open its market in 1985, the major consumer groups united in opposition, arguing that the program would sacrifice consumer protection to appease the USA. They fought most vigorously against agricultural liberalization, citing three primary concerns: liberalization would undermine food self-sufficiency, increase the risk of contamination or disease, and threaten the livelihood of farmers. The Japanese consumers' stance contrasts markedly with that of similar groups in other countries that have supported trade liberalization. Public opinion polls throughout the 1980s and 1990s have shown strong public support for agricultural protection. Consumer groups have also reinforced trade protection by demanding tough regulatory standards that effectively discriminate against imports. David Vogel has demonstrated that although consumer groups have pushed for tough standards for both domestic and foreign

products, they have been particularly zealous in blocking imported products (Vogel 1992).

Since the 1980s, economists, business executives, and political leaders have campaigned for **deregulation**, stressing that it could bring huge benefits for consumers. Yet the consumer groups themselves have been less than enthusiastic. They strongly opposed the privatization and deregulation of telecommunications and rail transport and other central pillars of the administrative reform program in the 1980s, and they resisted many elements of the deregulation drive in the 1990s. Of course, one would expect consumer groups to oppose the abolition of regulations designed to ensure the safety and quality of products. But Japanese consumers have also refused to support, and in some cases have directly opposed, the removal or relaxation of economic (price and entry) regulations – precisely the kind of deregulation that should benefit consumers the most. Consumer groups have even resisted retail deregulation, which should directly benefit consumers by bringing down retail margins. They argue that price is not everything, and that deregulation would not only hurt small retailers but could wipe out entire neighborhood shopping districts.

Particularly surprising, especially from an American perspective, is the consumer groups' strong opposition to marketing promotions such as gifts and coupons. These groups lobbied hard to restrict these promotions in the 1970s, and they have strongly fought off appeals to remove the restrictions in the 1990s. The US government has requested the removal of these restrictions, but consumer groups see this as US interference in Japan's internal affairs that would only give unfair advantages to those large firms that can afford promotions.

So why have Japanese consumer groups resisted market liberalization that should enhance their economic welfare? With the overwhelming drive to catch up with the West, Japanese consumers willingly subordinated their short-term interest in lower prices and greater choice to national goals of economic growth and military strength. Throughout the period of war mobilization, the Second World War, and recovery, the government actively sought to shape consumer preferences that would support these goals, organizing massive campaigns to increase savings (hence to suppress consumption) and to buy only domestic products (Garon 1997). And the consumer groups themselves actively collaborated in this effort. Through participation in national campaigns and other activities, moreover, consumer groups built up allegiances with other groups, including farm groups, trade unions, opposition parties, and environmental groups. Many of the local chapters of consumer organizations work directly with farm groups, especially the rural cooperatives, and thus feel bound by mutual ties of obligation. Other groups work closely with the traditional opposition parties. The Japan Women's Conference (*nihon fujin kaigi*), for example, is allied with the Social Democratic Party of Japan, and the New Japan Women's Association (*shin nihon fujin no kai*) with the Japan Communist Party. These groups have been especially reluctant to embrace measures such as trade liberalization and deregulation that might threaten labor unions, the core constituents of these parties.

The Japan Consumer Cooperatives Union (*Nisseikyo*), by far the largest consumer organization with 16 million members, is both a consumer group and a major retailer in its own right. Consumers join cooperatives to benefit from lower prices or to gain access to products, such as organic produce, but *Nisseikyo* plays a political role as well. It generally has not opposed trade liberalization – although it has not supported it either – and it does sell imported fruits and vegetables despite objections from other consumer groups. Yet when it came to liberalizing the rice market, *Nisseikyo* stood with the other groups, unified in opposition. In recent years, another network of consumer cooperatives, known as Lifestyle Clubs (*seikatsu kurabu*), has become active in politics, running its own candidates for local office and promoting political participation with an emphasis on local issues (Estevez-Abe and Gelb 1998).

To understand why Japanese consumer groups did not reverse Japan's "producer" system, we must recognize that consumer groups advocated policies that supported this system. They supported industrial investment by campaigning to increase savings; they complemented industrial policy by pushing for higher product quality standards; they reinforced trade protection by urging consumers to buy Japanese and by demanding health and safety regulations that discriminated against foreign suppliers; and they gave government ministries a pretext to limit competition and bolster corporate profits by advocating a heavy hand of regulation overall.

Signs of change?

In the early 1990s, consumer groups turned their attention to pushing through the Product Liability Law of 1994. The Consumers Federation of Japan (*Shodanren*), a liaison organization for thirteen of the biggest consumer groups, organized a special national liaison committee to mobilize public support and coordinate appeals to government ministries and political parties. Consumer groups were also influential in pushing through a US-style information disclosure law in 1999.

In recent years, consumer groups have begun to develop new attitudes, albeit very slowly. Most groups remain opposed to further agricultural liberalization, but they have shifted from staunch opposition to deregulation to a more nuanced stance: they welcome the elimination or relaxation of those regulations simply designed to protect industry, yet remain concerned that deregulation should not unduly disrupt social stability. Meanwhile, consumers at large have substantially altered their behavior in the marketplace. With the prolonged recession and the strong yen, Japanese consumers have become more price sensitive, fueling a boom in **discounters** and a real decline in retail prices. Although they did not support deposit interest liberalization or import liberalization, consumers have taken advantage of these changes in their savings and purchasing behavior. Over time, consumers' changing economic behavior appears to be affecting their political role, if ever so slightly, as they have become less staunchly opposed to market liberalization.

See also: consumption tax; Large Retail Store Law 1974; marketing in Japan; pricing practices; retail industry; superstores; trade barriers; trade negotiations

Further reading

Garon, S. (1997) *Molding Japanese Minds: The State in*

Everyday Life, Princeton, NJ: Princeton University Press.

Gelb, J. and Estevez-Abe, M. (1998) "Political Women in Japan: A Case Study of the Seikatsusha Network Movement," *Social Science Japan Journal* 1: 263–79.

Kokumin Seikatsu Kenkyu (People's Life Studies) (1994–6).

Maclachlan, P. (1999) "Turned Away at the Gate: The Politics of Postwar Japanese Consumerism," manuscript.

Vogel, D. (1992) "Consumer Protection and Protectionism in Japan," *Journal of Japanese Studies* 18: 119–54.

Vogel, S. (1999) "When Interests Are Not Preferences: The Cautionary Tale of Japanese Consumers," *Comparative Politics* 31: 187–207.

STEVEN VOGEL

consumption tax

The consumption tax is a Japanese version of the European value-added tax (VAT). It was introduced in 1989 by the Tax Reform Act of 1988 and has come to be one of the main taxes within the Japanese tax system, accounting for about 20 percent of total national tax revenue.

In order to cope with a budget deficit, the aging of society, and internationalization of the Japanese economy, fundamental tax reform had become inevitable since the middle of the 1980s. As part of the government's efforts to reform the tax system, the Tax Reform Act of 1988, one of the major tax reform acts, was enacted under the slogan of "tax reform to meet the time of aging society and internationalization of the economy." The main points of the Act were reduction and rationalization of the income tax burden, measures for more equitable distribution of the tax burden, reduction of the inheritance tax, fundamental reform of indirect taxes including the installation of the consumption tax, and reduction of the corporate tax. Besides coping with the problems touched upon above, the aims of the Act were to develop an optimal tax system, balancing income, consumption, property and other tax revenue areas, and to secure stable and sufficient revenue.

A fundamental reform of indirect taxes was needed in the context of social and economic developments such as the increase and the equalization of income standards, the diversification of consumption patterns, the larger share of service consumption, the aging of the population and so forth. In addition to these conditions, increases in expenditures and a budget deficit fostered the idea that a broader range of people should share the basic burden of paying for the maintenance costs of society. The consumption tax, which is supposed to bear widely and evenly for consumption, was considered to be a match for the idea and to ensure more stable tax revenue than do direct taxes such as income tax and corporation tax, under which revenue strongly fluctuates according to the business cycle.

Taxable items under the consumption tax are asset transfers made by enterprises within the country and imported goods (foreign goods received from bonded areas). Asset transfers includes sales and leases of assets, and provision of services. In other words, the tax is levied on consumption of goods and services and charged by sellers at the time of the sale of goods or services. Taxpayers are enterprises and importers and, periodically, they must total the tax collected on sales, deduct from this the tax paid on purchases and pay the balance to the tax authorities. As a result, consumers ultimately bear the tax. The tax bases are the counter-value of the transfers of assets and delivery value at the time of import. The tax rate is 5 percent, including a 1 percent local consumption tax. The rate was raised from initial 3 percent in 1989 to 5 percent in 1997 by the Tax Reform Act of 1994, which introduced the local consumption tax at the same time.

The following transfers of assets are exempted from taxation in terms of non-consumption or social policy: sales and leases of land, sales of securities and means of payments, interest on loans and insurance premiums, sales of postal and revenue stamps, fees for government services, foreign exchange, medical care covered under the medical insurance laws, social welfare services, burial and crematory services, educational services and so forth.

There are some special rules for small enterprises, which were introduced in order to weaken their opposition to the consumption tax. First, small enterprises whose taxable sales during the base period are less than ¥30 million are exempt from the tax. However, this rule is not applied to newly established corporations with equity capital of ¥10 million or more. Second, small enterprises whose taxable sales during the base period are ¥200 million or less can choose to use the product of the consumption tax associated with final sales and the deemed rate of purchases as the consumption tax associated with purchase. The deemed rates are 90 percent for wholesalers, 80 percent for retailers, 70 percent for manufacturers, 60 percent for others, and 50 percent for services. This rule, which was designed to decrease the task of tax filing for small enterprises, is called the simplified taxation system.

Since the consumption tax is a value-added tax levied at each stage of distribution of goods and services, the tax already paid in the former stage is deducted. In other words, the consumption tax paid on purchase is deducted from the consumption tax collected on sales by enterprises on the basis of its accounting records. It is has been said that using invoices is the most accurate method for determining the added value, and thus the amount of tax, and that this system also guarantees an open relationship between the tax authority, consumers, and distributors in terms of filing taxes and of incorporating the tax in prices. However, an accounting method that used bookkeeping without invoices was introduced in Japan in order to appease small enterprises that had feared their accounts would become too open, and also above board. The new method has attracted widespread criticism. According to Kato (1994), for example, the *Rengo* (Union of Japan Private Labor Unions) argued that under the new method it was difficult for the tax authority to ascertain if distributors were manipulating transaction records or keeping inaccurate records in their accounting books and not filing the taxes that consumers had paid. Although all taxpayers are required by the Tax Reform Act of 1994 to keep books plus business invoices, it is still said to be insufficient. In addition, the above-mentioned measures for small enterprises have made the consumption tax more opaque and problematical, because they may allow small enterprises to collect a "subsidy" or "profit tax" (*ekizei*) from consumers. When the issue of raising the consumption tax comes up in the future, the issue of transparency will certainly be raised again.

Further reading

Ishi, H. (1993) *Japanese Tax System*, 2nd edn, Oxford; Tokyo: Clarendon Press.

Kato, J. (1994) *The Problem of Bureaucratic Rationality: Tax Politics in Japan*, Princeton, NJ: Princeton University Press.

JETRO (2001) *Illustrated Guides: Taxation Laws*, Tokyo: Japan External Trade Organization.

Ministry of Finance (2000) *An Outline of Japanese Taxes*, Tokyo: Printing Bureau, Ministry of Finance.

—— (2001) *Outline of the Consumption Tax System*, http://www.mof.go.jp/english/zei/report/zc001e05.htm.

HITOSHI HIGUCHI

contract employees

Also known as non-regular employees (the common term in Japanese is *shokutaku shain*), the term can also be applied to part-time and temporary workers, though there are distinctions among the three types. Each type will be discussed in greater depth below. Contract employees are distinguishable from regular or permanent employees in that the former do not have full membership in the organization, that is, they do not have access to security (lifetime employment), seniority promotion or union membership. Moreover, the full range of **allowances and non-salary compensation** may also be outside their contracts. Contract employees constitute an important segment of the total work force in Japan. They often serve as a buffer within the labor force, their work hours expanding or shrinking based on the temper of the economy.

Contract workers usually work on one-year renewable contracts. Though they lack full access to the benefits of affiliation that permanent employees enjoy, it is the custom to receive a variety of allowances and benefits. Contracts are usually renewed automatically, and many workers have lengthy tenures with the firm. Except in extreme situations non-renewal of contract is a rare occurrence.

Temporary workers are those persons who work on contracts ranging from three to nine months. Their position in the firm is a level below that of contract workers. Contracts may be renewed somewhat automatically, but there tends to be greater mobility among this segment of the work-force, with some workers wanting greater freedom to move to other firms should a good opportunity present itself. During down cycles, these workers are much less likely to have their contracts renewed. Indeed, some firms in the manufacturing sector confronted with cyclical patterns of demand rely on temporary workers to buffer their permanent labor force.

Part-time workers are predominantly female and work less than forty hours a week, though it is not unusual for them to work more than forty hours per week during certain times of year or in response to short-term pressures. Part-timers are overwhelmingly female. An OECD study estimated that females comprise 75 percent of the part-time labor force. Part-timers are not to be confused with *arbuaito* (a Japanization of the German *"arbeit"*), a term which is generally applied to students working side jobs.

See also: lifetime employment; permanent employee

Further reading

Brown, C., Nakata, Y., Reich, M. and Ulman, L. (1997) *Work and Pay in the United States and Japan*, New York: Oxford University Press.
Tachibanaki, T. (1996) *Wage Determination and Distribution in Japan*, New York: Oxford University Press.

ALLAN BIRD

contracts

The contract comes into existence when a prior declaration of intention (an offer) is met by a posterior declaration of intention (an acceptance), regardless of whether consideration takes place or not. The validity is not affected either by an absence of contract under seal.

The liberty of contract refers to the right to freely choose the specific counterpart of contract and establish legal relation with it. Contracts vary in contents and characteristics. The civil code of Japan stipulates thirteen types: gift, sale, exchange, loan for consumption, loan for use, lease, contract of employment, contract for work, mandate, bailment, association, life annuity, and compromise. The civil code provides substituting rules for the case where concerned parties do not specify rules between themselves. When they do so, they may establish rules different from the civil code, on condition that their rules are not against public order and good morals.

A bilateral contract refers to a contract such as a sale, under which both parties assume a claim and an obligation. A unilateral contract is one such as a gift, under which only the donor is under obligation to transfer whereas the donee is exempt from obligation. Onerous contract relates to one with enumeration, and gratuitous contract without.

The consensual contract, the predominant form of contract, comes into existence once declarations of intention accord with each other. A contract in kind, on the other hand, becomes valid when the object is actually delivered, such as a loan for consumption, a loan for use, or a bailment.

The civil code is the general legal framework for contracts, but a number of laws are applied to specific types of contract. A sale between merchants is under the jurisdiction of the **Commercial Code**. Especially after the Second World War, a series of enactments and revisions have been undertaken to protect the economically weak and the interests of the consumer. Examples of such enactments and revisions include Land and Housing Lease Laws, Labor Standards Law, Usury Law, Door-to-Door Sales and Other Direct Sales Law, Installment Sales Law, the Consumer Contract Act, and the Law on Sales of Financial Products.

Further reading

Oda, H. (1997) *Basic Japanese Laws*, Oxford: Oxford University Press.

Uchida, T. (1997) *Minpou II* (The Civil Code, vol. II), Tokyo: The University of Tokyo Press.

Wagatsuma, S., Ariizumi T. and Mizumoto, H. (1997) *Shinban Minpo 2 Saikenho* (The Civil Code New Edition, vol. 2, Credit Law), Tokyo: Ichiryuusha.

KAZUHARU NAGASE

corporate finance

Fundamentally, corporations are financed with some combination of debt and equity. In Japan, there has been a tendency to use relatively large amounts of debt, much of it being loans via the banking system. Indeed, Japan has been characterized as having a bank-centered financial system compared with the more market-based system in the USA. Another notable characteristic is the substantial **cross-shareholdings** among Japanese corporations. Progressive deregulation of the Japanese financial system has led to forecasts that the strong role of banks would disappear and much of the cross-shareholding would be unwound. While there has been some movement, these traditional aspects of Japanese corporate finance have remained very important.

Debt financing

Debt comes in a variety of forms, including differing maturities, interest rates which may or may not be fixed over time, and a host of possible repayment provisions. A particularly important characteristic is whether the debt is a market-traded instrument such as a bond, or whether it is a loan (typically not tradeable). This distinction is important for the flexibility of terms on the borrowing. With a loan between a bank (or other financial institution) and some borrower, all the terms and provisions are potentially negotiable. For a bond or other market traded instrument (e.g. commercial paper), more standardized provisions are needed. In addition, provisions on market instruments are frequently the subject of governmental regulation, at least ostensibly, to protect investors (possibly individuals) who may be less sophisticated and have inferior information compared with financial institutions such as banks.

Indeed, the information which must be publicly disclosed for a bond issue may be sufficiently sensitive that a firm chooses to borrow via loans rather than disclose such information.

Another key distinction between loans versus market debt instruments is the ability of lenders to exercise control over a borrower's behavior. To a substantial extent, that ability depends on the number of lenders involved. With bonds or other market traded debt, there may be thousands of individuals as well as financial institutions which own portions of the debt. It is extremely difficult to coordinate such a large number of lenders, who also have potentially differing financial situations and motivations. In fact, a standard procedure for facilitating renegotiations of a firm's debt position is to buy up most (or all) of the market-traded debt so that there are a limited number of lenders involved in the negotiations. At the opposite extreme would be a situation where all a firm's borrowing is from a single source; for example, a bank. In that situation, the firm can reveal information to the bank on a confidential basis. The firm and bank can negotiate whatever borrowing terms are agreeable to both. Furthermore, such terms can be renegotiated in the future much more easily than if there are many lenders involved.

In Japan, an intermediate situation has evolved in the form of the **main bank system**. In essence, a firm develops a close working relationship with one bank (sometimes two), which is referred to as its main bank. The main bank performs a monitoring function regarding the client firm's behavior. This might involve bank access to confidential information regarding major proposed investments and strategic planning at the firm. The main bank may also provide advice on a wide range of financial issues, including the desirability and terms of potential market debt or equity issues. The intensity of the main bank's involvement is generally viewed as increasing with the indebtedness of the client.

Traditionally, other lenders such as other banks and insurance companies have relied on the main bank's monitoring to mitigate lending risks. Hence, they could lend to a monitored firm (with the main bank's concurrence) without having to acquire as much information. If the client firm got into financial difficulties, the main bank possibly bore substantial responsibility due to either inadequate monitoring or poor advice. This suggests a potential obligation for the main bank to compensate other lenders for its failures; a quasi-guarantee of their loans. Indeed, there have been spectacular examples where a main bank absorbed large losses due to a client's financial difficulties while other lenders were largely unscathed. On the other hand, there have been bankruptcies where the main bank apparently did not compensate other lenders. This illustrates that the main bank's obligation can vary dramatically and ultimately depends on acceptable business practice within the Japanese banking community.

It has been argued that the main bank system developed in response to severely restricted financial markets in Japan. Until the early 1980s, the typical Japanese firm was not allowed to borrow outside Japan. Moreover, it could not issue market debt instruments (e.g. bonds) in Japan without bank permission. There were also restrictions on equity issues which made them a relatively unattractive funding source. Rapidly growing firms tend to need substantial amounts of external funding to supplement their own retained profits, and many Japanese firms were growing rapidly from the 1950s until the mid-1970s. During this period, the banks controlled (directly or indirectly) funding for these firms. Even if this did not create the main bank system, it surely enhanced its strength and growth.

Around 1975, the average Japanese manufacturing corporation was over 80 percent financed with debt (less than 20 percent equity; see **debt/equity ratios**). Over the next fifteen years, growth rates were slower for most Japanese firms; and there was a sequential **liberalization of financial markets** in Japan. Access to offshore financing was also greatly enhanced, and it became an important funding source. This included not only loans from foreign financial institutions but large issues of bonds in offshore markets, particularly during the last half of the 1980s. Many of these bonds were convertible into equity shares or had attached warrants which allowed future share purchase (typically within four or five years) at a specified price. In 1987, a domestic commercial paper market came into existence, where large industrial

firms could borrow short term funds via market-traded instruments. That market proved attractive and rapidly grew to a substantial size. During the last half of the 1980s, there were also substantial equity issues. Thus by 1990, Japanese firms had a much broader set of funding sources available, had substantially lower debt/equity ratios, and overall were less dependant on the banking system.

Equity financing

Japanese equity markets have also provided some marked contrasts with the US situation. Prior to 1970, virtually all share issues were rights offerings to a firm's existing shareholders and priced at the stated par value for that firm's shares. Typically this par value (often 50 yen per share) was well below the current market price. Listing requirements, particularly on the Tokyo Stock Exchange, caused firms to pay (if at all possible) annual dividends of at least 10 percent of par value. From a cash flow perspective, these two requirements made equity issues an expensive financing mechanism since Japanese interest rates have typically been well below 10 percent as well as being fully tax deductible for borrowers.

After the Second World War, there was a confiscation and redistribution of shares from **zaibatsu**, large holding companies, to individuals. This resulted in Japanese individuals owning roughly 70 percent of all listed shares in 1950. However, this percentage has declined markedly and by 1990 was down to less than 25 percent. In contrast, holdings by financial institutions (primarily banks and insurance companies) as well as industrial firms has grown substantially. Often these shareholdings are reciprocal, with firms owning shares in each other. This includes industrial firms owning shares in banks and vice versa. Frequently, any one firm's holdings represent a small fraction of the other firm's outstanding shares. However, a group of such firms can collectively have a controlling fraction of the total shares. As a simplified illustration, suppose there is a group of 20 firms where each firm holds 3 percent of the shares issued by each of the other nineteen firms. Collectively, 57 percent of each firm's shares is held by other group members. This effectively blocks unfriendly takeovers and merger bidding contests such as seen in the USA.

The pattern of cross-shareholding in Japan is more complex than that simple illustration and is motivated by more than simply takeover deterrence. Cross-shareholding is prominent within *keiretsu*, groups of firms with common interests and /or heritage; for example, descendants of former *zaibatsu* groups. It has also been used to cement long-term customer and supplier relationships outside a *keiretsu*. The pattern also extends to banking relationships where client firms frequently hold shares in their main bank and other important lenders, with the banks holding shares in the firm (subject to a 5 percent legal limitation). Moreover, cross-shareholding relationships in Japan tend to be very long term and are even referred to as stable shareholdings.

Except for parent firms with a majority stake in a subsidiary, cross-shareholding positions are typically so dispersed that shareholders are in a weak position for exercising control over a corporation's management. This contrasts with the main bank's position described earlier. While the main bank is almost certainly a shareholder (typically about 5 percent), its power comes largely from being the firm's key lender. For substantial borrowers, the main bank may be providing a modest fraction (perhaps 25 percent) of the firm's debt; however, the bank's view on the firm's prospects is critical to obtaining other loans and floating bond issues. For firms with modest borrowing positions, the main bank's influence is substantially diminished and the firm's management has considerable autonomy from both lenders and shareholders.

After the crash

The Japanese stock market declined precipitously in 1990. This was followed slightly later by a similarly precipitous decline in real estate prices. Collectively, this has been referred to as "bursting" the **bubble economy**, which prevailed in the late 1980s with booming stock and real estate prices. The dramatic price declines altered the landscape for corporate financing in Japan. The number and size of new equity issues declined, with market price offerings virtually disappearing for a time. Real estate had frequently been used as collateral on bank loans, and this created serious problems for many industrial firms. In some cases, firms continued to make payments on loans whose principal amounts exceeded the current value of their assets. In other instances, borrowers defaulted. The effect on the banking system was disastrous, with virtually all banks suffering enormous losses which severely curtailed their ability to make new loans as well as to "roll over" existing loans.

In the aggregate, Japanese firms dramatically shifted their funding away from bank loans. In large part, they reduced their use of external funding, slowing their asset growth and relying more on internal funding (retained profits plus depreciation). They also relied more on the domestic bond market and, after the early 1990s, on foreign loans. The Japanese commercial paper market stopped growing, and offshore bond issues declined. The shift away from domestic bank loans reflects the difficulties experienced by the Japanese banking system. Clearly there has been a weakening of the main bank system. However, forecasting its demise seems quite premature. On the other hand, the growth of market-based financing has probably been healthy via providing a broader and more balanced range of financing alternatives for firms.

See also: banking crises; shareholder weakness

Further reading

Campbell, J. and Hamao, Y. (1994) "Changing Patterns of Corporate Financing and the Main Bank System in Japan," in M. Aoki and H. Patrick (eds), *The Japanese Main Bank System: Its Relevance for Developing and Transforming Economies*, Oxford: Oxford University Press, 325–49.

Hodder, J.E. and Tschoegl, A.E. (1993) "Corporate Finance in Japan," in S. Takagi (ed.), *Japanese Capital Markets*, Cambridge, MA: Basil Blackwell, 133–63.

Hoshi, T. and Kashyap, A. (1999) "The Japanese Banking Crisis: Where Did It Come From and How Will It End?" in B.S. Bernanke and J. Rotemberg (eds), *NBER Macroeconomics Annual 1999*.

JAMES E. HODDER

corporate governance

In its broadest sense, corporate governance refers to a complementary set of legal, economic, and social institutions that protect the interests of a corporation's owners. Systems of corporate governance vary widely across the industrialized economies, reflecting the fact that different countries answer the fundamental question, "To whom does the corporation belong?" in very different ways.

The Japanese system of corporate governance is based on the notion that a company is answerable to multiple stakeholders: creditors, employees, trading partners, and society. This emphasis on multiple stakeholders contrasts sharply with the shareholder focus of the Anglo-American system. The Japanese system, however, also diverges from other stakeholder-centered systems, such as that of Germany, in that the obligations of a corporation to its stakeholders stem from a set of normative understandings rather than law or ownership. While Japanese corporate law, codified in the **Commercial Code**, spells out a system of shareholder rights and corporate obligations, this system is largely a fiction, and bears little resemblance to actual practice. Japanese corporate governance works through a web of mutual obligations, minority ownership ties, business interests, and social norms.

The Commercial Code

The Japanese Commercial Code governs the structure and behavior of the corporation and outlines a system of corporate governance that, on paper, is very similar to that of the USA. At the core of the Commercial Code is the assumption that shareholders are the ultimate owners of the firm, and accordingly, the Japanese corporate law grants broad rights to shareholders. The shareholders' meeting, or *kabunushi sokai*, elects directors, or *torishimariyaku*, who then select management. Shareholders further elect statutory auditors, or **kansayaku**, who are required to monitor the board of directors, and assure that it operates in accordance with the law. The Commercial Code grants minority shareholders even greater powers than in the USA. Shareholders with a stake of 3 percent can demand that a board meeting be held, while a 10 percent stake gives a shareholder access to confidential financial documents (see **torishi-mariyakukai**).

Actual practice, however, diverges considerably from the spirit if not the letter of the Commercial Code. Shareholders' meetings tend to be short and incorporate little to no discussion. For many years, **sokaiya**, corporate blackmail artists, accepted payments from companies to stifle embarrassing questions from shareholders (though their activities have diminished over time). The shareholders' meeting is little more than a rubber stamp for board appointments, dividend payments, and other important decisions mandated by the Commercial Code. *Kansayaku*, with their obligation to monitor the board, are in fact appointed by the president, and are mostly insiders or outsiders with very close ties to the firm who play little to no real role in governance.

Stakeholder governance

Japanese corporate governance, as it actually works, bears little resemblance to practices outlined in the Commercial Code. Japanese managers balance the interests of banks, employees, trading partners, and society at large. In turn, all of these stakeholders play an important role in monitoring management. While key stakeholders of Japanese firms – its banks, buyers and suppliers, and other business associates – tend to be shareholders of the firm as well, their interests are in a firm's long-term growth and survival, rather than its ability to pay high dividends or maximize its stock price. In the 1980s, such stable shareholders held from 50–70 percent of a typical firm's equity.

At the core of this stakeholder system are the banks. Most Japanese firms have one (sometimes two) main banks (see **main bank system**). Main banks not only investigate corporate finances and strategy as a prerequisite for loan approval, but also intervene actively in corporate management. The role of the bank is most obvious in troubled firms. If a firm appears in danger of defaulting on its loans, a bank is likely to step in with a new management team, strategic direction, and financing. While banks are less vocal when it comes to high performing firms, they nevertheless keep a close watch on management to prevent a bailout from ever becoming necessary.

Certain conditions have enabled banks to play this role. Japanese firms, heavily dependent upon bank financing for much of the postwar period, have had little choice but to submit to rigorous bank monitoring. Banks may also exert influence by placing one or two of their own executives on a firm's board. By law, banks are forbidden to hold more than a 5 percent equity stake in a firm. However, a firm's other shareholders are likely to be related trust banks and insurance companies, and other firms closely related to the bank such as other members of the bank's *keiretsu*, or business group.

Employees are another cornerstone of Japanese corporate governance. In general, large corporations consider providing employment stability and career advancement to *seishain* (full-time employees, hired with an implicit promise of permanent employment) as a goal more important than maximizing share price. Under the permanent employment system, employees' career prospects are closely linked to the fate of the firm, and thus, they carefully monitor management. A president who fails to take employees' interests into account is unlikely to remain in that position for long. It is important to note, however, that unlike in Germany, where employee representation on the supervisory boards of large firms is legally mandated, Japanese employees have no legal right to board representation. Rather, their important role in the Japanese system of governance revolves on strong social norms concerning a firm's obligation to its employees.

A further set of stakeholders are buyers and suppliers. Like employees, buyers and suppliers often have a long-term stake in the survival of a firm, in particular if they have invested in relationship-specific assets that cannot be easily used elsewhere. A supplier that has built a factory next to its main buyer, or a buyer that has invested heavily in training a supplier's engineers in its manufacturing system, has a vital interest in the survival of its trading partner. Firms often hold minority equity stakes in their trading partners, often in conjunction with other members of their *keiretsu*. Buyers, in particular, often place one or more of their own managers on a supplier's board

to provide ongoing oversight. Even so, equity stakes in buyers and suppliers tend to fall short of levels that allow control. A firm's obligations to its buyers and suppliers, and the ability of buyers and suppliers to monitor each other, rests largely on a set of normative understandings concerning a firm's obligations to its trading partners.

Recent changes in corporate governance

Until the bursting of the **bubble economy** in the early 1990s, the Japanese stakeholder-oriented system of corporate governance was praised as a key to Japan's competitive strength. Patient capital – in the form of minority equity positions by friendly banks and trading partners – allowed firms to make long term investments rather than scramble to meet quarterly financial goals. Praise of Japanese corporate governance turned abruptly into criticism as the bubble burst, and the Japanese economy faltered during the 1990s. It was during the 1990s that the Japanese translation of the term corporate governance – *copureto gabanansu* or *kigyo tochi* – became widespread in the mass media and popular discourse. Poor corporate governance was blamed for everything from the excesses of the bubble economy to a spate of corporate scandals exposed in the 1990s. The stakeholder system was blamed for fostering insular thinking and lack of accountability. A debate emerged over whether Japan should adopt what was termed the "global standard" of Anglo-American corporate governance, or fine-tune the existing system.

While the causes of the bubble economy are complex, and it is not clear how much inadequate corporate governance was to blame, changes in the Japanese economy in the 1980s and 1990s did render the existing system less effective. Large firms, in particular, increasingly turned to **capital markets** rather than banks for funds. Banks had less reason to monitor firms, and firms had less reason to listen to banks. The banking crisis further diminished the credibility of banks as monitors and dispensers of managerial advice (see **banking crises**). While the institutions of permanent employment and long-term buyer–supplier relationships did not disappear in the 1990s, they were weakened through bouts of corporate **restructuring**. The web of mutual obligation that caused firms to put the interests of these stakeholders over returns to shareholders began to unravel. Another force in the transformation of corporate governance was the increasing influence of foreign shareholders. Ownership of Japanese shares by foreigners increased from about 5 percent in 1990 to over 13 percent in 1997 and ownership levels continued to grow through the end of the decade. These foreigners, largely US and European institutional investors and corporations, often had little ongoing business interest in the firms in which they invested, and began to demand that Japanese firms pay more attention to shareholder value.

The decade of the 1990s produced a number of changes in governance. In 1994, the filing fee for shareholder derivative suits was reduced dramatically. This increased the number of shareholders attempting to sue a company for real or alleged misbehavior. In 2000, shareholders won an ¥83 billion decision against the directors of Daiwa Bank for their role in trading improprieties in the USA. Managers of Japanese companies claimed that the real threat of shareholder suits made them far more cognizant of shareholder interests than ever before.

Other changes were implemented in board structure and compensation. Beginning in 1997, corporations were allowed to issue stock options to their board members and, by 2000, nearly 800 companies had done so (though a combination of a sinking stock market and very few options issues, made this incentive less than lucrative). A number of firms, beginning with **Sony**, reduced the size of their boards, often by more than half, by demoting board members with operating responsibilities to *shikko yakuin*, or corporate executive officers. This, it was argued, would enable the board of directors to behave more like a US corporate board, in overseeing the activities of top managers. The Ministry of Justice, urged on by the various interests of the **Ministry of International Trade and Industry**, Keidanren, and foreign investors, began the process of a major overhaul of the Commercial Code to mandate more effective and realistic governance practices. It was, however, by no means clear whether these changes were harbingers of convergence to Anglo-American governance, attempts to fine-tune the existing system, or window-dressing to please foreign investors.

Further reading

Aoki, M. (1988) *Information, Incentives, and Bargaining in the Japanese Economy*, New York: Cambridge University Press.

Aoki, M. and Patrick, H. (eds) (1994) *The Japanese Main Bank System*, New York: Oxford University Press.

Charkham, J. (1995) *Keeping Good Company: A Study of Corporate Governance in Five Countries*, New York: Oxford University Press.

Fukao, M. (1995) *Financial Integration, Corporate Governance, and the Performance of Multinational Companies*, Washington, DC: The Brookings Institution.

Gerlach, M.L. (1992) *Alliance Capitalism: The Social Organization of Japanese Business*, Berkeley, CA: University of California Press.

Shishido, Z. (2000) "Japanese Corporate Governance: The Hidden Problems of Corporate Law and Their Solutions," *The Delaware Journal of Corporate Law* 25: 189–233.

CHRISTINE L. AHMADJIAN

creative houses

Creative houses are specialized in activities related to **advertising**, a major area of marketing. The advertising industry in Japan was born during the Meiji era, when newspapers aimed toward ordinary citizens began to be published. At first they relied heavily on readers for sales and profitability, but they soon realized that charges for advertisements and various announcements in the paper were a much more stable source of revenue. As the economy grew a number of leading newspapers achieved increased circulation and volume, which in turn prompted a proliferation in firms seeking space for their advertisements.

Prior to the Second World War, the main function of advertising firms was limited to brokerage activities between newspapers and advertisement sponsoring companies. Although there were some ingenious examples of advertisement using other media such as magazines and periodicals, billboards, and publicity slips which were distributed with papers, the leading advertising firms handled only newspaper space.

In the 1950s, a number of independent radio stations began commercial broadcasting. The leading advertising firms in Japan today, such as **Dentsu** and Hakuhoudou, were quick to foresee the large potential of this new media, while those who neglected it never found a way to keep pace with the tremendous growth of the industry. Commercial messages on radio proved to be much more effective than more traditional media. But when television broadcasting started, the principal media for mass advertising shifted quickly from radio to television.

With the introduction of audience polls in both radio and television broadcasting, programs began to be rated according to the audience percentage they were able to track. However, they were rated from the standpoint of attractiveness and quality. Over time, firms gradually recognized that the advertising must be carried out in line with a comprehensive and coherent marketing strategy.

The advertising firms' function, hitherto limited to the brokerage of space and time, soon expanded to planning and production of effective commercial messages. The most important area of development was that of audio-visual messages on television, especially during the period when the entire nation became viewers following the period of **economic growth**.

Once the quality of commercial messages on television was put under careful scrutiny, literary and artistic components such as catchy copy, overall design, audio and visual effects gained importance. As a result, the contents of commercial messages were understood as a kind of synthetic, or total, art. Consequently, the section of advertising firms responsible for planning and production of commercial messages was renamed the "creative" section, in contrast to the sales section handling the traditional brokerage functions. The head of the creative section is now often called "creative director", and subordinates are known as "creators," the "creative team," or the "creative group."

Japan's leading advertising firms often carry out the substitute function of serving as the advertising section of several sponsors who are competing with each other. In order to avoid potential conflict of interests or leakage of secret information, the teams and sales force are grouped according to each client. In this regard, Japanese advertising firms are radically different from their Western counterparts, the advertising agencies that adhere to the principle of one client in one industry. Furthermore, the Japanese advertising firms' scope of operation includes a variety of related activities such as planning and conduct of marketing research or its arrangement on behalf of producers, inception and management of conventions and large development projects. Due to these characteristics, they are usually referred to as advertising firms (*koukoku gaisha*), rather than advertising agencies.

A recent trend in the advertising industry in Japan is to assume the entire marketing activities of producers, under the self-designation of "marketing agency." On the other hand, as an advertising firm's client companies become ever more international and foreign agencies make inroads in Japan, alliances and cooperative arrangements are actively pursued.

The total advertising expenditure in Japan, estimated by Dentsu, was ¥5.7 trillion in 1999. Advertising firms nationwide number approximately 3,500, but only sixty or so have annual turnover above ¥10 billion. Among the latter, Dentsu (based in Tsukiji, Chuo ward, Tokyo) is by far the largest with a turnover at ¥1.309 trillion in fiscal 1999. It is followed by Hakuhoudou (in Shibaura, Minato ward, Tokyo, ¥673.9 billion), Asatsu-D.K. (in Ginza, Chuo ward, Tokyo, ¥320.1 billion), Tokyu Agency (in Akasaka, Minato ward, Tokyo, ¥182.1 billion), Daiko (in Miyahara, Yodogawa ward, Osaka, ¥152.9 billion), and Yomiuri Koukokusha (in Ginza, Chuo ward, Tokyo, ¥110.5 billion).

Further reading

Nikkei Koukoku Kenkyujo (2000) *Koukoku Hakusho* (Advertising White Paper), Tokyo: Nihonkei-zaishinbunsha.

Saito, Y. (2000) *2002 Hikaku Nippon no Kaisha Koukoku Gaisha* (Comparison of Japanese Companies: The Advertising Industry), Tokyo: Jitsu-mukyouikushuppan.

Yamaki, T. (1994) *Koukoku Yougo Jiten* (Dictionary of Advertising), Tokyo: Toyokeizaishinpousha.

SHINTARO MOGI

cross-shareholdings

It has been a common practice in Japan for pairs of firms to exchange equity shares in each other, a practice called "cross-shareholding." Sometimes the firms have been in the same **industrial groups**, sometimes they are suppliers and customers, and sometimes creditors and borrowers.

Kabushiki mochiai (mutual aid shareholding) is the Japanese term for what is customarily translated as "cross-shareholding," that is, equity shares that two companies hold in one another. Cross-shareholding, in turn, is a subset of what is known as *antei kabunushi* (quiescent stable shareholding), which may be held in trilateral, multilateral, or otherwise stable arrangements among companies, usually based on group and/or transactional relationships. Together, the various forms of stable shareholdings comprise some 65 percent to 70 percent of all stock issued by publicly traded corporations in Japan. The remaining shares are freely traded on the stock exchanges.

Cross-shareholding in Japan, however, represents much more than a single-dimension ownership relationship. It often also reflects other understood but unstated obligations. As will be noted, cross-shareholding arrangements in the postwar era operated as tacit mutual pacts designed to insulate the management of both sides from any market threat of hostile takeover. The purpose of most cross-shareholding is to avoid rather than confer shareholder rights, so stable shareholding relationships function as a strategy of corporate management to limit shareholder governance of the firm.

Cross-shareholding may be divided into two categories: (1) cross-shareholding between members of a horizontal corporate conglomerate group, or *kigyo shudan*, the core of stable shareholding arrangements, and (2) cross-shareholding that reflects business relationships between suppliers and customers. In neither case is the cross-shareholding relationship intended to confer the owner-

ship rights inherent in the Anglo-American model of **corporate governance**. Cross-shareholding arrangements between suppliers and customers are primarily a franchise to do business, a method of cementing transactional relationships.

In 1992, Japan's Economic Planning Agency (EPA) responded to criticism raised by the United States in the Strategic Structural Initiative (SSI) trade negotiations that cross-shareholding promoted unfair trading practices and that Japan's cross-shareholding and **main bank system** specifically locked out foreign-owned banks. In its reply, EPA advanced three main economic justifications, among others, for cross-shareholding, characterizing them as "merits."

First, it argued that cross-shareholding provides a stable source of funding for businesses by ensuring that there will be partners who will be stable investors and who will buy new issues of stock whenever needed. Second, according to EPA, cross-shareholding strengthens the stability of corporate management by acting as a bulwark against the threat of hostile takeover. Such arrangements relieve management of the necessity of responding to excessive pressures from the **capital markets**, permitting it to develop operations according to a long-term perspective. Lastly, the EPA maintained, cross-shareholding stabilizes and strengthens business transactions between companies. The EPA White Paper of 1992 termed cross-shareholding a mutual "hostage" taking, which creates a captive relationship in the supply of goods or services and promotes long-term transactional relationships between cross-shareholding companies.

However, EPA accepted the point that group companies tend to do business mainly with each other, thus making it difficult for foreign investors to break into Japanese networks, and thus that extensive cross-shareholding among members of a corporate group could lead to exclusionary, anti-competitive business practices:

> Even though interlocking stockholding has the functions mentioned above, if it creates a relationship of 'conspiracy', business may become inefficient. What is more important, in selecting the customers, if it is taken into account whether or not they have interlocking stock-

holding unrelated to their individual products or substance of service, or cartel relations come into existence between competitors, competition may be limited.

(Japan Economic Planning Agency 1992: 181)

In addition, scholars in Japan have long criticized the practice of cross-shareholding as limiting shareholder governance, which they have characterized as among its major "demerits," particularly in terms of management accountability. In other words, without effective oversight by shareholders of corporate operations and managerial performance, Japanese managers had little incentive to seek to maximize profits. This is typically contrasted with the United States, where shareholders, at least theoretically, oversee the effectiveness of corporate management, and where the possibility exists of shareholders exercising their rights to change management if operations become too inefficient. Corporate management in the USA is thus given the incentive to focus on the more effective operation of the company for the benefit of the shareholders. In Japan, however, the mutual non-interference agreements generally implied in a Japanese cross-shareholding relationship gave Japanese corporate management an abundance of discretion in making business decisions and in regulating itself. This allowed inefficiencies to build up that produced a low return on equity. Until recently, declaring shareholder dividends had been neither a necessity nor even a priority concern of Japanese corporate managers. In recent years this view has been changing. Stable shareholders, in the absence of profits from capital gains, are now demanding dividends on their shareholdings.

Another significant demerit raised by critics in Japan is the potential for cross-shareholding agreements to damage and even defraud shareholders. Cross-shareholding represents an offsetting exchange of stock between companies, in most cases entailing no injection of new outside capital. For example, when a company issues ¥100 million in stock, the company uses the funds to acquire productive assets worth ¥100 million. Most often, in cross-shareholding arrangements, when a company issues stock to a partner, there are usually no net proceeds, just the receipt of new stock in exchange; such a transaction is purely a paper one.

Third-party investors in both firms might be made worse off in that their ownership share in the equity of the firm has been diluted by the increase in the number of shares without there being a corresponding increase in the earning capacity of the shares from investment. In addition, there has been an unspoken fear among third-party shareholders that any large-scale sell-off of shares into the market by a cross-shareholding partner (i.e., without either consultation or the replacement of that partner with another stable shareholder) could cause the collapse of the company's share price in the equity market.

The widespread practice of cross-shareholding has also been criticized as having negative effects on the stock market. As cross-held shares in a company are rarely traded on the exchange, the effective market in each company's stock is restricted to a fraction of the firm's outstanding shares. Thus, according to this view, speculators can manipulate the market price more easily. Such speculation by Japanese investors would tend to discourage outside investors, and, in overall terms, would dissuade participation of longer term investors.

Whether positive or negative on a net basis, the standard practice of enterprises holding substantial shares in other enterprises, owing primarily to the cross-shareholding phenomenon, creates an interdependency in the prices of shares. The shares of companies holding stock in other companies are more vulnerable to share price volatility the larger the holdings of such stock. The interdependency arises because when a firm has large holdings of shares in other companies, its own profits can depend to a significant degree on the price performance of those shares. If stock prices go up, the company earns "hidden profits" from those stocks; but if the prices of those stocks go down, they will have unrealized losses. As the market is at least implicitly aware of these unrealized gains and losses, it affects the first firm's own stock price. For example, Japanese companies that showed a steady rise in their core business income between 1985 and 1991, suffered unrealized losses on shares held in other companies when the stock market declined from 1989 to 1991. This resulted in a decline in their own company's stock price during those years, despite the core business profits, the effect being greater the greater the extent that they engaged in cross-shareholding.

The postwar cross-shareholding arrangements grew out of the dissolution of the *zaibatsu* in the initial period of the **American occupation** of Japan following the Second World War. The *zaibatsu* were holding companies, each of which held shares in and controlled a group of firms, many of which, in turn, had controlling interests in other firms (albeit often through a minority stake). The dissolution was intended to introduce "Western" principles of corporate democracy and to dismantle the industrial underpinnings of Japanese militarism. The divestiture by the *zaibatsu* of their corporate holdings under the Anti-Monopoly Act of 1949 led to an increase in stock ownership by individual investors. As a result, individual investors held 69 percent of all outstanding shares in 1949, a level that would fall dramatically as cross-shareholding was resurrected.

The cross-shareholding system as it existed by the 1990s was the result of three stages of major buildup: the first in the early 1950s, the second from the middle 1960s to early 1970s, and the third in the late 1980s. The corporate equity market in the early 1950s was characterized by active **take-overs** and free-wheeling shareholder meetings. During this period, speculators purchased stocks, which management bought back at a higher price (greenmail). Companies wanted to protect themselves by cross-shareholding. However, the provisions of the Anti-Monopoly Act prohibited stockholding by companies. Revision of the Act in 1953 allowed companies to invest in stocks of other companies, provided such stock holdings were not anti-competitive. The resurrection of cross-shareholding during this period was thus primarily intended to protect companies from unsolicited acquisition by speculators, who were particularly active after Japanese stock prices collapsed following the end of Japan's economic boom during the Korean War. The 1953 easing of the Anti-Monopoly Act also raised the upper limit of shareholdings by financial institutions from 5 to 10 percent.

This first stage in the development of cross-shareholding was also significant in that the former *zaibatsu* groups of **Sumitomo**, **Mitsui**, and **Mitsubishi** re-established themselves as a new form of grouping of companies, called *kigyo shudan* (corporate groups), horizontally organized conglomerates, with their **trading companies** and banks at the center of their groups (see below).

The second stage in the growth of cross-shareholding was precipitated by the collapse of share prices in 1964–5 and the first Yamaichi Crisis (1964), in which Japan's fourth largest securities company was faced with imminent bankruptcy. In order to boost the Japanese stock market, a special corporation, the Nihon Kyodo Shoken (Japan Cooperative Securities Co.), was set up by the securities industry with **Ministry of Finance** (MOF) **administrative guidance** to make major purchases of shares. Another major factor was Japan's having become a member of the Organization for Economic Cooperation and Development in 1964. As a condition of membership, Japanese capital markets were to be gradually deregulated, causing the MOF as well as business to become concerned about preventing hostile takeovers by foreign investors.

Once the Yamaichi bankruptcy had been averted, the Nihon Kyodo Shoken was able to sell the shares it had accumulated. Section 280 of the Commercial Act was revised so that boards of companies would be able to allocate newly issued shares to specified companies and individuals. Such allocations were made primarily to financial institutions and companies within their own group, resulting in further stabilization and concentration of stock ownership. This strengthened the aforementioned successors to the prewar *zaibatsu* groups and aided newly emerging *kigyo shudan*, centered around Sanwa, **Daiichi Kangyo Bank** (DKB) and Fuji Bank. As these shares were unlikely to be sold, it reduced the threat of hostile takeovers by either domestic or foreign investors.

The second stage of the growth of cross-shareholding ended with the introduction of a new policy to curtail the practice. After the first "oil shock" hit Japan in the fall of 1973, inflation rose and the price increases were seen as having been engineered by the corporations. This led, after much opposition, to adoption of the 1977 Anti-Monopoly Reform Bill, that reduced the allowed bank shareholding of company stocks from 10 to 5 percent. The implementation of this reform, however, was stretched over ten years.

The third stage in the growth of cross shareholding accompanied the "'bubble period" of the late 1980s, when corporations took advantage of high and rising equity prices and flooded the stock market with new issues as a way to raise funds. By itself, this would have increased the proportion of company shares that were actively traded, relative to the "quiescent stable shares." However, the issuance of new cross-held shares could prevent this, which was thus the primary purpose for the issuance of such shares in this period.

This was also a period of intensive *zaitech* (financial engineering) investment in securities by corporations, unrelated to investment for cross-shareholding purposes. That is, many companies sought to bolster their profits from gains in the rising stock market. The portfolio of the *zaitech* investor, like any unaffiliated investor, was strictly speculative, in anticipation of capital gains. Firms following this practice thus built up their portfolios of shares in other firms and if after several years these new shares were not traded, they would appear quite like traditional "stable" shares. Indeed, after the stock market crashed there was little incentive to sell these shares.

In fact, when analysts observed a reduction in corporate shareholding portfolios in the late 1990s, they measured the fastest rate of dissolution as being in the stable-shareholding (*antei kabunushi*) category. However, it is difficult to distinguish sales of shares that had actually been part of a firm's stable shareholding from sales of *zaitech* shares which it would have been timely to sell given that the Tokyo market had temporarily regained some strength as foreign buying increased substantially in the mid-1990s and again in 2000.

Much of bank–firm cross-shareholding in Japan has taken place within groups of interrelated firms, typically with a large bank at the center (see **main bank system**). Some economists suggest that the groups helped to manage risk in the Japanese economy (Nakatani 1984). Other analysts have been critical of bank–firm cross-shareholding, challenging this supposition. The shares cross-held by banks and firms became a matter of grave concern in the 1990s in part because most Japanese banks depended on the market value of stocks held in their portfolios to help satisfy capital adequacy standards. With the huge decline in the Tokyo stock market during the 1990s, at times falling to less than one-third of its 1989 peak level, banks had great difficulty in maintaining the level of capital required to meet the Basel Committee standards to operate internationally. The greatest part of bank-held shares have been in each bank's client firms.

Although there has been a decline in non-financial firms holding bank stocks, since many of these firms were importuned by their main banks to purchase their shares in the late 1980s so that the banks could meet the newly imposed capital adequacy standards, there has been little winding down of bank holdings of shares in current client firms. It is within the category of transactional relationships that one should view the shares of stock that a bank and its major client firms cross hold. The same is true for insurance companies and trust banks. They typically own shares in companies with which they do a significant amount of business, including selling insurance and pension fund products to the client firm and its employees. Such transaction-related shareholdings are considered to be separate and apart from any holdings of the client firm's stock that these financial institutions may have in their investment portfolios.

In the midst of these changes in Japanese (and global) financial systems, the prospects for bank–firm cross-shareholding are unclear. Japanese firms increasingly have market alternatives to banks for funds and depositors increasingly have market opportunities for placements of funds. Arm's length, market-related financial transactions seem less amenable to the kinds of relationships that bank–firm cross-shareholding characterized.

In fact, banks continued to acquire shares in firms that have newly become main bank clients. Asahi Bank and Tokai Bank (both with strong regional bases) and most recently firms in the Fuji group and in Sakura Bank's Mitsui group have also increased their holdings in order to strengthen their group's main bank. Business in Japan is typically conducted within highly contextualized sets of relationships and opaque rules that govern access and accountability. Thus far, there is little evidence of devolution in mutual shareholding arrangements on the part of banks, especially by regional banks whose clientele have very traditional notions of business relationships.

For the banks, we can conclude that two

significant purposes of cross-shareholding exist: to maintain stable business relationships, i.e., transactional relations between the cross-shareholding partner companies, in other words, as a franchise to do business with each other; and second, to maintain capital adequacy standards. Firms, on the other hand, are today buying bank shares generally only if they are in difficulty and need to preserve their relationship with a bank. Cross-shareholding thus continues to provide implicit relational contracts, a function that still has a role in Japanese business society.

Further reading

Iwao, N. (1984) "The Economic Role of Financial Corporate Grouping," in M. Aoki (ed.), *The Economic Analysis of the Japanese Firm*, North-Holland: Elsevier Publishing, 227–58.

Scher, M.J. (1997) *Japanese Interfirm Networks and Their Main Banks*, London: Macmillan, and New York: St. Martin's Press.

—— (1999) "Japanese Interfirm Networks: 'High Trust' or Relational Access?" in A. Grandore (ed.), *Interfirm Networks: Organization and Industrial Competitiveness*, London: Routledge, 303–18.

—— (2001) "Bank-Firm Cross-Shareholding in Japan: Why Is It, Why Does It Matter, Is It Winding Down?" Discussion Paper No. 15, United Nations Department of Economic and Social Affairs.

MARK J. SCHER

D

Daiei

Daiei, Inc. was established by Isao Nakauchi in April 1957 in Osaka. Shortly thereafter, Daiei expanded very rapidly to become a national general merchandising store chain. In March 1972, it outperformed Mitsukoshi and had the largest gross sales of any retailing company. Daiei is characterized by its low prices, mass sales policy, aggressive mergers and acquisitions strategy, business diversification, and organizational innovation. In September 1999, the company directly operated 317 stores, employing 15,603 staff. In the same year, the company was capitalized at ¥52,000 billion and the operating profit totaled ¥2.3 trillion.

Yoi moto o don don yasuku uru (Sell high quality goods inexpensively) is Nakauchi's mission and the corporate philosophy of Daiei. This mission is reflected in the company's pricing and store development strategies. Daiei adopted the low price and mass sales policy from the beginning, believing that low prices would stimulate sales and eventually increase profits. It has also extended its network of stores from Kansai to Kyuushuu, Touhoku, Kantou, Hokkaidou, and Okinawa to exploit economies of scale. In the 1990s, Daiei further expanded its network through mergers and acquisitions. In 1994 the company merged with three other retail companies. Three years later, Daiei acquired sixteen stores from Yaohan Japan. Daiei also expanded its business scale by building high-volume stores, expanding the average sales floor area from 1,500 square meters in the 1960s to over 5,000 square meters in the 1970s. This expansion enabled Daiei to include food, textile, and variety merchandise in its stores.

Daiei is also known for its rapid business diversification. In the 1980s, the Large Store Law was extended to cover supermarket chains and thus limit the expansion of Daiei. In response to this legal change, the company quickly developed other retail formats such as convenience stores (Lawson), discount stores (D-Mart), supermarkets (Maruetsu), specialty stores (Robella), and department stores (Printemps). At the same time, Daiei branched into hotel business, property development, finance business, restaurants, fast food business, travel, baseball, publishing and so on, turning itself into a large retail conglomerate.

To organize effectively for this rapid diversification, Daiei turned its divisions into nine independent companies, transferring most of the headquarters functions to each independent company, which could thus be more flexible in satisfying ever-changing customer needs. In December 1997, Daiei established the first holding company in postwar Japan in order to control its subsidiaries.

In 1998, the company recorded a ¥2,500 billion loss with a ¥260 billion debt. At the beginning of 1999, the company's chairman Nakauchi appointed Tadasu Toba, the former president of Ajinomoto and a corporate finance specialist as the company's president, hoping that Toba could improve the company's finance. In March 1999, Nakauchi's son suddenly resigned from the post of vice president. His unexpected resignation, it was said, has made the future of Daiei uncertain.

See also: retail industry

Further reading

Mizoue, U. (1998) *Daiei VS Ito-Yokado* (Daiei, Inc. and Ito-Yokado Co., Ltd), Tokyo: Baru Shuppan.

HEUNG-WAH WONG

daihyoken

Under the Japanese **Commercial Code**, at least one director must have the authority to represent the company to third parties and execute resolutions approved at the general shareholders meetings and the board of directors meetings (*torishimariyaku-kaigi*). Such directors, called *daihyo-torishimariyaku* (literally, representative director) are chosen from the members of the board of directors (Commercial Code 261-I). The board of directors or **torishimariyakukai** can dismiss *daihyo-torishimariyaku* anytime. *Daihyo-torishimariyaku* hold the right to represent and sign documents for all business activities of the company (Commercial Code 261-III). Thus, even if the board of directors imposes some restriction on this right, for example to restrict the right of *daihyoken* to represent only some operations or businesses of the company, the company is still liable to any claims made by third parties without such knowledge.

From a legal standpoint, there are only two classes of directors in Japanese firms, *daihyo-torisimariyaku* and *torishimariyaku*. However, most Japanese companies have their own internal designations for various classes of directors such as *kaicho* (chairperson), *shacho* (president), *fuku-shacho* (vice president), *senmu* (senior managing director), and *jyomu* (managing director). While these internal designations have no legal foundation and thus need not be officially registered, they are often mistakenly seen as titles to indicate the right to represent the company. In order to protect the public trust in *daihyo-torishimariyaku*, the company has an obligation to inform third parties without legal knowledge of *daihyoken* when it has business contracts with them (Commercial Code 262).

In most Japanese firms, only higher ranking directors such as the president and a few senior executives hold *daihyoken*. However, the number of directors with *daihyoken* varies by industry and size of company. In Japanese firms with both a president and chairperson, the president is usually the highest ranking director with *daihyoken*. The chairperson is a semi-retirement position for the previous president, often without *daihyoken*. Such chairpersons play the role of elder statesman, attending official functions, particularly those of industry and business associations. However, in some cases, chairpersons retain the right to represent the company and continue to exert strong influence over the management of the company as well as the appointment of the president. Thus, whether or not the chairperson holds *daihyoken* reveals the relationship between the chairperson and the president. The same can be said about who else holds *daihyoken* and their relationship within the board and other board members.

Further reading

Bird, A. (1988) *Nihon kigyo executive no kenkyu* (Research on Japanese Executives), Tokyo: Sangyo Noritsu Daigaku Shuppansha.
Charkham, J. (1994) *Keeping Good Companies: A Study of Corporate Governance in Five Countries*, Oxford: Clarendon Press.

TORU YOSHIKAWA

Daiichi Kangyo Bank

Daiichi Kangyo Bank (DKB) was established in 1971 as a result of a merger between Daiichi Bank and Nippon Kangyo Bank. Dai-Ichi Bank, which was established in 1887 as a national bank, was the oldest modern bank in Japan and had contributed to the industrialization of Japan. In 1896 it became a commercial bank. Nippon Kangyo Bank was established in 1897 as a special bank for promoting agriculture and industry. In 1948 it started national lotteries for public agencies. In 1950 it became a commercial bank.

Since the merger, Daiichi Kangyo Bank (DKB) has grown to be a major global bank. During the

1970s DKB began in earnest efforts to become more competitive and efficient, which ultimately led to the internationalization of its business. It was listed on the Amsterdam stock exchange in 1973 and on the London, Paris and Swiss stock exchanges in 1989, well ahead of its rival banks. During the 1990s DKB actively pursued the development of its information technology infrastructure in addition to investing in building its financial engineering capabilities, thus ensuring rapid internationalization.

In July 1997, DKB's reputation was dealt a serious blow when it was revealed that it illegally lent billions of yen to a racketeering group or **sokaiya** (corporate extortionists) at about the same time other scandals were being discovered (for example, **Nomura Securities**). The former chairman of DKB was arrested for violation of Japanese **Commercial Code** and the bank itself was prosecuted. In reaction to this devastating turn of events, the bank began a complete overhaul of its management, replacing all top management and attempting to renew an ethical corporate culture.

Finally, in September 2000, Daiichi Kangyo Bank, Fuji Bank, and the Industrial Bank of Japan began their three way merger process under a new holding company, Mizuho Holdings. This new colossal bank boasted some ¥130 trillion in assets, the largest in the world. Mizuho Financial group focuses its investment banking activities on the promotion of corporate mergers and acquisitions.

Further reading

Bremner, B. (1999) "Rebuilding the Banks: Mega-mergers are Just the Beginning; in Tokyo," *Business Week*, September 6: 48.

Ishizuka, M. (1997) "Japanese Firms' Sokaiya Ties Run Deep," *Asian Business* Vol. 33(8): 18.

SUMIHIRO TAKEDA

dango

Dango, loosely translated as "agreement through consultation," is the practice of price-fixing or bid-rigging. Even though Japanese law forbids such practices, *dango* arrangements have been uncovered in a range of industries and activities. A popular alias for *dango* is "shady cartel" (*yami karuteru*). In some cases, notably in bidding for public works contracts, *dango* arrangements take on a highly institutionalized and almost ritualistic form.

Some observers believe that *dango* is an offspring of the Japanese cultural proclivity for harmony and consensual decision making. While there may be some truth in such cultural explanations, it is well to note the existence of pecuniary incentives and political institutions that facilitate this shadowy behavior. For instance, the existence of well-organized industry associations enables close contact among executives of rival firms, thereby providing opportunities for would-be competitors to establish standards of "acceptable" market behavior and price-setting. Of course, this sort of behavior is not unknown in the United States and other countries, but Japan's industry associations tend to play a more extensive and significant role than do their counterparts in other Western countries. In the case of bidding for public works contracts, the Japanese government's procurement system facilitates price-fixing. In contrast to an "open bidding" system wherein all qualified firms are permitted to submit bids, the Japanese government employs a "designated bidder" system in awarding contracts for the vast majority of public works projects. Under this system, the contracting agency designates approximately ten "qualified" firms from which to accept bids on a project. The contract is awarded to the firm submitting the lowest "responsible" bid, as judged in accordance with a government-set anticipated ceiling price (*yotei kakaku*). In this way, the procurement system limits the sphere of competition for public works contracts. Defenders of the system argue that since public works are financed by taxpayers, it is important to ensure that they are carried out efficiently and that the work meets a high standard. In theory, only contractors who have a proven track record are designated to submit bids.

Dango is also facilitated by close, mutually beneficial interactions involving industrialists, politicians, and government bureaucrats. Here, too, the case of public works is instructive. In order to ensure that they are designated to bid on a project or to assist in settling disputes concerning which firm will be the "low bidder," construction contractors often appeal to influential allies in the political world. Mayors, prefectural governors, and members of parliament have been known to be the object of these appeals. The use of political influence in this context is known as the "voice of heaven" (*ten no koe*). Not surprisingly, large transfers of cash seem to accompany the invocation of heaven's will. In fact, it is known that certain politicians demand kickbacks in the form of a prescribed percentage of the total value of the project. Given the pecuniary incentives, it is somewhat surprising that relatively few bureaucrats from the contracting agencies – in particular, officials of the **Ministry of Construction** – are directly implicated in scandals involving bid-rigging on public works projects. Indirectly, however, the cost of bureaucratic involvement takes the form of providing "second careers" for retired officials, a practice known as ***amakudari*** (descent from heaven). Some observers believe that firms employing ex-bureaucrats benefit not only from their technical competence, but also appear to be rewarded with strategic leaks of information concerning the allegedly confidential government-set anticipated ceiling price. Obviously, prior knowledge of the ceiling price is a valuable asset when it comes time to rig bids on public works contracts.

Brokers (*dangoya*) play the part of determining how to apportion the illegal profits gleaned from price-fixing. In the case of public works contracts, brokers determine how much money will be transferred from the designated winner-to-be to the other members of the shadowy cartel. A popular device for accomplishing this aim is the "shady joint venture" (*ura jointo*). After bids are submitted on a project, the contract is awarded to the low bidder, Firm A. As the prime contractor, it is perfectly legitimate for Firm A to allocate segments of the project to specialized subcontractors. However, in a shady joint venture, the prime contractor transfers the contract to Firm B, which proceeds to pass it along to Firm C. Eventually, Firm D is hired as a specialized subcontractor. As prime contractor and subcontractor, Firm A and Firm D can lay just claim for services rendered. But, in a shady joint venture, Firms B and C also receive payment for service charges even though neither do any actual work.

Finally, Japan's weak penalties and lax enforcement of antimonopoly law do little to discourage would-be price-fixers from engaging in anti-competitive behavior. Indeed, until the early 1990s the maximum administrative surcharge imposed in those rare instances when violations of anti-monopoly law actually came to light was a mere 0.5–2 percent of ill-gotten gains; and the maximum fine for criminal activity was a paltry 5 million yen. In contrast, those convicted of price-fixing in the United States face treble damages and the very real possibility of incarceration. Under pressure from US trade negotiators, the Japanese government agreed to strengthen anti-monopoly penalties and their enforcement. The administrative surcharge was raised to 6 percent and the maximum fine was boosted to 100 million yen. These rather modest legal changes certainly give would-be price-fixers a bit more to think about, and they place Japanese penalties more in line with those found in some European countries. But many observers believe that the disincentives to price-fixing are not strong enough, and doubts persist about the ability of the Japan Fair Trade Commission to transform itself into anything more than a nearly toothless watchdog.

In sum, *dango* is deeply entwined in the mechanisms of political and economic power in Japan. The system serves the narrow concerns of vested interests while neglecting the general welfare. Industrialists reap ill-gotten gains, retired government bureaucrats secure second careers in the private sector, and politicians rake in political contributions. Of course, the cost of this anti-competitive activity is directly borne by Japanese consumers and taxpayers. Because of its shadowy nature, it is impossible to accurately estimate the cost of this price-fixing in Japan. In the case of spending on public works projects, estimates of the inflated price tag imposed by bid-rigging range from 15 percent to as high as 50 percent or more of the total contracted amount. And Japan's trade partners point to the *dango* system as non-tariff barrier that unfairly disadvantages foreign firms in their efforts to gain access to Japanese markets.

Further reading

McMillan, J. (1991) "Dango: Japan's Price-Fixing Conspiracies," *Politics and Economics* 3: 201–18.
Schoppa, L.J. (1997) *Bargaining with Japan: What*

American Pressure Can and Cannot Do, New York: Columbia University Press.

Woodall, B. (1996) *Japan Under Construction: Corruption, Politics, and Public Works*, Berkeley, CA: University of California Press.

BRIAN WOODALL

debt/equity ratios

The debt/equity ratio measures the amount of debt (bonds, bank loans, etc.) relative to equity used to finance a firm and is interpreted as an indicator of financial riskiness. Particularly during the 1970s and early 1980s, debt/equity ratios of many Japanese firms appeared extraordinarily high by US or UK standards. This led to questions regarding why Japanese financial institutions would lend to firms with high debt/equity ratios and how the apparent risks were controlled.

The debt/equity ratio is viewed as measuring financial leverage, with higher ratios indicating greater leverage. The physical analogy is that debt acts like a lever; and the longer the lever (more debt), the more weight (total assets) can be supported by a given amount of equity on the lever's other end. This suggests an accounting perspective where a firm's total assets must equal the sum of its liabilities (debt) plus net worth (equity). Hence, more debt allows a firm to have greater total assets for a given amount of equity.

Interest in Japanese debt/equity ratios was fueled by comparisons which suggested startling amounts of leverage for Japanese firms. Frequently these comparisons examined average values for broad groups of firms: for example, all manufacturing corporations. Often the statistic reported was the equity/total assets percentage. This statistic provides equivalent information to the debt/equity ratio when debt is interpreted as total liabilities. To illustrate, one could take the 1980 book value of total liabilities for all Japanese manufacturing corporations (reported by the Bank of Japan) and divide by their aggregate shareholders equity (net worth) to obtain a ratio of 3.85. Alternatively, one could divide net worth by total assets (net worth plus total liabilities) to obtain an equity/total asset percentage of 20.6 percent. In other words, these firms were financing roughly 20 percent of total assets with equity and 80 percent with debt: a debt/equity ratio of roughly 4. For US manufacturing corporations in 1980, the aggregate debt/equity ratio was 1.02 and the equity/total asset percentage was 49.5 percent. The difference across the two countries is striking. Moreover, these figures represent very broad averages and suggest a major systemic difference in borrowing patterns across the two economies.

An important aspect of leverage, particularly when it reaches high levels, is that it increases the risk of financial distress. The logic is that more leverage implies larger debt payments (interest and principal), which are obligatory. The larger these payments, the greater the chance that a downturn in a firm's revenue will result in not having enough income to make the required payments. The firm may still be able to meet the payments (for eample, using cash reserves); however, if revenues remain low or decline further, the situation may become critical. Even if the firm does not default on its obligatory debt payments, the prospect of financial distress can have very negative consequences. When default risk seems substantial, lenders may decline to renew maturing loans. Similarly, suppliers will be reluctant to extend trade credit (accounts payable) and instead demand cash-in-advance. Also, customers may be less willing to purchase products from firms that may not exist when replacement parts or service are needed. In addition, employees may leave for positions at other firms which seem to provide more job security. These are strong reasons to avoid even the appearance of a serious risk of financial distress. From this perspective, the Japanese debt/equity ratios appeared almost unbelievable.

There was considerable debate and analysis, particularly during the 1980s, regarding whether Japanese firms were really that highly leveraged. Several authors proposed adjustments for accounting differences across the two countries as well as using market values for the equity calculation. One motivation was that many Japanese firms had hidden assets (such as land and shareholdings) which were much more valuable than reflected in their accounting statements. Typically, such adjustments dramatically reduced the apparent leverage differences, at least on average. Some analysts concluded that after such adjustments there were no significant remaining differences. Others argued that there were still broad differences in leverage patterns and that some Japanese firms remained very highly leveraged by US standards. This naturally led to questions of why lenders would provide financing to such firms or, alternatively, how financial distress risks were being controlled.

Answers to such questions were typically attributed to the **main bank system**, where a large Japanese bank monitored and potentially intervened in the activities of highly-leveraged client firms. Moreover, there was an implicit quasi-guarantee that should a client firm get into financial difficulties, its main bank would organize a rescue. Thus, the main bank system was viewed as providing the mechanism for controlling financial distress risks and allowing firms to operate with high amounts of leverage.

The discussion of high debt/equity ratios for Japanese firms subsided considerably in the early 1990s. As suggested above, accounting and market value adjustments diminished the apparent book value differences. Also, book value debt/equity ratios for Japanese firms displayed a substantial decreasing trend starting in the mid-1970s and continuing into the 1990s. When coupled with accounting adjustments, this tended to make aggregate leverage differences between the US and Japan appear fairly minor by the early 1990s. Subsequently, discussion has focused more on the possibility that a high debt/equity ratio with main bank support can be disadvantageous if the main bank gets into financial difficulties. The banking crisis in Japan made this issue quite relevant for some firms (see **banking crises**).

See also: corporate finance

Further reading

Gibson, M.S. (1995) "Can Bank Health Affect Investment? Evidence From Japan," *Journal of Business* 68(3): 281–308.

Hodder, J.E. (1991) "Is the Cost of Capital Lower in Japan?" *Journal of the Japanese and International Economies* 5: 86–100.

Kester, W.C. (1986) "Capital and Ownership Structure: A Comparison of United States and Japanese Manufacturing Corporations," *Financial Management* 15(1): 5–16.

JAMES E. HODDER

Deming, W. Edwards

An American, W. Edwards Deming (1900–93) was one of the leading proponents of **quality management** in Japan and the west. With his emphasis on viewing organizations as systems and on understanding the implication of variation in processes, he is widely credited with having tremendous influence on the development of Japanese manufacturing excellence during the second half of the twentieth century. Despite Deming's technical background (Ph.D. in mathematical physics), his message was managerial, with simple statistical approaches advocated as useful tools to support business decisions (see **Ishikawa**).

During the 1930s, Deming, an expert in statistical sampling, was exposed to Dr Walter Shewhart's work on statistical process control (SPC). This sparked Deming's interest in quality management. Shewhart's focus was on applying SPC to production, to reduce scrap and rework. Deming recognized that the tools were more broadly applicable, to both manufacturing and services.

Immediately after the Second World War, Deming and others (including **Juran**) were invited to Japan by the Japanese Union of Scientists and Engineers (JUSE) to lecture on statistical methods. In addition to SPC, Deming covered managerial issues, laying the foundations for modern quality management. His experience in the USA led him to insist that the audience include top managers, in addition to engineers and designers. Deming was convinced that quality began at the highest levels of the organization, because improvement required substantial changes in processes, which only senior management could accomplish. He argued that over 90 percent of the potential improvement fell under the control of management, rather than workers. Thus, exhorting workers to produce better quality without changing the processes and systems in which they operated, was futile.

Deming's impact in Japan was far-reaching. Many credit him with changing the Japanese management approach from top-down to **bottom-up decision making processes**. The Deming Prize is Japan's highest quality award. In 1960, Deming received the Second Order Medal of the Sacred Treasure from the emperor. Very proud of this honor, he nearly always wore the lapel pin commemorating the award. Despite his stature in Japan, he made few inroads into Western management until the early 1980s, when Ford Motor Company and then General Motors engaged him to assist with large-scale corporate turnarounds. Ironically, US interest in Deming was driven by competition from Japanese firms that had adopted his suggestions in the 1950s.

Deming advocated a complete transformation of the traditional top-down approach to management. The transformation was to be based on considering the organization as a system and managing its interrelationships, understanding statistical variation to permit data-based decisions, focusing on internal and external customers, and creating "win-win" situations in place of debilitating competition. His book *Out of the Crisis* (1982) described fourteen points which should serve as the basis for the transformation. Deming then worked to develop a more theoretical approach, which resulted in his "system of profound knowledge," as described in *The New Economics for Industry, Government, Education* (1993). He asserted that the fourteen points would follow naturally in an organization whose management was guided by the four interrelated parts of profound knowledge: appreciation for a system, knowledge about variation, theory of knowledge, and psychology.

Deming emphasized that an organization is a network of interrelated components (e.g. departments) with a single aim of gain for everyone: stockholders, employees, suppliers, customers, community, and environment. Managing the interdependencies among the components is crucial, and necessary for optimization of the entire system. Independent optimization of individual components will result in suboptimization of the system. Success requires cooperation, rather than competition, among the components. Top management must guide the optimization of the system, with a focus on delighting customers, both internal and external to the organization.

Knowledge about variation

Two types of variation characterize all processes. Common cause (system) variation is that inherent in the process. Special cause variation is due to specific, generally identifiable, events. Special causes are often resolvable by workers close to the problem. Common cause variation is generally related to process design or the consistency of incoming material. Management must resolve these issues, as front-line workers have neither the authority nor the fiscal responsibility. Common and special cause variation demand different actions. Treating common cause variation as special leads to over-adjustment of processes, which increases the system variation. Treating special cause variation as common prevents the search for a resolvable problem. SPC is based on reducing the economic loss from these two errors.

A process with only common cause variation is statistically stable; only stable processes can be used for prediction. However, stable processes are not necessarily capable of meeting specifications. To achieve process capability, specifications should be established only after the process variation is understood. **Taguchi** loss functions can be used in place of specifications.

Theory of knowledge

Deming maintained that all management is based on prediction, and that prediction requires theory. Knowledge is then developed through systematic revision and extension of theory, based on comparing predictions with observations. Theory, which may be revised, is necessary for using information and creating knowledge. This relationship is demonstrated in Deming's Plan-Do-Study-Act cycle (which he called the "Shewhart cycle"), a systematic approach to problem solving.

Ultimately, organizations consist of people, and Deming emphasized the need to understand what motivates individuals. He stressed that managers must be aware of the different factors that motivate individual people, and understand that intrinsic (internal, individual) motivation is more important than extrinsic (external) motivation. According to Deming, the reward systems used in most organizations allow extrinsic motivation to smother intrinsic motivation, replacing simple recognition with money, and removing joy from work.

Further reading

Deming, W.E. (1982) *Out of the Crisis*, Cambridge, MA: CAES.
—— (1993) *The New Economics for Industry, Government, Education*, Cambridge, MA: CAES.
Latzko, W.J. and Saunders, D.M. (1995) *Four Days with Dr. Deming: A Strategy for Modern Methods of Management*, Reading, MA: Addison-Wesley.
Scherkenbach, W.W. (1986) *The Deming Route to Quality and Productivity: Road Maps and Road Blocks*, Washington, DC: CEE Press Books.

ELIZABETH L. ROSE

Dentsu

Dentsu is Japan's largest advertising agency with almost double the billings of its number two competitor, Hakuhodo. Dentsu has dominated Japanese advertising for a long time, and it has consistently accounted for one-quarter of Japan's total advertising billings. In the area of network television, Dentsu dominates to an even greater degree by buying half of the national prime time airtime. Dentsu is also ranked as one of the largest advertising agencies in the world.

Originally established in 1901 as a news telegraphic service, the name Dentsu literally means "telegraphic communications." Today, Dentsu is a full-service mass media advertising agency that also handles below-the-line services such as events, sales promotions, transit advertising, internet advertising, direct mail, and outdoor billboards, to name a few. These activities are in keeping with Dentsu's publicized strategy of providing "total communications services."

The majority of Dentsu's nearly 6,000 employees are based in Japan, where the agency has thirty-one offices nationwide. The slightly over 4,000 employees presently based in Dentsu's headquarters in Tokyo occupy ten buildings. These employees will be housed in Dentsu's new headquarters in the Shiodome ward of Tokyo, which is scheduled for completion in 2002. The remainder of Dentsu's employees in Japan are located in its five regional subsidiaries, and its affiliate and associate companies, which total 400 in number.

Dentsu also has many subsidiaries including film and video production companies, theme park and resort companies, real estate services, property management and insurance companies. Together with Young & Rubicam of the USA, Dentsu also has a joint venture ad agency named Dentsu Young & Rubicam that is focused exclusively on the Asia/Pacific region. In addition, Dentsu maintains six fully owned overseas offices, and has subsidiaries and affiliates in forty-seven cities in thirty-four countries worldwide.

Dentsu is privately held. The two largest shareholders are two of Japan's major news services, Kyodo News and Jiji Press. Dentsu has announced plans for a listing on the Tokyo stock exchange in 2002.

In Japan, Dentsu's several thousand clients include both **Toyota** and **Honda**, as well as all of Japan's major brewers. This is possibly due to the sheer size of Dentsu, particularly its number of employees, allowing the agency to physically separate the sections handling competing clients.

A major reason clients go to Dentsu is due to its clout with the media. The root of Dentsu's strength with the media lies in the fact that Dentsu has a history of assisting the various media during their launches. Dentsu helped establish the Tokyo Broadcasting System (Channel 6), and remains the network's largest non-financial shareholder. In addition, Dentsu holds minority interests in other television stations and owns a large percentage of Video Research, Japan's television rating service. Dentsu also conducts business with an unrivaled number of Japanese publishers. Besides creating and placing advertisements in the publishers' magazines, Dentsu's support extends to such activities as publicizing books and magazines and helping new publications secure a position in the media community.

SEAN MOONEY

department stores

Japanese department stores have a long history. The earliest stores began as kimono shops, eventually growing into other product categories. Matsuzakaya (founded 1611) originated as a Nagoya kimono shop. Shirakiya, which is now Tokyu Department Store began in Tokyo in 1662. Mitsukoshi (Echigoya) began in 1673. Daimaru (1717) Sogo (1830) and Takashimaya (1831) are some of the other early retailers. Six of the ten largest department stores in Japan originated before 1850. A second group of department stores originated as providers of daily necessities and operated in or near the railroad terminal. Their names, such as Seibu, are shared by railroad lines. Originally the terminal department stores were considered much lower status than the kimono shop stores, but gradually the newer terminal stores gained respect as full-line department stores.

Department stores represent tradition in Japan. They offer cradle-to-grave services for their customers. About one-third of a department store's total sales will occur during two Japanese seasonal gift-giving periods. Department stores provide gift-giving consultation, gift wrapping and home delivery. Selecting gifts from a prestigious department store provides assurance that the gift is appropriate.

Since the economic bubble burst in 1990, department store sales have declined dramatically. The top department stores in Japan in order of rank are Takashimaya, Marui, Seibu, Mitsukoshi and Isetan. The ranking of these top department stores changed little from 1990 to 2000.

Several characteristics of Japanese department stores set them apart from department stores in other parts of the world. First, Japanese department stores can be considered manufacturers' showrooms. Only about 10 percent of the merchandise in a Japanese department store is direct purchase; the other 90 percent is return-based purchases with no inventory responsibility (*shoka shire*) and consignment sales (*itaku shiire*). Second, sales employees are sent from the manufacturer and are compensated by the manufacturer rather than the retailer. These sales employees interact with consumers gathering market intelligence for the manufacturer. Major manufacturers sell their products in all the top ten department stores, so there is little to differentiate one department store from another. Third, department stores follow the manufacturer's suggested retail price. Little department store merchandise is direct purchase, so manufacturers maintain the right to set and maintain price throughout the season. Seasonal sales will be determined by the manufacturer, if they are held at all.

Japanese department stores expanded to Hong Kong, Singapore, Thailand, Taiwan, Indonesia, Vietnam and China. By 1989, the fourteen Japanese department stores in Hong Kong held 30 percent of the department store market. Ten years later, however, most of the Japanese department stores had left Hong Kong. Some stores such as Tokyu and Matsuzakaya simply withdrew and went home. Others such as Isetan used Hong Kong as a departure point for operations in China.

There are three environmental factors that make international markets attractive: (1) domestic competition from mass merchandisers; (2) government restrictions on expansion of large department stores; and (3) the high cost of labor and land in Japan. Japanese mass merchandisers, also called supermarkets, carry clothing, appliances, and often food. Although they carry the same merchandise mix as department stores, they are not brand name discounters. They carry merchandise with brand names different from those of the traditional department stores. Often the same manufacturer will produce brand-name merchandise for department stores and brand-name merchandise for supermarkets, but consumers do not associate the two brand names with each other. The difference between the positioning of the two store formats is that department stores carry a luxury image while mass merchandisers provide goods for everyday needs. The relaxation in the large-scale retail law has made the opening of these stores easier, and in addition the recession in Japan has made customers very price-conscious. Mass merchandisers such as Ito Yokado and Mycal have been trading up, reducing the distinction between mass merchandisers and department stores.

The domestic growth of department stores was limited by the Large-Scale Retail Store Law. This law required lengthy evaluation and approval of any new large store development, severely restricting the number of new department stores, but also reducing competition for the department stores that are already present in the market. The Large-Scale Retail Store Law motivated several Japanese department stores to use international expansion as a growth mechanism.

Land prices and construction costs in Japan are the highest in the world. There is no early return on investment in a new building project. It takes ten to twelve years for a new department store to become profitable in Japan, and fifteen to twenty years before it breaks even on investment costs. In places like Hong Kong, Singapore, Taipei and Bangkok, retail footage is expensive, but it is available.

Japanese department stores also have small branch outlets around the world to provide Japanese travelers the guarantee of nearly 300 years of tradition and service.

See also: discounters; distribution system; Ito-Yokado; Japanese business in China; Large Retail Store Law

Further reading

Sternquist, B. (1998) *International Retailing*, New York: Fairchild Press.
—— (2000) "Internationalization of Japanese Department and GMS Stores: Are There Characteristics of Profile Success?" in M. Czinkota and M. Kotabe (eds), *Japanese Retail Strategy*, London: International Thomson Business Press, 242–249.
Sternquist, B., Chung, J.E. and Ogawa, T. (2000) "Japanese Department Stores: Does Size Matter in Buyer-Supplier Relationship?" in M. Czinkota and M. Kotabe (eds), *Japanese Retail Strategy*, London: International Thomson Business Press, 64–80.

BRENDA STERNQUIST

depressed industries

In the course of a nation's industrial development, it is inevitable that some manufacturing industries will lose their competitiveness and enter into long-term periods of economic distress and decline. Industrial decline can stem from various causes, including rising costs of production, notably those of labor and other resource inputs such as raw materials and energy; outmoded and inefficient plant technology, especially relative to foreign rivals; or a shift in demand to other substitutes. Depressed industries generally lose competitiveness relative to foreign producers, and so are challenged by high levels of imports. Depressed industries are characterized by excess production capacity relative to existing demand, leading to great pressures for firms to exit the market, as well as high levels of **unemployment**.

Industrial decline can be divided into two stages: industrial distress, in which firms struggle to remain solvent in the face of underutilized capacity and depressed prices and profits; and true decline, in which the industry's problems are so overwhelming that exit of large numbers of firms is the only option. Thus far, most of Japan's declining industries have not yet entered this second phase.

Depressed industries in postwar Japan

Although more attention has been paid to Japan's growth industries in the postwar period, depressed industries have also been common. In the 1950s, for instance, industries such as coal mining and various parts of the textile industry (yarn and cloth production, weaving, etc.) had clearly lost their competitiveness, and were faced with excess capacity, bankruptcy and high levels of unemployment. Others, such as silk reeling and rayon production, found demand for their products superseded by other substitute goods. (Another entire sector of the economy, agriculture, has been inefficient for most of the postwar period. Similarly, a number of service sectors, including the **construction industry** and many industries involved in the **distribution system** have also suffered from a relative lack of efficiency.)

In the 1970s the rapidly rising price of oil following the twin oil shocks staggered a number of energy-intensive materials industries, including aluminum, petrochemicals and chemical fertilizers, synthetic fibers, and minimill steel. Others, such as the shipbuilding industry, suffered from the worldwide decline in demand for new ships. Still others, such as paper and paper pulp, cement, and plywood also faced deep industrial distress as the result of declining demand at home and abroad.

In the 1990s, former growth industries such as the integrated steel industry and the **automotive industry** have approached industrial maturity and have experienced periods of economic distress. These problems were exacerbated by the long recession of the 1990s. The economy's weak condition and rising levels of unemployment made more difficult the adjustment process for these new depressed industries.

Adjusting to decline: market-oriented and political solutions through the 1980s

All depressed industries in Japan have attempted to deal with their problems through market mechanisms, for instance by cutting the costs of production or by developing new sources of demand. Firms have also attempted to diversify into higher value-added production by shifting to more specialized, processed products, or into other, non-related businesses. Others have attempted to relocate production facilities abroad, either to tap into less expensive inputs (labor and raw materials) or to be closer to final demand.

Successful market-oriented adjustment to industrial decline, however, has been limited to the relatively large, capital and technology-intensive firms. Smaller firms, which have often had less access to capital and technology, have been much less successful in following these economic adjustment strategies. In addition, all industries have had a hard time in drastically reducing their labor forces. Most Japanese firms – including small ones – have made an implicit guarantee to their workers not to fire them at the first sign of industrial distress. Rather, firms have resorted to such measures as cutting working hours, retraining redundant workers, and transferring excess labor to other, related firms. Again, larger firms, especially those with *keiretsu* ties, have been better able to pursue these options; still, all firms in Japan have tried to shield their workers to bear the full brunt of adjustment.

In the past, depressed industries in Japan have also tried to deal with their problems through political, or collective, means. Rather than letting market forces weed out the less efficient firms,

which would entail long periods of depressed prices and profits for all, industries have organized to try to stabilize their industry's conditions. In general, these efforts have taken the form of trying to control or manage "excessive competition." In the short term, industries have attempted to form quasi-cartels, in which all firms in the industry consent to reduce their output levels by an agreed upon amount. These efforts at bringing production in line with demand have been aimed at stabilizing prices, and therefore profits. Above all, industries have sought to avoid cutthroat **competition** that would damage all firms. In the longer term, industries have also tried to reduce overall capacity using similar, collective means. Rather than relying on the market to force out the least competitive, industries have negotiated collective agreements in which all firms are expected to reduce a negotiated percentage of their capacity.

These collective efforts have usually been negotiated on a private basis, usually within each industry's political organization, the **industry and trade associations**, or *gyokai*. Within these associations, firms have been able to communicate, negotiate industry-wide agreements, and to some extent enforce their collective action. In periods of acute economic distress, however, industries have often found these private enforcement mechanisms to be insufficient to curb the problem of free riding common to any cartel. Rather, industries found external enforcement mechanisms to be necessary, and have often turned to the **Ministry of International Trade and Industry** (MITI) for help, either to discipline so-called industry "outsiders" (relatively competitive firms that refuse to cooperate with industry agreements), to regulate new entry into the industry or, in some cases, to impede rising levels of imports.

The Japanese government responded with a variety of measures, especially for those industries with political clout, as well as those that are deemed to be strategically important. MITI helped industries to coordinate production and capacity cuts, often through the formation of formal "recession cartels." In 1978 the government passed the Depressed Industries Law, which supported the capacity reduction efforts of designated industries, raised barriers to entry into the industry, and made further cartelization possible. The law also included specific provisions designed to prevent "outsider" firms from violating the industry's capacity reduction plans. The Japanese government has also supported efforts by industries to slow down the growth of foreign imports, which would undermine domestic attempts to stabilize prices and profits. In the textile industry, as one example, MITI used its powers of administrative guidance to importers and trading companies to avoid flooding the domestic market. While Japan has avoided overt protection of its domestic market, the Japanese government has also helped to negotiate informal agreements with competing textile industries in other countries, including China, Korea, and Pakistan, to maintain an "orderly market" in Japan, akin to the "voluntary" export restraints that the United States has negotiated with Japan. The government has also passed measures to cushion the costs of adjustment, for instance by encouraging labor retraining and relocation, and providing inducements for diversification.

Depressed industries in the 1990s

In large part because of foreign pressures, the Japanese government in the 1990s was less able to support industry efforts to deal with distress through collective or political means, especially when such actions served to impede imports. Japan's ability to impede imports through informal means has also come under heavier scrutiny. Recession and other types of government-approved cartels are less common today. Legislation specifically designed to help industries cooperate to reduce production or capacity levels have been made more generic over time. Still, Japan's depressed industries benefit from the many existing regulations that help them continue to stabilize their economic environment. Depressed industries have been powerful and vocal opponents of efforts to deregulate the domestic economy.

Depressed industries in the 1990s have thus had to rely more on market-oriented adjustment mechanisms. Some large firms have had success in diversifying at home or relocating production overseas. But all firms continued to struggle with the problem of shedding excess labor, and as a result have often been slow to adjust to changing market conditions. In the late 1990s, however,

many firms, including some of Japan's largest firms, saw no alternative but to lay off significant numbers of their core workers.

The rising level of foreign investment in Japan in the late 1990s has been a new and significant catalyst for adjustment. In the automotive industry, for example, foreign participation has led to a significant **restructuring** of the industry.

See also: bankruptcies; cartels; industrial policy; industrial regions

Further reading

Dore, R. (1986) *Flexible Rigidities: Industrial Policy and Structural Adjustment in the Japanese Economy, 1970–1980*, Stanford, CA: Stanford University Press.

Katz, R. (1998) *Japan: The System That Soured*, Armonk, NY: M.E. Sharpe.

Noble, G. (1998) *Collective Action in East Asia: How Ruling Parties Shape Industrial Policy*, Ithaca, NY: Cornell University Press.

Tilton, M. (1996) *Restrained Trade: Cartels in Japan's Basic Materials Industries*, Ithaca, NY: Cornell University Press.

Uriu, R. (1996) *Troubled Industries: Confronting Economic Change in Japan*, Ithaca, NY: Cornell University Press.

ROBERT URIU

Depressed Industries Law (1978)

In response to demands from a number of **depressed industries**, the Japanese government in May of 1978 passed this legislation, designed to help designated industries to cooperatively reduce their excess productive capacity. The Japanese economy in the late 1970s was still feeling the effects of the first oil shock, which forced many energy-intensive industries, such as aluminum smelting, synthetic fibers, and petrochemicals, to face rising production costs and the loss of competitiveness relative to foreign producers. Other industries, such as the shipbuilding industry, faced a drastic drop in foreign demand. All industries in Japan were also hurt by the 40 percent appreciation of the yen between 1977 and

1978, which further undermined their export competitiveness (see **appreciating yen**).

Under the provisions of the 1978 law (*Tokutei Sangyo Antei Rinji Sochiho*, or *Tokuanho*), two-thirds of an industry's firms had to agree to apply to the government in order to be designated as depressed. Designated industries were exempted from anti-trust laws, allowing the industry to formulate a "stabilization plan" specifying capacity reduction targets and methods. These plans were then approved by the **Ministry of International Trade and Industry**, but capacity cuts remained voluntary. Industries that could not scrap sufficient capacity could form an indicative cartel for the purpose of capacity reductions. The law also created a special trust fund that provided low-interest loans to the designated industries to finance capacity reductions. In addition, the government also passed separate legislation dealing with unemployed workers in depressed industries, and for designated depressed regions.

There was a strong consensus among industry leaders, politicians, and bureaucrats in favor of the *Tokuanho*. Depressed industries in Japan had been struggling with excess capacity for some years prior to the legislation. Rather than allowing the market to weed out the weakest firms, which would have led to periods of depressed prices and profits for all, industries had been trying to reduce capacity through cooperative industry agreements. Industries were finding, however, that these efforts were undermined by the problem of free riding: each firm hoped that it would be someone else who cut capacity or exited the market. The *Tokuanho* allowed industries to develop a more formal mechanism to reduce capacity across the board, and offered financial inducements for the disposal of capacity. Many of the depressed industries themselves were vocal advocates of the law, and in fact lobbied for provisions that would have given the government even greater powers to enforce their collective capacity-cutting efforts.

Japanese politicians, faced with growing criticisms for failing to act to deal with the economic crisis of the 1970s, were also in favor of the law. The new legislation promised to help some key industrial supporters deal with their problems. Bureaucrats from the Ministry of International Trade and Industry also saw the *Tokuanho* as a way to deal with the problems of industries under its jurisdiction. MITI was especially concerned with avoiding socially disruptive bankruptcies and rising **unemployment**, as this would have increased the politicization of its **industrial policy**. Some MITI officials were also concerned with a handful of industries deemed to be strategically important.

The legislation proved effective in helping some designated industries shed their excess capacity. In most cases firms had planned to scrap these facilities even before the law was passed, but the effect of the law was to ensure that scrapping occurred. The second oil shock hit Japan soon after the legislation went into effect, making recovery of the designated industries more difficult. In addition, a number of other industries became depressed in this period. The *Tokuanho* expired in June 1983, and was superseded by a similar piece of legislation, the Structural Improvement Law (*Tokutei Sangyo Kozo Kaizen Rinji Sochiho*).

See also: cartels; industrial regions

Further reading

Dore, R. (1986) *Flexible Rigidities: Industrial Policy and Structural Adjustment in the Japanese Economy, 1970–1980*, Stanford, CA: Stanford University Press.

Noble, G. (1998) *Collective Action in East Asia: How Ruling Parties Shape Industrial Policy*, Ithaca, NY: Cornell University Press.

Tilton, M. (1996) *Restrained Trade: Cartels in Japan's Basic Materials Industries*, Ithaca, NY: Cornell University Press.

Uriu, R. (1996) *Troubled Industries: Confronting Economic Change in Japan*, Ithaca, NY: Cornell University Press.

ROBERT URIU

deregulation

Deregulation refers to the reduction or elimination of government regulations over industry. It is most often used to refer to the reduction of economic regulations, such as price and entry restrictions, but may also be used to refer to the reduction of social regulations, such as health and safety codes. Most advanced industrial countries have experienced a broad deregulation movement since the 1980s that has redefined government–industry relations. The Japanese government's approach to deregulation diverged sharply from that of the United States or Britain in that it was much more cautious in promoting competition and reducing or devolving regulatory authority (Vogel 1996).

Popular commentators tend to use the term "deregulation" to refer to both the reduction of regulation and the promotion of competition, as if the two were necessarily associated. That is, they assume that less regulation necessarily means more competition. In the case of US airline deregulation, this is precisely what happened: the government reduced regulation and eliminated a major regulatory agency, and by doing so stimulated greater competition. But in many other cases, governments have actually strengthened regulation in order to promote competition. In telecommunications, for example, most governments have increased regulation in order to foster competition with the former monopoly service providers. Thus deregulation is often a misnomer for regulatory reforms which combine market liberalization with "reregulation," meaning the reformulation of existing regulations or the creation of new ones.

In Japan, the deregulation movement began with the Second Provisional Commission on Administrative Reform (known as the *Rincho*), which presented a report in 1982 recommending sweeping bureaucratic restructuring and deregulation. In practice, however, the *Rincho* and related reform commissions were more successful with privatization than with deregulation. In telecommunications, the government privatized **Nippon Telegraph and Telephone** NTT and opened the telephone market to competition in 1985. In transport, the government introduced second and sometimes third carriers on select routes through a meticulously planned series of barters in which **Japan Airlines** (JAL), for example, would open a new route on a specific All Nippon Airways (ANA) line, and ANA would open a new route on a JAL line in exchange. In finance, it gradually liberalized deposit interest rates from 1985 through 1994, and began the process of lowering regulatory barriers between different segments of the financial industry (such as banking, brokerage, and insurance) in 1992. In all of these sectors, the regulatory

authorities continued to manage competition after "deregulation," controlling new entry and minimizing exit from the market. They retained a discretionary regulatory style, and resisted the devolution of regulatory responsibilities to independent agencies outside the central government ministries. Some have argued that the failure to deregulate more thoroughly contributed to the Japanese economy's weakness in the 1990s.

The Japanese government accelerated its deregulation program in the 1990s in the face of a severe recession combined with a full-fledged financial crisis. Manufacturers began to press for deregulation in the utility and service sectors to lower their costs, and economists and journalists advocated deregulation to address structural inefficiencies in the economy. The government set up a new deregulation headquarters in the Cabinet Office in 1994, and developed a long-term plan for deregulation subject to annual progress reviews.

In the financial sector, Prime Minister Hashimoto announced the "Big Bang" reform package in December 1996, and the government began implementation in April 1998. The package includes the deregulation of brokerage commissions, the elimination of controls on many foreign exchange transactions, and the liberalization of the asset management market. It also allows banks, securities houses, and insurance companies to cross into each others' lines of business through holding companies.

In telecommunications, the Ministry of Posts and Telecommunications overhauled price regulation in 1994, creating new larger local dialing areas with higher initial call rates. The government then broke up NTT into one long-distance carrier and two regional carriers, although the three units remain joined within a single holding company structure. In 1998, it announced further deregulation, including the elimination of some price regulations and the reduction of interconnection charges (charges levied by NTT for other providers using its network).

In retail, the authorities phased in reforms gradually from 1990 through 1994, streamlining the approval process for large stores but still allowing the small merchants themselves to exercise considerable control. Then in 1998 the government replaced the **Large Retail Store Law** with a new regulatory regime (effective in 2000) that devolves authority to local governments. The new system is designed to promote competition while still allowing local authorities to promote social values such as preserving the environment. Critics argue, however, that it leaves considerable discretion in the hands of both the **Ministry of International Trade and Industry** (MITI) and the local governments, and that in practice it may actually constrain competition and increase regulation.

The Japanese government has sustained a commitment to deregulation from 1980 through to the present, yet progress has come slowly due to substantial political resistance from bureaucrats, regulated industries, trade unions and consumers.

See also: airline industry; competition; consumer movement; liberalization of financial markets; Ministry of Finance; retail industry

Further reading

Carlile, L. and Tilton, M. (eds) (1998) *Is Japan Really Changing Its Ways? Regulatory Reform and the Japanese Economy*, Washington, DC: Brookings Institution.

Management and Coordination Agency (various) *Kisei kanwa hakusho* (Deregulation White Paper), Tokyo: Okurasho Insatsukyoku.

Vogel, S. (1996) *Freer Markets, More Rules: Regulatory Reform in the Advanced Industrial Countries*, Ithaca, NY: Cornell University Press.

—— (1999) "Can Japan Disengage? Winners and Losers in Japan's Political Economy, and the Ties that Bind Them," *Social Science Japan Journal* 2: 3–21.

STEVEN VOGEL

DEVELOPMENT BANK OF JAPAN *see* Japan Development Bank

discounters

The term discounters relates to retailers who, by developing innovative distribution channels, sell commodities at a considerably lower price than the standard market price. In Japan, there have been several types of novel retailers that were designated as discounters, one after another.

The first renowned discounter in the post-Second World War period is **Daiei**, which opened its first store in 1957. Its founder, Isao **Nakauchi**, was firmly opposed to the then prevailing price maintenance practices that the leading producers administered. He deployed a large number of chain stores that provided strong buying power in regard to the existing wholesalers, and employed such innovative methods as bulk purchase by cash and direct purchase on site of production, in order to bypass the traditional **distribution system** and offer lower prices to customers.

As consumer needs increased rapidly throughout the postwar period of **economic growth**, a number of new entrepreneurs followed Nakauchi with the chain store strategy consisting of deployment of standardized stores, self-selection of merchandise in contrast to the traditional sales by clerks, and lower prices. They were generally called "super" or "supermarket" despite the fact that the Japanese outlets were much smaller than the US supermarkets and located, at this initial stage, in commercial districts rather than in suburban areas, and should fall into the category of **superstores**.

After the 1970s, a distinction began to be made between general merchandizing stores (GMS) and supermarkets (SM). GMS pursued a strategy of establishing branch stores nationwide, while SM, essentially focusing on fresh products (fish, meat, and vegetables), tended to focus on regional expansion. By the late 1980s, GMS and SM chains had become the dominant forms within the **retail industry**. At this time, however, a new type of discounter began to challenge GMS and SM, especially in the field of liquor retailing. The liquor tax law in Japan stipulates a number of restrictions in regard to the distribution of alcoholic beverages. These restrictions functioned to sustain a complex and lengthy channel composed of the producers, **tonya**, and retailers. The new discounters developed various methods to skip intermediary stages that allowed them to lower their prices.

In the 1990s, as a result of the US–Japan Structural Talks that opened the Japanese retail industry to foreign operators, some American and European leading retailers began to enter the country. Among them, Toys R Us, which opened its first store in Japan in 1991, is known to be the first example of a "category killer." Category killers are retailers with a chain network specializing in a specific type of commodity at discount prices. The term refers to the fact that this type of retailer aims to capture a large share of a particular category of commodities from traditional **department stores** and GMS. The term was then applied, in parallel with the term "discounters," to the roadside low-price chain stores specializing in such fields as home electronic appliances, men's clothing, shoes, and optical wares, and also to camera discounters located in high-traffic areas close to large railroad terminals.

Throughout the 1990s, this new type of discounter spread to other genres of commodities. Several power centers, composed of a handful of category killer stores along with a GSM or SM, were developed following the US model of Kmart and Wal-Mart. Toward the end of the decade, however, this second generation of discounters gradually lost novelty.

Since the turn of the century a new form of discounter has emerged, under the designation of the SPA (Specialty store retailer of Private Label Apparel) or SPA type retailer. UNIQLO, the brand and store name of First Retailing Company, is generally regarded as a pioneer of this type of discounting. The company designs all the clothes and related products in-house, orders production from overseas factories (especially China), and sells them exclusively in its own stores. The term SPA is also used to designate other commodity retailers that provide original products at low price, relying on **overseas production** in Southeast Asia and China. An example is Daiso, a retailer that sells a variety of commodities at a uniform price of ¥100.

See also: foreign companies in Japan; Large Retail Store Law; trade negotiations

SHINTARO MOGI

distribution system

Compared to its counterparts in the West, Japan's distribution system is complicated and difficult to navigate. Multiple vertical layers and multiple product or segment channels characterize the system. Compared with distribution systems in Europe or North America, it is often considered highly inefficient. However several unique geographic, physical and social aspects of the Japanese market help to explain how the system developed and why it is so complex. In the latter half of the twentieth century, and with increasing acceleration, significant changes have been taking place within the system. The most noteworthy of these are the appearance of discount retail outlets that have effectively bypassed several layers of the distribution system and the growing presence of foreign firms, a number of which have introduced innovative or more sophisticated approaches to distribution management.

With a population of over 125 million people living in an area slightly smaller than Sweden, the Japanese market is a large, but relatively compact one. Population density in the major urban areas of Kanto and Kansai ranks among the highest in the world. When combined with the historical development of the Japanese economy, the result is a complex distribution system. Most of the roughly 6 million business enterprises in Japan are small. This is particularly the case in the retail sector, where over 90 percent of retail outlets employ 10 persons or less, yet account for nearly 80 percent of all retail sales. These small retail outlets fall into one of four categories: (1) specialty shops or boutiques marketing niche products to a narrow market segment; (2) single brand stores or franchises with a very close relationship to a single manufacturer; (3) convenience stores, such as 7–11, Circle K or Family Mart; and (4) traditional "mom and pop" stores serving established neighborhoods. Many outlets are located away from major thoroughfares and lack the capacity to carry inventory. North American-style shopping centers or European-style hypermarkets are becoming somewhat more common. The density of the population and the high cost of land, however, have limited their growth.

Historical development

Several historical developments have influenced the structure of the distribution system. In the **Tokugawa period** (1603–1854), during which much of the commercial infrastructure developed, wholesalers and merchants established a craft-like orientation toward their distribution activities. Wholesalers would carry a specific product and service a defined geographical area. For example, a pickle wholesaler in the Asakusa area of Tokyo would handle only pickled or cured products and deliver them only to shops in the several kilometer area surrounding Asakusa Shrine. Similarly, a *wagashi* – tea cakes and candies – wholesaler would distribute only these goods, but within the same geographic region. Over time, wholesalers developed close relationships with each shop owner, leading to the establishment of highly individualized arrangements with regard to matters such as product returns and sales financing.

In the immediate post-Second World War era the emergence of large comprehensive consumer electronics and household appliance companies led to the establishment of brand or company stores. Companies such as Hitachi, **Toshiba** and **Matsushita** signed exclusive dealership contracts with pre-existing shops as well as helped finance the opening of new ones. In exchange for carrying only the products of a single company, these stores were allowed to sell the full range of products manufactured by that company. For example, a National (the domestic name for Matsushita products) dealer would sell everything from washing machines, refrigerators and air conditioners to home stereo systems, clock radios, televisions and VCRs to electric shavers, lamps, light bulbs and batteries. The manufacturers benefited from this relationship because it allowed them to create closed distribution channels, thereby enabling the removal of layers and associated margin costs. Closed channels also made it possible for large firms to maintain price controls on products, and to carefully monitor competition among brand retailers.

In the 1980s, with the advent of a maturing market, discount houses began to surface in major metropolitan areas. Although major manufacturers tried to prevent discounters from gaining access to their products, as consumer awareness grew this became increasingly difficult. In the early 1990s the US-based Toys R Us entered the Japanese market, further solidifying the position of **discounters**.

At this same time changes in consumer purchasing habits and tastes, combined with heightened competition, led to economic distress among many wholesalers in traditional product and market channels. Not surprisingly, many struggling wholesalers attempted to forestall bankruptcy by expanding into new geographic areas or by trying to take on new products.

The early 1980s also saw the emergence of television shopping and catalog sales, which further eroded the margins of struggling distributors, as growth in consumer purchases from retail outlets flattened. This was followed in the 1990s by the growth of the Internet and the emergence of **e-commerce** websites.

System structure

The postwar Japanese distribution system evolved into a multi-layer, multi-channel system. In the mid-1980s the average distribution channel had four layers. A manufacturer would hand off product to a primary wholesaler capable of distributing it nationwide or, at a minimum, to several major regions within Japan. The primary wholesaler would then transfer the product to a secondary wholesaler, who would cover a region of smaller geographic area. The secondary wholesaler would deliver the product to a tertiary wholesaler – often called a **tonya** – who would then deliver the product to a retail outlet. In short, the average product was handled four times, entailing four margins or commissions. By contrast, the average length of distribution channel in the USA was 1.5 layers and in France it was 1.25 layers. Each additional layer incurs an added cost, thereby making the distribution of product in Japan significantly more expensive for both domestic and foreign firms.

The Japanese system is also multi-channel. There are separate channels for separate products. Pet food is delivered through one channel, dry goods through another, soft drinks through a third and so forth. An average 2,000 meter^2 supermarket in Japan may be serviced by more than thirty different wholesalers. Interestingly, a single channel wholesaler would not be limited to a particular brand of product. So, for example, a personal hygiene products wholesaler would deliver to the same store competing brands of toothpaste, soap, shampoo and deodorant.

To some extent, the multiple layers and channels represent a historical artifact. However, **geography** also plays a role. Because most retail outlets are small, the tertiary wholesaler, or *tonya*, often acts as a warehouse for the retailer, holding inventory and delivering it to the store on an "as needed" basis. Additionally, the *tonya* often provides a financial service. Rather than the customary "thirty day due" payment arrangements common in North America and Europe, *tonya* use **promissory notes** to extend credit on deliveries up to 120 days. Payment arrangements are often individualized, such that a *tonya* may have a different billing scheme for each retail outlet to which he delivers. Additionally, return of unsold goods is an established practice, requiring the *tonya*, as well as secondary and primary wholesalers to move goods backwards through the channel.

Not surprisingly, the distribution system has often been targeted by foreign firms as a non-tariff barrier to their doing business in Japan. With established, long-term relationships to both retail outlets and manufacturers, wholesalers were historically reluctant to take on the products of foreign manufacturers. To handle foreign products was to run the risk of angering domestic manufacturers, who might in turn refuse the distribution of their products. Nor were many foreign firms adept at working with wholesalers in terms of financing arrangements or liberal returns.

The influence of foreign firms

Many significant changes in the distribution system have been brought about, either directly or indirectly, by foreign firms seeking to enter the Japanese market. There are several notable examples. When Coca-Cola entered the Japanese market in 1960, it sought to control its marketing channels, but required retailers to pay on the standard "thirty day due" terms it was accustomed to in the USA. Initial resistance was replaced by acceptance, as word of product sales spread among cooperating retailers. Although not widespread, this payment practice has continued to spread among other manufacturers and into other channels.

In a similar vein, L'Oreal and Wella introduced innovations into the beauty parlor and barbershop distribution channel by encouraging the retail sale of their hair care products. Formerly, wholesalers to this channel had delivered only large, institutional products for use by the barbers and beauticians. These two European firms showed wholesalers how they could increase their sales by also distributing customer-use size product for additional point-of-purchase sales. Again, over time this innovation spread to other products and to other channels.

A Japanese company, through its involvement with a US convenience store chain, introduced one of the most significant changes to the distribution system. 7-11 Japan was a US-licensed operation owned by the **Ito-Yokado** Group. In the 1970s it began opening 7–11s around the country. 7–11 pioneered the convenience store in Japan, competing directly against "mom and pop" neighborhood stores. By staying open for longer hours, carrying a wider variety of products and by restocking shelves more frequently, 7–11 effectively overwhelmed its more traditional counterparts. In the mid-1980s it borrowed Toyota's **just-in-time** concept and introduced a point-of-sale (POS) inventory that allowed them to track sales on an hourly basis. The innovation in distribution came about when the company began using its POS data to make more frequent and targeted deliveries. A typical, urban 7–11 received deliveries twice a day, once before the morning rush hours and once before the evening rush. As a result of its ability to keep high demand product fresh and on the shelf, by 1990 7–11 Japan had grown to become the fifth largest retail operation in the world. Following its lead, other convenience stores, grocery stores and supermarkets have attempted similar approaches in managing their distribution systems.

Although other discount houses had already established themselves, Toys R Us entered Japan as the first "category killer," that is, a large retail store that sells only one category of merchandise and often dominates competition. Its entrance was significant because Toys R Us competes on the basis of price, relying on direct purchases from manufacturers and the attendant cost savings from not having to pay wholesaler commissions. Discount houses adopt a similar approach, but generally carry a much wider range of products. By contrast, and of particular significance for the distribution system in Japan, Toys R Us sought to control only a single market segment. Its consequent overwhelming success had a devastating effect not only on toy retailers, but on the toy distribution channel. As with other distribution innovations, category killers in other market segments have moved into Japan.

The future of the distribution system

It is clear the innovations over the latter half of the twentieth century will continue to reshape the distribution system in the twenty-first century. Heightened competition is removing layers and blurring distinctions among channels. Moreover, the growth of catalog and on-line shopping will further erode the power and role of the wholesalers and the traditional distribution system. Nevertheless, the historical constraints of small outlets, limited inventory capacity, long-term relationships and specialized arrangements suggest that the Japanese distribution system will continue to retain greater complexity and appear more inefficient than its Western counterparts.

Further reading

Dodwell Marketing Consultants (2000) *Retail Distribution in Japan*, Tokyo.

ALLAN BIRD

Dodge, Joseph M.

Dodge was a Detroit banker who, as financial advisor to the **American occupation** of Japan from 1949–52, designed policies to end Japan's postwar hyperinflation, re-establish international trade, and restore the market mechanism in the Japanese economy. Dodge's severe austerity program, known as the "Dodge Line," dictated the balancing of the national budget, the reform of US aid policies, the reduction of government subsidies and direct economic controls, and the setting of a single yen–dollar exchange rate.

Dodge's deflationary policies were extremely unpopular and caused widespread fears of financial collapse before Korean War procurements buoyed Japanese industry in 1950–1. Nevertheless, the

Dodge Line was crucial in stabilizing the volatile postwar economy and restoring it to a firm peacetime footing. The financial discipline which Dodge imposed would continue to characterize Japanese fiscal policy until the 1960s.

Further reading

Tsutsui, W.M. (1988) *Banking Policy in Japan: American Efforts at Reform During the Occupation*, London: Routledge.

WILLIAM M. TSUTSUI

Dokoh, Toshio

Toshio Dokoh (1896–1988) was one of the leading Japanese business leaders responsible for revitalizing Japanese industry in the aftermath of the Second World War and for reforming the Japanese government and public corporations in the 1980s. Born in Okayama Prefecture in 1896, he graduated from the Tokyo Technical Higher School (subsequently named the Tokyo Institute of Technology) in 1920. Upon graduation he joined the Ishikawajima Shipyard Company (which was later renamed Ishikawajims Heavy Industries). He ascended to the presidency of the company in 1950, and held that position for ten years. During his tenure as president, he repositioned the company to take advantage of US procurement in Japan in support of US military involvement in the Korean War. During the latter part of his presidency he engineered the merger that created Ishikawajima-Harima Heavy Industries (IHI), and then became president of the merged company.

In 1965 Dokoh took over the reins of **Toshiba** and, as he had done at IHI, led another company to growth and profits. In 1972 he moved from president to chairman, retiring from that position in 1976. From 1974 to 1980 he also served as president of Keidanren, the Federation of Economic Organizations, one of the four most important business associations in Japan.

In 1981, Prime Minister Yasuhiro Nakasone asked Dokoh to head the Second Ad Hoc Commission on Administrative Reform. (The First Ad Hoc Commission on Administrative Reform operated from 1962 to 1964.) Though the commission reviewed a broad range of governmental administrative issues, the most significant related to what should be done with Japan's three largest public corporations: **Japan National Railways** (JNR), **Nippon Telegraph and Telephone** (NTT) and Japan Tobacco Corporation (JT). Under Dokoh's leadership, the commission recommended the privatization of all three, an action that began in 1983. Dokoh passed away in Tokyo in 1988.

ALLAN BIRD

dollar shock

The dollar shock in 1971, generally called the "Nixon shock" in Japan, was caused by President Nixon's announcement of his New Economic Policy that led to the collapse of the Bretton Woods system. Although the shock waves went throughout the world, Japan received the greatest shock. The reason was that the policy was viewed in Japan as an attempt to force Japan to revalue the fixed ¥360:$1 exchange rate established in 1949 that had been regarded as one of the institutional frameworks of the high-speed growth. In fact, the Nixon shock became a major turning point of the Japanese economy.

In order to cope with the dollar crisis, the policy included the suspension of convertibility of dollar into gold, an across-the-board 10 percent surcharge on imports, and a 10 percent reduction in **foreign aid** expenditure. The goals of the policy were: the suspension of dollar's convertibility into gold would initiate a multilateral currency adjustment; the import surcharge would force other countries to revalue their currencies (after which it would be lifted); the costs of maintaining the world order such as foreign aid and defense expenditures should be shared more properly among major countries. Ultimately, the policy sought to reduce the United States' balance of trade deficits, the situation that had caused the dollar crisis.

In his speech announcing the New Economic Policy on August 15, 1971, President Nixon stated: "Others should bear 'their fair share of the burden of defending freedom around the world' and agree to exchange-rate changes that would enable 'major nations to compete as equals.' There is no longer any need for the United States to compete with one hand tied behind her back." Three concessions were demanded of Japan: exchange rate adjustment (a large-scale revaluation of the yen), liberalization of domestic markets, and burden sharing of American global policy costs such as defense and ODA (Official Development Assistance).

In 1968, Japan became the second largest economy in the free world and its rapid increase in exports accelerated the expansion of the United States foreign trade deficit that deepened the dollar crisis, – in other words, the international monetary crisis – and led to the Nixon shock. As a result, the USA demanded that Japan share the maintenance costs of world order in a broad sense. However, Japan's response was delayed. With regard to Japan's delayed response, Angel (1991) pointed out, "Lack of response was interpreted in the United States and Europe as evidence of Japan's unwillingness to assume her share of the costs of maintaining the international economic system."

Nakamura (1981) notes that at that time there were misunderstandings between Japan and the rest of the world over Japan's international position and its economic power, namely, the gradually widening gap between the Japanese perception of their own economy as a small, backward latecomer, and its evaluation by the international community as an emerging economic power. This perception gap was an underlying source of Japan's delayed response and international economic friction as symbolized by the Nixon shock.

Having received the Nixon shock, the Japanese government was forced to respond to foreign pressure, especially American demands. Under the Smithsonian Agreement of December 1971, Japan accepted the upward revaluation of the yen from ¥360 to ¥308, a 16.88 percent appreciation against the dollar. The Japanese government's statement on the Agreement noted "there was an 'end to the postwar system' in the background of implementation of the multilateral currency adjustment," and "the time has arrived when we should, domestically, further increase welfare and, abroad, make still greater contributions to international society."

Japan also partly accepted liberalization of domestic markets, but showed a negative attitude toward sharing the costs of defense against the so-called communist world because of constitutional constraints, strong domestic opposition, and Asian neighbors' memories of Japanese imperialism in the prewar and wartime period. More positive actions by Japan included an expansionary fiscal policy to stimulate domestic demand and reduce the trade surplus. This led to a rapid increase in government spending on public works and social welfare.

At that time, the Japanese government had just confronted a three-pronged problem: foreign pressure, as noted above; a domestic recession that implied the end of high **economic growth**; and relatively meager social welfare provision compared to that of other major countries. In order to deal with these three problems simultaneously, the government adopted a system of policies centered on expansionary fiscal policy, which was supposed to expand social welfare and public works, recover the economy from the recession, and reduce the trade surplus. It was a plan that attempted a switch in growth pattern from export-led growth to fiscal policy-led growth.

After the Nixon shock, other major countries openly demanded that Japan accept the burden sharing of maintenance costs of the world order and Japan began to virtually share the burden. The "small country hypothesis" no longer held. In this period, however, an international discretionary coordination of macroeconomic policy to maintain the world economy had not yet appeared. Consequently, it is reasonable to argue that the Japanese response was an attempt at international monetary cooperation, in response to criticism that Japan was responsible for the rapid increase in trade surplus that was the cause of the international monetary crisis.

See also: income doubling plan

Further reading

Angel, R.C. (1991) *Explaining Economic Policy Failure: Japan in the 1969–1971 International Monetary Crisis*, New York: Columbia University Press.
Higuchi, H. (1999) *Zaisei Kokusaika Trends: Sekaikeizai No Kozohenka to Nippon No Zaiseiseisaku* (Fiscal Internationalization: Structural Changes of the World Economy and Japanese Fiscal Policy), Tokyo: Gakubunsha.
Kosai, Y. (1986) *The Era of High-Speed Growth: Notes on the Postwar Japanese Economy*, trans. J. Kaminski, Tokyo: University of Tokyo Press.
Nakamura, T. (1981) *The Postwar Japanese Economy: Its Development and Structure*, trans. J. Kaminski, Tokyo: University of Tokyo Press.
Uchino, T. (1978) *Japan's Postwar Economy: An Insider's View of its History and its Future*, trans. M.A. Harbison, Tokyo: Kodansha International.

HITOSHI HIGUCHI

Dore, Ronald

Ronald Dore was a British sociologist, author of many highly influential books on Japan, including *City Life in Japan* (1958), *Land Reform in Japan* (1959), and *Education in Tokugawa Japan* (1964). This historical and social research provided a strong grounding for his influential comparative study of work organization and industrial relations in a Japanese and a British manufacturing company, *British Factory Japanese Factory*. His model of the Japanese enterprise as community and his exposition of late development as an explanation for the differences between the Japanese and British patterns were very influential. His later work on relational contracting in the Japanese textile industry (1986) and his writings on the importance of the Japanese model of capitalism (1987) have made him the most influential European sociologist of Japanese business.

Further reading

Dore, R.P. (1973) *British Factory Japanese Factory*, Berkeley, CA: University of California Press.
—— (1986) *Flexible Rigidities*, Stanford, CA: Stanford University Press.
—— (1987) *Taking Japan Seriously*, London: Athlone Press.

ELEANOR D. WESTNEY

dual structure theory

The dual structure economy is generally understood as a national economy that has both modern capitalistic sectors and traditional non-capitalistic sectors at the same time. The term was first introduced by Hiromi Arisawa in 1957 in an Economic White Paper and was noted as one of the distinctive characteristics of the Japanese economic system. It was also believed that effective economic growth could not take place within such an economic structure. Indeed, in a White Paper published the previous year, the government declared, "The Japanese economy has passed its recovery process; the postwar period has ended." Elimination of the dual structure came to be viewed as the most critical issue in modernizing the economy through rapid growth.

The 1957 White Paper argues that the most obvious distillation of the dual structure could be found in the specific structure of the labor market: large numbers of family members continued to work as laborers in both agriculture and small industry/commerce. As a result, it was common for labor relations to be non-existent or pre-modern in those sectors and for wage differentials to be large and varied according to firm size within the industry.

As far as the manufacturing sector was concerned, the exact wording of the White Paper report referred to the dual economy as a "polarization between small industry and large industry." In 1957, large enterprises with more than 300 employees accounted for 44 percent of total manufacturing shipment but just 27 percent of employment, while small enterprises with fewer than 100 employees accounted for 39 percent of shipment, but 42 percent of employment. Furthermore, comparing these numbers with those of the USA and Britain, Japan was characterized by significantly larger numbers of small-and-medium sized enterprises and "mom and pop" business operations: 68 percent of all enterprises had fewer than 200 employees and 34 per cent had fewer than 20 employees. In the USA, the respective figures were 40 percent and 16 percent; in Britain they were 40 percent and 16 percent.

The data unquestionably confirm the presence of a dual economic structure. Nor is there any question that this structure developed over time from the Meiji era forward, largely as a result of government policies. However, there is controversy about what other factors contributed to its development and how it can be eliminated.

The most popular theory, espoused by Miyohei Shinohara, proposed that the most important factors of the dual structure were the split labor market and the Japanese banking system that had favored large-scale industries. As large-scale industries were able to invest huge amounts in capital-intensive equipment, even in its overseas operations, with long-term loans at favorable interest rates from both banks and the government, it was able to earn high returns with a relatively small number of laborers. Those who were not able to gain access to employment, or who were eliminated from, the large-scale capitalistic sector had no other alternative than to be absorbed into small and medium industry which offered lower income due to shortages of capital.

The typical Japanese labor system characterized by **lifetime employment** and a seniority system of wages has been adopted to a limited extent within large industry. Given this, Shinohara's explanation seems rational and persuasive. However, another school of thought challenges this conclusion. Daikichi Ito argues that, because the monopoly power of large industry has so thoroughly penetrated the economic system from top to bottom, there is really not a dual structure. Instead, the wage differentials of workers in smaller firms merely reflect the monopoly power that large firms hold over small firms, who are often their subcontractors. Other critics note that Shinohara's view, concentrating as it does mainly on labor and capital markets, does not take into consideration product markets in which prices are non-elastic in the monopolistic markets and vice versa.

While the positions were disputed by scholars, the government recognized the importance of providing more support to the huge number of small/medium industries that were very influential to the national economy and the people's life. Even before the first analysis in the 1957 White Paper, the government had already established the National Finance Cooperation, a bank for small and family businesses, in 1949. This was followed by the Finance Cooperation for Small and

Medium Enterprises in 1953, when democratization of the economy was in progress after the Anti-Trust Law was introduced by GHQ in 1947. Soon after the Income-Doubling Program was started in 1961, the government enacted the Minor Enterprise Law in 1963. "Modernization" was the key word for small/medium industry policy in that period. The government announced its intention to foster medium-sized enterprises that have both modern management and high technology.

Through the 1970s, the situation underwent many changes. First, when an abundant labor force abandoned the rural areas, wages rose even in small manufacturing firms and wage differentials diminished as a result. Ohkawa demonstrated that it was at this point that Japan passed Lewis's Turning Point. Second, many modern medium-sized enterprises emerged, and they were able to overcome, by means of high technology and skilled labor, the difficulties twice caused by oil crises. Although wage differentials still remain, as does the subcontracting system, it is difficult to argue that the dual structure still dominates the Japanese economy.

One opinion holds that a dual structure can be seen as a temporary phenomenon in the capitalistic development in latecomers. In fact, South Korea demonstrated a similar pattern in the 1970s, although the subcontracting system did not exist. Instead, the South Korean government promoted policies aimed at encouraging "organic linkages" to develop in the domestic economy. Similar cases may be emerging in other developing countries in Asia and Southeast Asia.

JO-SEOL KIM

E

e-commerce

In the latter half of the 1990s, as Japan struggled to recover from the recession that followed the collapse of the bubble economy, e-commerce was one of the few bright spots in the nation's economic landscape. Although Japan still lagged behind other industrialized nations in the everyday application and use of information technology (IT), Internet use and e-commerce were expanding rapidly. At the same time, these were evolving in somewhat different directions in Japan than elsewhere, reflecting the nature of the country's specific business and regulatory environment.

In Japan, as in other countries, IT, Internet use, and e-commerce have been and will continue to be marked by rapid and continuous change. This entry describes the state of e-commerce as it existed in Japan in the year 2000.

The development of the Internet in Japan

The Internet got off to a slow start in Japan, due in large part to excessive regulation on the part of the Japanese government. Japan's first Internet transmissions were sent not by Japanese but by American engineers working for US companies which had set up Internet services for expatriates working in Japan. During the early years of the Internet, the Japanese government placed higher priority on maintaining its highly regulated telecommunications system than on promoting the development of the new technology. Japanese companies seeking to enter the Internet market were blocked by the difficulty of obtaining the

necessary licenses from the Ministry of Posts and Telecommunications, and even when licenses were granted, the government allowed only narrowly defined applications of the Internet and was not supportive of efforts to broaden its usage.

An individual Japanese and a natural disaster are generally credited with reversing this situation. Jura Murai, often referred to as the "godfather of the Japanese Internet," fought with government officials over the right to bring the Internet into the country and, when faced with continuing opposition, went ahead on his own. In 1992, Murai and his colleagues created the Internet Initiative Japan (IIJ). IIJ's Internet system violated the Ministry of Posts and Telecommunications' rigid regulations, but was faster and more efficient than the government's own system. Helped by the fact that Internet access and usage is by nature difficult to monitor, Murai's efforts prevailed, and the government's attempts to monopolize the Japanese Internet ended. A further boost was given to Internet usage in the aftermath of the Kobe earthquake in 1995. At a time when other communications systems failed or were inadequate, Internet transmission served as a vital means of sharing information, and this helped convince government officials of the benefits of the new technology.

Although high access charges, the dominance of English on the Web, and the slow spread of personal computers for home use prevented Internet usage from growing as quickly as in some countries, Internet use in Japan increased steadily beginning in the mid-1990s. In 1995 it jumped by 41 percent, the highest rate of growth in the world at that time. By the end of 1997, Japan had 11.6 million Internet users and Japanese was the second-most commonly used language on the net. Japan's Internet population continued to grow, reaching 16.9 million by the end of 1998 and 27 million – 21.4 percent of the population – by the end of 1999. It was projected that 77 million people – 60 percent of the population – would be users by the year 2005. In 1998 there were 1 million Japanese web sites, the second highest number in the world.

Internet access in Japan

One of the biggest drags on Internet use and the development of e-commerce in Japan was slow and expensive access. In 2000, most of Japan's Internet users accessed the Web through the telephone network of Nippon Telegraph and Telephone Corporation (NTT), formerly a government monopoly. This meant paying not only Internet access fees to an Internet Service Provider (ISP) but also per-minute local telephone charges, which NTT had not reduced for twenty-three years. With Internet fees averaging around $20 per month for thirty hours of access and local telephone charges adding up to $100 or more for a heavy user, Internet use in Japan was quite costly by international standards. On top of this, many of Japan's small ISPs lacked the scale and resources needed to secure premium bandwidth, resulting in slow and poor connections. Faster and cheaper Internet service was becoming available, however, as ISPs were consolidating to secure better international connections and broadband alternatives such as cable television and ADSL (asymmetric digital subscriber lines), which allow vast amounts of data, including moving pictures and music, to travel through the net at very high speed, were starting to be offered. NTT was marketing a flat-rate ISDN (integrated services digital network) service in Tokyo and Osaka that provided faster access than phone lines, while Sony had announced plans to build a wireless network to provide low-cost, high-speed Internet access in large Japanese cities.

The Internet access mode that was growing at the greatest speed in Japan was wireless. In 1999 NTT DoCoMo, Inc., the country's largest wireless phone company, launched i-mode, an Internet connection service for mobile phones (*keitai denwa*). By May of 2000, i-mode and similar services had 10 million subscribers and NTT DoCoMo had become Japan's largest Internet service provider. Hundreds of Web sites were being created for tiny cell phone screens to support mobile e-commerce, or "m-commerce." The response rate to i-mode advertising was reported to be five times higher than that for ordinary Web ads.

The growth of e-commerce

The same type of hands-on approach that marked the Japanese government's early regulation of the Internet could be seen in its efforts to promote e-commerce, which by the late 1990s was seen as a major driver of economic growth in the twenty-first century. While the United States promoted IT through deregulation, Japan did the opposite: using government subsidies and intervention to try to push development of e-commerce and other IT sectors. For example, in 1996 the US government amended the nation's Telecommunications Law to remove barriers between telecommunications carriers and broadcasters in order to encourage competition, reduce connection charges, and support the growth of e-commerce. At the same time, the Japanese government set up the Electronic Commerce Promotion Council of Japan, which together with MITI invested $476 million to try to develop Japanese e-commerce technology; by 2000 this project had produced little in the way of results.

While government efforts floundered, Japanese companies and consumers gradually embraced e-commerce. According to a Ministry of Posts and Telecommunications White Paper issued in 2000, Japan's e-commerce market in 1999, including advertising, totaled more than $200 billion. B2B (business-to-business) transactions dominated, with consumer spending accounting for only $3.2 billion. E-commerce was projected to expand to $1.35 trillion per year by 2005, with $68 billion being spent on consumer goods. The explosive growth of cell phone-based Internet use was expected to stimulate sharp growth in the B2C (business-to-consumer) sector. In 1999 almost two-thirds of Japanese Internet users reported making purchases online; the major products and services being bought were consumer electronics and personal computers, automobiles, travel, office supplies, books, and software. By 2000, Japan had over 25,000 virtual shops, with new e-businesses being added at a rate of 500 to 800 per month. Online advertising expenditures totaled $68 million in 1998 but were expected to reach $1.26 billion by 2003.

Despite these figures, many industries had not yet been able to generate significant online sales. One reason for this was that Japanese consumers did not feel comfortable using credit cards online. This led to the development of alternative payment methods, including cash at physical stores for goods ordered online. Convenience stores, which are found everywhere in Japan, were also becoming a key site for e-commerce transactions. The 'Loppi' system, developed by IBM and installed in convenience stores, allowed shoppers to order thousands of items online – from concert tickets to software – far more than could be stocked in an actual store. 7-11 Japan was installing terminals in its convenience stores for those who did not have Internet access at home and was teaming up with NEC, Sony, Japan Travel Bureau and other leading Japanese firms to set up an e-commerce market which integrated the convenience of online shopping with in-store payments and merchandise pick-up capabilities.

One factor which slowed the growth of e-commerce in Japan was the lack of a national, comprehensive IT policy, like that of Singapore, which in 1997 built a high-bandwidth telecommunications network to connect the country to the rest of the world, and Malaysia, which promoted e-commerce by enacting "cyber laws" that recognize electronic signatures and protect privacy. Another issue was fear that e-commerce could cause job losses, by cutting out the middlemen in Japan's traditional multi-tiered distribution system. The Japanese preference for face-to-face contact with suppliers and customers also tended to hamper e-commerce.

Other factors were working in e-commerce's favor, however. Women, who made up 40 percent of Japan's Internet users, were being seen as a major engine for future e-commerce growth; female Web users were more willing to shop online than men, and appreciated the convenience of use, access to foreign companies, and new entertain-ment services offered by the Internet. The environment for creating new e-businesses was also improving, with the launching of the Mothers and NASDAQ Japan stock markets for start-ups and the financing and incubation of new e-commerce ventures by companies such as the venture capitalist and Internet holding company Softbank, Inc. Numerous Internet data centers – facilities where corporate customers can locate their servers and connect them to the Internet and which provide security from hackers and natural disasters like earthquakes – were being set up in Japan. And every day, Japan's business press carried announcements of new e-commerce initiatives: by companies large and small, old and new, and in areas from banking, computers, and entertainment to kimonos, food, and online education.

Elements of both careful, hands-on planning – characteristic of the traditional Japanese approach to business – and the more freewheeling, spontaneous nature of dot.com entrepreneurship in California's Silicon Valley could be seen in the various e-commerce start-up communities that were emerging in Japan. Representative of the former was Kyoto's highly organized Kyoto Research Park (KRP). Established by Osaka Gas Corporation, KRP provided space, service, and support for Internet start-ups in return for stock, and had built a reputation as one of Japan's top incubators. At the other end of the spectrum was the Bit Valley Association and organic start-up community of Tokyo's Shibuya district. The Bit Valley Association was started in 1999 by two Tokyo Internet pioneers as a weekly meeting/party held in a Shibuya cafe. It soon attracted thousands of participants and inspired many people, including salaried workers from large established firms, to jump into Internet businesses and establish e-commerce start-up funds.

Given the nation's history of success in business and the eagerness of Japanese to purchase and try out new technologies, often available earlier in Japan than in other countries thanks to the leadership position enjoyed by major Japanese technology firms, it seemed certain that Japan would remain at the forefront of e-commerce well into the twenty-first century.

Further reading

Coates, K. and Tiessen, J.H. (2000) *Canadian Firms, Electronic Commerce and the Japanese Market*, Toronto: The Canada-Japan Trade Council.

TIM CRAIG

economic crisis in Asia

In the early 1980s the Japanese economy was booming. However, the economic bubble then burst, leading to an economic crisis in Japan that reverberated throughout Asia. Japan's productive capacity began to exceed demand and a recurring trade surplus developed. The Japanese government was forced to adopt policies aimed at boosting internal demand and restraining production. Mandatory cutbacks in rice acreage were imposed, and voluntary restraints were applied to exports. The bursting of the **bubble economy** shows that supply and demand cannot be balanced by relying on a bureaucratic-led drive to stimulate domestic demand and keep the economy going. GDP growth began to decrease from 6.2 percent in 1988 to 4.3 percent in 1991 and −1.1 percent in 1992. There was also a long slump in the stock market beginning in 1990 and continuing for several years. Deflation (*defure* in Japanese) led to a decrease in consumer prices and a price revolution, *kakaku hakai*, that came to be known as Heisei Recession. Declining corporate profits and adverse business conditions were due in part to the **appreciating yen**. This was also a time of lowering real estate prices and low interest rates.

Job offers also decreased in Japan, although **unemployment** remained unchanged at less than 3 percent for many years. The ratio of job offers to job seekers was 1.02 in 1988 and 0.76 in 1993. This was a recession without layoffs. Between 1992 and 1994, 8.5 percent of Japan's companies with 1,000 or more employees cut an average of 130 new jobs. Between 1992 and 1995, manufacturing employment decreased by 8 percent. Companies said that this was accomplished by dismissing part-time and temporary workers (6 percent), reducing overtime (24 percent), reassignments, *hai-ten* and *shukko* (18 percent), hiring freezes (13 percent), voluntary retirement (20 percent), and extended holidays/vacations (4 percent).

In 1990, the Nikkei Index (the Japanese stock market) went from a high of 38,915 to a low of 19,781, a drop of 49 percent. It had not been below 20,000 since 1987. Large companies' share prices fell (for example, **Nissan** by 44.6 percent, **Toshiba** by 23 percent, **Sony** by 19.6 percent, **Honda** by 18.2 percent, and **NEC** by 15.6 percent), while banks and real estate firms were even harder hit (Mitsubishi Estate Co. fell by 63.7 percent, Sumitomo Bank by 56.1 percent, and **Daiichi Kangyo Bank** by 46.5 percent). This first occurred in isolation, but over time the entire economy of Japan and then the economy of the entire Asian region was affected. Minister of Finance Hashimoto closed the Tokyo Stock Exchange for a day and announced a market-rescue plan. Japanese real estate firms began to sell their holdings in the United States because Japanese banks were nervous and increased interest rates. This affected not just the USA and Europe, but the rest of Asia as well.

Many economists hold that deregulation is key for economic recovery. The Japanese government must restructure the economy, stimulate demand, and reform the political system. Japanese companies must upgrade their operations and lower their production costs. Prime Minister Morihiro Hosokawa's economic policies were not planned in advance, but developed as a result of the economic crisis. Called "Hosonomics," this policy placed an emphasis on small government, deregulation, consumerism, deficit spending, and business-oriented government policies.

In 1996, according to a study by **Dentsu** Advertising, 34.5 percent of Japanese consumers believed that the economy was on course to recover. However, consumers wanted lower prices, and were willing to accept "good enough" quality rather than "best quality." In other words, they were still cautious about spending money. In 1997, leisure businesses such as theme parks and department stores were still showing large losses. By the end of that year, the economic problems in Japan were even worse.

The Japanese recession may have positive implications for small and medium enterprises (SMEs) and the service industry (see **small and** medium-sized firms). Some things that small businesses could not do during the 1980s could be done during the recession because of lower real estate prices and lower interest rates. Labor and other resources were also now available and affordable. However, the SMEs were hard hit by the crisis and are still negative about an economic recovery.

To decrease expenses, temporary work and employment of women on a part-time basis is increasing. To decrease production costs, Japanese companies moved manufacturing operations overseas to the rest of Asia, which was also hit by the economic crisis. This allowed Japanese firms to import lower cost products. Japanese real estate firms began selling off overseas holdings. This too affected not only the United States and Europe but also the rest of Asia.

In 1997, Japan was still in a recession and the currency crisis began in Asia. There was a slowdown in growth for all ASEAN countries in 1997–98. The ASEAN four – Thailand, Indonesia, Malaysia and the Philippines – were at the center of the crisis but other Asian countries were also hard hit including Korea, Taiwan, Singapore, Hong Kong and China. Hong Kong had its worst economic crisis since the Second World War. The Hong Kong stock market lost more than 80 percent of its value in one year, and real estate prices plunged. Hundreds of businesses went bankrupt and unemployment doubled to greater than 4 percent (a fifteen-year high).

In all of Asia, wages were hit by the crisis. The devaluation of the Thai baht caused workers' monthly wages to fall from US$164 in June 1997 to $90 in July 1997. In Indonesia and Malaysia, wages fell by about half. Currency devaluation led to a 30–50 percent decrease in automobile prices. In order to try to prevent a recession, many governments raised taxes and increased prices on government-controlled industries and goods, such as electricity and gas. In 1998, the Korean government increased fares on airlines, buses and railways. The Malaysian government increased prices of sugar, flour, milk and other government-controlled items. However, the recession continued. Companies in Thailand, Malaysia, Korea, and elsewhere in Asia laid off employees. Many

businesses shut down operations due to decreased demand and consumption in the region.

Japanese firms were hit hard by the crisis in the region. The cost of imported raw materials rose, while demand for finished products decreased. Many companies put expansion plans on hold. The Japanese government supplied financial aid, primarily through the IMF, to assist the countries in crisis.

By 2000, the economies of the region had finally begun to recover. The ASEAN countries and Korea showed growth in their gross domestic products in 1999. The consensus is that the Asian economy is on the mend, but appropriate government policies are needed to reinforce infrastructure and create jobs in order to keep growth on track.

See also: business ethics; Heisei boom

TERRI R. LITUCHY

economic growth

The postwar Japanese economy attained high growth. Annual growth rates of gross domestic product on average for the periods of 1955–60, 1960–65 and 1965–70 were 8.9 percent, 9.0 percent and 10.9 percent respectively. These rates declined somewhat to 4.4 percent and 4.1 percent in the 1970s and 1980s. However, in the 1990s (1990–97), the economy slowed to 1.6 percent. The sections below consider the features and fundamental factors underlying the high growth periods in light of several theoretical perspectives and then discuss problems that the Japanese economy faces now.

Features and theoretical background of high economic growth in Japan

The high growth of the Japanese economy accompanied rapid changes in industrial structure. In particular, industries such as metal, machinery and chemicals, grew dramatically. These heavy and chemical industries comprised 20 percent of Japanese total product of manufacturing industries in 1955, but 75 percent in 1990. The machinery industry now comprises the largest share of Japanese exports. In the process of industrialization, a rapid concentration of the population in urban areas has been observed. At present the two largest metropolitan areas, Tokyo and Osaka, account for nearly half of the total population in Japan.

Neoclassical economic growth theories explain the processes of capital accumulation and economic growth based on the saving behavior of households and the investment behavior of companies. The smaller the amount of installed equipment, the higher the return on investment for a company. Thus, aggressive investment in equipment is observed in the earlier stages of economic growth, and this lifts interest rates in the capital market. In contrast, households increase future income by consuming less and saving more when interest rates are high. Large savings by households finance large investments in equipment. In this way, a higher economic growth rate is attained. As capital accumulates and income increases, returns on investment fall. Investment and saving decline and consumption increases. The process of economic growth is thus completed.

Traditional growth models, however, cannot fully explain the cases of postwar Japan and other Asian economies in recent years. Traditional growth models predict higher growth rates in an economy with lower income levels. Hence, the difference in per capita income among economies should converge in the long run. In reality, however, the difference has been diverging rather than converging. To explain this phenomenon, two factors have been explicitly introduced into new economic growth models.

Firstly, focus has been placed on capital goods other than equipment. The accumulation of human capital, which is acquired through educational investment, plays a particularly crucial role in economic growth. Differences in economic growth rates can be explained to some extent by this factor.

Secondly, scale economies have been explicitly introduced into new growth theories. Scale is effective in heavy and chemical industries. In other words, the size of an industry has a positive external effect on the productivity of the companies within that industry; the larger the scale of the industry, the more productivity increases. This characteristic is opposite to the diminishing returns

that are assumed in traditional economic growth theories. To establish such industries, a huge investment in equipment is necessary in the initial stages.

There are two stable equilibriums in an economy where scale merits operate: an equilibrium in which no investments are made and income levels remain low; and an equilibrium in which industries with scale economies are successfully established and high income levels attained. The former is called a "poverty trap." In the latter equilibrium, scale economics result in the geographical concentration of capital and the labor force. With these new growth models, it is possible to explain the persistent income gap among nations. We can also say that economic growth in Japan is a "jumping process" to a better equilibrium.

However, this jumping process cannot be achieved automatically. Sufficiently large markets, entrepreneurship, positive expectations for the future, an abundant labor force, and appropriate economic policies are all indispensable. The following is an analysis of these factors in the postwar Japanese economy.

Large domestic market

Industries with effective scale economics cannot be established until huge investments in equipment are made. Markets large enough to pay for this investment are essential. Foreign markets have played a significant role in the recent industrialization of Asian economies. In Japan, however, the domestic market is more important than foreign markets. The Japanese economy had been growing since the middle of the nineteenth century. Light industries, such as textile and foods, were the leading sectors in prewar Japan, and accordingly, income levels were not particularly low. Furthermore, drastic reforms such as farmland reform after the Second World War mitigated income inequalities. These factors created potentially large domestic markets for durable consumer goods.

Positive expectations for the future

To establish an industry with scale economies, several companies must simultaneously invest heavily in equipment. Of course, investments are made in anticipation of future profits. In industries with scale economies, however, companies will make investments only if they do share positive expectations regarding the future size of their market. Then, a balance of coordination and competition among the companies is needed. Once the investments are made, productivity and income, and therefore the market size, increase. As a result, initial investment can produce a profit and positive expectations become self-fulfilling. The market expands more and more, which leads to new companies entering the industry. In this way, a competitive market is achieved, and this leads to further economic growth. This process can be observed in the postwar Japanese economy, especially in the 1960s. In contrast, pessimistic expectations depress investment. Income and markets never grow, and pessimistic expectations thus become self-fulfilling. This process is a vicious circle in which investment for industries with scale merits is never made.

Appropriate economic policy stances

Protective trade and **industrial policy** are often said to have supported Japan's industrialization and economic growth. However, these did not play as important a role as they are said to have. Several Latin American nations also attempted industrialization that relied on protective policies, but failed. Their domestic markets were too small for scale to be fully realized. The expectation of perpetual protectionism and limited entry also hampered the development of entrepreneurship. In Japan, however, abundant demand and resources, as well as the efforts of the private sector, were the basic factors behind high growth. The trade and industrial policies implemented in Japan were far smaller in relative scale and were intended to be temporary. From this, we can conclude that the policies were not essential.

However, it can be said that some policies played an important role in coordinating economic activities and in improving some incompleteness of financial markets. The **Ministry of International Trade and Industry** may have contributed by causing companies to share positive expectations for the future and regulating them to prevent excess competition. Public finance

companies such as the **Japan Development Bank** have financed huge investments of heavy and chemical industries.

Abundant labor force

In order to establish and develop industries with effective scale economies, it is necessary to mobilize a large labor force in a short period. A huge number of young and inexpensive workers were supplied from rural areas and absorbed into the newly growing sectors in urban areas. In this way, rapid changes in industrial structure and high growth of the Japanese economy were attained. Japanese company management systems were the mechanisms used to organize the labor force efficiently.

The concentration of population in cities increased the demand for durable consumer goods. When labor force migration stopped, wages began to increase, and companies began substituting equipment for workers, which increased the demand for machinery. These growing markets promoted industrialization and sustained high growth.

Summary and recent issues

Through the factors we have examined here, the Japanese economy was able to attain high growth and catch up with the Western industrialized countries. The Japanese company management system, the relationship between the private and public sectors, and the education system operated very efficiently based on Japan's potentially large domestic markets and abundant young labor force.

The situation today, however, is drastically different. Which industries will grow is not as clear as it once was. Unclear and pessimistic expectations for the future deter companies from investment. In financial markets, many commercial banks have not yet disposed of the huge bad debts caused by overheated speculations and investments in the **bubble economy** era. This is a negative factor for a standard Japanese company that heavily depends on indirect finance. Because of these negative factors in both demand and supply sides, investments in new industries cannot grow. The supply of young and inexpensive workers which would allow rapid changes in industrial structures has dried up. Rapid aging of the population is fundamentally changing the Japanese company management system.

Goods, financial and labor markets all face problems. Abuses of the once-beneficial relationship between the private and public sectors are also coming to light. In goods markets, with industrial policies to promote not only process innovation but also product innovation, large new foreign markets can be created. Aging may create potentially large domestic markets of new types of goods and services. In financial markets, public financial organizations are still influential. When financial markets are incomplete, the public sector should finance huge investments of growing industries. At present this duty should be transferred to competitive markets. However, though direct participation may not be called for, indirect participation by governments is necessary. The nature of incomplete financial markets and the types of appropriate government participation is currently the focus of much theoretical and empirical investigation.

It is essential for these Japanese systems to change in ways that will allow them to utilize the middle-aged and older labor force and the female labor force efficiently. Japanese company management systems such as employment and promotion systems are drastically changing. Appropriate social security systems to enforce these movements will also be indispensable.

Further reading

Barro, R.J. and Sala-I-Martin, X. (1995) *Economic Growth*, New York: McGraw-Hill.

Grossman, G. and Helpman, E. (1991) *Innovation and Growth in the Global Economy*, Cambridge, MA: MIT Press.

Krugman, P. (1991) *Geography and Trade*, Cambridge, MA: MIT Press.

Mankiw, N.G., Romer, D. and Weil, D.N. (1992) "A Contribution to the Empirics of Economic Growth," *Quarterly Journal of Economics* 107: 407–37.

Murphy, K.M., Shleifer, A. and Vishny, R.W. (1989) "Income Distribution, Market Size, and Industrialization," *Quarterly Journal of Economics* 104: 537–564.

—— (1989) "Industrialization and the Big Push," *Journal of Political Economy* 97: 1003–26.

HIROKI KONDO

economic ideology

Japan's extremely rapid rise to economic power in the postwar period brought with it a much sharper interest in the Japanese economic system. As observers both within and outside of Japan sought to explain the success of Japanese capitalism, explaining the ideological underpinnings became increasingly important. However, for both Japanese and non-Japanese alike, explaining ideology has not been particularly easy. For observers weaned on free-market, neoclassical economics, Japan's economic system often seemed a paradox. The lessons of neoclassical theory are to let flexible prices in deregulated markets delineate where resources go; this ultimately leads to greater efficiency and growth. However, Japan grew amazingly quickly in the postwar period with capital, labor, and product "markets" influenced heavily by government and inter-firm relationships.

The implication of neoclassical economic theory is that the Japanese economy could have grown *even faster* during the postwar period had it looked more like a laissez-faire economy with flexible price signals. By the 1980s, however, this began to ring hollow as many US and European industries lost significant ground to the Japanese. Attention increasingly turned to how capitalist systems can differ in their evolution and in a particular moment in time, as well as what can be learned from those differences. Furthermore, with the collapse of the Soviet Union in the 1990s, the Cold War pressure to view capitalism monolithically – without historical, institutional, and cultural differences – diminished. Given recognized differences, the question now for capitalist economic systems is what form they should take during different stages of development.

Ironically, the early 1990s also marks the moment when the Japanese **bubble economy** burst, and the drawn-out struggle to revive Japan's economy has made literature pinpointing and trumpeting the reasons for Japan's success somewhat less compelling. The urge to define and learn from Japanese economic ideology has arguably decreased in the face of Japan's stagnation. Indeed, the pendulum swung in the other direction in the 1990s, with many outside and inside Japan arguing for major structural reform of the economy, structural reform that gives free markets a more central role. This parallels the German experience in the 1990s as the USA and Britain boomed while Germany struggled. Interestingly, like their US counterparts in the 1980s debating the relative merits of **industrial policy**, policy makers and others in Japan and Germany are similarly engaged with whether, when and how to allow convergence towards more Anglo-American practices such as a shareholder model of corporate control (see **corporate governance**).

Japan's economic ideology draws some inspiration from Anglo-American neoclassical theory, but it is also clear that the German schools of thought have had particular influence. German schools of economic thought and philosophy such as the historical school stress the role of the government in a "national" economy oriented towards production. Actors in a system like this engage collectively in production to increase a nation's power. Production strengthens national power while consumption weakens that power. Japan's economic ideology has been labeled "developmentalism" by those focused on the primacy of the Japanese government in economic activity. Chalmers **Johnson** is perhaps the best known of the Western scholars for his exposition of developmentalism. Principles characterizing developmentalism in Japan include the importance of strategy and the government in directing resources, a production rather than a consumer orientation, restraint of excessive price competition, and the premium on long run firm growth and productivity rather than profit. Also distinctive is the focus on the concrete *processes* of production, distribution, exchange, and consumption. Japanese developmentalism is relentlessly pragmatic and not bound to any one universalistic economic theory. As such, it is relativistic, flexible, and grounded in the contemporary conditions of economic life.

Johnson and other scholars have pointed out that Japanese capitalism evolved as the country sought to industrialize rapidly due to the Western threat of superiority, and that this urgency affected ideology. For the Japanese, the goal in the nineteenth century was immediate: strengthen the nation's power in international competition. In contrast, Anglo-American capitalism was gradually nurtured in a cultural context of individualism during the Enlightenment. In Japan, industrialization was borrowed from the West, but the laissez-faire mindset stressing the autonomy of the individual was not. In the twentieth century, a military form of developmentalism had emerged in full force in response to the Great Depression and the First World War. This was later challenged by the democratic reforms under MacArthur, but instead of resulting in a liberal free market economic system, the economy evolved into a form of developmentalism centering on trade.

This is one view of a fairly well-known school of thought on Japanese economic ideology; there are other schools, some focusing on the critical role of corporations, or of human resources, or of the market. At this point, it is safe to say that debates over capitalist economic ideology – even debates within a country over what that ideology is – are not about to end. The Japanese developmentalist model – however "stylized" it may be – remains important as a point of reference. This is especially the case for the developing world. The Russian experience provides a sobering case study in the potential pitfalls of universalist neoclassical solutions quickly administered. Deregulating Russia through Western style "shock therapy" proved to be nothing short of disastrous. The Japanese approach to development – which is more incrementalist, strategic, and sensitive to institutional and historical context – widens the constellation of possibility and enlivens the challenge of increasing economic and social welfare in all countries.

Further reading

Gao, B. (1997) *Economic Ideology and Japanese Industrial Policy*, New York: Cambridge University Press.

Johnson, C. (1982) *MITI and the Japanese Miracle*, Stanford, CA: Stanford University Press.

WILLIAM BARNES

education system

The Japanese education system has provided the foundation for twentieth-century Japanese economic success by producing an adaptable, productive work force and has become a model for developing countries, particularly in East Asia. Growing out of roots in the **Meiji restoration** and modeled after the German, French and American education systems, it is a unitary system dominated by the Ministry of Education in Tokyo and its affiliated prefectural branches. The Japanese education system is renowned for providing a strong education to all students, particularly in mathematics and science, but has been criticized by Japanese teachers and politicians for inhibiting creativity and causing extreme stress in some students.

The education system in Japan is structured along the American model, with six elementary school years, three middle school years, three high school years and four university years. Elementary and middle school are mandatory. Students with physical and mental handicaps attend separate schools, creating greater educational uniformity. Over 99 percent of children of compulsory school age are enrolled in school, and approximately 95 percent of students complete the equivalent of high school. The Japanese school year begins in early April and is organized in trimesters that run from April to July, September to December, and January to March. Japanese students receive an average of approximately 200 days of classroom instruction.

The Ministry of Education (MOE) exerts the strongest influence on the school system, prescribing curricula, standards, and requirements; approving textbooks; providing guidance and financial subsidies accounting for nearly half of total educational expenditures; authorizing the establishment of colleges, universities, and private schools; and operating national universities, junior colleges, and technical colleges. Each prefecture also has a board of education, appointed by the prefectural governor. Prefectural boards appoint the prefectural superintendent of education with the consent of the MOE; operate prefectural high schools; license teachers; and make appointments to schools. Finally, each municipality has a board of education appointed by the mayor. Municipal boards operate municipal elementary and middle schools; choose textbooks from the MOE's approved list; and make recommendations to the prefectural board of education on the appointment and dismissal of teachers.

Historical development

Historians describe two educational revolutions in Japanese history. The first occurred during the Meiji restoration in the late nineteenth century when Japanese leaders worked to tear down neo-Confucian educational structures and attitudes and institute modern educational practices, roles, and structures imitated from the United States, Germany, and France. From France, Meiji leaders imitated a centralized educational system run by a national Ministry of Education. Following the German model, they created a system that sorted students from the time they entered primary school into discrete career tracks. They borrowed basic curriculum from the United States. During the 1920s, teachers pressed for American-style reforms inspired by John Dewey, such as "liberal education" and "life-in-education." The rise of the military during the 1930s, however, ensured that the centralized, state-oriented system continued.

The second educational revolution occurred after Japan's defeat in the Second World War. The American occupation attempted to create a more decentralized, egalitarian, and above all democratic Japanese education system. At the urging of Occupation authorities, the Japanese Diet created a single-track 6–3–3–4 system to replace the pre-war multi-track system. Occupation authorities also mandated the establishment of neighborhood schools instead of merit-based school recruiting; established locally elected school boards; and limited the authority of the MOE to issuing outlines, suggestions, and teaching guides.

While political liberals and the national teachers' union embraced the reforms, Japanese political conservatives bitterly opposed them. After winning control of the government in 1955 when the **Liberal Democratic Party** was created, conservatives began an educational "reverse course," passing legislation gutting the authority of local school boards, making MOE curriculum nationally mandatory, requiring that all school texts be approved by the MOE review boards, and finally striking at the single-track system by creating vocational high schools. Elementary schools, however, remained largely untouched.

In the 1980s, Japan entered a national debate on education reform. Spurred by widely reported incidents of student violence, increasing reports of bullying, and a sharp rise in "school refusers," children psychologically unable to attend school out of fear or stress, Prime Minister Yasuhiro Nakasone created the National Ad Hoc Council on Education Reform to further diversify the single-track system, improve the high school and university entrance examination system, increase emphasis on moral and physical education, promote internationalization of education, and improve the quality of teachers. Despite strong public interest, pervasive media coverage, support from Nikkeiren and Keidanren, and the prime minister's personal attention, the council failed to recommend structural changes, only endorsing increased moral education and internationalization. Radical change to the educational system appears unlikely.

Elementary schools

Japanese elementary schools emphasize personal development and an experiential approach to learning, seeking to build students' motivation and confidence, as well as personal and social skills. In particular, elementary schools stress the ability to work well in small groups through structures such as *han*, classroom workgroups. *Han* members must work together to perform academic tasks, such as making presentations and doing research, as well as non-academic tasks, such as serving lunch and cleaning the classroom and school.

Elementary students remain with the same *kumi*, or class, for the entire academic year. Elementary school teachers' top priority is to engage students in learning, not to fill their heads with facts. Accordingly, teachers emphasize process, engagement, and commitment rather than discipline and outcome. At the same time, teachers work to provide students with fundamental academic skills, particularly in Japanese language and mathematics. However, no academic tracking takes place,

and teachers deliberately mix students of differing academic ability in *han* and go to extreme lengths to ensure that all students proceed together through lessons.

Secondary schools

In contrast to elementary schools, Japanese secondary schools focus on preparing students to enter the workforce. High schools and to some extent middle schools track students and teach increasingly specialized curricula. They also stress the central importance of hard work and diligence through required moral education courses and structures such as the entrance examination system.

Like elementary schools, middle schools are neighborhood schools. Students remain with the same *kumi* for at least a year, while teachers specializing in an academic area rotate classrooms throughout the day. Students learn the same MOE-mandated curricula, use the same MOE-approved textbooks, and take the same classes: mathematics, Japanese language, English, science, history, moral education, and physical education, with occasional art and music classes.

Middle school students' concerns become increasingly dominated by the prefectural high school entrance examination. The examination is written to ensure that students have mastered three years of middle school course material and is dominated by facts and specifics. In order to excel, students must spend hours studying and memorizing. Proponents of the system argue it teaches students the importance of hard work, diligence, and perseverance. Based on the results of the entrance examination, a student may enter (in decreasing prestige): an elite private school, a public university prep school, a public vocational school, a general private school, or a public night school.

Education in Japanese high schools varies widely according to the type of school. In university prep schools, the mood is serious and behavior is oriented toward the national university entrance examination. Teachers are expected to pour information into students by lecture to prepare them for the university entrance examination. Students in vocational schools have fewer hours of the core academic subjects to allow them to study nursing, cooking, practical business skills, etc., and emphasis falls on those vocational skills. In night schools, teachers emphasize basic coping skills.

High school students are expected to continue to learn to work in groups, continuing to stay with the same *kumi* for a year, though *han* are much less prominent than in elementary school. Instead, students participate in mandatory after-school sports or culture clubs, where students learn to work within the *sempai-kohai,* or senior-junior, relationships that will become important during their university and work lives.

Juku and *yobiko*

Juku encompass a large and diverse range of private, for-profit tutorial, enrichment, remedial, preparatory, and cram schools. On average, students attend *juku* after school two and a half times per week for a total of five hours. The majority of students attending *juku* study English and mathematics, most in preparation for the high school or university entrance examination.

Yobiko are *yuku* specializing in intense training for university entrance examinations, often tailored specifically to the requirements and examinations of individual schools. *Yobiko* particularly cater to the 200,000 *ronin* in Japan, students who have failed the exams for their first-choice schools and who have elected to spend a full year preparing to take the examinations again. Because so many university students have had the *ronin-yobiko* experience, education in Japan has been called the 6–3–3–1–4 system. Most *ronin* and *yobiko* students are male, outnumbering female students by more than 10 to 1.

Higher education

Approximately 20 percent of high school graduates enter a four-year university, about 10 percent enter a two-year junior college, and another 25 percent enter a vocational program, usually a continuation of studies begun at vocational high schools. Admission to universities and colleges is determined almost exclusively by the results of the national entrance examination, and admission to the most prestigious universities such as **Tokyo University** is extremely competitive.

Once admitted, however, almost 75 percent of university students graduate in four years and almost 90 percent graduate eventually. Coursework demands drop off significantly from high school and most students take part-time jobs. Japanese universities have been criticized for their relatively lax instruction and poor attendance, leading to their reputation as merely credentialing institutions.

Graduate students are concentrated in a small number of elite public and private universities and make up only 4 percent of total university enrollment. Graduate studies are considered strictly in-service training for careers in academia since most Japanese employers prefer to train university graduates in-house.

Strengths and weaknesses

The Japanese education system generates graduates with a high average level of capability. On the whole, Japanese students are well-disciplined and motivated. They routinely score at or near the top of international test comparisons in mathematics and science. Over 97 percent of Japanese are functionally literate, despite the demands of using a non-phonetic writing system. The Japanese education system achieves these results even though Japan spends only 2.3 percent of its GDP on primary and secondary education, much less than other industrialized countries such as the United States.

Critics of the Japanese education system argue it is too centralized and regimented. With textbooks, curricula, and examinations set by MOE bureaucrats, relatively little discretion for local innovation exists. In addition, the lock-step educational approach disadvantages the brightest and slowest students and marginalizes handicapped students. The system also lacks institutionalized emotional and psychological support beyond teachers, often failing to support troubled students. Finally, critics argue that the examination system puts too much pressure on children at too young an age, resulting in over-stressed and unhappy children. The continuing problem of bullying as well as the rise of school violence since the 1980s are symptoms of these weaknesses.

Further reading

Beauchamp, E.R. (ed.) (1991) *Windows on Japanese Education*, New York: Greenwood Press.

Leestma, R. and Walberg H.J. (eds) (1992) *Japanese Educational Productivity*, Ann Arbor, MI: Center for Japanese Studies, University of Michigan.

Marshall, B.K. (1994) *Learning to Be Modern: Japanese Political Discourse on Education*, Boulder, CO: Westview Press.

Rohlen, T. and Björk, C. (eds) (1998) *Education and Training in Japan*, 3 vols, London: Routledge.

United States Study of Education in Japan (1987) *Japanese Education Today*, Washington: Government Printing Office.

KEITH A. NITTA

electronics industry

Japan's electronics industry includes world-leading firms in consumer electronics, semiconductors, computers and telecommunications. Most of these firms were established long before the Second World War, but came into international prominence during the 1950s and 1960s when they began large-scale exports of transistor radios, television sets, calculators and semiconductors. The industry continued to thrive through the 1980s, as Japanese consumers became increasingly affluent, but with the end of Japan's **bubble economy**, was faced with a number of problems: relatively slow growth in domestic markets, high wages, and increasing competition from newly industrialized Asian competitors. In the late 1990s and early 2000s most of the leading Japanese electronics firms began restructuring in response to these pressures.

Origins of the industry

After Japan was opened to the West in the mid-nineteenth century, the Japanese were quick to master the advanced technologies of the time. Telegraph service was inaugurated between Tokyo and Yokohama in 1869. In the 1870s the government established a university-level program in electrical engineering and electrical research laboratories. By the end of the nineteenth century

Japanese had built electric power plants, begun producing electric light bulbs, and introduced telephone service. In 1905, the Japanese Navy used wireless telegraphy to defeat a Russian fleet in the Russo-Japanese War.

The origins of modern electronics engineering in Japan are commonly dated to 1925, when radio broadcasting began. By this time Japanese researchers were amongst the most advanced in the world in some areas of electronics. Yagi Hidetsugu and Uda Shintaro invented the Yagi antenna in 1926. The Yagi became the most widely used radio and television antenna in the world. That same year, Takayanagi Kenjiro was one of the first in the world to produce an all-electronic television image (Japanese sources credit Takayanagi with being the first).

Foreign firms were deeply involved in the early Japanese electronics industry. Western Electric established a Japanese subsidiary in 1899 that later became today's **NEC**. In 1905 General Electric (GE) took a controlling interest in Tokyo Electric Lighting, which used GE technology to become Japan's leading producer of light bulbs. Five years later, GE exchanged heavy electrical equipment technology in return for 24.5 percent of the equity of Shibaura Electric Works. This helped Shibaura to become Japan's largest producer of generators and other heavy electrical equipment. Tokyo Electric and Shibaura later merged to form Tokyo Shibaura Electric, today's **Toshiba**. Westinghouse Electric, a US firm, worked in partnership with **Mitsubishi** to establish Mitsubishi Electric in 1921. Similarly, in 1923 Germany's Siemens and Furukawa Electric formed Fuji Electric. A Fuji spin-off, Fujitsu, later became one of Japan's "big five" firms in the industrial electronics industry.

Other major Japanese electronics firms that were established before the Second World War remained independent of foreign interests. Hitachi was established in 1908 as a shop repairing electric pumps and other equipment at a mine. It became a separate firm in 1920. **Matsushita** (the consumer electronics giant which also uses the National, Panasonic and Quasar brand names) was established in 1918. **Sharp** was initially established in 1912 as a metal processing firm. Its founder invented a mechanical pencil (the "Ever Sharp") from which the company eventually took its brand name. The company began making radio sets in 1925.

During the late 1930s the foreign firms were forced out of Japan. One consequence of this was that Japan had less access to foreign technology. The Japanese electronics firms were also required to stop producing home appliances and to concentrate on military electronics.

The electronics industry after the Second World War

New opportunities contributed to the explosive growth of the Japanese electronics industry after the Second World War (see **post-Second World War recovery**). First of all, the **American occupation** authorities promoted the rapid introduction of commercial radio (and later television) broadcasting, believing this would help foster the development of democracy. Secondly, large numbers of talented electronics engineers were suddenly available to work on commercial products. The military research institutions had been closed down and research on radar and other technologies that could contribute to remilitarization was banned. Finally, much of the technology developed in the West during the 1930s and 1940s suddenly became available to the Japanese. By 1949 nearly 200 Japanese firms were producing radios. Two former naval researchers started Tokyo Telecommunications Engineering (Totsuko) to repair radios and to make various electrical devices. In 1958 Totsuko changed its name to **Sony**.

As the demand for radios approached saturation, television provided another big boost for the Japanese electronics industry. Television broadcasting began in 1953, and in January of that year Sharp marketed the first Japanese-made television set. Sharp was not alone. Nearly forty Japanese firms had signed technology transfer agreements with RCA, then the leading source of television technology (see **export and import of technology**).

In 1953 Sony signed an agreement to import transistor technology from Western Electric. Most of the other Japanese electronics firms soon signed their own agreements. Although US firms were ahead of Sony in marketing transistor radios, Sony offered a combination of price and size that almost instantly attracted a huge market. By 1959 more than one hundred Japanese companies were making transistor radios. In 1960 transistor radios generated more export earnings for Japan than any other industry except shipbuilding.

Japanese firms also began the production of transistors. At the time transistor production was highly labor-intensive and Japanese companies were able to hire thousands of young women, "transistor girls," to manufacture the transistors at approximately ten cents per hour. This helped Japan to become the world's largest transistor producer.

As Japanese consumers became more affluent in the late 1950s, demand increased for a variety of electrical and electronic products: rice cookers, electric fans, washing machines, refrigerators, and stereos. The utilities needed heavy electrical equipment and there was unprecedented growth in telephone service.

Challenges and growth in the 1960s and 1970s

Although Japan continued its rapid **economic growth** through the 1960s and into the early 1970s, special challenges faced the electronics industry. New transistors were developed that eliminated low labor cost as a major competitive advantage. This and the later development of the integrated circuit (IC) shifted competitive advantage in semiconductors from Japan to the United States. Meanwhile, the most important consumer product in Japan, the black and white television set, was reaching market saturation. By the early 1960s, about 90 percent of Japanese households had television sets.

The electronics firms quickly made the transition to the production of color television sets. Although the sets produced in the mid-1960s may have been inferior to those available in Europe and the United States, the Japanese market was protected until Japanese firms could catch up with their foreign competitors. In 1970 color television sets accounted for one-third of total electronics industry sales. As this market, in turn, moved towards saturation the consumer electronics firms began introducing new products such as video tape recorders. In the case of monochrome and color televisions, the Japanese had trailed the USA and Europe by several years. Now they were in the vanguard in introducing a major new consumer electronics product to world markets.

In 1969, another key product for the Japanese electronics industry was introduced. Sharp began selling a Large Scale Integrated Circuit (LSI) calculator. Some fifty other Japanese firms quickly brought out their calculators beginning what became known as "the calculator wars." Only two firms survived the resulting competition. Just as the transistor radio had supported the birth of a Japanese semiconductor industry, the calculator supported the next phase of development of the industry. Although the LSI and later Very Large Scale Integrated Circuit (VLSI) technologies had been developed in the United States, US firms developed increasingly complex forms of this technology for use in defense applications. The Japanese concentrated on simpler, cheaper, more reliable integrated circuits that served especially well in consumer applications. The Japanese government played some role in nurturing the development of the technological capacities of the semiconductor industry. In a controversial piece of policy it delayed the entry of Texas Instruments into the Japanese market. It also orchestrated the formation of **research cooperatives**, such as the **VLSI Research Cooperative**, to speed the development of technology.

The 1980s: years of triumph

During the 1980s it seemed as though the progress of Japanese industry was unstoppable. Although Japan no longer enjoyed the economic growth of earlier decades, Japan was now the world's second largest economy and had passed the United States to lead the world in per capita GDP.

By 1985 Japanese firms and their affiliates produced some 80 percent of the world's video recorders. Sony's Walkman, introduced in 1979, was a worldwide hit through the decade and later. Throughout the 1980s lists of the world ten largest semiconductor products typically included five or six Japanese firms. Indeed, by the late 1980s Japanese firms had more than half of the world market for semiconductors. The Japanese also moved to an early lead in the development and use of computer-aided machine tools, industrial robots and other factory automation technologies.

There were problems, however. Wage costs which had been a source of competitive advantage, were now a competitive weakness for Japan. Trade frictions with the USA and other countries made it politically impossible to sustain export growth. Some Japanese firms had built or bought off-shore production facilities in the 1970s, and in the 1980s this became a growing trend.

The 1990s and 2000s

In the 1990s the Japanese electronics industry faced severe difficulties. The collapse of the bubble economy at the end of 1989 undermined consumer confidence. Domestic markets for consumer electronics goods were largely saturated. Competitors were beginning to emerge in other parts of East Asia. The **economic crisis in Asia** in the late 1990s further aggravated the situation. During the 1990s sales of consumer electronics products dropped in half. This weakness in demand was also devastating for the semiconductor firms, which still relied on consumer products to take one-third of their output.

The trend towards offshore production continued. By 1998 Japan's electronics firms had some eight hundred production facilities in other parts of Asia and an additional four hundred in other parts of the world. Only about 10 percent of the color television sets produced by Japanese firms were actually made in Japan, and only about one-third of the video recorders.

The "big five" Japanese industrial electronics firms, Toshiba, NEC, Hitachi, Fujitsu and Mitsubishi Electric, and the largest consumer electronics firm, Sony, were all experiencing new difficulties. Toshiba, for example, experienced its first losses in nearly a quarter of a century. The large vertically integrated giant Japanese electronics firms that had seemed unstoppable in the 1980s were now seen as unwieldy and poorly focused because of their size. Many of them were re-structuring and entering into international alliances, most often with US partners.

Further reading

Anchordoguy, M. (1989) *Computers, Inc.: Japan's Challenge to IBM*, Cambridge, MA: Harvard University Press.

Aoyama, Y. (1991) *Kaden* (Home Electronics). Tokyo: Nihon Keizai Shimbun.

Lynn, L. (1998) "The Commercialization of the Transistor Radio in Japan: The Functioning of an Innovation Community," *IEEE Transactions of Engineering Management* 45(August): 220–29.

Methe, D. (1991) *Technological Competition in Global Industries*, New York: Quorum.

Nathan, J. (1999) *Sony: The Private Life*, New York: Houghton-Mifflin.

Partner, S. (1999) *Assembled in Japan: Electrical Goods and the Making of the Japanese Consumer*, Berkeley, CA: University of California Press.

LEONARD H. LYNN

enterprise unions

There are two kinds of workers in the world: employees and independent craftsmen. Employees are organized into unions according to their plant, establishment or enterprise. Furthermore, employee trade unions usually include enterprise-based organizational units within their organization. Can such enterprise-based organizational units of unions be called "enterprise unions?" If so, every trade union in the world, with the exception of craft unions, can be termed an enterprise union. In order to avoid confusion, it is necessary to provide a definition of enterprise union. Enterprise unions are those unions which are organized on the basis of enterprises or establishments and which are more or less autonomous with regard to national unions. Organizational autonomy of the enterprise union, *vis-à-vis* the national union applies to collective bargaining, finance and staff.

Types of enterprise union

Enterprise unions can be classified into two types according to their degree of autonomy with respect to national unions: highly-autonomous unions and partially-autonomous unions, referred to here as HAEU and PAEU, respectively. Such autonomy depends on the power-relations among enterprise unions affiliated with the national union and with the national headquarters of their national union.

Various characteristics determine the organizational structure of trade unions. The most important of these are degree of concentration in industry, government regulation, and path dependency during the formative years.

Zensen Doumei (Textile Workers Union) is an example of a highly centralized national union, whose affiliated enterprise unions are PAEUs. Jidousha Souren (Automobile Workers Union) is a loosely-structured national federation of enterprise unions and so its affiliate enterprise unions are HAEUs.

Overview of major trade unions in Japan

Incorrect images of Japanese trade unions are widespread in the world, even among industrial relations professionals. One such popular but erroneous view is that most trade unions in Japan are "enterprise unions." The second incorrect stereotype is the view that "enterprise union" is a sugar-coated phrase for "company-dominated union," a union which is essentially obedient to and cooperative with management. The former stereotype is examined first.

In 1999, there were twenty-three national unions in Japan that had over one hundred thousand union members:

Jichirou (Local Government Employees Union)	1,017,000
Jidousha Souren (Automobile Workers Union)	768,000
Denki Rouren (Electrical Equipment Workers Union)	740,000
Zenken Souren (Construction Workers Union)	715,000
Zensen Doumei (Textile Workers Union)	585,000
JAM (Metal Machinery Workers Union)	500,000
Nikkyouso (Teachers Union)	365,000
Seiho Rouren (Life Insurance Workers Union)	351,000
Jouhou Rouren (Communications Workers Union)	266,000
Denryoku Souren (Electrical Power Workers Union)	257,000
Jichi Rouren (Local Government Employees Union – left wing)	249,000
CSG Rengou (Chemical Workers Union)	214,000
Nippon Ih Rouren (Hospital Workers Union)	172,000
Tekkou Rouren (Steel Workers Union)	170,000
Kokukou Rouren (Central Government Employees Union)	160,000
Sitetsu Souren (Private Railway Workers Union)	167,000
Zentei (Postal Workers Union)	155,000
Zenginren (Bank Employees Union)	149,000

Zenkyou (Teachers Union – left wing)	143,000
Unyu Rouren (Trucking Workers Union)	136,000
Shougyou Rouren (Retail Workers Union)	124,000
Zousen Juki Rouren (Shipbuilding and Heavy	
Machinery Workers Union)	123,000
Shokuhin Rengou (Food and Drink Workers Union)	110,000
Total number of members	7,644,000

There were approximately 11,706,000 union members in 1999, with an estimated union density of about 22.2 percent. The ratio of major national union members to total union members is 65.3 percent, and the trade union movement in Japan has been much more vigorous in the public and the highly concentrated private sectors than in the less concentrated private sectors where small firms are dominant. Enterprise unions do not exist in the public sector at all because public corporations were largely privatized in the 1980s and public sector enterprises as such do not yet exist. One-third of all organized workers are public employees and have "enterprise unions". The third largest union in the private sector, Zenken Souren (Construction Workers Union), is a craft union whose members are skilled craftsmen such as carpenters or plumbers. Craft unions are not enterprise unions. In Japan, pure enterprise unions are very few. Most enterprise unions belong to national unions and are allied with other enterprise unions within the same national union in their struggle against management and government. The national union is an alliance of enterprise unions within the same industry.

Which type of union is more numerous, the HAEU or PAEU? In postwar Japan, wage negotiations, and consequently wage determination, have been highly centralized. Therefore, enterprise unions are not very autonomous in their negotiations with employers, these being coordinated at the national level by the headquarters of their national unions or by the national federation of national unions. Since 1955, wage negotiations in Japan have been concentrated in the spring and synchronized and/or coordinated at the national level. This wage determination practice has been called "spring offensive." The wage negotiations themselves are conducted mostly at the enterprise level, and collective agreements are signed firm by firm, and by the leaders of the respective enterprise

unions and management. However, these enterprise-level negotiations are coordinated by the concerted actions of both parties at the national level. Under these circumstances, enterprise unions are unable to maintain a high degree of autonomy and in this sense PAEUs are more dominant than HAEUs in Japan.

The pure enterprise union is the exception in Japan. Affiliated enterprise unions are very similar to union locals affiliated with national unions in the US. Are there any distinctions between the Zen Toyota Rouren (an enterprise union), which is affiliated with the Jidousha Souren (a national union), and the GM Department (an enterprise union) of the UAW (a national union)? In terms of organizational structure there does exist a slight difference.

Unique characteristics of Japanese enterprise unions

Generally speaking, industrial societies are becoming similar, an indication that the convergence theory of history is also valid in the field of industrial relations. But national uniqueness does not disappear so long as it is appropriate for and does not hinder the economic and societal development of the society. In terms of organizational structure, Japanese enterprise unions have a few unique features compared with similar labor organizations of foreign countries. Firstly, enterprise unions in Japan are distinctive in regard to membership eligibility. In Japan, both white-collar and blue-collar workers join the same enterprise union, without exception. In the case of blue-collar workers, members retain their union status until they are promoted to general foremen and white-collar workers usually lose membership eligibility when they are promoted to *kachou* (section chief). In the Republic of Korea, the bottom organizations of national unions are enterprise unions but white-collar employees do not usually join these unions. In the USA, white-collar workers are organized separately.

The second distinctive feature of enterprise unions in Japan is the alignment of union members. Enterprise unions are organized according to the organizational structure of the enterprise or company. Skilled tradesmen or professionals do not have their own organizational chapter within the enterprise union. For example, a medical doctor (company doctor or company clinic doctor) belongs to the hospital or clinic section of the enterprise union; there is no separate branch within the organization for professional people in the enterprise union. Medical doctors, nurses, technicians, clinic clerks and janitors join the same union chapter and meet at the same union conference.

The third feature that is characteristic of most Japanese enterprise unions is their dual role in relation to management. Enterprise unions engage in collective bargaining with management and at the same time take part in joint consultation committees as partners to make the enterprise more competitive and to enhance its profitability. This two-faceted nature of the enterprise union raises serious questions for both practitioners as well as scholars of industrial relations in Japan and abroad. Collective bargaining is a process for resolving antagonism and disputes between employers and employees, and it presupposes the existence of adversarial relations between the parties. But union participation in management or the decision-making process and partnership between employers and employees rests upon an opposite philosophy, namely that the parties share mutual interests and are like "a crew in a life boat" (*Gemeinschaft* in German). Enterprise unions in Japan engage in wage negotiations annually and sometimes strike to win their demands. At the same time, enterprise unions meet and discuss managerial matters with employers at least four times a year at the *roushi kyougi kai* (union-management conference).

Controversy over the nature of the enterprise union

Enterprise unions play a balancing act between their roles as collective bargaining agents and management collaborators. Is it possible for a union to do that? There have been heated controversies about this in postwar Japan. Some practitioners and scholars assert that enterprise unions are not *bona fide* unions, that they are company-dominated labor organizations in nature, and that they must be destroyed and replaced with *bona fide* trade unions. This type of leftist opinion is

called *dappi ron* (casting off argument) and one of the slogans of such proponents is "towards industrial unionism." Other practitioners and scholars evaluate union participation in management highly, and praise enterprise unions as the most advanced organizational form of trade unionism today. This type of participationist view is called *yougo ron* (defense of enterprise union).

Today, practitioners are losing interest in the debate but industrial relations scholars and labor historians are enthusiastically discussing the problem. After the collapse of the Soviet Union, Marxists are becoming even less influential among intellectuals and at the same time such radical opinions of trade unionism are fading even among academics.

Past, present and future of enterprise unions

Enterprise unions were hastily organized in the latter half of 1946, with the strong support of the Occupation Army. SCAP (Supreme Commander of Allied Powers) ordered the government of Japan to enact labor legislation for the democratization of Japan, and the Diet (Parliament) rapidly enacted the Trade Union Act in December of 1945. The Act was implemented in April of 1946. During the war, workers had been organized in enterprise-based patriotic organizations called *sanpou*, short for Sangyou Houkoku Kai (Industrial Patriotic Association). *Sanpous* were the forerunners of enterprise unions. Blue-collar as well as white-collar workers joined the *sanpou*, which was engaged in both negotiation and participation. The reason that the trade union movement in Japan was able to deeply take root in enterprises in a short period of time was the historical good luck of the War and the Occupation, times during which employers' were easily deprived of their management prerogatives. Enterprise unionism was one of the "war babies."

The enterprise union is the most appropriate type of organization for a trade union playing the double roles of negotiation and participation. Recently, the Dunlop Commission in the USA recommended the introduction of enterprise-union organizations to promote union–management co-operation. The enterprise union is one institutional model of present-day industrial democracies in which worker participation and employment security is growing increasingly important. The enterprise union provides unions with three organizational advantages: (1) participation in the creation of rule-making for work; (2) enhancing employees' career development; and (3) maintaining employment security.

Further reading

Koike, K. (1977) *Shokuba no Rodo Kumiai to Sanka* (Workplace Labor Union and Participation).

Oukochi, K. (ed.) (1956) *Rodo Kumiai no Seisei to Soshiki* (Formation and Organization of Labor Unions), in *Sengo Rodo Kumiai no Jittai* (Realities of Postwar Labor Unions), Tokyo: Tokyo University Press.

Roshi Kankei no Nichibei Hikaku (Comparative Labor Relations in Japan and the US), Tokyo: Toyokeizai Shinpo Sha.

Shirai, T. (1979) *Kigyoubetsu Kumiai* (Enterprise Unions), Tokyo Chuo Koron Sha.

SUSUMU HAGIWARA

environmental and ecological issues

Alternately described as an environmental outlaw or an environmental performance leader, Japan's record with regard to the natural environment has been filled with a complex mix of environmental tragedies and triumphs. During its high economic growth years of the 1950s and 1960s, Japan experienced environmental degradation that was without historical precedent. While Japan continues to be criticized for such practices as whaling and importation of tropical hardwoods, Japan also merits recognition for its subsequent achievement of world-class performance on several environmental measures. Recently, the involvement of Japanese business in environmental issues has been undergoing a notable transformation as it attempts to shift from a reactive orientation to a more proactive stance. During the late 1990s and early 2000s in particular, leading Japanese companies have actively worked to improve their environmental performance through greener technology,

purchasing, operations, accounting and other means. At the same time, the Japanese economy as a whole continues to face considerable challenges in achieving environmentally sustainable development.

History

While medieval Japan had experienced instances of severe forest depletion and watershed erosion, the first major case of industrial pollution began in the 1880s with the Ashio Copper Mine in Tochigi, where mining wastes poisoned the region's rivers and lands. Though other cases of industrial pollution continued to emerge throughout Japan, one that eventually attracted worldwide attention was Chisso Corporation's discharge of mercury compounds into Minamata Bay. Eventually, thousands of Minamata residents suffered debilitating effects or even died due to mercury poisoning from eating contaminated fish. Though human cases were first reported in 1956 with the probable cause determined soon afterward, cover-ups and denials by Chisso with the backing of the **Ministry of International Trade and Industry** (MITI) delayed an official confirmation of Chisso's responsibility until a 1968 announcement by the Ministry of Welfare. In the meantime, outbreaks of several other pollution-related diseases occurred, including *itai-itai* disease from cadmium poisoning in Toyama, Yokkaichi asthma named after the city by that name and its smog-emitting petrochemical industrial complex, and yet another case of mercury poisoning in Niigata prefecture. The severity of widespread pollution led one international observer to liken Japan to a test case of unrestrained industrialization that the rest of the world was watching, much as coal miners once watched the canary in the cage.

Increasing public concern during the 1960s about widespread air and water pollution eventually resulted in government action, with the 1967 passage of the first basic environmental protection law. Due to industry pressure, however, this law contained a clause that environmental protection was to be pursued in "harmony with sound economic development." Intense public concern continued, however, and led to a special Diet session in 1970 that passed fourteen strict environmental laws and abolished the "harmony" clause. Japan's Environment Agency was established soon afterward in 1971. With the later passage of more laws and the creation of a number of innovative regulatory approaches, the 1970s and 1980s can be characterized as a period of active technocratic environmental policy for pollution abatement and energy conservation, though industry pressure did win some later concessions. Air pollution levels for sulfur dioxide fell from their 1967 peak to become the lowest per capita among OECD nations. Such improvements were due to a combination of energy conservation, fuel conversion, economic structural change, and technology investment. At its peak in 1975, investment in pollution control accounted for 20 percent of capital investment, several times higher than other OECD nations. By 1989, Japanese companies operated three-fourths of the world's desulpherization and denitrification units. Spurred by the "oil shocks" of the 1970s and with the guidance of MITI, Japanese industry also achieved the world's highest level of energy efficiency. Energy consumption and carbon dioxide emissions remained nearly level from 1970 to 1987 even while the index of industrial production increased by 70 percent, with a majority of this effect attributable to improved energy efficiency (Watanabe 1997). As a result of R&D and investments in energy conservation and pollution control, Japan came to be a world leader in many environmental technologies.

Recent issues

The 1990s marked a new era for Japan and the environment. At the international level, Japan was increasing its environmental diplomacy efforts and attempting to position itself as an environmental leader in the global community. Domestically, a new wave of environmental legislation was passed, including an ambitious new basic environmental law. In the years afterward, several additional laws were enacted dealing with packaging, energy conservation, recycling of automobiles and household appliances, pollutant release and transfer registration, and the creation of a "sustainable recycling-based society" (*junkan-gata shakai*). In 2001, Japan's Environment Agency was raised to ministry status. During the 1990s, the Japanese

business community also experienced a shift in its environmental stance, as being "green" became an increasingly important business issue. Symbolizing this was Keidanren's release of a Global Environmental Charter in 1991 (later updated in 1996) that notes the responsibility of corporations to protect the global environment and its resources. By the late 1990s and early 2000s, the Japanese business press was regularly reporting on corporate environmental initiatives and companies touted their accomplishments in frequent press releases.

Representing this rise in Japanese corporate environmentalism was the "ISO 14000 boom," referring to the intense interest shown in the international standard for environmental management systems released October, 1996. Certification activity was initially highest among export-oriented industries such as consumer electronics, but quickly extended to other industries and even local government bodies. As of January 2001, Japan's number of certifications ranked highest internationally at 5,338, double the number for the next highest country, Germany, and nearly four times that of the UK or USA.

Besides corporate image and meeting market requirements, improving eco-efficiency is another motivation behind this activity, as companies try to reduce wastes and resource consumption. A number of Japanese firms, including Kirin Brewery, **NEC** and Honda, have announced that their plants have achieved "zero emissions," where practically all the waste stream is recycled in some way rather than hauled to a landfill. Some firms are increasing their efforts at recycling and remanufacturing parts for reuse in new products. Fuji Xerox, for example, first modeled its remanufacturing efforts after Xerox in the USA, but reports that it has since improved upon and overtaken Xerox. Also, stricter laws on packaging and recycling are motivating companies to design products with lower end-of-life costs.

Forming the subject of MITI's Eco-Vision report, environment-related businesses have been another area of activity. Many firms have established divisions or subsidiaries to provide environmental services and others have increased their efforts at developing and marketing clean technologies and systems. Besides green process technologies, many firms have also been successful in developing market-leading green products. Japanese firms lead in such areas as battery technology, hybrid cars, solder-free electronics products, and consumer goods with ultra-low power consumption.

Corporate environmental reports, though rare in the early 1990s, are now becoming *de rigueur*. Also, by 2000, one in five firms surveyed by Nikkei had initiated environmental accounting. Though savings are achieved in some areas, early reports generally showed overall environmental costs several times larger than environmental savings. In addition, a Nikkei survey showed nearly one in four companies as having established environmental criteria for procurement decisions. Also, Japan's first eco-funds for investors began in the summer of 1999, with Toyota, NEC, Sony, NTT, Matsushita, Fujitsu, and Ricoh among the more popular companies for investment.

Challenges

Japan has achieved a dramatic turnaround from the 1960s and 1970s when it was known as a "showcase for industrial pollution." Nevertheless, its progress is far from complete. Development and public works projects routinely take precedence over nature conservation. Biodiversity faces serious threats. Reports of illegal dumping of wastes are not uncommon. A reliance on incineration of wastes has led to dioxin levels far higher than other countries. Also, due to its high population density and relative lack of natural resources, Japan will continue to face the challenge of sustaining its economic well being. According to a 2001 cross-national comparison conducted by the World Economic Forum, Japan ranked behind most industrialized nations on its index measuring environmental sustainability at twenty-second, with Finland ranking first, Canada third, Australia seventh, USA eleventh, Germany fifteenth, and the UK sixteenth. Yet another study from the 2000 Living Planet Report compared the ecological footprint of various nations: the land and sea area necessary to meet their consumption of food, materials, and energy. According to this study, Japan's eco-footprint on a per capita basis was among the smallest of the industrialized nations due to relatively efficient use of resources. The

challenge, however, is that Japan's own biological capacity to provide those resources was less than one-sixth of that required.

Further reading

Environment Agency (2000) *Kankyo Hakusho* (Quality of the Environment in Japan) Tokyo: Gyousei.

Ishizu, T., Ichie, M. and Shimizu, M. (1993) *Japanese Corporate Response to Global Environmental Issues*, Japan Development Bank Research Report No. 36, Tokyo: Japan Development Bank.

Nikkei Ecology, Tokyo: Nikkei Business Publications (monthly).

Tsuru, S. (1999) *The Political Economy of the Environment: The Case of Japan*, Vancouver, BC: UBC Press.

Tsuru, S. and Weidner, H. (eds) (1989) *Environmental Policy in Japan*, Berlin: Edition Sigma Bohn.

Watanabe, C. (1997) "The Role of Technology in Energy/Economy Interactions: A View from Japan," in Y. Kaya and K. Yokobori (eds), *Environment, Energy, and Economy*, Tokyo: United Nations University Press, 199–231.

SHANE J. SCHVANEVELDT

environmental regulations

Before the 1970s, Japan's environmental policy focused on anti-pollution measures by directly controlling emissions from factories and power plants. Rapid growth in Japan in the 1970s and 1980s, however, led to increased pollution. Domestically, Japanese businesses were criticized for being concerned only for growth and for being the cause of pollution and ecological destruction. The attitude of Japanese firms led to lawsuits by victims of pollution. In the 1980s the focus of environmental policies shifted to automobiles and other vehicles. The Japanese government introduced several laws and regulations to deal with pollution caused by automobiles. There were also tougher regulations on diesel engine emissions. In 1993, new pollution laws and environmental regulations were introduced. These environmental regulations covered everything from air pollution and soil pollution to solid waste management treatment systems and hazardous waste emissions systems.

Not surprisingly, these new regulations have also led to rapid growth in the Japanese environmental system industry. Total production has been over ¥1.5 trillion in recent years. This is due to strong demand for replacement of environmental facilities constructed in the 1970s and for new systems that improve the quality of the environment. Solid waste treatment systems account for 40 percent of this demand. The market is dominated by demand from the government for new recycling technologies and by laws on recycling packages and containers. This has caused the Japanese industry for environmental systems to be a showcase for the most advanced technologies in the world, although US controls on hazardous emissions are tougher than the controls in Japan.

The Japan Environmental Association uses a life-cycle assessment (LCA) to determine if products are environmentally friendly. The Association considers products friendly when they use few resources, emit no waste during production, save energy, and are easily broken down to permit recycling. In 1996, the Association revised its "eco-mark" system to promote production and use of products that are environmentally friendly. Products that meet the LCA are allowed to display this new mark on their packaging.

In 1997 new recycling legislation was passed. The law divides responsibility for the separation and collection of containers and packaging between local government, businesses and consumers. Due to increasing household garbage, discarded cans, bottles, and plastic containers account for over 60 percent of garbage by volume and must now be recycled. By 2000, businesses using containers and packages must treat and recycle packages and containers. PET (polyethylene terephthalate) bottles are a problem since the government does not yet have the technology to recycle them, although some cities and municipalities already have separate collections of PET bottles (from 1.8 percent of container waste in 1995 to 14 percent in 2000, and expected to rise to a rate of 27 percent in 2005).

Dioxin pollution is another major environmental issue in Japan. Ninety percent of dioxin pollution comes from the incineration of garbage such as plastics (PCBs). The dioxins enter the atmosphere as soot particles falling into soil, rivers and oceans. They enter the food chain through drinking water, and fish and livestock used for human consumption. New legal regulations on dioxin emissions from refuse incineration were established in 1997 amending both the Waste Disposal Law and the Air Pollution Control Law.

Eco-business has seen new opportunities in Japan due to these environmental protection regulations. The **Ministry of International Trade and Industry** (MITI) predicts rapid growth in environmental support, waste and recycling, environmental conservation, environmental friendly energy, and environmental friendly products. By 2010, MITI expects eco-business in Japan to be a ¥3.5 trillion market.

See also: business ethics

TERRI R. LITUCHY

export and import of technology

Japan's rapid economic expansion, both in the years between the **Meiji restoration** (1868) and the Second World War and in the first three or four decades after the war, is often credited to its efficient utilization of technologies developed in the West. Japan is still the world's largest importer of technology. As Japan became a technology superpower in the 1970s, it also began to emerge as a significant exporter of technology. Today it is second only to the United States in the value of technology exported.

Prewar imports of technology

Japan began systematically importing technology in the seventh century when it brought in weaving, pottery, lacquer ware, mining, metallurgy and farming technologies from China. Technology was also acquired from Korea. In the late sixteenth century the Portuguese brought Western guns and artillery to Japan. The Japanese quickly developed the ability to produce their own firearms and even introduced some refinements.

During much of the Tokugawa Period (1603–1868) contact with the outside world was severely restricted. Foreign books (except for those on Christianity) however, could be brought in beginning in 1720. Since the Dutch were the only Westerners allowed to trade with Japan, it was Dutch-language books on Western science and technology that were imported. A government official produced a Dutch-Japanese dictionary in 1745. In 1774 a book on anatomy was translated into Japanese. The book demonstrated the universality of Western science and inspired translations of books on astronomy, physics, chemistry, and botany. In 1808 the government established a special office for the translation of Western books.

In 1853 and 1854 a US naval squadron under Commodore Perry visited Tokyo Bay to pressure the Japanese government to open Japan to trade. The squadron demonstrated such achievements of Western technology as the steam engine and the telegraph. The obvious military advantages that technology gave the Westerners caused both the central Tokugawa government and the regional rulers to strive to absorb military and related technologies as quickly as possible. Some ninety young Japanese were sent abroad to study Western technology and institutions. The Tokugawa government requested Dutch and French help to build facilities to make iron and build ships.

Efforts to assimilate Western technology reached a fever pitch during the Meiji Era (1868–1912). By 1873 some 250 young Japanese were abroad studying Western technology and administrative practices. The Ministry of Industry (Komusho, also called Ministry of Engineering) played a key role in the adoption of foreign technology from 1870–85. The Ministry and other parts of the Japanese government hired some two or three thousand foreign technical experts in the late nineteenth century. Englishmen were put in charge of Japan's rail and telegraph systems, and Germans served as experts on medicine and medical education. Large numbers of American and French technical advisors were also hired.

The foreign experts had the highest salaries in the Japanese government at the time. Providing for their transportation, housing and entertainment was also very expensive. By 1879 the high cost of the foreigners, plus the desire of the Japanese to become as independent as possible, led the government to move aggressively to replace the foreigners with Japanese who had studied technology abroad or who had been trained by the foreign employees.

The Japanese often found it necessary to make major adaptations before they could use foreign technology. In 1897, for example, the Japanese government planned a world-class integrated iron and steel works at Yawata. Since Germany had the world leading blast furnace technology at the time, Germans were hired to design the construction of the blast furnace and supervise its construction. German foremen and workers were also hired to supervise operations. The technology, however, was not suited to the types of coke available in Japan and the plant was forced to shut down. The Germans were sent home and Japanese successfully redesigned and operated the steel works. Japan's growing mastery of imported Western technology was further demonstrated in 1905 when the Japanese navy used wireless telegraphy to decisively defeat a Russian fleet.

Despite these successes, the Japanese sometimes had to rely on on-going foreign support to effectively use imported technology. In the electrical industry, for example, Japanese firms relied heavily on the capital, patents and technical guidance of Western firms. General Electric provided technology and took a stake in Toshiba. Mitsubishi Electric was formed with the participation of Westinghouse. Fujitsu was formed as a joint venture between Fuji Electric and Siemens.

Japan imported far more technology than it exported in the decades before the Second World War, but there were some consequential Japanese technology exports. Perhaps the best known of these was the sale of patent rights for the Toyota Automatic Loom to Platt Brothers of Great Britain in 1929. The proceeds financed Toyota's entry into the automobile business. Other prewar Japanese technologies, notably the Yagi antenna (invented in 1926), also came to be used widely around the world.

Despite the strong realization that Japan needed foreign technology to maintain its economic and military security, the Japanese periodically became concerned about the risk of being overly dependent on foreign technology. In 1896, for example, Japanese shipyards were forbidden to use imported ship parts. During the 1930s foreign firms such as

General Electric, Western Electric, and Westinghouse were forced to turn their Japanese operations over to their Japanese partners.

Postwar technology import control policies

In the years following the Second World War, Japan's leaders were again convinced that Japan needed to import technology to catch up with the West. At the time Japan suffered from chronic balance of payments deficits, and the government tightly controlled foreign currency. Firms wanting to import technology during the 1950s and 1960s had to get the foreign exchange to pay for it from the government. Approval was required from the most relevant Ministry, most often the **Ministry of International Trade and Industry** (MITI). Government staff reviewed the proposed agreements to ensure that the Japanese buyer was not paying too much or being unduly restricted in using the technology, and that the agreement was beneficial to the Japanese economy. Government controls were substantially eased in the 1960s as Japan joined the OECD and changed its status in the IMF, but the currency control laws remained in effect until 1980. Since then Japanese government controls over technology trade have been closer to those in other developed countries.

There is a long-standing controversy over whether the restrictive controls in the 1950s and 1960s benefited or harmed the Japanese economy. Some observers conclude that government intervention in technology import must have been harmful. They cite **Sony**'s import of transistor technology. MITI delayed Sony's agreement to import the technology from Western Electric because Sony was then a small and unknown company. While Sony did successfully import and commercialize the transistor, some argue that it might have done so more quickly and at lower cost without government intervention. They further suggest that there may have been other firms that failed to surmount bureaucratic barriers, costing Japan even greater economic success in the 1950s and 1960s. The Japanese-language literature mentions another instance where government intervention apparently raised costs to Japanese importers of technology. In 1958, two firms signed agreements to import polypropylene production

technology from Italy. MITI did not approve the agreements. When Japanese firms finally did import the technology the cost was substantially higher.

Those arguing that the technology import control policies benefited Japan point out that government intervention allowed a pooling of the limited experience of Japanese firms with international agreements, put government pressure on the side of the Japanese negotiators, kept Japanese firms from bidding against each other (raising the price of a technology), encouraged foreign firms to sell technology to Japanese firms (because of government guaranteed payments), and kept Japanese firms from using technology agreements to monopolize the Japanese markets. These claims are supported by well-documented cases in the steel and computer industries. It has also been pointed out that only two or three example of apparent harm caused by the policies have appeared in the literature.

Japan's technology imports

During the 1950s the Japanese government approved more than one thousand "A" technology import agreements (in which the effective life of the agreement was more than a year and payment was to be made in foreign currency). US firms were the technology suppliers for two-thirds of these agreements. About half the agreements were in just three industries: electrical/electronics, chemicals and steel/non-ferrous metals. The USA continues to supply about two-thirds of Japan's technology imports, though today most of the imports are in electronics and computer software.

Japan's postwar technology exports

Japan's technology exports were relatively stagnant through the 1950s, and overwhelmingly concentrated in Asia. In 1960 the Japanese steel industry achieved a breakthrough by signing its first major contract for the export of technology. The recipient of the technology was a Brazilian company, which paid nearly six million dollars for technical guidance in building a steel plant. In 1963 Japanese steel makers made their first technology exports to advanced Western countries, and in 1974 steel became Japan's first industry to achieve a technology trade surplus. The steel industry continued to generate large revenues for its technology as Japanese firms entered into technology agreements with firms in the United States and elsewhere. The construction and textile industries also enjoyed surpluses during the 1970s, but Japan had huge technology trade deficits in electronics, telecommunications and transportation.

By the late 1970s, Japan was second only to the United States in R&D spending and Japan's technology exports continued to increase during the 1980s and 1990s. In 1983 Japan achieved a surplus in automotive technology trade, and in 1993 in electronics. By the mid-1990s Japan had passed the UK to become the world's second largest exporter of technology after the USA. In the late 1990s Japan's annual technology exports were valued at about 70 billion dollars, compared to nearly five times that amount for the USA. Nearly half of Japan's technology exports (44 percent) went to the United States, but 34 percent went to Asia (especially Taiwan, South Korea, China and Thailand, which accounted for 22 percent of total exports). Some 85 percent of the exports were in automobiles and electrical goods/electronics.

There has been controversy over the benefits of Japan's technology export practices compared to those of other advanced nations. Hatch and Yamamura (1996) argue that Japanese firms carefully control the transfer of technology to other parts of Asia, allowing only the slow transfer of relatively old technologies. The result is an ever-widening gap between Japan and other Asian countries. Yamashita (1998) agrees that Japanese firms exercise more control in technology transfers, but characterizes this as allowing a more efficient transfer that benefits the recipients.

See also: industrial policy; science and technology policy

Further reading

Hatch, W. and Yamamura, K. (1996) *Asia in Japan's Embrace*, Cambridge: Cambridge University Press.

Lynn, L. (1982) *How Japan Innovates: A Comparison with the U.S. in the Case of Oxygen Steelmaking*, Boulder, CO: Westview Press.

—— (1998) "Japan's Technology-Import Policies in the 1950s and 1960s: Did They Increase Industrial Competitiveness?" *International Journal of Technology Management* 15(6/7): 556–67.

Ozawa, T. (1974) *Japan's Technological Challenge to the West, 1950–1974*, Cambridge, MA: MIT Press.

Partner, S. (1999) *Assembled in Japan: Electrical Goods and the Making of the Japanese Consumer*, Berkeley, CA: University of California Press.

Peck, M. and Tamura, S. (1976) "Technology," in H. Patrick and H. Rosovsky (eds), *Asia's New Giant*, Washington, DC: Brookings Institution, 525–85.

Samuels, R. (1994). *"Rich Nation, Strong Army:" National Security and the Technological Transformation of Japan*, Ithaca, NY: Cornell University Press.

Yamashita, S. (1998) "Japanese Investment Strategy and Technology Transfer in East Asia," in H. Hasegawa and G. Hook (eds), *Japanese Business Management*, London: Routledge, 61–79.

LEONARD H. LYNN

Export-Import Bank of Japan

Originally called the Japan Export Bank, Export-Import Bank of Japan (Nihon Yushutsunyuu Ginkou) was one of the principal government-funded financial institutions in Japan. Headquartered in Tokyo, it provided wide ranges of services, engaging primarily in overseas investment financing and trade financing.

The Japan Export Bank was established in 1950, but changed its name in 1952 to the Export-Import Bank of Japan when it expanded its activities to include import financing. The bank's principal activity was the provision of low-cost loans to support corporate growth. Such activities included, for instance, credits for exports of heavy industrial products and imports of raw materials in bulk as well as financing ships and industrial plants in order to promote the export of Japanese products. In the 1960s the bank provided loans to Japanese ventures for overseas investments and expanding of overseas resources. The Export-Import Bank of Japan also provided yen loans to developing countries in order to allow them to import from Japan, these loans in particular constituted a large portion of the bank's activities. The bank limited the uses of its loans to Japanese investors to three general purposes: (1) to finance the equity of ownership in overseas ventures; (2) to provide debt capital to overseas ventures; and (3) to finance the purchase of plants and equipment from Japanese firms, to be installed in overseas ventures.

The Export-Import Bank of Japan came under growing pressure from other countries, particularly from the United States, to make changes to its one-sided trade policies and its growing trade surpluses. As a result of foreign pressures, the bank began to develop some programs to assist in management of the global economy. In 1986 it began to work with the World Bank and the Asian Development Bank in co-financing loans to developing countries.

In October 1999 the Export-Import Bank of Japan merged with the Overseas Economic Cooperation Fund of Japan, forming the Japan Bank for International Cooperation (JBIC), a government financial institution facilitating cross-border economic cooperation. The purpose of the Japan Bank for International Cooperation is to contribute to the development of Japan and the international economy and community through undertaking lending and other financial operations. Among these operations are the promotion of Japanese exports, imports and Japanese economic activities overseas, the development of stability of the international financial order and the economic and social development of economic stability in developing areas. The Japan Bank for International Cooperation functions in accordance with the principle that it shall not compete with commercial financial institutions and has taken the general responsibility for: (1) financing to contribute to the promotion of Japan's exports or imports and overseas economic activities, and to the stability of international financial order; and (2) financing to contribute to economic and social development and the economic stability in overseas developing regions. It will also combine the knowledge and enterprise, which the two institutions have accumulated, and the synergy effect of the merger will hopefully prove beneficial to the Japan Bank of International Cooperation.

ALEXANDRA COHEN

F

Fair Trade Commission

Japan's Fair Trade Commission (FTC) is the country's sole **competition** policy agency, responsible for the enforcement of the nation's Antimonopoly Law as well as two additional statutes promoting protection of small business and consumers. The FTC, created in 1947 according to the mandate of occupying American forces after the Second World War, is based on the US independent commission-style of government agency. Its powers appear broad on paper, and include quasi-legislative (rule-making powers) and quasi-judicial functions (independent hearing and appeal procedures) in addition to its administrative role. In spite of its powers, however, the agency has been buffeted consistently by opposing forces for much of its history, thereby having a deleterious effect on the overall importance of competition policy in Japan.

Organization and function

Organizationally, the FTC is headed by a commission of five members appointed by the prime minister and confirmed by the Diet for five-year terms, one of whom acts as the chairman of the FTC. Since the early 1950s, appointments to the Commission traditionally have been made from former officials of a select group of government ministries. These patterns of appointments are widely perceived to have compromised the agency's independence. By the mid-1990s, however, these appointment patterns changed so that the industrial and finance ministries no longer had a dominant presence on the Commission. The agency is staffed by career civil servants who undertake the day-to-day work of the agency, although a small but significant number of these employees also have come from other ministries.

Japan's Antimonopoly Law has features similar to other such laws in advanced industrialized countries, including prohibition of private monopolization, unreasonable restraints of trade (cartels, boycotts, etc.), and unfair trade practices. The former two are punishable by administrative or criminal measures and, in the case of restraints of trade, by fixed surcharges on illegal activity. Measures against unfair trade practices are limited to orders to cease illegal activities and take appropriate remedies. The Antimonopoly Law was passed with additional provisions unique to Japan's competition policy regime, such as a ban on holding companies to prevent the re-formation of industrial groups, or *zaibatsu*.

The FTC also enforces unfair business practice laws. One helps provide small business with some protection from larger companies in their business dealings, and another protects consumers from misleading advertising and aggressive advertising promotions. It should be noted that the restrictions on promotions and premiums, while playing some consumer protection role, also appears to have limited competition in the retail sector.

History

The FTC has had a difficult history for much of its existence, even having been threatened with complete abolition from time to time, particularly during periods when Japan's conservative **Liberal Democratic Party** (LDP) has held a strong majority in the Diet. The introduction of US-inspired antimonopoly legislation in 1947 directly challenged pre-Second World War and in particular wartime industrial practices of government and industry-led control associations, turning Japan's industrial, political, and bureaucratic elite against the agency and its legislative mandate. The US Occupation's anti-*zaibatsu* program, including dissolution and restrictions under the Antimonopoly Law, also was an additional factor.

Conservative forces began consistent efforts from the late 1940s to emasculate competition policy through efforts such as weakening the Antimonopoly Law, drawing up legal exemptions to the Law, and circumventing the Law through the formation of cartels among businesses to be led by bureaucrats in other agencies. The FTC survived complete abolition through the 1950s and 1960s by weakening its standards, failing to take on high-profile cases, and appealing to small business and other groups to support the agency and its role.

The FTC re-emerged during the early 1970s when inflation and suspected price rises by cartels became an important political issue. The FTC took on a high-profile case against oil companies in the wake of the 1973 oil shock and followed with an active anti-cartel campaign. The attention enabled a strengthening of the Antimonopoly Law in 1977, including the addition of mandatory surcharges on cartel activity. As inflation faded and as the LDP emerged again as the dominant party in the 1980s, the FTC de-emphasized active enforcement in favor of a defensive program to encourage compliance with the law.

The rise of Japan's industrial might by the late 1980s brought international scrutiny of Japan's industrial structure and business practices that were perceived to keep foreign companies out of Japan's domestic market. Strong pressure was brought to bear on Japan by the United States to strengthen measures against anti-competitive practices. As a result, the FTC again emerged with a stronger profile. Cartel surcharges were raised, among other measures. The FTC also began stronger efforts to enforce the law, including intermittent use of referrals of criminal acts to Japan's Public Prosecutors Office. By the end of the 1990s, the dissolution of the Left in Japanese politics and an economic downturn enabled the repeal of the ban on holding companies. The FTC nonetheless remained able to continue with a cautious but moderate level of enforcement of the Law.

Current status

The FTC's overall profile in the Japanese government today is much improved from its position during the 1950s and 1960s. However, the agency remains among the more cautious competition policy agencies in advanced countries for a variety of institutional as well as political reasons. The fact that the FTC has been embattled for much of its existence has had a critical impact on the attention that Japanese companies have paid to competition policy in their overall business activities. This is particularly relevant because the agency, until very recently, effectively has controlled access to, interpretation of, and remedies and punishments under the Antimonopoly Law. Direct access to the courts to file Antimonopoly Law grievances now is allowed for lesser violations under unfair methods of trade provisions.

Further reading

Beeman, M. (1997) "Public Policy and Economic Competition in Japan," D.Phil Thesis, University of Oxford.

Hadley, E. (1970) *Antitrust in Japan*, Princeton, NJ: Princeton University Press.

Iyori, H. and Uesugi, A. (1994) *The Antimonopoly Laws and Policies of Japan*, New York: Federal Legal Publications.

Matsushita, M. (1993) *International Trade and Competition Law in Japan*, New York: Oxford University Press.

Tilton, M. (1996) *Restrained Trade*, Ithaca, NY: Cornell University Press.

MICHAEL BEEMAN

firm strategies for technology

Firm strategy for technology is roughly divided into goal setting in technology development and the formulation of the means to obtain the goals set. Setting a goal in this context means the selection of a technology domain to which firm resources are allocated. To formulate the means to acquire technologies, alternative methods such as in-house development, alliances with other companies, license contracts and acquisitions of companies are considered. In addition, the approach to innovation – whether a company achieves its targeted performance through means of radical innovation or by accumulating incremental innovations – could be included in the formulation of means.

Selection of technology domain

The key characteristic of Japanese companies in terms of the selection of technology domain is homogeneity with its competitors. Many companies tend to select a similar domain to that of their competitors. As a result, many unremarkable companies may compete against each other in the same industry. This occurs because firms believe that by mimicking competitors' technologies and products they can avoid being in a weak position in the market. This strategy seems to run contrary to the general theory of strategic management, which proposes that firms should accumulate distinct technical resources, and introduce differentiated products in the market. Lacking distinctive or differentiated products, Japanese firms often compete on the basis of price. But intensified price **competition** with homogeneous competitors is likely to decrease company profits, and hurt a company's ability to make long-term investments as well. In this sense, Japanese firm strategy is often regarded as irrational.

However, Japanese firms have succeeded in some industries by using a mimic strategy. For example, the Japanese color television industry was successful by adopting homogeneous technologies. As changes in televisions production technology began to occur with the adoption of transistors and integrated circuits, Japanese firms copied one another, while American firms did not follow suit. Led by Motorola, only a few US companies adopted these technological innovations early on. But the leading companies in Japan – **Matsushita**, **Sony**, **Toshiba**, and others – followed the

innovation of Hitachi immediately. As a result, intense competition in the product market occurred, and Japanese companies boosted their frequency of new **product development** in order to compete in a tough market. In turn, the cost performance of Japanese products was remarkably improved, leading to the defeat by Japanese companies of US competitors in US markets. Although the selection of similar technology can intensify competition in an industry, it can also lead to mutual learning among competitors and the development of related industries. As a result, products and manufacturing processes can be improved quickly in comparison with foreign competitors.

The matter of the homogeneous selection of technologies has sparked interest from a different direction in more recent times. The adoption of a unified technical standard in an industry, particularly in high-tech industries, has become important. The underlying reason for this tendency is the spread of products connected to the diffusion of its complementary goods, such as application software for personal computers (PCs). To produce these types of products, companies prefer developing and manufacturing products with a unified standard as opposed to having to compete among companies with different standards in the same market. A good illustration of competition over a technical standard is the well-known case of a videocassette recorder (VCR) standard among Japanese companies. In the 1970s the Betamax standard developed by Sony and VHS standard promoted by Matsushita and JVC competed head-to-head in the consumer VCR market. Though considered technologically inferior to Betamax, the VHS standard eventually won out. The major factor in VHS's predominance in the market was the spread of VHS-complementary goods: software and product. The VHS standard defeated the Betamax standard, even though it was introduced to the market much later than Betamax.

Means of technology acquisition

The means to acquire technology are: in-house development, alliances with other companies, license contracts and the acquisition of a company that has valuable technologies. From the end of the

Second World War to the 1960s, technology introduction by means of license contracts was the primary means by which Japanese firms accomplished their technology development goals. After the 1970s, however, the rate of in-house technology development was increased, which is preferable in terms of the long-term growth prospects of companies. In fact, new products developed by Japanese companies, such as the consumer VCR and facsimiles, have increased remarkably. Also in the field of intermediate goods, such as LCD and industrial robots, Japanese technology developed in-house has surged ahead of other countries.

However, in the 1980s and 1990s, companies began to focus on technical alliances and acquisitions. The speed of technology development has increased, while the ability to develop technology in-house remains relatively unchanged due to the long time it takes to develop technological capabilities in-house. Increasingly, Japanese firms have sought alliances with firms outside Japan. For example, a Japanese drug manufacturer, Takeda Chemical Industries, Ltd, tied up with Abbott Laboratories and succeeded in developing a new medicine for prostate cancer, Leuplin. However, compared with the behavior of firms in the United States, these methods are not as widespread in Japan.

Approach to technical innovation

In terms of their approach to technical innovation, Japanese companies focus on incremental innovation rather than radical innovation. With regard to technical innovation, although the introduction of epoch-making technology often attracts great attention and is viewed as being central to technological progress, the accumulation of incremental innovations often brings great progress in technological advances as well. Frequent introduction of new products with incremental innovations has the advantage of making use of the "learning by using" of customers and the experience of manufacturing in contributing to the progress of technology.

Many studies tend to view the technology orientation of Japanese firms as an inevitable consequence of Japanese institutions and customs, rather than that of deliberate strategic choice by corporate executives. Thus some researchers express doubts about the innovation capability of Japanese companies, especially with regard to their ability to achieve radical innovation. They argue that the Japanese system of training engineers, the labor market, the corporate culture and other features of the Japanese system create obstacles to pursuing a technology strategy that focuses on new radical technology development. However, it cannot be easily determined that one is better for the progress of technology than the other, and the tendency of adopting an incremental approach does not necessarily mean a low ability for technical innovation.

Further reading

Finan, W. F. and Frey, J. (1994) *Nihon no gijutsu ga abunai* (Japanese Technology at Bay), Tokyo: Nihonkeizai Shinbunsha.

Porter, M.E. (1985). *Competitive Advantage: Creating and Sustaining Superior Performance*, New York: The Free Press.

Rosenbloom, R. and Cusumano, M. (1987) "Technological Pioneering and Competitive Advantage: The Birth of the VCR Industry," *California Management Review* 29(4): 51–76.

Shintaku, J. (1994) *Nihon kigyo no kyoso senryaku* (Competitive Strategy of Japanese Corporations), Tokyo: Yuhikaku.

YASUO SUGIYAMA

5S campaign

The 5S campaign is a technique used by Toyota and other Japanese firms to establish and maintain a quality environment in the organization. The name stands for five Japanese words: *seiri, seiton, seiso, seiketsu,* and *shitsuke.*

Seiri means structure or organize. An example would be to throw away rubbish. *Seiton* means systematize or neatness. A typical example would be the quick retrieval of a document. *Seiso* means sanitize or cleanliness. It is an individual's responsibility to keep the workplace clean. *Seiketsu* is standardize or standardization. *Shitsuke* means self-discipline, in other words, following the 5S's daily.

TERRI R. LITUCHY

foreign aid

In line with postwar Japan's emphasis on non-military contributions to international society, Japan's foreign aid has been limited to official development assistance (ODA) and disaster relief aid. Since its origins in early postwar bilateral reparation agreements, Japan's foreign aid grew to be the single largest aid program in the late 1980s, and it retains that status as of 2001 despite growing domestic pressure for budget cuts.

The Potsdam Declaration (1945) which set the Allied Powers conditions for peace with Japan called on the latter to pay war reparations to all victims of Japanese wartime aggression. The San Francisco Peace Treaty (1951) narrowed this by limiting Japan's reparation obligation only to countries that suffered losses as a direct consequence of Japanese occupation. As postwar Japan re-established ties to its Asian neighbors, the reparation obligation in each case became a key initial hurdle to normalized bilateral relations.

Japan's situation at that time played a critical role in determining its reparations policy and subsequent ODA policy. As a war-devastated country seeking to rebuild its industrial base and recapture export markets, Japan decided to make reparations in kind, not in cash. Reparations would typically come in the form of industrial plant and equipment. This assisted the recipient's industrialization and generated export orders for Japanese industry. The Japanese government also adopted a request-based system. This required the recipient country to submit specific project requests to Tokyo for review. But because the reparation countries often did not have the technical expertise to identify and design industrial projects, in practice Japanese businesses active in these markets would fill this void.

Japan joined the Development Assistance Committee (DAC) of the Organization for Economic Cooperation and Development (OECD) in 1961. DAC was formed at American initiative to coordinate the Western countries' economic assistance efforts and raise its effectiveness. Japan's reparation programs were recognized as economic assistance, but they came under critical scrutiny within DAC because of their thinly veiled export promotion emphasis. Pressure was put on Japan to make new aid commitments that were more concessional and genuinely beneficial to the recipient economy. Over the years the DAC and its members have played a key role in moving Japan's ODA away from its original character.

Through its aid programs Japan has offered developing countries valuable access to its high quality industrial products and engineering services. In return for granting this benefit Japan has been able to gain recipient cooperation in addressing Japan's problems of foreign resource dependence and competitiveness in a global economy. Over the years Japan has used aid projects to secure stable long-term supplies of critical energy resources, raw materials, and food resources. With the emergence of the borderless economy Japan has used its aid to help Japanese firms globalize production by helping developing countries build industrial parks and regulatory environments hospitable to Japanese firms seeking to move production overseas.

Japan also offered its aid program to the West as an alliance contribution during the Cold War. Starting from the mid-1960s Japan offered aid as support for US containment policy in Asia. In the 1970s and 1980s it offered rapid growth in its aid spending as a non-military contribution to winning the Cold War and as a salve for trade friction with its western trading partners. In the 1990s Japan attempted to use its aid to gain a larger role in international security matters by promulgating new aid principles in 1991 that conditioned ODA upon the recipients' development, procurement, and exports of weapons. It followed this up with a symbolic and temporary cut in grant aid to China after that country's nuclear bomb test in 1995. In the aftermath of the Asian financial crisis of 1997–8 Japan made new funding pledges for Asian currency stability. At the start of the new millennium, Japan is emphasizing the use of its aid to help narrow the so-called digital divide and to address problems of the heavily indebted developing countries.

On the domestic front, the Japanese government has confronted widening calls for greater ODA transparency and reform from the late 1980s to the present. It attempted to deal with this by producing an ODA Program Outline in 1992 that laid down a broad and flexible set of policy principles. In response to pressures for increased effectiveness and breadth of concern Japan moved to include non-governmental organizations (NGOs) in the identification and implementation of aid projects and programs, and aid to address environmental problems became more salient in aid policy in the 1990s. Continuing aid scandals and revelations of misuse, however, along with tightening budgetary constraints throughout the 1990s led to the first ever ODA budget cut in 1997. The prospect at present is for arrested budget growth and perhaps a gradual decline in real spending terms.

Japan's aid administration has long been noted for its opaque and bureaucratic character. The Foreign Ministry has the role of representing Japan's aid policy to external actors. Behind this window, however, the realities of policy making are more complicated. Aid policy is coordinated inside the domestic political system by four central government bureaucratic actors, i.e., the Ministry of Foreign Affairs, the **Ministry of Finance** (MOF), the **Ministry of International Trade and Industry** (MITI), and the Economic Planning Agency. In addition, some fourteen other main government ministries and agencies play more specialized roles in those aspects of aid that fall into their respective areas of competence. With respect to policy implementation, the Japan International Cooperation Agency (JICA) administers most of Japan's grant aid and the Japan Bank for International Cooperation administers the bulk of loan aid.

In 1999 net ODA disbursements totaled $15.3 billion with almost two-thirds allocated to countries in East and South Asia. This regional distribution reflects Japan's traditional pattern of aid-giving. In other respects, however, the breakdown of Japanese aid has changed. The balance of bilateral and multilateral aid has shifted from roughly a 2:3 ratio to a 3:4 ratio in the 1990s, reflecting perhaps some degree of Japanese disappointment at its weak leadership role in multilateral institutions relative to the size of its financial contributions. With respect to bilateral aid, the share of technical aid has increased markedly to over 30 percent while the share of loans has decreased to little more than 40 percent. This reflects a shift in emphasis away from heavy infrastructure projects toward debt relief, technical training, and programs to improve the welfare of poorer population segments.

Further reading

Arase, D. (1995) *Buying Power: The Political Economy of Japan's Foreign Aid*, Boulder, CO: Lynne Rienner.

Development Assistance Committee, Organisation for Economic Cooperation and Development (annual) *DAC Journal: Development Cooperation Report*, Paris: OECD.

Economic Cooperation Bureau, Ministry of Foreign Affairs (annual) *Japan's ODA Annual Report*, Tokyo, Japan: Ministry of Foreign Affairs.

DAVID M. ARASE

foreign companies in Japan

The history of foreign companies in Japan parallels the development and transformation of Japan's economy, and also serves as a proxy for its increasing openness to foreign ideas and cultures. Very few foreign companies were active in Japan prior to the Second World War, since Japan made few efforts to open itself to foreign products, its consumers or middle class were very small and not very exposed to non-Japanese cultures, and Japan's distance from other markets made the conduct of business there difficult. Nevertheless, a few companies did persist in at least establishing relationships and business in Japan. Of those, many were invited to Japan to provide specific know-how or product knowledge that Japan could not provide for itself. For instance, the Swiss food giant Nestlé first opened a representative office in Yokohama in 1913 in order to provide milk products to Japan's populace. Other foreign companies operating in Japan during the 1920s and 1930s, but which had origins in the countries allied against Japan in the Second World War, were shut down or were effectively banished from Japan during the war.

After the war, foreign majority ownership of Japanese companies was prohibited by law, but the presence of military government and soldiers from the victorious powers influenced the growth of an environment of admiration for foreign lifestyles and, as a result, for foreign products. Many of the largest and most profitable foreign companies in Japan today, for example, first set up operations in Japan or began exporting to Japan in the two decades following the war.

As Japan's society grew increasingly affluent in the 1950s and 1960s, interest in Japan among globalizing foreign companies grew, and during many of those years Japan ran a trade deficit. But Japanese companies and government policies designed to completely protect key domestic industries (such as agriculture and distribution) combined to ensure that foreign companies would not be able to dominate specific industries and destroy their mostly smaller domestic competitors. For example, a 1956 Department Store Law protected small retailers and strengthened their ability to keep unwanted competitors out of their community. And revisions to Japan's *Shogyo Ho*, or **Commercial Code**, during the 1960s encouraged domestic companies to issue new shares and place them with friendly customers, suppliers and companies in their **industrial groups**. Not only would this strengthen *keiretsu* ties, but it would also provide insurance against unwanted foreign takeover attempts. As a result, the few foreign companies that were allowed to set up wholly-owned subsidiaries in Japan, such as IBM in 1960, were forced to license most or all of their basic patents and technologies to their eventual Japanese competitors as a condition of doing so. Or, like the foreign oil companies, they were allowed to set up operations for the specific purpose of ensuring Japan's access to essential commodities and supplies. Other successful major foreign companies formed **joint ventures** in Japan, such as Hewlett-Packard with Yokogawa Electric and McDonald's with Fujita. A number of Chinese and Korean-owned businesses also set up operations in Japan during this time; today they account for the majority of foreign companies in Japan.

Many foreign companies soon learned that the dynamics of **competition** in Japan were different from those they were used to in their home markets or other markets where they competed. The willingness of Japanese companies to accept lower

profits in order to obtain greater market share, the existence of exclusionary buying networks among Japanese producers and suppliers, the existence of a host of "non-tariff" or administrative barriers to trade and investment, the existence of a complex and multi-tiered physical **distribution system** for many different types of products, the often greater importance of relationships, quality and service (instead of price) in buying decisions, and opaque and often arbitrary regulatory guidance and decision making, have all combined to cause difficulties for a variety of foreign companies seeking to grow their businesses in Japan. Occasionally these problems attained a high profile or became entangled with domestic politics, as in the case of the Lockheed bribery scandal that caused the resignation of the Japanese prime minister in 1976, but more frequently foreign companies like Procter & Gamble grew to appreciate the need to modify or design their products specifically for Japan, or manufacture in Japan rather than try to import. Or in the case of General Motors, to put the steering wheel on the right rather than the left.

In the 1970s and 1980s, certain foreign products and brands grew popular with Japan's middle-class society, including German luxury cars such as BMW, French and Italian beauty and fashion brands such as Louis Vuitton and Gucci, and US consumer and food brands like McDonald's and Coca-Cola. Increases in tourism abroad by Japanese families, and a strong yen, helped expose Japanese families to foreign brands for the first time. But Japan's growing affluence in the 1980s, its trade surplus with the rest of the world, and its increasing acquisitions or establishment of operations in its traditional export markets, increased the interest of other countries in stimulating structural changes in Japan's domestic market that would stimulate domestic consumption, increase importation of foreign goods, and lower the trade surplus. This resulted in many cases of friction between Japanese and foreign companies competing in the same industry, and also between foreign governments and the government of Japan. Negotiations between governments and among governments and specific industries often resulted in explicit agreements by Japan to increase imports, loosen regulations or 'non-trade barriers, open specific industries for foreign investment, reduce restrictions on foreign ownership, protect intellectual property, curtail exports, or implement reforms to give foreign companies a 'level playing field' when competing in Japan. A variety of such negotiations, involving numerous industries ranging from textiles in the early 1980s to Internet access in the late 1990s, have taken place over the past two decades and continue today, and have collectively had a major impact on the ability of foreign companies to enter and grow their companies in Japan.

Japan's capital market development also played a role in foreign companies' Japan strategies (see **capital markets**), as foreign firms such as IBM which had major Japanese operations took their Japanese units public in the 1970s and early 1980s as a way of emphasizing their dedication to the local market and solidify their ties to customers and suppliers. The popularity of listing in Japan died down in the early 1990s as Japan's stock market fell, but picked up again in the late 1990s as technology companies such as Oracle listed shares of their Japan operations on the local market. Today, the existence of NASDAQ Japan demonstrates the involvement of foreigners in Japan's capital market institutions.

At present, foreign companies are entering and growing in Japan in a variety of ways, using numerous strategies and tactics to increase their prospects of success. Smaller firms or those with niche products, technologies or services often contract with middlemen of various kinds (such as agents, representatives, distributors or webmalls). Larger companies (such as General Motors, Starbucks, and Unisys) are able to arrange partnerships and alliances in Japan, which may or may not include the formation of joint ventures or the taking of equity in their Japanese partner. For companies seeking to acquire major positions in the Japanese market immediately, mergers and acquisitions or transactions which provide operating control of an already existing Japanese company (such as Renault with Nissan) have become far more frequent, and the availability of distressed companies (or those excessively burdened by their debt) and those open to management buyouts has increased markedly in recent years (companies such as Cargill, Merrill Lynch and General Electric have made outright acquisitions of major bankrupt companies in recent years).

Foreign companies (such as AutoLiv and other global automotive systems suppliers) are also increasingly using relationships established first in their native regions with Japanese manufacturers operating abroad, to expand into Japan with customer relationships already established. Those wishing to establish new operations on the ground are able to take advantage of the availability of qualified native staff, as well as lower costs for **advertising**, office space, travel, staff and entertainment. Still other companies like US-based Boeing have established and maintained significant Japanese business while successfully avoiding the creation of Japanese competition, by making potential Japanese competitors like **Mitsubishi** and Kawasaki Heavy Industries significant suppliers to their commercial airplane manufacturing operations.

Foreign companies can rely on a variety of organizations and programs to support their operations and employees in Japan. Japan is the only major economy whose government has established an agency whose specific objective is to increase the level of imports to Japan, encourage foreign direct investment in the country, and otherwise provide assistance to foreign companies seeking to do business in Japan. The **Japan External Trade Organization** (JETRO) was initially created to promote Japanese exports, but now operates offices around the world and all over Japan to assist foreign companies and help them make the contacts they need to increase their Japanese business. Among its various actions, it promotes the existence of specific "foreign access zones," which offer incentives for foreign companies which choose to establish operations in specific, often rural, prefectures. It also provides temporary office space, library facilities, and other services helpful primarily to small and medium-sized foreign companies. Other Japanese national government bodies, such as Japan Development Bank, provide financing or offer specific programs, incentives and discounts designed to encourage investment by foreign companies, including large manufacturers, in Japan. And individual prefectures and municipalities often sponsor their own programs designed to ease the entry or investment of foreign companies in their regions.

Many of the countries whose companies have come to Japan in significant numbers have themselves established both government and/or non-profit support organizations and chambers of commerce in Japan. Organizations such as the American Chamber of Commerce in Japan (ACCJ), the European Business Community Organization in Japan, and Deutsche Industrie und Handelskammer in Japan (DIHKJ) are examples of membership organizations providing information services, programs and events for their respective business communities in Japan. In addition, often specific states, regions or provinces of a country establish offices in Japan, both to promote the Japan business interests of their home companies, as well as to seek Japanese investment in their state and prefecture abroad.

Today, certain foreign companies dominate their industries in Japan. Coca-Cola obtains fully 20 percent of its global operating profit from Japan, despite a host of competitors in Japan's various beverage markets. Microsoft holds greater than a 90 percent share of the PC operating system market in Japan. American Family Life Assurance Company (AFLAC) receives more than 80 percent of its business from its Japanese sales of cancer and other specialty health insurance. Service industries such as healthcare, nursing, eldercare, financial services, Internet, and environmental technology are in many cases wide open and solicitous of foreign technology and investment. Early in 2001 a British company, BS Group, made an acquisition in one of Japan's largest yet most traditional industries, that of *pachinko*, and it is rare today to find a Japanese industry in which foreign companies do not participate at least marginally.

On the other hand, certain Japanese industries have proven too difficult or inaccessible for foreign companies to make significant inroads to date. These include the **construction industry**, the **telecommunications industry** dominated by the Japanese government through its (until recently) majority ownership in dominant telephone carrier **Nippon Telegraph and Telephone** (NTT), and the agriculture industry. In automobiles, foreign car brands still only achieve (as of 2000) 6 percent share of all vehicles sold in Japan. In fact, foreign companies play a much smaller overall role in Japan's economy, and account for a much smaller proportion of total employment, than in other developed economies in which they compete.

Nevertheless, because of relatively low share to date in Japan, and the recent weakness of an increasing number of previously formidable domestic competitors, foreign companies may find Japan's enormous market to be one of their last great growth markets as the new century dawns.

JAY NELSON

foreign workers

Japan continues to have the most homogeneous population of all major industrial nations in the world. Approximately 3 percent of Japan's overall population could be described as other than culturally, ethnically, and racially Japanese, and this 3 percent is made up primarily of Koreans and Chinese. Both Taiwan and Korea were long-term colonies of Japan until the Second World War, and many of these Chinese and Koreans in Japan today were forced to migrate to Japan with the labor shortage during the war. Most of these people have remained in Japan in subsequent generations but continue to hold Korean or Taiwanese citizenship, partly because of Japan's highly restrictive naturalization laws.

The number of foreign workers in Japan, however, has been growing in recent years. At first the increase in foreign workers was induced by the economic boom of the 1980s. Although Japan is currently experiencing a severe economic recession, this trend persists; the number of foreign workers is now over 600,000, or about 1 percent of the nation's working population. To a large degree, the need for foreign workers persists even during Japan's long economic stagnation from the early 1990s because, as is common with advanced industrial nations, the more affluent and well-educated Japanese population is unwilling to perform unattractive jobs which are characterized by the so called 3Ks: *kiken* (dangerous), *kitanai* (dirty), and *kitsui* (demanding). Japan faces a looming crisis because of a rapidly aging population due to a serious drop in the birth rate and an increasing life expectancy that has already put

Japan ahead of all other nations. This looming labor shortage crisis is made more critical for Japan's future because typical solutions of immigration and increased female labor participation are culturally resisted in Japan.

Immigration

During the mid-1980s and 1990s Japan began exporting jobs to Southeast Asia as the yen dramatically increased in value. If Japan is to keep existing factories and offices operating in Japan and stop short of moving most production to other countries, the immigration of foreign workers into Japan would seem the most logical solution. This is a solution all of the advanced industrial nations in Europe and North America have followed to at least some degree. But it is a solution that creates extensive resistance among the Japanese people. Japanese government surveys continue to show that Japanese people are uncomfortable among foreigners and the unfavorable treatment many foreign workers have received in Japan in recent years has caused public conflict.

When Japan experienced a serious labor shortage during the period of rapid industrialization of its economy in the mid-1960s, there was a strong demand to import foreign workers from countries such as Korea and Taiwan. However, the Japanese labor minister at the time argued against this idea, since he feared that the importation of foreign laborers might deter the nation from promoting the welfare of domestic workers and improving working conditions. Then again the same decisions were made by subsequent labor ministers in the 1970s. Japan managed without importing foreign laborers, partly thanks to the massive introduction of labor saving technologies in various industries, as well as a large labor pool in rural areas. There is growing awareness, however, that sooner or later the looming labor shortage because of the "baby bust" will demand more foreign workers.

By the late 1980s, the Japanese Diet approved several amendments to its Immigration Control and Refugee Recognition Law that became effective in 1990. The new law expands the number of job categories for which the country will accept foreign workers; from eighteen categories to a total of twenty-eight categories. These

are mostly professional categories such as lawyers, accountants, medical personnel, and researchers. However, the law also attempts to tighten up regulations and control the inflow of unskilled and semi-skilled foreign workers. It imposes sanctions on those who try to recruit or hire illegal unskilled foreign workers. The increase in the number of legal residence and work categories allows a variety of professional workers as well as the descendants of Japanese immigrants abroad, up to the third generation, to work and reside legally in Japan for a specified period of time.

In terms of controlling illegal immigration, the new law has had a temporary deterrent effect. Before the law took effect, about 30,000 illegal workers left Japan for fear of arrest. The new visa agreement made it very difficult to obtain a visa, and contributed to the reduction of the number of visitors.

The new law also allows some unskilled labor in through the following categories: (1) company trainees, which has become a way for employers to bring in low-wage foreign workers for unskilled, manual labor jobs where little training is involved; and (2) students of post-secondary (except for university) institutions, including language and vocational schools. They can work for a limited number of hours per week.

Under this law, the only group of foreigners who can legally work full-time in simple labor jobs in Japan is *nikkeijin*, foreigners with Japanese ancestry. The legal status of *nikkeijin* workers led to the replacement of illegal foreigners with *nikkeijin* by many companies. Even with these provisions created for employers to obtain unskilled workers, Japan still maintains the position that the nation does not allow unskilled laborers. Thus, the new law has been criticized because it does not directly address the labor shortage in unskilled labor jobs.

Further reading

Kitagawa, T. (1992) "Social Research on Japanese South American Immigrant Workers in Oizumi-machi, Gunma Prefecture: The Settling Down Motivation and Infrastructure for Acceptance," in K. Yamashita (ed.), *Hito no Kokusaika ni kansuru Soogooteki Kenkyuu* (Comprehensive Research of

Internationalization of People), Tokyo: Department of Sociology, Tokyo University.

Komai, H. (1991) "Are Foreign Trainees in Japan Disguised Cheap Laborers?" *Migration World Magazine* 20: 13–17.

Morita, K. and Sassen, S. (1994) "The New Illegal Immigration in Japan 1980–1992," *International Migration Review* 28: 153–63.

Murashita, H. (1999) *Gaikokujin Roodoosha Mondai no Seisaku to Ho* (Government Polities and Laws Regarding Foreign Worker Problems), Osaka: Keizai Hooka Daigaku Shuppan Bu.

MEIKA CLUCAS

Fuji Photo Film

Fuji Photo Film Co., Ltd was established on January 20, 1934. Fuji Photo began as a division of Dainihon Celluloid Company. At that time, Dainihon Celluloid was attempting to cooperate with Kodak, Inc. of the United States in order to learn new techniques of film production and processing, because it lacked the technological sophistication necessary to compete. However, Kodak refused to help, and Fuji Photo went on to learn how to produce photo film on its own. As the company grew and developed, it diversified into many film-related businesses, globalized and became the one of the largest photo film companies in the world.

Currently, Fuji Photo is a global company with over 37,551 employees worldwide, distributed across ninety-two subsidiaries. Fuji Photo's capital stands at ¥40,363 million as of March 31, 1999, with net sales ¥1,437,810 million and net income of ¥71,540 million for the fiscal year ending March 31, 1999. Fuji Photo's businesses include imaging systems, photo finishing systems and information systems. These activities are spread across divisions: general photo and imaging, advanced photo systems, camera and movie film, digital photo systems (Fuji developed the first digital camera in 1988), recording media (including video tapes and CDs), office imaging information systems, printing systems, medical instruments, and high-functional industrial material.

Within the global photo film industry, Fuji Photo holds the largest market share in Japan (70 percent) and ranks second in the world. Its international success started over fifty years ago when Fuji Photo began an optical products export business in 1949. Fuji Photo began exporting photo film to Asia and South America in 1954, slowly developing its overseas markets. During this time, Fuji Photo took on the role as exemplar for other Japanese companies that followed its lead in internationalizing operations and services. By taking a leadership role, Fuji Photo dominated the photo film market in Japan by 1960. In 1962, Fuji Photo Film developed a partnership with Xerox UK to form what is now considered to be one of the most successful joint venture companies in the history of business, Fuji Xerox. This joint venture project helped Fuji Photo to solidify its international presence and reform its image over the next few years.

Future growth for Fuji Photo will depend on the strength of their existing operations around the world. It plans to expand its digital based business as part of a drive to dominate "imaging and information." So far, success within this growth industry has been mixed. Fuji Photo has 20 percent market share in digital cameras in the world, which, although high, places it third compared to its Japanese rivals, Olympus and **Sony**. Fuji Photo's goal for the future is to be number one in the world in the digital imaging business.

Further reading

Arai, T. (1995) *The Real Ability of the Lion, Fuji Film,* The Nikkan Kogyo Shinbun, Ltd.

Barron, D. (1997) "Integrated Strategy, Trade Policy, and Global Competition," *California Management Review* 39(2): 145.

Fuji Photo Film Co., Ltd. (1984) *50 Years History of Fuji Photo Film,* Tokyo Fuji Shoshun Fuirumu Kabushiki Kaisha.

OGIWARA TAKESHI
MARGARET TAKEDA

Fukuzawa, Yukichi

Born in 1835 in southern Kyushu, Yukichi Fukuzawa was perhaps the most influential man of the Meiji era who did not serve in government. He was trained in "Dutch Learning," the study of Western society, literature and science through books and materials introduced into Japan via Dutch traders who had restricted trade with Japan on a small island at Nagasaki. After teaching Dutch in Edo (present-day Tokyo), he switched over to a study of English in response to the influx of foreigners involved in trading at Yokohama. In 1860 and 1862 he accompanied embassies to the USA and Europe respectively. Upon his return he founded a school in Edo which, in time, became **Keio University**, the leading private university in Japan in terms of educating top business leaders. He subsequently published, in 1875, *The Encouragement of Learning*, which laid out his ideas on education. More than 700,000 copies of the book were sold.

ALLAN BIRD

G

GAISHIKEI KIGYOU *see* foreign companies in Japan

genba-shugi

Genba-shugi literally means "shop-floorism." This is a management philosophy that dictates that, as far as possible, the process of production of goods and services must be controlled at the shop-floor level by shop people. The set of policies and practices designed for implementing this idea is called the shop-floor approach, and is commonly observed in Japanese factories. *Genba-shugi* includes a variety of participative and bottom-up approaches used for managing the process of production based on empowerment of the shop workers and delegation of decision-making authority to the shop-floor level. *Genba* indicates the "actual site" where all important processes take place, and people who run the *genba* are considered to have full power and responsibilities for controlling what is going on there. Therefore, to successfully implement this idea, systematic delegation of authority from management and engineering sections to *genba* leaders and workers is indispensable. Also important is empowerment of the shop through extensive training of *genba* workers in the skills and knowledge of production management, and sharing day-to-day business and production-related information with them. In other word, systematic human resource development at the shop-floor level and extensive information sharing by managers and engineers with shop people constitute critical conditions for practicing *genba-shugi* successfully.

The power exercised by production teams in Japanese shops is not derived from the institutionalized group autonomy embedded in the work group which seeks to maintain independent authority relative to management, as is the Scandinavian model of autonomous work groups. Rather, power is delegated by management to the shop-floor level on the basis of established accountability of the shop, and in terms of policies and targets set by management. Thus, *genba-shugi* works effectively when management deploys set policies with clear goals of production to which *genba* teams commit. In this sense, *genba-shugi* is a method of shop management co-operation for the accomplishment of goals of production.

In Japan, the tradition of corporate unionism helped co-operation between management and the shop develop very quickly after the Second World War, based on the idea *of genba-shugi*. The concept also facilitated a "win-win" spirit within the firm between management and employees. Both parties recognized that responding to market needs quickly by providing reliable products with relatively low costs was essential to winning and growing in competitive markets. Therefore, all parties concerned in the firm – managers, engineers, technicians, and operating workers – started to explore methods for responding to market needs by studying through **quality control circles** and experimenting based on ***kaizen*** activities at the shop-floor level. The fruits of their co-operation were shared through the other components of the Japanese style of management, namely **lifetime employment**, seniority-based wage increases and promotion, biannual bonuses, welfare provisions and so forth.

In Japan, the *genba* is recognized as the ultimate source of competitive strength and all efforts are placed on improving production processes in order to perfect *genba-shugi*. Consequently, the shop sometimes experiences increasing pressure, and stress increases. When this happens, the weight of expectations associated with *genba-shugi* will become excessive for team members and work will become overwhelming (see **karoshi**)

Organization for the practise of *genba-shugi*

Hanada and Yoshikawa (1991) characterize the organization for *genba-shugi* practices in Japan as being soft, having flexible boundaries, sustained by face-to-face communication networks and implementing extensive on-the-job training, compared to the hard, hierarchical, manual-based and occupational skill-based organizations of Western society. In other words, in order to practice *genba-shugi*, the organization of factories must be constructed by overlapping roles in which task-related skills, knowledge, information and responsibilities can be shared extensively, so that all people concerned particularly managers, foremen and operators, can co-operate easily through efficient interpersonal communication networks. Likewise, Wakabayashi and Graen (1991) demonstrated that a transplant organization developed by a company in the **Toyota** group in the USA was based on empowered teams with technical and information support provided by supervisors, managers and staff engineers. They pointed out that human resource development for establishing effective team-based factory organization in the cross-cultural context was a key to successful transfer of the **Toyota production system** (TPS) to the USA.

Commonly, a team consists of one team leader, one or two sub-leaders and ten to fifteen operating workers called associates. One supervisor or foreperson supervises several teams. Roughly 20–30 associates work under the supervisor. Since a team leader and sub-leader(s) are synonymous with *hancho* and *kumicho* of the home plant respectively in terms of position roles and functions, developing a *genba* organization with a Japanese-style team structure was considered to be the foundation on which further technology transfer would take place

in order to practice *genba-shugi* production in the USA.

To effect a transfer of *genba-shugi*, this firm first categorized knowledge and skills considered mandatory for running the *genba* shop and then organized them into a team structure as follows (see Table 1)

The above arguments suggest that empowerment of a team comprised of qualified team members is a key to this type of shop-floor approach. Particularly, a powerful leader must possess appropriate qualifications of extensive quality control skills and management knowledge, problem-identifying and solving skills, long-range planning skills, all practical skills related to work subordinates are conducting, skills of training subordinates, writing manuals, conducting *kaizen* improvement, handling emergencies and so forth. It is clear these skills overlap with those of engineers and managers. Therefore, engineers and managers must be able to work closely with shop sub-leaders and associates in order to run the shop smoothly. *Genba-shugi* is impossible without teams empowered with management authorities through delegation, competent team leaders and qualified team members organized into a soft and overlapping work system. In particular, continuous development of team members through extensive knowledge-sharing and skill is essential for successful implementation of a shop-floor approach.

Practices associated with *genba-shugi*

Practices conducted at the shop-floor level are closely associated with policies and goals set by management. *Houshin-kanri* (policy deployment) is one of the methods by which management policies and specific goals of production are delivered to the shop, with the provision of necessary resources and authority for achieving them. Managers, supervisors and engineers monitor the production process and assist the *genba* workers in realizing policies and goals. Normally, quality improvement and cost reduction are the two major areas where policies and goals are set.

First, *genba-shugi* must be initiated through empowerment of team members. To build team capabilities, members are developed through a multi-job-holding program where, theoretically

Table 1: Qualifications for team associates and a team leader for *genba-shugi*

Knowledge and skills	Associates	Sub-leader	Team Leader
Knowledge	Basic SQC skills; fundamental job process/ knowledge	Standard method of work and basic knowledge of management	Knowledge of SQC and plant operation: broad knowledge of management
Judgement	Give proper solution to normal problems	Can solve routine problems; think of effects on other departments	Analyze and solve non-routine problems; consider effects on company
Planning	Makes suggestions for improvement	Implement small suggestions and ideas	Implement long range plans that affect other areas
Interpersonal relations	Effective communication with peers and supervisors	Solve problems with peers and supervisors	Communicate effectively at all levels for problem solving
Skills	Can perform varied procedures with standard quality	Perform complicated and varied procedures with high precision	All skills required within the work unit
Direction/ Training	Self-direction and training	Train subordinates under supervisor's direction	Train associates and sub-leaders
Example of work	Operate complex machinery, problem finding and improvement suggestions	Handles emergency, identify quality problems and directs tasks for associates	Write operating manuals, promote improvement, handle emergencies and train/direct others

speaking, everybody becomes capable of handling everyone else's job by going through a planned job rotation and on-the-job training. Multiple job holding by multi-skilled workers makes possible interchangeable job assignment. It also helps each person detect mistakes made by others, and encourages fixing them before the process is completed. These practices also lead to members feeling a sense of belonging to an effective team and further nurturing a team spirit.

Second, maintaining *genba* in a clean and orderly manner becomes an important responsibility for each team member. Typically, the 5Ss are practiced for this purpose: *seiri* (orderliness), *seiton* (aligning), *seisou* (sweeping), *seiketsu* (cleanliness) and *shitsuke* (discipline). These 5Ss constitute preconditions for

implementing further cost saving and quality production programs in *genba-shugi* (see **5S campaign**).

Third, a variety of team-based small group activities can be practiced for quality improvement and cost reduction at the shop-floor level. QCC (quality control circle) and *kaizen* (incremental improvement) activities are two common ones. These programs become engines and foundations for the more extensive TQM (total quality management) or TQC program for the entire firm, which must be rooted within team activities at the shop-floor level.

Fourth, entire production systems such as Toyota's TPS that incorporate **just-in-time** and **kanban** practices must depend on the *genba-shugi* philosophy. Since the ultimate goal of TPS is deploying policies and empowering teams to enable them to satisfy market needs in technical and cost-related issues by improving the quality and reducing *muda* (waste) of all kinds (materials, energy, defects, efforts, time, transport, etc.), *genba-shugi* must be pursued to its maximum benefit. Moreover, what is known as *jidouka* (self-control) systems in TPS involving FMS (flexible manufacturing systems), fail-proof devices, an *andon* (lantern) line-stop mechanism all depend on initiatives of empowered teams at the shop-floor level.

Finally, in future, *genba-shugi* practices will increase in importance because employees are becoming more and more empowered and organizations are becoming flatter. Management is talking more directly with employees at the shop-floor level. Moreover, information technology and the evolution of new organization systems are changing the nature of the shop and *genba-shugi*.

MITSURU WAKABAYASHI

general trading companies

General trading companies (*sogo shosha*) are traditionally defined as integrated international trading enterprises engaged in importing and exporting a wide range of merchandise. *Sogo shosha* themselves like to claim that an increasing proportion of their profit comes from investment in various projects around the world, undertaken not only to boost trading relationships but also for pure capital gain. This shift to investment is the latest in a series of business transitions by *sogo shosha*, who have been declared obsolete in every decade since the 1960s but have so far managed successfully to reinvent themselves, with only a few casualties along the way.

Although *sogo shosha* are usually considered to be unique to Japan because of the range and scale of their business activities and their pivotal role in each *keiretsu*, many Japanese business scholars prefer to point out their similarity to Western trading companies and multinationals in general, both past and present. It is important to remember that *sogo shosha* are by origin trading, not manufacturing conglomerates. They have close links to

other manufacturers in their *keiretsu*, however, and often have joint venture manufacturing companies with these manufacturers. *Sogo shosha* supply other *keiretsu* members with raw materials and sell their finished and semi-finished products on the domestic and international markets. Thus, as they react to the changing needs of their clients, their patterns of overseas expansion and business development have many parallels with other multinationals. There is some evidence that their *keiretsu* ties are weakening, however, due to post-**bubble economy** restructuring and mergers.

Partly as a result of their ties with *keiretsu* companies across a range of key industries, *sogo shosha* are also heavily intertwined with the fate of the Japanese economy, to the extent that Japanese GNP growth is often the most statistically significant predictor of their trading transactions growth rates. *Sogo shosha* still handle a major proportion of Japan's international trade, coordinating 30 percent of Japan's exports and 50 percent of its imports. This sense of 'representing Japan' permeates their business strategy and has prevented them from becoming truly global operations, in the sense of having key clients and senior managers originating from outside Japan. This is illustrated by the surprisingly large proportion of turnover represented by domestic transactions. According to the Japan Foreign Trade Council, the combined sales of the eighteen *sogo shosha* are around one trillion dollars a year, of which 12 percent comes from exports, 15 percent from imports, 24 percent from offshore trading and 49 percent from domestic trading. Although the scale of their trading transactions has led to the top five *sogo shosha* being named as some of the world's largest companies, their market capitalization would not justify this claim. Furthermore their net profits are only a fraction of a percentage of their turnover and their employee totals worldwide are not much more than 10,000, even for the largest companies.

There are around 8,000 import/export companies in Japan, but only eighteen are recognized as *sogo shosha* by the Japan Foreign Trade Council (which represents Japanese trading companies). The more common interpretation includes only the nine largest companies: **ITOCHU** Corporation, Kanematsu Corporation, **Marubeni** Corporation,

Mitsubishi Corporation, **Mitsui** & Co Ltd., Nichimen Corporation, Nissho Iwai Corporation, **Sumitomo** Corporation and Tomen Corporation. Recently, however, Kanematsu has been excluded from this group, following a restructuring which halved its staff and sold off its textiles and energy businesses. The remaining nine smaller companies are: Chori Co, Ltd., Iwatani International Corporation, Kawasho Corporation, Kinsho-Mataichi Corporation, Nagase & Co Ltd., Nissei Sangyo Co. Ltd, Sumikin Bussan Corporation, Toshoku Ltd. and Toyota Tsusho Corporation. The latter is the only trading company that is growing rapidly, and has ambitions to enter the ranks of the top five trading companies by acquiring or taking a stake in other failing trading companies. Okura and Co was also part of the official group of *sogo shosha* until it filed for bankruptcy in 1998.

General trading companies are engaged in all industrial sectors from resource development to advanced technology, including energy such as oil and gas; metals such as iron and steel and nonferrous metals; machinery including automobiles, ships, airplanes and industrial machinery and equipment; chemicals including petrochemical products; general merchandise, sporting and leisure goods, medical equipment, construction and property development, and information and communications including satellites and mobile phones, software and services such as retailing. In addition to trading and business investments, general trading companies also offer services such as financing, transportation and logistics, research and consulting, marketing and project coordination.

Employees

Due to their pivotal role in the Japanese economy, the variety of work and possibility of international postings that *sogo shosha* offer, they are a highly popular employment choice for Japanese university graduates. *Sogo shosha* employees are therefore well represented amongst the alumni of Japan's elite universities, and consequently have high level contacts ranging across government and business circles. These contacts further enhance their usefulness as facilitators for entry into the Japanese market for foreign companies.

Sogo shosha are also well-known for their benevolent, perhaps overwhelming care of their employees, in excess even of Japanese high standards. As well as the usual fringe benefits of dormitories, subsidized accommodation and lifetime employment, many *sogo shosha* offer employee marriage bureaux, higher than average salaries and retirement packages and very generous expatriation benefits. With the latest restructuring, however, some of these benefits are being cut and the complex hierarchies associated with lifetime employment are being de-layered. It is noticeable too that trading companies have been slipping down the student employer popularity rankings in the 1990s, largely due to being identified with the "old" and failing Japanese economic structure.

History

Most general trading companies started merchant businesses during the Tokugawa period (1623–1853) but formally established themselves in the Meiji era (1868–1912) as specialty trading companies: Mitsui as a silk and rice merchant, Sumitomo as a copper refining and sales company, Mitsubishi as a shipping and shipbuilding company, and so on. In fact the use of the term *sogo shosha* to describe trading companies only became popular in the mid-1950s, when foreign trade was resumed after the Second World War and the Japanese economy began to revive. Indeed, many of the prewar specialty trading companies only became general trading companies in the first two decades after the war.

The early specialties were a reflection of the status of some of the trading companies as *seisho*, or merchants who used their close contacts with politicians to take advantage of the Meiji government's industrial promotion policy. The trading companies took up the challenge of wresting control of Japan's trade from the foreign merchants who had a near monopoly on Japan's foreign commerce and shipping after the enforced opening of Japan, following two centuries of isolation. The earlier trading companies were given licenses to export the products in which Japan had a comparative advantage, such as silk, rice and tea. Latecomers such as Mitsubishi concentrated first of all on fighting off P&O for shipping lines out of

Japan and then on transferring technology from Britain for shipbuilding, in order to reduce dependency on foreign ship purchases. The trading companies quickly diversified into mining, manufacturing and transportation, evolving into **zaibatsu**. These various divisions were spun out into separate companies, with the sales divisions becoming the prewar predecessors of the post war *sogo shosha*.

The First World War proved a major boost to some of the trading companies and a disaster for others. Those who speculated heavily in metal and did not control their finances failed, such as Masuda, Shimada, Furukawa, Kuhara, Mogi, Yuasa, Takada and Suzuki Shoten. Mitsui Bussan by contrast avoided speculation and maintained a steady and high profit level, profiting from the shortage of goods and ships in wartime. Mitsubishi Shoji's period of growth and consolidation did not come until the 1930s, however, when its strengths in heavy industry drew it into the rearmament and Asian expansion of Japan. These two companies were the nearest to a prewar form of *sogo shosha* in terms of range of products and international presence. By 1938, Mitsui Bussan and Mitsubishi Shoji employed 7,000 people and had trading transactions of ¥2bn ($560m) each.

The trading companies were dissolved, along with their fellow *zaibatsu* member companies, by the Supreme Command of the Allied Powers as holders of excessive economic power in 1947. Historical ties were never completely severed, however, and with the pressures of the Korean War, they were allowed to regroup in the 1950s. Mitsubishi Shoji was the first to become a true *sogo shosha*, opening offices around the world to cover a range of products in 1954–5. Mitsui Bussan was slower to regroup, with its final merger taking place in 1959. Marubeni, Itochu and Sumitomo were specialty trading houses until the 1960s.

The 1960s were supposed to herald the "setting sun" for *sogo shosha*, as the liberalization of Japan's trade meant that specific categories of trade were no longer allocated to them by the government, so they would have to compete for business. In fact, the 1960s were a time of vigorous expansion for *sogo shosha*, with their combined annual sales growing over 900 percent between 1960 and 1973. This was partly due to mergers, inflation

and yen reevaluations but also because of their ability to diversify into news industries and to integrate their businesses upstream and downstream.

In the 1970s *sogo shosha* facilitated the overseas investments of Japanese manufacturers, often taking a stake in their foreign subsidiaries, or setting up joint ventures for distribution and warehousing. They also became conduits for Japan's increasing Overseas Development Assistance projects in Africa and the Middle East.

Sogo shosha's *raison d'etre* was questioned again in the 1980s, a decade which was supposed to be a "winter" for them. In the early 1980s, the second oil crisis and the Iran-Iraq war had a serious impact on their growth and profitability, as did the depressed state of the Japanese economy. The development of the **bubble economy** from the mid-1980s revived their fortunes, however, and led them to direct their resources into *zaitech* and other financing functions.

The 1990s have largely been a decade of restructuring and writing off of bad debts arising from *zaitech* failures, although there have been some new initiatives in information technology, retailing and Asian investment.

Function

Sogo shosha use their international networks to collect and analyze information, which they then pass on to their headquarters or even to government agencies. This latter activity has sometimes led *sogo shosha* to be accused of espionage, particularly by US politicians and journalists. The importance of the information gathering function has necessitated major investments in information and communication technology, including satellite communication and dedicated electronic networks. Unsurprisingly, *sogo shosha* have recently combined their knowledge of information and communication technology and trading to become involved in setting up e-commerce networks and business-to-business exchanges.

The traditional function of *sogo shosha* is the procurement and distribution of goods. This function has its roots in Japan's status as a resource poor country and a major importer of raw materials. The importation of fuel, iron ore, foods and so on into Japan has led to the logical extension of their business into actual investment and development of coal mining, oil fields, and agriculture overseas. *Sogo shosha* often act as the coordinators of these highly complex projects, as well as acting as financiers. Whereas in previous decades investment had been undertaken as a way of securing scarce resources or boosting trading relationships with major customers, investment activity is increasingly looked on by *sogo shosha* as a profit center in its own right, for pure capital gain. *Sogo shosha* are therefore starting to compete more directly with Japan's struggling banks and investment houses in areas such as mergers and acquisitions and investment funds.

Further reading

Arai, S. (1991) *Shoshaman: A Tale of Corporate Japan*, Berkeley, CA and Los Angeles: University of California Press.

Yonekawa, S. (ed.) (1990) *General Trading Companies: A Comparative and Historical Study*, Tokyo: United Nations University Press.

Yoshino, M.Y., and Lifson, T.B. (1986) *The Invisible Link: Japan's Sogo Shosha and the Organization of Trade*, Cambridge, MA: MIT Press.

Young, A.K. (1979) *The Sogo Shosha: Japan's Multinational Trading Companies*, Tokyo: Charles E. Tuttle Company.

PERNILLE RUDLIN

geography

Japan is made up of a chain of four mountainous islands: Honshu, the main island, Hokkaido in the north, Kyushu to the south, and Shikoku the smallest off the coast of southern Honshu, together with several hundred lesser islands. The total landmass of Japan is about 145,000 square miles; its elongated nature is revealed by the fact that although Japan stretches over 1,800 miles from northeast to southwest (from 25 to 45 degrees latitude), no point in Japan is more than seventy-five miles from the sea. Until the modern era, Japan was relatively isolated physically from the

Asian mainland, left free to develop its own cultural system.

In considering geography and its relationship to social and historical factors, Britain and Japan offer some interesting similarities. Both are made up of large islands and have between 100,000 and 150,000 square miles of territory; both are located off the coast of continents, which are home to long civilized traditions. Both have received influence from those traditions, but have been isolated enough to retain a distinct identity. They share basically similar climates and both were the first in their respective areas to industrialize. The two nations have used the sea with unusual effectiveness for military and commercial pursuits. But the similarities only hold in a very general comparison.

Climate in Japan is more varied than the climate of Britain, more reminiscent of the climate along the US eastern seaboard. Hokkaido has quite cold winters and mild summers. The weather in the center of Japan near Tokyo is quite like that of the Washington, DC area, cool to cold in winter, with muggy hot days in late summer. Okinawa, the southernmost part of Japan, is Japan's winter playground.

Japan is far more isolated from its continent than Britain. By contrast, Japan lies approximately ninety miles off the Korean Peninsula. For humans to swim from England to France is a challenging but completely possible undertaking. Japan is also very close to some Russian held islands in the north, but cultural influences have never come from those places. From Japan to the main body of its nearest historical contact, Korea, there is more than a hundred miles of ocean. In terrain, as well, the British Isles and the Japanese islands are quite dissimilar. Britain is relatively flat, while Japan is more like a larger version of Switzerland, with dramatic stretches of mountainous terrain in many interior areas, with smaller mountains and hills covering all areas with the exception of a few interior valleys and relatively small coastal plains.

For several hundred years, Japan's population has been about double that of Britain; early in the twenty-first century it stands at a little over 125,000,000. Japan has, on the other hand, less than half the arable land for farming that Britain has, and although the Japanese employ intensive farming techniques and some of Japan's soil is quite fertile, Japan imports a high percentage of its food products, being self-sufficient only in a few products such as green vegetables and rice.

The Japanese islands are situated on the western edge of what has been called the "Ring of Fire," an area of seismic volatility stretching from the Philippines up along the Asian mainland, across the Aleutian Islands and down the west coast of North and South America. There are more than sixty active volcanoes in Japan, and modest quakes of 2.5 or less on the Richter scale occur somewhere in Japan almost daily. Large quakes causing loss of life and great destruction have been recorded throughout Japanese history, including the catastrophic Great Kanto Earthquake of 1923 which brought enormous damage to Tokyo and environs and cost the lives of over 100,000 people, and the more recent Great Hanshin Earthquake which struck the city of Kobe in 1995.

With only two navigable rivers (and both of those for less than one hundred miles), aside from fresh water fishing, rivers have not played an important role in Japanese life. The ocean, on the other hand, is deeply woven into Japanese culture in many ways. It has served to protect it from foreign military power, provided a considerable percentage of the Japanese diet, and throughout history has been a chief medium for moving people and things. It is interesting to observe that because of the mountainous terrain and proximity of ocean waterways, the Japanese, unique among sophisticated societies, never developed any practical system of animal-pulled carriages.

The human population of Japan is not as spread out over the land as is that of Britain. A few areas are extremely densely populated, and others, for example the long arm of northern Honshu called by the Japanese the *Tohoku* region, are considered to be underpopulated. A corridor about 350 miles long, but only forty miles wide, running from northeast of Tokyo, down the Pacific coast through the city of Nagoya, and then on southwest to and including the three cities of the Kansai area – Osaka, Kyoto, Kobe – is home to almost half of the entire Japanese population, even though in land mass it represents just one-fiftieth of the nation.

As late as the end of the Second World War, less than half the population of Japan lived in urban areas, with very rapid urbanization occurring since

that time. Partly because of events which occurred during the **Tokugawa period**, the capital city of Tokyo plays a role similar to that of Paris or London in their respective societies. It has the largest concentration of population in the industrialized world, and while Osaka, Sapporo, Kyoto, and Fukuoka together with a few other cities are important centers of culture and commerce, Tokyo is the center of political, economic, entertainment and international activity of the nation.

See also: Kansai culture

Further reading

Noh, T. and Kimura, J.C. (eds) (1989) *Japan: A Regional Geography of an Island Nation*, Tokyo: Teikoku Shoin.

Reischauer, E.O. (1981) *The Japanese*, Rutland, VT: Tuttle.

Trewartha, G. (1990) *Japan, a Geography*, Madison, WI: University of Wisconsin Press.

JOHN A. McKINSTRY

giri

Ethics and morality in Japan are not as tied to universal concepts of good and bad as in societies which have been influenced by monotheistic religions such as Christianity and Islam. For the Japanese, behaving properly relates less to absolute rules of conduct than in the West, and is more tied to how well people fulfill obligation within relationships. A highly developed sensitivity to duty and obligation owed to others has resulted in a specialized vocabulary of terms relating to such phenomena. *Giri* is one of those terms.

Introducing *giri* to people not familiar with Japan carries with it the danger of exaggeration. *Giri* is real, and its effects on relations between people and institutions are real, but its imprint on contemporary Japanese society is quite subtle; in fact, hardly noticeable until one gets well beneath the surface of everyday life. The word *giri* is heard frequently. But used for its traditional meaning, to refer to a somewhat more conscious and formalized sense of obligation to people and organizations, the term is not actually used often in Japan today. When it is used that way, it is often employed in a negative sense, such as referring to someone who is judged not trustworthy as in *giri shirazu no hito*, literally, a person who does not know *giri*. The reason for its frequent use is simply because it has over the past seventy or eighty years come to be the most popular word for "in-law;" a wife's mother is referred to as *giri no okaasan*, and a husband's older sister as *giri no oneesan*.

It is not exactly clear which came first: *giri* with the *samurai*, later filtering down to influence more general cultural themes, or in the reverse direction, *giri* as a more general cultural theme which the *samurai* formalized. Whatever the answer to that question is, we know that what *giri* came to mean in Japanese life was first articulated in the fourteenth century, a time when the warrior elite began to eclipse the court nobility in Kyoto as the dominant force in Japan. But it is quite possible that the basic idea of *giri*, in a more diffuse and less formal sense, was an important part of the way people and communities establish order and at all levels as far back as there has been anything recognizable as Japanese society. Any human group, in order to function in a cooperative way over time, has to be tied together with some kind of basic outline of ethics and morality. In societies which came to be dominated by monotheism, the agents and interpretations of God serve much of this purpose. Societies such as China and Japan that have not had significant experience with a single, prescribed set of guides for behavior and relationships have to rely on something else. In China, bonds of kinship and extended clan ties have traditionally been the anchors of ethics and morality. For the Japanese, it seems that a conscious type of mutual obligation, both ascribed by formal social roles, and achieved through deeds of behavior, has served more typically than elsewhere to underlay the rules of morality.

The fifteenth and sixteenth centuries in Japan were a time of desperate struggles for power and dominance in various regions throughout the country. Survival of any *han*, the autonomous mini-states of feudal Japan, depended on military prowess, and the virtues of loyalty, devotion, faithfulness, honor, sacrifice, together with skill in swordsmanship and other forms of combat, came, by natural selection, to constitute the special culture of *bushido*, the way of the warrior (see **samurai, role of**).

Four terms relating to the formal sense of duty arose from *bushido*. *Gimu*, similar to *giri*, usually used in regard to an abstract entity such as the state. *On*, a related concept, referred to formal obligation owed to persons and institutions in an ascribed sense, for example to one's feudal lord, and to parents. During the Meiji period, Japanese were taught that they owed obligation to the nation, symbolized by *on* owed to the Emperor. *Giri* was obligation owed because of some service or help rendered. One owed *giri* to a teacher of calligraphy or swordsmanship, or to someone who rendered assistance in battle. The fourth term, *ninjo*, was the feelings of affection and longing pulling in the opposite direction, feelings which if acted on could cause a samurai to violate the code of *bushido* by failing to carry out his duty. Japanese drama through the centuries institutionalized the pull of affection against the demands of duty. The dilemma of the *giri/ninjo*, in which *giri* always wins, has been the subject of Japanese drama through the ages, from *kabuki* through to modern motion pictures.

Ethics and morality continue to be somewhat less tied to universal concepts of good and evil, and more directed toward connection to people and organizations. Words such as *on* and *giri*, which in the twentieth century came to be used more or less interchangeably, sound old-fashioned to people in contemporary Japan, but their force can still be discerned in the sensitivity Japanese have to what is owed to other people. In Japan the lessons of reciprocity are given a special importance. Gifts must always be repaid with concomitant worth. The first words uttered upon subsequent meeting of someone who has hosted a person in any way are, *Kono aida wa domo*, "Thank you for the (nice) time." For any adult to neglect to do so would be more than impolite, it would represent for many Japanese, a breach of decency.

See also: business ethics

Further reading

Benedict, R. (1946) *The Chrysanthemum and the Sword: Patterns of Japanese Culture*, Boston: Houghton Mifflin.

Keene, D. (1961) *Major Plays of Chikamatsu*, New York: Columbia Univesity Press.

Nakane, C. (1970) *Japanese Society*, Berkeley, CA: University of California Press.

JOHN A. McKINSTRY

guilds

The earliest Japanese guilds (*za*) were formed in the eleventh century, while trade associations (*nakama*) were established during the **Tokugawa period** (1603–1868). These farmers' and merchants' associations formulated and enforced market rules for their industries in a growing economy to create trade in the absence of legal institutions and to safeguard market participants from deception and fraud. Thus, guilds and *nakama* are predecessors of today's trade associations. Their early formation and sophisticated organizational structures reflect both the vigor and drive of the Tokugawa-period economy and the merchants' vital contributions to creating and maintaining their own markets.

Early history: *Za*

The earliest groupings that can be considered cooperatives were the *mujin*, groups of farmers in the Heian period who submitted dues so that a few group members could go on a pilgrimage to the Ise Shrine every year (something no farmer could have afforded on his own). The first records of a merchants' guild date from the year 1092, when a group of merchants in Kyoto established market hours and rules. As the economy began to develop in various regions of the country, the *za* grew stronger. They had exclusive membership, created barriers to entry, and set product prices on their markets. During the continuing wars and territorial disputes of the fifteenth and sixteenth centuries, the *za* became increasingly powerful by assuming control over regional tax barriers and domain borders.

In 1603, Oda Nobunaga (the first of the three unifiers) assumed military control over Japan. He understood that one primary source of power and wealth of the local landlords were the guilds. To weaken these landlords, Oda instituted a policy of *rakuichi-rakuza* (free the markets, open the *za*). Under this policy, all *za* were prohibited, except for those with special permission, such as the mints (the gold *za* or *kinza*, the silver *za* or *ginza* – located in what today is central Tokyo – and the copper *za* or *zeniza*). The new Tokugawa government also introduced a division of society that put merchants at the bottom of the hierarchy and created a new leadership class of administrative officials (the former *samurai*) who had money to spend and wanted products to buy. In the absence of laws and courts, associations surreptitiously re-emerged to design mechanisms of enforcing trade agreements. After 1670, the Shogunate gave up on its attempts to outlaw the groupings, and *nakama* (literally, "among those who know each other") flourished.

The earliest full-fledged *nakama* we know of were the wholesalers and shippers (***tonya***) along the Tokaido, followed by public bath-houses (1650), hairdressers (1659) and money changers (1679). All of these were awarded licenses (*kabu*, literally "shares") by the government because they were considered to play important social roles (maintaining public hygiene, banking). From the entrepreneurs' perspective, the licensing system enabled them to control their markets. Outsiders were not allowed to practice in the profession. This meant that all stationary and successful entrepreneurs were members of a trade association.

Nakama organization

The organizational structure of the *nakama* was remarkably similar to that of today's trade associations. At the biennial general meeting (*sokai*), members elected directors. There was one standing (long-term) director, resembling today's senior administrative director, as well as annual and monthly directors. The main tasks of a board of directors were: (1) to collect taxes and donations to the Shogunate and domain chiefs from members; (2) to evaluate and admit new members; (3) to punish transgressions of *nakama* rules (typically, by prohibiting the infringer from producing or trading for a certain period); (4) to maintain contacts with other associations about the good standing of merchants; (5) to establish quality controls in the industry; (6) to set uniform prices for the industry's products or services; and (7) to hold social functions such as arranging gifts to shrines and temples or end-of-the-year parties.

To engage in a certain business, an entrepreneur had to become a member of the *nakama*. Once admitted, the member had to move into the *nakama*'s quarter. Living in one area facilitated the monitoring of a member's business behavior, creditworthiness, and pricing.

Economic functions

Nakama engaged in trade-enhancing activities, ranging from structuring market rules to guaranteeing the creditworthiness of their members. Specifically, by establishing fixed and regular market hours, *nakama* brought merchants of different trades together. By limiting markets to members and monitoring their behavior, *nakama* kept markets clear from charlatans and swindlers. Because a member's standing was guaranteed by its *nakama*, a credit economy could develop. In Osaka this even led to the establishment of a rice futures exchange in 1730, where trading positions were kept on the books and settled at the end of a three-month trading period. Not only did these settlement systems make things easier, in many instances they made trade possible in the first place, thus leading to the creation of new markets. By enforcing quality controls, the *nakama* further reduced the potential for fraud on the marketplace. In the event of deception, the *nakama* had rules for settlements and punishment. Social stigma was attached as well, as most *nakama* had an elaborate code of honor. Finally, *nakama* often administered the widespread apprenticeship system and enforced rules against the poaching of apprentices by competing merchants.

In addition to enhancing the trade mechanisms of the time, the *nakama* also ensured that their members would be profitable by limiting competition. In particular, most *nakama* enforced a "fair profit" system, whereby the directors described binding product prices that enabled merchants to earn a stable, but not exorbitant, profit margin. By way of their organization, *nakama* also established barriers to entry. In many cases, the number of outstanding *kabu* for *nakama* was limited, and only after an incumbent member had quit or died could a new merchant enter the group. Even groups that

did not issue *kabu* were very careful in selecting as new members only merchants who would not undermine the group's standing. Moreover, *nakama* imposed strict boycott rules: members were not allowed to trade with merchants that were not a member of a *nakama*. Occasionally, an additional entry barrier was employed in the form of minimum requirements that were set so high that only incumbent firms could fulfil them (e.g., a certain shipping volume was required before a wholesaler could enter a shipping *nakama*).

By inviting and enabling sophisticated trade practices, creating markets, restricting access, and ensuring stable profit margins, the *nakama* contributed greatly to the economic development of Japan. Businesses grew steadily, and markets developed around the country. On the downside, precisely because the *nakama* were so protective and restrictive, they hindered technology transfer among industries and often served to slow technological progress and innovation. This became apparent when Japan opened up in the 1860s: some basic artisan trades were world-class, but the country lagged behind in many industrial areas.

Shogunate policies towards *nakama*

In the course of the **Tokugawa period**, the Shogunate changed its policies towards trade associations several times. This was particularly visible during the three major economic reforms of 1720, the 1780s, and the 1830s.

In 1720, Shogun Tokugawa Yoshimune faced huge budget deficits and inflation in most products other than rice. To realign finances and prices, he embarked on major fiscal reforms and officially licensed all *nakama*. By issuing *kabu* to the associations, he could charge licensing fees and taxes to increase the goverment's tax revenue. He also asked the *nakama* to set or maintain certain prices, and in particular to increase the price for rice while curbing inflation elsewhere. This was the first time that trade associations were used as an instrument of public policy implementation.

The effects of Yoshimune's reforms were short-lived. Pro-business policies after his reforms granted associations more freedom to regulate their own markets, and in turn the *nakama* were charged ever higher taxes and fees. The *nakama* passed these taxes on to their customers by way of higher prices, which severely affected the *samurais'* standard of living. The Kansei Reform of the 1780s was also aimed at fiscal restructuring. To curb the increasing influence of business and cut their monopolistic pricing powers, the largest *nakama* were dissolved. However, since small associations were allowed to continue and the previous groups soon reassembled, these attempts at breaking up industry association once again proved futile.

The Tempo Reform of the 1830s brought about an interesting real-world experiment with market institutions, as it rested on the complete abolition of all trade associations, with the goal of curbing merchants' influence and power. What the reformers had overlooked was that this move halted all the trade-creating and trade-supporting mechanisms supplied by the *nakama*, and thus toppled the pillars of the market system. The policies were revised in 1857 when *nakama* were allowed to operate again, albeit with open membership and free market access.

Modern associations

This last policy move coincided with the opening of the country after 1853. The Meiji Restoration of 1868 led to a complete reorganization of government. All *nakama* were asked to dissolve. Again, because this significantly limited trade in an increasingly uncertain environment, many associations continued to operate surreptitiously. The new Meiji government did not pass a new Commercial Code until 1893, but, understanding the merchants' plight, it began to actively support the formation of local Chambers of Commerce and trade associations in the 1870s. As some of the modern industries grew at the beginning of the twentieth century, the large firms began to found their own, large-firm trade associations, plus over-arching federations, such as the predecessor of Keidanren in 1917. A distinct differentiation of trade associations into small-firm cooperatives and large-firm groups emerged during the Taisho years (1911–25).

As Japan moved towards a war economy in the 1930s, trade associations and cooperatives were increasingly called upon to gear their industries towards the war effort. However, the government's attempts at complete economic control and rationing were consistently undermined by circumvention on the black market. To enforce production and distribution controls, the Key Industries Association Ordinance of 1941 established control associations (*toseikai*) in every narrowly defined industry. The *toseikai* were headed by the leading businessmen in their industries, and their function was to implement input and output plans and punish any deviation from these plans. In 1942, the Transfer and Administrative Authority Law even gave official legal authority to the *toseikai* to punish violations.

Interestingly, while the *toseikai* were an attempt to increase government controls over industry, in the end they only increased industry's controls over itself. By receiving official enforcement rights, the *toseikai* leaders could structure their own rules while upholding the appearance of cooperation with the government.

Beginning in 1945, the US Occupation Forces demanded that all *toseikai* be dissolved. Many of the existing groups simply adopted slightly different names but maintained staff and directors. While a purge of business leaders by the Occupation affected many executives in the leading firms, their proteges, who had also been active in the associations before, assumed leadership and continued many of the old policies. In 1947, the USA helped Japan draft and pass a new Antimonopoly Law as well as a highly restrictive Trade Association Law. This law was so prohibitive that business lobbied very heavily to have it abolished as soon as the Occupation ended in 1953. Some of the competition rules for trade associations were subsumed in the revised Antimonopoly Law of 1953, but in much more lenient form. This more lenient wording and interpretation of anti-trust statutes allowed trade associations to continue significant industry self-regulation throughout the postwar period.

Further reading

Miyamoto, M. (1958) *Kabu nakama no kenkyu* (Research on *Kabu Nakama*), Tokyo: Yuhikaku.

Okazaki, T. (1999) *Edo no shijo keizai* (The Market Economy of Edo), Tokyo: Kodansha.

Schaede, U. (1989) "Forwards and Futures in Tokugawa-Period Japan: A New Perspective on the Dojima Rice Market," *Journal of Banking and Finance* 13: 487–513.

—— (2000) "The Historical Development of Self-Regulation by Japan's Trade Associations," in U. Schaede, *Cooperative Capitalism: Self-Regulation, Trade Associations, and the Antimonopoly Law in Japan,* Oxford: Oxford University Press, ch. 7.

Sheldon, C.D. (1958) *The Rise of the Merchant Class in Tokugawa Japan 1600–1868: An Introductory Survey,* New York: Russell & Russell.

Yamamura, K. (1973) "The Development of *Za* in Medieval Japan," *Business History Review* 47: 438–65.

ULRIKE SCHAEDE

habatsu

Habatsu, or "clique," refers to a significant component of the social organization in Japanese companies. Japanese organizations are structured primarily around small groups for decision making, socialization, **organizational learning** and career development. These small groups reflect both the cultural and historical roots of modern Japanese organization. For example, it is theorized that Japanese small group decision making is an indirect derivative of rice paddy culture, in which all members of the community play a role within a system of small groups (Hayashi 1988). Others argue that it is the historical significance of feudal governance which has influenced the strong adherence to group allegiance within organizations (Whitehill 1991). In any case, it is clear that the small group as a unit of decision making is a cornerstone of Japanese social organization. *Habatsu* represents one version of this small group phenomenon.

Habatsu represent informal groups within organizations to which membership is mandatory and loyalty is paramount. Membership in the *habatsu* means for employees that they must obey habatsu rules and seek to achieve *habatsu* goals, even in the case when *habatsu*-related goals are contradictory to overall company goals. Thus, *habatsu* can be both a constructive and destructive force in the organization. *Habatsu* membership influences employee and management decision making on such things as overall company policy, strategic goals, personnel policy and even budgetary decisions. The *habatsu* influence is often unspoken and implicit, yet it is felt very clearly and strongly by management and employees alike.

So, who becomes a member of a *habatsu*? In Japanese organizations most employees belong to one informal group or another. But, whereas cliques in American companies are often based upon common interests, sports or community activities, Japanese *habatsu* are based upon unalterable criteria. Examples of *habatsu* membership criteria include graduating from the same university, growing up in the same prefecture (state), or coming from the same hometown. Because these criteria are unchangeable for the employee, *habatsu* membership is considered to be involuntary as well as permanent.

As mentioned, *habatsu* can be a powerful force within the power structure of Japanese organizations. Since they have their own internal, vertical hierarchy, they can disrupt attempts at company-wide programs aimed at employee development, such as career planning, employee development and or promotion systems. They can influence company wide long-term planning, budgetary decision making and even marketing strategies. Depending on the longevity of the *habatsu* in the organization and the power with which members exercise their desires, *habatsu* are sometimes considered the invisible power structure (operating like an underground or parallel economy) within the Japanese organization (Whitehill 1991).

Habatsu can also have a direct impact on company strategy. A powerful *habatsu* can influence the outcome of major organizational decisions, through its implicit support or defeat. Since members of *habatsu* can be fiercely loyal to their leaders, it is in the highest interest of upper management to gain the support of *habatsu* leadership on any major decision facing the organization.

One of the most enduring forms of *habatsu* in Japanese organizations is the *gaku-batsu* or university clique. *Gaku-batsu* members are fiercely loyal to the alumni of their university and offer preferential treatment for their members. In some Japanese organizations, hiring, staffing, promotion and even compensation systems are heavily influenced by *gaku-batsu* membership, making this form of clique more than just an informal influence on the organization. These systems can be so rigid that even in the cases of exceptional ability, talent or effort by a non-member of a powerful *gaku-batsu*, rewards (promotion, extra compensation) are not forthcoming. Only those who are members of the powerful *gaku-batsu* can expect to be treated favorably and provided career advancement.

Recently, the increasing level of foreign competition in Japan has begun to erode the strong tradition of *habatsu* power in Japanese social organization. Japanese companies are beginning to embrace human resource management practices which are contradictory in nature to the *habatsu* system. One example is performance management, which relies on the objective assessment of employee contribution to company goals in order to determine promotion and pay. In this merit-based, professionally oriented system there is no room for feudal like preference for special groups solely based upon fixed membership criteria.

Habatsu may even impact globalization attempts by Japanese companies. According to Rosalie Tung (1991), Japanese organizations cannot professionalize their operations while clinging to outdated social mechanisms like *habatsu*. Since professionalism is the foundation for globalization efforts (standardization of practices, performance management systems based upon fair, unbiased criteria), informal small group structures such as habatsu may act as an impediment to the long-term competitiveness of Japanese companies.

Still, *habatsu* continue to thrive in many of the larger, established Japanese firms. As evidence of this, the importance placed upon entry into top universities in Japan is still largely a function of the effect of *gaku-batsu* membership on career success for Japanese employees. Acceptance to, graduation from and then membership in a top university *gaku-batsu* is still believed to be the key ingredient for success in Japan. Until these *gaku-batsu* lose some of their power and influence, it may be difficult for Japanese companies to professionalize their management systems.

Further reading

Hayashi, S. (1988) *Culture and Management in Japan*, Tokyo: University of Tokyo Press.

Ouchi, W. (1981) *Theory Z*, New York: Addison-Wesley.

Rohlen, T. (1974) *For Harmony and Strength*, Berkeley, CA: University of California Press.

Tung, R. (1984) *Key to Japan's Strength: Human Power*, Lexington, KY: D.C. Heath and Co.

Whitehill, A. (1991) *Japanese Management: Tradition and Transition*, London: Routledge.

MARGARET TAKEDA

Hayakawa, Tokuji

Hayakawa, the inventor of the snap belt buckle and the mechanical pencil, was an entrepreneur and founder of **Sharp** Corporation. Born in Tokyo in 1894, Hayakawa set up his first business, a metalwork business employing two other people that produced a snap belt buckle, the "Tokubijo." Hayakawa came up with the idea after being annoyed in a theatre by a man sitting nearby who kept playing with his belt. Three years later, in 1915, he invented the "Ever Ready Sharp" pencil. This was the original mechanical pencil and quickly acquired the nickname "Ever-Sharp" because it did not requiring sharpening. At this time Hayakawa also founded the Hayakawa Electric Industry Co., Ltd, the predecessor of the current Sharp Corporation.

On September 1, 1923, Hayakawa's entire manufacturing facility was destroyed in the Great Kanto Earthquake. In December of that year he relocated to Osaka and set up Hayakawa Metal Works and undertook research on radio technology. Two years later, in 1925, he built his first crystal radio set. Mass production of radio sets began shortly thereafter. By 1930 the company had pioneered numerous product innovations and established itself as a leading electronics manufacturer.

Hayakawa carried his creative capabilities onto the production floor. His mass production facilities developed a reputation for quality and efficiency. Masaru Ibuka and Akio **Morita** credit their visit to his factory floor with helping them hone their own manufacturing skills when the fledgling **Sony** (then known as Totsuko) was first getting off the ground.

In 1970, Hayakawa stepped down as president and became chairman. In 1980, the company formally changed its name to Sharp Corporation in honor of his "Ever-Sharp" pencil. Hayakawa died in 1981 at the age of 86, after building the Sharp Corporation into a world leader in electronic products. The company's creativity and dedication to quality reflect his core values as its founder.

ALLAN BIRD

Heisei boom

The Heisei boom refers to an expansion of the Japanese economy that began in November 1986 and lasted until roughly July 1991. The economic expansion was one of the longest in Japan's postwar economic history. It was marked by extraordinary growth, peaking at 5.6 percent in 1990. The high growth came to halt in 1991, and was followed by three years of macroeconomic stagnation and subsequently by economic recession through the end of the decade. The Heisei boom subsequently came to be called the "bubble boom" or the **bubble economy**. The name "Heisei" derives from the name of the imperial era in the Japanese calendar during which the most dramatic rises in the economy occurred.

In Japan's postwar history, there have been three significant periods of economic expansion. The first took place from 1958–61 and was known as the Iwato boom. The second boom took place between October 1965 and July 1970. The **Izanagi boom** (named after a mythical Japanese figure) saw fifty-seven months of uninterrupted economic expansion, and came to an end shortly before the International Exposition opened in

Osaka. The third significant period was the Heisei boom.

Although similar to the other two in several respects, there were also significant differences. Property prices rose during and then slumped after all three booms. However, the drop in land values was extreme in the Heisei boom. So inflated were land values during this period that several economists noted, in theory, one could purchase the entire state of California, including all of its buildings, plants and equipment, in exchange for the plot of land on which the imperial palace was situated.

A second similarity is found in the high level of investment in plant and equipment during each of the three booms. However, again the Heisei boom differed in that much of the financing for this investment derived primarily from the issuance of stock, rather than by obtaining financing through banks and other lending institutions. Stock issues reached a peak of ¥8.848 trillion in 1989, but dropped precipitously to ¥3.792 trillion in 1990. The decline continued on a downward trend hitting ¥807.7 billion in 1991 and ¥419.9 billion in 1992. In short, there was a drastic decline in the rate of capital increase.

Finally, the Heisei boom remains significant because of the length of the recession that followed it due to a snowballing effect of loss of confidence that rippled through the economy. The longest postwar recession previously took place over a thirty-six-month period from March 1980 to February 1983, following the second oil shock. The Heisei boom broke that record, and the Japanese economy struggled through the remainder of the 1990s.

See also: economic crisis in Asia

ALLAN BIRD

history of the labor movement

The term "labor movement" can be generally understood as a sustained and organized joining together of employees, or wage earners, to advance common interests. By joining together, employees increase their power and their ability to bargain with employers over employee concerns such as wages, working hours, and working conditions. Labor unions – identifiable, permanent associations of employees engaging in collective action – are often the result of labor movements, but not always. Strikes and labor disturbances, for example, are much older than unions.

In Europe, then the USA, and then Japan, the labor movement was primarily sparked by the Industrial Revolution, a time of great economic and social upheaval. Labor unions first started with small associations of craft employees threatened by new mass production methods. Craftsmen such as printmakers and metalworkers faced the prospect of being undercut by lower cost production methods and of passing into permanent wage earning status. For these skilled employees working under the supervision of a master hoping to later become masters of a craft themselves, the new mass production methods represented an unpalatable loss of autonomy, status, and creativity, and unions represented a way to counterbalance these losses.

Paralleling the spread of mass production, the labor movement and the formation of unions occurred first in Europe, primarily Britain, where labor was plentiful and land and capital equipment were scarce. To increase their relative value, employees in Europe quickly learned the power of acting collectively. In the USA, with abundant land, there was ample opportunity for individuals to seek self-employment when there was dissatisfaction with wage employment. This meant that individual employees, with more alternatives, had more bargaining power than their European counterparts, and unionization did not arrive in the USA as soon or with as much intensity.

In both Europe and the USA, as mass production and markets continued to spread and to nationalize, unions began to nationalize as well, with industry-wide and national unions becoming commonplace by the mid-1800s in the USA. By the mid-1900s, the AFL-CIO was a huge national union representing over 15 million employees in a large constellation of industries including auto and steel. The tendency to organize across employers and industries in the USA and in Europe continues to this day. By the end of the twentieth century, a common Western view was that meaningful unions are organized across employers within an industry. With anything less, the power of collective action is diminished and unions are more at the mercy of particular employers. Because of this belief, many Western observers have been critical of the Japanese propensity to unionize by employer in **enterprise unions**, and not by industry.

Japan's labor movement has waxed and waned like other labor movements, and there are several distinct phases that are important. Interestingly, the later phases are really when the labor movement and labor management relations took on a cast commonly seen as "Japanese," characterized by **lifetime employment**, seniority wages, and enterprise unions. Before 1900, early craft workers in Japan – accustomed to autonomy and applying their skills in different settings – were not inclined to appreciate the discipline of factory work, similar to their Western counterparts. They also had significant power because management still needed their skills and had not learned how to direct labor in an organized way. Management therefore had to rely on these relatively skilled workers to do a wide variety of jobs dependably and well, even though many workers were not willing to commit themselves to one organization. Furthermore, there was also little job security for them. Although there were attempts to organize a union movement towards the end of this period, it was largely unsuccessful.

Around the beginning of the twentieth century, coincident with increased specialization of work in Japanese large manufacturers, management began to try to impose a more coherent, authoritarian form of control on employees, coupling this with the rhetoric of "beautiful customs" such as paternal care and worker obedience. Typical company strategies at this point included greater control over the work process, more efficient labor, and cultivation of foremen who would identify with the long-term fate of the company. Initial paternal practice was largely rhetorical, but increased in substance during periods of strong labor challenges. Employers were still wrestling with problems of high turnover, and this, coupled with occasional union pressure, led to wage hikes, bonuses, and welfare programs such as retirement pay, all designed to promote commitment to the firm. From this point, through the First World War and up to the Second World War, the groundwork for more stable patterns of labor management was laid. Employee expectations of job security, wages based on seniority, and employer expectation of commitment from employees emerged in this period. However, actual practice differed from expectations, and it was only after the Second World War that this gap narrowed.

There was significant labor strife in this period, particularly around the First World War. Like unions in other countries, Japanese unions gained economic strength from the expanded demand for labor as the economy boomed. Strike activity increased, and the growing economic strength of unions helped lead to political concessions. However, union leaders were also routinely incarcerated. By the early 1930s, union membership as a percentage of the industrial workforce peaked at 8 percent. By the late 1930s, the Japanese government had imprisoned many of the labor leaders with socialist leanings, and by 1940 independent labor unions were abolished completely, organizing unions into company by company political cells. These cells preempted the formation of autonomous labor unions in order to suppress disputes and advance the war effort.

After the Second World War, the Supreme Commander of Allied Powers (SCAP) imposed labor laws that initially strengthened and led to a more democratic labor movement. The Labor Union Law enacted in 1945 officially recognized labor unions and their right to strike. Two other laws, the Labor Relations Adjustment Law and the Labor Standards Law, further elaborated the rights of unions and employees and curtailed the power of employers to break up independent unions. Unionization increased rapidly from this period, climbing to 55 percent of the workforce by 1949. The union desire for consistent and fair treatment by managers echoed concerns voiced before the war. These legal and newly powerful labor unions helped to bring fundamental change to the structure of labor relations in the first postwar decade, building on the past.

However, it was also during this period that radical elements of the labor movement rose up and were forcefully put down, with the help of SCAP. Ultimately, the labor movement was effectively split by management, and the resultant labor relations version that arose – now characterized as the **three sacred treasures** – was

management-led. At the same time, however, workers did become a much greater part of the organization and were accorded a status that they did not have before. With job security, seniority wages, and enterprise unions, coupled with rapid **economic growth**, many blue-collar employees were able to achieve their broader goals of stability and middle-class status, something that did not exist for them before.

Further reading

Gordon, A. (1985) *The Evolution of Labor Relations in Japan: Heavy Industry, 1853–1955*, Cambridge, MA: Harvard University Press.

Taira, K. (1970) *Economic Development and the Labor Market in Japan*, New York: Columbia University Press.

WILLIAM BARNES

Honda Motor

Established in 1946 by Soichiro **Honda**, Honda Motor is the leading manufacturer of motorcycles in the world. It is also one of Japan's top five automobile manufacturers. Its reputation is built on excellence in engineering and design of engines. Along with **Sony**, Honda has been one of the fastest growing companies in the post-Second World War era. It rose to prominence in Japan in the 1950s when it grew from having a 20 percent share of the domestic market to a 44 percent market share, surpassing the former leader Tohatsu.

The company's major breakthrough in international markets came in 1962, when Honda successfully penetrated and then captured the US motorcycle market. With its innovative advertising campaign and the slogan, "You meet the nicest people on a Honda," it transformed the perception of motorcycles from that of a wild machine favored by rebels to that of an economical, mainstream mode of transportation. In the 1980s it moved aggressively into the three-wheel and all-terrain vehicle (ATV) markets. It is also a strong competitor in the small engine market of lawn mowers, portable generators, and other similar products.

Honda is one of the most widely known Japanese companies in the world. In the early 1960s Honda committed to an overseas production strategy that it has consistently implemented, first with motorcycles, later with automobiles and small engines. As a result, Honda has generally experienced less criticism from host country governments than its Japanese automotive and motorcycle counterparts, many of which set up production facilities only reluctantly. Honda's Marysville, Ohio plant for example, was established in 1982 as the first Japanese automotive facility in the United States.

Honda is consistently rated among the top ten companies preferred to work for in Japan. It also has a reputation for innovation in both its products and its managerial policies. The foundation for this reputation is the company's commitment to excellence in engineering through individual initiative and experimentation. One example of this is the company's annual inventor's fair. Employees working on their own time and with modest support from Honda, compete as individuals and teams to create new and unusual products.

In 1992 Honda became embroiled in a scandal in the United States involving illegal payments of cash and gifts totaling $50 million over a fifteen-year period. At that time, Honda fired key executives implicated in the scandal. Between 1994 and 1997, eighteen former executives were convicted. The scandal grew out of the effects of the voluntary import restraints placed on Japanese automotive makers in 1981. The demand for Honda's cars rose precipitously, creating a situation in which dealers were coerced to make illegal payments in order to get shipments.

See also: automotive industry

Further reading

Lynch, S. (1997) *Arrogance and Accords: The Inside Story of the Honda Scandal*, Dallas, TX: Pecos Press.
Nelson, D., Moody, P.E. and Mayo, R. (1998), *Powered by Honda: Developing Excellence in Global Enterprise*, New York: John Wiley & Sons.
Otsuki, S., Tanaka, F. and Sakurai, Y. (1996) *Good Mileage: The High-Performance Business Philosophy of Soichiro Honda*, New York: Weatherhill.

ALLAN BIRD

Honda, Soichiro

Soichiro Honda (1906–91) was a Japanese inventor and automobile executive, and founder of **Honda** Motor Company, the world-famous manufacturer of motorcycles and automobiles. Honda was born in 1906 in a small town near Hamamatsu in Shizuoka Prefecture, where his father was a blacksmith. As a child he was fascinated by machinery, and when the first automobile appeared in his village during his primary school days, he decided that he would one day build cars himself. At the age of fifteen, Honda became an apprentice at an automobile repair shop in Tokyo. Pressed into intensive on-the-job training when the 1923 Tokyo earthquake forced most of the shop's employees to return to their homes, he became an accomplished mechanic, and in 1928 he opened his own auto repair shop in Hamamatsu.

Honda's skills as an inventor became evident when he began building racing cars in his spare time. Through innovations such as tilting the engine to the left so that the car could more easily negotiate left turns, improving engine cooling by adding an extra radiator, and fashioning the valve seats out of heat-conducting metal, his cars won many races. Although a crash at the finish of the 1936 All-Japan Speed Rally ended his career behind the wheel, Honda's interest in racing continued, leading to the success of Honda motorcycles and racecars in international racing competition in later decades.

In 1937, Honda decided to try his hand at manufacturing piston rings. Studying metal casting on his own, Honda developed a piston ring and tried to sell it to **Toyota**, but was turned down. He refused to give up, however, and after two hard years of trials and failure he was finally able to produce piston rings that met Toyota's quality standards. His company became a supplier to Toyota in 1940.

When the Second World War ended, Honda sold his company to Toyota and used the proceeds to buy a large drum of medical alcohol. This he installed in his home, where he made whiskey and spent a year partying with friends and playing the *shakuhachi* (Japanese flute).

In 1946, refreshed, Honda established the Honda Technical Research Institute, the forerunner of Honda Motor Company, in Hamamatsu. His new company began by modifying the small engines that the Japanese military had used for radios and attaching them to bicycles. He then began producing his own engines, and went into the production of motorcycles. In 1949 he teamed up with Takeo Fujisawa, who became co-founder of Honda Motor Company. The two worked together as equal partners until their retirement in 1973, with Honda in charge of technological development and Fujisawa responsible for management of the company.

Further reading

Otsuki, S., Tanaka, F. and Sakurai, Y. (1996) *Good Mileage: The High Performance Business Philosophy of Soichiro Honda*, New York: Weatherhill.

Sakiya, T. (1982) *Honda Motor: The Men, The Management, The Machines*, Tokyo: Kodansha International.

TIM CRAIG

human relations management

Human relations management refers to the type of work system found in Japanese companies, in particular, how Japanese companies manage their personnel. The human relations approach relies on the assumption that an employee enters the company as a "clean slate." Thus, human relations management focuses upon interpersonal skill development, teamwork, flexibility and generalist knowledge. The study of human relations management focuses upon the functional divisions of management, namely, the work system, recruitment, training, compensation and labor relations.

The work system in Japanese companies is structured around small group activities and decentralized decision making. The primary focus in this approach is upon the promotion of cooperation among workers in order to sustain an internal workforce over the long term. Small group activities serve as a tool to involve employees in decision making while promoting interpersonal conflict resolution and close personal relations. Additionally, small group activities promote group level learning, which improves implicit communication and company specific knowledge development. Therefore, the work system facilitates the building of a "company mindset" and strong corporate culture (Nonaka and Takeuchi 1998).

Recruitment in the human relations system is based upon long-term external relationships with the company. The system of recruiting only new school graduates is still the norm in Japan. Recruitment into a Japanese company most often centers on achieving a fit between the personality of the individual and the company culture. This is because recruitment is designed to provide stable human capital for the long term versus short-term (strategic) skill or knowledge. Males and females are recruited for different roles in the organization, as are white-collar (university graduates) and blue-collar (high school or junior college graduates) employees, but the delineation among employees is confined mainly to these categories.

Training and development in the Japanese system emphasizes an evolutionary process of education and training designed to mold an individual into the ideal corporate employee. On-the-job training, or OJT, is the primary method of training for the Japanese employee. OJT is learning by observing and doing, with little or no systematic measurement or evaluation. This system of knowledge development is sometimes supplemented by education and training for employees outside the company, as in study abroad scholarships or technical training assignments, but is largely confined to company-specific employee development.

Compensation and promotion are based upon a seniority system. The seniority system assumes a slow, steady progression of employee development which occurs at roughly the same time for all employees. Thus, the length of employment determines the amount of change in pay and or status of the individual. This is in direct contrast to a performance-based system in which individual effort and output determine the amount of compensation and the rate of advancement. Although the seniority system has often been criticized as promoting mediocrity and dampening innovation in the organization, its main purpose, to maintain harmonious relations among employees, has been successful over time.

Labor relations in a human relations management system relies on the family structure of Japanese organizations to allow a unique "company union" system to persist. Whereas in the Western labor union tradition there is an adversarial relationship between management and workers, Japanese managers and line staff are members of the same union. Again, the focus of Japanese unions is to promote quality or work-life issues much more than the traditional Western unions which negotiate mainly on issues of compensation and safety.

Further reading

Abegglen, J.C. and Stalk, G. (1985) *Kaisha: The Japanese Corporation*, New York: Basic Books.

Inohara, H. (1990) *Human Resource Development in Japanese Companies*, Tokyo: Asian Productivity Organization.

Nonaka, I, and Takeuchi, H. (1998) *The Knowledge Creating Company: How Japanese Companies Create the Dynamics of Innovation*, Oxford: Oxford University Press.

Whitehill, A.M. (1991) *Japanese Management*, London: Routledge.

MARGARET TAKEDA

Ie

There is perhaps no more evocative word in the Japanese language than *ie*, most literally "family," which encompasses a range of meanings from simply "kinsfolk" to "dwelling" to a value-laden sense of "household." Historically shaped by Confucian familial rights and obligations, the word *ie* today still connotes the social basis of one's fundamental relationships: to parents and off-spring, to community and workplace. By purposefully extending the household collective beyond relationships bound purely by blood, the *ie* has continued to serve from Japanese medieval times to the present as the basic unit of a cohesive social structure that eventually built the "Japanese economic miracle."

The *toyo kanji* (ideograph) for family, *Ie*, shown in Figure 1, illustrates its roots. The ideograph consists of two elements: a roof over a pig, a domesticated animal in a dwelling. This image succinctly symbolizes the importance placed upon the household's economic role over the human aspects of a conjugal nuclear family. The conjugal nuclear family is subordinate to the Ie. The *Ie*'s significance as an economic collective has, in fact, brought added relevance to the word's other meanings.

The *ie* concept of the household unit may be traced back to ancient times and has its earliest roots in the cooperative nature of traditional agricultural production. Later, in the seventh century, Confucian concepts were imported from China and adapted by the elite classes, providing fundamental support for the *ie* ideology. The focus of Confucian doctrine was the cult of the family. In

Figure 1

general, it prescribed: the hierarchical relations between members; personal loyalty consisting of reciprocal duties and obligations; ritual observances of these reciprocities; contractual arrangements between groups patterned after family relationships. Diffusion of Confucian ideas to all social orders did not occur until much later, during the **Tokugawa period**. Until then, peasant family members were scattered as serfs among the noble classes within the feudal order.

Buddhism also had a profound effect on Japanese culture. Its social impact, through an emphasis on the cultivation of humility and the subordination of individual ambition for a collective good, cannot be overestimated, particularly in regard to its implicit support for key Confucian values. Confucianism and Buddhism were complementary to the *ujigami*, patron deities of the native Shinto local god system. Together the three evolved into a family religion, commonly referred to as ancestor worship, which was virtually universal in Tokugawa Japan. The brief daily ceremony before the family shrine was a constant reminder to household members of their obligations to the *ie*.

The *ie* was the most basic economic, political, and social collective unit of a society that was itself governed by precepts of **giri**, obligations and duties to superiors, and *on*, benevolence to inferiors. Within the *ie*, the most important criterion by which to evaluate action and behavior was how well it served the group. In such a collectively oriented society, the individual hardly existed as a distinct entity, and failure to fulfill one's obligations was considered selfish, or even cowardly. This *ie* ideological system suited Japan's oligarchic feudal system quite well. The *daimyo* (feudal lord) was referred to as *shushin* (lordparent) and the followers as *ienoko* (children of the family). First adopted by the warrior class, the *samurai*, the *ie* house system later informed the business and social practices of the merchant and the artisan classes as these groups increased in economic importance.

The *giri* psychology of moral obligation and duty provided stability to the two and one-half centuries of peace and tranquillity of Tokugawa Japan, following a hundred years of civil wars. After the Battle of Sekigahara in 1600, Tokugawa hegemony was established and a class structure imposed that was to become largely immutable. Its rigid hierarchy, popularly known as the *shinokosho* (warrior, farmer, artisan, merchant classes), declared the peasants second only to the *samurai* in the social pecking order, although they ranked last economically.

By the mid-1700s the whole of Japanese society was comprised of economic units based on households reinforced by a religious cult of the family. During this *Pax Tokugawa*, every effort was made to suppress change in order to maintain the social structure. Tokugawa government policy sought to settle peasants permanently in stable villages and establish the *ie* as the basic unit of society. During the seventeenth and eighteenth centuries, land and tenant rights were promulgated among the peasantry making it possible for individual farming households to establish themselves. Family units could then remain intact through successive generations. Thus formalized by law, the peasantry began to adopt the family values of the *samurai* household codes.

The *ie* was seen first and foremost as an ongoing enterprise rather than as a sanguineous family unit.

Once an *ie* was established, its continuity through successive generations was of major concern to its members. If there was no son, a daughter's husband would be adopted into the household to assume the family name and eventually inherit the household. If there were no children at all, a son or daughter would be adopted and, with his or her spouse, carry on the household. Kinship blood ties were not as important as the suitability of the candidate to manage the affairs of the household, particularly in a merchant family. Although a son would normally be considered first choice to inherit, if unsuited to the task he might be sent to establish his own branch household while a longtime faithful employee would be chosen as successor, married to a daughter, and adopted into the household.

Although the laws of inheritance allowed for only one heir so as to preserve the property of the household, custom provided for the establishment of branch households for additional offspring and loyal apprentices who had become part of the *ie*. It is these last two attributes, the adoption of a non-blood member as heir and the indivisibility of inherited property, that distinguishes the Japanese institution of the *ie* from other East Asian family/kinship enterprise systems, such as in China and Korea.

The harsh living conditions of the Tokugawa period made the division of property among offspring nearly impossible, so that only the wealthiest families were able to bestow any assets on a second or third son. However, high mortality rates during the Tokugawa period and into the modern period meant that second or third sons could be adopted into other households in the same or neighboring villages.

It was most common that, in the formative stages of the household enterprise, the direct management of the *ie* was in the hands of family members for the first two generations. As the business grew in stability and size, however, often by the third generation, competent managers who had grown up in the *ie* from early childhood and had been promoted from *detchi* (apprentice) to *tedai* (salesperson) and then **banto** (manager), were ready to assume the management operations of an expanded business. It was often at this stage in the development of the *Ie* that management of the *mise* (store) became physically separated from the *oku* (back living quarters), symbolically marking the progression from a nuclear family business to an extended family business. For *ie* that had grown to a very large scale, such as **Mitsui**, it was imperative that non-family member managers be given authority since there could not possibly be a sufficiently large talent pool within the Mitsui family itself.

The *banto* was permitted to marry at age twenty-five and was then provided by the master with a *bekke* (separate house). Those who continued to work within the *honke* (main house) were guaranteed their livelihood after retirement. Those *bekke* that operated a business were financed and given a share of the goodwill by the *honke*, whether in the same or a different type of business. Apprentices for the main house were selected from among the sons of the *bekke*, thus maintaining the fictive kinship relationship.

The successful collectivist centered development of the Japanese firm differed sharply from the weakened role of the household firm in Western Europe, which was superseded by the creation in early seventeenth century England and the Netherlands of the joint stock company form (see **joint stock corporation**).

The Japanese family firm in the *ie* system was able to develop many of the attributes of a Western-style corporation while retaining the motivational aspects of a household business: (1) perpetuation of the firm by training of suitable successors from within the *ie*; (2) securing the loyalty of management to the household by the use of fictive kinship status; (3) the indivisibility of the *ie* and its assets, which tended to constrain the ability of any one individual stakeholder to act on his own against the overall interests of the household.

The origins of the **zaibatsu** and its successors the *keiretsu* (vertically grouped companies) and *kigyo shudan* (horizontally grouped corporate firms) are found in the establishment of the merchant family houses of the Tokugawa period. The extended household enterprises or family associations, such as the Konoike, Sumitomo, and Mitsui groups, were all engaged in different types of businesses and strategies. They were active in developing the capital resources and a household enterprise management system during the early Tokugawa

period that enabled them to continue to prosper during the industrialization era of the Meiji period.

The management style which enabled the development of the merchant household style business was based on a distinctive concept of kinship, namely, of non-blood, fictive kinship-based economic units. In a household style business non-blood related individuals function together as a simulated kinship group. Even when the internal structure of a modern industrial enterprise grows beyond a small-sized business, traditional patterns of *on* and *giri* continue. Subsidiaries and sub-units assume the traditional obligations to their employees. Similarly, the traditional distinctions between insider and outsider are in play in the modern notion of the "lifetime employee," a modern-day embodiment of the traditional apprentice, an adoptive member of the *ie* (household). In the postwar period the most sought after jobs for new university graduates are those not only with a prestigious company but also with a secure "family" culture. Although, only some 30 percent of Japanese industrial workers were considered to have "lifetime" status; an employee would still be classified as "temporary " or "part-time" even after working twenty years for the firm. The so-called temporary employee remains outside the network of reciprocities, without share in the *ie* or job security.

The attributes of the postwar Japanese style management, such as the **lifetime employment** system, **seniority promotion**, and a paternalistic policy towards employees, have their historical basis in the annals of medieval seventeenth century merchant households. *Ie* household codes governing the management of family businesses contained specific regulations on the theory and practice of long-term employment, seniority, and the good treatment of employees.

The process of modernization in Japan may be viewed, in some very fundamental aspects, as the continuous development of native institutions rather than as the result of the abrupt introduction of Western ideas in the Meiji period of the late nineteenth century. The values and beliefs associated with the *ie* household concept are alive not only in family-operated businesses but are reflected in the relationships and practices within firms and within **industrial groups**. The concepts that came to be inherent in *ie* provided foundation for the transformation of Japanese household enterprise across the centuries into the present day forms as member firms of large corporate enterprise groups (*kigyo shudan*) and *keiretsu*. *Ie* prepared the way for the great trading houses and their commercial banks, known as the *zaibatsu* in the prewar period. Finally, *ie* "house" practices not only prefigured the relationship for the *kigyo shudan*, of today, but, more significantly, the development of Japanese firms as group entities, prototypic of the formation of relationships between industrial groups, both big and small, throughout Japanese society and its economy.

Further reading

Nakane, C. (1970) *Japanese Society*, Berkeley, CA and Los Angeles: University of California Press.

Scher, M.J. (1997) *Japanese Interfirm Networks and Their Main Banks*, London: Macmillan, and New York: St Martin's Press.

MARK SCHER

Ikeda, Hayato

Hayato Ikeda was born in the Hiroshima prefecture in 1899. In March 1925, he graduated Kyoto Teikoku University (presently Kyoto University) Department of Law, and entered the **Ministry of Finance**. He became the chief of National Taxation at the Ministry of Finance in 1941, and the Vice-Minister of Finance in 1947. In 1952, he became Minister of International Trade and Industry

In 1960 the First Ikeda Cabinet was formed, and the government set the *Shotoku-Baizo-Keikaku* (Double Income Policy). The success of this policy formed the basis of Japan's phenomenal economic growth during the next few decades. Japan formally became a member of the Organization for Economic Cooperation and Development (OECD) in April, 1964.

In September of that year (1964), Ikeda entered the National Cancer Center. In October, he announced his resignation, and the entire Ikeda

Cabinet resigned in November. He passed away on August 13, 1965. He was awarded the Grand Cordon of the Supreme Order of the Chrysanthemum that same year.

Further reading

Ito, M. (1985) *Hayato Ikeda and His Times*, Tokyo: Asahi Shinbun-sha.

Kobayashi, K. (1989) *Hana mo Arashi mo: Prime Minister Hayato Ikeda's Ambitions*, Tokyo: Kodan-sha.

MARGARET TAKEDA
AKI MATSUNAGA

Inamori, Kazuo

Born in 1932, Kazuo Inamori is the founder of two multibillion dollar companies: **Kyocera** Corporation, which is the world leader in manufacturing ceramic casings for semiconductors, and DDI Corporation, the second-largest telephone company in Japan. He is viewed by many as one of the greatest entrepreneurs of post-Second World War Japan along with Akio **Morita** and Soichiro **Honda**.

As a student, Inamori failed to get into any of the prestigious high schools, colleges, or companies. He later received a degree in chemical engineering from Kagoshima University and in 1955 went to work for Shofu Industries, a Kyoto-based manufacturer of electronics. In 1959, at the age of twenty-seven, he quit Shofu because the company management would not pursue his vision of a ceramic business, and started Kyocera with seven colleagues .

Inamori's business philosophy has strong religious overtones. For example, Kyocera's corporate motto is "respect the divine and love people." His teachings are a mixture of Zen, Zig Ziglar and motivational speaking. He has written two books that have been translated to English: *A Passion for Success* and *For People For Profit*.

DAYO FAWIBE

income doubling plan

The National Income Doubling Plan (*Kokumin Shotoku Baizo Keikaku*) decided by the Ikeda Cabinet in 1960 has been called the "Income Doubling Plan" and is the most famous government economic plan in post-Second World War Japan. The then Prime Minister, Hayato Ikeda, taking a hint from Professor Ichiro Nakayama's theory of wage-doubling, announced that his government would double national income within ten years from 1961 to 1970.

The political and economic background of the plan was the following. On the one hand, 1960 was the year for renewal of the United States–Japan Security Treaty concluded in 1951, which gave the United States the right to station troops and maintain military bases in Japan. The treaty renewal, which did little to change the basic situation, gave rise to strong opposition and political turmoil. After Prime Minister Kishi Nobusuke's resignation in 1960, he was succeeded by Ikeda, who tried to overcome the political crisis, which had also been triggered by the Mitsui-Miike Coal Mine Strike, the postwar period's largest labor–capital confrontation. In this context, the announcement of the plan had an aspect of political appeasement.

On the other hand, the Japanese economy, though reconstructed after the destruction of the Second World War, was still weak and fragile domestically as well as internationally. Although rapid growth had begun in 1955, achieving full employment and balancing international accounts were still the biggest challenges facing Japan. The Ikeda plan also had to address these challenges.

The plan stated its goal as follows: "the ultimate aim is to move toward a conspicuous increase in the national standard of living and the achievement of full employment. To that end, the maximal stable growth of the economy must be contrived." The target set in order to maximize stable growth was to double national income and GNP within ten years. The target level for GNP in 1970 was set at ¥26 trillion (at 1958 values), double the GNP for 1960. Therefore, average annual growth had to reach 7.2 percent over the decade. In actuality, the plan called for an average annual rate of 9 percent for the first three years.

Five major problems had to be solved in order for the plan to reach this target. First, infrastructure bottlenecks that impeded further growth had to be solved by increasing government investment. The expansion of the private sector was creating bottlenecks due to lack of roads, harbors, factory sites and so forth. Second, in order to achieve economic independence, the modernization of national industrial structure had to be promoted. This called for the Americanization of Japanese industry, or in other words, the introduction of Fordism. Third, the promotion of international trade and cooperation had to be increased. Fourth, the improvement of human capabilities and advancement of science and technology was emphasized and promoted. For example, one approach was to set up a number of new colleges of science and engineering. Fifth, mitigating the negative side effects of the dual structures of the economy (see **dual structure theory**) and securing social stability was established as a major focus. This was a response to problems that accompanied rapid **economic growth**: the need to reduce wage differentials between large and small companies, to reduce income gaps between agricultural and manufacturing sectors, and to diminish regional income disparities. The type of approach embodied in the income-doubling plan can be viewed as one element of Japanese-style welfare state.

The plan's policies can be broken down into two main thrusts: economic growth and appeasement. Although it is difficult to evaluate the full effects of the plan itself, the Medium-Term Economic Plan introduced by the Sato Cabinet in 1965 replaced the plan halfway through its lifespan. The Japanese economy continued to grow at the highest rate of any major economy in the world and, as a result, exceeded the target of ¥26 trillion, reaching nearly ¥40 trillion in 1970. The actual average annual growth rate in the period from 1961 to 1970 was 11.6 percent.

Due to its high rate of growth, Japan attained almost full employment and economic independence in the middle of 1960s, mitigating to some extent the dual structure economy and becoming the second largest economy in the free world. However, the high rate of growth caused distortions in the economy such as price increases, overpopulation in urban areas and depopulation in rural areas, pollution, and so forth. Indeed the main objective of the above-touch behind introducing the Medium-Term Economic Plan was to correct these distortions.

Japan's economic planning, as carried out officially by the Cabinet, began with the five-year plan for economic self-support put forward in 1955. Since that time the government has introduced fourteen further plans. The most recent plan is called the Ideal Socioeconomy and Policies for Economic Rebirth (1999–2010).

Japan's economic plans possess three basic characteristics. First, they indicate the "desired direction of economic and social development;" second, they indicate the policy direction the government should take in order to achieve these ends; third, they indicate behavior guidelines for people and for business. On the whole, the planned figures fall somewhere between predictions and guidelines. Few government or business leaders consider the national economic plan as a rigid, binding plan that must be followed by the government. Instead it is viewed as a long-term forecast, with some flavor of wishful thinking by the plan-makers.

Especially in the case of the Income Doubling Plan, Komiya (1990) suggests that the "announcement effect" or "propaganda effect" on economic growth seems to have been quite substantial. Ikeda and the plan pulled together a national consensus for economic growth and defined the era of high growth that had already begun.

See also: dollar shock

Further reading

Komiya, R. (1990) *The Japanese Economy: Trade, Industry, and Government*, Tokyo: University of Tokyo Press.

Kosai, Y. (1986) *The Era of High-Speed Growth: Notes on the Postwar Japanese Economy*, trans. J. Kaminski, Tokyo: University of Tokyo Press.

Nakamura, T. (1981) *The Postwar Japanese Economy: Its Development and Structure*, trans. J. Kaminski, Tokyo: University of Tokyo Press.

Uchino, T. (1978) *Japan's Postwar Economy: An Insider's View of its History and its Future*, trans. M.A. Harbison, Tokyo: Kodansha International.

HITOSHI HIGUCHI

industrial efficiency movement

The industrial efficiency movement (*nouritsu undou*) was a series of initiatives starting in the period 1910–20 that aimed to modernize labor and production management practices in Japanese industry. Inspired by American models, and especially by Frederick Winslow Taylor's theories of scientific management, Japanese reformers sought to systematize and rationalize inefficient, customary production methods. Adapting imported theories to Japanese conditions, the proponents of industrial efficiency pioneered managerial ideologies and techniques which would become the hallmarks of Japanese-style management (**Nihonteki keiei**) after the Second World War.

The age of efficiency

Japan's industrial efficiency movement paralleled similar drives to modernize factory management practices in the United States and Europe. Taylor's work on the systematic rationalization of production was a crucial catalyst in this international effort and his classic book, *The Principles of Scientific Management*, was published in Japanese only two years after its American release in 1911. Taylorite methods and the broader notion of efficiency captured the imagination of many in industrializing Japan, from engineers to academics to the general public: new books and journals dedicated to management issues proliferated, many universities introduced courses on Taylorism, and expositions featuring the latest managerial advances attracted thousands of interested spectators.

Although the Japanese mania for efficiency seemed to some a passing fad of the 1910s, important figures in private industry and the government embraced the Taylorite message and actively promoted the adoption of techniques such as time-and-motion study, standardization and incentive wages. During the 1920s, thanks in part to the work of Yoichi **Ueno** and other early management consultants, scientific management spread steadily through Japan's modern industries, especially textiles, electrical goods and the national railways. Reformers encountered opposition from some intellectuals and labor groups that criticized Taylorism as dehumanizing, exploitative and excessively materialistic. Nonetheless, Taylorite practices appear to have engendered significantly less hostility from shop-floor workers in Japan than was the case in either the USA or Europe. An important reason for this was the fact that Japanese management reformers, sensitive to their nation's particular economic and cultural conditions, sought to adapt Taylorism ideologically and methodologically to Japanese realities. Tempering scientific management's mechanistic rationality and managerial elitism with more concern for the well-being of workers, proponents of industrial efficiency endeavored to develop a more humane Taylorism for application in Japan.

Depression and war

After the onset of the Great Depression, Japan's management reformers were increasingly integrated into the industrial rationalization movement (*sangyou gourika undou*), a major government-sponsored program to increase productivity, limit competition and stabilize industry during the global economic crisis. As part of this broader effort, the industrial efficiency movement, which during the 1920s had been a loosely organized, uncoordinated and largely private sector initiative, became more centralized, streamlined, and professional. With official subsidization and encouragement, a series of new campaigns aimed at the modernization of factory management were launched during the 1930s.

Despite the early achievements of the industrial efficiency movement, proponents recognized that much improvement was still possible, especially as labor productivity in Japan continued to lag behind US and European levels. Some ambitious reformers even looked toward the establishment of Fordist mass production, a dramatic extension of the logic and methodologies of Taylorism. Yet such a dream remained beyond the reach of prewar Japanese industry, which lacked adequate markets, capital and technology to make the leap to

American-style assembly lines. Indeed, even incremental Taylorization proved impossible for many Japanese employers: under the straightened circumstances of the depression, mass layoffs and work intensification seemed easier solutions than the scientific analysis of production.

The coming of the Second World War and the realization that industrial power was as important as military might in modern "total war" brought an unprecedented surge of interest in efficiency and management reform. Japanese Taylorites were readily mobilized and the application of scientific management was trumpeted as the patriotic duty of manufacturers. But despite heightened appreciation of Japan's need for managerial modernization, actual progress on the shop floor was slow in an environment of constant dislocation, endemic shortages and imperfect central planning. Standardization and specialization proved elusive through the war and, in the end only a few industries realized even limited assembly line production. Nonetheless, wartime developments did lay sound foundations for the sweeping reform of management practices and the attainment of mass production in the postwar years: most importantly, as the number of trained, professional managers swelled during the war, the vision of a humanized recasting of Taylorism was widely embraced as a specifically Japanese approach to modern production and labor management.

Legacies

Although the industrial efficiency movement is usually taken to have ended with Japan's defeat in 1945, its intellectual and methodological legacies suffused the major management reform efforts of the postwar period. For example, Taylorite ideologies – including the assumption that prosperity would neutralize class conflict and the abiding faith in apolitical managerial expertise – came to characterize the productivity movement, a US-sponsored drive to modernize Japanese industry and labor relations. Meanwhile, familiar Taylorite practices such as time-and-motion study became the technical building blocks of the famed **Toyota production system** and were widely embraced as Japan made the postwar transition to a modern, mass production economy.

Japan's particular heritage of scientific management may have had its greatest impact, however, on the postwar quality control movement. Over a decades-long process of trial and error, quality advocates sought to realize the vision of a humanized Taylorism, fusing the scientific remaking of the workshop (through statistical analysis and rigorous standardization) with new means for engaging and motivating labor such as **quality control circles**. The distinctive patterns and conspicuous successes of Japanese **quality management** – and, indeed, of contemporary Japanese production and labor management as a whole – derived in large part from the formative influence of the industrial efficiency movement.

See also: Japan Productivity Center for Socio-Economic Development

Further reading

Okuda, K. (1985) *Hito to keiei: Nihon keiei kanrishi kenkyuu* (Men and Management: Research in Japanese Managerial History), Tokyo: Manejimento-sha.

Sasaki, S. (1987) "Scientific Management Movements in Pre-War Japan," in S. Yasuoka and H. Morkiawa (eds), *Japanese Yearbook on Business History: 1987*, Tokyo: Japan Business History Institute.

Tsutsui, W.M. (1998) *Manufacturing Ideology: Scientific Management in Twentieth-Century Japan*, Princeton, NJ: Princeton University Press.

WILLIAM M. TSUTSUI

industrial groups (*keiretsu*)

Keiretsu is a Japanese word that defies exact translation. A literal rendering into English might be "succession," in the sense of a sequence of entities joined together, as links in a chain. The word *keiretsu* is used to refer to business groups including (1) the six groups centered around the large Japanese banks (also called financial groups, financial *keiretsu*, or horizontal *keiretsu*), (2) the groups of firms centered around the forty or so largest industrial companies of Japan (also called enterprise groups or vertical *keiretsu*), (3) the

subcontracting groups that are an important component of several of the groups centered around the large industrial companies, and (4) directed marketing channels (also called distribution *keiretsu*). This entry is confined to the first two of these, which we will refer to respectively as the financial *keiretsu* and the enterprise groups. Both are also called industrial groups.

Financial *keiretsu*

The financial *keiretsu* are the postwar reincarnations of the prewar *zaibatsu*. After the end of the Second World War, the **American occupation** authorities directed the dismantling of the *zaibatsu*. These measures included the divestiture of share interlocks, dissolution and abolition of holding companies, and appropriation and disbursement of shares held by the *zaibatsu* families. Soon after the Occupation ended, and continuing until about 1960, many of the firms previously affiliated with the major *zaibatsu* or the successors of such firms re-established their old shareholding interlocks. The large commercial banks among these firms became major stockholders in most of the other members of their respective reconstituted groups. Besides the progeny of the big four *zaibatsu* – Mitsui, Mitsubishi, Sumitomo, and Fuyo (formerly Yasuda) – the six financial *keiretsu* include the Dai-Ichi Kangyo group, consisting mainly of former members of the smaller Kawasaki and Furukawa *zaibatsu*, and the Sanwa group that had no prewar antecedent.

There are different ways of ascertaining which companies belong to which financial *keiretsu*. The clearest evidence of affiliation is appearance on the roster of monthly "presidents' club" meetings of any one of the six respective groups. These rosters are public, though the agendas of the meetings are not. A few companies belong to more than one presidents' club – Hitachi belongs to three of them – but these are the rare exceptions. The rosters of the presidents' clubs exhibit little change from one year to the next, and the changes that do occur are mostly the result of mergers. Altogether, the members of the six presidents' clubs in 1995 numbered 185 companies, including most but not all of the largest companies in Japan. Some of the large companies not on the rosters of presidents' clubs include Honda Motor, Matsushita, Sony, and Fuji Film.

The presidents' club companies span a wide selection of industries. In fact, the economist Miyazaki Yoshikazu famously characterized the financial *keiretsu* as organized on the basis of the "complete-set principle" (*wan setto shugi*); that is, each of them comprised of at least one company in each major industry. In industry after industry, the members of the differing financial *keiretsu* compete with one another. For instance, Toyota, Mitsubishi Motors, Nissan, Daihatsu and Isuzu are each affiliated with a different *keiretsu*. Kirin Brewery belongs to the Mitsubishi presidents' club, but Sapporo Breweries belongs to the Fuyo presidents' club. There are many other similar examples. The financial *keiretsu* are not simply cartels, coalitions of suppliers of similar products. Rather, they represent suppliers of differing products, and in many instances, fellow members of the same presidents' club trade with one another. Japan's Fair Trade Commission has periodically surveyed the extent of transactions between fellow members of same presidents' clubs. In 1980 it reported that 20 percent of the sales of presidents' club manufacturing firms were to fellow members of the same clubs, and 12 percent of purchases were from fellow club members. These are all very large companies, most of whose transactions are probably with smaller firms, outside the presidents' clubs, so the Fair Trade Commission data does suggest a disposition towards trade between fellow members of the same financial *keiretsu*.

Presidents' club members borrow principally but not exclusively from fellow members. The single largest lender to each of them is usually the city bank that belongs to the same presidents' club as the company itself. In the usual pattern, loans from the presidents' club city bank account for 10 percent to 20 percent of any other fellow presidents' club member's total outstanding debt. The presidents' club trust bank holds another 5 percent to 10 percent of each fellow member's debt and the life insurance company 1 percent to 5 percent. The balance of a typical presidents' club company's total borrowing is from outside the group, including borrowing from financial members of other presidents' clubs than the one of affiliation. Presidents' club members also borrow

from the three long-term credit banks, the city banks not affiliated with the six financial *keiretsu*, and from the regional banks. Since 1980, large Japanese companies have been allowed access to international financial markets as a source of funds, but still rely quite heavily upon domestic loans.

Another visible linkage among fellow presidents' club members is cross-shareholding. The average fractions of outstanding shares held within the respective presidents' clubs in 1997 were Sumitomo (22.2 percent), Mitsubishi (27.3 percent), Dai-Ichi Kangyo (11.3 percent), Sanwa (15.8 percent), Mitsui (15.1 percent), and Fuyo (15.5 percent), but about half of these shares were held by financial institutions of the respective groups. The Antimonopoly Law of Japan limits the extent of shares that banks and insurance companies may hold in any one company. Since 1987 these limits have been set at 5 percent for banks and 7 percent for insurance companies. Few banks or insurance companies hold share interests approaching these limits. The shareholding of banks in the companies to which they lend is an important aspect of Japan's bank-centered system of financial intermediation.

About one-third of the (non-ordered) pairs of nonfinancial companies belonging to a same presidents' club are directly linked with one another by cross-shareholding, and in about half of these instances, the cross-shareholding is reciprocal. Typically, the share interest of any one presidents' club company in another lies around 1 percent. In other words, the cross-shareholding ties are usually insufficient to confer a controlling interest. Cross-shareholding between nonfinancial members of differing presidents' clubs is unusual.

The financial *keiretsu* occupy a sizeable niche in the Japanese economy. Together, the six presidents' clubs in 1997 accounted for about one-eighth of the sales of nonfinancial businesses in Japan, one-seventh of the paid-in capital, and one-eighth of the net profit.

Enterprise groups

The groups of firms centered, respectively, around a number of the largest industrial companies are also referred to as *keiretsu* and as industrial groups. There is no standard term of reference for them but here let us refer to them as enterprise groups.

The prominent examples are listed in Table 2 below. Quite a few of the forty firms identified there as leaders of enterprise groups are themselves members of a *keiretsu* presidents' club.

The enterprise groups generally include myriad subsidiaries as well as independent subcontractors and other suppliers, and some also include whole-salers and retailers of the group's products. Trading ties within the respective enterprise groups may be presumed to be much more extensive than is generally true in the financial *keiretsu*. Also the shareholding of the enterprise group leader in the other members is typically strong enough to confer *de facto* control, not merely a silent financial interest. The enterprise groups are more tightly knit than the financial *keiretsu*.

The combined assets of the forty enterprise groups listed in Table 2 approached 10 percent of the total assets of all industrial firms in Japan, in 1994. In other words, the scale of the forty largest enterprise groups roughly corresponds to that of all the industrial members of the presidents' clubs of the six financial *keiretsu*.

Business scholars have offered various conjectures regarding the fundamental rationale behind Japan's industrial groups. The financial *keiretsu* owe something to their *zaibatsu* antecedents. The companies' long history of profitable trade and cooperation with one another has engendered a mutual sense of trust within the respective financial *keiretsu*, and enhanced their shared reputations in dealings with outsiders. These reputations represent a true business advantage and one that the companies are loathe to abandon. If the companies' early histories had not included the fact that each lay within the control orbit of the same respective *zaibatsu* then these advantages of group affiliation might never have been realized and perpetuated. The Sanwa financial *keiretsu*, unlike the others, has no prewar antecedent but from its origin it imitated the proven success of the others and so required their example.

Bank dominance of financial intermediation in Japan is another factor buttressing the financial *keiretsu*. Regulations and other factors that inhibited companies from raising external funds in securities markets gave rise to the main bank system in Japan, in which banks supplied the greater share of external funds and also therefore developed close relationships with loan clients. The main bank for any one member of a financial *keiretsu* was naturally the main bank for all because given the various group members' active commerce with one another, information about each one's credit-worthiness also bore on that of the others. This very fact further inclined the companies to perpetuate their special ties with one another; the implied information spillovers lowered their costs of borrowing.

The enterprise groups represent a form of economic organization that is less vertically integrated than some conceivable alternatives. In the market economy, vertical integration will proceed further when the costs of transacting through the price system are greater and the costs of administering a directed system of production are lower. Factors bearing on transaction costs include the extent of the market, the weight of reputation effects, the sophistication of contracts and the degree of government interference with private contracts. The large scale of the Japanese market, the durability of trading ties in Japan, and the laxity of Japan's anti-trust laws all contribute to the organization of production into enterprise groups rather than into fully vertically integrated enterprises.

Table 2 Companies that head the forty most significant enterprise groups. Presidents' club memberships are stated in parentheses.

1801 Taisei (Fuyo)
2503 Kirin Brewery (Mitsubishi)
2914 Japan Tobacco
3402 Toray Industries (Mitsui)
3407 Asahi Chemical Industry (Dai-Ichi)
3863 Nippon Paper Industries (Mitsui, Fuyo)
4010 Mitsubishi Chemical Industries (Mitsubishi)
4204 Sekisui Chemical (Sanwa)
4452 Kao Corp.
4502 Takeda Chemical Industries
4901 Fuji Photo Film
5001 Nippon Oil Co.
5108 Bridgestone Corp.
5201 Asahi Glass (Mitsubishi)
5401 Nippon Steel
5404 NKK (Fuyo)

5711   Mitsubishi Materials (Mitsubishi)
5802   Sumitomo Electric Industries (Sumitomo)
6326   Kubota (Fuyo)
6501   Hitachi (Fuyo, Sanwa, Dai-Ichi)
6502   Toshiba (Mitsui)
6503   Mitsubishi Electric (Mitsubishi)
6701   NEC (Sumitomo)
6702   Fujitsu (Dai-Ichi)
6752   Matsushita Electric Industrial Co.
6758   Sony Corp.
7011   Mitsubishi Heavy Industries (Mitsubishi)
7201   Nissan Motor (Fuyo)
7203   Toyota Motor (Mitsui)
7267   Honda Motor Co.
7751   Canon (Fuyo)
8031   Mitsui (Mitsui)
8058   Mitsubishi (Mitsubishi)
8263   Daei
8264   Ito-Yokado Co.
8591   Orix (Sanwa)
8801   Mitsui Estate development (Mitsui)
9501   Tokyo Electric Power Co.
9613   NTT
       JR-Higashi Nihon

Source: T.Y. Keizai (1996) *Kigyo keiretsu soran* (Handbook of *Keiretsu* Enterprises), Tokyo.

Further reading

Flath, D. (1996) "The Keiretsu Puzzle," *Journal of the Japanese and International Economies* 10: 101–21.

Gerlach, M. (1993) *Alliance Capitalism: The Social Organization of Japanese Business*, Berkeley, CA: University of California Press.

Hadley, E. (1970) *Antitrust in Japan*, Princeton, NJ: Princeton University Press.

Miyazaki, Y. (1967) "Rapid Economic Growth in Post-War Japan – With Special Reference to 'Excessive Competition' and the Formation of 'Keiretsu,'" *The Developing Economies* 5: 329–50.

DAVID FLATH

industrial policy

Industrial policy consists of government actions to influence the economic behavior of specific industries, firms, and other economic actors, for the achievement of broadly defined political goals. Industrial policy is designed to affect specific industries differentially, and so is distinct from general economic policies that influence the economy as a whole, overall aggregate demand, economic welfare, and the like. In general, industrial policy involves actions that anticipate or at times contradict market signals, with the goal of channeling resources to (or away from) selected industries, leading to developmental outcomes that would not have occurred had market forces been allowed to operate freely. Industrial policy generally operates on the supply-side, influencing private investment decisions in directions consistent with broader political goals. A key concept in industrial policy is the creation of comparative advantage: rather than maximizing efficient production while taking existing factor endowments as a given, a government can use industrial policy incentives to change a country's factor endowments.

In the postwar period the Japanese government has provided a range of policy incentives, both positive and negative, to influence private sector behavior. Industrial policy was designed first to help the Japanese economy recover, and then to foster the development of industries with high growth potential, particularly those that embodied advanced technology. In general, Japan's industrial policy has focused on the promotion of capital and technology-intensive production, and has sought to shift the country's entire industrial structure in these directions. Another focus of Japan's industrial policy has been on international trade: many policies have sought to increase the export competitiveness of Japanese products, and at times have shielded domestic industries from international competition.

Scholars do not agree on the nature of Japan's industrial policy goals, and the extent to which the state has been insulated from political and societal pressures. Many have argued that state bureaucrats have been able to define and pursue relatively coherent national-level goals such as improving Japan's international power position through rapid industrialization or achieving national economic and technological autonomy. Others stress the economic motivations behind industrial policy, such as raising factor productivity and national incomes, and overcoming so-called "market failures."

Still others argue that industrial policy has been more politicized, subject to the influence of political actors or affected industries. An academic consensus is emerging that describes Japan's industrial policy as the product of a negotiated balance between the goals of the state and the sometimes conflicting interests of the private sector.

Japan's early industrial policy

Japan's rapid industrialization in the Meiji era is often associated with the industrial policies followed by the new government. The Meiji leadership recognized that Japan lagged behind the European countries in terms of industrial strength, technology, and military capabilities. Unless Japan could rapidly increase its national strength it would be unable to protect its national sovereignty or preserve its economic autonomy, and thus would be vulnerable to the fate that was befalling many others in Asia: imperialism. The Meiji leadership, under the slogan *fukoku kyohei*, or "rich nation, strong army," thus embarked on a sustained effort to upgrade Japan's industrial capabilities and to achieve economic and military parity with the West.

In addition to the government's massive effort to create a modern government administrative structure, the state also took the lead in using industrial policy to modernize the Japanese economy. The government realized that Japan was an economic "latecomer," and that the private sector lacked adequate capital, technology, and entrepreneurial skills to create crucial large-scale and capital-intensive industries. Rather than relying on market forces, the Japanese government intervened in the market by creating a number of state-run "model firms" in such industries as textiles, steel, and shipbuilding. These firms were in part designed to induce private Japanese entrepreneurs to create firms of their own, and most were soon sold off to private sector entrepreneurs. Other government industrial policies included the promotion and financing of the import of advanced technology, and the development of exports, particularly in the textile industry.

In subsequent decades, the government's industrial policy role became more indirect. State policy continued to promote exports and to encourage investment in strategic industries, and especially those deemed to be important for Japan's military capabilities. In the 1930s and then during the Second World War, the Japanese government became increasingly involved in the economy, especially in order to direct resources to war-related industries. During the war, the government semi-nationalized a number of industries through the so-called control boards (*toseikai*), in an effort to sustain the war effort.

Japanese industrial policy during the era of rapid growth

The government's direct involvement in the economy was drastically reduced following Japan's defeat in the war. In the postwar period the Japanese government has not relied heavily on public or state-owned firms. Rather, industrial policy has relied on more indirect measures, including inducements, guidance, and threatened punishments, to influence private sector behavior.

In the postwar period industrial policy has been the responsibility of the **Ministry of International Trade and Industry** (MITI), created in 1949. (Prior to this, MITI was known as the Ministry of Commerce and Industry, or MCI; in January 2001 the ministry was renamed the Ministry of Economics, Trade and Industry, or METI.) The creation of MITI ushered in a period of rapid industrial development and growth. Between 1950 and 1973, the country's gross national product grew by an average of more than 10 percent per year, a record of sustained development that was unprecedented, in Japan or anywhere. At the same time, Japan's industrial structure shifted from agriculture to manufacturing and services, and from light to heavy industry. By the end of this period a growing number of Japanese industries had reached the forefront of international competitiveness, and Japan had become a highly successful exporter. These achievements can be attributed at least in part to industrial policy, although analysts still disagree on the extent.

The decades of fast economic growth up through the oil shocks of the 1970s, the period of the so-called "Japanese miracle," can be considered industrial policy's "golden age." During this period the Japanese government enjoyed a number of advantages, particularly the benefit of a national consensus on economic growth and control over scarce resources and policy tools, that allowed it to design and implement a relatively coherent industrial policy.

The national consensus on the need for economic recovery permeated Japanese society during the first two decades following the war. Not only government officials, but also the conservative politicians, small and large businesses, and labor, all generally agreed on the need to focus the country's energy on economic growth. Opponents of a focus on industrialization had been weakened either during the war or in the period of the US occupation.

Japan's industrial policy was also more effective in this period because the state controlled access to a number of scarce resources that the private sector desperately needed. Particularly in the early postwar years, most Japanese industries faced acute shortages of critical resources, especially capital and technology. It was the government's ability to influence the availability of these resources that gave it some early leverage over the behavior of the private sector.

Most importantly, the state was able to control to an extent the flow of capital. The government at the time had control over foreign exchange, and was able to allocate this scarce resource to favored industries. The government was also able to use a system of "industrial finance" to favor selected industries. MITI, working with the **Ministry of Finance**, was able to use government loans from the **Japan Development Bank** (JDB) as a signal to the private sector. These JDB "policy loans" amounted to a government stamp of approval; industries that received these loans could then usually borrow all that they needed from the private sector. MITI also was able to offer low-interest loans to selected industries through the annual Fiscal and Investment Loan Plan (FILP), which were drawn from Japan's huge national **postal savings** system. This system of savings represented a pool of capital that the government could direct to the private sector on relatively easy terms

The closed nature of the Japanese economy in this period also made industrial policy more effective. The government's role has been referred to as that of a "gatekeeper," with some influence over what was allowed to enter and leave Japan. The government was able to restrict the import of competitive manufactures through relatively high industrial tariffs and quotas. These allowed Japan to protect its targeted industries and in particular the so-called "infant industries" that would have been overwhelmed if exposed to open competition with more established, more efficient foreign competitors. The Japanese government was also able to influence to an extent access to foreign technology. MITI in particular tried to encourage the import of technologies deemed essential and to discourage those that were not. In addition, MITI played a critical early role in helping to "untie" technology, using its ability to restrict access to the Japanese market to allow Japanese firms to obtain foreign technology without permitting inward investment.

Japan's industrial policy also focused on the promotion of exports. In addition to early "infant industry" protection, export sectors were provided with incentives such as tax exemptions and direct and indirect subsidies. State support was often withdrawn once the industry was able to compete on its own in international markets. The Japanese government was also active in compelling, or allowing, key export industries to become more concentrated through mergers. Japan's industrial policy thus influenced the country's industrial structure in two ways: the shift to capital- and technology-intensive industries, and the shift toward an oligopolistic structure within each industry.

A final factor that made Japan's industrial policy more coherent was the so-called "advantages of a follower:" Japan could use the example of the industrialized nations as a blueprint for its own industrial development. Early on, it was clear to government officials, politicians, and the business community that Japan needed to rebuild some basic infrastructure industries. One of the earliest postwar industrial policy efforts was the "priority production plan" in which the government helped rebuild four key industries: electric power, coal mining, steel, and shipbuilding. In ensuing years it was also clear to most that Japan needed to develop certain basic industries, notably steel, chemicals and energy-related industries. It was also clear which would be the "industries of the future," not only in terms of high levels of income and value-added, but also in terms of their "strategic" importance to the industrial economy. In subsequent decades the state provided support to a broad range of industries, including general and precision machinery, automobiles, and consumer electronics. Most of the chosen industries were those that enjoyed high growth potential or were deemed to be potentially competitive in international markets.

Industrial policy after the oil shocks

Many of the factors that made industrial policy seemingly coherent in the high-growth era were gradually breaking down over time. By the time of the oil shocks of the 1970s, which ushered in a period of stable growth, Japan's industrial policy had become less coherent and more politicized.

First, as Japan caught up with the industrialized nations, the consensus on growth gradually broke down. By the 1960s many in Japan had come to recognize the costs of high-speed industrialization, most notably industrial pollution. In addition, the population increasingly demanded that more attention be paid to general quality of life issues such as improving housing and public infrastructure. At the same time, a growing number of industries clamored for industrial policy support from the state, including many small and medium-sized firms and **depressed industries** that had lost their international competitiveness. Many of these less-favored firms relied on support from politicians to press their demands on industrial policy bureaucrats.

As the result of these changes, Japan's industrial policy after the oil shocks became less "strategic" and more redistributive in nature. Industrial policy in this era continued to focus on high-growth industries and the promotion of exports, but now also was involved in improving housing, welfare-related infrastructure, and regional development. In addition, a growing portion of industrial policy efforts was now devoted to propping up the less efficient sectors in the economy.

Japan's industrial policy was also less effective in this era because industries were no longer as dependent on the resources the state had to offer.

As the Japanese economy grew, many of Japan's industries were able to develop their own sources of capital and technology. As a result, many industries had become less dependent on, and thus less receptive to, the inducements offered by the state's industrial policy.

At the same time, the Japanese government was in the process of losing many of its industrial policy tools, largely because of external factors. As the condition for joining the international economic organizations, Japan was forced to substantially lower its tariffs on imported goods, and was later compelled to liberalize its foreign exchange laws. Another important change in this period was the rising level of international scrutiny of Japan's industrial policy. In the early postwar period Japan, as a "small economy" whose actions did not have a great impact on its trading partners, was able to make its industrial policy without much outside interference. But as the Japanese economy gained in export competitiveness, its actions now clearly impinged on its trading partners. Foreign governments now put growing pressures on Japan to refrain from using its industrial policy to give unfair advantages to Japanese industries.

Japan's industrial policy in this era also was made more complicated because many of its industries had reached the forefront of technology. Without the advantages of a follower, it was less clear which industries of the future were the most promising or strategic. One key shift in this period was the support of the "knowledge-intensive" industries. In particular, MITI became involved in public-private research and development efforts, for instance the VLSI (Very Large Scale Integrated) Circuit project (see **VLSI Research Cooperative**). The Japanese state continued to provide incentives for future technologies, but with a more mixed success rate. Although industries such as semiconductors and computers developed in part because of state support, industrial policy was less successful in industries such as aerospace and computer software.

Reassessing industrial policy after the bubble

The long period of stagnant growth in the 1990s has led many scholars to reassess the nature and effectiveness of Japan's industrial policy. Many have noted that Japan's earlier industrial policy was not infallible, often citing MITI's failure to recognize the future competitiveness of firms such as Sony and Honda, and its failures in industries such as aerospace. Others have argued that Japan's industrial policy has led to a chronic problem of excess capacity in that it has been more effective in inducing firms to invest, but less effective in forcing firms to divest or exit the industry. Rather, industrial policy more recently has often been used to shield industries suffering from excess capacity from the costs of economic adjustment, leading to a Japanese economy that is less efficient and competitive.

Most recently, Japan's industrial policy practices have been at the center of the ongoing debate on **deregulation**. Many of Japan's industrial policy regulations, which at one time served to nurture and protect infant industries or to stabilize competition in the domestic market, are now being blamed for stifling innovation and preventing the Japanese economy from regaining its competitiveness. Industries that benefit from these regulations – often the less competitive, inward-oriented sectors – have been very powerful opponents of substantial deregulation. On the other hand, complaints about excessive regulation have come not only from Japan's trading partners but also from many of Japan's more competitive, export-oriented industries. Industrial policy bureaucrats thus find themselves in a dilemma as to which side of Japan's dual economy to support.

The current emphasis on the problems and failures of industrial policy is perhaps as exaggerated as the earlier belief that industrial policy was a main reason for Japan's economic success. Scholars still disagree in their assessment of the effectiveness of Japan's industrial policy. Many have argued that industrial policy was especially effective in its earlier phases, as it helped Japan recover from the devastation of the war and get back on the high-growth track relatively quickly; counterfactually, we need to consider whether the economy would have grown as fast as it did *without* the industrial policy that Japan followed. But as the Japanese economy matured and reached the frontiers of technology, the coherence and effectiveness of its industrial policy was already beginning to decline even before the economy stagnated

in the 1990s. Japan's more recent economic problems have bolstered the position of those who stress the potential downside risks of government intervention in the market.

See also: administrative guidance; amakudari; cartels; competition; declining industries; Fair Trade Commission; industry and trade associations; industrial regions; Johnson, Chalmers; shingikai

Further reading

Calder, K. (1995) *Strategic Capitalism: Private Business and Public Purpose in Japanese Industrial Finance*, Princeton, NJ: Princeton University Press.

Callon, S. (1995) *Divided Sun: MITI and the Breakdown of Japanese High-Tech Industrial Policy*, Stanford, CA: Stanford University Press.

Johnson, C. (1982) *MITI and the Japanese Miracle: The Growth of Industrial Policy, 1925–1975*, Stanford, CA: Stanford University Press.

Katz, R. (1998) *Japan: The System That Soured*, Armonk, NY: M.E. Sharpe.

Noble, G. (1998) *Collective Action in East Asia: How Ruling Parties Shape Industrial Policy*, Ithaca, NY: Cornell University Press.

Okimoto, D. (1989) *Between MITI and the Market: Japanese Industrial Policy for High Technology*, Stanford, CA: Stanford University Press.

Samuels, R. (1994) *Rich Nation, Strong Army: National Security, Ideology, and the Transformation of Japan*, Ithaca, NY: Cornell University Press.

Tilton, M. (1996) *Restrained Trade: Cartels in Japan's Basic Materials Industries*, Ithaca, NY: Cornell University Press.

Uriu, R. (1996) *Troubled Industries: Confronting Economic Change in Japan*, Ithaca, NY: Cornell University Press.

ROBERT URIU

industrial regions

There are three primary industrial regions in Japan. In order of size and importance they are the Tokyo-Yokohama regions, the Osaka and greater Kansai region, and Nagoya and the Chubu region. These three regions stretch consecutively along the eastern side of Honshu (the largest island in the Japanese archipelago) beginning in the north with Tokyo and extending down to Osaka. Taken as a whole their combined geographic area is also home to roughly 30 percent of the Japanese population.

Tokyo is the largest city in Japan with a population in its twenty-three wards exceeding 8 million. The larger metropolitan area has a population of 11.9 million. It is the national capital and ranks number one among all cities for number of corporate headquarters. Not surprisingly, it is the hub of the Kanto region. Tokyo harbor is the third largest seaport in Japan, and Narita International Airport is the largest airport in terms of passenger and cargo. In addition to the nearly thirty other towns that comprise the remainder of the Tokyo metropolitan region, the six prefectures surrounding Tokyo – Chiba, Gumma, Ibaraki, Kanagawa, Saitama and Gumma – are also considered part of this industrial region. They are home to thousands of large, medium and small manufacturers, assembly plants and warehouses.

The other hub of this industrial region, in Kanagawa prefecture, is Yokohama, situated on Tokyo Bay 30 kilometers southwest of Tokyo. With a population approaching 4 million, it is Japan's second largest city and possesses the largest seaport in Japan. It handles roughly 15 percent of Japan's foreign trade. This is not surprising given its historical importance. In 1859 it became the most influential seaport in all of Japan as a result of its proximity to Tokyo, the national capital. Yokohama soon attracted a large number of foreign residents, most of them connected with European and American trading and shipping companies. For that reason, Yokohama has tended to have a more international atmosphere than its big sister, Tokyo, nearby.

The Kanagawa region immediately surrounding Yokohama became the site of major manufacturing facilities, which used the nearby port for exporting their products overseas and even domestically within Japan. As a result, the area around Yokohama ranks near the top in terms of manufacturing output for general and electrical machinery.

The second major industrial region is located in the Kansai region and has as its main hub the

historical commercial capital of Japan, Osaka. The two other large cities in this region are Kyoto, the imperial capital of Japan for more than a millennium, and Kobe, a second major port city to the region. The six prefectures surrounding Osaka – Hyogo, Kyoto, Mie, Nara, Shiga, and Wakayama – encompass the second largest concentration of industrial capacity after the Tokyo-Yokohama region.

Osaka is the third largest city in Japan and is the site of the second largest stock market, again after Tokyo. From the ninth century until well into the twentieth century, Osaka was the commercial center of Japan. It was the birthplace of five of Japan's **general trading companies**: **ITO-CHU**, **Marubeni**, **Mitsui**, Nissho Iwai and **Sumitomo**. It is also home to **Matsushita** Electric Industrial, the largest electrical appliance manufacturer in the world. The Osaka region's chemical and petroleum industries rank number one in terms of production capacity, and the steel industry ranks second only to the Tokyo region.

From the **Meiji restoration** (1858) onward, Osaka witnessed an erosion of its commercial importance as business activity shifted to Tokyo and the munificent government contracts that marked the era of Japan's push toward rapid industrialization in the latter half of the nineteenth century. Mitsui typified this exodus from Osaka to Tokyo when it moved its corporate headquarters in 1873. The trend of Osaka firms moving corporate headquarters to Tokyo has continued for well over 100 years. It was given additional impetus in the immediate postwar era, as the **American occupation** had a tendency to further concentrate power and control of resources in Tokyo.

In the past decade, however, the region's fortunes have taken a turn for the better. For one, the Tokyo-Yokohama region simply ran out of room for further significant industrial expansion. Because of its well-developed infrastructure and historical position, the Osaka became the heir apparent for future growth. This shift has been buttressed by several aggressive development projects. The first of these was the Kansai International Airport, built on a man-made island in Osaka Bay. The project was the culmination of a thirty-year project by government and business leaders to significantly upgrade the commercial and cargo air facilities in the region. The airport opened in 1994 and its impact on bringing more foreign investment into the region appears significant. A second major project involved a joint business-government effort to build a cluster of large high-tech research parks and government research centers in a completely new city. Kansai Science City can be considered a Kansai counterpart to Tsukuba, the Kanto city known for its government and corporate research facilities. In many respects, Kansai Science City represents an effort by the central and local governments to replicate the success of Tsukuba in the Kansai region.

Nagoya and the Chubu region, locating roughly midway between Tokyo and Osaka, are the third major industrial region of Japan. Nagoya is Japan's fourth largest city with a population of approaching 2.5 million. It is located in Aichi prefecture and is considered the main city of the Chubu region, which includes the surrounding prefectures of Gifu, Mie, Nagano and Shizuoka. Because **Toyota**, **Honda**, **Mitsubishi** and Suzuki are headquartered in the region and have their major manufacturing there, the Nagoya region accounts for over 50 percent of all vehicles manufactured in Japan. Just as Toyota City is a key automotive producer, two other cities claim similar honors in two other industries. Seto is an established center for ceramics, which explains why Noritake and several lesser fine china manufacturers are headquartered in the region. Ichinomiya, in nearby Gifu prefecture, is a major center for textiles.

See also: Kansai culture

ALLAN BIRD

industry and trade associations

Trade associations (*jigyosha dantai*) have played an important role in Japan's early economic development (see **guilds**). In the control economy during the Second World War, existing industry groups were transformed into "control associations" (*toseikai*). In every industry a control association was in charge of designing and implementing the rationing of input materials and output quotas. After the war, a large number of associations

continue to be importantly involved in **industrial policy** and regulation (interacting with bureaucrats), lobbying and policy planning (interacting with politicians), as well as intra-industry and inter-industry negotiations on joint product development, production curtailment, and self-regulation.

Over time, the pendulum of government involvement in trade association activities has swung back and forth. During the Edo period, the Shogunate at times ignored the guilds and at other times used them for its policy purposes. The Meiji period saw more active government interest in business affairs, and the Taisho period less. The immediate postwar years were a period of particularly high government involvement, so much so that it often looked as if the ministries unilaterally imposed policies onto industries. Because in those years the interests of the bureaucrats and those of industry were often intertwined, it was difficult to determine whether bureaucrats were bending to industry pressure in designing certain policies, or industry was shaped to the interests of government. This may have led to an exaggeration of the role of ministries in industrial policy design and implementation. When the ministerial leverage over industry by way of **administrative guidance** and **industrial policy** began to decline in the 1980s, the pendulum of government involvement in industry also began to swing back, and trade association activities of self-regulation became increasingly important and visible.

Data

The wartime control associations were based on very narrowly defined industries, often by product category. Although these control groups were forced to dissolve under the Occupation, many of them simply changed their names and continued to exist to support the recovery of their member firms. As a result, there are more trade associations in Japan than in many other countries. For instance, even in the 1990s, there were separate associations for pens, pencils, ballpoint pens, fountain pens, highlighting pens, and white-out ink.

As of 1997, a total of 15,437 trade associations were registered with Japan's **Fair Trade Commission** (FTC). Of these, roughly 2,100 were "incorporated" (*zaidan hojin*), i.e., they held a license from their cognizant ministry and had to submit annual reports. In contrast, 9,700 were "voluntary", with no immediate ties to a regulator, while 3,500 were cooperatives based on special small-firm legislation that exempted these associations from certain anti-trust rules.

In a sample of 1,200 trade associations in 1990, the median (representative) association had eighty member firms, four staff, twenty directors, and a budget of 70 million yen; these numbers were similar to US associations except for budget, which was, on average, more than five times larger in Japan (Schaede 2000). Given that budgets are financed through membership dues and Japanese firms are typically members of several associations, Japanese companies incur significant expenses from association membership.

Organization

The governing body of every trade association is the "general meeting" (*sokai*). Typically, once a year all members meet to vote on general issues such as changes in the by-laws. Very large associations also hold annual conventions (*taikai*) which are high-profile events and often feature as speakers representatives from the cognizant ministries and politicians. Substantial policy decisions are delegated to the board of directors (*rijikai*), which meets monthly. The directors (*riji*), as well as the association's president, are member company presidents who are officially elected at the general meeting and are usually the presidents of the largest firms in the industry.

Directly under the president, the staff of the association is headed by one senior administrative director (*senmu riji*) who is a member of the board of directors but as a long-term employee provides institutional memory among the rotating directors. This person also acts as a liaison between the member firms, the association, and the outside world. In those associations that hire retired government officials or "old boys" for closer contacts with their regulators, this person typically assumes the position of senior administrative director.

Below the senior administrator, a number of staff people are in charge of administrative functions, including: organizing committee and sub-committee meetings (which occur in large numbers at frequent intervals); publishing a newsletter; collecting industry statistics; conducting research on foreign market access; collecting opinions on policy issues and contacting related associations; organizing educational programs and seminars; organizing trade shows and other industry promotion; and processing information from the cognizant ministry for distribution to member firms. In large associations, several of the staff are *shukko*, employees from member firms on a two-year secondment. During the stints at the association, *shukko* learn about their industries and meet a large number of people with whom to maintain networks as their careers develop.

Functions

Trade associations fulfil a wide range of functions which require different organization. For instance, for influential lobbying, associations must be large, but for effective cooperation they should be small. Japanese industries have addressed this tradeoff between size and effectiveness by creating a pyramid with focused, small associations at the bottom, industry umbrella associations in the middle, and large, over-arching federations, such as Keidanren, at the top. Thus, different types of associations specialize in different functions within the political economy. In general, there are three categories of functions: (1) administrative (information exchange), (2) economic (self-regulation and ministry/business relations), and (3) political (lobbying and politicians/business relations). While all associations engage in information exchange, large federations typically engage more in lobbying, whereas the focused industry-based associations are more concerned with economic functions.

Studies in corporate management attest to the importance of information and knowledge for businesses to reduce uncertainty in strategy decisions, avoid duplication, and cooperate on new technologies. In particular, if firms want to cooperate, the most important condition for a sustainable agreement is the frequent exchange of information, because it facilitates monitoring. Understanding this, Japan's trade associations have crafted systems of institutionalized information exchange through committee meetings at various junior and executive levels. These frequent meetings provide formal and informal opportunities to interpret complicated signals from competitors and related markets, and to respond to them. Japanese anti-trust law does not require that a lawyer be present at these meetings, and because the anti-trust authority has never interfered with the extensive and multi-layered committee structure, the exchange of critical data, including prices and costs, appears to be quite customary in some industries.

Trade associations and regulation

The fundamental economic function of trade associations is to ensure a constant flow of discussion between officials at the ministries and the associations they regulate. Activities that formalize these contacts include long-standing deliberation councils (**shingikai**), holding joint seminars on special policy issues, or a ministry paying the association to undertake a feasibility study for their industry.

As for what ministries do for associations, at the most basic level the bureaucrats structure a bargaining situation and assume the role of referee for the negotiation. A well-known example of an outcome of this process are **research cooperatives**. Upon discussion with all affected industries and companies through their associations, MITI may formulate the basic plan and offer subsidies as incentives for a group of firms to engage in joint research (importantly, Japanese ministries rarely offer subsidies to individual firms). Since firms do not typically like to disclose technology-related information, without a referee they may be unable to agree on a project. Another example can be found in maturing, or structurally depressed, industries. By creating negotiations among firms regarding capacity reductions, a ministry can fulfil its own goals of phasing in unemployment in the industry.

From the perspective of the regulating ministries, trade associations are important and helpful both in formulating and implementing regulation. First, the understaffed ministries need associations to provide them with aggregate information on industry, such as sales, investments, or inventory, as well as industry-specific knowledge of products,

standards, etc. Because many trade associations collect data on foreign markets, ministries often use them as informants in international trade negotiations. Second, rather than contacting individual firms, the regulators typically negotiate policy issues with the association. This is particularly useful when the ministry is drafting **administrative guidance**, which does not need cabinet approval but is negotiated just between the regulator and the industry. Third, trade associations are instrumental in monitoring compliance with informal regulation. As Japan does not have specific supervisory agencies (except for the financial industries since 1998), the ministries are at the same time responsible for policy formulation and enforcement. In most industries, understaffed ministries rely on the trade associations for administering industry self-enforcement.

Finally, trade associations also engage in autonomous self-regulation, without the involvement of ministries. "Self-regulation" refers to a process by which a trade association designs the rules of trade for that industry and enforces these rules through self-designed sanctions. What types of rules associations create depends on the specific circumstances and competitive environment of their industries. Fundamentally, these rules can be either "administrative" and trade-enhancing (for example, through standard or quality requirements, or rules on advertisement and ethical behavior), or they can be "protective" and trade-restricting (through price agreements, restricting markets or customers, restricting market access, or an exclusive distribution system). Although industries differ in the extent and types of their self-regulation, the practice is widespread. One reason is that the boundaries between administrative and protective self-regulation are difficult to define, and even protective self-regulation is not necessarily always found to be in violation of the anti-trust statutes.

Lobbying

Trade associations participate in the policy-making process in various ways. At the formal level, association representatives often participate in the government's deliberation councils. More informally, business tries to influence political decisions through informal meetings and small gifts. For instance, large associations typically procure the best tickets to *sumo* wrestling bouts or *kabuki* and *no* performances, to give them to politicians who hold influence over their industry.

Above all, trade associations play a major role in party donations. To the extent that comparative data are available, the ranking of sources for political donations in Japan are almost the opposite from the USA. Whereas in the mid-1990s, donations to US parties came primarily from individuals with corporations only contributing 6 percent of the total, in Japan individuals accounted for 10 percent of all party financing whereas corporations provided more than 30 percent. Importantly, Japanese companies channel their contributions through their trade associations. The associations in turn give directly to the party up to the legal limit of 100 million yen per year, and also channel funds to the ultimate umbrella organization, Keidanren. Under the LDP one-party rule between 1955 and 1993, all industries were most interested in lobbying the LDP, and Keidanren was continuously one of its strongest supporters. The system was interrupted when the LDP briefly lost its majority in the Lower House in 1993.

Outlook

The decline in ministerial leverage over industry due to deregulation and market liberalization is further increasing the importance of trade associations in Japan's political economy. Whereas associations have always self-regulated to a significant degree, their activities are becoming more important as antitrust authorities allow significant exchange of information and rule-making by associations, while many ministries do not strictly supervise or monitor their industries. Some industries self-regulate to open their markets and expose their member firms to full competition, whereas others create entry barriers to protect incumbent firms. Many of these firms have been able to weather the extended recession of the 1990s thanks to the activities of their trade associations.

Further reading

Procassini, A. (1995) *Competitors in Alliance: Industry Associations, Global Rivalries, and Business-Government Relations*, Westport, CT: Quorum Books.

Schaede, U. (2000) *Cooperative Capitalism: Self-Regulation, Trade Associations, and the Antimonopoly Law in Japan*, Oxford: Oxford University Press.

Young, M. (1991) "Structural Adjustment of Mature Industries in Japan: Legal Institutions, Industry Associations and Bargaining," in S. Wilks and M. Wright (eds). *The Promotion and Regulation of Industry in Japan*, New York: St. Martin's Press, 135–66.

ULRIKE SCHAEDE

internal labour markets

A central premise behind the idea of "internal labour markets" (ILMs) is that many of the rules determining economic outcomes for employees are written inside the firm rather than outside in an external labor market. When employees work for long time periods in one firm, understanding internal firm rules becomes critical if one wants to understand the organization of work, wages, how and why employees change jobs, and other labor outcomes. Of course, the internal rules may vary substantially across individual firms, industries, national boundaries, and time periods.

Early literature on internal labor markets was US based. Clark Kerr – who focused on US labor market institutions in the 1950s – first made the point that there was a central boundary between what was happening in the firm and the activity in "external" labor markets. His distinction was important because prevailing neoclassical economic theory implied that the boundary was not significant: the laws of supply and demand in the labor market affect everyone in the same way. Kerr and others began to argue that this is not necessarily the case; the internal, firm-specific rules affect internal employees in ways that are independent of an external labor market. John Dunlop, who originally coined the term "internal labor markets" in the 1960s, first focused on the job ladders that he saw within US firms. Much of this early research was narrowly focused on detailing ILMs within blue-collar, union-dominated manufacturing industries in the USA. More recent work has focused on the differences between ILMs in different manufacturing work models, between manufacturing models and services, and across national boundaries. This is particularly true in the last two decades as US, Japanese, and European firms set up transplants and joint ventures. In the USA in Freemont, California, the NUMMI joint venture between **Toyota** and General Motors generated extreme interest because of its early success with a significantly different model of work using US employees.

Because of the longer documented job tenure for Japanese employees relative to their Western counterparts, analyzing and understanding internal labor markets has been a primary concern of those studying Japanese labor markets. James **Abegglen** and Ronald **Dore** were among the first non-Japanese scholars to document Japanese style employment practices that characterize ILMs, including the "three pillars" of **lifetime employment**, **seniority promotion** and wages, and **enterprise unions**. The stylized facts on Japanese and US ILMs are now very familiar. Kazuo **Koike** and many others have been careful to point out that comparisons can often be misleading, and the differences revolve around degree. Some of the more common stylized differences are: (1) executive and manager pay vs. average employee pay is more compressed in Japan; (2) job security for core employees at large Japanese firms is greater than in their US counterparts; (3) job rotation, employee participation, and training is emphasized much more strongly; and (4) the delineation between blue-collar and white-collar work tends to be more ambiguous, with movement from blue-collar ranks to white-collar work.

The study of Japanese internal labor markets has recently become much more fine-grained, with scholars increasingly concerned about what we can learn from different ILM systems. Early comparative work was often static and described Japanese ILMs as uniquely Japanese. Even if seen as efficient and effective in the Japanese context, many argued that particular ILM practices could not be transferred across national culture. However, the weight of opinion now sees ILM practices as dynamic and in a constant state of evolution within particular countries. Also, cross-national diffusion of differences can and often does occur.

At the same time, there is growing agreement that the rules making up a particular internal labor market "model" do tend to have a self-reinforcing logic and should be evaluated and understood as a whole. For example, narrow job classifications, wage attachment to a specific job, and few restrictions on the ability of the firm to lay off workers are practices that tend to be mutually reinforcing. Broader job classifications, wages attached to individuals rather than a job, and greater job security are also practices that are self-reinforcing. The former model is essentially a traditional American model, while the latter is commonly associated with Japanese firms and particular US and other non-Japanese firms modifying their traditional work systems (now commonly labeled as "high-performance work systems").

In the post-Second World War period, many observers saw the character and smooth functioning of internal labor markets within Japanese firms as a source of relative economic strength. To encourage cooperation and commitment from employees, flexibility in job assignments in the firm, and effective employee participation in on-line problem solving, Japanese firms provided firm-specific training, relatively high job security, and compressed wages based largely on seniority. More effective on-line problem solving and a commitment to the firm ensured rising productivity and product market success for Japanese firms.

Japan's internal labor markets worked well in the context of a high and stable growth environment with tight labor markets, and few cyclical disturbances. With high growth and scarce labor, it makes good sense to build an internal labor market system that attracts, trains and keeps good workers. Rapidly growing firms also allow quick promotion internally for qualified employees committed to firm success. With no large, unexpected declines in demand, the relative expense of guaranteeing employment and training employees is low. This is especially the case with a corporate landscape dominated by firms utilizing the same strategies.

Sustained lower growth in Japan during the 1990s has increased pressure to de-regulate "rigid" internal labor markets and to increase the efficiency of external labor markets. With low growth, Japanese firms with relatively permanent employment guarantees can quickly become top-heavy. The temptation to cut expenses by reducing employees has increased as traditional options such as farming out core employees to subsidiaries (**shukko**) are exhausted. Meanwhile, those employees who are let go are finding it harder to find work in a weak external labor market.

How, then, will Japan's labor markets change? Many Japanese firms are still reluctant to give up the benefits of an internal labor market that effectively encourages firm specific skill acquisition and meaningful employee participation. Even as non-Japanese firms continue to appreciate Japanese ILM practices, Japanese firms continue to search for ways to adapt to a persistently difficult economic environment. This search includes experimentation with more "Western" practices like performance-based pay, less overall security for employees, and a firm decision matrix that gives shareholders more power. However, to what extent practices like these should be and will be adopted remains unclear.

Further reading

Abegglen, J.C. (1958) *The Japanese Factory: Aspects of its Social Organization*, Glencoe, IL: The Free Press.

Dore, R. (1973) *British Factory, Japanese Factory*, Berkeley, CA: University of California Press.

Gordon, A. (1985) *The Evolution of Labor Relations in Japan: Heavy Industry, 1853–1955*, Cambridge, MA: Harvard University Press.

Koike, K. (1988) *Understanding Industrial Relations in Modern Japan*, New York: St. Martin's Press.

WILLIAM BARNES

Ishikawa, Kaoru

Kaoru Ishikawa (1915–89) was a pioneer in the development of **quality management** in Japan, with a particular impact on the spread of **quality control circles**. He emphasized company-wide participation in quality, and worked to develop a set of simple statistical tools, usable by workers at all levels of the organization. Making invaluable contributions to the implementation of concepts introduced by **Deming** and **Juran**, Ishikawa promoted the careful collection of process-related data, and its presentation using charts and diagrams. He developed the widely-employed cause-and-effect (fishbone) diagram for understanding relationships in processes; it is often called the "Ishikawa diagram." Ishikawa espoused an holistic view of quality, arguing that it is much broader than simple product quality, but rather an all-encompassing way of managing people and processes.

Further reading

Ishikawa, K. (1976) *Guide to Quality Control*, Tokyo: Asian Productivity Organization.

ELIZABETH L. ROSE

ISO issues

ISO is a group of five standards set by the International Organization for Standardization that are generic guidelines and models for ensuring the quality of a company's goods and services. Some companies see ISO as a management tool, while others see it as a trade barrier.

ISO 9000 and total quality are not the same thing. However, ISO 9000 can be part of a larger total quality management (TQM) environment. Organizations that have achieved a high level of quality may already have the criteria for ISO 9000 in place. This is the case in Japan. It is a major reason why Japanese firms have not adopted ISO 9000 to the extent that businesses in other countries have. Many Japanese firms do not see the need for ISO 9000 certification since the Japanese are known for quality and already have many of their own quality processes in place. The Japanese also have their own awards for quality such as the Deming Award. Some researchers believe firms such as **Toyota** would have little to gain from ISO certification since their products are recognized as world class in terms of quality. Many Japanese firms set their sights on one of the best-known quality awards, the Deming Prize. Deming Prizes are almost exclusively won by Japanese firms, with three exceptions (Florida Light &

Power, Taiwan Tube, and Lucent Technology). In Japan, five years after a company has received the Deming Prize, it is eligible to compete for the Japan Quality Control Prize. Only a few organizations, including Toyota, have won this award, thereby showing their commitment to continuous quality improvement.

Today, the new versions of ISO 9000 include principles of total quality management and continuous improvement from Japan. Quality Improvement and therefore ISO 9000 is important from organizations' and suppliers', as well as customers' perspective. At a time of increasing globalization, ISO 9000 provided an international standard for quality. For example, European Union (EU) members made ISO 9000 compliance part of their safety laws and many EU companies require suppliers to be ISO certified. However, there are no laws requiring ISO certification to export or sell to Europe. Nevertheless, it is a competitive advantage. The standards do not apply to products or services themselves, but rather to the process. They are an assurance that the certified firm has in place a quality system enabling it to meet its stated quality. As Japanese companies continue to move manufacturing facilities to developing countries, they have become more interested in having their subsidiaries as well as their suppliers ISO 9000 certified.

In the summer of 2000, ISO standard officials from 46 countries met in Kyoto, Japan to sign off on revisions to the year 2000 version of the ISO series. However, Japan as well as France voiced objections to these new standards. The new standards are streamlined and focus more on tracking processes, on continuous improvement, and on customer satisfaction.

In addition to global recognition of the importance of high-quality products and services is the growing worldwide concern for the environment. ISO 14000 is a newly established certification system of environmental standards. The ISO Committee developed an environmental management system that could be applied to firms around the world. It provides companies with a structure for an environmental management system that will ensure that all operational processes are consistent and effective and that will achieve the stated environmental objectives of a given organization. It

attempts to balance socio-economic and business needs with environmental protection and pollution prevention.

In Japan, with environmental issues becoming a public issue and with growing governmental regulations around environmental issues, firms are looking into ISO 14000 certification as a way of demonstrating their commitment to the environment, to be "good corporate citizens" and as a competitive advantage. Firms such as Toyota and Denso have sought ISO 14000 certification in their plants in Japan and abroad.

It is important to note that Japanese companies are not trying to modify existing operations to implement ISO 14000. Instead, they are creating new operations that meet the ISO 14000 criteria. As of 1999, more than 2100 Japanese companies have already been certified. According to one report, about 1000 Japanese companies per year are applying for certification. Overseas, Japanese firms such as **Sony** and Toyota in the United States have made public commitments to ISO 14000 standards.

Japanese companies are also starting to recognize suppliers who are more environmentally friendly. For example, Witt (1999) states that **Matsushita** Electric has a program of "green sourcing." It gives priority to companies with ISO 14000 certification. These suppliers do over $2 billion in business with Matsushita.

In the United States, Sony and Toyota, as well as Ford, have made public commitments to ISO 14000 standards. Additionally, numerous Japanese firms have stated that they plan to have all of their overseas operations both ISO 9000 and ISO 14000 certified in the future.

Further readings

Witt, C. (1999) "ISO 14000 revisited," *Material Handling Engineering* 54(11): 22.

Zuckerman, A. (2000) "Start Preparing for Revised ISO 9000 Standards," *Metal Center News* 40(11): 5–6.

TERRI R. LITUCHY

Ito-Yokado

Ito-Yokado Company, Ltd was established by Masatoshi Itou, currently Ito-Yokado group's honorary chairman in Tokyo in April 1958. Masatoshi successfully developed the company into a retail conglomerate over the next forty-two years. Ito-Yokado is characterized by its profit-oriented policy and scientific management. In February 2000, the company directly operated 176 stores, employing 16,514 staff. In 1999, the company was capitalized at ¥46,674 million and sales totaled ¥1,490,709 million.

In the 1960s, Ito-Yokado aggressively expanded its supermarket chains. In contrast with **Daiei**'s nationwide expansion, Ito-Yokado chose to build its new stores in the Tokyo area to maintain the company's domination there. It became the second largest retailer in Japan in terms of total sales in 1981.

Ito-Yokado also operated its own department stores (for example, York Matsuzakaya), discount stores (Daikuma), specialty shops (Merian), supermarkets (York Benimaru), and convenience stores (7-11 Japan). 7-11 Japan in particular has been very successful. It was named York Seven Inc. when Ito-Yokado reached a licensing agreement with the Southland Corporation to run the convenience store business in Japan in 1973, and was renamed 7-11 Japan in 1978. In 1996, 7-11 Japan became the first company to record profits of ¥100,000 million in Japan.

Ito-Yokado also branched out into restaurants (Denny's Japan), mail order (Shop America Japan), food production (Aiwai Foods), real estate (Urawa Building), and finance (Union Lease). However, the company is still less diverse than Daiei.

In the 1980s, Ito-Yokado could no longer increase its profit simply by building new stores because of the introduction of the Large Store Law. The company, unlike Daiei with its diversification strategy, decided to fundamentally reform its management system. In 1982, Ito-Yokado formed an operation reform committee to carry out a five-stage reform to improve its profitability. The first and second stage aimed at improving the inventory, increasing the stock turnover, and reducing the opportunity losses. In the third stage, Ito-Yokado introduced the POS (point of sale) system to implement "item-by-item inventory control," which enabled the company to detect sales trends for each item of merchandise and subsequently develop a selling strategy which would then be tested again using sales data. The fourth stage was to develop new products. Ito-Yokado adopted the concept of "team merchandising," whereby the company, based on the sales data, came up with product ideas and then worked with manufacturers, wholesalers, and other collaborators as a team to develop new products.

The company started to expand again in the final stage. First, Ito-Yokado started to extend its store network to western Japan, building stores rapidly in the Kansai area from 1995. The second expansion took place overseas. In 1996, Ito-Yokado established a joint venture with a Chinese retail company in China, aimed at building a nationwide store chain there. Simultaneously, the company allied with Wal-Mart and Metro Group to develop new merchandise.

See also: retail industry

Further reading

Mizoue, U. (1998) *Daiei VS Ito-Yokado* (Daiei, Inc and Ito-Yokado Co., Ltd), Tokyo: Baru Shuppan.

Okamoto, H. (1998) *Yokado guruupu: koushuueki no shisutemu kakushin* (Yokado Group: System Reform For High Profit), Tokyo: Baru Shuppan.

HEUNG-WAH WONG

ITOCHU

In 1858, at the age of fifteen, Chubei Ito began work as a linen trader. In 1872 he established "Benichu," a fabric shop in Osaka. From this humble beginning emerged one of Japan's largest *sogo shosha* (general trading company). Building upon its strengths in the burgeoning textile industry in late nineteenth-century Japan, Ito expanded the business into thread and yarn. In 1914 he formally re-organized under the name C. Itoh & Company, and the firm came to insinuate itself into all aspects of the textile trade, from threads and yarns to finished goods, from arranging for the purchase, shipment and delivery of milling machines to the export of textiles worldwide. In 1918 Ito divided the company, forming a second trading company, **Marubeni**.

During the Second World War, C. Itoh & Co. merged with Marubeni and several manufacturers, including Kureha Cotton Spinning and Amagasaki Nail. However, as part of the **American occupation**'s policy of breaking up *zaibatsu*, in 1949 C. Itoh, Marubeni, Kureha and several related firms were separated.

In the postwar era, C. Itoh established itself as an aggressive sales company. It has consistently led its industry in sales. In 1992, to reflect a more international identity it formally changed its name to ITOCHU. As of 2000 the company was organized into seven divisions: textiles; automobile industrial machinery; aerospace, electronics and multimedia; energy, metals and minerals; chemicals, forest products and general merchandise; food; and finance, realty, insurance and logistics services.

As with other general trading companies, ITOCHU has been involved in numerous large-scale projects around the world. It achieved particular visibility in the early 1980s when, at the height of Japan-US trade friction over automobiles, it facilitated a joint venture between General Motors and **Toyota** which became the NUMMI operation in Fremont, California.

See also: general trading companies

ALLAN BIRD

Iwasaki, Yataro

Born December 11, 1834 in Inokuchi Village, Shikoku island, in the Tosa clan domain (now Kochi Prefecture), Yataro Iwasaki was the founder of the **Mitsubishi *zaibatsu***. Frustrated by discrimination because of the family's status as low-ranking *samurai* and appalled by the way Japan's trade was subordinated to foreign concerns, he swiftly gained a reputation for being impetuous and aggressive but also possessing a shrewd business sense and excellent negotiating skills. Iwasaki was imprisoned for six months in 1856–7 for libeling the government, after his father had been beaten up by an Inokuchi village headman.

His abilities were nonetheless recognized by a leading Tosa clan figure, Yoshida Toyo, who became his teacher in 1858 and recommended Iwasaki for a commercial post in Nagasaki, in 1859. In Nagasaki Iwasaki first came into contact with scholars of Chinese classics, doctors of Western medicine and foreign technology. His lack of languages frustrated him in his quest for knowledge, so he returned home before he was supposed to, and was discharged from his post by the Tosa clan as a punishment.

Despite this setback he was able to reacquire a higher ranking title for the family in 1861, and in the following year he married Kise, with whom he had five children; Masaya, Yasuya, Masako, Hisaya and Haruji. Iwasaki reclaimed rice fields and managed forests in Inokuchi until 1867, when he was reappointed as a clan official and transferred to the Nagasaki branch. It was in Nagasaki that he came to deal with later business partners such as Thomas Glover, buying steamships and munitions from them. Iwasaki became head of the clan's Osaka branch in 1869, which was then separated from the Tosa clan management and set it up as a private firm, Tsukumo Shokai, in 1870. Some historians date this as the beginning of the Mitsubishi *zaibatsu* although Iwasaki was not officially the head of the company at that time. The company was renamed Mitsubishi Shokai in 1873, taking the name from the three water chestnut diamond-shaped leaves that formed the Iwasaki family crest. This change in name probably marks the point at which Iwasaki gained full control over the company.

Iwasaki saw the spirit of contributing to the company's prosperity as the same as contributing to the nation's prosperity. This philosophy led to Iwasaki volunteering his ships for delivering munitions for the Japanese government's Taiwan Expedition in 1874. Until 1881 Iwasaki could be considered to be a *seisho*, a merchant who made use of government contacts to build a commercial empire. Iwasaki's particular government support was from Toshimichi Okubo and other progressive bureaucrats. In 1875 he petitioned the Japanese government for a loan to buy the Shanghai Line of the Pacific Mail, which was granted on Okubo's recommendation, as part of the government's shipping promotion policy. In 1876, when another powerful rival appeared, the Peninsular and Oriental Steam Navigation Company of the United Kingdom, Iwasaki reduced his own salary by half, made sixteen workers redundant and cut the salaries of his executives by a third, in order to engage in a rate cutting war. P&O eventually withdrew their Yokohama-Kobe line in August 1876, and Iwasaki celebrated his victory by inviting them and other foreign shipping companies to a lavish banquet, where he asked for their future cooperation.

Iwasaki also helped the government suppress the Satsuma Rebellion in 1877 through providing transport for troops and munitions, from which he made a tidy profit and further consolidated his shipping monopoly. On July 8, 1878 the government decorated Iwasaki with the Fourth Order of Merit with the Grand Cordon of the Rising Sun, the first time a non-bureaucrat had received such an honor.

However, after the assassination of Okubo in 1878, Iwasaki had only one protector left in the government, Shigenobu Okuma. Okuma's faction fell from power after senior ministers decided not to accept his radical democratic ideas for a constitution. The new faction in power suspected Okuma, Iwasaki and other allies of plotting to overthrow them. Iwasaki found himself being shadowed and his house watched by spies. He became so incensed by what was happening that he declared in 1881 that his staff should no longer be involved in politics.

Nonetheless the attacks continued and the government established a new steamship company to compete against Mitsubishi in 1882. Iwasaki stated his view that having two large companies competing with each other would only weaken Japan's nascent maritime industry but decided not to campaign publicly to stop the formation of the new company. Instead he paid off the remainder of the loans from the government for ship purchasing, cut costs and upgraded the shipping services, in order to ready the company for a price war. This war ended with the merger of the new company with Mitsubishi's shipping activities in 1885, to form the Nippon Yusen Kaisha, several months after the death of Iwasaki, aged fifty.

Mitsubishi was able to continue throughout Iwasaki's frequent illnesses in the 1880s thanks to the able staff whom Iwasaki had hired. Iwasaki was encouraged in scholarly activities by his literary family as a child and this respect for intellect undoubtedly made Iwasaki keen to hire educated people for his company. This habit of hiring intelligent, independent-minded staff rather conflicted with Iwasaki's autocratic style. He outlined his official position in his *Rissha Teisai* (The Style of Establishing the Company), where he stated that all key decisions were to be made by the president. Nonetheless, Iwasaki sometimes found himself overruled, as in the instance of his close friend and famous educationalist, Yukichi Fukuzawa, collaborating with Iwasaki's younger brother Yanosuke and another Mitsubishi employee, Shoda Heigoro, to persuade Iwasaki to buy the failing Takashima Coal Mine in 1880. It was businesses such as this which Iwasaki's heirs were to build up into the diverse conglomerate for which the Mitsubishi name became famous.

See also: general trading companies

Further reading

Hensankai (ed). (1967) *Iwasaki Yataro Den*, Tokyo: University of Tokyo Press.

PERNILLE RUDLIN

Izanagi boom

The Izanagi boom (October 1965–July 1970) refers to the postwar unprecedented prosperity that lasted for fifty-seven consecutive months. This period saw the second-highest level of economic growth in Japanese history. Under the Eisaku Sato Administration, the Japanese economy grew rapidly mostly due to dependence on exportation and the power of Japanese financial standing in Asia and the world. Also, the Japanese economy was recovering from a period between 1956–65 in which economic growth was restricted by the deterioration of international income and expenditure. The substantial growth rate reached 11.6 percent (the average between 1966–70) and GNP grew to third place among capitalist countries (behind only West Germany and the USA).

During this period, individual consumption,

investment in private facilities, and exporting worked together toward a balanced expansion for the economy. Consumer electrical products such as cars, air conditioners, and color televisions expanded into mainstream use, thus fueling a boom in the consumer **electronics industry** in which Japanese companies were poised for success: the market expansion for autos was 17 percent per year, air conditioning equipment 5 percent, and color televisions 25 percent. The color television was at the height of popularity during this period. And air conditioning systems were fast becoming staple household and industry items, coming into wide use in department stores around 1970.

The profitability due to trade income increased to its high point and then the tide shifted away from high growth, mostly due to the maturing of the Japanese economy. By the time of the International Exposition hosted in Osaka in July 1970, the Izanagi boom was over. The peak price of the average Japanese stock was ¥2,534 in April 1970, and it is said that the decline of the stock market during the three months prior to the Exposition signaled the end of the Izanagi boom.

The Izanagi boom was a period during which steel production doubled along with the volume of oil refined and the output of aluminum. But these increases took place without any change in the methods of production, meaning a corresponding increase in the amount of waste created. Pollution became and still is a huge problem, with cases being brought to court one after another, spurring the creation of the first laws on environment pollution control. The Japanese government understood the need for industry to invest in environmentally friendly technology, and a new position, that of Director General of the Environment Agency, was established.

Further reading

Hitomi, H. (1996) *Nihonsi-B Yougosyu*, Tokyo: Yamakawa-syuppan.

Ikeda, Y. (1997) *Seiji EKeizai* (Political Economy), Tokyo: Shimizushoin.

MARGARET TAKEDA
IPPEI ICHIGE

J

Japan Airlines

Japan Airlines Company Ltd. (JAL) was founded on August 1, 1951, as Japan's national flag carrier. Exactly two years later, on August 1, 1953, the so-called JAL Law was passed by the Japanese government and, on October 1 of the same year, it provided half of the new company's capital investment. Government support continued until November 18, 1987, at which time the government sold its 34.5 percent stake and JAL became a fully privatized company.

During its initial start-up phase, JAL flights operated only on domestic routes. On February 2, 1954, the first international route was inaugurated between Tokyo, Honolulu, and San Francisco. Six years later, on August 12, 1960, JAL entered the jet age when a DC8-32 made its inaugural non-stop flight between Tokyo and San Francisco. JAL's international route expansion continued the following year with the introduction of a trans-polar route which linked Tokyo, Anchorage, Paris and London. Five years later, the Tokyo–San Francisco flights were extended to New York.

From 1970 forward, JAL remained positioned with the most technologically advanced aircraft to meet the challenges of both domestic and international competition. During the decade-long recession of the 1990s in Japan, as well as in the rest of Asia, its revenues steadily eroded. Moreover, the deregulation of the aviation industry in Japan resulted in greater domestic competition with the creation of two new domestic airlines in Japan. Subsequently, Japan's aviation laws were revised on February 1, 2000 and this resulted in additional domestic competition as carriers were allowed to set their own ticket prices.

The introduction of technologically advanced aircraft, the computerization of the flight management systems in both air and ground environments, and the highly competitive deregulated business environment have required JAL to undertake a thorough review of its human resources training and productivity. By 1994, JAL had initiated massive cost-cutting measures by reducing its full-time workforce by nearly 4,300 and by hiring, on a limited contract basis, part-time non-Japanese flight attendants. Another strategy employed by JAL to cope with the highly competitive business environment was to use its low-cost subsidiaries: JAL Express (JEX) for domestic flights and JAL-ways for international flights.

In June 1998, Isao Kaneko became the first JAL president and chief executive officer to advance from the labour management division, thus signifying a major change in the selection of JAL leaders who have traditionally come from the sales and corporate planning departments.

Further reading

Japan Airlines (1999) *A More Competitive JAL Group*, Tokyo: Japan Airlines.

Norris, G. and Wagner, M. (1996) *Boeing 777*, Osceola, WI: Motorbooks International.

Orlady, H.W. and Orlady L. (1999) *Human Factors in Multi-Crew Flight Operations*, Aldershot: Ashgate.

Ujimoto, K.V. (1997) "Changes, Challenges, and Choices in the Japanese Aviation Industry: The Development of Crew Resource Management in

Japan Airlines," in H. Millward and J. Morrison (eds), *Japan at Century's End*, Halifax: Fernwood, 150–60.

Yamamori, H. (1993) "Keeping CRM is Keeping the Flight Safe," in E.L. Wiener, B.G. Kanki and R.L. Helmreich (eds), *Cockpit Resources Management*, New York: Academic Press, 399–420.

VICTOR K. UJIMOTO

Japan Association of Corporate Executives

Founded in 1946 by eighty-three business leaders seeking to contribute to the reconstruction of the economy, the Keizai Doyukai (Japan Association of Corporate Executives) is distinctive among business associations in Japan. Its membership in 2000 included 1,500 senior executives from over 900 large corporations. A distinguishing characteristic of Keizai Doyukai is that members are expected to participate in association affairs as individuals, letting go of their corporate identities. A second characteristic is that members are expected to adopt a far-reaching and long-term perspective in addressing issues that span a range of political, economic and social matters. In striving to maintain an independent position with the larger business and social community, Keizai Doyukai conducts its own in-depth studies, research projects and discussions. It also actively pursues a dialogue with government officials, labor organizations, political parties and other business organizations. It is one of the most influential business organizations in Japan and, along with the Japan Chamber of Commerce and Industry (Nihon Shoko Kaigisho), the Japan Federation of Employer's Associations (Nikkeiren), and the Federation of Economic Organizations (Keidanren), is one of the four "voices of business" in Japanese society.

For purpose of research, discussion and coordination, the association is structured into three basic areas. Policy committees address a host of primarily domestic matters. As of 2001, there were fifteen standing committees. These were as follows: Committee on Corporate Management; Committee on Employment Issues; Committee on Finan-

cial Markets; Committee on Fiscal and Tax Policy; Committee on Public Administration: Economy; Committee on Social Security Reforms; Committee on Political Affairs; Committee on Judiciary Reforms; Committee on Education; Committee on Environment, Resources and Energy; Committee on Issues Concerning Metropolitan Areas; Committee on Foreign Relations and National Security Issues; Committee on Socioeconomic Principles for the Twenty-First Century; Committee on E-Economy; and Committee on New Technology Strategies. As is evident from the committee names, the interests of the association include but also extend well beyond business and economic matters and address a host of important political and social matters.

A second group of committees within the association fall under the title, International Affairs Committees. The groups, of which there are five, focus on geographical regions and their relation to Japan. Finally, a third grouping of activities falls under the title of Discussion and Study Programs. These include the following: Industrial Discussion Groups; Seminar on Current Topics; Global Forum; Committee for the Future; Senior Executives' Discussion Group; and Discussion Group of New Members.

Keizai Doyukai has been criticized as being elitist and exclusive. It has also been criticized as a "harmonizing voice" in support of Keidanren. There is no doubt that its membership, comprised as it is of very senior executives from the largest corporations, reads like a Who's Who list. It is also true that a comparison of the membership of the two organizations has a high degree of overlap. At the same time, the association has taken positions at variance with Keidanren on a number of matters. Perhaps more importantly, Keizai Doyukai, with its unique purpose and perspective, provides a venue where individuals have room to speak their own minds. Whether those minds have become inextricably entangled with the corporation mindset from whence they come will, in all likelihood, remain a point of debate. What is not debatable is the large influence that the association wields within the Japanese business community.

ALLAN BIRD

Japan Automobile Manufacturers Association

The Japan Automobile Manufacturers Association, Inc. (JAMA) or Jikoukai was established on April 3, 1967, with the objectives of encouraging the development of the Japanese **automotive industry** and contributing to the progress of society (the first Japan-US automobile meeting was held in the same year). The former Automotive Industrial Association and Midget Motor Manufacturers' Association of Japan were merged into one association, Jikoukai. Since then the organization has been the leading association of the automobile industry in Japan.

The purpose of founding JAMA was to enable the industry to address a host of issues as a unified entity. The impending liberalization of capital was a particularly pressing matter, and as JAMA's activities would also include the promotion of exports, issues of traffic safety, exhaust emissions and international trade were also points which needed to be considered.

The new association's membership did not include all the members of the two previous organizations. Many members of the Midget Motor Manufacturers' Association of Japan entered into a new cooperative relationship with JAMA, while other companies, especially chassis manufacturers actually merged into JAMA.

JAMA consisted of the fifteen founding member manufacturers: Aichi Kikai, Isuzu, Kawasaki, Suzuki, Daihatsu, **Toyota**, Toyo Kogyo, **Nissan**, Nissan Diesel, Hino, Fuji Heavy Industries, Bridgestone Cycle, **Honda**, Mitsubishi Heavy Industries, and Yamaha. The first chairman of JAMA was Katsuji Kawamata, president of Nissan Motor Co., who had also served as chairman of the Automotive Industrial Association, JAMA's predecessor. Since then, either the chief executives of Toyota or Nissan have been elected as chairman. Some elected executives of the thirteen domestic motorcycle and automobile member manufactures have been installed in the board of directors, which is comprised of a chairman, five vice-chairmen, a president, an executive vice-president and a secretary general.

JAMA has been the contact organization regarding the export, overseas developments and the internationalization of the automobile industry in Japan since its inception. JAMA opened branches abroad to deal with these matters: the Paris office was opened in 1969; the New York office was opened in 1970; the Washington office was opened in 1976; Japan Automobile Manufacturers Association of Canada was opened in 1986; and the European office was opened in Brussels in 1990. A commerce mission was dispatched to the Association of Southeast Asian Nations (ASEAN) in 1995 in response to the advance of Japanese manufacturers into ASEAN. In 1996 a Singapore office was opened.

JAMA has standing general committees and special vehicle committees. The general committees consist of the technical administration committee, the safety and environmental technology committee, environment committee, the traffic affairs committee, the distribution committee, the taxation committee, the international affairs committee, the parts & materials committee and the electronic information exchange committee, and these committees deal with various issues in the automobile industry. The special vehicle committees consist of the mini-vehicle committee, the motorcycle committee, and the heavy vehicle committee. These committees deal with the matters based on type of car, such as exhaust emission standards.

JAMA has an administration under the supervision of a vice-chairman and associates. The administration is divided into the administration department, the planning and coordination office, the traffic affairs department, the business affairs department, the technical department, environment department and the international department. The administration regularly issues several publications, provides information, helps to adjust different opinions in the industry, holds international conferences, helps negotiations and carries out industry research.

JAMA's activities under the general committees and the administration were: (1) research projects related to production, distribution, trade and consumption of automobiles; (2) the rationalization of automobile production, setting and promoting policies concerning improvements in manufacturing techniques; (3) setting and promoting policies concerning the automobile trade and international exchanges; and (4) other projects in order to achieve its objectives. Concretely, JAMA carries out the following:

- production of yearly, quarterly, monthly and other publications to provide information about the automobile industry and international trade;
- provision information about traffic safety, fuel reduction, environmental preservation, and so on;
- participation in international conferences related to automobiles;
- joint research and information exchanges about automobiles, auto parts and auto materials, as well as global environment issues with various organizations in many countries;
- cooperation in the attainment of international agreements regarding various automobile standards such as those relating to safety and the environment;
- research in order to set future roles in the automobile industry and to set future directions in international society;
- opinion adjustment concerning global environment problems in the broader industrial world as a whole;
- issuance of position statements on behalf of the automobile industry in Japan;
- compilation of statistical data related to the automobile industry in Japan and the announcement of the result of statistical analyses;
- research and investigations related to the automobile industry in Japan, and the publication of research results.

In addition to these activities, JAMA set up a meeting for the study of a reduction in working hours in 1992 in order to deal with the problems of fatigue caused by overwork and economic stagnation. Consequently, the application for employment adjustment subsidies started in 1993. Since the early 1990s JAMA has dealt with environmental and safety matters, and has promoted exchange and discussion of different opinions with American and European makers about supplying materials to Japanese makers.

With the improvement of automobiles' efficiency and reliability, the progress of environmental measures concerning exhaust emission standards, recycling, and waste disposal has received increasing attention. In addition, taking steps to cope with safety problems has recently taken on increased importance. JAMA seeks to shape these developments in ways that lead to automotive innovations being in harmony with society.

In response to increasing concerns about various environmental issues, Japanese automobile manufacturers have sought to solve these issues by introducing new technologies such as electronics. They also conduct research and develop new materials for automobile manufacture and also develop alternative energy sources. For instance, Japanese manufacturers are experimenting with new perspectives such as establishing internal organizations to deal exclusively with specific issues and developing charters for comprehensive environmental action. Their objective is to carry out decisive, effective measures across the spectrum, from development and design, through manufacturing and sales, to the eventual scrapping and recycling of their products.

In this context, JAMA established forums in its organization to comprehensively assess and address these issues. Since the 1970s JAMA has promoted collection and salvage of discarded automobiles. Since the late 1980s it has dealt with global pollution of the environment, such as greenhouse gas emissions. Moreover, in 1994 an environment department was established to address environmental problems on behalf of the automobile industry. The organization also considers traffic safety owing to an increase in the number of traffic accidents. While various measures to promote traffic safety have been introduced by the government, requiring the cooperation of vehicle users with respect to, for example, the mandatory use of seatbelts and helmets, Japanese manufacturers have also been actively pursuing programs to ensure traffic safety.

The JAMA action plan which is now being carried out demands further improvements in automobile safety features, new traffic safety campaigns and educational activities, improvement of driving conditions such as road infrastructure development, and close government-industry cooperation on traffic accident analysis through the Institute for Traffic Accident Research and Data Analysis, founded jointly by the government and public sectors in 1992. JAMA has carried out its activities broadly: it sets up various kinds of new committees and meetings regarding traffic safety, implements various traffic safety campaigns, studies the actual nature of vehicle uses, prepares and publishes statistical data, and conducts public relations to deepen understanding of the automobile industry.

While economic internationalization is progressing, Japanese automobile companies have developed export activities to various countries as well as improving their local production in those countries. Since the 1960s, Japanese automobile manufacturers have been asked for assistance in the import of materials and the development of self-subsistence capabilities in several countries. To cope with these requests, JAMA assists Japanese makers and foreign makers in mutual understanding at the private sector level by offering a venue for the exchange of opinions and affording opportunities to negotiate with one another.

At the government level in Japan and the United States, the Japan-US automobile meeting was held in 1967; two Japan-US summit meetings took place in 1992; and the Japan-US auto parts meeting was held in 1993. From 1981 to 1994 voluntary export restraints (VER) for the US market were carried out. At the private sector level, however, significant efforts have also been made to resolve automobile trade issues between Japan and the United States. JAMA also serves as a mediator between Japan and the United States at the private sector level.

In terms of local parts procurement, Japanese makers are actively promoting industry-level cooperation. In 1977, and also in 1980, JAMA dispatched a mission to the United States to promote the purchase of auto parts. In 1987, the first JAMA-MEMA Liaison Committee Meeting was held in Tokyo to exchange opinions concerning the purchase of US-made auto parts. Fifteen meetings had been held as of 1995. A series of general conferences and discussion meetings organized by the Japan Automobile Manufacturers Association (JAMA), the US Motor and Equipment Manufacturers Association (MEMA) were first held in 1987 for the purpose of promoting US auto parts to Japanese manufacturers.

In 1990 the first One-on-One Auto Parts Business Development Meeting, co-sponsored by JAMA and MEMA, was held in Las Vegas for the purpose of promoting negotiations between US parts makers and Japanese automakers. Five meetings had been held as of 1995. In 1991 a report on "Replacement Parts for Japanese Vehicles in the US" was released, and in 1993 a meeting was held in Tokyo for the purpose of promoting closer cooperation between the US and Japanese auto industries. In the meeting, eleven Japanese automakers announced voluntary plans to purchase US-made parts. These meetings have led to the implementation of specific initiatives aimed at establishing closer business ties between Japanese manufacturers and US parts suppliers, including joint committees, the publication of materials explaining the "design-in" process of Japanese manufacturers, the compilation of industry contact lists, and the organization of special events designed to enhance cooperation and mutual awareness.

In Europe, JAMA-mediated negotiations have led to adjustments between Japan and Europe. JAMA held Japan-UK automobile meetings on twenty-three occasions from 1975 to 1992, and held a meeting with European automobile manufacturers in Paris in 1985. In the late 1980s, the rapid advance of Japanese manufacturers into the European market brought about problems concerning the rate of self-subsistence in the field. For these kinds of situations, JAMA has promoted adjustments and negotiations between Japan and Europe at the private sector level.

Japanese manufacturers are actively promoting industry-level cooperation to obtain local parts. In 1995 JAMA held a joint conference with the European Automotive Components and Equipment Industries Association (CLEPA) in Paris, where decision makers from eighty selected European suppliers met with representatives of Japanese manufacturers to explore potential business opportunities. Japanese manufacturers are also working hard to expand business ties with automotive parts firms in Canada, Europe, Asia and Australia with JAMA's assistance. Some of their initiatives have been outlined in the JAMA Action Plan for International Cooperation released by the Japan Automobile Manufacturers Association in June 1995.

MASANORI YASUMOTO

Japan Chamber of Commerce and Industry

The Japan Chamber of Commerce and Industry (JCCI) or Nihon Shoko Kaigisho is the overarching association to which all local and regional chambers belong. Its membership consists of the 523 (as of 1999) local chambers of commerce, whose collective member firms total 1.64 million. It operates as the primary representative of the concerns of small and medium-size enterprises throughout the country. It is, in many respects, the counterpart of Keidanren, which represents primarily the interests of large corporations. JCCI coordinates discussion among local chambers and formulates concerns and recommendations that it then proposes to government ministries and agencies. It also assists in the implementation of initiatives growing out of those recommendations. Other functions of JCCI include the dissemination of information on government policies and programs affecting chamber members, human resource training and development programs, and information sharing and coordination of joint efforts with business organizations outside of Japan with similar interests and concerns. It is one of the most influential business organizations in Japan and, along with the **Japan Association of Corporate Executives** (Keizai Doyukai), the **Japan Federation of Employers' Associations** (Nikkeiren), and the Federation of Economic Organizations (Keidanren), is one of the four "voices of business" in Japanese society.

The first local chambers of commerce and industry in Japan were established in Tokyo, Osaka and Kobe in 1878. In the next few years, enterprises in other cities followed suit. Fourteen years after the first local chambers were established, fifteen of them met in Tokyo to establish the Japan Chamber of Commerce and Industry.

Local chambers in Japan are designated as "corporations with special status" and operate under the Chambers of Commerce Act. Under this special status, local chamber membership is open to companies both large and small. However, the bulk of active chamber membership is among small and medium-size firms. Chambers are also required to maintain political neutrality and are prohibited from engaging in political activities. They are also prohibited from for-profit activities. The local chambers are independent and self-governing; they do not operate under the direction of the JCCI.

JCCI supports about 5,500 business consultants who are located in the local chambers to provide counsel and guidance to small and medium-sized businesses on a host of matters including advances and innovation in management practices, financial issues, and tax matters. In support of these consultants, JCCI carries out various research projects and field studies which it disseminates to the local chapters.

JCCI also works to assist business members of the local chambers in recruiting and training skilled employees. It offers standardized certification tests in English, bookkeeping and accounting, word processing, salesmanship and abacus-based calculation. Annually, JCCI tests roughly two million people.

Beginning in the 1980s and expanding rapidly in the 1990s, JCCI has worked with the local chambers to enhance its services in helping Japanese firms find foreign partners and vice versa. In 2000, JCCI handled over 15,000 inquiries from abroad regarding potential trade opportunities with business outside Japan. In support of its international activities, it published the quarterly *JCCI Business Guide*. It also provides assistance by helping local chambers in the issuance of certificates of origin, of which over 1 million are issued each year. As small and medium-size Japanese firms have expanded their activities into foreign markets, the role of JCCI within the larger Japanese business and economic community has grown, as has its influence.

ALLAN BIRD

Japan Development Bank

The Japan Development Bank (JDB) was chartered in 1951 and is the modern incarnation of the many specialized public policy-based banks which were created at the end of the nineteenth and beginning of the twentieth century to promote economic development and implement the policies of the

Ministry of Finance under the long tenure of the autocratic Meiji Finance Minister, Matsukata Masayoshi.

The JDB's most immediate predecessor was the Reconstruction Finance Bank (RFB) (1947–9) which was the only financial institution in the immediate postwar period capable of helping to revive key industries such as the coal, iron and steel, electric power, and chemical industries. The chief failing of the FRB was that, because its funding came directly from the Bank of Japan, repayments of loans to the FRB were at interest rates far below the hyperinflation rate of the postwar period. In effect, the loans made by the FRB became a form of government grants to private industry outside the scrutiny of the Allied occupation forces, or, for that matter, parliamentary authorities.

The problems of the FRB reflected the fact that postwar reconstruction had to be placed on a more sound financial footing which would provide long-term credits to industry. The creation of JDB, as well as the chartering of long-term credit banks in 1952 (see **banking industry**), were designed to address this need through their authority to provide intermediate long-term funds by the issuance of five-year debentures. In JDB's case, most of their debentures in the early years were purchased by the Ministry of Finance's Fiscal Investment Loan Program (FILP) whose main source of funds was from deposits from the **postal savings** system, as well as postal pension schemes and government pension plans.

The chief mechanism in directing funding for targeted industries was by the so-called "cow-bell effect" in which JDB led the private sector banks to join in lending to the targeted industry and/or specific firms. Although it was rarely the majority supplier of funds within any given syndicate of loans for a particular enterprise, JDB was able to organize support as a result not only of its diligent project appraisal and credit analysis of the enterprise, but also because of an implicit government guarantee of JDB's policy-based initiatives and the ability of the Ministry of Finance (MOF) to bestow upon cooperative banks favorable consideration in regulatory matters. Of equal, if not greater, importance to the participation of private sector banks in the lending syndicate was the

opportunity for these institutions to reap considerable main bank rewards with a lesser commitment of their own funds to the client firm (see **main bank system**). JDB as a government-owned institution is prohibited from taking deposits or serving as a main bank.

Over the years the national policy mission of JDB, as determined in an inter-ministerial government agency committee, changed with the development of Japan's economy. Initially, in the early 1950s JDB provided funding for reconstruction of the electric power, coal mining, ocean shipping, and iron and steel industries. In the late 1950s to the early 1960s the emphasis shifted to catching up with advanced countries in the synthetic fiber, oil refinery, nuclear power generation, machinery, and electronics industries. By the late 1960s and into the early 1970s policy emphasis was directed towards social welfare and environmental considerations in urban and residential land development, pollution prevention, welfare facilities, private railroads, and further development of new technology. In the late 1970s and early 1980s energy policy received priority with lending directed towards energy conservation and the development of alternative energy sources. In the late 1980s and early 1990s JDB's key mission was directed towards promoting the structural adjustment of industry and industrial research and development.

Lending policy in the present period is targeted towards livelihood and lifestyle, the improvement of living standards, social welfare-related facilities, regional revitalization, urban transportation, information and telecommunications, and the fostering of new businesses. The name of the bank has also been changed to the Development Bank of Japan (DBJ). This change in part reflects the bank's assumption of remnants of the Hokkaido Takushoku Bank, a failed city bank with a strong regional base in northern Japan. This bank's demise was due to its extensive exposure in non-performing real estate loans, dating back to the bubble period of the late 1980s. It is a testament to the due diligence of JDB that it suffered only one-tenth the rate of non-performing loans that still continue to plague the entire private commercial banking sector.

Further reading

Scher, M.J. (1996) *Japanese Interfirm Networks and Their Main Banks*, London: Macmillan and New York: St. Martin's Press.

MARK J. SCHER

Japan External Trade Organization

Japan External Trade Organization (JETRO) or Nihon Boeki Shinkokai, is comprised of JETRO headquarters in Tokyo, JETRO Osaka, thirty-six local offices throughout Japan, and eighty offices in fifty-eight countries. JETRO is Japan's official trade promotion organization. Originally established in 1951 as the Japan Export Research Trade Organization, its original purpose was to collect and distribute information on foreign markets to Japanese manufacturers and exporters. In 1954, the institution was restructured into the Japan External Trade Recovery Organization with cap-abilities to display Japanese products at trade exhibitions, providing overseas market research and providing a trade inquiry service. At this time the **Ministry of International Trade and Industry** (MITI) began to oversee JETRO's activities. JETRO attained its current status as a public corporation in 1958 when a law was passed that officially outlined its functions and its opera-tional framework. As a result of this legal transition, 25 July 1958 is said to be the year JETRO was established.

JETRO's role changed as Japan's global com-petitiveness increased. In the early 1980s, JETRO began to implement a variety of programs to encourage imports and expand foreign investment in Japan. In 1985, the Made in USA Fair was organized in Nagoya along with other exhibitions in Tokyo, Yokohama, and Kitakyushu. In 1993, JETRO's first Business Support Center was established in Tokyo to be followed by centers in Yokohama, Nagoya, Osaka, Kobe, and Fukuoka. These facilities function as temporary offices for foreign companies needing support while doing market research and establishing contacts in Japan.

JETRO publishes extensive English periodicals, marketing reports, fact books, business guides, and numerous other materials to assist foreign business executives in doing business in and exporting to Japan. JETRO organizes large trade exhibitions on behalf of foreign companies in such areas as healthcare and environmental equipment in Japan. Product import specialists in the information technology and consumer products sectors are sent to overseas markets for individual consultations with companies regarding export potential for the Japanese market. JETRO also organizes seminars on Japan's economy, business trends and assists foreign business development missions. In addition, JETRO maintains extensive business libraries in Tokyo, and in overseas offices, which are open to business executives. JETRO's presence on the internet includes regularly updated market reports, background information, current articles from periodicals, and instructions for participation in JETRO programs.

In the United States, JETRO staffs regional offices in New York, Chicago, Los Angeles, San Francisco, Houston, Denver and Atlanta. Addi-tionally, "Senior Trade Advisors" are assigned to work directly with state trade officials in a number of states, and with individual companies to facilitate local efforts to trade with Japan.

JETRO merged with the Institute of Developing Economies (IDE) in July 1998. IDE's focus on economic research on the developing economies of Asia complements JETRO's extensive global busi-ness development activities.

RALPH INFORZATO

Japan Federation of Economic Organizations

The Japan Federation of Economic Organizations or Keidanren (an abbreviation of its name in Japanese, Keizai Dantai Rengokai) was established on August 16, 1946. Its membership as of 2001 stands at 1,007 firms (sixty-five of these firms are non-Japanese) and 118 industry and trade groups representing all of Japan's key industrial sectors. Keidanen's primary purpose is to coordinate the discussion and subsequent resolution of major pro-blems confronting the Japanese business community, whether domestically or abroad. Given its large size and broad scope of purpose, its work is structured around committees that focus on specific industry sectors as well as particular topics. It is one of the most influential business organizations in Japan and, along with the **Japan Association of Corporate Executives** (Keizai Doyukai), the **Japan Federation of Employers' Associations** (Nikkeiren), and the **Japan Chamber of Commerce and Industry** (Nihon Shoko Kaigisho), is one of the four "voices of business" in Japanese society.

Keidanren was established as part of the effort to reorganize the business sector of Japanese society in the postwar era. As its influence grew, in 1952 it absorbed the Japanese Industrial Council, in a move that increased its membership and expanded its influence. In addition to its close interaction with Japanese government bureaucracy, it was also active in the political realm and is credited with playing an important role in the creation of the **Liberal Democratic Party**, which was established in 1955. Its participation in the political arena was significant until 1975, when political contributions became more tightly regulated. Its influence has also waned as Japanese companies have become global players and the influence of non-Japanese firms within Japan has grown.

Leadership of the organization is drawn from among the largest and most influential companies in Japan. Among its past chairmen are such business leaders as Toshio Dokoh (CEO of both Toshiba and Ishikawajima-Harima Heavy Industries) and Akio Morita (CEO of Sony). In addition to position papers and policy statements, Keidanren also develops charters which it encourages member firms and organizations to sign. A recent example is the Keidanren Global Environment Charter, which sets forth guidelines and standards for environmentally responsible economic activity. The organization is involved in an array of public relations efforts, including seminars and conferences. It also publishes position papers and several periodical and occasional publications. This range of activities is directed at both gathering *and* shaping public opinion on matters pertaining to business and the economy in Japan.

As Japanese companies have become more active within the world economy, and as the Japanese economy became increasingly influential within the world economy, especially during the 1980s, Keidanren has sought to develop ties with influential business and economic organizations outside of Japan. At the same time, it has increased its efforts to build closer relationships with various groups including labor, consumer and special interest non-profit organizations domestically.

ALLAN BIRD

Japan Federation of Employers' Associations

The Japan Federation of Employers' Associations or Nihon Keieisha Dantai Renmei, more commonly known as Nikkeiren, was established on April 12, 1948. Founded in a context of frequent labor disputes, Nikkeiren was launched to promote solidarity among employers and better relationships between labor and management. One of Japan's four key economic organizations and identified as part of the *zaikai*, Nikkeiren has historically wielded considerable clout with the government over the postwar period. The organization's membership is comprised of sixty industry associations and forty-seven prefectural employers' associations. Member associations represent the whole range of industries.

Activities

Nikkeiren's activities include the articulation of policy proposals, requests to the government, and position statements based on the conclusions reached at regular meetings and on findings from survey research. The organization presents these to member organizations and corporate employers, the government, political parties, and related ministries and agencies and works to have these policies implemented. Nikkeiren also sends representatives to government deliberation councils to ensure that managerial views are reflected in the development of government policy. The organization furthermore publishes a number of periodicals, including a weekly newsletter, the *Nikkeiren Times*, and a monthly journal, *Monthly Keieisha*.

Nikkeiren has been well represented on the government's Labor Legislation Council. The organization also maintains close ties with the **Ministry of Labor** and the Ministry of Health and Welfare, and has had an influential voice in the selection of the Labor Minister. Nikkeiren furthermore maintains close ties to the Labor Subcommittee of the LDP's Policy Committee and to the Social Welfare Committees of both houses in the Diet. The association holds frequent informal meetings with government officials and politicians as well.

Since 1951, Nikkeiren has served as the official voice of Japanese employers in the International Labor Organization (ILO) and one of Nikkeiren's Policy Board members serves simultaneously as a member of the ILO Governing Body. Nikkeiren has also actively participated in the activities of the International Organization of Employers (IOE) and taken part in the work of the Organization for Economic Co-operation and Development (OECD) through the activities of the OECD's Business and Industry Advisory Committee (BIAC). In addition, Nikkeiren's International Cooperation Center furthers human resource development abroad by bringing managers from overseas for training in Japan.

Evolution of role

In its early years, Nikkeiren was regarded as the most powerful and unified of Japan's four main business organizations. This unity came about because of greater agreement in the business community in the 1950s and 1960s over the need to confront labor than on other aspects of economic activities. Nikkeiren was highly sensitive to the activities of those political parties supporting labor, and especially to the activities of the Communist Party. The association was then known as "fighting Nikkeiren" since it focused its efforts on addressing labor offensives.

Leaders of Nikkeiren helped play a role in the 1955 establishment of the Economic Reconstruction Council, an organization that pooled political contributions from *zaikai*. This council was intended to strengthen the *zaikai*'s position *vis-à-vis*

the leftist movement while at the same time helping to prevent the political scandals often arising out of close relationships between individual companies and individual politicians. Nikkeiren and the other business organizations – arguing that national economic viability was contingent on a stable political situation – were furthermore very influential in pushing for a merger between the Liberal and Democratic Parties to form the **Liberal Democratic Party** (LDP) in 1955.

Since the 1960s, Nikkeiren's emphasis has focused more on the promotion of cooperation between labor and management. In 1974, when Japan was confronted with economic difficulties arising from the first oil crisis, for example, Nikkeiren established a task force to study repercussions in the area of labor relations. Nikkeiren's efforts since have focused in particular on human resource development, management ethics, orderly and harmonious relationships within corporations, and social and economic progress through corporate activities. The organization has been particularly active as a voice in articulating management concerns in regard to changes in the employment, personnel, social security and education systems.

Spring labor negotiations

Every year, Nikkeiren's Committee for the Study of Labor issues a report in January examining the current Japanese economy and labor issues. This report then serves as the basis for spring wage negotiations, also known as the "spring labor offensive" or *shunto*. Major changes in the industrial and employment structures, record high unemployment rates, and a widening of the gap between strong and weak firms within particular industries have changed the character and needs of labor negotiations since the latter 1990s, however.

Management and labor in individual companies settle labor negotiations and wage agreements. Yet, in the past, unions demanded identical wage increases and simultaneous replies from management. In a context of economic growth, long-term employment within a single firm, and a seniority system of promotions, this strategy seemed to work well. Since the 1990s, however corporate earnings have come to vary widely, even within the same industry. As a result, it has become increasingly difficult for industry unions to make unified demands. At the same time, employers are switching to pay systems that emphasize merit over seniority. As a result of these developments, the traditional negotiating practice between Nikkeiren and labor unions has become increasingly outdated and the need for annual labor negotiations questioned. In twenty-first century Japan, it is no longer as desirable or feasible to work towards the adoption of uniform wage and working conditions across companies or industries.

Nikkeiren's position in the 2001 spring labor negotiations reflected adjustment to this changed environment. Opposing uniform wage increases, Nikkeiren called instead for individual companies to raise their labor expenses to appropriate levels. The organization also proposed that work sharing should be introduced as an issue in the negotiations and that priority should be placed on stable employment over wage increases.

Challenges to labor–management relations in recent years

Other dramatic changes in the economic and business environment in the 1990s posed additional challenges to labor–management relations. The prolonged economic downturn led companies to rectify high cost structures through cuts in employment. Growing labor mobility arising from the change in industrial structure, corporate restructuring, diversification in the modes of employment and changing employment expectations have also been an outgrowth of the economic downturn. Notably, the number of temporary employees has grown steadily since the introduction of the Manpower Dispatching Business Law in 1999. These changes have spurred *Nikkeiren* to work together with **Rengo** (the Japanese Trade Union Confederation) to determine what kinds of labor–management relations might best serve Japan in this transitional period.

Nikkeiren's activities have focused increasingly on working to expand skill training to enhance employability. The organization is engaged in building an information network to enhance labor mobility and enable companies to better meet employment needs. In addition, Nikkeiren advo-

cates deregulation in the economic and labor fields and the establishment of private sector leadership in the economy as a means of creating jobs. A declining birthrate and aging population will also change Japan's labor force participation rate in the future and thereby affect labor supply trends. In response to concerns over the tendency towards declining consumption that typically accompanies a declining population, Nikkeiren has spoken out in favor of relaxed immigration laws.

Finally, a number of corporate and management scandals in the 1990s raised the profile of business ethics in Nikkeiren's activities. The organization has advocated the establishment of higher standards of behavior. At the same time, however, Nikkeiren has expressed alarm at rulings in 2000 concerning the responsibility of corporate directors for failure to carry out proper risk management, seeing the burden of responsibility placed on Japanese management as excessive.

Merger with Keidanren

For many years, Nikkeiren and the **Japan Federation of Economic Organizations**, Keidanren, proved complementary. Although there was considerable overlap in memberships, the division of labor was fairly clear: Nikkeiren was the leading player in shaping corporate policies regarding labor and wages while *Keidanren* focused on other business issues. In the 1990s, however, Keidanren became increasingly concerned with social security and social welfare issues such as pension reform and medical insurance programs, areas that had traditionally been the domain of Nikkeiren. The increasing overlap in issue area focus, combined with the declining role for Nikkeiren in annual labor negotiations and calls for restructuring and streamlining of business organizations in line with similar trends in corporate Japan, eventually resulted in pressure for the two organizations to merge. In September 2000, Nikkeiren and Keidanren announced their plans to create a more unified voice to articulate Japanese business interests. The merger, to be carried out in 2002, will result in a new organization called the Japan Business Federation.

Some regional employers' associations have expressed opposition to the merger between

Keidanren and Nikkeiren. Nikkeiren membership at the local employers' association level includes some small and medium-sized firms whose interests have not traditionally been represented in Keidanren. Keidanren's primary members tend to be large companies with headquarters located in Tokyo. Local employers' associations are also wary of the trend towards centralization of power in Tokyo and fear that region-specific concerns may become increasingly overshadowed by national or Tokyo-centered concerns.

The different legal status of the two business organizations also complicates the merger process. While Nikkeiren operated as a voluntary body, Keidanren operated as an incorporated association. To carry out the merger, Nikkeiren will be dissolved and then absorbed by Keidanren, a process that to some symbolizes the likely overshadowing of the Nikkeiren elements by Keidanren elements in the new organization. The merger is expected to have some clear positive benefits, however. In addition to bringing a potentially greater business influence over the formation of government policies and eliminating redundancies in the respective activities of the two groups, the merger is expected to lead to an increased volume of information available to members.

Further reading

Chitoshi, Y. (1968) *Big Business in Japanese Politics*, New Haven, CT: Yale University Press.
The Current Labor Economy in Japan (annual), Tokyo: Japan Federation of Employers' Associations.
Nikkeiren Position Paper (annual), Tokyo: Japan Federation of Employers' Associations.

JENNIFER AMYX

Japan, Inc.

"Japan, Inc." is a widely used phrase in referring to Japan's industrial system, with a changing meaning that reflects the changing views of Japan's economy over several decades. Apparently first used in an article in *Fortune* magazine in the mid-1930s, the term vanished from the business vocabulary until the mid-1960s when it was given currency in

several speeches and articles. It served usefully as a brief description of the generally supportive interaction between government and business, with relations rather like that in a conglomerate, Japan, Incorporated, whose businesses were free to compete within the broad limits of common overall goals and consensus. Audiences still at that time had little knowledge of Japan's economy and still only marginal interest. "Japan, Inc." was a useful way of describing Japan's economic management system to naive audiences.

As Japan's industrial growth continued and as trade frictions with the United States intensified, the phrase began to take on a more sinister tone, and became a way of encapsulating what was seen as a conspiratorial Japan in which business entities marched in unison to instructions from an all-powerful central government. This view was very much reinforced as some US academic studies provided legitimacy to the view that the **Ministry of International Trade and Industry** (MITI) was the entire determinant of Japan's industrial structure, competitive frameworks and trade policy. "Japan, Inc." became the quick reference to this unfair conspiracy, which served to explain Japan's success. This was for business and government in the United States at least a much more palatable explanation for Japan's competitive success than different levels of competence in the market place, and appealed to widely held paranoid feelings of being attacked by a sinister enemy.

Much of the rapid and wide currency of the phrase no doubt derived from a US Department of Commerce publication, *Japan, The Government-Business Relationship: A Guide for the American Businessman*, issued in early 1972. The Japanese translation, *Kabushiki Kaisha Nippon*, appeared in Tokyo only a few months after the US edition. The book provided a very good definition of the Japan, Inc. phrase, using the conglomerate analogue, and describes most positively government–business interaction in Japan. The three detailed industry case studies in the book, of computers, autos and steel, similarly give little support for the more sinister and conspiratorial echoes.

Even now, after so long a time, "Japan, Inc." remains a very much used, and misused, phrase. Perhaps it is distance that blurs complexity and makes a simple (and misleading) phrase useful to newsmen and others when speaking of Japan. Unfortunately, the negative nuances of the phrase are also long-lived, serving as one measure of how little we seem to have learned about the intricacies of Japan's business systems.

Further reading

Kaplan, E.J. (1972) *Japan, the Government-Business Relationship. A Guide for the American Businessman*, Washington, DC: U.S. Government Printing Office.

Shomushohen, B. (1972). *Kabushiki Kaisha Nippon*, Tokyo: Simul Press.

JAMES C. ABEGGLEN

Japan National Railways

Japan has long placed great emphasis on its railway system, believing it to be an important means of fostering economic development. As early as 1872, an opening ceremony was held for a rail line running between Shimbashi, near Tokyo, and Yokohama. By 1874, service between Osaka and Kobe began. Three years later, the service was extended from Osaka to Kyoto. By 1880, railways were running in the northern-most island, Hokkaido. In 1882, service opened between Shimbashi and Nihombashi, and in 1889, the Tokaido line between Shimbashi and Kobe began. In the same year, the Kyushu Railway Company began operations between Hakata and Chitosegawa.

The 1890s saw continued expansion of Japan's rail system. Kyushu Railway Company opened another line from Moji to Kumamoto in 1891, the same year that Nippon Railway Company began running trains between Ueno in Tokyo and Aomori. Japan's first steam locomotive was produced in Kobe in 1893, with the Kyoto Electric Railway opening in 1895. At the end of the decade, the Kansai Railway Company line between Nagoya and Osaka began. In the new century, Japan continued to develop its rail system. The Sanyo Railway Company began to operate between Kobe and Shimonoseki in 1901, and the Kobu Railway Company began running electric

and steam locomotives between Iidamachi and Nakano from 1904.

Up to then, the railways had been privately owned. To create more cooperation between the lines as well as put government backing behind them, the National Railways Law was passed in 1906, with private railways taken over by the government in the following year. Throughout the next several decades the national railways continued to make progress in new trackage and in technical developments. Some of the developments during this time were electric locomotives, colored signal lamps, automatic couplers for passenger cars, ticket vending machines and automatic door openers. Japan's first subway was introduced in Tokyo at this time, as well as a number of tunnels being built.

In 1949, following the devastation of rail lines during the Second World War, the rail system was reorganized with the creation of Japan National Railway (JNR). In the years that followed, JNR continued to develop the nation's rail system. In 1956, the Tokaido line between Tokyo and Kobe was electrified. In 1964, at the time of the Tokyo Olympics, the Tokaido Shinkansen (high-speed service) line opened between Tokyo and Osaka. Other high-speed lines followed: Osaka to Okayama in 1972, Okayama to Hakata in 1975, Nigata to Omiya and Morioka in 1982, and Omiya to Ueno in 1985. By this time, there were five types of railway operating organizations in Japan: JNR, local government railways, private railway companies (*mintetsu*), joint local government and private railways known as the third sector, and Teito Rapid Transit Authority for local commuters.

In 1987, Japan National Railways was privatized. At that time, there were about 27,600 km of railway lines, and 345 billion passengers per km. Freight transportation was about 21 billion tons per km. The reason for the privatization was JNR's tremendous operating and accumulated deficits and labor problems. At the time of privatization, accumulated deficits were written off, and labor cuts were made. As a result of the privatization, JNR was split into six passenger companies, one freight company and other organizations. The passenger companies were regionally based: Hokkaido, East, Central, West, Shikoku and Kyushu. Since they were no longer government-owned,

National was not included in their names. For instance, the northernmost regional company was named Hokkaido Japan Railways.

Further reading

Noda, M., Harada, K., Aoki, E. and Oikawa, Y. *Japanese Railway: The Establishment and Development*, Railway History Series, Tokyo: Nihon Keizai Shinbunsha.

ROBERT BROWN

Japan Productivity Center for Socio-Economic Development

The Japan Productivity Center for Socio-Economic Development (JPC-SED) is a private, non-profit tripartite association of management, academics and labor circles. As its organizational mission, JPC-SED seeks to further strengthen the productivity movement in Japan and abroad. It came into being in 1994 when the Japan Productivity Center (JPC) merged with its sister organization, the Social and Economic Congress of Japan (SECJ). Established in 1955, JPC was a major channel for acquiring advanced management technology from the USA and Europe and disseminating it throughout Japan. SECJ was established in 1973 to develop a national consensus by addressing social and economic macro-issues. The new organization combines SECJ's expertise in research with the productivity techniques that JPC has developed. Although the Japanese government played a major role in the initial establishment of the two organizations, it was not involved in their evolution beyond that point.

JPC-SED's major role is the study and formulation of policy proposals concerning three major issues: reform of various social systems, productivity enhancement and structural economic reform, and development of the international economy balanced with conservation of the global environment. Its most significant accomplishment has been its promotion of the productivity movement in Japan. A significant difference between JPC-SED and other similar organizations abroad is that the former employs a human resource-centered approach, while the latter often advocate a technology-centered perspective. Additionally, JPC-SED acts as a human resources development organization. Through various seminars and outreach programs, it educates managers of Japanese companies about the latest techniques and trends of corporate management and economics. The fees from these seminars are the major source of income for JPC-SED. Consequently, JPC-SED is not dependent financially on other organizations.

In order to propose solutions to the problems that the Japanese society and economy face, the JPC-SED has formed committees consisting of leaders and experts from various fields such as management, economics, and sociology. There are fifteen committees that carry out studies and surveys on issues such as social policy, welfare, employment, management innovation, and society in the information age. Although typically long term, these committees are not permanent, but change according to the issues that emerge. The members of the committees disclose the results of these studies to the public in the form of policy proposals. These proposals are typically presented to the prime minister's cabinet, appear in the leading mass media, and often are compared to the proposals made by **Ministry of International Trade and Industry** (MITI).

JPC-SED disseminates its knowledge and experiences to overseas countries. It is the national representative to the Asian Productivity Organization, an inter-governmental regional organization established in 1961 to increase productivity in the countries of Asia and the Pacific region. Also, JPC-SED instituted the Japan Quality Award in 1995, an annual award that recognizes excellence of management quality in companies.

See also: industrial efficiency movement

Further reading

Japan Productivity Center Staff (1989), *New Paradigm of Productivity Movement in Japan,*. Portland, OR: Productivity Press Inc.

GEORGIOS GIAKATIS

Japanese business in Africa

In contrast with other regions, Japanese business have only an insignificant presence in Africa. This situation can be attributed to both the lackluster economic performance of the region, and the physical distance between Japan and the African continent. However, two significant trends can be noticed: the uneven presence of Japanese businesses within the various African countries, and the adoption of certain distinctive aspects of Japanese management practices.

Japanese businesses are concentrated in a few African countries, while a large number of countries have a negligible presence, if not a total absence, of Japanese enterprises. Within the Sub-Saharan African countries, the largest number of Japanese businesses and investment can be found in South Africa. In northern Africa, Egypt has the largest number of Japanese businesses and investment. The other countries that have a relatively significant share of Japanese presence include Kenya, Tanzania and Ethiopia in eastern Africa, Zambia, Namibia and Swaziland in southern Africa, and Senegal and the Ivory Coast in West Africa. The Japanese businesses found in Africa are mostly found in the natural resources, manufacturing and commercial services sectors. Investments in natural resource extraction and processing are in such product areas as agricultural products, copper, and other precious metals. Businesses in the manufacturing sector are mainly involved in transport equipment, electrical machinery, and electrical appliance assembly and manufacturing. The branches of some of the more established and larger Japanese trading companies dominantly represent commercial businesses.

Two clear issues emerge with regard to the uneven distribution and relatively insignificant presence of Japanese businesses in Africa. First, the African region is still not a favorable recipient of Japanese investment. Second, business between the region and Japanese companies is still conducted through international trade. The presence of branch offices of major Japanese trading companies in the capitals of many African countries attests to the fact that Japanese business in Africa is still by and large at an explorative or information collection stage. This is more so for the countries having a negligible presence of Japanese corporations. It can also be noticed that some of the Japanese trading and manufacturing companies use their presence in one African country as a strategic position for gauging the regional economic trends. A case in point is that of companies based in South Africa, Kenya and Egypt, which use these strategic vantage points to gauge the economic trends within the larger regions of southern Africa, eastern Africa, and northern Africa, respectively.

In sharp contrast to the negligible presence of Japanese business in Africa, it is quite common to find certain elements of the Japanese management style practiced by both foreign affiliates and indigenous firms in various African countries. This is true for both the manufacturing and service industry. The use of Japanese management practices can be largely attributed to the branch offices of one international consulting company. This consulting firm had previously learned the Japanese system of management for use in their European division. While jointly working with their European counterparts, the firm's African division consultants became interested in the Japanese management system. This interest finally culminated in the adoption of the Japanese management system into the consulting firm's product portfolio. This has resulted in the wide use of certain aspects of the Japanese management system in Africa, albeit with varying levels of success.

The most commonly found aspects of the Japanese management system are quality control systems, *kaizen* activities to reduce waste, elements of the just-in-time production system, factory layout changes, and multi-skill training for shopfloor workers. Adoption of the Japanese quality control system can be found in large manufacturing enterprises in a number of African nations. Clearly discernible are the quality task groups and the new concept that quality starts at the beginning of the production process with raw material acquisition, rather than at the end of the production line. There are also a number of manufacturers that have changed their factory layout by introducing cells and bringing machines closer together. Even though the lack of a community of parts and components suppliers has prohibited the complete adoption of the just-in-time system of production, many manufacturers use the *kanban* system to organize production activities in their factories. Against the background of production inefficiency and rampant wastage, many factories have found *kaizen* to be an appealing method for reducing wastage and effecting incremental small changes in the entire production process. Another aspect of the Japanese management style that many African factories have found quite appealing, is the human resource management system for factory floor workers, placing emphasis on multi-skill training. However, there has been mixed performance in the adoption of the Japanese management system, with the emphasis on failure; generally, the performance has been very dismal. This can be attributed to management failure in several areas: poor approach to quality issues, resistance from middle management and the workforce, unreliable suppliers and poor quality of parts and components, and short-term output maximization at the cost of preventive maintenance.

In the future, an increase in the presence of Japanese business will largely depend on positive economic performance, political tranquility and a generally favorable investment climate in Africa. It is also an interesting fact that in the last half of the 1990s there have been a number of Japanese delegations visiting a few African countries (South Africa, Kenya, Ethiopia and Zambia) on fact-finding missions on the general investment climate in Africa. Such visits may signal a relative increase in economic exchanges and possibly be followed by direct investment from Japanese companies. As such, any significant presence of Japanese business in Africa will follow a pattern in which certain favored first-in-line countries will act as a window from which the strategic monitoring of both national and regional economic conditions and opportunities will be undertaken. Nevertheless, it is quite difficult to project as to when there will be any significant Japanese investments in Africa.

Further reading

Kaplinsky, R. and Posthuma, A. (1994) *Easternization: The Spread of Japanese Management Techniques to Developing Countries*, London: Frank Cass.

NATHANIEL O. AGOLA

Japanese business in Australia

Japan is Australia's most important business partner in terms of both inward investment and overall trade. Japanese business interests in Australia are also substantial and represent 5 percent of Japan's total global investment (see **Japanese investment patterns**), making Australia the third largest recipient of Japanese foreign direct investment (FDI) behind the USA and the UK. Japanese business in Australia has been concentrated in agriculture, mining, automobiles and finance with a recent growth of investment in real estate and tourism.

The development of offshore operations in Australia has taken place in a series of waves. In the 1960s and early 1970s Japanese business investment in Australia was mainly "resource seeking" and was focused around raw material extraction, with Australia traditionally being Japan's largest supplier of iron ore and coking coal. In the 1970s "market-seeking" FDI intended to offset **trade barriers** saw substantial Japan investments in the Australian automobile and electronics industries with the establishment of local manufacturing operations by major Japanese companies including **Toyota**, Nissan, NEC, Sanyo and later **Mitsubishi**. These investments preceded by almost a decade similar investments in the USA and Europe. Japanese business investment in Australia from the mid-1980s to the early 1990s witnessed a new wave of investment in real estate, tourism, and services, making Australia the largest recipient of Japanese investment in these categories next to the USA. Australia also became one of the top 10 recipients of Japanese finance-related investment as Japanese banks established a succession of affiliates in Australia.

Over 700 Japanese business firms operate in Australia and directly employ more than 45,000 local workers or about 0.5 percent of the workforce. In addition, some 180 Australian subcontractors and major suppliers to Japanese businesses employ an additional 263,000 workers, making a total of 308,000 people employed in Japanese or Japanese-related companies. This represents 3.7 percent of Australia's total full-time workforce. Japanese manufacturing firms, while representing only 15 percent of Japanese investment in Australia employ 34 percent of all direct employees, high-lighting the contribution of Japanese firms to employment in the local manufacturing sector. Japanese business operations in primary industries such as mining, energy and agriculture involve a relatively small number of Japanese companies handling a large volume of exports. Conversely, in secondary industries such as manufactured goods and industrial production a large number of Japanese companies handle a relatively small volume of exports.

Of Japan's nine *sogo shosha* (see **general trading companies**) in Australia, four rank in the top ten list of Australia's exporters. Combined export revenue in 1995–6 of the nine *sogo shosha* was US$15.8 billion, representing 21 percent of Australia's total merchandise exports in the same year.

Almost half of all Japanese manufacturing firms in Australia were established before 1980, although the last decade has witnessed a rapid growth in the number of Japanese multinational enterprises (MNEs) operating sales and production facilities. The establishment of financial services and tourism firms is much more recent and generally after 1988.

Japanese financial, trading and manufacturing firms have a long history of involvement in the Australian economy (Purcell 1981). Most Japanese firms have pre-FDI involvement in Australia through representative offices or joint venture. The beginnings of Japanese business in Australia go back almost 150 years to the late **Tokugawa period** when Akiyama Teiji, the first Japanese trader to reside in Australia, arrived in Sydney in 1850 to attend the International Exhibition and later opened a store in Melbourne selling Japanese wares. The real beginnings of Japanese business in Australia, however, began in 1890 when Kanematsu Fusajiro established Kanematsu Shoten, the forerunner of the great Kanematsu Trading Company, based around the export of Australian wool to Japan. By the early 1920s more than thirty Japanese companies operated some fifty branch offices in Australia. The group included Japan's seven great *sogo shosha* including **Mitsui** Bussan and **Mitsubishi** Shoji plus a variety of smaller, more specialized operators and an ancillary group of banking, shipping and insurance firms including the Yokohama Specie Bank.

Nearly all of Japanese businesses in Australia are wholly-owned subsidiaries. Since the mid-1980s more than 80 percent of new Japanese businesses have been greenfield investments, of which two-thirds are wholly owned subsidiaries. Japanese banks and tourism firms are overwhelmingly (92 percent) wholly-owned, greenfield operations.

Japanese manufacturing firms came to Australia principally to supply the Australian domestic market, while financial firms came to mainly service their parent's Japanese clients or other Japanese firms in Australia. Japanese tourism firms came to service the burgeoning Japanese tourism market. Japanese manufacturing firms rank the need to adapt to local customer requirements, political stability, tariff duties and energy costs as the most important reasons for selecting Australia as an investment location (Nicholas *et al.* 1996).

Japanese businesses in Australia have also adopted many of the organizational practices of Japanese firms in Japan, including the wide application of work practices related to product and process technology such as **quality control circles**, ***kaizen***, **just-in-time** production systems and formal on-the-job training practices (Purcell and Nicholas 1999). In the banking and trading sectors, which contain the highest levels of Japanese ownership and where the density of Japanese expatriates and Japan-related business is highest, Japanese management style in Australia tends to be most intense and subsidiaries more "clone-like" in appearance. Where the ratio of local employees is high, such as in manufacturing, firms tend to be much more hybrid in appearance, characterized by the adoption of Japanese organizational practices on the one hand but accompanied by more local labour market incentives on the other.

See also: Japanese investment patterns; Japanese multinational enterprises; Japanese business in the USA

Further reading

Australian Institute of International Affairs (ed.) (1999) *Australia and Japan Beyond 2000, Proceedings of the 20th Australia-Japan Relations Symposium*, Canberrra: AIIA.

Nicholas S., Merrett, D., Whitwell, G. and Purcell, W. (1996) "Japanese FDI in Australia in the 1990s: Manufacturing, Financial Services and Tourism," *Pacific Economic Papers* 256: 1–24.

Purcell, W. (1981) "The Development of Japan's Trading Company Network in Australia, 1890–1941," *Australian Economic History Review* 22(2): 114–32.

Purcell W. and Nicholas S. (1999) "The Transfer of Human Resource and Management Practice by Japanese Multinationals to Australia: Do Industry, Size and Experience Matter?" *International Journal of Human Resource Management* 10(1): 72–88.

Toyama, Y. and Tisdell, C. (eds) (1991) *Japan-Australia Economic Relations in the 1990s*, Osaka: Centre for Australian Studies.

WILLIAM PURCELL
STEPHEN NICHOLAS

Japanese business in Canada

Canada has a small, open economy, highly dependent on international trade and foreign direct investment (FDI). International trade accounts for over 40 percent of Canada's gross national product. Inward foreign direct investment has always played a large role in Canadian economic development. More recently outward FDI has grown very rapidly, to the point where it now exceeds inward FDI. In 1998, the stock of inward FDI amounted to $217 billion Cdn and outward FDI was $240 billion Cdn. Canadian FDI in Japan is still relatively insignificant, but it is growing in importance. Japan ranks fourth in terms of Canadian inward FDI, following the United States, the United Kingdom and the Netherlands. The Japanese share of the stock of Canadian inward FDI was about 4 percent or $8.3 billion Cdn. As a percentage of Japanese outward FDI, it was under 2 percent.

Early post-Second World War Japanese FDI in Canada aimed at securing raw materials for the resource-poor Japanese domestic economy. The first investments were in mining, both energy and minerals. In 1983 these totaled $726 million dollars Cdn. They peaked in the mid-1990s at over $1 billion Cdn and in 1998 fell back to $783 million

Cdn. FDI in wood products, including pulp and paper, was still relatively small in 1983 at less than $100 million Cdn, but it grew rapidly to a maximum in 1996 of $1,250 million Cdn and in 1998 stood at $972 million Cdn. Combined, these two industries (resources) accounted for over one-fifth of Japanese FDI in Canada.

Manufacturing became the largest component of FDI by the early 1980s. Unlike the FDI in raw materials, this sector's FDI was aimed at serving the North American market. It began with a handful of consumer and industrial investments such as **Matsushita** producing color televisions and NTN turning out ball bearings. In 1983 combined Japanese inward investment in food processing, chemicals, electrical and electronic production, construction and communications stood at only $84 million Cdn rising to $1.511 billion Cdn in 1998 or about 18 percent of total Japanese FDI in Canada. (This is the grouping according to Statistics Canada, which includes some non-manufacturing businesses.)

However, the largest investments in manufacturing are those in the **automotive industry**. This reflects the strong competitive advantage that Japanese auto companies have had over their rivals from the early 1980s. Statistics Canada classifies automotive investment in the machinery and transportation equipment category. From a 1983 level of $368 million Cdn, Japanese FDI in the industry grouping rose to $3.148 billion in 1998 Cdn and has increased considerably since. In 1998, this sector accounted for nearly 38 percent of Japanese FDI in Canada, compared to only about 14 percent of overall Canadian inward FDI. Hence, Japanese companies are much more concentrated in this sector than are other foreign investors.

The automotive investment began in the mid-1980s when the Japanese auto assemblers decided to build plants in North America to avoid both import quotas resulting from the voluntary restraint agreement they were forced to accept, and also to avoid being subject to North American import tariffs. As part of their North American expansion, Honda and Toyota decided to select Canadian sites in Ontario (in addition to their United States operations). Suzuki, a smaller Japanese manufacturer, followed by forming a joint venture with General Motors known as CAMI. Although these plants served the Canadian market, their output was primarily destined for the United States. Canada was chosen for several reasons. These included the lure of duty rebates offered by the Canadian government as well as incentives provided both by the federal and provincial governments. There was also an available easily trainable labor force. Lower wage rates in Canada and the payment of medical insurance by the Canadian government were other incentives. In addition, energy and land prices were attractive and, given that the United States market was quite close, transportation costs were not high. Finally, other things being equal, firms like to produce in markets where they have substantial sales.

The **Honda** and **Toyota** operations were originally small, even sub-optimal. However, they were expanded partly as a result of the duty free access to the United States market provided by the Canada-United States Free Trade Agreement in 1989 (and subsequently provided by the North American Free Trade Agreement of 1994 that added Mexico to the free trade zone). A rapid descent of the Canadian dollar relative to the United States currency in the 1990s further enhanced the attractiveness of expanding the Canadian plants. In 1997 Toyota opened a second plant at its site and Honda likewise in 1998. In 1998 Honda began to produce its new Odyssey minivan and Toyota its Camry Solera coupe in Canada. In 2000, Honda launched production of its new sports utility van (SUV), the Acura MDX. Soon a sister vehicle, a Honda SUV, will be added. Toyota is now gearing up to assemble the first Lexus produced outside of Japan, the RX300 SUV. The total investment in the three operations is expected to be $5.1 billion Cdn by 2003 (Honda 1.1, Toyota 2.1, and CAMI 1.0). Aside from these plants, there are also in Canada forty Japanese auto parts, materials and machine shop operations associated with the automotive industry. Over half of these are joint ventures with Canadian partners. Total employment in 2000 was over 9,000 in vehicle production and more than 10,000 in parts manufacturing.

Japanese automotive companies recently increased their competiveness versus their US-based rivals by winning a case that Japan had brought

before the World Trade Organization. Effective February 2001, General Motors, Ford and DaimlerChrysler (the Big Three) can no longer import vehicles from their factories outside of North America duty-free. For example, Saabs produced in Sweden, Mercedes assembled in Germany by DaimlerChrysler, and Volvos and Jaguars manufactured in Sweden and England, respectively, will have to bear the same 6.1 percent tariff that is levied on motor vehicles imported into Canada from outside of North America by other manufacturers. Canada will no longer be able to discriminate in favor of the Big Three, who were party to the 1965 Canada-United States Auto Pact.

Turning to Japanese FDI in finance, including insurance, there is a rapid increase in the period 1983 to 1998, from $150 million Cdn to $1.31 billion Cdn. In the case of services including retailing, the trajectory is far less steep, climbing only from $350 Cdn to $614 Cdn over the same period. The small investment in services is indicative of Japan's comparative disadvantage in this sector. While Japanese auto assemblers, especially Honda and Toyota, excel in manufacturing vehicles, the service sector in Japan lags its Western counterparts.

What is the likely future of Japanese FDI in Canada? Most probably, the automotive investments will continue to grow if Toyota and Honda are able to gain market share in North America against the Big Three. There is also likely to be more FDI in technologically advanced industries, as Canada becomes a more knowledge-focused economy.

Further reading

Canadian Embassy Tokyo, DFAIT/Asia-Pacific & Coordination, Investment Section (2000) *Japanese Investment Fact Sheet 2000*.

Industry Canada (2000) *The Trade and Investment Monitor*, Fall/Winter 1999–2000.

Japanese Automotive Manufacturers Association of Canada (JAMA) (2000) http://www.jama.ca.

Statistics Canada (2000) *Canada's International Investment Position from 1926 to 1999*, Ottawa: Statistics Canada.

BERNARD WOLF

Japanese business in China

The People's Republic of China has become an important destination country for Japanese business in recent years. Over 50 percent of Japanese FDI in emerging markets goes to China. Although Japan and China had a long history of diplomatic and trade relations, and although China began opening up to the world in 1979, most of Japan's FDI has taken place in the 1990s. Of almost 2,000 Japanese subsidiaries in China in 1996, only 4 percent were in China before 1987. As of 1997, there were almost 2,000 Japanese subsidiaries in China; over 77 percent are joint ventures, and 20 percent are wholly-owned subsidiaries. China is also the primary country into which Japanese SMEs are moving their production operations.

Reasons for locating in China include geographic and cultural proximity. The main reason for choosing China, however, is the potential of the domestic market. Over 56 percent of companies surveyed by the **Japan External Trade Organization** in 1997 chose China for this reason. The country is a particularly attractive market for electronic firms as well as automotive companies such as **Toyota** and Denso. At present, however, most of the products manufactured by Japanese companies in China are for export. Exports represent 91.3 percent of all Japanese production. In the case of audio component systems, China holds the number one position in terms of reverse imports to Japan.

China has also been expanding its sales to Japan of inexpensive mass-produced clothing made with low-cost labor. In the 1990s, the Japanese textile industry set up operations in China mostly through the establishment of joint ventures with Chinese companies. Japan's reverse imports of textiles reached ¥2.8 trillion in 1996, a 52 percent increase over 1993, most of which originated in China.

Japanese businesses in China are doing reasonably well. Approximately 70 percent reported a profit in 1992. However this number decreased to 50 percent in 1997. Sales to Chinese consumers, however, have not taken off. Furthermore, exports to China in 1999 were a record high at 16.5 percent. At the same time, imports from China increased to 16.2 percent, also a record high.

Local procurement is modest in China. The number of firms that source over 50 percent of their raw materials and parts locally totaled only 16.4 percent. Firms in China that source no more than 20 percent of procurement locally reached a level of 67.2 percent. Most firms also did not have local boards of directors (86.8 percent).

The export of electronics and IT-related parts and materials from Japan to China has been increasing in recent years. There has also been an increase in imports of consumer electronics from China to Japan as well.

See also: Japanese business in Southeast Asia; economic crisis in Asia

TERRI R. LITUCHY

Japanese business in Germany

A history of the Japanese presence in Germany

While the Japanese corporate presence can be found all over western and southern Europe, most Japanese corporate operations are concentrated in the United Kingdom, Holland, and Germany (in that order). Within Germany, corporate offices and personnel are primarily in the Dusseldorf area. During the early 1990s Germany had the second highest concentration of Japanese firms. Since then the Netherlands has moved ahead of Germany. When Japanese corporations began moving into Europe in large numbers from the 1970s, the Dusseldorf area was a favored location for several reasons. Dusseldorf is located in the Ruhr area of Germany, in the *länder* (state) of Nordrhein-Westfalen, known since the 1800s as the industrial heartland of Germany. The nearby city of Duisburg also has one of the biggest inland seaports in Europe, with easy access to the Atlantic through the Rhine River. Furthermore, the Dusseldorf area is centrally located in Western Europe, giving foreign corporations easy access to all of the biggest industrial centers of Western Europe.

Before the Second World War, the Japanese presence in Germany was concentrated in the northern port city of Hamburg. But from the mid-1950s the returning Japanese corporations were moving mostly to Dusseldorf. There was one Japanese person registered as living in Dusseldorf in 1950, but 300 by 1960, 2,000 by 1973, and 7,443 by 1992. In 1966 the Japanese Chamber of Commerce in Dusseldorf was founded, representing sixty Japanese companies in the area. By 1968 the number of Japanese companies had grown to 100, then 200 by 1973, and 300 by 1980. Japanese companies first began production in the area in 1971. In 1990, Japan was behind only the United States and the Netherlands in levels of direct investment in Nordrhein-Westfalen, and Nordrhein-Westfalen accounted for half of all Japanese investment in Germany. In 1980 the Japanese direct investment in Nordrhein-Westfalen totaled slightly more than DM 1 billion; by 1990 it had grown to over DM 5 billion. In 1990, however, the number of Japanese companies' production facilities in the Dusseldorf area had still only reached 30 and began to decline from this time forward.

From 1992 the number of Japanese corporations of all industries in Dusseldorf began a slow decline because of: (1) the economic slowdown in Japan; (2) slow movement to Berlin after Berlin was designated the new capital of united Germany; and (3) slow movement out of Germany along with more economic activity in nearby Holland. As of late 1998 there were just over 23,000 Japanese living in Germany, and 1,110 Japanese corporations with some kind of operations in Germany. Just over 4,500 Japanese lived in the Dusseldorf area in 1999, down from 7,443 in 1992.

By the late 1990s there were also only 520 Japanese companies in the Dusseldorf area. A 1991 survey by the Japanese Chamber of Commerce in Dusseldorf found about 75,000 Germans employed by 1,099 Japanese corporations in Germany, with more than DM 100 billion in profits in Germany. These numbers have been cut almost in half since 1991, but as noted above there are still 1,110 Japanese companies with at least some business in Germany. But by the late 1990s there were almost no Japanese production facilities in the Dusseldorf area, or anywhere else in Germany. Still, Dusseldorf remains the center for Japanese business activity in Germany. By the late 1990s some Japanese firms that had moved out of the area (and especially to Berlin) began moving back to Dusseldorf because of the infrastructure and support from a well-established Japanese community with a Buddhist center and good Japanese schools. But there has continued to be a reduction of Japanese corporate offices in the Dusseldorf area due to movement out of Germany since the early 1990s, and especially to neighboring Holland. The movement out of Germany has been stimulated mostly by high labor costs and labor laws. The European Single Market, realized in 1993, has eliminated barriers to capital flow and trade, producing strong locational competition for the whole EU market, making it more and more difficult for Germany to hold on to such direct foreign investment.

German labor laws

Even at the high point of Japanese investment in Germany, during the early 1990s, only 10.1 percent of the Japanese corporations in all of Germany were involved in manufacturing, while the vast majority were active in sales, service, and the financial industry. The Japanese corporations involved in manufacturing were almost exclusively electronic firms. Interviews with the top executives of thirty-four randomly selected Japanese firms in the Dusseldorf area and officials of the Japanese Chamber of Commerce confirmed that the primary reasons few Japanese corporations have manufacturing plants in Germany are labor costs, taxes, powerful German labor unions, and the strict German labor laws. These are also among the reasons most often given for the movement of Japanese corporations out of Germany and into other European countries such as the Netherlands. German workers continue to enjoy the highest wages and benefits in the world, and the German Works Constitution Act, passed soon after the Second World War (and expanded during the early 1970s, also referred to as "co-determination laws") gives German employees extensive influence and rights in the work place. These German work laws apply to all corporations hiring a significant number of German employees while in Germany. Most importantly, these German work laws require companies to allow for the election of employees to fill the "works council" which must be consulted on all matters involving the interests of employees in the company, including the hiring and firing of employees at all levels, wages and other compensation, and even changes in work organization and working hours. The larger the number of employees in the company, the larger the works council, whose members must be given paid release time to take care of employee interests. Corporations can try to go against the recommendations of the works council in such matters as the hiring and firing of employees, but they do so at their own peril. There is a system of labor courts to back up the German work laws and a company can be tied up in court, unable to implement changes challenged by the works council, for months if not years. Powerful German labor unions add to the influence of German employees by focusing on industry-wide issues and politics while the works council members take care of employee interests on every shop floor and office. The philosophy of the German government after the Second World War in passing the Works Constitution Act was that employees of companies have just as much right to influence major decisions of the company as stockholders. This is why German laws also require that almost all major corporations reserve half the positions in the boards of directors for representatives elected by the employees of the company.

Despite such rigid labor laws and powerful unions, which Japanese managers find in extreme contrast to their working environment in Japan, research has found that respect for German labor appears to remain very high among Japanese executives in Germany. There is little history of significant labor conflict in Japanese corporations in Germany, and German labor union officials have confirmed that Japanese executives have at least as much respect as executives of German corporations. Before the middle 1990s, Japanese executives said they would remain in Germany despite high labor costs, regulations, and taxes because German labor is the most skilled, productive, and quickest to train of any country. This ratio of costs and benefits of doing business in Germany, especially for those with production facilities apparently began to change by the end of the twentieth century. Japanese executives often state they are in Germany now because they must be there primarily for sales, service, and finance. There are, however, signs of gradual change in the influence of labor in the German economy. Despite the election of Gerhard Schroeder to head the German government in 1998 with a "green-red"

coalition government of the Social Democrats and Green Party (both traditionally most supportive of labor), there has been a slow erosion of labor influence, support for the welfare state, and high corporate taxes. This is also in spite of considerable evidence by social scientists and labor research institutes (such as the Institut für Arbeit und Technik in Gelsenkirchen) in Germany that the high productivity of German labor is related to their rights and co-determination required under these German work laws.

Lack of trust of foreign employees and the position of German middle managers

While labor conflict within Japanese corporations in Germany has been comparatively low, there is, however, a major employee-related problem for Japanese corporations in Germany, a problem found in Japanese corporations with foreign operations all over the world. There is a rigid "glass ceiling" for foreign employees in Japanese corporations. A simple indicator of the situation is the Japanese Chamber of Commerce publication in Germany listing all Japanese corporations and their top managers in Germany: There is almost a complete absence of non-Japanese names among these executives. Foreign managers in Japanese corporations know that they are seldom given the full trust of Japanese higher management or given authority on major company decisions. (And in this sense it can be said that German employees on the shop floor have more legal, and perhaps actual influence than do German middle managers of a Japanese company in Germany.) The lack of opportunities for career promotions within the company mean that these Japanese corporations have difficulty hiring and keeping talented German middle managers. This problem is crucial because, given the rigid German work laws, the common practice is for Japanese executives to rely extensively on German middle managers. Japanese executives in Germany, as elsewhere, are expected to spend only a few years away from Japan, often returning to the home office in Japan after two years. These Japanese executives do not typically understand the full meaning of German work laws, nor do they speak fluent German. Thus the German middle manager is most often a "go-between," a representative of German employees to Japanese management and at the same time a representative of Japanese management to the German employees. Thus, especially in Germany, with the crucial role played by German middle managers under German work laws, the mistrust and lack of promotions for foreign managers in a Japanese corporation proves to be especially harmful to Japanese corporate interests.

Further reading

Kerbo, H.R. and Strasser, H. (2000) *Modern Germany*, New York: McGraw-Hill.

Kerbo, H.R., Wittenhagen, E. and Nakao, K. (1994a) *Japanische Unternehmen in Deutschland: Unternehmensstruktur und Arbeitsverhaeltnis*, Gelsenkirchen: Veroffentlichungsliste des Instituts Arbeit und

—— (1994b) "Japanese Transplant Corporations, Foreign Employees, and the German Economy: A Comparative Analysis of Germany and the United States," *Duisburger Beiträge zur Soziologischen Forschung*, Duisburg.

Lincoln, J.R., Kerbo, H. and Wittenhagen, E. (1995) "Japanese Companies in Germany: A Case Study in Cross-Cultural Management," *Journal of Industrial Relations* 25: 123–39.

Thelen, K.A. (1991) *Union of Parts: Labor Politics in Postwar Germany*, Ithaca, NY: Cornell University Press.

Turner, L. (1991) *Democracy at Work: Changing World Markets and the Future of Labour Unions*, Ithaca, NY: Cornell University Press.

HAROLD KERBO
PATRICK ZILTENER

Japanese business in Italy

At the close of the twentieth century, Japanese direct investments in Italy amounted to ¥5.2 billion, less than 0.2 percent of the total Japanese foreign direct investment (FDI) in Europe. When compared to Japanese FDI in the UK (45.4 percent), the Netherlands (40.1 percent), France (4.4 percent), Germany (2.5 percent), this figure points out the marginal involvement of Japanese companies in Italy. Developments during the 1990s confirm this situation. In fiscal year 1989, Japanese FDI in Italy accounted for ¥42.2 billion (2.1 percent of total investments in Europe). In 1991 it reached a peak of ¥44.2 billion (3.4 percent of total Europe). Between 1992 and 1998 they decreased from ¥28.2 billion (3 percent) to ¥14 billion (0.8 percent). The weakness of the Italian position is confirmed by the fifteenth survey on Japanese-affiliated manufacturing companies in Europe conducted by the **Japan External Trade Organization** (JETRO). According to JETRO data, even if the number of Japanese manufacturing companies in Italy has steadily increased from twenty-eight to fifty-seven in the ten-year period between 1989 and 1998, the last figure accounts for only 6.5 percent of the 883 Japanese companies operating in Europe (JETRO 1999). As of 1998, nineteen Japanese enterprises in Italy had design centers or R&D facilities, again accounting for only a small percentage (5 percent) of the total number of such facilities in Europe.

Japanese FDI in Italy has some peculiar features. First, the majority of Japanese companies are mainly sales subsidiaries; they involve mostly trade-related activities and manufacturing and only in very few cases of finance and insurance services. Second, the manufacturing companies are concentrated in traditional and specialized supply industries, such as textile, clothing, machinery and machine tools, where Italian companies are highly competitive. With regard to the fifty-seven Japanese manufacturing companies operating at the end of 1998, thirteen were in chemical and petroleum products, nine in general machinery industry, seven in transport machinery parts, six in electrical machinery and five in apparel and textile products, with the remainder in various other industries (JETRO 1999). Third, with respect to mode of entry and capital structure, **joint ventures** are preferred over wholly-owned, green-field investments. This may be due to several reasons. Italian subsidiaries of Japanese firms are of relatively recent age. The first cases of Japanese manufacturing companies in Italy were YKK Italia, which began to operate in 1968; **Honda**, which was established as a joint venture (IAP Industriale) in 1971; Alcantara, which was originally a joint venture between ENI and Toray

Industries (1974); and Tessitura Tintoria Stamperia Achille Pinto, a joint venture between an entrepreneurial Italian company and Toray Industries, established in 1974. Additionally, the majority of Japanese companies were established in Italy during the 1980s and 1990s. A second reason may be the fact that in the first phase of Japanese FDI Italian companies took on the role of developers of the Italian market. Finally, in many joint ventures, there is the presence of an Italian partner who often owns the majority of capital, and is an entrepreneurial firm having peculiar creative capabilities. For the Italian partner, the joint venture represents a way both to gain access to competencies, technologies and assets which could not be developed autonomously and rapidly, and to enter new markets, especially in Asia, through co-operating with a strong competitor (Molteni *et al.* 2000). Conversely, for the Japanese partner, the joint venture provides an opportunity to obtain rapid access to the Italian market, to overcome legal or trade barriers, to take advantage of fiscal incentives, and to gain access to the peculiar know-how of the Italian partner, which complements the Japanese partners' range of competencies. The most striking cases of joint ventures between big Japanese and Italian companies are, for example, those established by Fiat and Hitachi, Olivetti and Canon, Fiamm and Nippon Denchi, Eni and Toray, FAI and Komatsu, Piaggio and Daihatsu.

With regard to the transferability of Japanese management and production systems to Italian subsidiaries, it usually has taken place with adaptation of Japanese management principles to the local context. In particular, according to a study carried out in 1993 on Japanese manufacturing companies in Italy, local management style seemed to predetermine Japanese management principles. This result may be due to the fact that the research involved a significant number of joint ventures with entrepreneurial Italian companies (Songini and Gnan 1995). A similar study carried out in 1997 pointed to a combination of Japanese and local goals, organizational mechanisms and management styles (Songini and Gnan 1998). This study identified a more significant role of the Italian subsidiaries than in 1993. In fact, Italian subsidiaries seemed to have stronger R&D and product policy autonomy and to be responsible for a wider range of value-chain activities. They pursued long-term goals, both typical of Western companies (profitability) and peculiar to Japanese firms (growth and quality); adopted both formal, vertical and Western organizational mechanisms and some peculiar Japanese ones, those devoted to developing human resources competencies. The size, the shareholding structure, the older age and a wider range of core activities influenced the degree of transferability of Japanese management. As far as headquarters control over foreign subsidiaries was concerned, Japanese multinationals coordinated and controlled Italian subsidiaries by both substantive control systems, based on the centralization of strategic resources and decisions at the parent company, and administrative control mechanisms, based on planning and control systems. Moreover Japanese headquarters involved Italian subsidiaries in most strategic decisions concerning innovation, pricing and production levels.

The transferability of Japanese management to Italy points out that Japanese management has to be adapted to the local context to be effective. In the green-field, wholly-owned investments, often in depressed areas, such as for example **Sony** and **Honda**'s transplants, Japanese technology and management were transferred more effectively due to the fact that this choice favored the selection of young workers more willing to create employment relationships similar to those used in Japan. As far as joint ventures are concerned, in some cases they achieved satisfactory results in terms of production efficiency, profitability and knowledge creation, due to the fact that they stimulated the development of synergies between the partners. However, in other cases the transferability of Japanese management and production systems found significant obstacles and resistance due to the Italian system of labor market regulations, the resistance of labor unions and management, the language and cultural barriers, the difficulties of Japanese companies in attracting the first-class Italian graduates and technicians.

Further reading

JETRO (1999) *The 15th Survey on the Operations of Japanese-affiliated manufacturing Companies in Europe and Turkey*, Tokyo: JETRO.

Kidd, J.B. (1998) "Knowledge Creation in Japanese Manufacturing Companies in Italy," *Management Learning* 29(2): 131–46.

Molteni, C. (1996) "Japanese Manufacturing in Italy," in J. Darby (ed.), *Japan and the European Periphery*, London: Macmillan, 132–48.

Molteni, C., Conca, M.G. and Zara, C. (2000) "Japanese Manufacturing Activities in Italy: Characteristics and Management Issues," in L. Songini (ed.), *Political and Economic Relations between Asia and Europe*, Milano: EGEA, 121–36.

Songini, L. and Gnan L. (1995) "Management Styles of Japanese Companies in Italy," *Management International Review* 2: 9–26.

—— (1998) "Japanese Management in the Nineties: New Features and Their Transferability Abroad," paper given at the AIDEA 3rd International Conference, Lugano, Switzerland.

Songini, L., Gnan, L. and Kidd J. (2000) "A Comparison of Management Styles of Japanese Manufacturing Firms in the UK and in Italy," in L. Songini (ed.), *Political and Economic Relations between Asia and Europe*, Milano: EGEA, 147–81.

LUCREZIA SONGINI

Japanese business in Korea and Taiwan

The operations of Japanese-affiliated companies in Korea and Taiwan are characterized by a relatively high degree of **localization** of top managers at overseas subsidiaries, as well as by a considerable level of implantation of the Japanese management system in terms of institutions and form. However, there are considerable differences between these firms and manufacturing plants at home in Japan in more substantive aspects, such as the degree of employee participation in management and the development of a wide range of skills among workers. In the future, Japanese-affiliated companies in Korea and Taiwan will need to strive to narrow these gaps with Japanese plants, and at the same time to learn from the advantages of local companies accruing from their local business climates.

The process of entry

The advances of Japanese companies into Korea and Taiwan, which began in the 1960s, came largely in response to the import-substitution industrialization policies adopted by those governments. Like other developing economies, Korea and Taiwan imposed high tariffs on imported manufactured products in order to protect and nurture their own industries. Japanese and other foreign companies then began local production in order to surmount the high tariff barriers and capture markets. Most of the local production projects were launched in the form of **joint ventures** with local firms because of restrictions on foreign ownership. In particular, the Korean government imposed severe restrictions on the entry of foreign companies, and as a result, Japanese direct investment in Korea took off later and on a more reduced scale than in Taiwan.

A major turning point in Japanese investments into the two economies came from the late 1960s through the 1970s. Behind this change were both "pull" and "push" factors. The "pull" factor was the fact that both economies had switched to export-oriented industrialization policies, under which they sought industrialization through the promotion of exports by attracting foreign companies. Specifically, they set up "export processing zones" where foreign companies were allowed to establish 100 percent-owned units and were granted preferential tariff treatment for the importation of parts and production facilities, but were required to export the products they made there. The first of the "push" factors was that after going through its period of high economic growth, Japan had lost its suitability as a location for labor-intensive industries as wages rose to match those of European countries. As a result, Japanese companies headed toward Korea and Taiwan, which then had cheap and ample labor, as well as to Singapore and Hong Kong. This grouping was called the newly industrialized countries (NICs) (they are now referred to as the newly industrializing economies (NIEs)). The second "push" factor was undoubtedly the growing trade friction between Japan and other advanced economies, which prompted Japanese companies to search for bases from which to "detour" their exports. These factors combined to push Japanese companies to establish exclusively export-oriented wholly-owned factories, mainly in labor-intensive industries or processes such as textiles, electrical and electronics, and leather.

At first, this mode of industrialization was criticized as degrading Korea and Taiwan into mere subcontractors for Japanese companies and for ultimately subordinating them to the Japanese economy. In reality, however, the advance of Japanese firms and transfers of technologies from Japan contributed to lifting the levels of both technologies and income in the two economies. This then made possible the transfer of higher levels of technologies from Japan, and in turn encouraged the development in Japan of higher value-added products. In summary, a virtuous cycle was created where the advance of Japanese firms and the accompanying technological transfer made possible and promoted the transfer of higher levels of technologies.

The second turning point came in the latter half of the 1980s. The rapid industrialization raised income levels in both Korea and Taiwan, bringing about broad democratization ranging from politics to intra-company organizations (though there were differences in that demands for democracy were more radical in Korea than in Taiwan). This far-reaching democratization resulted in sharp rises in wages. At the same time, the two economies faced trade frictions with the United States, and were criticized for the perceived undervaluation of their currencies against the US dollar. Eventually, Korea's won and Taiwan's new Taiwan dollar were substantially revalued *vis-à-vis* the US dollar. The sharp rises in wages and the revaluation of the currency exchange rates prompted Korean and Taiwanese companies to invest in ASEAN (the Association of Southeast Asian Nations) states, while Japanese companies also shifted their main export bases to ASEAN countries, centering on Thailand and Malaysia, and then to China in the 1990s. This is not to say, however, that Japanese direct investment into Korea and Taiwan completely dried up. While the value of new investment did decline, the flow continued in qualitatively higher sectors. Thus, Japanese firms molded a relationship of intra-company divisions of labor: the mass production of products with high value-

added was done in Japan, the output of mass-produced goods with low value-added in ASEAN and China, and the production of many varieties of products in small lots in Korea and Taiwan.

The wave of digitalization that swept through electronics and other industries in the latter half of the 1990s dramatically altered the intra-company divisions of labor in a short period of time. Japanese firms gained the ability to almost simultaneously begin turning out nearly equivalent finished products in Japan, ASEAN and China, thus lessening the importance of Korea, and of Taiwan to a greater extent, as production bases. However, a new, functional relationship of intra-company divisions of labor is already being developed. This new relationship calls for Japan to focus on R&D activities and the production of products with frequent model changes or high value-added products for the domestic market, for ASEAN and China to export volume-products, and for plants in Taiwan, Singapore and other NIEs to serve as mother plants, providing technical support for plants in ASEAN and China.

Specific features of management

The management styles of Japanese companies in Korea and Taiwan share common institutional and organizational formulas with Japanese domestic plants. They include low barriers separating job categories, wage systems in which rates are not determined by job categories, and the fact that responsibility for quality control is given to the workers at manufacturing plants. The introduction of these organizational characteristics is a prerequisite for the building of versatile skills, coordination between divisions, and high operational efficiency in areas where Japanese firms are strong, such as quality control, production of many varieties of products, and parts inventory management. The first reason the Japanese system has taken root in Korea and Taiwan is because, unlike the other advanced industrialized economies such as the United States and European nations, they had no established systems to hamper the introduction of the Japanese formulas. Secondly, they had certain similarities with Japan in organizational features and in the way they dealt with workers, as exemplified by low institutional barriers between job categories, and in their wage systems.

Another feature of the management of Japanese-affiliated firms in Korea and Taiwan is the relatively high degree of localization of management. In comparison with subsidiaries in industrialized countries, they have lower ratios of Japanese expatriates to total payrolls. In comparison with subsidiaries in ASEAN and other host countries with similar ratios of Japanese expatriates, those in Korea and Taiwan have more locally-recruited top executives. Many of the firms are joint ventures with local firms that themselves have relatively long years of operations. But as the same can be said about subsidiaries in ASEAN, these factors alone cannot explain the larger number of locally-recruited chief executives. The more fundamental reason for the greater localization of top management lies in the existence of local managers in Korea and Taiwan who have a deep understanding of Japanese management style. This can be traced to the institutional, social and cultural similarities between Korea and Taiwan and Japan, including education. Also many local managers have a fluent command of the Japanese language.

However, there are differences, which cannot be neglected, between Japanese domestic plants and those in Korea and Taiwan. The extent of employee participation in management is smaller, as seen in the lack of enthusiasm for small group activities. Therefore, regardless of whether the top management is led by Japanese or local executives, subsidiaries there have a stronger tendency toward top-down management than those in Japan. It can be said there are gaps between the formal introduction of the Japanese management style and the conditions of its actual implementation. These gaps stem in part from the higher separation rates (tendency for workers to quit their jobs) than in Japan and large promotion gaps based on educational backgrounds.

The differences between Korea and Taiwan are also important. The strong point of Japanese-affiliated plants in Korea is management's ability to achieve high productivity and high quality levels while precisely observing the stipulated work and quality standards within relatively large operational organizations. In Taiwan, which compares unfavorably to Korea in quality and other management

abilities, there are subsidiaries that excel in the intermediate fields between hardware and software, or in creating a wide range of added value for products. Meanwhile, subsidiaries in Korea have a higher dependence than their counterparts in Taiwan on the procurement of parts from Japanese firms or Japanese parts makers operating in Korea, reflecting the weakness of supporting parts industries in Korea. In the localization of top executives, however, Korea has an upper hand over Taiwan. One reason for this is that the joint venture partners there are all manufacturers, while in Taiwan the partners are quite often non-manufacturers, such as distribution firms. Another reason that cannot be overlooked is the greater intensity of anti-Japanese sentiments in Korea, a fact that is traceable to differences in Japan's colonial rule in the two economies.

In the future, Japanese-affiliated plants in Korea and Taiwan will have to increase the stability of core personnel and strive to narrow their gaps with Japanese plants in such areas as the acquisition of versatile skills and coordination between divisions. At the same time, they need to selectively learn the advantages of local companies accruing from the local business climate. In Taiwan, for example, subsidiaries need to introduce a sharp-witted management style to enable them to promptly discover business areas with high earnings potential and to assemble products by gathering parts and components with high cost performance.

See also: Japanese investment patterns; Japanese multinational enterprises; overseas production

Further reading

Itagaki, H. (ed.) (1997) *The Japanese Production System: Hybrid Factories in East Asia*, London: Macmillan.

Suehiro, A. (2000) *Kyacchi-appu-gata kogyoka-ron: Ajia keizai no kiseki to tenbou* (Catch-Up Style Industrialization: Tracks and Prospects of Asian Economy), Tokyo: Nagoya Daigaku Shuppannkai.

Tokunaga, S., Nomura, M. and Hiramoto, A. (1991) *Nihon kigyo/sekai sennryaku to jissenn: dennshi sangyo no gurobaru-ka to nihonn-teki keiei* (World Strategy and Practices of Japanese Companies: Globalization of the Electronics Industry and

Japanese-Style Management), Tokyo: Dobunn-kann.

HIROSHI ITAGAKI

Japanese business in Latin America

Japan has had a long history of doing business in Latin America. Japan's relation with Latin America dates back to the 1600s when traders brought goods from Spanish colonies to Japan. More than any other country other than the USA, Japan exerts political and economic leverage in this region of the world through its substantial amounts of development assistance and international business (trade, **joint ventures**, subsidiaries and affiliates). This may be because Latin America is rich in the natural resources that Japanese industry needs. An additional motive for close ties between Japan and Latin America is the benefit of foreign direct investment (FDI) in the regions. Historically, Latin America has had comparatively inexpensive labor, low overall productions costs, and lax environmental standards, and has provided a geographically proximate export platform for delivering goods to North America and Europe.

Hundreds of Japanese firms have been attracted to Latin America, especially to Colombia and to Mexico's US border cities. In addition, FDI in Latin America is a logical way to access US market as a result of the North American Free Trade Agreement (NAFTA). Although NAFTA involves only one Latin American country – Mexico – along with the USA and Canada, it is expected that future modifications to the agreement will incorporate other countries in the region, most likely Argentina, Brazil and Chile.

Within the context of modern trade relations, there has been an imbalance between Japan and Latin America. Japan has been seen as more important to Latin America than the other way around. Eight percent of all Latin American exports go to Japan. Conversely, Japanese exports to Latin America are relatively small, and are mainly in industrial goods. The most significant level of activity is in Japanese FDI in the region.

Although Japanese firms have maintained a presence in the region since the early 1900s, Japanese FDI in Latin American grew most significantly during the decade of the 1980s, and has dropped since then. In Brazil, for example, 86 percent of current Japanese subsidiaries were established prior to 1990. Comparable figures hold for Argentina and Mexico, where the rates were 74 percent and 64 percent respectively.

Direct investment grew in the 1990s due to the formation of the NAFTA and MERCOSUR economic alliances. The Southern Common Market (MERCOSUR) was established in 1988 as a customs union between Argentina and Brazil. It subsequently expanded to include Uruguay, Paraguay, Bolivia and Chile. After its formation, MERCOSUR countries saw an almost immediate increase in Japanese FDI, particularly in the automotive, electrical appliance, communications equipment and food processing industries. Not including Mexico, Japanese FDI in Latin America grew from US\$3.628 billion in 1990 to US\$5.231 billion by 1994. Between 1993 and 1994 alone there was a 55.2 percent increase in Japanese FDI.

The economies of Latin America plunged into recession in 1998 and 1999. Most of countries in the region saw initial signs of economic recovery by the first quarter of 2000, when GDP grew by 0.9 percent in Argentina, 3.1 percent in Brazil, 2.2 percent in Colombia, 5.5 percent in Chile, 7.9 percent in Mexico and 8.5 percent in Peru. Latin American exports of goods and services rose in 1999. Despite these positive economic signs, Japanese exports to Latin America fell 8.1 percent in 1999 to US\$17.79 billion, mostly in transport equipment, electrical machinery and general machinery. At the same time, however, Japan's imports from the region rose to US\$9.25 billion, an increase of 3.6 percent from 1998.

As Latin American economies continue to grow, and with the expansion of MERCOSUR to include more countries in the near future, analysts expect Japanese FDI to grow. In a similar vein, trade between Japan and the region is also expected to increase.

See also: Japanese business in Mexico; Japanese business in the USA

TERRI R. LITUCHY

Japanese business in Mexico

Beginning in the early 1980s and extending over the next twenty years, Japanese corporations have made significant foreign direct investment (FDI) in Mexico. Mexico has often been seen as a geographically convenient platform for the manufacture and assembly of products destined for the large market of Mexico's northern neighbor, the USA. With the emergence in the 1990s of a growing middle class and the establishment of a stable political climate, in the twenty-firstst century Mexico is becoming an attractive market in its own right.

The primary attraction for Japanese foreign direct investment (FDI) has been the opportunity to establish *maquiladoras*. These are factories situated in the US border region which manufacture products for export to the US using primarily US parts and components that are assembled by Mexican workers. **Matsushita**, Sanyo, **Sony** and **Hitachi** were the first major Japanese MNCs to establish *maquiladoras* in this region. They are also Tijuana's largest private employers. Sony has over 6,400 employees, Sanyo has 5,000 and Matsushita has 4,000. Hundreds of other Japanese manufacturers and suppliers followed these firms not only into Baja California, but also located throughout Mexico. In Tijuana alone, there are over 515 Japanese *maquiladoras*.

With the signing of the North American Free Trade Agreement (NAFTA), Mexico has become an even more attractive site for Japanese FDI. NAFTA created a customs union among Canada, Mexico and the USA. It called for steps to abolish tariffs for goods made in North America. For products to be classified as "Made in North America," they must meet one of the following criteria: (1) produced using materials produced in North America; (2) changed in tariff classification in the process of production in North America when using materials not produced in North America; or (3) achieve a certain level of local content even when not meeting condition 2. In general, the local content level is 60 percent (when using the transaction price), or 62.5 percent for automobiles. In addition color television sets and some electronics must have key components made in North America and textiles must have North American fibers. As many Japanese MNCs already had manufacturing and assembly facilities in the USA, the effect of NAFTA was to encourage them to maintain existing manufacturing operations in the USA but to shift assembly to plants in Mexico.

The Japanese experience in Mexico has not been without its problems. In addition to the usual challenges of adjusting to different business practices and business related cultural values, Japanese firms have struggled with crime, including kidnapping and extortion. In 1997, for example, the president of Sanyo Video was kidnapped and held for a $2 million ransom. In 1999, another Japanese executive was killed in a botched carjacking. In response to the growing problem, Sony, Sanyo and several other major Japanese employers met with Mexican President Ernesto Zedillo in the spring of 2000 to express their concern over safety and security issues.

Japanese firms have also taken measures to respond to crime in Mexico. Many Japanese executives working along the US border area of Tijuana–San Diego live on the US side and receive armed escorts to and from work in Tijuana. Additionally, firms have hired their own plant security staffs and worked with organizations such as the Latino Peace Officers Association to conduct in-house training on personal protection and safety. Finally, it is well known that Denso chose Monterrey, in the interior of the country, as the site for its automotive parts manufacturing facility because it felt the area was safer than the US border region.

See also: Japanese business in Latin America; Japanese business in the USA

Further reading

JETRO (various years) *JETRO White Paper on International Trade*, Tokyo: Japan External Trade Organization.

TERRI R. LITUCHY

Japanese business in Southeast Asia

While Japanese investment has flowed into Southeast Asia for decades since the **post-Second**

World War recovery, this FDI (foreign direct investment) picked up considerably from the mid-1980s. With Japanese economic power on the rise around the world from the early 1980s, and with North American and European nations growing more critical of Japanese economic power and investment in their countries, FDI from Japan was increasingly directed closer to home. Some have charged this investment flow to Southeast Asia has been an attempt by Japan to build a self-sustaining Asian centered economy with Japan in the powerful center. The immediate stimulus for the increased flow of FDI into Southeast Asia, however, was the rapid rise of the yen compared to other world currencies after the Plaza Accord in 1985. Japanese goods quickly became more expensive around the world and to cut costs many Japanese corporations began seeking cheaper labor in Southeast Asia. Some authors argue that it was this influx of Japanese investment which began the economic boom in many Southeast Asian nations. But it must also be recognized that many countries in Southeast Asia had already entered boom years from the early to middle 1980s, leading Japanese firms to implement strategies to tap into the expanding consumer markets of Southeast Asia. For example, the sale of automobiles in Thailand was increasing at a rate of 30 percent or more annually during the late 1980s and early 1990s, leading all of the major auto companies in Japan to set up plants to build and then distribute automobiles in Thailand. By the mid-1990s Japanese auto firms accounted for some 90 percent of all autos made or sold in Thailand.

During the mid-1990s, Japan accounted for more FDI than any other country in each of the industrializing countries of Southeast Asia except one, the Philippines, a former colony of the United States and still dominated by FDI from the USA. Japan accounted for just over 20 percent of FDI in Indonesia, 32 percent in Malaysia, 23 percent in Singapore, 29 percent in Taiwan, and 34 percent in Thailand. With *doi moi* (economic liberalization) in Vietnam from the late 1980s, Japan has been moving investments into Vietnam as well. In many of these countries the Japanese economic presence seems even greater because of the concentration of Japanese plants in huge industrial parks around the main cities. Of the many large industrial parks around Thailand, for example, more than half of the hundreds of factories display the corporate logo of Japanese firms. As of 1999 the Japanese Chamber of Commerce in Thailand listed 1,166 Japanese firms with operations in Thailand. And while Vietnam is far behind other Southeast Asian countries such as Thailand, Malaysia, and Indonesia in establishing such industrial parks, it has also begun to establish them. During 1995, FDI from Japan to Vietnam exceeded the $1 billion mark, with much going to facilities in new industrial parks around Hanoi and Ho Chi Minh City. Japan remains behind South Korea and Taiwan in terms of FDI in Vietnam, but is gaining on both countries.

The most "troubled" countries of Southeast Asia, particularly Cambodia, Laos, and Burma (Myanmar), have received very little FDI from Japan, or any other country for that matter. There has been discussion of Japanese investment in Laos, but little action, especially since the Asian economic crisis of 1997 reduced costs in other, more attractive Southeast Asian countries and took away economic incentives to move investments to even lower cost countries in the region. The change in economic incentives can be easily seen in the history of the Thai baht. Before July, 1997 the Thai baht was pegged at around 25 baht to 1 US dollar, falling to 55 baht to 1 US dollar six months after the Asian economic crisis hit (see **economic crisis in Asia**), then stabilizing at just under 40 baht to the dollar through the fall of 2000.

The Asian economic crisis of 1997, as might be expected, slowed the movement of Japanese FDI into Southeast Asia, and even led to steep drops in investments. By the end of the twentieth century, most nations in the region have shown significant recovery from the crisis and Japanese FDI in the region has begun to pick up. However, concerns about the strength of the Southeast Asian recovery remain, particularly because many of the needed reforms, especially in Southeast Asian financial institutions, and how long it can be sustained. Southeast Asian nations have lost export share to rich countries such as the United States because countries such as China and Mexico have increased their exports significantly since the Asian economic crisis of 1997. Thus, FDI in Southeast Asian nations remains below pre-1997 levels both in terms of actual dollar amounts (over $20 billion for 1997 but less that $14 billion for 1999) and in share of worldwide foreign direct investment.

Labor relations

Labor relations for Japanese corporations in Southeast Asia are reported to be generally good, despite the negative view of the Japanese in many of these countries because of the Second World War. Studies report there is very little labor union representation in Japanese corporations around Southeast Asia, but in none of these countries have labor unions been allowed to grow very strong by governments in the region. While there are reports in the mass media of exploitation of Southeast Asian workers by American and Japanese corporations, it is important to note that the larger and well-known corporations from the United States and Japan generally provide higher wages and better benefits than do domestic corporations in each of the countries in Southeast Asia. These wages and benefits are certainly low compared to standards in North America, Europe, or Japan, but certainly not by Southeast Asian standards. There are foreign corporations paying poverty or below poverty wages in Southeast Asia, but these tend to be small foreign firms able to hide from negative attention or corporations such as Nike that work mainly with small local companies to out-source their production. One large study of major American and Japanese corporations in Thailand, for example, showed firms from both countries to have comparatively high levels of work satisfaction among Thai employees, and these employees claimed that wages and benefits were above those of Thai corporations.

In most of the major Southeast Asian countries where studies have been conducted, however, there are some common complaints directed toward Japanese corporations and their managers, especially by the local white collar and management employees. As in other countries around the world, Japanese executives are known for their lack of trust in foreign employees. Compared to corporations from other nations, Japanese corporations send more executives to oversee operations in Southeast Asian nations and hire fewer local employees for top positions in the local operations.

Japanese transplant corporations in Southeast Asia as elsewhere in the world, have been found to promote fewer local managers to top positions than transplants from other countries, and in Southeast Asia the percentage of Japanese executives per corporation was actually increasing through the 1990s. Studies document complaints that Japanese managers, compared to managers from North America and Europe, do not allow their local managers to become involved in decision making, and some Japanese executives have even admitted to having secret meetings of Japanese only managers for decision making. Not surprisingly studies of Japanese corporations in Southeast Asia have found local employees stating they feel a lack of trust on the part of the Japanese executives. Further, while Thai employees of Japanese corporations report that wages and benefits are above local levels, they also state they prefer working for American rather than Japanese corporations for the above reasons.

Japanese management styles

One of the most interesting issues related to Japanese transplant corporations in Southeast Asia is the extent to which famous Japanese management techniques such as **quality control circles**, rotation of workers, and *kaizen* are put into effect by Japanese corporations in the region. Studies of Japanese transplants in North America and Europe report that individualistic oriented Western employees require that Japanese transplants alter their typical management styles and work organization. The common assumption, however, is that Japanese transplants in East and Southeast Asia would be more likely to follow traditional Japanese management styles and work organization given "common Asian values." There is some research on this issue, but far more is needed to arrive at firm conclusions. The little research that exists remains somewhat contradictory. Some report success for Japanese corporations in using their traditional management styles and work organization. This seems to be the case more often in the auto industry. The large **Toyota** plant in the Bangkok area of Thailand, for example, is the second most productive and efficiently run Toyota plant in the world. Interviews in Toyota plants in

Thailand find both Japanese and Thai management claiming to fully implement the work organization of the home factories in Japan. But other studies indicate more mixed results, with many Japanese firms admitting they have given up trying to implement Japanese work organization with Southeast Asian employees.

It seems most likely the success of Japanese management styles and work organization in Southeast Asia is affected by type of industry and varies by the nation where Japanese transplant corporations are in operation. Contrary to popular assumption, there is considerable cultural variation within Southeast Asia, and most likely more cultural variation than can be found across North America and Europe. Vietnam, for example, despite the years of communism, remains more Confucian, with high respect for authority and group cooperation, while the Thais are noted for their greater individualism and independence in the work place. The Thai corporation is usually described as authoritarian and dominated from the top much like an old feudal domain. However, while Thai employees are expected to defer to superiors as would be expected in Asian collectivist societies, Thai employees are noted for their lack of loyalty, jumping from employer to employer in a rather un-Japanese fashion. With the rich mixture of cultural variation throughout Southeast Asia, we find an interesting opportunity for research on the effects of culture and differences in social organization in the cross-cultural work place.

Further reading

Dobson, W. and Yue, C.S. (eds) (1997) *Multinationals and East Asian Integration*, Singapore: Institute of Southeast Asian Studies.

Elger, T. and Smith, C. (eds) (1994) *Globalization Japan: The Transnational Transformation of the Labour Process*, London: Routledge.

Hatch, W. and Yamamura, K. (1996) *Asia in Japan's Embrace: Building a Regional Production Alliance*, Cambridge: Cambridge University Press.

Kerbo, H. and Slagter, R. (2000) "The Asian Economic Crisis and Decline of Japanese Economic Leadership in Asia," in F.-J. Richter (ed.), *The Asian Economic Catharsis: How Asian Firms Bounce Back From Crisis*, Westport, CT: Quorum Books, 33–54.

—— (2000) "Thailand, Japan and the East Asian Development Model: The Asian Economic Crisis in World System Perspective," in F.-J. Richter (ed.), *The East Asian Development Model: Economic Growth, Institutional Failure and the Aftermath of the Crisis*, London: Macmillan, 119–40.

Slagter, R. and Kerbo, K. (2000) *Modern Thailand*, New York: McGraw-Hill.

HAROLD KERBO

Japanese business in the Middle East

Japan's exports to the Middle East (including North Africa) were $12.2 billion dollars in 1999, which accounted for 2.9 percent of Japan's total exports. About 80 percent of exports to the Middle East were machinery. Transport machinery, electric machinery, and industrial machinery account for 46 percent, 13 percent and 19 percent, respectively. Oil-exporting countries were Japan's main export markets in the Middle East, accounting for about 70 percent of total exports. Saudi Arabia was the largest market (27 percent) and UAE was the second (21 percent). Exports to non-oil exporters (excluding Israel) are usually affected by the oil producers' economic situations, which are influenced by oil prices.

Japan's imports from the Middle East were $31,261 million in 1999, which accounted for 10.1 percent of total imports. Most of the imports were mineral fuel, mainly crude oil.

Japan's direct investments to the Middle East have been absolutely small and unstable compared with its economic size. The amount of Japan's direct investments to the Middle East accounted for only 1.6 percent of the world total in 1998. According to a research by the *Oriental Economist*, only about seventy Japanese companies were operating in the six Persian Gulf countries (Saudi Arabia, Kuwait, United Arab Emirates, Bahrain, Iran and Oman) in 2000. About one-third of these firms are trading companies. The others are electric machine companies, electronic parts companies, industrial machine companies, construction and engineering companies and so forth. For the most part, these companies consist solely as sales or service/maintenance companies.

Saudi Arabia

Japan's exports to Saudi Arabia amounted to $3.97 billion and imports $7.1 billion in 1998. Transport machinery accounted for 69 percent of total exports, and industrial machinery, electric machinery and steel products 11 percent to 13 percent respectively. Mineral fuel such as crude oil accounted for 96 percent of total imports. Saudi Arabia is the second largest mineral fuel supplier to Japan. Although it is also a main supplier of chemical products such as ethylene glycol, styrene and methanol, its share of imports is only 3 percent of Japan's total. Construction and engineering companies represent the largest number of Japanese firms in Saudi Arabia. There are also local subsidiaries of manufacturing firms, but their activities are mainly in sales and service.

In the early 1980s, manufacturing companies such as National Pipe Co. (steel pipe), Saudi Methanol Co. (methanol), and Eastern Petrochemical Co. (Petrochemical) were founded as large Japanese companies attempted to secure a Saudi market that appeared to be expanding indefinitely. However, investment activities have been stagnant since the mid-1980s owing to a long-lasting recession.

A chronic **unemployment** problem among young people has continued to be a serious issue in Saudi Arabia since the latter half of the 1980s. In an effort to ameliorate this problem, Saudi government and business circles have asked that Japan increase investments in Saudi non-oil sectors. In turn, the Japanese government asked **Japan External Trade Organization** (JETRO) and other government affiliates to find potential investment projects, which resulted in the foundation of several joint venture companies such as the Saudi Arabian-Japanese Pharmaceutical Co. (medicine), the Red Sea Prawn (aquaculture) and several joint venture agreements in the fields of firebricks, printing ink and textile goods. Despite all of these Japanese efforts, the Saudis have complained about the low level of investments by Japanese companies and this may have resulted in the expiry of

Arabian Oil's oil concession in the Saudi part of the Neutral Zone.

United Arab Emirates

Japan's exports to the United Arab Emirates amounted to $1.9 billion and imports were $8.7 billion in 1999. Transport machinery accounted for 38 percent of total exports and machinery in total was 74 percent. Mineral fuel such as crude oil accounted for 98 percent of total imports. The UAE is the largest supplier of crude oil and liquefied petroleum gas to Japan. More Japanese local affiliates are located in the UAE than in any other country in the Persian Gulf region. Electric/ electronic machinery manufacturers, industrial machinery manufacturers, automotive manufacturers and transport/distribution companies have UAE-based affiliates, which handle sales, transport, and distribution activities throughout the Gulf area via Dubai.

Iran

Japan's exports to Iran amounted to $576 million and imports $3.1 billion in 1999. Transport machinery, industrial machinery, and metal products accounted for 20 percent to 25 percent of total exports respectively. Mineral fuel, mainly crude oil, accounted for 97 percent of total imports. Iran is Japan's third largest mineral crude oil supplier. The Iran-Japan Petrochemical joint venture (IJPC) was founded in 1973. Shortly thereafter, Japanese companies (including medium-size companies) undertook investment in Iran throughout the 1970s. After the Iranian Revolution in 1979, the situation changed owing to widespread political and socio-economic confusion. Japanese participants withdrew from the IJPC and Japanese investments to Iran decreased drastically.

The Iranian government, in principle, did not approve any new entry of foreign capital until the Rafsanjani administration adjusted foreign policies, increasing Iran's openness toward new investment. As policies became more positive Iran also enacted the Free Zone Act, which granted special tax and investment breaks to foreign companies in special processing zones. The government subsequently introduced a bill on inward foreign direct investment but it stalled in the face of strong resistance by religious conservatives.

Rafsanjani and the current president, Moham-mad Khatami, are positive about the acceptance of official development aid (ODA). In response to Iranian requests, the Japanese government has granted yen loans to support hydroelectric projects and other infrastructure development initiatives. Although the US government has imposed sanc-tions on Iran, the Japanese government believes that aid will help ease the Iranian government's entry back into the world community. During President Khatami's visit to Japan in November 2000, both governments agreed on economic cooperation plans in several areas, including oil development projects and petrochemical projects.

Most Japanese local affiliates in Iran are trading companies at present. Recent reports are that Kobe Steel has undertaken a feasibility study on the building of a steel mill in a "free zone," which may be a sign that Japanese firms have started to resume investment in Iran.

TETSUYA IWASAKI

Japanese business in the UK

Although most attention has been paid to the rapid increase in Japanese manufacturing investment in the UK since the 1980s, Japanese companies have had a presence in the UK since the late nineteenth century. Furthermore, the bulk of investment activity, both then and now, has been in the service sector (particularly financial services), rather than the manufacturing sector.

Undoubtedly much of the recent investment in manufacturing was due to Japanese companies wishing to gain a foothold inside the single European market in a way that would avoid further tariff impositions and anti-dumping actions against them. The UK has attracted the major portion of this kind of Japanese investment over the past two decades, but it is debatable whether this trend will continue. Japanese companies have been expressing concern over the high sterling exchange rate, following the UK's refusal to join the first wave of euro membership and uncertain prospects for its future membership.

Statistical overview

US firms are still the largest foreign employers of UK labor but Japanese foreign direct investment in the UK since the 1980s showed fastest growth rate of any country, increasing fivefold from 1987 to 1996 and reaching an annual total of $9.79 billion in 1998. Conversely, investment by British compa-nies in Japan has rarely reached even 10 percent of this level.

Over 280 Japanese companies have invested in manufacturing in the UK, accounting for more than 40 percent of Japanese total investment in the European Union, with 65,000 associated jobs (**Japan External Trade Organization** in 1997 claimed 100,000 jobs or 2.5 percent of the British manufacturing labor force derive from Japanese affiliates in the UK). Individual investments have become more capital intensive over the 1980s and 1990s, however, and the average employment per firm has shrunk. Total real fixed assets reached just under £4 billion by 1996. Of increasing impor-tance is the investment by Japanese companies in R&D in the UK; there are now over 150 such operations by Japanese companies.

Reasons for investing in the UK

The reasons most cited for Japanese companies favoring a UK location over other countries in the European Union are the English language, the size of the UK market, low direct labor costs, good employment relations, high-quality workforce, political and economic stability, solid infrastructure and legal system, well-established parts industries, stable local financing and low corporate taxes. There are also less openly cited, but influential factors such as the Japanese interest in British culture (including golf and whisky) and the long-standing historical ties between Japan and the UK.

Many of these advantages were emphasized by the Conservative government which came to power in 1979 and showed a very welcoming attitude towards Japanese investment in the 1980s, which has continued with successive governments in the 1990s. The Conservative government's restructuring of the British economy led to highly localized pockets of skilled manual unemployment and trades unions which were only a shadow of their former militant selves. Generous regional grants, the above-mentioned Japanese strategy of setting up operations in the EU and other factors favorable to the UK led to the nice coincidence of Japanese plants being set up in areas of Britain with strong historical ties to Japan.

Nissan's opening of a £350m greenfield car plant in Sunderland in 1986, near to where ships had been built for Japan since the mid-nineteenth century, was a catalyst for other Japanese manufacturers to set up nearby. Another cluster developed in Wales following **Sony**'s 1973 investment in television manufacturing in Bridgend. Other major investments have included **Toyota**'s £700m car plant in Derbyshire, which was opened in 1992, **Honda**'s £300m car plant in Swindon and Fujitsu's £400m semiconductor facility in the Northeast.

Japanization of British industry

The establishment of these plants in areas of high unemployment partly explains the high degree of attention paid to them by the British media and academia, relative to investments by other foreign companies. The other noteworthy feature was that they were concentrated in relatively few sectors, either ones in which the UK had lost any preeminence, such as automobile manufacture, or sectors where Japan had become famously strong, such as semiconductors and electronics. Japanese companies brought their manufacturing and human resource management techniques with them to the UK, with resultant successes such as Nissan's plant in Sunderland, which is now widely seen as being the most efficient car manufacturing operation in Europe.

There was therefore a strong sense that British management and manufacturing could learn from Japan, either to revive failing industries or to enter the new high technology sectors. Much debate amongst academia, the private sector and the government ensued from the late 1980s into the 1990s, about the degree and desirability of "Japanization" in British industry. Concepts such as **just-in-time**, *kaizen*, *kanban*, total quality control, flexible working, **enterprise unions** and so forth were introduced into British-owned factories, with varying degrees of success and sincerity.

Service sector investment

Japanese service sector companies established operations in the UK a good century before Japanese manufacturers arrived. Japanese sailors started settling in London and the Northeast, and Japanese marine engineers arrived on extended study tours from the 1860s onwards, often setting up trading companies or boarding houses. The first major Japanese company to start operations in the UK was probably Okura, a Japanese merchant house, which established a London office in the early 1870s. Over the next two decades other commercial companies such as **Mitsui**, Takata, Tokio Marine Insurance Company, the Nippon Yusen shipping company and the Yokohama Specie Bank all opened operations in London to support Japan's attempt to regain commercial rights over its exports such as rice, silk, and tea.

These firms faced a struggle to survive, however, until the First World War, when many more Japanese companies arrived in London. They were aiming to take advantage of Japan's limited involvement in the war on the Allied side by making up the shortfall of European products available worldwide. Trading companies such as Suzuki and Furukawa were also tempted by the shortages of wartime necessities such as steel, and began speculating in scrap. Few purely speculative ventures survived the end of the war, the 1920 recession in Japan, the 1923 Kanto Earthquake and the 1927 Japanese financial crisis. Consequently, the number of Japanese companies in London began to decline in the 1920s.

Those London offices that survived, such as those of the trading houses Mitsui and **Mitsubishi**, began to evolve into regional headquarters, using London's status as a world commodity trading center to coordinate the export of raw materials to Japan, as well as importing items into Europe such as canned fish and oils from Japan's colonies in Asia. This role continued after the Second World War until the boom in Japanese manufacturing investment in Europe and the consolidation of the City of London as a world financial capital in the 1970s and 1980s brought a second wave of Japanese financial companies to London.

Japanese banks and securities houses had a dramatic impact on the City, buying prime London real estate at the height of the boom in the late 1980s and paying extravagant salaries and bonuses to their locally hired staff. Japan's economic problems in the 1990s, particularly the collapse of several banks towards the end of the decade, have brought about a withdrawal or contraction of London operations. At the same time, many of the persistent issues surrounding the management of Japanese overseas operations were once more uncovered, in a series of sex and racial discrimination cases and other incidents pointing to a lack of risk management and localization.

The future of Japanese companies in the UK

Unless London loses its status as a world financial centre, it is unlikely that there will be any further significant decline in Japanese commercial and financial companies operating in London. Of more concern to the British government is the impact that the UK's non-membership of the euro, the high sterling exchange rate relative to the euro and uncertainty over the UK's future position inside the European Union will have on Japanese manufacturers. Japanese manufacturers may relocate British operations in Eastern Europe or Asia, or choose such locations for any new investments. The signs are mixed: Fujitsu closed its semiconductor factory in Durham in 1999, but this was as much due to the worldwide slump in semiconductor prices as any local disadvantages. Mitsubishi Electric closed its television factory in Scotland in 1998, but is increasing European investment in mobile phones. The UK government claims the number of Japanese UK-based investment projects increased 15 percent from 1999 to 2000. The future of the Nissan Sunderland plant is in question now that Renault has a strong say in Nissan's European production, following Renault's purchase of a 36.8 percent stake in Nissan in 2000. Clearly factors such as links to continental Europe (both transportation and commercial/political) as well as the availability and cost of a highly educated and skilled workforce to support new, higher value-added production are going to be critical in

maintaining the UK's position as main recipient of Japanese manufacturing investment in the EU.

Further reading

Aaron, C. (1999) *The Political Economy of Japanese Foreign Direct Investment in the UK and US: Multinationals, Subnational Regions and the Investment Location*, London: Macmillan.

Conte Helm, M. (1989) *Japan and the North East of England from 1862 to the Present Day*, London: The Athlone Press.

Morris, J., Munday, M. and Wilkinson, B. (1993) *Working for the Japanese: The Economic and Social Consequences of Japanese Investment in Wales*, London: The Athlone Press.

Newall, P. (1996) *Japan and the City of London*, London: The Athlone Press.

Oliver, N. and Wilkinson, B. (1992) *The Japanization of British Industry: New Developments in the 1990s*, 2nd edn, Oxford: Blackwell.

Warner, F. (1991) *Anglo-Japanese Financial Relations: A Golden Tide*, Oxford: Blackwell.

PERNILLE RUDLIN

Japanese business in the USA

Japan and the United States have had a long and difficult history of trade and foreign direct investment. According to the **Japanese External Trade Organization** (JETRO), economic and trade relations between the USA and Japan have been calm since the auto trade agreement reached in 1995. However, the Asian financial crisis in 1997 caused the US once again to be concerned over the growing size of its trade deficit with Japan.

Beginning in the late 1980s and into the early 1990s, a large number of Japanese firms set-up production facilities in the United States. These "transplants," especially in the **automotive industry** were sometimes seen as a way for Japan to work around the 'voluntary' import quotas on auto exports, while others see Japanese manufacturing plants as jobs for Americans. By 1990, there were over 300,000 Americans working in Japanese businesses in the USA. Japanese FDI exceeded $50 billion. Many of the largest, well-known

Japanese firms have manufacturing facilities in the United States, including companies such as **Sony**, Epson, **Mitsubishi**, **NEC**, **Toyota**, **Nissan**, Isuzu, Mazda and Sanyo. There were more than 600 Japanese businesses in California alone in 1990.

As a result of this dramatic growth in the Japanese presence, many Americans were concerned with Japanese takeovers of US companies, technology, and real estate. Sensitive to this concern, several Japanese companies formed **joint ventures** to break into the US market, such as specialty steel manufacturers.

At the same time that one segment of the US population was concerned about rising Japanese investment, another segment was actively courting Japanese joint ventures and strategic alliances. In the high-technology area, many small US venture firms struggling to attract US venture capital were happy to get capital from Japanese firms instead. In return, Japanese firms obtained access, to and control of, cutting-edge technologies and processes. Japanese firms acquired four banks and several large pieces of California real estate. In two of the most visible acquisitions, Sony purchased Columbia and **Matsushita** bought Universal Studios. Some people feared that Japan was taking over the United States. The concern was short-lived, as the bursting of the **bubble economy** forced many Japanese companies to sell off their US holdings.

Despite the economic recession in Japan, the US trade deficit with Japan grew 14.7 percent from 1998 to 1999, reaching US$73.4 billion. Japan imports decreased due to the slow pace of its economic recovery while exports increased due to a booming economy in the USA. Japan's FDI (foreign direct investment) in the USA has been decreasing from 53.3 percent ($26,128 million) in 1990 to 34.5 percent ($17,331 million) in 1994. In other words, investment from Japan accounted for 38.7 percent of all FDI received in 1990 and dropped to 12.9 percent in 1994.

Around this same time, in the automotive industry, Japanese firms developed relationships with American automotive manufacturers and suppliers and related fields such as hardware and software, thereby creating more jobs as well as procurement of local (American) parts. In addition to transferring manufacturing plants, the Japanese firms have transferred management and technological know-how. Joint research and development as well as cooperative sales programs have grown as a result of these relationships.

In the **electronics industry**, the USA has led in innovation and entrepreneurship while Japanese firms have led in quality and overall competitiveness. These complementary competencies have led to joint ventures in manufacturing as well as research and development. Similar arrangements have been developed in the chemical industry and **pharmaceuticals industry**. These relationships have been beneficial to firms on both sides of the Pacific. Banks and the US government have both strengthened the relationship between Japanese companies located in the US and local firms. In addition to the federal government, particularly the Department of Commerce, many US states have offices in Japan to promote trade, including California, Georgia, Illinois, Kentucky, North Carolina, Tennessee, Oregon and Washington

Japanese investment has not been without its critics. While providing in excess of 300,000 jobs, observers note that there were no Americans in top management positions in these firms. Moreover, at most of companies there were communication problems, in some cases quite severe. Most Japanese managers have limited English skills, while only 10 percent of the American employees speak Japanese at any level of fluency. In recent years the number of local employees able to communicate in Japanese has been on the rise.

Japanese managers, although they usually only remained in the United States for from three to five years, brought Japanese management techniques with them. Decision making by consensus, **lifetime employment**, and other practices widely used in Japan appeared to work for the Japanese but often the Americans felt left out. For example, many American employees lacked any knowledge of their firm's mission statement. Most Japanese firms in the United States try to duplicate the Japanese model of management, but this is not always possible, due to differences in culture and values.

Japanese companies of all sizes and all industries are doing business in the United States. In 1972, the Maruchan division of Toyo Suisan Kaisha opened its first instant ramen production facility in the United States; by 1997 it had three factories. In 1991 there were 1,563 Japanese manufacturing plants in the USA employing over 300,600 employees. By 1996, the number of plants had increased to 1,709.

See also: overseas education; overseas research and development; trade barriers; trade negotiations

Further reading

Laurie, D. (1990) "Yankee Samurai and the Productivity of Japanese Firms in the United States," *National Productivity Review* 9: 131–9.

TERRI R. LITUCHY

Japanese Industrial Standards

Japanese Industrial Standards (JIS) refer to technical standards established for the purpose of improving the quality of industrial and mineral products and for facilitating their efficient production, distribution, and usage. Similar to ANSI in the USA or BS in the UK, JIS are voluntary national standards that are established or revised on the basis of a consensus between producers, consumers and related parties. JIS and other standardization efforts at the national, industry and company level are credited with making significant contributions to Japan's successes in quality and productivity improvement. At the same time, some technical standards have been viewed as non-tariff **trade barriers** by foreign companies.

At the end of 2000, there were 8,764 Japanese Industrial Standards in force, which reflected activity during the year of 621 newly established standards, 464 revised standards, and 309 withdrawn standards. While JIS are classified into nineteen different technical areas ranging from civil engineering and architecture to management systems, they fall into three major types: (1) basic standards which specify terminology, symbols, units, etc. (roughly 30 percent of all JIS); (2) method standards which specify procedures for testing, analysis, inspection, measurement, etc. (20 percent); and (3) product standards which specify the shape, dimension, function, and so forth, of products (50 percent). Two JIS of particular note

are the JIS Q 9000 series and JIS Q 14000 series, which are the identical Japanese equivalents of the ISO 9000 and ISO 14000 international standards for **quality management** and environmental management systems.

Organizations with responsibilities for JIS include the Japanese Industrial Standards Committee (JISC; see www.jisc.org) and the Japanese Standards Association (JSA; see www.jsa.or.jp). Based on the Industrial Standardization Law originally passed in 1949, these two bodies work together to establish and promote JIS. JISC is affiliated with the Ministry of Economics, Trade and Industry (formerly MITI) and serves as the national standards body with membership in the International Organization for Standardization (ISO) and the International Electrotechnical Commission (IEC). Among other things, JISC has responsibility for deliberating and approving draft standards that have been submitted to it. Initial drafting of most standards is done by **industry and trade associations**, with a small number done by consumerist groups and government entities. JSA's responsibilities include facilitating the creation of draft standards and publishing and disseminating approved JIS, as well as promoting standardization and quality management activities in Japanese industry.

Certain designated products meeting the relevant JIS standards may be authorized to display the "JIS" mark, based upon an examination of the product prototype and the production facility involved. As of March 1999, the number of certifications for JIS marks were 14,976 domestically and 354 in foreign countries. Other product certification and marking schemes in Japan include the JAS (Japanese Agricultural Standards) mark for agricultural and forestry products, as well as the S mark and SG mark for product safety.

See also: standard setting

Further reading

Japanese Industrial Standards Committee (1991) *Industrial Standardization in Japan*, Tokyo: JISC.
Japanese Standards Association (2000) *JIS Yearbook*, Tokyo: JSA.
Krislov, S. (1997) *How Nations Choose Product*

Standards and Standards Change Nations, Pittsburgh, PA: University of Pittsburgh Press.

McIntyre, J.R. (ed.) (1997) *Japan's Technical Standards: Implications for Global Trade and Competitiveness*, Westport, CT: Quorum Books.

SHANE J. SCHVANEVELDT

Japanese investment patterns

For many years, Japanese foreign direct investment (FDI) consisted mainly of investment that was related to Japan's worldwide trading activities, at manufacturing industries in Asia and at resource development. In the 1980s, however, a major shift occurred in these investment patterns as the Japanese manufacturing industry changed its strategy from exports to local production within the industrially advanced countries. Non-manufacturing industries such as finance and insurance also began to energetically pursue FDI. In examining the stages and changes in investment patterns of Japanese FDI, it is helpful to classify this development into four periods: prewar expansion, postwar economic recovery through the 1960s, strategic changes in the 1970s and 1980s, and finally, globalized management in the 1990s. Furthermore, since Japanese FDI is regulated by the Japanese Foreign Exchange and Foreign Trade Control Law (FEFTCL), the FDI includes the acquisition of foreign securities reflecting 10 percent or more of stock or invested capital, the establishments of branch offices or factories and the period of investment exceeds one year.

Before the Second World War: investment related to trade and colonies

There was a rapid surge in Japanese FDI in the 1980s, in fact the roots of Japanese investment overseas date back to before the Second World War. Most of this pre-war investment was related to trade and it was largely in the four areas of trade, banking, insurance, and shipping. The *sogo shosha* acted as middlemen, facilitating exports and imports, as well as the transfer of technology (importing factories, creating licensing agreements, introducing investment opportunities in Japan) and

as collectors and providers of news and information about foreign markets and societies. Banks provided the financial support necessary for Japan's foreign trade. The insurance industry helped to absorb the risks associated with ocean transport and of course, the marine shipping industry, carried manufactured products and raw materials back and forth between Japan and its trading partners. The earliest of the *sogo shosha* to venture abroad was **Mitsui** & Co., Ltd. It opened a branch office in Shanghai in 1877, followed by one in Paris in 1878 and then in New York in 1879.

In the period between the First and Second World Wars, direct investment expanded in the Japanese colonies in Manchuria, China, on the Korean Peninsula, and in Taiwan as well as in those regions under the general sphere of influence of the Japanese Imperial Army. In all of these areas, investment was directed not only at those industries specifically engaged in trade, but also at the railroad, mining, and manufacturing industries. During and following the Second World War, Japan lost its overseas foreign assets, the majority of which were located in Asia, after they were either frozen or seized.

From the Second World War until the 1960s: resumption

The second period in the development of Japan's FDI was from the end of the Second World War until the 1960s. The Japanese government began to regulate FDI when it enacted the Foreign Exchange and Foreign Trade Control Law in 1949. In the beginning, the Ministry of Finance reviewed applications for FDI on an individual basis, granting permission in those cases where it felt that there was a positive impact on Japan's balance of payments as well as clear merit for the economic benefit of the Japanese people. During this period, FDI patterns were essentially the same as before the war. In other words, those industries which contributed to the promotion of trade, namely *sogo shosha* and banks, became the major recipients of investment, which was applied to regions throughout the world including North America, Asia, Central and South America, and Europe. Moreover, in the developing nations, particularly in Asia, this investment was directed mainly towards the extraction of natural resources as well as towards local production by the manufacturing industry in response to foreign governments' policies for promoting their own industrialization through import substitution. However, in contrast to the prewar activities, there were no longer any political or military objectives associated with this investment. This investment was implemented by private sector industries and carried out not only in East Asia but in Southeast Asia as well.

The 1970s and 1980s: strategic shift from export to overseas production

The third period in the development of Japanese FDI was the two decades spanning the 1970s and 1980s. Particularly in the latter decade, the level of FDI increased and there was a fundamental shift in the pattern of this investment. This was partly the result of changes in strategies for internationalization as well as a shift from the manufacturing industry's export-led initiatives towards one that relied increasingly upon local overseas production. There was also diversification among the types of industries in the non-manufacturing sector that carried out FDI. No longer were participants limited to those involved in trade-related activities; now these included the real estate industry as well as non-trade-related businesses in the financial and insurance industries. Furthermore, while overseas investment had been traditionally weighted in favor of the developing countries, now investment in North America and Europe began to become more numerous.

The factors underlying these changes included the liberalization of FDI, trade friction between Japan and the other industrially advanced nations, and the dramatic appreciation of the yen. Between 1969 and 1978, the Japanese government carried out FDI liberalization in five stages. In the third stage, which was implemented in 1971, the limit on the amount of investment eligible for automatic approval was lifted. This is not to say, however, that the change in policy suddenly resulted in a massive increase in FDI. Since the end of the Second World War, the Japanese manufacturing industry had developed its overseas markets in accordance with a fundamental export-oriented strategy. Business

leaders had little confidence that distinctive management and production systems, such as **lifetime employment** and the **Toyota production system** which had developed in Japan, would take root in foreign countries, especially in North America or Europe. Although some Japanese companies had ventured overseas in the 1950s and 1960s, these were the rare exceptions. By far the majority of enterprises elected to stay at home and tread the path of "internationalization" on the basis of exporting their manufactured products from Japan.

However, it was during this period that two compelling reasons began to emerge for Japan's manufacturing corporations to switch their strategies from export to FDI. The first of these was trade friction with the industrially advanced countries, and the second was the appreciation of the yen beginning 1985. Trade friction between Japan and the USA first appeared in regard to textile fibers, followed by iron and steel, color televisions, semiconductors, and automobiles, in that order. Trade friction with the European countries also occurred, although it lagged slightly behind that that developed with the United States. The policy for eliminating trade friction was one of voluntary export restrictions on the part of the Japanese exporters. The manufacturing industries offered their vigorous response to the policy for voluntary export restrictions through local overseas production. In regard to yen appreciation, the rise in the export price of Japan's manufactured products resulted in a decrease in exporters' price competitiveness. To avoid this effect, exporters had no choice but to pursue **overseas production**. As a result of these two factors, the switch away from an export-led strategy became inevitable, as Japan's manufacturing corporations grudgingly began to tread the path towards local overseas production. In the case of industries in the non-manufacturing sector, the applicability of Japanese-style management practices in a foreign environment was also an issue of some concern; however, the obstacles were not as great as they were for manufacturers.

FDI by Japanese corporations increased steadily through the 1970s and 1980s, and particularly from 1986 until 1989. In 1972, it reached $2.3 billion, exceeding the $2 billion mark for the first time. In 1984 it surpassed $10 billion and in 1986

$20 billion for the first time, reaching a level of $47 billion in 1988. In the three years from 1986 to 1988, cumulative Japanese FDI reached $102.7 billion, exceeding the cumulative FDI for the twenty-five-year period from 1951–85, of $83.6 billion. Finally, in the year 1989 alone, Japanese FDI posted an amazing $67.5 billion, an annual record that holds to this day.

Among the rest of the industrially advanced nations, Japan's FDI in the 1980s ranked at the very top, reflecting the extent to which investment patterns had changed. In addition to the dramatic surge in the amount of investment, two other salient characteristics were, industrially advanced nations now outnumbered the developing nations, among the nations which were the target of this FDI, and there was a notable diversification among the types of industries that were carrying out the investment, spanning a variety of industries from the manufacturing to the non-manufacturing sectors.

The 1990s to the present: global management

The fourth period in the development of Japanese FDI began in the 1990s. It was during this decade that the Japanese economy was burdened with the task of managing the non-performing loans that had accumulated as a result of the asset-inflated **bubble economy**. Nevertheless, the high level of Japanese FDI persevered and Japan maintained its position as the leading provider of FDI in the world. In the latter half of the 1980s, the dawn of the age of globalized management, the patterns of Japanese FDI, in terms of regions and industries, became more distinct. In other words, on a cumulative basis, the industrially advanced countries of North America and Europe received the highest proportion of investment, followed by Asia and then Central and South America.

By industry, and from a global perspective, the manufacturing industries carried out 30 percent of the total investment, and the non-manufacturing industries 70 percent. Among the non-manufacturing industries, and again from a global perspective, the finance and insurance industries carried out the bulk of the investment, followed by real estate, services, and commerce, in that order.

The composition ratio of Japanese FDI in North America was very close to global trends. However, in Europe, the finance and insurance industries represented an even larger proportion of investment than the global average, followed by the manufacturing sector. In Asia, on the other hand, nearly 50 percent of the investment comes from the manufacturing industries, reflecting the increased investment in China that took place in the 1990s. In Central and South America, finance and insurance were the largest targets of investment, followed by shipping. In summary, whereas the North American pattern closely resembled the average global pattern for Japanese FDI, Europe received a higher proportion of investment in the finance and insurance industries than in the case of other countries, while FDI in China was predominantly directed at the manufacturing industries.

See also: Japanese multinational enterprises

Further reading

Basu, D.R. and Miroshnik, V. (2000) *Japanese Foreign Investments 1970–1998: Perspectives and Analyses*, Armonk, NY: M.E. Sharp.

Encarnation, D.J. (ed.) (1999) *Japanese Multinationals in Asia: Global Operations in Comparative Perspective*, New York: Oxford University Press.

Hollerman, L. and Myers, R.H. (eds) (1996) *The Effect of Japanese Investment on the World Economy: A Six-Country Study, 1970–1991*, Stanford, CA: Hoover Institution Press.

Mason, M. (1997) *Europe and the Japanese Challenge: The Regulation of Multinationals in Comparative Perspective*, New York: Oxford University Press.

Wilkins, M. (1994) "More than One Hundred Years: A Historical Overview of Japanese Direct Investment in the United States," in T. Abo (ed.), *Hybrid Factory: The Japanese Production System in the United States*, New York: Oxford University Press, 257–83.

HIROSHI KUMON

Japanese multinational enterprises

Theories that attempt to explain Japanese multinational enterprises (MNEs) fall into two broad categories: those that adhere to the Development Stage Model and those that follow the Japanese MNE Model. According to the former, Japanese MNEs developed later than those in the Western economically advanced nations and were characteristically immature and backward. The Japanese MNE model, however, contends that Japanese MNEs incorporated Japanese-style management and organizational features into their overseas subsidiaries, giving rise to a new model of MNE that differed from its Western counterparts. To be sure, the characteristically high ratio of Japanese expatriates, which is evidence of a certain immaturity, as well as the concentration of authority in the home country, are changing as Japanese corporations gain experience in international business. In this respect, the Development Stage Model presents an undeniably persuasive argument. However, compared with their US counterparts, Japanese MNEs' conspicuously high ratio of expatriate employees, as well as their tendency to leave much of the strategic and business decision-making in the hands of the parent companies, is fundamentally unchanged despite their increased experience in international business. Consequently, the following explanation will emphasize the Japanese MNE Model.

The fundamental characteristic of Japanese MNEs lies in the paradox between their high-performance operational efficiency, as reflected in quality control and inventory management, on the one hand, and their low-performance profitability on the other. Why is it that Japanese MNEs have achieved a fairly decent operational efficiency but are unable to realize a level of profitability that is comparable with the overseas subsidiaries of Western MNEs? The key to unraveling this paradox lies in the organizational features of those Japanese corporations that emphasize the accumulation and utilization of managerial resources to increase operational efficiency, such as technology and the human resources that possess skill and know-how. The paradox of simultaneously high operational efficiency and low profitability and the type of business management that values the accumulation and utilization of managerial resources are characteristics that Japanese corporations at home and abroad share. Moreover, those features that have come to be considered char-

acteristic of Japanese MNEs, such as the high ratio of expatriates, a head office-oriented managerial style, and the importance of informal information networks, can also be explained by this paradox, and by a style of management that accumulates managerial resources.

High-performance operational efficiency

The competitive advantage of Japanese corporations lies in their operational efficiency. Basic multinational theory teaches that Japanese MNEs must introduce their competitive advantage, namely their operational efficiency, to the host countries in which they operate.

This operational efficiency is the result of a quality control capability that ensures a high level of quality in finished products, a level of production control that allows a diverse range of products to be manufactured in the same plant and on the same production line, inventory management that minimizes the stock of parts and materials, and a maintenance system which assures that all of the manufacturing equipment is running smoothly and kept in good condition. Foreign subsidiaries of Japanese companies have achieved fairly good results in regard to this operational efficiency, as documented by Takamiya (1979), Abo (1994), and Itagaki (1997). Their research has provided evidence that foreign subsidiaries of Japanese firms in the UK or the USA, as well as their export factories in Asia, have succeeded in achieving a level of product quality that is almost on par with products manufactured in Japan. Furthermore, while most of the Japanese subsidiaries operating in the US are less efficient than their mother plants in Japan, they boast a higher productivity than their local rivals. To realize this high operational efficiency, Japanese corporations have introduced a variety of systems and innovations. For example, they have adopted quality control innovations that improve quality during the manufacturing process instead of simply rejecting defectives at the final stage, and have implemented a **just-in-time** (or similar) inventory system that minimizes the stock of parts and materials. In terms of the Japanese manufacturing system, this is referred to as the international transfer of its functional core. In other words, Japanese MNEs have succeeded to a remarkable degree in achieving a high operational efficiency, as well as in transferring the functional core of their manufacturing system to their overseas subsidiaries.

Organizational features and low profitability

Specific organizational features of Japanese corporations as they exist in Japan, and which are necessary to attain a high operational efficiency, include the following: First, the tendency to a long-term commitment to the enterprise. This means setting up various types of business and accumulating core technologies within the corporation, as well as improving the ability of the corporation to respond to the ever-changing and increasingly challenging business environment. Second, a priority for management participation by and information sharing among all of the many different classes of employees, as well as an inter-departmental capacity for coordination. This feature supports a rapid and flexible response to a variety of unanticipated problems concerning matters such as quality or equipment maintenance. Third, long-term training and methods for cultivating human resources that possess a wide variety of skills. The formation of these skills supports a managerial approach that places emphasis upon information sharing and coordination between departments. Fourth, a personnel management system with the type of wages and opportunities for promotion that can attract employees to remain with the company for longer-term employment. Long-term employment is a basic premise for the cultivation of multi-skilled employees. Fifth, harmonious labor relations are widely seen throughout Japan and are a foundational characteristic that promotes management participation and information sharing.

Although such organizational features are common in Japan, are they common in overseas subsidiaries? There are two things that the overseas subsidiaries have in common with companies in Japan: their long-term commitment to the enterprise and their unwillingness to easily resort to layoffs. This was clearly revealed by the behavior of Japanese firms in the face of the 1997 Asian economic crisis. According to a survey conducted by the **Ministry of International Trade and**

Industry (MITI), as little as 3 percent of Japanese companies with manufacturing operations in the NIEs or ASEAN countries withdrew their investment and less than 10 percent of the companies with plants in ASEAN countries laid off any of their regular employees. For example, neither Toyota's subsidiaries in Thailand nor in Indonesia laid off any regular employees despite production cutbacks. On days when plants were not operating, they held training sessions or sent large groups of employees to Japan for training.

Finally, to encourage employees' participation or sharing of information, a number of subsidiaries have introduced small-group activities, various types of meetings, and cooperative labor-management conferences. However, the introduction of such organizational features is to a large extent influenced by the business environment that obtains among the host countries and in general, their international transfer is more restricted than in the case of the functional core. Compared to the situation in Japan, overseas subsidiaries experience a lower degree of employee participation in management, and for many subsidiaries employees have only a narrow range of skills. Factors that obstruct the international transfer of organizational features include pre-existing systems in the host countries (e.g. the wage system in the USA and in continental Europe), social inequality stemming from factors such as education (in Asia and Europe, including the UK), a management style that emphasizes job specialization (USA and Europe), and high employee turnover ratios (common among many host countries).

A number of supplementary features have allowed overseas subsidiaries to achieve high operational efficiency despite their insufficient transfer of organizational features. The first of these was the presence of Japanese expatriates among their personnel. At many subsidiaries, these personnel were used to fill gaps between different jobs or to assist with coordination between departments. This is one of the reasons that the ratio of expatriate staff at Japanese subsidiaries was higher than at US or European counterparts. It is also important to give credit to the continual transfer of know-how from Japan, such as the results of **kaizen**. This represents the transfer of the products of organizational features, rather than the transfer of those features themselves. It also helps to explain one of the factors behind the strict authority maintained by the mother plants and head offices in Japan. It should be noted that the authority and influence of the mother plants, which are at a similar rank in the managerial hierarchy as the overseas subsidiaries, were in some cases even stronger than that of the headquarters. This is because the source of the technology and know-how, which is related to operational efficiency, exists at the mother plants in Japan. This also helps to explain characteristics of the Japanese MNEs such as the importance of informal information networks and the weak function of regional head-quarters. Finally, the quality and inventory control aspects of the subsidiaries' operational efficiency is due to the presence of Japanese parts manufac-turers who established their own operations in host countries in tandem with Japanese MNEs. This situation is frequently referred to as the "mini-Japan" form.

According to data accumulated by the Japanese **Ministry of Finance** and by the US Department of Commerce, the ratio of return on foreign direct investment by Japanese MNEs is conspicuously lower than that of US MNEs. Similarly, if the rates of return on investment from European and Japanese MNEs operating in the USA are compared, those of Japanese MNEs are also lower, as a rule. To be sure, these organizational features, which protect and sustain diverse managerial resources over the long term, are extremely effective in coping with continued changes in an increasingly challenging business environment and in raising operational efficiency. In contrast, however, this means that at any given point in time there exist superfluous managerial resources that do not contribute to the return on investment. This is the fundamental factor behind the low profitability that characterizes Japanese plants at home and abroad. Especially when economic conditions are poor, the excess of managerial resources is magnified and there is a stronger tendency to further aggravate declining profits. In the case of overseas subsidiaries, there are also additional factors such as the high ratio of expatriates, the relatively short plant operating experience, and employee education programs including the dispatch of a wide variety of

personnel to Japan for training, all of which drive costs up further. Finally, the reliance upon Japanese parts suppliers also puts upward pressure on costs.

Prospects

For Japanese overseas subsidiaries, achieving high operational efficiency, which gives them their competitive edge, is a prerequisite for success. Neglecting their operational efficiency in the pursuit of short-term profits may likely sacrifice the very basis of their competitiveness. However, focusing on operational efficiency while the transfer of organizational features remains incom-plete is hazardous and entails not only increased costs but a variety of other attendant risks as well. Japanese MNEs face the dilemma of having to choose between operational efficiency and higher costs and risks on the one hand, or undermining their competitive advantage by sacrificing effi-ciency and reducing costs and risks, on the other. It is interesting to consider how the Japanese MNEs will attempt to solve this dilemma in the particular case of the Japanese expatriates.

A high ratio of Japanese expatriates and the large role they play not only increases costs for the overseas subsidiaries, but also risks damaging the motivation of local employees and encouraging the best employees to seek work elsewhere. This may create a vicious circle where it becomes even more difficult to reduce the degree of dependence on expatriates, and talented local employees are further encouraged to leave. However, unreason-ably decreasing the number of expatriates will reduce operational efficiency and possibly obstruct the transfer of technology in the longer term. Even if the need for Japanese MNEs to reduce their dependence on expatriates is a given, it may be better to consider this a long-term objective. Perhaps the key for the success of Japanese MNEs is to discover a talented local manager who understands the importance of accumulating and utilizing the characteristic Japanese managerial resources and then to put the reins of management into that person's hands. In fact, among successful Japanese MNEs, there are already examples where this has taken place.

To gradually reduce the degree of dependence upon Japanese expatriates, it is necessary to systemize and standardize the skills and know-how required to increase operational efficiency. In many host countries where there is a high employee turnover ratio, the proportion of "core" multi-skilled employees is smaller than it is in Japan. To that extent the systemization and standardization of these skills and know-how becomes even more important. While some Japanese MNEs are grappling with this task themselves, in most cases the process of systemizing and standardizing these skills and know-how is left either to the mother plant or to personnel dispatched from Japan. To make full use of the standardized know-how that has accumulated at subsidiaries in each host country, it may be necessary to organize a horizontal information-sharing network among the various subsidiaries. Once that is accomplished, it will be possible to share the authority that is currently over-concentrated in the mother plants and headquarters.

Finally, in the long term, it is possible that the stability of employees in Japan and their degree of participation in management will both gradually begin to decrease. At such time, it will become necessary to transfer to Japan the know-how accumulated by overseas plant management about organizing a highly mobile workforce. When that happens we may see a Japanese MNE-style international, horizontal network that supports the mutual learning and exchange of information between mother plants and their overseas subsidiaries as well as among overseas subsidiaries themselves.

See also: Japanese investment patterns; overseas production

Further reading

Abo, T. (ed.) (1994) *Hybrid Factory: The Japanese Production System in the United States*, New York: Oxford University Press.

Bartlett, C.A. and Ghoshal, S. (1989) *Managing Across Borders: The Transnational Solution*, Boston: Harvard Business School Press.

Beechler, S. and Bird, A. (eds) (1998) *Japanese Multinationals Abroad*, New York: Oxford University Press.

Campbell, N. and Burton, F. (eds) (1994) *Japanese Multinationals: Strategies and Management in the Global Kaisha*, London: Routledge.

Itagaki, H. (ed.) (1997) *The Japanese Production System: Hybrid Factories in East Asia*, London: Macmillan.

Kenny, M. and Florida, R. (1993) *Beyond Mass Production: The Japanese System and its Transfer to the U.S.*, New York: Oxford University Press.

Kojima, K. (1978) *Direct Foreign Investment: A Japanese Model of Multinational Business Operations*, London: Croom Helm.

Takamiya, M. (1979) "Conclusions and Policy Implicationsm," in S. Takamiya and K. Thurley (eds), *Japan's Emerging Multinationals: An International Comparison of Policies and Practices*, Tokyo: University of Tokyo Press.

HIROSHI ITAGAKI

Johnson, Chalmers

Born 1931, in Phoenix, Arizona, Johnson taught political science at the University of California, Berkeley from 1962–88. In 1988 he moved to University of California, San Diego. Since 1994 he has served as president of the Japan Policy Research Institute.

Johnson is the most prominent non-Japanese theorist of the politics of Japanese capitalism. His work analyzes the Japanese bureaucracy's use of **industrial policy** to promote economic development. Johnson explains how the industrial planning bureaucracy operates internally, how it works with business to develop and implement plans, and how it has been supported politically.

See also: competition; industrial policy; Ministry of International Trade and Industry

Further reading

Johnson, C. (1982) *MITI and the Japanese Miracle: The Growth of Industrial Policy, 1925–1975*, Stanford, CA: Stanford University Press.

—— (1995) *Japan: Who Governs? The Rise of the Developmental State*, New York: W.W. Norton.

MARK TILTON

joint stock corporation

The joint stock corporation is one of four types of company form in Japan. These are: (1) the *gomei kaisha* (commercial partnership where partners have unlimited liability to creditors); (2) the *goshi kaisha* (limited partnership that has limited and unlimited liability partners, of which the unlimited partners represent the company); (3) the *yugen kaisha* (limited liability company, where the total contribution is no less than ¥3 million, the number of members is no more than fifty, and the contribution per member is no less than ¥50,000); and (4) the *kabushiki kaisha* (joint stock corporation with a total contributed capital of no less than ¥10 million).

In 1998 there were a total of 27,000 *gomei kaisha* and *goshi kaisha*, 850,000 *yugen kaisha,* and 800,000 *kabushiki kaisha*. Of these 800,000 joint stock corporations about 2,000 are listed on the first and second sections of the Tokyo Stock Exchange, and another 800 or so are traded on the over-the-counter (OTC) market. In 1995 there were about 1,200,000 joint stock corporations and fewer limited liability companies than in 1998. The minimum capital stock for *kabushiki kaisha* was raised to ¥10 million, in 1991. As there were many joint stock companies that could not meet this new requirement within the five years that were allowed as an adaptation period, in 1996 many *kabushiki kaisha* were converted to *yugen kaisha*.

The majority of Japanese companies in general as well as the joint stock corporations in particular, are **small and medium-sized firms**. At the beginning of the twenty-first century, the two largest Japanese joint stock corporations are NTT Docomo with a total capitalization of about ¥19 trillion, and **Toyota** Motors with a capitalization of about ¥16 trillion.

History

The modernization of the Japanese economy, starting with the establishment of a modern financial system, was a major goal for the Meiji government from its establishment in 1868. Therefore in 1869 the government founded the **Ministry of Finance**. The Commercial Company (Tsuushou Gaisha) and the Exchange Company (Kawase Gaisha), set up in the same year, could arguably be called the first joint stock corporations. Their fund suppliers received interest and shared in the profits, but did not enjoy limited liability. The first joint stock bank, and joint stock corporation in the true sense of the word, was the First National Bank (Dai-ichi Ginkou), which was established in 1873. Finally in June 1878 the Tokyo Stock Exchange was established in order to enable companies to raise capital outside the banking system. At that time, regulations for investor protection were still virtually non-existent.

The Commercial Code as it was implemented in 1893 provided rules for the establishment of companies, and offered some basis for creditor protection and accountability towards stockholders. The Securities and Exchange Law (SEL) of 1948 was enacted to contribute to "the proper operation of the national economy and the protection of investors." In accordance with the Securities and Exchange Law, the stock exchanges themselves provide detailed regulations for listing. The "Ministerial Ordinance regarding the disclosure of corporate information" stipulates the rules for disclosure of information towards shareholders. The Ordinance is part of the Laws pertaining to the SEL.

Establishing a joint stock corporation in Japan

Chapter 4, paragraph 1 of the Commercial Code stipulates the rules for establishing a joint stock corporation. The articles of incorporation should include the company's purpose, firm name, the number of authorized shares, par value of the shares (if applicable), a breakdown of par value and non par-value shares issued, the company's address, the method of public announcement, and the names and addresses of the sponsors. Par value of the shares shall be no less than ¥50. At the time of the establishment of the company, the stock issued shall be no less than one fourth of the authorized capital. In case non par-value stock is issued at the time the corporation is established, the minimum value shall be ¥50,000. Total capital stock shall be no less than ¥1 million. A director and a statutory auditor shall be appointed at the inaugural meeting.

See also: Commercial Code

CARIEN VAN MOURIK

joint ventures

Before the FDI liberalization in the mid-1970s, joint ventures were the typical mode of entry into Japan. Even today, when full control is the preferred option, it is still used by many foreign enterprises as a means to reduce cost of entry, minimize risk, and gain quick access to market knowledge and infrastructure. For Japanese firms, joint ventures offered a shortcut for accumulating knowledge, or minimizing the risk of going abroad. Outward joint ventures peaked in the 1980s during the Japanese investment expansion to Southeast Asia, while in the US and Europe the preferred option was always 100 percent owned entity.

There are four types of joint ventures between Japanese and foreign enterprises, based on their strategic and knowledge-creation contexts: complementary, learning, resource, and competitive.

A *complementary joint venture* is formed when partners with complementary strategic intent join forces to exploit their existing resources or competencies – by linking different elements of the value chain, for instance. A typical complementary joint venture in a Japanese market would be an alliance in which a Western firm contributed its technology and the local partner facilitated entry into a local market. While most joint ventures are typically defined as complementary in opening public relations statements, a shift in partnership orientation must be expected.

A *learning joint venture* can develop from a complementary alliance when both partners share an interest in enhancing their individual competencies, whether through an exchange of existing knowledge, or the development of new knowledge where the partners jointly participate in the same value chain activities. An example of learning alliances is the former Fuji–Xerox joint venture in Japan. Originally set up to facilitate Xerox's penetration of the Japanese market, it served for many years as a critical source of competency development for the Xerox worldwide. Compared to complementary alliances, learning alliances require more interaction, shared work and interface management.

Resource joint ventures have been the traditional way to minimize risk or deal with closed markets. This is changing as markets open up. But they are still a useful vehicle when competitive pressures such as resource constraints, political and business risks, or economies of scale lead competitors to join forces. It can help minimize the risks in a particular aspect of the business by getting others to participate. When Japanese car companies began to advance in the USA in the mid-1980s, their suppliers did not have much choice but to follow suit. For most of them the investments required to enter the USA were too big and too risky, so many decided to join forces with US companies in the same business.

Finally, *competitive joint ventures* are formed between companies who are otherwise competitors. One of the best-known examples is NUMMI, a 50–50 joint venture between General Motors and **Toyota**. This venture was nominally designed for the joint production of small cars for the North American market, but at the same time it was intended to serve as a 'learning laboratory' for the two competitors. General Motors gained insights into Toyota's manufacturing system, and Toyota learned how to operate a US-based manufacturing facility. In a competitive alliance, it is not just fast learning that matters but also its speed and effectiveness relative to the partner; maintaining learning parity is the key to sustaining such a relationship.

None of four types of joint ventures is "better" than another. Joint ventures in all four quadrants can enhance a firm's competitive advantage. However, the management challenges associated with each type of a joint venture are different. Problems occur when the company does not know what kind of alliance it has entered or – because joint ventures are by their nature dynamic and transitory – when it does not respond appropriately to early signals that the nature of the alliance is changing. For example, in a complementary venture, a Western company can rely on the Japanese partner to recruit and train the alliance workforce since the loyalty factor may not be an issue – at least in the short run. However, in a competitive venture such an approach could prove costly in the event of subsequent conflict between the partners.

Contrary to a popular metaphor, a joint venture is *not* like a marriage: longer alliances are not necessarily better. Joint ventures are not forever; most either die early or evolve, just as any other business enterprise. Joint venture stability is a contradiction in terms. Joint venture success cannot be measured by its longevity, but the degree to which the alliance helps the firm to improve its ability to compete in the marketplace. In this respect, a good question to ask is, "how successful were the joint ventures with the Japanese, in particular those in the Japanese market combining Western technology with the market know-how and distribution capabilities of the Japanese?"

The bottom line is that the track record of many joint ventures in Japan is poor. By the early 1990s most were dissolved or taken over by the Japanese partner who rapidly absorbed new technology without ceding much in market access. For the Japanese, the "market-for-technology" swap exchange created valuable opportunities to upgrade their competitive capability. The strategic intent of many of the Japanese partners was to learn as much as possible about the technology contributed by the Western firm. A carefully implemented human resource strategy secured rapid diffusion and assimilation of the know-how to the Japanese parent.

Western firms did not pay sufficient attention to the competitive aspects of the joint venture relationship and were not prepared for the possibility of changes in the relative power of their Japanese partners. Western partners saw their joint ventures as "defensive," established primarily to save resources, or simply to supplement the competency they lacked. Because of a lack of systematic investment in learning, very little local knowledge filtered back to the Western parent. Without such local knowledge, the Western firm's freedom of action in the Japanese market was greatly reduced.

Successful joint ventures were only those that were "offensive" in building a common competitive and learning culture. The partners embarked jointly on a "race to learn," using the joint venture as a mutual tool for faster and broader gains in competitive capability through investments in competency development. In Japan, as in many other markets, the rule for joint venture success is simple: "There is no free lunch."

VLADIMIR PUCIK

Juran, Joseph M.

A US-based pioneer in **quality management**, Juran (1904–) was invited to Japan by the Union of Japanese Scientists and Engineers (JUSE) in 1954. Like **Deming**, he gave lectures to managers on the need to promote quality in both processes and products.

Juran's focus has been on management, stressing managerial responsibility for quality, with quality integral to managerial duties. He promotes planning for quality, with goal-driven agendas, and defines quality as "fitness for use," rather than compliance with specifications. Based on work by economist Vilfredo Pareto, Juran developed the "Pareto principle," which states that large proportions of problems are generated by only a few causes. Often cited as an "80/20" split, the Pareto principle emphasizes the separation of the "vital few" from the "useful many" when allocating resources to fixing problems.

Further reading

Juran, J.M. (1988) *Juran on Planning for Quality*, New York: The Free Press.

ELIZABETH L. ROSE

just-in-time

As articulated by its principal architect, Taiichi **Ono** of Toyota Motor Corporation, a just-in-time (JIT) system produces only the necessary items, at the necessary time, and in the necessary quantity to meet customer demand. The underlying philosophy is to seek manufacturing excellence through the elimination of waste in all aspects of the production system, with particular attention placed on reducing excess levels of in-process and finished goods inventories. Common usages of the term can be confusing, however, because in varying instances

JIT is used to refer to the generic philosophy of manufacturing management noted above, to a specific mechanism of production and inventory control called **kanban**, or to the overall **Toyota production system** (*Toyota seisan hoshiki*) which includes other aspects.

Though Toyota did not develop the methods for realizing just-in-time production until the 1950s under Ohno, the term was used as early as the 1930s by Toyota founder, Kiichiro Toyoda, as an English phrase with Japanese pronunciation (*jasuto in taimu*) (see Fujimoto 1999). Within Japan, the terms "just-in-time" and "JIT" are still used with a Japanese pronunciation rather than a native Japanese language equivalent. In an interview, one Toyota executive commented that the phrase "just-on-time" may have been more appropriate, so as to emphasize the synchronized, clockwork nature that is intended, rather than a "barely in time" connotation. In the West, while other terms such as stockless production and zero inventory have been used, JIT remains the commonly accepted, though imprecise, term.

Under Ohno's leadership, Toyota developed its JIT system using *kanban* during the 1950s and gradually implemented it throughout Toyota plants. By the late 1960s, Toyota was also extending it to its suppliers, with the result that not only Toyota, but also its first-tier suppliers, were able to dramatically decrease their inventory levels. The cost and quality advantages that Toyota achieved through JIT and its company-wide quality control approach (see **quality management**) are credited with buoying Toyota through the economic turmoil following the 1973 "oil shock." Toyota's success prompted many other Japanese manufacturers to learn from its JIT methods at that time. By the late 1970s and early 1980s, JIT was the object of intense interest worldwide.

Concepts and support factors

A notable aspect of JIT is that it focuses on inventory reduction not only as an end, but also as a means to enable broader improvements throughout the production system. High inventory levels are viewed like deep water that hides various problems and inefficiencies below the surface. Reducing inventory levels, therefore, exposes problems so that they may be acted upon for improvement. At the same time, it must be recognized that reducing inventories without also improving the production system can result in a system stoppage as the buffering function of the inventory is eliminated.

For this reason, Toyota and other companies emphasize **kaizen** and effective quality management to assure that parts are defect free, as there is little or no buffer inventory to replace them. One approach that JIT uses to achieve defect-free production is the use of *jidoka*, sometimes translated as autonomation. The original meaning of *jidoka* is to stop a machine automatically when abnormal conditions are detected so as not to produce defective parts. Extensions of this idea are the use of *poka-yoke*, or mistake-proofing devices, and visual control systems such as *andon* light boards that indicates to workers when and where a problem has occurred so that corrective action can be taken. Along with this, failure-free equipment is necessary so that a machine breakdown in one area does not force a shut-down of the entire system. To improve equipment reliability, approaches such as total productive maintenance are often used.

In order to effectively implement JIT, several other supporting factors must be in place, including smoothed production schedules, rapid setup or changeover times, multiskilled workers, and highly reliable processes. *Heijunka*, or smoothing of the production schedule to achieve uniform plant loading, is critical for JIT implementation. With *heijunka*, Toyota attempts to even out the production quantities of each item in the final assembly schedule. This minimizes the variation in the quantities of parts needed and enables the upstream stages to produce each part at an efficient, constant rate. In addition, the production schedule is smoothed in terms of product variety. In other words, if several models are scheduled for production then the quantities of each model are divided up and evenly dispersed throughout the day, rather than producing large batches of each model in succession. The ultimate goal is to have a production system so flexible and responsive that products can be made in a batch size of one and scheduled according to the market's demand rate. This is also called one-piece flow production.

To make such small batch sizes feasible, it is

important that setup or changeover times be short for all processes, with a common goal being to reduce setup times of all processes to less than ten minutes. Toyota consultant Shigeo **Shingo** is known for a number of techniques for achieving rapid setup. Also, in a one-piece flow production environment, it is possible that each succeeding item might require different operations to be performed. For this reason, the development of a flexible, multiskilled workforce is necessary. Cross-training also makes it possible for a worker to be responsible for several machine tools and to be flexibly reassigned to keep both worker and machine utilization high.

Production and inventory control methods

Another typical aspect of JIT is the use of a pull method, such as the *kanban* system, for coordinating production and inventory throughout the system. In a pull system, production is initiated only to replenish what has been actually used at the next stage of the production system. This is a reversal of a push system in which parts are produced in anticipation of future demand. A *kanban* system functions as a pull system due to the way that it uses *kanban* (literally meaning card or sign) and returnable parts containers to control the production and movement of materials between two stages of the production system. The production of additional parts is authorized only when a worker at the downstream stage begins to use an existing full container of parts and takes the appropriate *kanban* card back up to the upstream process as authorization to produce another full container as replenishment. The total amount of inventory in the production system is determined by the number of *kanban* cards and containers in circulation between any two stages of the system. Consequently, inventory levels can be reduced by removing some of the *kanban* containers from the system. Sometimes this is done as a purposeful way of stressing the system in order to identify the weak points that are exposed when the inventory buffer is removed.

Kanban systems are not appropriate for all situations, however. Toyota itself uses several alternate methods for coordinating production and material flows. For low consumption parts, Toyota uses a push method called *chakko-hiki*, or schedule-initiated production. In this method, the production and delivery of parts is determined in advance based upon the final assembly schedule and bill of materials. For large components and parts such as engines and seats, another method called *junjo-hiki*, or sequence-synchronized production, is used. With this method, the production and delivery of each part is synchronized with the individual vehicles in the final assembly schedule, rather than waiting for a *kanban* card to signal production of the part.

See also: supply chain management in Japan

Further reading

Enkawa, T. and Schvaneveldt, S.J. (2001) "Just-in-Time, Lean Production, and Complementary Paradigms," in G. Salvendy (ed.), *Handbook of Industrial Engineering*, 3rd edn, New York: Wiley, 544–61.

Fujimoto, T. (1999) *The Evolution of a Manufacturing System at Toyota*, New York: Oxford University Press.

Kuroiwa, S. (1999) "Jasutuo In Taimu to Kanban Hoshiki" (Just-In-Time and Kanban System), in T. Enkawa, M. Kuroda, and Y. Fukuda (eds), *Seisan Kanri no Jiten* (Handbook of Production Management), Tokyo: Asakura Shoten, 636–46.

Monden, Y. (1998) *Toyota Production System: An Integrated Approach to Just-In-Time*, 3rd edn, Atlanta, GA: Institute of Industrial Engineers.

Sugimori, Y., Kusunoki, K., Cho, F. and Uchikawa, S. (1977) "Toyota Production System and Kanban System: Materialization of Just-In-Time and Respect for Human System," *International Journal of Production Research* 15(6): 553–64.

SHANE J. SCHVANEVELDT

K

kaizen

Kaizen, continuous improvement, is one of a full set of the Japanese-style production practices, but, in a sense, a word to reveal the most essential aspect of the overall Japanese management and production systems. *Kaizen* in itself is simply bit-by-bit improvement in practices and day-to-day accumulation of the results which are implemented as participative activities at worksites of Japanese companies. It is not a strictly defined concept by academic people but a conventional one that has been used in broad meanings by worksite people at companies, the leaders at practice institutions such as the Japanese Union of Science and Engineers (JUSE), and only by some researchers. *Kaizen* has not clearly been defined in dictionaries, there is room for various kinds and levels of definitions.

Historically, the above characteristic features of *kaizen* practices by Japanese firms, small to large, in their technology and skill improvements have broadly been seen in Japan, compared with the science-led, breakthrough type innovations, often seen in western, especially American, firms. The reasons are several. First Japanese people are generally stronger in practice-oriented inductive ways of doing research and development than in theory-oriented deductive ways. Second, the Japanese also have a distinct inclination for working together in cooperative ways within a team, rather than as individuals in division of labor. Finally, a worksite-oriented style of management has become popular at the company level, integrating the above into *kaizen* innovation activities.

There are three different dimensions of *kaizen* activities. Two types are seen at the shopfloor level. The first encompasses broader day-to-day improvement practices carried out on the shopfloor by all members. This would include practices such as **quality control circles** focused on maintaining better productivity, quality, and so forth as well as activities aimed at promoting worker motivation and improving work procedures, as reflected in practices incorporated in the **Toyota production system** (TPS). The second type of *kaizen* covers activities that are both narrower and deeper, and more technology-oriented. These are carried out primarily through activities led by groups of engineering and maintenance specialists. A third type of *kaizen* activity is found within management or at the overall company level. At the company or factory level, *kaizen* initiatives are led by top management and focused on evolutionary changes through total quality control (TQC) and total production management (TPM).

Theoretically, at any levels, the essence of *kaizen* is an overarching philosophy of requiring all management personnel to be responsible for motivating all employees to improve steadily the existing state of conditions. It is interesting to note the international diffusion of *kaizen* and its feedback to Japan of *kaizen* activity. Modifications and adaptations to local managerial environment are reflected in the ISO 9000 and Six Sigma initiatives originated in Europe and North American respectively. Both can be understood as modified and developed quality improvement models adopted from Japanese style worksite-oriented organizational learning activities to more American style top-down and specialist-led methodologies.

Further reading

Cole, R.E. (1999) *Managing Quality Fads*, Oxford: Oxford University Press.

Fujimoto, T. (1999) *The Evolution of a Manufacturing System at Toyota*, Oxford: Oxford University Press.

Toyota Motor Corporation (1996) *The Toyota Production System*, Nagoya.

TETSUO ABO

kanban

Made famous by the **Toyota production system** (TPS) and **just-in-time** (JIT), the term *kanban* simply refers to a card or ticket used to control production and inventory of a given item. *Kanban* cards typically indicate such information as the relevant part number, process name, and number of parts per container. In a *kanban* system (*kanban hoshiki*), these cards are used in combination with returnable containers that hold a designated number of parts. Together they form a means to authorize and coordinate the production and movement of materials between stages of a manufacturing system so as to prevent excess production and inventory.

Taiichi **Ono** of Toyota Motor Corporation is credited with leading the development of the *kanban* system. He, in turn, credits American supermarkets as being an inspiration in the sense that they put additional items on the shelf only to replenish the number of items pulled off by customers. When Toyota originally developed the *kanban* system in the 1950s, Toyota called it the "supermarket system" and adopted the *kanban* name some years later. Toyota first implemented *kanban* on a plant-wide scale in 1959 and extended it company-wide in 1962. In 1965, Toyota began extending the *kanban* system to its suppliers.

There are various types of *kanban* cards and systems. In the most basic form of *kanban* system, the production of more parts is authorized only when a worker begins to withdraw parts from an existing full container of the part, at which time the worker takes the appropriate *kanban* card to the upstream process that makes the part. In due time, the upstream process will use that card as authorization to produce another standardized container full of the part to be ready for the downstream process. The number of *kanban* cards and containers in circulation between the upstream and downstream processes can be adjusted to control the total number of parts in the system. Since the production of more parts is initiated only when they are being used in the downstream process, a *kanban* system is considered to be a "pull system:" demand downstream pulls or triggers the production of more parts from the upstream processes. If the usage of a part slows or stops downstream, then its production upstream will correspondingly slow or stop. In this way, *kanban* functions as a sort of self-regulating, manual system for controlling the flow of materials from upstream stages, including outside suppliers, through final assembly.

Although the term *kanban* system is sometimes used synonymously with just-in-time or Toyota production system, it should be recognized that *kanban* is merely a mechanism to help achieve the goals of JIT and is only one aspect of TPS. Also, successful implementation of a *kanban* system requires that many supporting factors be in place, including leveled production schedules, high-quality levels, rapid equipment set-up times, multi-skilled workers, and so forth.

Further reading

Fujimoto, T. (1999) *The Evolution of a Manufacturing System at Toyota*, New York: Oxford University Press.

Monden, Y. (1998) *Toyota Production System: An Integrated Approach to Just-In-Time*, 3rd edn, Atlanta, CA: Institute of Industrial Engineers.

Ohno, T. (1988) *Toyota Production System*, Portland, OR: Productivity Press.

SHANE J. SCHVANEVELDT

Kansai culture

In ancient Japan around the twelfth century, *Kansai*, which literally means "west of the barrier", referred to the whole of western Japan, west of a major barrier station located in today's Mie Prefecture in the middle of Honshu Island. *Kanto*, "east of the barrier", referred to eastern Japan. Today, the areas of both Kansai and Kanto are much more limited. Kanto indicates Tokyo and its several surrounding prefectures, and Kansai covers three major cities in the west, Osaka, Kyoto, and Kobe, and a few surrounding prefectures. Kansai and Kanto have been noted as two major central areas in the history of Japan, although in the post-war period, Kanto has been increasingly dominant politically, economically, and culturally.

Even though the term "Kansai" is widely used in Japanese daily living, it is hard to say that there is a common "Kansai culture," as the area that Kansai covers consists of a wide variety of subcultures. Values, customs, communication styles, and so on are significantly different, even among the above-mentioned central three cities.

Kyoto has a long history of noble culture. The imperial family had resided there for over 1,000 years before moving to Tokyo in the late nineteenth century. Osaka has developed since the sixteenth century as a center of Japanese commerce and industry. In contrast, Kobe has a relatively short history. It was founded in the late nineteenth century, but its historical significance, parallel with that of Yokohama in Kanto, as a major international trade port of Japan has been notable. Therefore, Kobe has been known as a city with an international atmosphere because many Westerners and Asians have settled there since the beginning of the city's history. In addition to these three cities, the city of Nara, the ancient capital of Japan before Kyoto, can be also included as part of Kansai, thus adding to the diversity of Kansai culture.

In terms of economic status, the three major city areas are absolutely dominant in Kansai. However, since Osaka has been outstanding economically and in terms of population, the focus is exclusively on that city. Osaka began to play a major economic and industrial role in the history of Japan in the late sixteenth century. The city of Sakai, in the southern part of Osaka, emerged as a major international center of commerce and industry in the late sixteenth century, when Japan was torn by civil wars among *daimyo*, the *samurai* lords. The mer-

chants in Sakai traded internationally with Westerners and Chinese. They also provided major *daimyos* with guns, which were then new weapons. Guns were initially brought to Japan from Portugal in the mid-sixteenth century, but soon thereafter were being made by Japanese artisans. Sakai was a center of the gun industry at the time. Even today, the specific skill and expertise developed in making guns survives in the production of high-quality bicycle parts and cooking knives, which are exported overseas in addition to having a large domestic market share.

Toyotomi Hideyoshi, a peasant-born *samurai*, finally put an end to a half-century of civil war toward the end of the sixteenth century. He built a huge castle in Osaka to rule Japan and dramatically increased the commerce of Osaka. Tokugawa Ieyasu reigned in Japan after the death of Hideyoshi and even after he settled his shogunate government in Edo (now Tokyo) in the early seventeenth century, Osaka continued to be the center of commerce for over two centuries during the **Tokugawa period**.

Japan's modernization started after the Tokugawa period ended in the late nineteenth century. Even though modern Japan's capital is Tokyo, Osaka played a central role in modernizing Japan. From the end of the nineteenth century until the 1930s, Osaka was the center of the spinning industry in Japan, the tractor of the industrial revolution. Toyobo, one of the major spinning companies based in Osaka, was the largest such facility in the world in the early 1930s. Thus, Osaka was said to be the "Manchester of the Orient."

The chemical industry and **pharmaceuticals industry** also developed in Osaka in modernizing Japan, as Osaka merchants had dealt with Chinese and even Western medicine in the Tokugawa period. Many of Japan's major pharmaceutical companies originated in Osaka and still operate there.

Osaka also witnessed the founding of seven out of nine *sogo shoshas*, large-scale trading companies in Japan, including **Sumitomo**, **ITOCHU** and **Marubeni**. Only two others, **Mitsubishi** and **Mitsui**, started in Tokyo. Japan's representative electric appliance makers, **Matsushita** and Panasonic, also originated in Osaka. The former's founder, **Matsushita** Konosuke, said to be the

"God of Management" in Japan, was trained to be a merchant in Senba, a small region in Osaka, historically known as the mecca of commerce. **Sharp** also started in Osaka, although the founder came from Tokyo. In addition, major securities houses such as **Nomura Securities** and Daiwa have roots in Osaka.

Since the Second World War, Tokyo has had an increasingly greater presence economically as well as politically, whereas Osaka's presence has declined significantly. However, the tradition of centuries of commerce and industry can also be seen in the culture of the daily way of living and the values of Osaka people.

If one were to characterize Osaka culture, it would be as a culture of the people. This appears in various aspects of Osaka people's behavior. An individual is evaluated by his personality and ability, not by his birth, formal authority or political power. This consciousness can be traced to Toyotomi Hideyoshi, who ruled Japan in the sixteenth century. He is still a hero in Osaka because he was a peasant-born man of great ability, who made his way from the bottom to the top of society. The Osaka anti-establishment attitude can also be seen in the tradition of public entertainment. For example, unlike such Japanese traditional performing arts as the *no* play and *kabuki*, whose performers are hereditary, in the *bunraku* puppet play, which developed in Osaka in the Tokugawa period, birth is not important. Recruits are found in the general public and trained to be performers.

The Osakan consciousness of anti-authority and power sometimes manifests itself as an anti-Tokyo attitude. Unlike many other areas in Japan, what is trendy in Tokyo is not necessarily so in Osaka, where people tend to assert their own taste.

Osaka's tradition of commerce is also manifested in the people's face-to-face communication style. In negotiation, for example, a delicate technique of communication is used by which one expresses his opinion and feeling quite honestly, but in a way that avoids hurting the opponent's feelings. Conversely, even in cases where an opponent is too aggressive or offensive, an adroit, often humorous defensive response is given on an ad hoc basis.

One outcome of such a culture of communication is that Osaka is noted as a centre of comedy. Many comedians who have come from Osaka or been trained there have become famous nationwide.

NORIYA SUMIHARA

kansayaku

The *kansayaku* is equivalent to an auditor in Western companies, and a mandatory organ for any kabushiki kaisha (**joint stock corporation**). The *kansayaku* monitors the management of the **torishimariyakukai** and audits the accountings of joint stock corporations with more than ¥100 million of capitalization. The former function is not assumed in case of joint stock corporations with ¥100 million of capitalization or less. The *kansayaku* is not mandatory for *yugen gaisha* (limited liability corporations), and if there is one, assumes only an auditing function. In either case, the general assembly of stockholders or members of the corporation elect *kansayaku*. The **Commercial Code** stipulates that *kansayaku* are not eligible to serve as *torishimariyaku*, general managers, or as employees of the corporation or its subsidiaries (article 276).

More than three *kansayaku* must be elected for a stock corporation with outstanding common stock of ¥500 million or more or total liabilities of ¥20 trillion or more, and more than one is required to be chosen from outside the corporation. The *kansayaku* must then set up a *kansayakukai*, auditing board.

Kansayaku can request that anyone in the corporation at any time report to them about the corporation's operations, and are entitled to survey the practices and properties of the corporation (article 274 clause 2). *Torishimariyaku* must promptly report to *kansayaku* in cases where a danger that might cause asubstantial damage to the corporation has been identified (article 274–2). *Kansayaku* at a parent company, if it is deemed necessary for them to carry out their duties, can exercise these same rights in regard to subsidiaries, and are required to mention in the auditors report the methods and results of their auditing in regard to subsidiaries (article 281).

Projects and papers drafted by *torishimariyaku* for submission to shareholders at the general meeting of shareholders must be scrutinized by *kansayaku* prior to submission. If *kansayaku* find violations of law or violations of the articles of association of the corporation, or a matter of substantial inadequacy, they must declare this at the general meeting (article 275).

Kansayaku are entitled to request that *torishimariyaku* cease actions that are either beyond the purpose of the corporation or that amounting to a violation of law or the articles of association that may lead to substantial damage to the corporation (article 275). An extension of this function of the *kansayaku* is that, in case of legal disputes between the *torishimariyaku* and the corporation, the *kansayaku* represents the latter (article 267 clause 1). Prosecution of the responsibilities of *torishimariyaku* is also brought to trial by *kansayaku* (article 275–4).

See also: bubble economy; business ethics

Further reading

Kishida, M. (2000) *Zeminaaru Kaishaho Nyuumon* (Introductory Seminar on Corporate Law), Tokyo: Nihon keizai shinbunsha.

Maeda, H. (2000) *Kaishaho Nyuumon* (Introduction to Corporate Law), Tokyo: Yuuhikaku.

Oda, H. (1997) *Basic Japanese Laws*, Oxford: Oxford University Press.

KAZUHARU NAGASE

Kao

Tomiro Nagase founded Kao in 1887, creating the first soap business in Tokyo. Throughout its history, the company changed its name nine times and made seven changes in its logo, indicating how the company has tried to adapt to the changing tastes of society in Japan. The current president, Takuya Goto, has led the company through major structural and cultural change in order to become the leading company in the household products industry in Japan. Kao sells over 600 consumer products, from household detergents to floppy disks. In addition, the company is now trying to globalize and has so far established foreign operations in Asia, North America, and Europe. Consolidated sales for 1999 were ¥924.5 billion with a net profit of ¥98 billion.

Kao has grown to 6,086 employees worldwide, excluding related subsidiaries and joint venture companies. Of that total, almost a quarter of the workforce are involved in research and development. Even with this extraordinarily high percentage of employees devoted to R&D, former president Maruta Yoshiro said that half of the employees in the future would be involved with research and development. By focusing on innovation and new products, the company has remained at the forefront of basic chemical research.

Kao has announced that its strategic goals are to invest in technological development, develop marketing through new distribution systems, and maintain a state-of-the-art information system. Kao's increasing sales and profit could not be explained without discussing its marketing information system (MIS). The "free access to information" computer system introduced in the organization allows anyone at Kao to access the sales system, marketing information system, production information system, and even the distribution information system. This unique system provides the user full access to real time company data, giving all employees firsthand business knowledge regardless of their position in the company.

Another strength of the Kao management system is its distribution system, which has been evaluated as the best of any Japanese corporation. The Tokyo Distribution Center runs at such a high capacity that deliveries of Kao products can be made to as many as 6,000 retail stores located at metropolitan areas by the next day following receipt of an order.

Kao has established its consumer products and chemical products as the pillars of its business activities, and is striving to expand its operations in each business segment and in the global marketplace by providing consumers throughout the world with superior products and services.

Further reading

Nonaka, I. and Takeuchi, H. (1995) *The Knowledge-Creating Company*, New York: Oxford University Press.

Noriaki, O. (1985) *Kao's Astounding Strategy VAN*, Tokyo: Chukei.

MARGARET TAKEDA

TETSU MORISHIMA

karoshi

At time of writing, there is a great deal of debate in Japan regarding sudden death among Japan's white-collar workers. This phenomenon is called *karoshi*, or sudden death syndrome. The Japanese officially recognized *karoshi* as a fatal illness in 1989. Its symptoms include high blood pressure and asthma-like problems. Most of the victims, in their prime working years in white-collar occupations, die from subarachonodial hemorrhage (stroke) or myocardial infarction (heart attack).

The cause of *karoshi* can be attributed to the fundamental nature of the Japanese-style work week, which consists of twelve-hour days and work-filled evenings. The Japanese work such long hours because in many organizations, working overtime has become a ritual of obedience and subservience. This is in spite of the fact that there is rarely any work-related reason and there are no improvements in productivity for the company. In addition to the long working hours, there is social pressure which discourages employees from taking vacations.

Consequently, many Japanese workers feel mentally and physically fatigued every day, and many are afraid of dying from overwork. This high level of work anxiety often results in poor work performance for those employees, causing other employees to take up the slack. The resulting redundancy means that the some employees are doing the work of up to four people. Those overworking employees cannot manage the heavy workload within normal time frames and so they work extra long hours in order to give the appearance of efficiency. The result is a self-fulfilling destructive cycle of anxiety, overwork, and death.

To illustrate the extent of the *karoshi* phenomenon, a study conducted by the Fukoku Life Insurance Co. found that:

- 80 percent of Japanese workers want to sleep more;
- 70 percent feel stressed;
- 44 percent feel constant fatigue;
- 42 percent fear death from overwork;
- 28 percent lack creativity and motivation;
- 23 percent feel a frequent desire to call in sick.

Fundamental changes in the employment environment are taking place, however, which should have a favorable impact and minimize *karoshi*. The rise of the *shinjinrui* (new workers), the new generation of Japanese born into affluence, is changing work habits and transforming Japan into a consumption-driven economy. Employees are no longer willing to sacrifice their lives for the good of the company, or try to give the appearance to that effect. Employees are resisting pressure to stay at work when there is no actual work to be done. They are choosing to spend more time at home with their families, and are even taking vacations.

Although the Japanese government has finally acknowledged that *karoshi* claims an estimated 10,000 workers each year, it still does not officially recognize its existence and does not maintain comprehensive statistics. However, the Japanese Labor Ministry said it would introduce a new medical insurance program meant to prevent *karoshi* or death from overwork. Workers believed to be at greatest risk – those who are obese, have high blood pressure, high blood sugar and high blood lipid levels – would get free medical checkups under the plan.

Further reading

"A Kinder, Gentler Workplace" (2000) *New York Times*, January 30, 3(4): 1.

Brown, W., Lubove, R. and Kwalwasser, E. (1994) *Karoshi: Alternative Perspectives of Japanese Management Styles*, Greenwich, CT: Business Horizons.

Palumbo, F. and Herbig, A. (1994) "Salaryman Sudden Death Syndrome," *Employee Relations*, 54–61.

Smith, P. (1998) "Tougher than the Rest," *Management*, 42–7.

MARGARET TAKEDA

Keio University

Keio University (in Japanese, Keio Gijuku Dai-gaku) was founded as Fukuzawa's Dutch Studies School in Edo (present-day Tokyo) in 1858 by Yukichi **Fukuzawa**. It is the oldest institution of higher learning in Japan and, with Waseda University, one of Japan's two leading private universities. Historically, it has been a primary source of many of Japan's top business leaders, a position that it continues to hold to the present.

The name "Keio" was adopted in 1868 and comes from the Japanese name for that era. In 1871 the university moved to its present location in Mita, a southern section of Tokyo. At present it also maintains two large branch campuses: one in Hiyoshi, a suburban area roughly midway between Tokyo and Yokohama, and one in Fujisawa, about forty minutes by train west of Tokyo on the coast.

Keio's prominence as a university and its influence within Japan is twofold. First, early on the university established a reputation for educating business leaders. As school-based *habatsu* – i.e. *gakubatsu* – became established in larger firms, a powerful dynamic was created to enhance this reputation. Within a firm, the Keio *gakubatsu* helped advance the careers of its members who, in turn, encouraged the hiring of Keio graduates, who joined the company thereby strengthening the influence of the *gakubatsu*. In some organizations, Keio graduates accounted for an influential portion of the overall managerial cadre. For example, at **Mitsukoshi**, the top department store chain, as late as 1990, approximately one-fourth of the *torishimariya-kukai*, or board of directors, were Keio graduates.

Second, having been founded by one of Japan's most influential and revolutionary educators, it has continued to pioneer many educational initiatives. As far back as 1898 it created what amounted to a vertically integrated educational corporation by establishing elementary and secondary schools. This meant that a student could begin the very first year of formal education within the Keio system and continue all the way through to university graduation in that system. With the postwar establishment of a Keio pre-school, when combined with its graduate and doctoral programs, an individual could pursue what might be called a "cradle to corporation" educational experience at Keio.

Keio University has maintained its position as Japan's leading educator of business managers in several ways. In 1978, it became the first university in Japan to offer an American-style Master of Business Administration (MBA) degree. In a partnership with Harvard Business School, it introduced a full-time MBA program modeled on Harvard's curriculum and employing the distinctive case method pedagogy. It subsequently introduced Executive MBA courses. With the growth of executive education, lifelong learning and distance education trends to Japan, Keio University's role as a leading business educator continues to expand.

ALLAN BIRD

Kirin Brewery

Kirin Brewery is Japan's largest brewer. Kirin has dominated the Japanese beer industry for most of the postwar period on the strength of its flagship Kirin Lager brand and a strong supporting production and marketing strategy.

Kirin's origins go back to Japan's first brewery, Spring Valley Brewery, which was established by an American in Yokohama in 1870. In 1885, Spring Valley was reorganized into Japan Brewery Company, Ltd, with financial backing from several of Japan's leading industrialists, including Yanosuke Iwasaki of the **Mitsubishi** business group. Under the guidance of German brewmasters, Japan Brewery offered a German-style lager beer named "Kirin," after a dragon-like creature from Chinese legend. (A picture of a *kirin* adorns the Kirin beer label.) In 1907, the company again changed hands, and was renamed Kirin Brewery Company.

Japanese breweries proliferated and thrived during the early twentieth century, but with the 1929 stock market crash, the worldwide depression of the 1930s, and the Second World War, demand plummeted and many breweries closed or consolidated. By 1948 only two beer makers remained in Japan: Kirin and Dai Nippon Breweries, which had been built over a forty-year period through the merging of numerous independent brewers. In 1949, Dai Nippon was declared in violation of

Japan's new anti-monopoly law and split in half along geographical lines, with its operations in western Japan becoming today's Asahi Breweries and those in eastern Japan becoming today's Sapporo Breweries. At the time of Dai Nippon's breakup, Sapporo held 38.6 percent of the market, Asahi 36.1 percent, and Kirin 25.3 percent.

Over the next thirty years, Kirin surpassed its rivals and came to dominate the industry. Kirin's success is attributed to several factors. First, the breakup of Dai Nippon into Sapporo and Asahi left Kirin as the only brewer with a nationally recognized brand name and a nationwide sales network, until the others could expand their operations. Second, Kirin anticipated growing demand for beer and aggressively built new production capacity, at a rate of one new brewery every two years. Third, Kirin targeted the home consumption market, which expanded rapidly in the 1950s and 1960s as refrigerator use became widespread. Fourth, the strong, bitter taste of Kirin Lager was right for the times; the diet in postwar Japan was poor and bland, leading consumers to crave strong taste where they could get it. Finally, the company effectively stressed Kirin's superior taste in its advertising, leading the public to equate Kirin with beer.

In 1979 Kirin's market share reached 63 percent, prompting Japan's **Fair Trade Commission** to consider splitting the company into two separate entities. In the end, Kirin remained intact, though it suspended advertising for a time to dampen sales growth and deflect charges that it was a monopoly. The company also began diversifying into other product areas, including wines, soft drinks, restaurants, and pharmaceuticals.

During the 1990s, Kirin lost ground in the beer market to Asahi, whose Super Dry brand became Japan's top selling beer. But with two strong-selling brands in Kirin Lager and Ichiban Shibori, Kirin still held the industry's largest market share at around 40 percent in 2000. Kirin is a member of the Mitsubishi business group.

Further reading

Craig, T. (1996) "The Japanese Beer Wars: Initiating and Responding to Hypercompetition in New Product Development," *Organization Science* 7(3): 302–21.

TIM CRAIG

Koike, Kazuo

Koike (1932–) is the most influential labor economist in postwar Japan. His contributions to the field of labor research lie mainly in three areas: economic development, industrial relations theory and the economics of skill formation.

Koike has bitterly criticized the popular theories of Japan's economic development, especially the unlimited supply of labor and the dualist approach to Japanese industrial organization. He advocates the latecomer theories of economic development proposed by Alexander Gerschenkron and Ronald **Dore**.

Japan began to industrialize one hundred years after the UK. The lack of strong craft unionism as a result of late industrialization encouraged the internalization of the labor market and fostered the development of **enterprise unions**. The distinction between blue-collar and white-collar almost disappeared in postwar Japan. Koike conceptualized this development as "white-collarization of blue-collar."

Koike's most important contribution lies in the economic analysis of on-the-job-training (OJT) and career development. The recent progress of information technology requires OJT-based, more intelligent skills which can be formed through intra-firm career development.

Further reading

Koike, K. (1977) *The Economics of Work in Japan*, Tokyo: LTCB International Library Foundation.
—— (1988) *Understanding Industrial Relations in Japan*, London: Macmillan.
Koike, K. and Inoki, T (1991) *Skill Formation in Japan and Southeast Asia*, Tokyo: Tokyo University Press.

SUSUMU HAGIWARA

Komiya, Ryutaro

Ryutaro Komiya (1928–), professor at Aoyama Gakuin University and emeritus professor at University of Tokyo, is one of the leading Japanese international economists. He served as the director of MITI /Research Institute of International Trade and Industry from 1987–97. He has argued that the cause of the large trade surplus of Japan is not due to the exclusive nature of the Japanese markets toward imports but due to the fact that the amount of saving exceeds investment. He also argues that the situation of the United States is just the opposite, and if the United States does not adopt a policy of increasing the saving rate, managed trade measures to correct the imbalance are meaningless. Furthermore, he believes that the Maekawa Report, which made a formal commitment to the right of the Japanese to maintain a trade surplus, was a mistake.

Further reading

Ryutaro, K. (1990) *The Japanese Economy: Trade, Industry, and Government*, Tokyo: University of Tokyo Press.

SUMIHIRO TAKEDA

konbini

Konbini (convenience stores) constitute a dynamic segment of the Japanese **retail industry** that has a major impact on distribution channels for food and daily necessities and, increasingly, for products and services based on information technology. They are a ubiquitous presence on the urban Japanese landscape and an iconic trend in popular sociology. Convenience stores were introduced to Japan from the United States in the 1970s, and the term *konbini*, a contraction of "convenience," first gained popularity around 1990.

Konbini are medium-sized, brightly-lighted, streamlined shops, usually open twenty-four hours a day and generally located in high-traffic sites. The stores sell ready-to-eat and simple packaged foods, beverages, magazines, toiletries, and basic household goods. Initially, *konbini* were popular primarily with young adults and commuters, but their appeal has spread widely and their numbers have grown enormously.

There currently are estimated to be over 40,000 *konbini* throughout Japan, many of them franchised stores affiliated with large national chains. Several of these chains have thousands of outlets, including the largest chain 7-11 (over 8,000 stores), Lawson's, Family Mart, Circle-K, and am-pm. *Konbini*s first carved out their niches as purveyors of take-out food, snacks, beverages, and magazines, but their repertoire has expanded enormously. They have become general stores – touted as "lifestyle centers" – for young, mobile, free-spending Japanese consumers. Current *konbini* staples include computer software; copying and fax services; music CDs; postage stamps and telephone cards; tokens for toll expressways; ordering flowers for delivery; and rail and airline reservations.

Food remains their mainstay, however. *Konbini* benefit from long-established patterns in Japanese shopping behavior – frequent shopping trips for small quantities – which reflects some combination of consumer preference for fresh food products with practical limitations on domestic storage space in densely populated Japanese cities. Traditionally urban neighborhoods were dotted with small-scale shops that enabled residents to shop quickly, often, and close to home. *Konbini* are heir to this shopping and retailing pattern. *Konbini* derive one-third of their sales from the sale of box lunches (*bento*) and prepared foods, according to statistics reported in October 2000 by the Ministry of Economics, Trade and Industry (METI, formerly Ministry of International Trade and Industry, MITI). Packaged foods, beverages, and snacks account for another third. Magazines, media, and services make up the final third of their sales. Electronic services constitute only about 4 percent of total sales, but this is the fastest growing segment, increasing approximately 10 per cent over the previous year. Sales for top-of-the-line *konbini* locations average approximately ¥600,000 per day.

During the enduring Japanese economic slump since the late 1980s, *konbini* chains have increased their market share *vis-à-vis* other categories of large-scale retailers such as supermarket chains and **department stores**. In 2000, the *konbini* retail sector had an estimated sales volume of ¥6 trillion, roughly 70 per cent of the total sales of department stores and 40 per cent of supermarket sales. Profit margins for *konbini* tend to be higher than those for other large-scale retailers.

Some national *konbini* chains are subsidiaries of major retail corporations. 7-11, for example, is owned by **Ito-Yokado**, a major supermarket and discount chain which itself purchased the Southland Corporation, the US founder and disseminator of the franchise. Lawson's, the second largest Japanese *konbini* chain, is owned by another major supermarket and discount retailer, **Daiei**. An initial reason why large-scale retailers actively developed *konbini* was as a strategy to work around the restrictions on the size and scale of retail stores (under the **Large Retail Store Law**) which effectively prevented the expansion of supermarkets and department stores into many commercial districts and most residential neighborhoods. The small size of *konbini* (usually well under 100 square meters) set them outside the scope of the restrictive law, and major retailing firms were able to engineer ultra-sophisticated distribution and inventory systems appropriate to dense networks of small-scale outlets.

7-11, in particular, is noted for pioneering a retail "**just-in-time**" distribution and inventory system, which relies on deliveries daily or more often. Their system incorporates sophisticated real-time point-of-sale data collection for inventory control and ordering, as well as consumer analysis and market forecasting. The aggressive use of information technology by *konbini* has also enabled the major chains to become major providers of a wide (and increasingly wider) range of electronic services. *Konbini* provide automated teller machines; process many kinds of routine bill payments for utilities and insurance companies; make reservations and sell tickets for concerts, sports events, and travel; operate as drop-off and delivery points for express services (*takkyubin*); and download software updates for consumers. *Konbini* have developed a pivotal role in **e-commerce**, through links made with major Japanese manufacturers and merchandisers. *Konbini* serve as a customer's point for picking up and paying for products that consumers order over the internet directly from other companies. The advantages for consumers are that they do not have to use a credit card over the internet and that they can arrange for delivery at a time and place convenient for their daily commute.

In response to government mandated social welfare programs, one major chain has developed a system for daily deliveries of meals to senior citizens. Government agencies are considering possibilities for distributing bureaucratic forms to the general public and accepting routine information, such as social services applications, via *konbini* networks.

The extensive technological know-how and infrastructure provided by large *konbini* chains has been a critical factor in their successful marketing of franchises to local business people, many of whom have converted old-line specialized retail shops – corner grocers, rice shops, or liquor stores – into *konbini*. Small-scale family owned shops have been a major feature of the urban retail, wholesale, and service sectors for generations. Many family-owned businesses occupy valuable commercial locations, but in the past generation this small-scale sector of the economy has faced enormous labor difficulties, between the aging of the population engaged in family enterprises and the reluctance of children to follow in parental footsteps and take over the businesses. *Konbini* therefore offer many small-scale family businesses a good opportunity to capitalize on real estate assets and to retain ownership of a local business, much of the management of which is embedded in the technical know-how and efficiently engineered distribution systems of the large franchise chains (see **distribution system**). These systems reduce the need for hands-on management by local proprietors and enable the stores to be operated largely with relatively low-cost, low-skilled labor. Many stores rely to a great extent on part-time labor, for example from college students and housewives.

Konbini have become a major social phenomenon in their own right, and there is an enormous amount of pop sociological analysis of their impact and appeal. Some critics of *konbini* see them as garishly intrusive shops that destroy local retail competitors and push aside local production and distribution networks in favor of highly centralized major corporations. This economic trend has the side effect of hollowing out the social infrastructure of regional and community life. Other opponents see *konbini* as purveyors of a highly impersonal popular culture of consumption that especially targets alienated teenagers and young adults. Still other detractors decry the impact of *konbini* on nutrition and cuisine: the pejorative term "*konbini* housewives" labels young women who lack culinary skills and depend on the ready-made dishes of their local convenience stores.

Regardless of the criticisms, *konbini* have clearly established themselves as a major category of Japanese retailing, with wide consumer appeal and a significant impact on future developments in merchandising and services. They appear well-positioned to continue to expand their influence.

THEODORE BESTOR

Kyocera

Kyocera Corporation was originally founded as Kyoto Ceramics Ltd. in April 1959 by Dr. Kazuo **Inamori** and seven colleagues as a company specializing in fine ceramic components. Today, it is the world leader in the manufacture of fine ceramic components, semiconductor components (circuit boards), electronic components (liquid crystal displays, LCD), information equipment (printers), telecommunication equipment (cellular phones) and optical equipments (single-lens reflex).

Most of Kyocera's growth is due to mergers and acquisitions. Some of its subsidiaries include Kyocera International Inc., which was established in the United States in 1969 as a sales company, Feldmuhle Kyocera Elektronische Bauelemente GmbH, a joint venture with Feldmuhle AG of West Germany to manufacture semiconductor packages, and Kyocera Hong Kong, which supplies electronic components and equipment to Southeast Asia. In 1979, Kyocera acquired Cybernet Electronics Corporation, a manufacturer of citizen-band radios and equipment, in order to expand the company's base outside of ceramic packaging. In 1988, as part of a major expansion to bolster overseas operations, Kyocera set up head offices in Asia, the United States, and Europe (based in Germany). Also in 1990, it spent $250 million to acquire Elco corporation, a maker of electrical connectors, and $560 million in 1991 to acquire AVX Corporation, a manufacturer of multi-layered ceramic and tantalum capacitors used in semiconductors, based in South Carolina. In 1995, it expanded into multimedia with the establishment of Kyocera Multimedia Corporation. Later the same year, it established Shanghai Kyocera Electronics Co. Ltd to manufacture electrical components in China. In 1996, it merged with Dongguan Shilong Kyocera Optics Co. Ltd to manufacture and sell consumer optical instruments such as cameras, lenses, and stroboscopes.

As of March 2000, Kyocera had 13,746 employees, capital of ¥115,703,320,000 and $7,779 million in sales. Its largest sectors in terms of sales are electronic equipment (33.4 percent), telecommunications equipment (20.7 percent) and semiconductor parts (18.8 percent) respectively. It is traded on the Tokyo, Osaka and New York stock exchanges.

DAYO FAWIBE

L

Large Retail Store Law, 1974

The *Large Scale Retail Store Law* (which was enacted in 1973 and took effect in 1974, was amended in 1978, and abolished in May 1998) was the latest in a succession of Japanese laws over the last sixty years that imposed bureaucratic obstacles to the establishment of large stores. The Department Store Act of 1937, which was suspended in 1947 and then reinstated in 1956, required approval of the national government (Ministry of Commerce and Industry, prewar/Ministry of International Trade and Industry, postwar) for the opening of new department stores anywhere in Japan. In 1974 the Large Scale Retail Store Law replaced the Department Store Act and made the extent of floor space of proposed stores, rather than the nature of the stores, the criterion for necessitating MITI approval. The cutoffs were 3,000m^2 in the largest cities and 1500m^2 everywhere else; in fact, almost all stores with more floor space than these cutoff limits had been department stores. In 1978 this law was completely revamped so as to broaden its coverage to include all proposed new stores with floor space above 500m^2. In May 1998, the Diet replaced the old law with a new one (actually with three new laws) that place all details of the regulation of large stores under the control of the prefectural governments. Some prefectures may enact more severe restraints on the opening of large stores, and others may remove the restraints altogether.

Prior to 1998, the process of securing MITI approval to open a large store was tortuous, and, if successful, typically required two years or longer from the time approval was first sought. The process involved hearings before local panels that included owners of existing stores whose businesses would have suffered if the particular proposed large store was established. These panels tended either to recommend against MITI approval or else propose restrictions on the hours or days of the week that a new large store could operate. In many cases they proposed onerous requirements such as the requirement that the large store offer classes in cultural activities like calligraphy or floral arrangement, at prices that failed to cover costs. MITI tended to adopt these recommendations and proposals. Consequently, following the adoption of the 1978 amendments to the Large Store Law, the number of applications to open new stores dropped to a mere trickle in 1984, with less than 500 applications for permission to open stores with floor space in excess of 500m^2 in all of Japan, a nation of 120 million persons (see Larke (1994) for the details of the process of gaining approval to open a new large store).

In 1989, the US government identified the Large Store Law as a "structural impediment" to the sale of US-made consumer products in Japan, arguing in trade negotiations with the government of Japan for repeal or relaxation of the law. Whatever the merits of the claim that expansion of the number of large stores in Japan would expand commercial opportunities for American businesses, the government of Japan did agree to expedite the process of approving the opening of large stores. But the law remained in force and the actual numbers of large stores showed little signs of increase. Then in 1998 the Diet repealed the Large

Store Law, in effect shifting control of such regulations to the prefectural governments (who may actually perpetuate similar restrictions to those embodied in the old law). The Large Store Law is the essential reason why Japan, at least for now, has far fewer department stores per person than the USA while at the same time it has far more of most other kinds of stores per person (McCraw and O'Brien 1986). Nevertheless, the Large Store Law and its antecedents are almost certainly not the fundamental basis for Japan's multiplicity of small stores.

The proliferation of retail stores benefits households but at the same time raises the logistical costs of the distribution sector itself. It is more costly to restock numerous small stores than a few large stores. Put differently, as stores proliferate some of the burden of transporting goods from point of production to point of consumption are shifted away from households and on to the distribution sector. Just how far such shifting will go depends upon the households' and distribution sector's relative efficiencies at storing and transporting goods. This is because new stores can be profitable only if the added benefits their presence confers are greater than their costs. Factors such as scarcity of living space, that raise all households' costs of storing goods lead households to offer higher price premia to retailers who locate closer to their dwellings. This makes a greater profusion of stores profitable. Similarly, factors that lower retailers' costs render it more profitable for them to accommodate households' preferences for shorter shopping trips and increase the profitability of a profusion of stores. Sorting out the various influences on Japan's density of retail stores which include the Large Store Law, scarcity of household storage space, geographic centricity, cost of maintaining personal vehicles, and population density requires careful statistical investigation. To this point there have been only a few such studies (Flath (1991), Potjes (1993), and Flath and Nariu (1996)), but their findings support the tentative conclusion that regulation matters less than the other factors just mentioned.

Government policies that transfer income encounter less strenuous political opposition if the deadweight losses they impose are small in relation to the net subsidy. Given that small stores are already ubiquitous in Japan for the reasons mentioned in the previous paragraph, regulations that protect small stores from competition by large stores imply only small economic distortions and encounter little effective resistance. If small stores did not already predominate, the Large Store Law could not have survived in Japan's political marketplace. Geographic factors in the USA have favored large chain stores, and slanted the political marketplace in favor of regulations that benefit them instead. Government limitations on large stores can survive the give-and-take of political competition in Japan but not in the USA. For local zoning that favors large stores over small ones the reverse is true. In each case, regulation ends up exaggerating the inherent tendencies rather than fundamentally influencing them.

The Large Store Law of Japan and its antecedents have protected small stores from competition with larger ones. Government regulations in the USA have tended to favor large stores. Local zoning in almost every city in America has had the effect of separating residential and commercial activities, which promotes car ownership and favors large stores over smaller ones. Many scholars and others have correctly deplored Japan's Large Store Law as imposing unnecessary constraints on the marketing of goods in Japan, but have perhaps both exaggerated the extent to which Japan's marketing system reflects the heavy hand of government regulation, and overlooked the extent to which America's marketing system and those of other nations are also influenced by government regulations.

Japan's fragmented and complex distribution sector is uniquely suited to its own particular geography. The scarcity of living space in Japan, and the inconvenience of owning and operating a car, enhance Japanese households' willingness to pay for the added convenience of next-door shopping. And Japan's geographic centricity and highly developed transport system lower the costs of a distribution sector that accommodates this preference, a distribution sector having a proliferation of retail outlets that must be continually restocked through complex logistical arteries. These factors combine to make a proliferation of stores in Japan not only inevitable, but desirable. And given this, regulations like the Large Store

Law that protect small stores from competition by large ones imply only minor economic distortions and encounter little effective political resistance. The Large Store Law more reflected than shaped the structure of Japan's distribution sector.

References

Flath, D. (1991) "Why Are There So Many Retail Stores in Japan?" *Japan and the World Economy* 2: 365–86.

Flath, D. and Nariu, T. (1996) "Is Japan's Retail Sector Truly Distinctive?" *Journal of Comparative Economics* 23: 181–91.

Larke, R. (1994) *Japanese Retailing*, London: Routledge.

McCraw, T.K. and O'Brien, P. (1986) "Production and Distribution: Competition Policy and Industrial Structure," in T.K. McCraw (ed.), *America Versus Japan: A Comparative Study*, Boston: Harvard Business School Press, 77–116.

Potjes, J.C.A. (1993) *Empirical Studies in Japanese Retailing*, Tinbergen Institute Research Series no. 41, Amsterdam: Thesis Publishers.

DAVID FLATH

Liberal Democratic Party

As the dominant political party of Japan, the Liberal Democratic Party (LDP), known in Japanese as Jiyu Minshu To or simply Jiminto, has been in power throughout the post-Second World War era except for two brief periods. It was established in 1955 as the result of a merger between the Democratic Party (DP) led by Ichiro Hatoyama, the then prime minister, and a dissident group of the Liberal Party (LP) led by Shigeru Yoshida, Hatoyama's predecessor. The party was largely meant to be an anti-socialist coalition, as socialist candidates had won more and more seats of the House of Representatives in the successive elections in 1952, 1953, and 1955. The establishment of the LDP was prompted by the reunification of the Social Democratic Party (SDP), the largest socialist party, which had split in 1951.

In the second half of the 1950s, the LDP consisted of two major groups. Most of the former DP members had been in politics since the prewar period, and tended to be critical of the new constitution drafted in 1947. As they outnumbered the former LP members, the new party's platform called for constitutional reforms, which contributed to the "reactionary" and "right-wing" character of the LDP. In contrast, the former LP members were generally more consenting to the new constitution, under which they had started their political careers.

The postwar political structure of Japan is sometimes referred to as a two-party system controlled by the LDP and the SDP, or the "1955 regime." In fact, however, it was an exemplary model of the predominant-party system, consistent with the definition laid out by Giovanni Sartori, a leading Italian political scientist. The LDP secured the position of the first party in all general elections for more than three decades (1958–90), and stayed in power throughout the period of Japan's **economic growth** and **bubble economy**. Its defeat in the general elections in 1993 put the party, for the second time in its history, in opposition. But the next year the LDP came back to power in a coalition government with its arch-rival the SDP, and has managed to stay as the central force of successive coalition governments since then.

However, the end of the Cold War makes it extremely difficult for the LDP to retain its initial, and essential, identity as an anti-socialist coalition. Being created as the central pivot against the danger of socialist revolution, and almost nothing else, the LDP has become a catch-all party. The party was split in 1993 precisely because of different ideologies among members.

Leaders and achievements

Ichiro Hatoyama was elected the first president (*Sosai*) of the LDP in 1956. As the prime minister since December 1954, he wished to reverse his aristocratic predecessor Yoshida's pro-US foreign policies. One result was the termination of the belligerent status between the former USSR, with which diplomatic relations were normalized in 1956. On the other hand, Hatoyama tried, and failed, to revise the constitutional clause, Article Nine, that calls for the abandonment of arms.

After a brief interval, Nobusuke Kishi, who as a

leading official had been purged on suspicion of being a war criminal, took office in 1957. Kishi also was critical of Yoshida's foreign policies but, as his nickname *Ryogishi* (literally, "both-sided") indicated, he was a genuine realist. He aimed at what he thought would be the real independence of Japan, free from the US influences in the sphere of international politics, and adopted pro-US policies precisely for this reason. The Japan-US security treaty, concluded by Yoshida in 1951, provided no duty on the part of the US military forces based in Japan to protect it, which, from the prewar politician's viewpoint, was an offense to Japan's sovereignty.

However, if Kishi wanted an equal partnership with the USA, Japan would be obliged to accept a reciprocal obligation to assist the USA in case of war, but use of military means is explicitly denied by the 1947 constitution. Kishi's goal then became to revise both the constitution and the security treaty with the USA.

Not only the SDP and **Sohyo**, the largest labor organization at that time, but many ordinary citizens, still living with wartime memories, rejected Kishi's idea. On May 19, 1960, Kishi suddenly resorted to a forcible voting motion for ratification of the new security treaty with the USA. The news made headlines nationwide and violent demonstrations took place demanding his resignation and rejection of the treaty. After a few days, during which the Diet was surrounded by tens of thousands of protestors, the new treaty was ratified, but Kishi was forced to resign.

His successor, Hayato Ikeda, was also a former high-ranking official, but a faithful disciple of the so-called "Yoshida School". Yoshida, his political teacher, had served as prime minister under the occupation of Japan by the General Headquarters and the Supreme Commander of Allied Powers (GHQ/SCAP), instituted the 1947 constitution and concluded the peace treaty at San Francisco, as well as the former security treaty, although he rejected the idea of rearmament of the country. Yoshida had put more emphasis on postwar recovery. It was he who brought Ikeda and his aides, Masayoshi Ohira and Kiichi Miyazawa, into political careers and advised them on various occasions. Ikeda launched the famous **income doubling plan**, but at the same time introduced a new style of premiership described as "taking a low profile" or "tolerance and patience." His administration put aside the constitutional revision and honored the new security treaty with the USA, but built up *de facto* military strength. Ikeda is generally regarded as the statesman who established the postwar Japanese conservative politics. Japan enjoyed the economic growth throughout the 1960s, which consolidated LDP's position as the ruling party.

Ikeda's successor, Eisaku Sato, was in office for seven years and eight months, the longest premiership in postwar Japan. Sato was also a graduate from the "Yoshida School," but a younger brother of Kishi by birth. The fact made him a personification of the two founding parties' ideologies (LP and DP). Sato's premiership was described as the politics of waiting, as he usually did not wish to intervene with sensitive political issues and preferred to wait until the opportunity ripened. But Sato was a shrewd manipulator of appointments. He placed his confidential fellow politicians in cabinet posts and the principal party posts, in order to have them carry out what he wished.

One of the few issues on which Sato took an initiative was the return of Okinawa from US governance, which he deemed as his most important task. Already Yoshida, his teacher in politics, and his natural brother Kishi had provided him with examples to follow: the principle of give and take. Yoshida extended help to the USA in the first half of 1950s, when it badly needed behind the front-lines activities supporting its war efforts in the Korean Peninsula. Kishi also supported the USA when it was challenged by the USSR with supremacy in rocket technologies in the latter half of the 1950s. In the 1960s, Sato firmly supported the US commitments to Vietnam, and Okinawa was returned to Japan in 1972. However, some problems were left untouched, such as the suspected secret agreement with the USA that allows the bringing of nuclear weapons into Japanese territory in cases of emergency.

In the 1972 presidential election held within the LDP, Kakuei **Tanaka** defeated Takeo Fukuda. By then, many Japanese had grown weary of prime ministers who came from the elite central bureaucracy such as Kishi, Ikeda, and Sato. In this regard Fukuda, a graduate of the University of Tokyo and a former **Ministry of Finance** official, was not an attractive candidate in popular eyes. Tanaka, who had held a seat in the House of Representatives since he was first elected at the age of twenty-nine in 1947, was an experienced politician. Such prominent statesmen of the "Yoshida School" as Yoshida himself, Ikeda, and Sato had trained him in politics. But the fact that he had graduated only from an elementary school and had been in business in civil works contracting presented a sharp contrast to the profiles of established political figures.

Tanaka's premiership was heralded at first, as it symbolized postwar Japan where the prewar feudalistic social restraints no longer applied and democratic values, as well as equality of economic opportunities regardless of one's birth or origin, were a reality. Although a score of prime ministers after Tanaka were again from the central bureaucratic circles (Fukuda, Ohira, and Miyazawa), the image of the Japanese prime minister changed irrevocably with Tanaka. Thanks partly to his talent for oratory, Tanaka enjoyed popularity for most of his term, but his politics were always accompanied with an image of plutocracy. His approach was, critics said, centered on raising and distributing money in order to make political gains such as winning elections and forming and maintaining his faction; in short, a money politics. His greatest achievement was the normalization of relations with the People's Republic of China in 1972. Despite this diplomatic success, he is generally regarded as the one who coined the legacy of money in Japanese politics.

Tanaka's term was two years and five months. The oil shock shattered his ambitious policy of economic expansion. In December 1974 he resigned due to financial scandals. Two years later, suspected of accepting bribes from Lockheed Corporation, he was charged with violation of foreign exchange regulations. Although found guilty, Tanaka retained a strong political influence until he died in 1985.

During the 1970s and 1980s, the LDP continued to remain in power under successive presidents. After Tanaka, Takeo Miki, Fukuda, Zenko Suzuki, Yasuhiro Nakasone, and Noboru Takeshita held the post of prime minister, each for about two years. Exceptionally, Nakasone was in

office for five years, from 1982–7. Until 1985 Tanaka and his loyal members of parliament, called the "Army of Tanaka," exerted decisive influence in choosing LDP presidents, hence the prime ministers of Japan. The credo of the Tanaka faction was, as they themselves advocated, that holding a majority meant holding power. The LDP managed to rule Japan as the economy shifted from one of high growth to one of slow growth.

In hindsight, many Japanese tend to regard the 1990s as a "lost" decade, filled with legacies of money but devoid of agenda. Not only the LDP but its archrival the SDP and other new parties were suspected of being incapable of guiding the nation to overcome the social and economic challenges that have arisen since the collapse of the bubble economy. A question, then, is why the LDP has lost its dominant role. This question, in turn, leads to another: why did the LDP succeed in riding out the economic ups and downs and social changes throughout the postwar period? As an old adage goes, the cause of LDP's failure lies in its very success.

LDP power structure

There are four main reasons for the LDP's long governance. Firstly, the opposition, especially the SDP, was, and still probably is, weak and never really ready to be in power. Secondly, the long history of the LDP as the ruling party provided a strong reason for the electorate to vote for its candidates.

Thirdly, the LDP was the only party fit to the medium constituency system. Under this system, the country was divided into 130 districts, where on average four members of parliament were elected. Since the House of Representatives consisted of 512 seats, it required a party aiming for an absolute majority to nominate more than two candidates in all districts. Only the LDP was able to gather that number of candidates.

On the other hand, however, more than two candidates with the same party affiliation had to contest with each other in the same constituency. One difference between the LDP candidates lay in affiliations to factions within the LDP, not the party itself. The LDP was, and still is, composed of five or six factions. Election campaigns were run by factions and candidates' local supporters organizations, but not by the party itself. Another difference lay in the candidates' popularity among the voters, which it was critical to win. Typically, each potential candidate, regardless of whether he or she were actually seated in the parliament, would be present at every ceremonial occasion to "sell" their face with a gratuity (now illegal), called **giri**. When elected, members belonging to a faction asked their boss to approach the ministries and agencies on behalf of their local supporters, called **nemawashi**. The boss, in need of the party members' votes when he would run for the LDP presidency, accordingly approached bureaucrats and assisted his followers' supporters looking for subsidies to build bridges, roads, railways, and so on.

This method of systematically canvassing for votes is said to have been developed by Tanaka. But this system required much money to be spent by politicians, not supporters. For example, members of parliament hired, at their own expenses, private secretaries to be in charge of handling the various requests of their local supporters, or "clients." Since the late 1980s, LDP faction bosses one after another suffered from money scandals, which aroused indignation among the voters. In the face of demands for political and electoral reforms, the medium constituency system was replaced in 1994 with the single-member constituency system for 300 seats and the proportional representation system for the remaining 200 seats. Subsequent general elections, taking place in 1996 and in 2000, however, have not yet produced the two-party system that the reform had anticipated.

The fourth reason for the LDP's long governance was an "iron triangle" relationship between the LDP, the central bureaucracy, and business. At first, the LDP was an agrarian party. Newly created independent, small-scale farms provided strong support. The farmers' interest group, the National Federation of Agricultural Cooperative Associations (Nokyo), functioned as the most loyal election machine of the LDP, as well as an organ to promote the policies laid down by the Ministry of Agriculture, Forestry and Fishery. In return, LDP leaders ensured that the Ministry would extend various assistance to villages.

The same triangle can be found in every industrial sector. For example, the LDP and the **Ministry of International Trade and Industry** are closely connected with each other through the petrochemical industry, and the party holds a close relationship with the transportation industry, which is under the auspices of the Ministry of Transport. Business makes financial contributions to the party, which is useful in having the ministries and agencies grant licenses and promote policies fit to their needs. LDP gives aspirant bureaucrats a chance of becoming a statesman. This system, however, often works to protect vested interests that are in search of an executive's help to be shielded from free competition (referred to as "convoy guard practices"). In this regard, the LDP is neither liberal nor democratic, but may be similar to a social democratic party, which stands by the weak.

Such a system will not survive as Japan enters the age of global mega-competition, which requires openness and fairness. The LDP also faces changes in the nation's social and demographic structure. If the LDP clings to its traditional old "customers" in local areas, it will run the risk of being rejected by new potential clients, especially the urban electorate. If the LDP regards the latter as important, the former will no longer regard the party as their representative. The party today faces an unprecedented dilemma.

Further reading

Curtis, G.L. (1971) *Election Campaigning Japanese Style*, New York: Columbia University Press; trans. S. Yamaoka as *Daigishi no Tanjo* (Birth of a Politician), Tokyo: Saimarushuppankai, 1971.

Hayasaka, S. (1993) *Oyaji to Watashi* (Reminiscences of Kakuei Tanaka), Tokyo: Shuueisha.

Ishikawa, M. (1995) *Sengo Seijishi* (Political History of Post-War Japan), Tokyo: Iwanami Shoten.

Sato, S. and Matsuzaki T. (1986) *Jiminto Seiken* (LDP in Power), Tokyo: Chuuoukouronsha.

TSUTOMU TSUZUKI

liberalization of financial markets

The liberalization of financial markets involves the introduction of greater **competition** into the financial system. In general, therefore, the liberalization process centers on abolishing or relaxing regulations that stifle competition. In the early stages of industrialization, a nation's financial system tends to be particularly vulnerable and countries typically place heavy regulation or controls on the movement and investment of capital. As a nation's financial system develops and the national economy becomes increasingly integrated into the global economy, however, the costs and benefits of heavy regulation change, and controls stifling competition tend to be dismantled. Politics and the structure of political and administrative institutions play a critical role in the timing and nature of the reform process.

Competition-suppressing characteristics of Japan's financial system

Japan had a relatively laissez-faire financial system in the 1930s. In the immediate postwar period, however, the Japanese financial market was heavily regulated as a means of promoting economic reconstruction and growth. Japanese authorities established a system intended to promote financial system stability and facilitate the allocation of scarce capital from the private sector to the corporate sector, and to critical industries in particular. This system had a number of characteristics that suppressed free market-based competition.

One of the most prominent features of this system was the presence of numerous price controls. Artificially low interest rates on loans regulated the cost of capital for industry. At the same time, the Interest Rate Control Act of 1947 capped interest rates on deposits at below market rates, thereby guaranteeing banks significant profit margins on making loans. Interest rate regulations also applied to the bond-issue markets.

Importantly, these price controls took place on a backdrop of capital controls. Under the Foreign Exchange and Control Law, the government limited cross-border financial transactions. In their international financial dealings, Japanese banks faced restrictions on their net foreign exchange positions, on the banks' issuance of certificates of deposit abroad, on the amounts of foreign assets held by institutional investors, and on long-term Euroyen loans. Only a single bank – the **Bank of**

Tokyo – was permitted to engage in foreign exchange transactions.

Segmentation of the financial system also stifled competition. Not only was the banking and securities business legally divided, but banks were also subdivided into ordinary, trust, long-term credit, and foreign exchange banks. Crossing over into other areas of business was strictly prohibited, as were financial holding companies. Other regulations also served to offer support for bank-centered financing over the development of **capital markets**.

Strict limits on market entry and exit furthermore stifled competition. The **Ministry of Finance** (MOF) rarely issued new licenses for banks, brokerages, or insurance companies and kept a tight lid on the expansion of retail branches. A so-called "convoy approach" to regulation at the same time ensured that no actor moved forward so fast as to leave another actor behind. Financial institution failure was circumvented by the government's implicit guarantee of all banks and its arrangement for "rescue mergers" in cases of dire financial institution distress.

These formal regulations were not the only impediments to competition, however. In fact, much of financial system regulation was informal in nature. **Administrative guidance** – that is, extra-legal directives given by government authorities to companies – was one of the most prominent features of regulation of the financial sector. These directives also helped ensure that competition never became "excessive."

Pressures for liberalization

Many of the regulations that served to protect and stabilize the Japanese banking system in the early postwar years became obstacles to efficiency as time progressed. Pressures for the liberalization of Japanese financial markets began to emerge in the 1970s, and continued to rise in the decades thereafter. These pressures arose primarily in response to changing opportunity structures for domestic actors – both public and private – and to pressures from abroad.

As large Japanese firms became internationally active, they were able to circumvent high bank fees by raising funds abroad. By the 1970s, many multinational corporations procured funds in the Euromarkets rather than borrowing from banks. Thus, at the wholesale end, banks had incentives to support deregulation. In the area of retail banking, however, deregulation was slower because bank customers had fewer exit options. Nonetheless, with many more assets to invest and the threat of a loss to purchasing power which inflation in the 1970s had brought, Japanese firms and households became increasingly more sensitive to interest rate levels. By the late 1980s, the MOF had begun to allow interest rates on deposits to approach market levels.

Increased budget deficits in the 1970s also placed pressure on authorities to liberalize financial markets, as the financial system was hard-pressed to absorb increasing amounts of public debt in the absence of liberalized bond markets. The city (large commercial) banks played a large role in underwriting government bond issues. When the volume of government bond issues was small, Japanese banks could absorb these issues. After the oil shocks, however, debt issues reached such a level that banks could no longer absorb government debt or tolerate the losses this entailed. Pressure on the government to change controls on Japan's capital markets thus emerged from the banking sector. In 1978, financial institutions were permitted to commence the sale of government bonds in the secondary market. Banks also pushed for the right to expand into a wider range of services and products and the **Banking Act of 1982** represented a move in this direction.

Through the US-Japan Yen-Dollar Committee of 1983–4 and other pressures on Japan for reciprocity, foreign pressure also played a role in propelling reforms in the direction of a more open financial system. The overseas activities of Japanese banks became increasingly prominent in the 1980s, while the virtual absence of foreign banks in Japan was likewise conspicuous. This disparity led the US government to complain that the Japanese financial market was closed and push for deregulation that would enable foreign banks to enter. The USA threatened to limit opportunities for Japanese banks in the USA if Japan failed to open up its domestic financial sector.

Impediments to financial liberalization

In these ways, fiscal deficits, profit pressures on banks, and foreign pressure served as impetus for the commencement of financial liberalization in Japan. Interests were divided within Japan over the pace of this liberalization, however. Politics would control the pace of the transformation, helping to make the Japanese process of financial liberalization distinctively slow in comparison to liberalization in other advanced industrial countries such as the USA or the UK. The Ministry of Finance was the primary arena for mediating pressures for change and deliberating reforms but its own organizational interests had become entrenched in this system. Thus, Japan's path of financial liberalization would reflect consideration of the ministry's own preferences, as well as the preferences of domestic industry and the industry's political advocates.

Because interest rate levels were integrally tied into profits of financial institutions, liberalization of interest rates could be expected to squeeze financial institution profits. This anxiety for banks, however, might have been relieved by permitting banks to engage in other areas of financial services and thereby shifting away from exclusive reliance on bank loan spreads as the primary basis for profit-making. Yet, granting banks permission to expand into new business areas – and into the securities business, in particular – drew strong protests from brokerages. Rather than moving forward with financial system reform, therefore, the ministry followed a less conflictual route of alleviating profit pressures through loose monetary policy. In the process, financial liberalization was replaced in the latter half of the 1980s by the inflation of a speculative asset bubble.

Japan's deposit insurance system was also poorly equipped to handle liberalization. The introduction of greater competition would inevitably mean the need to deal with some financial institution failures. Although a Deposit Insurance Corporation (DIC) had been established in 1971, it lacked sufficient funds to pay off depositors in even a second-tier regional bank. Yet, banks resisted the imposition of higher deposit insurance premiums, preferring instead to rely on informal ad hoc means of solving problems that they perceived to be less costly.

Big Bang financial reforms

As a result of the political impediments faced in the 1980s, the final stages of Japan's financial liberalization would be postponed until the 1990s and the first decade of the twenty-first century. The 1993 Financial System Reform Law allowed banks to enter the securities business in a limited way through subsidiaries but postponed their entry into stock trading. Far-reaching reforms would not take place until the emergence of political leadership and reform elements within the Finance Ministry.

In 1996, Prime Minister Ryutaro Hashimoto announced a plan to push forward with liberalization of the Japanese financial market. The reform program, nicknamed the "Japanese Big Bang," was touted to make Japan's financial system "fair, free, and global." The plan resembled in many respects the major reforms undertaken in the UK some years earlier. Commencing in 1998 and scheduled for completion in 2001, the reforms were intended to revitalize the Japanese economy by making the management of over 1,200 trillion yen in household financial assets more efficient. In essence, the Big Bang reflected the completion of the liberalization process begun – but delayed – in the 1980s.

The Big Bang reforms include three major components: the promotion of competition between the securities and banking markets, the improvement of Japan's capital market infrastructure, and the promotion of investor confidence in Japanese capital markets. The first goal required the liberalization of cross-border capital transactions – that is, the repeal of foreign exchange controls – and was carried out in April 1998. This goal also necessitated promotion of competition among various financial intermediaries and the promotion of competition in the domestic market.

Reforms taken to improve Japan's capital market infrastructure included the elimination of legal obstacles to securitization, the promotion of small business financing through the securities market, and the diversification of financial instruments used by corporations. Procedures for issuing securities have also been simplified and accounting standards reformed as well. Other integral measures include improvement of the settlement system and the implementation of tax reforms.

To promote greater investor confidence in Japanese capital markets, the Big Bang reforms have improved disclosure by financial institutions and the quality of supervision by regulators. Early warning systems designed to detect serious problems with asset quality before financial institutions reach the point of insolvency have also been introduced in the form of Prompt Corrective Action measures. Finally, the reforms aim to improve the safety net for depositors, investors, and insurance policyholders.

The heavy reliance on informal relations-based regulation over most of the postwar period means, however, that true liberalization also involves a redefinition of the relationship between financial firms and their regulator. Legislation implemented in April 2000 in the form of a new Ethics Law for National Public Civil Servants has helped effect this needed shift.

Implications of financial liberalization

The liberalization of Japanese financial markets – and the Big Bang financial reforms, in particular – have had a number of implications. Most notably, the ongoing liberalization has led to a surge in foreign direct investment into the Japanese financial sector. Liberalization has also effected changes in the relationships between banks and their borrowers, serving to further weaken the **main bank system** and encourage firms to diversify their sources of fund procurement. Finally, while liberalization has meant the need to reduce or eliminate profit-padding regulation, it has meant the need to establish new prudential regulations to ensure that financial institutions do not act recklessly with their newfound freedom.

Further reading

Hamada, K. and Horiuchi, A. (1987) "The Political Economy of the Financial Market," in K. Yamamura and Y. Yasuba (eds), *The Political Economy of Japan: The Domestic Transformation*, Stanford, CA: Stanford University Press, 223–60.

Toya, T. (2000) "The Political Economy of the

Japanese Financial Big Bang: Institutional Change in Finance and Public Policy Making," Ph.D. dissertation, Stanford University.

Vogel, S. (1996) *Freer Markets, More Rules: Regulatory Reform in Advanced Industrial Countries*, Ithaca, NY: Cornell University Press.

JENNIFER AMYX

lifetime employment

The lifetime employment system, known as *shushin koyo*, is well known as one of the "three sacred treasures" of Japanese management, the other two being the seniority system and company unions. Although lifetime employment is not actually protected by law, it is an institutionalized practice which is engrained in the industrial structure of the country. Lifetime employment refers to the widespread practice of employing salaried workers for the duration of their working life within the same company family. In some cases an annual contract is continuously renewed, but in the majority of cases an employment relationship is understood to be for an indefinite period, with nothing put into writing. This long-term relationship between company and employee is offered mainly to salaried, college-educated males who are recruited from university campuses each year in the springtime. The lifetime employment system does not extend itself to part-time, female, or non-salaried workers (often called peripheral workers) except in a few cases. However, even without the implicit contract of lifetime employment, most people expect to work for the same company for the duration of their career, reflecting the importance of group memberships and company affiliation in Japanese society.

For Japanese employers, the notion of lifetime employment is a practical way to solve labor shortage problems during economic expansions. For Japanese employees, it provides the job security they had long demanded through their enterprise unionization.

Studies of Japanese mobility suggest that implementing the lifetime employment system differs by organizational type and size. Some studies assume that lifetime employment is limited to large firms (at least 500 employees), suggesting that under 20 percent of industrial workers take part in the system.

The lifetime employment system is closely linked to the seniority system in Japan, or *nenko*. In the seniority system, the length of service (years working for the company) heavily determines both wage increases and promotions. Without a long-term employment relationship between the employee and company secured in some way, it would be impossible to maintain such a system. Thus, without lifetime employment, the seniority system would fail.

The lifetime employment system, as mentioned previously, is not offered to all workers in Japan. A dual structure of employment exists in which "core employees" are protected by the lifetime employment practice, but all other employees (often called "peripheral" or "non- regular") are not. These core employees are predominantly male university graduates who are expected to be the future managers and leaders of the organization. Education, training and employee development programs are most often designed exclusively for the "core employees." Thus, company investment is high for this "core" group of employees who will be retained for the extent of their working life.

The "peripheral" workforce includes all non-core employees, such as women, part-time, contract, junior college graduates, foreign employees and other "non-regular" hires. The peripheral workforce provides the labor flexibility the company requires to maintain its lifetime employment system for the core employees.

"Peripheral" employees do not have job or wage security, and thus are a more flexible feature of the Japanese employment system. Investment in peripheral employees is low, and when employment restructuring is necessary, the "peripheral" workforce is more easily adjusted. However, even with these "peripheral" workers the Japanese company maintains a level of long-term commitment much higher than its Western counterpart. Firing is difficult given that the role of the company is that of "caretaker" for the employee. Although peripheral workers are not endowed with the same rights and privileges as the core group, they still have a relatively high degree of job security compared to their Western counterparts.

The history of the lifetime employment system

In pre-First World War Japan, workers were highly mobile. The labor market was structured upon occupational skill and knowledge, not upon company affiliation. Differences in labor mobility depended upon whether or not the occupation was a traditional Japanese craft or based upon a Western-style skill. The wage system was based upon the classification of these occupations, and an individual worker would stay within the same wage classification as long as they stayed in the same job, regardless of their years of service. In this system, the only way to increase status or pay was to move jobs. Thus, if there was dissatisfaction with either the pay or the company, there was little disadvantage to moving. This ability to move around in order to increase one's individual wealth helped to strengthen a worker's self-respect and independence, making it difficult for employers to control their workforce. Thus, this system was good for the individual worker, but not necessarily the company.

In the post-First World War era, this system began to be replaced during a period of "rationalization" which centered around creating large enterprises capable of supporting the development of the Japanese economy and military. The government of Japan played an active role in the configuration of industry, management of organizations and development of human capital (labor). Production processes in large companies were divided into simplified jobs which made the old system of skilled labor unnecessary. Company personnel policies were developed to reflect the increasing focus on large enterprise development and workforce control, including the hiring and training of their own new labor force. The old system of masters training unskilled students was replaced with companies training unskilled new recruits, with the guarantee of lifetime job security in return for company loyalty. Company management assumed the responsibility for skill development, which was usually exclusive to the needs of the company. Therefore the laborers' skills became non-transferable. This system of skill development, along with long-term compensation packages which reflected increasing wages over time, effectively replaced the old system of highly mobile and independent labor.

After the Second World War, the *zaibatsu* (family group of companies) system was abolished under the new constitution and immediately replaced by an almost identical *keiretsu* family system of companies and shareholders. This system has been characterized as the "industrial policy model" in which government and business act together in order to meet societal economic goals (Abegglen and Stalk 1985). Within this system, Japanese companies began to operate at a much broader level to maintain their costly lifetime employment system by developing a two-tier wage system. In this system, higher wages would always go to the "core employees" (white-collar college graduate males) at the expense of "peripheral workers" (women, part-time, contract workers, retirees). Japanese companies used the foundation of commitment between employee and organization to structure a complete system of lifetime rewards (employment, security, bonus, retirement).

Over the period between 1914 and 1945, Japanese companies created the now famous Japanese management system, in which lifetime employment is a key feature. Although the lifetime employment system has never formally applied to more than 30 percent of the working population, it nevertheless is prevalent in most large companies today. Over the years, employees put in long hours and are loyal to their employers. In turn, their future is secure and income is adjusted to their needs. Salaries grow progressively, regardless of individual performance. Younger employees are underpaid, and older ones receive more than their contribution to the company.

This system has worked well for the past fifty years, as long as companies maintained high profits, strong export growth, and were able to hire a sufficient number of new university graduates every year. But this system is costly to maintain in a low-growth, highly competitive environment. Thus, the lifetime employment system has distinct advantages and disadvantages in today's competitive global business environment.

Advantages and disadvantages of the lifetime employment system

The lifetime employment system has distinct advantages for the company. First, it retains the services of employees in times of labor shortage. In this system, no matter what the market circumstances may be, there is little chance of the employee finding a better position outside of his current company. In addition, the company maintains optimal control over the individual and their training, career development and compensation. This reduces the high level of uncertainty and risk that comes with more fluid labor markets. Finally, the company is able to plan for the long term and invest in its human resources accordingly, allowing it to develop a strong future workforce.

For the employee, the system has the advantage of job security in times of labor surplus and commitment from the organization toward the future development of the employee's knowledge and skills. More importantly from a cultural perspective is the fact that the company provides the whole social existence, or community, from which employees derive their identity and their self-worth. As a community, the company exercises shared authority and control in a society based upon group norms and social structure.

Thus, the lifetime employment system provides many cushions both economically and socially. Layoffs are scarce, wages are steady on the whole (but can rise and drop dramatically for the individual who is either promoted, demoted or transferred outside the headquarters), and a constant source of human capital is readily available.

Challenges to lifetime employment

The lifetime employment system worked best in an environment of steady economic growth, limited imports and controlled competition. Recently, several factors have arisen which have had an impact on the lifetime employment system in Japan: the high yen, the collapse of Asian markets, the aging population, and increasing global competition.

During the 1990s, the strengthening yen forced Japanese companies to significantly increase the amount of their overseas investment, especially within Asia. Trade with other Asian nations now exceeds trade with Europe and the United States combined. Supported by the high yen, imports have risen significantly, exceeding export growth.

This has eroded the local profit margins which once helped Japanese companies finance their overseas expansion and fuel growth at home. Although Japanese companies were able to remain competitive, it made many jobs in Japan redundant. However, with an institutionalized long term employment system, it has been close to impossible to reduce labor costs by downsizing.

The second major factor to challenge the lifetime employment system has been the far-reaching effects of the collapse of Asian markets. Both the Japanese government and Japanese companies relied heavily on the strong growth in Southeast Asia during the 1980s and 1990s as a foundation to their global manufacturing systems. With the collapse of currencies and even whole markets (Indonesia), Japanese investments turned into losses. Japanese companies not only lost billions of yen, but were forced to cancel long-term investment projects, and in many cases, close down whole operations. In the short term this forced Japanese companies to repatriate thousands of overseas managers, and over the long term has resulted in widespread economic turmoil in Japan. Thus, an era of employment restructuring had finally begun in Japan.

A third challenge to the lifetime employment system is the aging workforce in Japan. There is now only one future worker for every two employees currently employed in Japan. This means that over time all institutions will be affected by a shortage of labor at one end, and a surplus of welfare recipients (retirees) at the other. When companies experience such a shortage within the lifetime employment structure, it means that they can no longer rely on the long term strategy of human resource development. Fewer workers will have to produce the higher output to remain competitive, which means increasing the skills and abilities of workers at a faster rate, and at the same time trying to control spiraling labor costs. Thus, the lifetime employment may have a negative effect on employee productivity and company performance.

Finally, the effect of global competition on the Japanese employment system has been to challenge the long-term nature of employee development. New technologies and the skills required to develop and manage them are all changing at increasingly rapid rates. Companies no longer have the luxury of slow, internally focused and incremental skill development for their employees. They will need to attract employees at all levels of the organization and be able to recruit the necessary knowledge, skills and abilities to remain competitive. The system of lifetime employment, which includes annual university recruiting and long-term seniority wages, may be too slow and inflexible to respond to the rapid change of the global marketplace.

The future of lifetime employment

Job changes in the labor market are becoming polarized, or in some cases, even more fragmented. Companies are creating smaller "cores" and increasing their peripheral workforce (specialists, irregular hires, and term hires). Jobs are diversifying and job change for peripheral workers is on the increase. Thus, some conclude that the lifetime employment system will slowly become a thing of the past.

Conclusion

The Japanese lifetime employment system has a long tradition in Japan. This system of long term commitment between employee and company serves as both social and economic foundation for the industrial system in Japan. However, this system may be changing in order for Japanese companies to adjust to contemporary market realities. There remains an open debate as to whether or not the positive aspects of this system will outweigh the negative when it comes to maintaining a competitive labor market for Japanese companies competing in the global economy.

Further reading

Abbeglen, J. and Stalk, G. (1985) *Kaisha: The Japanese Corporation*, New York: Basic Books.

Cheng, M. and Kalleberg, A. (1997) "How Permanent Was Permanent Employment?" Thousand Oaks, CA: Work and Occupations.

Clark, R. (1979) *The Japanese Company*, New Haven, CT: Yale University Press.

Hayashi, S. (1988) *Culture and Management in Japan*, Tokyo: University of Tokyo Press.

Inohara, H. (1990) *Human Resource Development in Japanese Companies*, Tokyo, Japan: Asian Productivity Organization.

Ministry of Labor (1994) *White Paper on Labor: Tasks for Enriching Working Life Based on Stable Employment*, Tokyo, Japan: Japan Institute of Labor.

Okimoto, D. and Rohlen, T. (1988) *Inside the Japanese System*, Stanford, CA: Stanford University Press.

Okuchi, K., Karsh, B. and Levine, S. (1988) *The Japanese Employment Relations System*, New York: Routledge.

MARGARET TAKEDA

localization

Localization is known as *genchika* in Japanese. One meaning of localization refers to the gathering of as many production facilities at one geographical location as possible in order to increase efficiency. Usually, however, *genchika* is used in the context of the international management practices of Japanese multinational corporations that have overseas sales and production subsidiaries. Often such overseas subsidiaries operate under the aegis and direct control of their parent company in Japan. *Genchika*, on the other hand, refers to loosening the control of the parent company, so that the subsidiary becomes more independent in order to be regarded in the host country as a local rather than a foreign company. The *genchika* process consists of the following three elements: an increase in the percentage of local capital, an increase in the supply of raw and industrial materials for production within the host country, and the appointment of native managers to top posts.

With the rapid postwar economic development, many big Japanese corporations became multinational and began to do business all over the world. Much of their investment has been in Asia, North America and Western Europe. In general, *genchika* has been encouraged by pressure from the host countries, not by the internal motivation of Japanese corporations themselves.

In Asia, many nations gained their independence from Japan after the Second World War and had to develop their own economies. At first, these nations had strong protectionist policies to protect their natural resources and native businesses from the inflow of products from advanced nations. However, in order to modernize, they opened their gates to foreign multinationals in an effort to utilize foreign capital and advanced technology for their own national economy. Developing nations in Asia invited multinational corporations of advanced nations, including Japan, to set up local subsidiaries. Japanese multinationals established both sales and production subsidiaries because both cheap labor and developing markets were available to them.

In terms of capital, developing nations in Asia have demanded that foreign companies establish joint ventures with native investors. They have also demanded an increase in the local supply of production materials. The same is true for human resources. Asian nations expect foreign companies to develop native technicians and also to appoint native managers to high posts.

In general, *genchika* by Japanese multinationals has advanced significantly in terms of capital and production materials in Asia. In these two aspects, Japanese multinationals have met the laws and expectations of the host nations. But when it comes to personnel management, very few Japanese multinationals have opened their doors for native employees to take top executive posts. In the vast majority of Japanese multinationals, Japanese men who are sent directly from the parent companies in Japan have occupied the highest posts. Japanese multinationals have been very reluctant to have local people as top managers in their subsidiaries, because the parent companies fear that locals will not be as obedient as Japanese managers.

The fact that Japanese multinationals have been reluctant to appoint local people as top managers in Asia has nothing to do with Japanese prejudice against non-Japanese Asians. The same is true of Japanese multinationals in North America and Europe, although the background of *genchika* in those areas is somewhat different.

Japanese corporations' multinationalization in North America, especially in the USA, and Europe was largely driven by protectionist sentiment in those nations based on trade friction. Ever since the late 1960s, Japan has maintained a positive balance of trade with the USA, and the gap has increased enormously up to the present. Therefore, Japan has imposed restrictions on its exports to the USA. In the 1970s, Japan restricted the export of textiles and color televisions, and in the 1980s of automobiles, semiconductors and manufacturing machinery. Thus, a major motivation for establishing local production and sales subsidiaries for most Japanese companies was retaining market share in the USA.

Unlike their Asian subsidiaries, there were very few Japanese factories in North America before 1975, but since the late 1970s, the number has shot up like "bamboo shoots after rain." The Plaza Agreement in 1985 especially accelerated this tendency as the value of the yen rose drastically after the agreement. In addition, the long-lasting recession of the US economy in the 1970s and 1980s, and the accompanying de-industrialization of the USA provided an atmosphere of welcome for Japanese companies. At the turn of the twenty-first century, more than 600,000 Americans are employees in Japanese subsidiaries in the USA.

Japanese corporations' multinationalization in Europe was also driven by the same motivation, retaining market share in the face of a protectionist tendency. However, this tendency is reinforced by the historic unity of the European Union among Western European countries.

The three aspects of *genchika* in the USA and Europe display a pattern that is slightly different from that in Asia. In both the USA and Europe, there is little restriction on the percentage of capital, so Japanese companies can own 100 percent of their subsidiaries. However, just as in Asia, a certain percentage of production materials must be sourced locally; in the USA, this is in order to comply with what are known as "local contents" laws. As for the personnel issue, there is a strong expectation from local employees in the USA and Europe that the top managers be native people. However, Japanese parent companies remain very reluctant to hire non-Japanese local employees as top executives. The parent companies assume that local people are hard to control and less obedient because they do not know the inner working of the parent company. On the other hand, local employees who are not familiar with how Japanese management works, tend to assume that the subsidiary president and all top managers should be natives. This view fails to recognize how drastically subsidiary management would be affected by such a change.

Although *genchika* consists of such elements as capital, supply of local materials and human resources, the concept can also include other aspects such as the transfer of management know-how cross-nationally. Host nations and the local employees do not necessarily expect foreign corporations to operate just like a local company. If they sense that there is a "better" element in the foreign approach to management, they naturally want it to be retained in the local subsidiary.

Research (Sumihara 1999) in a Japanese-owned subsidiary in North America suggests that both Japanese expatriates and American employees refer to *genchika* or localization as a "good mixture of Japanese and American management," although they did not reach an agreement on what a "good mixture" is. As a reflection of this thinking, some American employees were sent to the parent company in Japan for over a year in order to become familiar with how the parent company operates. In other words, the concept of *genchika* may even include socializing natives into the company's Japanese way of doing things.

Further reading

Sumihara, N. (1999) "Roles of Knowledge and 'Cross-Knowledge' in Creating a Third Culture: An Example of Performance Appraisal in a Japanese Corporation," in S. Beechler and A. Bird (eds), *Japanese Multinationals Abroad: Individual and Organizational Learning*, New York: Oxford University Press, 92–106.

NORIYA SUMIHARA

Long-Term Credit Bank of Japan

The Long-Term Credit Bank of Japan (LTCB) was a government-run, long-term credit bank in Japan. LTCB was established in 1952 as a semi-governmental institution. It succeeded the long-term financial business of Nihon Kangyo Bank and

Hokkaido Takushoku Bank. After becoming a private financial institution in 1961, LTCB emphasized offering large amounts of capital for investment by the heavy chemical industry. The LTCB also contributed to the modernization of medium-sized and small businesses. LTCB raised funds by selling debentures.

During its high growth period of the 1970s, the LTCB expanded its business to include the financing of social development projects, such as resource and energy projects. The LTCB also began expanding its activities to include international finance and the security business. During this period, it opened overseas branches in London, New York, and Los Angeles. In the 1980s, the LTCB opened branches in Asian markets such as Singapore and Hong Kong, while diversifying even more into mergers and acquisitions and even aviation finance.

During the slowdown of the Japanese economy in the 1990s, the LTCB emphasized expansion of its business to security and derivatives trading and infrastructure development. The LTCB supported the overseas expansion of Japanese companies, but also encouraged foreign companies to enter the Japanese and Asian markets. In 1997, the LTCB entered into an alliance with Swiss Bank, and began an investment bank business. But, in October 1998 LTCB failed due to bad loans totaling ¥5 trillion ($46 billion) and was temporarily nationalized by an emergency act of parliament. The LTCB was then sold in February 1999 for ¥121 billion to a consortium led by the US-based Ripplewood Holdings and renamed and relaunched to become Shinsei (meaning "rebirth") Bank in June 2000.

Further reading

"Finance and Economics: Serious Long-Term Problems" (1998) *The Economist*, May 2, 69.

"Finance and Economics: Unforgiven" (2000) *The Economist*, July 1, 73.

Sender, H. (1999) "Old Habits Die Hard," *Far Eastern Economic Review* 162(26): 42.

SUMIHIRO TAKEDA

M

madogiwa zoku

Literally "window-side tribe," the term *madogiwa zoku* refers to salarymen (see **salaryman**) who have been shunted off the **seniority promotion** career track and who now have jobs of relatively little consequence and, therefore, sit by the window rather than with a work group. Salarymen moved to a window-side position have almost no hope of future promotion, but instead must resign themselves to handling matters of small import until they either choose to resign or reach the age of retirement.

Japanese office layouts are often arranged around workgroups. A typical workgroup will have the desks of all its members arranged together in the middle of the room, with the group leader's desk at the head or located immediately nearby. Such an arrangement affords ease of communication among the group and encourages increased interaction. In this sense, *madogiwa zoku* employees have been moved literally to the periphery of the workplace and the organization. A *madogiwa zoku* move is a polite, but clear signal by an organization about that employee's future with the organization. In some respects it also reflects an organization's recognition that the employment agreement has not worked out as hoped, but that "permanent employment" compact must be honored nonetheless.

With the bursting of the **bubble economy** in 1989, Japanese firms have found it increasingly difficult to maintain the practice of *madogiwa zoku* assignments. The economic costs of retaining unproductive employees in essentially "make-work" jobs is difficult to support in the economy of the 1990s. Firms have pared down their *madogiwa zoku*, moving in two directions. One direction has been to find ways to enhance the productive capabilities of unproductive workers. The other has been to engage in *shukko* and **outplacement**.

ALLAN BIRD

madoguchi shido

Madoguchi shido, or "window guidance," was an extra-legal means of quantitative credit control employed by the **Bank of Japan** (BOJ) from the 1950s through 1991. It involved indications by the Bank of Japan to banks of the amount of lending it deemed proper. As such, window guidance supplemented more conventional methods of controlling the monetary base. Although the BOJ was strongly influenced by the **Ministry of Finance** in the setting of the discount rate and in other aspects of its operations, the central bank had relative autonomy in giving window guidance.

The effectiveness of window guidance as a tool of influence over banks was inextricably linked to the practice of overborrowing and overlending by the nation's banks. Companies borrowed from banks well beyond their capacity to repay or beyond their net worth. Large commercial banks without a deposit base large enough to meet loan demands borrowed, in turn, from the central bank to meet this demand. Through the 1950s and 1960s, the city (large commercial) banks borrowed over 10 percent of their total funds from the BOJ. The overloan phenomenon thus made the banks dependent on the guarantees of the BOJ. Importantly, however, overborrowing also profited the banks because funds from the BOJ were a cheap and convenient source of capital. The discount rate at which funds were borrowed from the BOJ was lower than private sector lending rates elsewhere. Thus, banks risked endangering their profitability if they ignored the BOJ's guidance.

The dependence of Japanese industry on bank-centered financing and the underdevelopment of Japanese **capital markets** heightened the effectiveness of window guidance as a tool of monetary policy. The BOJ could employ window guidance to expand or contract the tempo of economic activity in response to the international balance of payments or other considerations. Scholars have debated the degree to which window guidance served as a means for qualitative credit allocation but recent studies suggest that the guidance focused on aggregate loan levels rather than on the composition of loan portfolios.

It is clear, however, that window guidance was another aspect of the "convoy approach" to regulation, wherein no financial institution was permitted to move forward at a pace that would leave another financial institution behind. This was because window guidance was carried out individually with each bank and not only served to regulate the monetary base but also served to ensure that no bank grew appreciably faster than another. Estimates of deposit base growth and expected growth, and estimates of fund demands served as the basis for ceilings set on the quarterly rate of increase in bank loans.

The BOJ's window guidance also affected the relationship between banks and their borrowers. When the BOJ reduced available funds, thereby tightening monetary policy, banks necessarily cut lending. Banks tended to pass this tightening of credit on to those borrowers for which it did not serve as a main bank (see **main bank system**). Thus, the practice provided incentives for firms to establish relationships with a main bank.

Window guidance was used most frequently in the late 1960s and applied almost exclusively to city (large commercial) and long-term credit banks until the 1970s. Its was heightened by the segmented nature of the loan market but, as time progressed, lending through agent banks began to erode the barriers in the loan market. Thus, from the 1970s, the BOJ began applying guidance to a wider range of financial institutions, and to regional banks in particular. Foreign banks remained outside the scope, however.

As the financial system became more market-oriented, window guidance declined in importance. Its effectiveness relied on the need or desire of private banks to rely on supplemental borrowing from the central bank to fund overloans. With a change in industrial structure, however, came a shift in demand for credit from the private sector.

Window guidance also led to perverse incentives for banks. Increases in lending were typically calculated as percentages of the existing lending base. Thus, to maximize the lending base in future quarters, banks had to lend to their maximum quota in each quarter, regardless of the worthiness of projects. The imprudent behavior this policy fueled became evident in the "bubble" period of the latter 1980s. From mid-1991, the BOJ abolished the window guidance system and focused instead on exercising influence over credit flows via market interest rates.

Further reading

Calder, K. (1993) *Strategic Capitalism*, Princeton, NJ: Princeton University Press.

Hamada, K. and Horiuchi, A. (1987) "The Political Economy of the Financial Market," in K. Yamamura and Y. Yasuba (eds), *The Political Economy of Japan, Volume 1: The Domestic Transformation*, Stanford, CA: Stanford University Press, 223–60.

Horiuchi, A. (1980) *Nihon no Kinyu Seisaku* (Monetary Policy in Japan), Tokyo: Toyo Keizai Shimposha.

Patrick, H. (1962) *Monetary Policy and Central Banking in Contemporary Japan*, Bombay: Bombay University Press.

Teranishi, J. (1994) "Japan: Development and Structural Change of the Financial System," in H. Patrick and Y. Park (eds), *The Financial Development of Japan, Korea, and Taiwan*, New York: Oxford University Press, 27–80.

JENNIFER AMYX

main bank system

The term "main bank" generally describes the relationship of a primary lender among a lending hierarchy of several banks to a single firm. The main bank system, as it later came to be called in the 1980s, is said to have its origins in the 1930s when Japan's wartime economic planners sought to insure that companies deemed essential to the military economy received adequate funding for the uninterrupted production of munitions. The system was later adapted to and reshaped by the requirements of postwar reconstruction as part of a diversification strategy of loan syndication to industry in the postwar credit crunch period. Historically, the special attributes which are an inherent part of the main bank relationship were a cornerstone of bank–firm relationships among members of the *zaibatsu* group (see **banking industry**). Before the modern period, main bank-style relationships can be traced back to the exchange houses and lending practices of the great merchant households (see *ie*) of the Tokugawa period.

In the early 1990s the main bank system was hailed as a governance model to be emulated by developing economies. Based on a highly stylized theoretical model, the main bank was seen as a significant corporate governor and monitoring agent over the activities of the client firm, not only on behalf of other creditors, but also for the shareholders of the firm, as the main bank typically held shares in the firm (see **cross-shareholdings**). This view of the role of the main bank was an expansion upon Nakatani's thesis, which held that one of the functions of Japanese industrial groups is risk-sharing among their members. In the case of the main bank, the long-term implicit contractual role of the group bank as risk-insurer for the other group members was interpreted as the chief mechanism enabling risk-sharing. Building on principal–agency theory, their model of the main bank emphasized the role of the bank as the governance and monitoring agent of the firm for its fellow creditors and shareholders. According to economists adopting this model, it purportedly achieved benefits in the following three areas: (1) efficiencies of capital derived from the delegated cost of monitoring by affirming the continued creditworthiness and financial viability of its client

firm to other creditors and shareholders, the so-called signal function; (2) main bank assistance to firms in financial distress, the so-called rescue function; and (3) the main bank role in corporate governance. The credibility of these hypothesized functions of the main bank was questioned by scholars, mainly in Japan but also elsewhere, who had been studying the main bank system.

Among the criticisms leveled against the agency interpretation of the role of the main bank was the absence of supporting evidence based on bank practices. Often treating the bank as a "black box," the agency literature emphasized the main bank's hypothetical agency role to the exclusion of considering what the role of the "main bank" meant in fact to the main bank and the firm. The main bank relationship is the bank's greatest source of profits. The liberalization of interest rates in recent years has made large corporate lending the least profitable aspect of the banking business. Similarly, the competition between bank securities subsidiaries in underwriting corporate bonds has proven to be a low profit area, and likewise is considered by bankers as a "loss leader" necessary for maintaining client relationships. By contrast, the main bank will ordinarily receive many lucrative benefits from its status as lead main bank to a company. The main bank expects to be given the main deposit accounts of its client, and it will require, as well, that the client firm hold a standing low or non-interest compensating balance account. The client may also be expected to maintain low interest-bearing time deposits at the bank for some off-balance sheet favor such as a business introduction. In addition, the main bank receives a disproportionately larger share of fee-based transactions such as transfers, foreign exchange, and derivative products, an important area of bank profits, than the other banks in the client firm's lending hierarchy. Finally, whether the client is large or small, the bank also expects to receive the advantage of the company's employee pool as its customers and with it the opportunity to supply a host of lucrative retail services to this captive client base.

The personal accounts of employees of client firms represent one of the greatest rewards to the main bank in the relationship and are an important source of low-cost depository funds. The extent of the main bank's efforts to maintain its relationship with the client firm is often directly proportional to the size of the captive employee base. Companies will "request" all of their personnel to open accounts at the main bank for the direct deposit of their salary. A large base of employee accounts means a significant amount of business for the bank in the retail sector, a high profit-margin area which includes consumer transactions, in the form of electronic transfers, consumer lending, personal lending, credit cards, mortgages, and so on. The commercial banking sector's large share of personal accounts has steadily eroded throughout the 1990s banking crisis as depositors seeking greater safety have shifted their personal savings into Japan's postal saving system (see **postal savings**).

Although the main bank system is no longer driven by large corporate bank borrowing, it has found new fuel in a host of bank products and services, thus maintaining profitability for the main bank and for the second, third, fourth, and even fifth bank in the lending hierarchy as well. On the other hand, firms expect to be able to rely on the bank's offices to supply business information, consulting services, and, especially for the medium-size firms, the ever-important bank introductions to prospective clients or suppliers. The client corporation thus has its own reasons to protect the hierarchical standing of its lead main bank. Such relationship banking practices are not restricted nor exclusive to the lead main bank, however. The second and third lending banks of that company will attempt to provide similar services, as will even the fourth and fifth banks in the lending hierarchy, which may be composed of upwards of 20–30 banks if the corporation is large. Preservation of that hierarchy in a highly competitive environment is of paramount importance to the lead main bank, particularly since it receives a disproportionately larger share of profits from the client than the other institutions in the hierarchy. In fact, when the top five lending banks typically supply only 50 percent of the firm's borrowed funds, they can still expect to receive almost 100 percent of the firm's fee-based transactions, such as foreign exchange, letters of credit and other trade or business related credit guarantees, leasing and underwriting to their non-bank financial subsidiaries. The opportunity for banks below the top five to acquire profitable business with the client

outside of lending has become quite remote, principally because corporations themselves are attempting to rationalize their relations.

The overriding characteristic that distinguishes the main bank from the second and third banks is that it is by custom the creditor of last resort for the firm in financial distress and is expected to initiate any rescue plan among the other banks. The degree to which the rescue function exists is more a matter of perception on the part of the client than contractual. Bankers report that they are loath to make even an implicit commitment.

A key agency assumption of corporate governance by the bank is based on the so-called bank rescue function. However, evidence reveals that such rescues generally have been effected only when the bank determined that a client's difficulties were a result of a liquidity problem rather than a solvency crisis. The bank then acted out of its own interest, if not just for its own profit. Bank officers often report they were the last to know of an imminent financial crisis when the client firm was intent on evading bank oversight. If the main bank rescue function really did exist, such calculated evasion by failing client firms would have been pointless at the very least, if not counterproductive. In cases of insolvency, "rescue" most often means overseeing the dissolution of the firm's assets and the distribution of collateral to its chief creditors, namely, the banks. Typically, for a small or medium-sized firm this means that the bank will ask some member company of their corporate group to take over the company or find some other enterprise to merge with the troubled company. Only in those limited cases deemed by governmental authorities to be in the interest of the nation's welfare, such as a large failing firm with many employees, does the **Ministry of Finance** (MOF) "request" a main bank to deliver a rescue package. Implicit in the bank's willingness to provide funds to a sunset industry is the understanding that MOF will reward the bank by granting it some concession in another area.

Bankers report that the main bank was often the lender of "last resort" to a firm only because the other creditors had been able to accomplish a rapid retreat, thereby increasing the burden of the main bank. According to agency theorists, other creditors take their cues by observing the "signals" of the main bank's actions, as the firm's largest creditor. The question is whether the signal "sent" is necessarily an accurate representation of the client firm's actual internal affairs. Often the signal is distorted by the main bank's own strategic considerations and needs in maintaining a particular client relationship. Any hint of trouble, signaled by a decrease in lending by the firm's main bank, would be noted by the other creditors, typically setting off a chain reaction of retreat by those banks which benefit least from their relationship with the ailing firm. Main banks are, therefore, very keen on not sending any signal which would lead to the collapse of the firm's lending syndicate. That is why competing banks prudently make their own independent credit assessments.

The primary vehicle for carrying out the main bank relationship is the bank team assigned to large client firms. Monitoring of the client firm by the bank team is often cited as one evidence of the existence of such an external governance function. In the case of a large corporation, a bank team, typically headed by a relationship manager, is intimately involved in the affairs of the client, visiting the firm's offices and other facilities on a daily basis. However, the nature of the team's mission is essentially sales-oriented. The team's purpose is to try and obtain information about the firm's future plans in order to promote the bank's services. The second and even the third banks of a major corporation will also assign teams to service a larger client.

A bank's ability to exercise any form of outside governance arises exclusively from its position as a major creditor and only when there are no other options for the client firm to access other banks, outside money markets, or internal sources of funds. However, given the competitive nature of the banking industry, other banks competing with the firm's main bank are usually only too eager to grant a new loan in an effort to improve their position in the relationship hierarchy and the increased access that it affords. During the "**bubble** period" of the 1980s, the mission of the bank teams was primarily to boost bank assets by issuing new loans, which were often used for speculative purposes by the client. This lending/sales function was in obvious conflict with agency theory notions of monitoring a client firm's creditworthiness, which the bank could do only to a very limited extent in any case.

The main bank's leverage is therefore quite low over firms listed in the First Section of the Tokyo Stock Exchange (generally large capitalized firms) and even for Second Section firms (generally large to medium capitalized firms), because firms in both categories have direct access to money markets and thus can circumvent the need for bank finance. Indeed, it is difficult for banks to monitor the activities of many such firms due to these firms' large scope of operations, business locations, and the multitude of other banks a firm may deal with. Furthermore, only the largest corporations merit their own bank teams. Medium and small-sized firms receive only the occasional attention of already overburdened junior officers whose ability to monitor their client firms is often limited to tracking the cash flow into the client's main deposit account.

Agency economists' assumption of firm monitoring by former bankers, the retirement or **shukko** (transfer of employees) process, is similarly flawed. *Shukko* serves as an outplacement mechanism under Japan's **lifetime employment** system and reflects the primarily fiscal necessity of the bank to find early retirement positions for high-salaried senior bank executives. Bankers readily acknowledge that their continued influence over their former employees was extremely limited, especially when a conflict of interest arose between the bank and its client firm. The necessity to retire senior bank employees has accelerated in pace since the over-hiring of junior personnel during the "bubble period." However, as Japanese firms also continue to downsize there are fewer and fewer positions available in client firms for retirement *shukko* from the banks.

In considering the role of banks in corporate governance, banks are not acting as monitors in the agency sense, that is, as agents for fellow shareholders, since the bank's own credit exposure to the client far exceeds its own equity position in the client firm. Even from a creditor's standpoint, the bank's ability to monitor is limited. The prolonged banking crisis in Japan has also painfully revealed the banks' lack of ability to evaluate the creditworthiness of clients when money was lent to pursue land and stock speculations in the 1980s "bubble economy." In the ever-rising economy which had been characteristic of Japan in the postwar era, the validity of agency assumptions of bank governance, and the main bank's "rescue function," implicit or otherwise, had not been seriously tested until the 1990s. The elements of the agency theory approach have been largely demythologized since then by the ongoing banking crisis. As Japan still continues to suffer its first profound postwar recession, questions of corporate financial efficiency are being starkly confronted. The prolonged recession has been characterized with increasing frequency as a governance recession.

The main bank relationship is rooted in the history of the postwar reconstruction of the Japanese economy, and prior to that in the role of the bank within the prewar *zaibatsu* groups. Indeed, many of its present-day practices stem from that history and also bear within them a strong component of traditional group relationships endogenous to Japanese society. Nonetheless, we cannot escape the fact that the functionalist practices of the main bank relationship are to seek competitive advantages in a system in which the relationship itself is a key source of bank profits.

Further reading

Aoki, M. and Patrick, H. (eds) (1994) *The Japanese Main Bank System: Its Relevance for Developing Economies*, Oxford: Oxford University Press.

Scher, M.J. (1996) *Japanese Interfirm Networks and Their Main Banks*. London: Macmillan and New York: St. Martins Press.

—— (1998) *Mainbank shinwa no hokai* (Collapse of the Main Bank Myth), Tokyo: Toyo Keizai Shimposha.

—— (1999) "Japanese Financial Institutions as Information Intermediaries," in H. Albach, U. Goertzen and R. Zobel (eds), *Information Processing as a Competitive Advantage of Japanese Firms*, Berlin: Sigma Publishing.

MARK SCHER

marketing in Japan

For the majority of Japan's post-war history, marketing in Japan traditionally focused on the fight for market share rather than on meeting consumer needs. In Japan's rapidly developing economy, consumer demand was so strong that quality products sold as soon as they hit the shelves. This led to the prevailing belief that the Japanese were homogeneous, and that individual tastes and concerns were not that important. The theory was that since any member of the firm producing a product was a representative of the target consumer, focus group interviews and consumer surveys were unnecessary.

At best, Japanese firms considered marketing as a function of everyone in the organization, rather than a specialized pursuit. Thus the Japanese corporate custom of hiring entry-level college graduates en masse, and subsequently rotating them through various positions, accounts for the fact that many individuals assigned to marketing departments have little or no formal training.

From the beginning of Japan's economic resurgence during the postwar era until the late 1980s, Japanese consumer demand for products outpaced supply. A good product from a reputable corporation was almost guaranteed success. During this producer-driven economy, the more products a firm could produce to fill retailers' shelves, the higher the chance for success. The keys to a product's success were considered to consist of a good corporate image, technological expertise, and a strong distribution channel. This led to a style of advertising that focused on building the corporate brand, rather than espousing product merits, or building product brands. Not surprisingly, in this atmosphere, the discipline of marketing was not considered an instrumental function to a product's success.

This product-driven approach worked well until the bursting of Japan's **bubble economy** in the early 1990s, and the subsequent recession. As consumer purse strings tightened, product manufacturers found themselves vying for consumer attention. Consumers began exercising personal choice, forcing companies to concentrate their attention on consumer needs.

Forced by the shift in the market to accept the importance of marketing in Japan, many major corporations looked for guidance from across the seas, resulting in a proliferation of Western marketing books translated into Japanese. More telling is the heavy investment Japanese corporations are making in marketing, by sending up-and-coming staff to overseas universities to pursue marketing degrees or MBAs.

Recognizing the importance of marketing, more Japanese companies are now tracking consumer preferences through point-of-sale data and consumer research, and tailoring their products to those findings. Many companies have also begun segmenting their markets by values and lifestyles, rather than relying on demographics alone. Furthermore, the importance of the product brand has come to be recognized, with the result that more emphasis is put on building the brand through advertising. As Japanese firms realize that their success depends increasingly on their marketing strategy, marketing staffs and budgets are being increased.

SEAN MOONEY

Marubeni

The company that later became Marubeni Corporation was founded in 1858, the year in which the company's founder, Chubei Itoh, began to sell Omi linen. In 1872, Chubei opened Benichu, a drapery shop, in Osaka, and in 1883 began using the Beni mark as the store's logo. The Beni mark is the origin of the name Marubeni. The company expanded into Osaka, Kobe, and Kyoto through the nineteenth century.

In 1914, the company was reorganized from a proprietorship into C. Itoh & Co. (see **ITOCHU**). In 1918 the limited partnership was divided into Itochu Shoten, with the main store and Kyoto store as its core, and C. Itoh & Co., with the yarn store and the Kobe Branch at its center. These two companies were the forerunners to Marubeni Corporation and ITOCHU Corporation, respectively.

As a result of the post-First World War slowdown in commodity markets, Itochu Shoten merged with Ito-chobei Shoten, which had remained under sound management, to form Marubeni Shoten in March 1921. At that time the company, which had only one branch in Kyoto, was a textiles wholesaler handing silk and wool fabrics. In 1931, the Osaka branch was established. This branch began to concentrate on trading, eventually opening branches and offices throughout China and in India. It also expanded the goods it handled to include construction materials, machinery, sundries, food products, and so on, in addition to textiles. The Osaka branch's sales grew rapidly and in 1937 exceeded those of the main store, accounting for 62 percent of overall sales.

As the business performance of Marubeni Shoten, C. Itoh & Co. and others recovered, the move to reunify all of the Ito family business strengthened. In September 1941, three companies (Kishimoto Shoten, a steel trading company; Marubeni Shoten and C. Itoh & Co.), merged to form Sanko Kabusiki Kaisya. Soon after, however, the Second World War erupted and this limited the company's trading to China and Southeast Asia.

In September 1944, Sanko Kabusiki Kaisya merged with Daido Boeki Kaisha and Kureha Cotton Spinning Co. (also established by Chubei Itoh) to form Daiken Co. The combined entity now had 103 affiliated companies inside and outside of Japan and interests in shipping and delivery of textiles, heavy industry and chemical industry products, grains, fertilizer, etc., and also provided materials to the military. With the ending of the war, however, the company lost all of its overseas assets.

In February 1948, Daiken Co. was designated as being one of those subject to the Law for Elimination of Excessive Concentrations of Economic Power, a measure designed to break up the *zaibatsu* which dominated Japan's economy at that time. Daiken was divided into four companies: Marubeni Co., C. Itoh & Co., Kureha Cotton Spinning Co., and Amagasaki Nail Works.

On December 1, 1949, Marubeni Co. was formally established with headquarters in Osaka, was capitalized at ¥150 million, and had 1,232 employees. When established, the company did not have a single overseas office, but new regulations allowing imports and exports were just starting. The first financial results after establishment (December 1949–March 1950) showed sales of ¥5 billion, 80 percent of which were from textiles.

Although its commodities businesses collapsed after the Korean War, the company opened its first overseas office in New York in April 1951. By the end of 1954 the company had twenty-two overseas subsidiaries. The government decided that the trading companies needed to be strengthened to expand the country's trade and so established a policy to do so. Because the trading company Iida & Co., the forerunner of Takashimaya Department Store, had sustained a large loss from the collapse of the soybean market, that company's main bank, Fuji Bank, decided that a merger with another trading company was the only way to restructure that company and asked Marubeni to cooperate. Marubeni agreed to the merger, judging that it was in accordance with the country's policy to strengthen the trading companies. On September 1, 1955, Marubeni and Iida & Co. merged to form Marubeni-Iida Co., now a true general trading company (*sogo shosha*).

In line with Japan's accelerating growth at the time, Marubeni-Iida established a chemicals department in 1957, expanded into polyethylene production, and in 1958 started automobile exports to the United States on behalf of Nissan Motor Co. In April 1966, Marubeni merged with Totsu Co., which was a trading company specializing in metals and one of the sales agents of Nippon Kokan K.K. (now NKK). Sales of heavy and chemical industry products, such as metals, machinery, and chemicals, now accounted for more than 50 percent of Marubeni-Iida's sales. Tokyo effectively became the company's headquarters.

In 1966 the Fuyo Conference consisting of the presidents of Fuyo group companies (all affiliated with Fuji Bank) was started, and a *keiretsu* was formalized. On January 1, 1972, the company changed its name from Marubeni-Iida Co. to Marubeni Corporation, and moved to the newly constructed Marubeni Building in the Takebashi district, which is still its headquarters today.

The Iranian Revolution in 1979 caused a temporary stoppage in crude oil production and oil prices rose. During this time the company's energy and chemicals division sales increased greatly and came to account for nearly 23 percent of sales, the same as the machinery and metals division.

In the early 1980s, Japanese trading companies faced criticism for their size and power in the economy, while manufacturers they had previously served moved to bypass them in favor of direct export. The company suffered high write-offs from the reorganization of affiliates, and relied heavily on asset sales to maintain profit levels. The businesses that did expand during this period were exports for power systems, energy, chemicals, etc., and exports of steel pipe for oil producing companies. In particular, large orders for power systems were received from around the world, and this proved to be a major profit source for the company from the 1980s through the first half of the 1990s. By fiscal 1990, the company had largely recovered, and reflected sales of ¥19.156 trillion and ordinary income of ¥54.8 billion, both record figures.

Throughout the 1990s the company reorganized and integrated some subsidiaries and affiliates and liquidated others, while continuing to expand in many areas, including information and electronic businesses and high-cost projects such as fiber optic submarine cables to Europe and the USA. As a result of appraisal losses on its bank and other stock portfolio, in fiscal 1997 Marubeni posted a net loss of ¥30.8 billion, the company's first loss since fiscal 1951. In the late 1990s it actually sought to reduce employee headcount through early retirement, attrition, buyout programs, and selected layoffs. Restructuring continued in 2000 and 2001 and the company is now focused on four business areas: retail, information and telecommunications business and electric power infrastructure, high value-added materials and materials processing and sales, and resource development and trading. Given their common roots, many observers believe Marubeni and ITOCHU Corporation will eventually merge again, as they have at previous times in their history.

See also: general trading companies

JAY NELSON

Maruyu

Maruyu is a system of tax breaks for small savers which was introduced in 1963. Investors could earn tax-exempt income on a total of ¥14 million ($US 140,000) in savings. Of that amount, up to 3 million yen could be deposited in tax-free bank accounts; 3 million yen in postal savings, 3 million yen in government bonds; and 5 million yen in special accounts for buying a house. The system spawned tax evasion on a huge scale.

After April 1988, the law was changed to limit access to the *maruyu* system. Eligibility for *maruyu* was limited to people sixty-five years or older; those who received a survivor's annuity; people who received a widow annuity or single mother annuity; mothers whose children receive childcare support allowance; and those who received a handicap annuity.

Further reading

Holloway, N. (1988) "Conflicting Accounts – Banks Scramble as Japan Ends the Small Saver's Tax Break," *Far Eastern Economic Review* 99–100

SUMIHIRO TAKEDA

Matsushita Electric Industrial Corporation

Matsushita Electric Industrial Co., Ltd (MEI) is a diversified manufacturer of industrial and consumer electronics/products, both assembled goods and components. MEI's predecessor firm, Matsushita Electric Appliance Factory (MEAF), was established in 1918 in Osaka, Japan by Konosuke **Matsushita**, and incorporated as MEI in 1935. MEI is the core firm in the Matsushita Group. In fiscal year 1999 its consolidated sales were in excess of $63 billion, and its total worldwide employment was over 282,000. It sells under the National, Panasonic, Technics, and Quasar brand names. In the late 1990s, MEI and its subsidiaries had a very broad product line that included components, home appliances, consumer electronics, and many industrial electronics products.

In 1918 MEAF brought out its first product, a double-ended electrical socket. Another important early product was a battery-powered bicycle lamp that was introduced in 1922. MEAF grew quickly in the 1920s and 1930s by selling household electrical products such as irons and, later, radios, fans, light bulbs, and various electric appliances. An early instance of the firm's willingness to move

beyond conventional business practices occurred during the Japanese Depression. In December 1929, to reduce inventory to avoid layoffs, MEAF put all workers on half-day work with full salary, eliminated holiday pay, and asked all the workers to sell the excess inventory. By February 1930 everyone was back to their regular shifts. In 1930 MEAF began its first sales of radios, which were defective; in 1931 the radios were redesigned and won first prize in a Nippon Hoso Kyokai (Japan Broadcasting Corporation or NHK) contest. By 1942 Matsushita was the largest radio producer in Japan.

In 1933 MEAF was one of the first firms in Japan to introduce a divisional structure based on product families, the goal of which was to delegate more authority to the divisions. Although General Motors had adopted a divisional structure as early as 1921, Matsushita does not appear to have been influenced by General Motors. The divisional structure created clear profit responsibilities, with the divisions operating almost like independent corporations. These divisions continue to be powerful and independent. At the end of the Second World War MEI had forty-nine separate subsidiaries.

In the aftermath of the war, MEI was declared a *zaibatsu* and five factories were seized by the occupation authorities. Initially MEI executives were scheduled to be purged; however, after a considerable lobbying effort this order was rescinded. Only in 1950 was Matsushita relieved of *zaibatsu*-related controls. In the 1950s MEI expanded rapidly, broadening its product lines to include black-and-white televisions, transistor radios, stereos, tape recorders, air conditioners, washing machines, and other products. It introduced its first television in 1952. MEI acquired majority ownership in Japan Victor Corporation (JVC) in 1954, but JVC continues to operate independently.

MEI was also an early entrant into global markets. Matsushita Electric Trading Company was established in 1935 and operated throughout Asia. During the Second World War MEI established production facilities throughout the expanding Japanese Empire. In the immediate aftermath of the war, thirty-nine overseas factories were confiscated. In 1948 the Dutch firm Philips approached Matsushita to reestablish their prewar business relationship. In 1951 Konosuke Matsushita visited firms in the USA and also Philips in Holland. By 1952 the two firms had created a joint venture for the Japanese market, and in 1954 they opened a plant in Osaka to produce picture tubes, vacuum tubes, transistors, semiconductors, and other electric components. In 1953 MEI opened its first overseas liaison office in New York City. In 1959 Matsushita Electric Corporation of America was founded in New York, becoming its first overseas subsidiary. The same year MEI opened its first overseas production facility, National Thai, in Thailand, and since then Matsushita has opened many subsidiaries around the world. Global sales, marketing, and production continues to be a high priority. In 1974 MEI purchased Motorola's consumer electronics division, which retailed under the brand name Quasar, but closed the last Motorola television factory in 1995. In 1990, MEI purchased a US entertainment and movie firm, MCA, for $6 billion, but then sold it in 1995 to Michael Bronfman for $5.7 billion. By 1999 MEI had 223 manufacturing and sales subsidiaries globally and operated in over 160 countries.

From its inception, MEI's business strategy has focused on being a fast follower: it has introduced improved versions at lower prices. In contrast to many Japanese firms, MEI has often purchased other companies as a method of entering a new business. An important strategy it had developed already in the 1920s was to promote brand names, particularly its National brand. MEI aggressively built a distribution and sales *keiretsu* before the Second World War, and as of 1999 it has the strongest retail distribution network in Japan, consisting of approximately 25,000 retail distribution outlets nationwide. These shops are the backbone of Matsushita's leading market share in Japan.

MEI's strength has been its emphasis on efficiency and quality mass production. In 1958 MEI received the Deming Award for quality. In contrast to the large general electric manufacturers, such as Hitachi and Toshiba, before the war MEI did not invest in research and development, preferring to improve upon existing products. However, after the war the relative backwardness of Japanese technology became clear to Konosuke Matsushita, as did the necessity of purchasing

technology from foreign firms. To remedy these shortcomings, in 1953 MEI created its Central Research Laboratory in Osaka, and MEI has continually increased investment both at the central laboratory and in divisional research and development laboratories.

See also: electronics industry; Sony

Further reading

Kotter, J.P. (1997) *Matsushita Leadership: Lessons from the 20th Century's Most Remarkable Entrepreneur*, New York: The Free Press.
Matsushita, K. (1988) *Quest for Prosperity: The Life of a Japanese Industrialist*, Tokyo: PHP Institute Inc.

MARTIN KENNEY

Matsushita, Konosuke

Konosuke Matsushita (1894–1989) was the founder of **Matsushita** Electric Industrial Co., Ltd. Japan's largest consumer electronics manufacturer. Known in Japan as the "god of management," Matsushita is credited with pioneering numerous managerial innovations, including the division system and the five-day workweek, and his books on management as well as broader social and philosophical issues continue to sell well even after his death.

The early years

Matsushita was born in 1894 in Wakayama Prefecture, south of Osaka, the youngest of eight children in a wealthy farming family. When he was four, his father lost everything while speculating in the rice futures market and the family was thrown into poverty. This was the beginning of a long series of trials that Matsushita would face, including poor health, the early deaths of all his siblings and his only son due to illness, and numerous business setbacks. Overcoming such adversity was to be a recurrent theme throughout much of his life.

When Matsushita was nine, he was sent to Osaka where he worked for six years as an apprentice in a bicycle shop. When he was sixteen, he got a job at the Osaka Electric Light Company and became an installation technician, wiring homes and businesses for lighting. At age nineteen, he was put in charge of large projects, with dozens of employees under his supervision. He was further promoted to inspector, but was unhappy in this position because it provided too many idle hours and not enough "serious work." In his spare time, Matsushita worked on designing a light socket that was better than the one his company used. When he had devised a socket that he had confidence in, he showed it to his boss, but his boss was not interested. At this point, Matsushita decided to quit the company to manufacture light sockets himself.

In 1917, at the age of twenty-two, he started a business with 100 yen, setting up operations in a two-room tenement house with five workers, including himself and his wife. None had a high school education, so they worked long hours to overcome their lack of technical expertise. Their first product did not sell well, and soon the company was down to just three employees.

Matsushita's first successful product was a double outlet adapter that screwed into light sockets. Since Japanese houses generally had just one electrical outlet, this enabled them to double their capacity: the adapter could accommodate a light bulb plus one other electrical appliance. Matsushita's small company continued to introduce one or two new products per month. He initially designed the products himself, but gradually came to rely on others. All of his products were improved versions of existing products, sold at prices below the competition.

In 1922, Matsushita developed a bullet-shaped bicycle light that was more durable and burned longer than existing bicycle lights. When he had trouble persuading skeptical retailers to carry the light, he came up with an innovative marketing strategy: he had salesmen leave samples at bicycles shops with one lit lamp on display, and asked to be paid only if the lamps sold. When retailers saw that the demonstration lamp worked for fifty hours on a single set of batteries, they were impressed, and began recommending the lights to customers. Sales took off. Matsushita continued to expand his product line, and by 1931 his company had 140 patents and was manufacturing over 200 products, including radios, lighting, batteries, and electric irons. In 1935, the company was reorganized into a public corporation and renamed Matsushita Electric Industrial Company (MEI).

Innovation in management

By the 1930s, several of the distinctive characteristics of Matsushita-style management were becoming evident. Matsushita rarely came out with an entirely new product category; instead the company improved existing products, making them better and/or cheaper than those offered by competitors. Costs were kept low by hard work and relentless pursuit of manufacturing efficiency. New and creative marketing methods were used, such as the promotion of the "National" brand name through aggressive nationwide advertising. Close and cooperative relationships were established with suppliers and retailers, in contrast to the arm's-length dealings that were then the norm in Japan. Matsushita also set up its own distribution channels, following a conflict with a sales agent for bicycle lamps. Many of these practices are now taken for granted in Japanese business, but at the time Konosuke Matsushita first introduced them they were rare.

Matsushita was also a pioneer in company–employee relations. When the stock market crash of 1929 sent the Japanese economy into depression, Matsushita's sales were cut in half. Matsushita responded by cutting production by half, but did not lay workers off. Instead, unneeded production workers were shifted into sales, to help reduce excess inventories. Thus, during the 1930s when other companies were laying off employees and bringing out few new products, Matsushita did the opposite. This predated by three decades the **lifetime employment** system and the practice of moving workers into other jobs to avoid lay-offs, policies for which Japanese companies became well known but which were not widely adopted until after 1960. Matsushita was also the first Japanese company to introduce the five-day work week, in 1960. As founder and "hands-on" president of Matsushita Electric, Konosuke Matsushita was the man responsible for all of these management innovations.

Matsushita was also willing to take the risk of moving quickly into mass production, even when the market for a product was still small. Inspired by the pricing strategy used by Henry Ford with the

Model T, Matsushita understood the concept of expanding the market for a new product by mass producing it at an early stage, thereby reducing per-unit production costs through economies of scale, and then translating the reduced costs into lower prices, making the product affordable to more consumers. In 1931, Matsushita made the unusual move of purchasing a critical patent and making it available free of charge to all radio manufacturers, to help stimulate growth of the radio market. Matsushita applied this market expansion model repeatedly. One of the best examples was with videocassette recorders (VCRs) in the 1970s and 1980s. When Matsushita adopted the VHS format (which had been developed by JVC, a Matsushita subsidiary), he aggressively built up production capacity in anticipation of growing worldwide demand, and licensed the VHS technology to other manufacturers. The result was falling production costs, falling prices, rapid expansion of the VCR market, and the establishment of the VHS system as the industry standard over the competing Sony Betamax format. By the mid-1980s, VCRs accounted for almost 30 percent of Matsushita's total sales and around 45 percent of its profits.

The division system

In the Japanese business world, Matsushita Electric is especially well known for its division system. In a division system, the different units of a company are organized primarily by product or product group, with each product division operating more or less autonomously, much like an independent company. Matsushita first adopted a division system in 1933, about the same time that Pierre du Pont was pioneering a similar divisionalized organization in the United States. His goals in devising this organizational structure were to delegate authority and train business managers (particularly as Matsushita himself suffered from chronically poor health); to give product units the customer closeness and flexibility of small companies; and to prevent employees from becoming too specialized and losing sight of the goals of satisfying customers and earning profits.

Matsushita initially divided his company into four divisions: radios, lamps and batteries, wiring

and electrical fixtures, and electrical heating appliances. The company then continued to add new divisions as it expanded into new product areas. Each of Matsushita's product divisions is in charge of its own R&D, engineering, production, and sales; at the same time, the accounting, recruitment, and basic employee training functions are centralized to maintain a degree of consistency and corporate control. The head of a division is held responsible for performance; divisional profitability is made public within the company, and when a division fails to meet its profit target for two consecutive years, the division head is replaced. Over the years, Matsushita alternatively tightened and loosened corporate control over the divisions, in response to market conditions and to maintain a balance between divisional autonomy and cooperation among divisions.

During and after the Second World War

During the Second World War Matsushita Electric, like all Japanese industrial companies, manufactured products for the Japanese military. After the war, the Occupation authorities designated Matsushita a *zaibatsu*, ordered it to cease production, and announced that its top management, including Konosuke Matsushita, would no longer be allowed to work for the company. Arguing that Matsushita was not a *zaibatsu* but a young, founder-led company which had been pulled into the war by the military, Matsushita fought hard to have the Occupation rulings reversed, making over fifty trips to Allied Headquarters in Tokyo to plead his case. The company's labor union helped too; at a time when many labor groups were petitioning to have their business leaders removed from office, Matsushita's union gathered over 15,000 signatures from union members and their families asking that Konosuke be allowed to remain as president. These efforts were successful; Allied Headquarters announced in 1947 that Konosuke Matsushita and all his executives could continue to work for the company, although it was not until 1950 that all of the postwar restrictions on the company's business activities were removed.

In the 1950s, Matsushita put his company on the road to "internationalization." In 1951 he visited the United States, where he was impressed by the sophistication and dynamism of American business, and in 1952 he signed a licensing and technology exchange agreement with the European electronics giant Philips. Matsushita's first overseas company, Matsushita Electric Corporation of America, was set up in New York in 1959, and this was followed over the next four decades by the establishment of dozens of sales offices, manufacturing plants, research facilities, and training centers in countries all over the world.

Spiritual values

Konosuke Matsushita is also revered in Japan for the philosophical side of his management philosophy. Throughout his career, Matsushita emphasized the importance of establishing and sharing with his employees clear management objectives and slogans to guide business decisions and actions. In 1929, he laid down his company's "basic management objective" (*koryo*), which states: "Recognizing our responsibilities as industrialists, we will devote ourselves to the progress and development of society and the well-being of people through our business activities, thereby enhancing the quality of life throughout the world." His thinking was further influenced through an encounter with a popular religious movement in 1932 which led him to feel strongly that people need a way to connect their work lives with society. This idea, along with his own business experiences, shaped the continuing development of his management philosophy. Concerning the relation between business, society, and profit, he said: "A business should quickly stand on its own, based on the service it provides to society. Profits should not be a reflection of corporate greed but a vote of confidence from society that what is offered by the firm is valued. When a business fails to make profits it should die – it is a waste of resources to society" (Pascale and Athos 1981).

Another famous part of the Matsushita management philosophy is the "water philosophy:" Konosuke's declaration that manufacturers should strive to make all products as "inexhaustible and as cheap as tap water." Matsushita was the first company to have its own song and code of values, which were sung and recited by all company employees every morning before starting work.

Included in the code of values and ingrained in every employee are Matsushita's "Seven Principles:" national service through industry, fairness, harmony and cooperation, struggle for betterment, courtesy and humility, adjustment and assimilation, and gratitude. Matsushita's philosophy shaped his company's approach to human resource development as well. Unlike many large Japanese companies, Matsushita does not rely heavily on recruitment of graduates from elite universities to fill management-track positions; instead, the company focuses on getting "extraordinary results from ordinary men." All employees receive thorough and continuous training, both in business skills and in Matsushita values. As one often-heard company slogan goes, "Matsushita makes people before it makes products."

Konosuke Matsushita served as president of Matsushita Electric until 1961, when he was made chairman. In 1963 he moved into a more "hands off" executive advisory position as he sought to develop the next generation of company leadership. Even as advisor, however, he was quick to become involved when a crisis arose. Matsushita was also a prolific author, writing forty-six books between 1953 and 1990.

Further reading

Kotter, J. (1997) *Matsushita Leadership*, New York: The Free Press.

Matsushita, K. (1988) *Quest for Prosperity: The Life of a Japanese Industrialist*, Kyoto: PHP Institute.

Pascale, R.T. and Athos, A.G. (1981) *The Art of Japanese Management*. New York: Simon and Schuster.

TIM CRAIG

Meiji restoration

The **Tokugawa period** was followed by the first era of modern Japan, the Meiji period (1868–1912). It was established by a rebellion against the Tokugawa regime led by low-ranking *samurai* from feudal estates far from the capital at Edo. In theory it was not actually a revolution, but a "restoration of Imperial rule." With a breathtaking series of fundamental changes, leaders of the Meiji restoration quite literally designed a new Japan. It stands as one of the most comprehensive and rapid transformations of any society in world history. Within the space of thirty years, Japan was transformed from an agriculture-based feudal economy and social system into a modern world power.

The Tokugawa regime was the supreme authority in Japan for more than two and one-half centuries, finally coming to an end in 1868. There were signs that the end was near even before events occurred which forcefully brought the regime down. Physical isolation of the country, one of its main ideological pillars, was under mounting attack from Britain, Russia and the United States. The warrior elite from feudal estates outside those favored by the regime were becoming more openly restive, and the question of why the Emperor was not the actual head of government, rather than a mere ornament of history, had become a common focus of discussion among groups of *samurai*, even including some within the ruling Tokugawa clan itself. When a small American fleet steamed into Edo Bay in June of 1853, under the very walls of the Shogun's castle, with orders demanding that Japan open ports to allow foreign ships to take on coal and provisions, the beginning of the end was at hand. A year later the Shogun's representatives were forced to open ports to several nations, and to suffer the humiliation of tariffs dictated to it by foreigners, and even to surrender a measure of sovereignty over areas where foreigners lived and worked.

It took another fourteen years for the regime to finally be replaced, a period called *bakumatsu* in Japanese, "last years of the military government," during which endless debate about what to do was carried out both inside and outside governmental circles. As the foreigners came in increasing numbers, their technological and military superiority was undeniable, and although many Japanese hated their presence, fearing the country would be reduced to semi-colonial status as had China, they came to realize that they were in no position to deal with the foreigners on an equal footing. Fortunately for Japan, this crisis brought to the fore a cadre of remarkable men who were eventually able to put aside *han* rivalries, suppress individual egos, learn from that very West that they

feared so much, and establish a new regime which, although imperfect and requiring many adjustments as time went on, successfully brought Japan into the modern world to an extent no non-Western nation has ever been able to do.

The young men who did all this (the oldest was a mere forty-one), were mainly lower ranking *samurai* from what the Tokugawa regime had always considered "outsider" *han*, those kept physically distant from Edo, and never allowed to participate in the deliberations of running the nation. They were joined by a progressive faction of young court nobles in Kyoto. Especially prominent in what finally culminated in the Meiji Restoration were *samurai* of Choshu in extreme southern Honshu and of Satsuma in southern Kyushu, who championed the idea of removing, by force if necessary, the entire Shogunate system of government and replacing it with a government established on western lines with the Emperor as a kind of spiritual rallying point. The young *samurai* from Choshu and Satsuma rallied a few thousand other *samurai* to their cause, confronting the forces of the Shogun for the first time in three centuries. The rebels were victorious in a short military struggle which produced surprisingly few casualties. The Shogun abdicated, was never harmed, and in fact was later granted a lifetime pension. The old regime was thus swept away, and now a group of idealistic young men faced the daunting task of building a modern nation on the ruins of an agriculture-based feudal autocracy.

The first task at hand for the new leaders was to establish trust and the image of authority over a confused population, and the way these young men used the imperial institution to do that reflected their cleverness and farsightedness. They decided to keep the seat of political power in Edo, but in a calculated move to symbolize the revolutionary nature of the new order, the Shogun's enormous castle was transformed into the home of the Keio Emperor, a lad recently turned fourteen, and the city itself was renamed Tokyo, "eastern capital." To further enhance the sense of newness of the regime, the Emperor's reign name was changed to Meiji, "enlightened rule." 1868, the start of a new modernizing Japan, thus became the first year of the Meiji period.

Building a new Japan: the first quarter-century

No emperor for a thousand years of history to that date had actually been a ruler in Japan, and the young Meiji Emperor certainly was not made one. In theory, on the other hand, getting rid of Shogunate rule was for the purpose of "restoring" the emperor – the sacred emperor – to his rightful place as head of the Japanese polity. In almost all respects, the young emperor had no real idea of what was going on, but the Meiji leaders controlled his seal. All edicts in a whirlwind of fundamental changes across society were proclaimed in his name. Ordinary people had no difficulty accepting the explanation the new government put forth that the Shoguns had been usurpers, and that Japanese society was at long last back on its original course with the Emperor at the helm. The Imperial institution was effectively used not only as a rallying point and a source of legitimacy, but actually as a way to put beyond criticism, even beyond serious review, many changes that were being made.

Designers of the new regime were themselves *samurai* and court nobles, but they understood that the old order would have to be completely dismantled if Japan was to be able to protect herself from domination by western powers through modernization. Meiji leaders adroitly placated the old elite by subsuming them into the new order. Important *daimyo* and central figures at the former Kyoto court were given titles in a new, European-style nobility. The classification of *samurai* was officially discontinued; *samurai* costume and sword-wearing were declared illegal. In compensation, former *samurai* were given cash payments together with government bonds, valuable only if the Meiji government continued to exist. From now on, except for the titled nobility and the Imperial family itself, all Japanese were to be considered part of a population of equals.

The new social order was not instituted without some resistance. An uprising of sorts, led by a charismatic man who had himself helped to overthrow the Tokugawa regime, broke out in Kyushu, pitting *samurai* against a new Western-style conscript army. The *samurai* fought valiantly and became somewhat canonized in legend, but more significantly, soldiers of the Meiji military achieved complete victory, indicating that without a doubt the new regime was firmly in place.

The West, especially Germany, Britain, France and the United States, became in a real sense classrooms for the young men of the new regime. Under conditions that must have been extremely trying, dozens of those young men agreed to actually go to Western countries and examine in detail "how things were done." Industrial techniques, especially shipbuilding techniques were examined in Britain. Military organization and artifacts were studied in France. The railroad system of the United States, the most comprehensive in the world at the time, was of special interest, and Meiji leaders turned to Germany for a model of modern government. Engineers and technicians were lured to Japan with two to three times the salaries of their previous employment, a great drain on the new regime's modest resources.

The earmarks of industry appeared within a few short years in the form of electric power in Tokyo, a railway line stretching from the central part of the capital some seventeen miles to Yokohama harbor, and a silk-weaving factory using steam power. At first the government tried to build modern industries by itself, but as funds ran out, it was decided to sell off enterprises to private owners. With the exception of a few wealthy merchants who had prospered during the late Tokugawa period, the only people with available cash were former samurai, who, if they pooled what money they had, could in some cases buy entire industries from the government. This formed the beginning of the ***zaibatsu*** groups which were to dominate the economic life of the nation for the next seventy years.

Enormous progress in building a new society was achieved during the first twenty-five years. A modern military system was established and the seeds of an industrial economy had begun to bear fruit. A constitution was issued (as a gift from the Emperor) in 1889, and a year later an elected national legislature met for the first time. A great landmark was reached in 1894, when first Britain and then the other Western powers signed new treaties with Japan, ending the unequal status Japan had been put under and had endured for forty years.

The later Meiji period

Late in the nineteenth century the original Meiji leaders began to die off. Their passion had been to build a nation strong enough to ward off the West. The second generation of Meiji leaders was determined to go farther, to see Japan itself as a full-fledged member of the community of great powers. Nationalist ideology, a blend of the sacredness of the Emperor with a new version of national Shinto, became a part of the school curriculum in an education system as widespread as any in Europe at the time. Political parties emerged, and eventually parliamentary government began to challenge the power of entrenched, non-elected bureaucracy.

In foreign relations, Japan looked more and more like an aggressive military power. Aware of the way England and France exploited other people to their economic advantage, a plan was hatched by a triad of political, economic and military leaders to expand Japan's authority beyond her traditional boundaries. A war was provoked with China in 1895 which the newly industrialized Japan easily won, giving it concessions and control over parts of the Asian continent. Early in the new century expansionists in Japan turned their attention to Korea, and eventually rivalry over control of the Korean peninsula resulted in the Russo-Japanese war of 1904–5. At great sacrifice Japan prevailed in the war, an outcome with rather profound significance. Since the beginning of the Industrial Revolution no society outside the orbit of European-based culture was able to confront on equal footing the technology and military power of the great European powers. It was assumed by most people in the West that such a thing could never happen. Japan proved them wrong, and the set of assumptions underlying European superiority were fatally weakened.

Further reading

Akamatsu, P. (1972) *Meiji 1868: Revolution and Counter-Revolution in Japan*, New York: Harper & Row.

Fukuzawa, Y. (1966) *Autobiography of Fukuzawa Yukichi*, trans. E. Kiyoka, New York: Houghton Mifflin.

Kosaki, M. (1978) *Japanese Thought in the Meiji Era*, Princeton, NJ: Princeton University Press.

Pyle, K.B. (1969) *The New Generation in Meiji Japan*, Stanford, CA: Stanford University Press.

Reischauer, E.O. and Craig, A.M. (1988) *Japan, Tradition and Transformation*, Boston: Houghton Mifflin.

JOHN A. McKINSTRY

Men in charge of MOF (mofutan)

Meaning literally "in charge of," the *tan* is a special company employee responsible for relations with the cognizant ministry in a system of informal regulation. *Mofutan* is a specialized Japanese expression referring to those who work with the Ministry of Finance. Almost every large corporation designates at least one employee to be in constant contact with the bureaucrats in the regulating agencies (for example, the **Ministry of Finance** (MOF) and **Bank of Japan** for banks, the Ministry of Health and Welfare for pharmaceuticals, etc.). The more regulatory discretion the cognizant ministry exercises over a firm, the more relevant the company's ability to affect the regulatory outcome through individual lobbying. In this respect, the *tan* are the junior-level equivalents of the "'old boys," senior-level company employees often hired upon retirement from civil service to facilitate the flow of information with the ministry.

Objectives

The most important goal for a company in designating a *tan* is to ensure a regular, immediate flow of information between the company and the cognizant ministry. While trade associations facilitate access to information on generic, industry-wide concerns, companies aim to ensure company-specific lobbying with the cognizant regulator. Even companies not necessarily close to their regulator often designate a *tan* in what can be called "regulatory competition:" if one competitor continuously lobbies its interests, all other firms in the industry will also dispatch a *tan* in order not to lose out.

The need to designate a *tan* increases with the ministry's leverage over a single company. One example is the voluntary export restraints (VER) demanded by the USA in the automobile trade negotiations of the mid-1980s. The VER meant that each company had to limit its exports according to a quota, which was officially set by MITI. While in practice the quota agreement was reached among the firms based on their existing market shares, MITI had the power to change these quotas. To represent their interests, even the most independent auto makers sent out their *tan*.

Implications

The overall effects of the *tan* system are twofold. On the positive side, the *tan* serve to increase the flow of information between government and business in a very direct, cost-effective manner. Since individuals interact repeatedly and openly, the civil servant is supposedly informed of all events in the industry under his jurisdiction and can identify low-cost solutions to any problems. The *tan* system also reduces the actual costs of regulation, since it replaces on-site inspectors and other monitoring by the ministry. Moreover, the *tan* system helps overcome one potential regulatory problem inherent in the rotation-on-the-job system, which also applies to ministries. As civil servants are moved to new positions every other year, they have to learn from scratch about the new industry's opportunities and challenges. The company and trade association *tan* provide free training to the incoming regulator. Of course, this also means that the industry lobbies the regulator from the beginning.

On the negative side, the *tan* system increases the opacity of Japanese regulation. In industries that are predominantly regulated through **administrative guidance** and where direct lobbying is therefore particularly effective, the institutionalized *tan* representation of large firms is a disadvantage to both smaller and foreign firms. The system also obfuscates the process of policy making and can lead to regulatory disinformation of outsiders. Moreover, the system helps to cloak accountability.

In cases of management mistakes, a ministry may choose to withhold negative information, possibly to the detriment of the affected shareholders and trading partners.

The finance industry

One industry where the *tan* system has been of particular importance is banking. Until 1998, the MOF held a wide scope of regulatory responsibilities and relied heavily on situational, informal regulation. Regulating banks is subject to special requirements in all countries. For instance, to avoid a bank run that could destabilize an entire financial system, governments sometimes opt to withhold critical information in the hope of limiting the damaging ripple effects of a bank failure. In Japan, however, bank regulation based not on objective inspections but instead on an excessive reliance on behind-the-door problem-solving may have largely contributed to the banking crisis of the 1990s. The full extent of bad loans held by the country's banks remained undisclosed, and even after a new agency had conducted thorough inspections beginning in 1998, the scope of the bad loan problem remained unclear.

Another instance highlighting the negative effects of the system was the August 1995 case of Daiwa Bank. The bank's New York branch incurred enormous losses which allegedly were duly reported to Japan's MOF. Because several defaulting Japanese banks were threatening the financial stability of Japan at the same time, the MOF decided not to inform US officials and did not make a public statement. US regulators were livid and demanded termination of all of Daiwa Bank's international business.

In response to these crises, the MOF was reorganized by transferring banking regulation to the new Financial Supervisory Agency, and an abolition of the *tan* system was demanded. Banks and other companies had to abolish the designated positions and terminate individual lobbying. In banking, this was strictly enforced beginning in 1995.

Outlook

Problems with this abolition soon became painfully obvious because the informal mechanisms of regulation were not replaced with formal ones.

The positive effects of smooth and efficient regulation were lost, and regulators had less access to information about their industries. In particular, formulating regulation became impossible without inside knowledge of new banking products. Quietly, some of the old relationships were re-established, especially through trade association *tan*. Whether the *tan* system will continue in the future depends on whether supervisory agencies will be established in industries other than banking, as these would obviate extensive personal communication with the ministry.

ULRIKE SCHAEDE

Ministry of Construction

The Ministry of Construction (Kensetsusho or MOC) is one of twelve ministries in Japan's central government bureaucracy. The ministry is charged with developing, operating, and maintaining roads, highways, sewerage, water resources, parks, and other public facilities; implementing river improvement, erosion control, and coastal preservation projects; planning for cities; promoting the construction and real estate industries; establishing building standards; and constructing and maintaining government buildings.

The Ministry of Construction was established on 10 July 1948. Even though it was a creation of the early post-Second World War period, the ministry inherited certain elements of its mission, structure, and personnel from other ministries. Most importantly, MOC absorbed the Civil Engineering Bureau of the once powerful Home Ministry (Naimusho), which was dissolved as part of the Occupation's efforts to demilitarize and democratize Japan. From the War Recovery Bureau (Sensai Fukko In), MOC incorporated the tasks of reconstructing and maintaining public sector facilities, supervising infrastructure development, and overseeing public works projects. MOC's immediate organizational predecessor was the short-lived Construction Institute (Kensetsu In), which was created in January of 1948.

The Ministry of Construction is organized around a headquarters office, several institutes, and a network of regional bureaux. Located in Tokyo's Kasumigaseki district, MOC's headquarters office is subdivided into a Minister's secretariat and five bureaux that administer functionally specific policies for cities, rivers, roads, housing, and economic affairs. The ministry oversees the Public Works Research Institute, Building Research Institute, Geographical Survey Institute, and the Construction College. Much of MOC's work is carried out through eight construction bureaux located in the Tohoku, Kanto, Hokuriku, Chubu, Kinki, Chugoku, Shikoku, and Kyushu regions. Only Hokkaido and Okinawa, which are overseen by agencies under the auspices of the Office of the Prime Minister, are excluded from the ministry's administrative embrace. In addition, MOC and its regional bureaux carry out their functions through hundreds of work offices and branch work offices located across the country.

The Ministry of Construction is charged with spending a sizable share of Japan's general accounts budget and a major portion of allocations from the Fiscal Investment and Loan Program (Zaisei Toyushi Keikaku), the so-called "second budget." MOC's spending power is reflected in the fact that Japan's ratio of public works expenditure to gross domestic product tends to be two to four times greater than that of other advanced industrial countries such as France, the United States, Germany, and the United Kingdom. Increased spending on public works – largely financed by the issuance of construction bonds (*kensetsu kokusai*) – is a popular artifice whereby the Japanese government seeks to stimulate economic growth. For these reasons, MOC is considered one of Japan's most powerful spending agencies. Nevertheless, some observers contend that MOC is among the most politicized of Japan's central governmental ministries, allegedly manipulated by the **Liberal Democratic Party**. However, some observers believe that the Construction Ministry wields relatively more power over Japan's enormous **construction industry** than the **Ministry of International Trade and Industry** does over client industries in its administrative bailiwick.

Construction bureaucrats

The human element of the Ministry of Construction consists of a trio of political appointees who head up a vast corps of meritocratically selected civil servants. At the apex of MOC's formal organizational hierarchy are the Minister of Construction (*kensetsu daijin*) and two Parliamentary Vice-Ministers of Construction (*kensetsu seimu jikan*). As with all of the ministries and agencies of Japan's central government bureaucracy, these are MOC's only political appointees. The paucity of political appointees in Japan's government bureaucracy contrasts starkly with the dozens, sometimes hundreds, of politically selected functionaries in each of the various agencies of the federal government in the United States. Most of those appointed to the top political posts at MOC spend only a brief time in the position. In fact, from 1948 to 2000 the average length of tenure in the Construction Minister post was only about nine months. Among other things, this means that the political appointees must depend heavily upon the good will and expertise of the career bureaucrats in carrying out their duties of overseeing the ministry. While a few individuals, such as Ichiro Kono (Construction Minister, 1962–4), come to be known for strong-handed control, there is little evidence to suggest that ministers exert any appreciable long-term influence over major policy and personnel decisions at the Ministry.

At the time of its creation, slightly less than six thousand civil servants were employed in the Construction Ministry's internal sections, affiliated organs, and local branches. The total rose precipitously until the mid-1960s when the Ministry employed more than 35,000 individuals. But the number has declined steadily ever since, with the 1998 figure standing at 23,674 employed officials. As with all central state ministries in Japan, MOC's officials fall into two distinct categories, depending upon whether they entered the Ministry after passing the Class A or the much less demanding Class B segment of the Higher-level Public Officials Examination. The former are referred to as "career" officials, while the vastly more numerous latter group is known as the "non-careers," a distinction akin to that between commissioned and non-commissioned military officers. The non-career officials tend to lack the educational pedigree of their career counterparts, and their promotional prospects are severely limited.

MOC's career bureaucrats may be divided into two groups, each with its own peculiar career path leading to the post of administrative vice-minister (*jimu jikan*), the foremost post for career civil servants. As with other ministries, the majority of MOC's "generalists" (*jimuya*) are graduates of the law and economics faculties, with prestigious universities such as the University of Tokyo supplying a disproportionate share. But MOC is unique among Japan's central government ministries in that "technical specialists" (*gijutsuya*) – individuals trained in civil engineering, architecture, and other technical fields – are permitted to hold the post of administrative vice-minister. Aside from wielding considerable administrative power within the Ministry, these technical specialists perform a larger sharer of the design services involved in public works projects than do their counterparts in commissioning agencies in countries such as the United States.

The balance of power between generalists and technical specialists is a postwar phenomenon. Indeed, technical specialists in the prewar Home Ministry's Civil Engineering Bureau were not promoted above the rank of section chief in the Ministry's headquarters or head of the civil engineering department in the regional branches. Owing to the combination of several forces, including the faith of Occupation planners in "scientific administration" (for which, presumably, technical specialists would be ideally suited), Tadayasu Iwasawa, a civil engineer, became the MOC's first administrative vice-minister and the first technical specialist to ascend to the post. Despite the triumph of the technical specialists, Masami Nakata, a generalist, became administrative vice-minister upon Iwasawa's resignation in March of 1950. This initiated what has become an unwritten, and nearly inviolable, law at the Ministry of Construction: that the top administrative post will alternate between technical specialists and generalists.

While the dual-track personnel system has become institutionalized at the administer/vice-minister level, there is no alternation with regard to the penultimate posts in the respective career ladders, deputy vice-minister for administration (*daijin kanbo cho*) and vice-minister for engineering affairs (*kensetsu gikan*). Generalists invariably serve as directors of the minister's secretariat, economic affairs, and city bureaux, while technical specialists hold the director posts at the river and road bureaux. The only exception is the directorship of the housing bureau, where generalists and administrative specialists alternate in the director's post. For the most part, the top posts in the Ministry's eight regional construction bureaux, auxiliary organs, and local branch offices are held by technical specialists.

MOC exerts influence over the construction bureaucracy at the local levels through **shukko**, the practice of temporarily "loaning out" mid-career officials. These loaned-out officials typically spend from two to fours years in positions attached to prefectural or municipal bureaucracies. In addition, MOC "loans" a number of mid-career officials to public corporations, particularly those entities under the ministry's jurisdiction, such as the Hanshin Highway Public Corporation.

Descent from heaven

Upon retirement from the government service, usually between the ages of fifty and fifty-five, most upper bureaucrats "descend from heaven" into a "second career." This re-employment of ex-officials, known as **amakudari** (descent from heaven), takes several distinct forms. The most widespread and controversial form of *amakudari* is the re-employment of retired MOC officials in private-sector construction firms. The ostensible reason that firms hire ex-bureaucrats is to obtain the administrative and technical expertise that these individuals possess. Yet many observers believe that the most important reason behind the practice of re-employing retired MOC bureaucrats in construction firms involves their personal connections to the government bureaucracy. Specifically, some observers believe that firms employing ex-bureaucrats are rewarded with access to confidential information concerning bidder designation and secret leakages of information concerning the government's confidential anticipated ceiling price (*yotei kakaku*) for public works projects. In this way, *amakudari* is said to be entwined with **dango**, the institutionalized, albeit illegal, system of price-fixing on public works projects.

A second form of *amakudari* is termed "side-slip style descent from heaven" (*yokosuberi gata amakudari*). This denotes the re-employment of ex-bureaucrats in upper administrative positions in quasi-governmental corporations, foundations, financial banks, and similar organizations. It is said that a large share of the top positions in these public entities are "hereditary" in that their occupants tend to be drawn almost exclusively from the ranks of retired government officials, particularly those from the agency which oversees the corporation. In some cases, these positions involve relatively high salaries, few duties other than ceremonial functions, and various other perquisites. MOC is in the enviable position of controlling a number of "progenitor posts" in a dozen or so public corporations, such as the Japan Housing Public Corporation. Some former MOC bureaucrats have been known to "migrate" through as many as five side-slip posts.

Finally, the Construction Ministry is well represented among members of parliament. The first construction bureaucrat to descend into parliamentary politics was Tadayasu Iwasawa, MOC's first administrative vice-minister, who won election to the Upper House in 1950. Over the years a number of former MOC officials have trodden up the fabled red carpet of the National Diet Building. The vast majority have claimed membership in the Liberal Democratic Party. It is believed that much of the electoral success enjoyed by former MOC bureaucrats derives from the potent campaign support provided by the "construction machine" (*kensetsu mashiin*), a somewhat shadowy apparatus designed to turn out the vote for candidates favored by the ministry.

In this way, *amakudari* is the glue that binds together MOC, the construction and real estate industries, and influential allies in the parliamentary world. Most importantly, *amakudari* facilitates mutually beneficial interactions and the exchange of information.

"Construction friction" and beyond

In the mid-1980s the Ministry of Construction became engulfed in heated trade friction with the United States and other countries concerning the closed nature of Japan's construction market. The first salvo in this trade dispute involved demands to include American firms in bidding for projects connected with the construction of the new Kansai International Airport. Eventually the dispute widened to include demands for reform of the designated competitive bidder system – whereby the contracting agency designates which firms will be permitted to submit bids on public works projects – and strengthening of Japanese antimonopoly law. A particularly contentious episode in this dispute followed the revelation that from 1984 to 1987 Japanese contractors rigged bids on construction projects at the US Naval Base at Yokosuka. Issues relating to US–Japanese "construction friction" were incorporated into the Bush administration's Structural Impediments Initiative and the Clinton administration's Framework Talks. Given the enormous size of the Japanese construction market and the difficulties faced by foreign firms attempting to gain access to it, construction friction likely will be a nagging irritant in Japan's foreign economic relations.

Further reading

Brooks, R.A. (ed.) (1990) *Opening Japan: The Construction Market*, Washington, DC: The Heritage Foundation.

Cutts, R.A. (1988) "The Construction Issue: Japan Slams the Door," *California Management Review* 30: 46–63.

Kensetsusho (annual) *Kensetsu hakusho* (Construction White Paper), Tokyo: Okurasho Insatsu Kyoku.

Ministry of Construction Home Page, http://www.moc.go.jp/eng/eng/index.htm.

Woodall, B. (1996) *Japan Under Construction: Corruption, Politics, and Public Works*, Berkeley, CA: University of California Press.

BRIAN WOODALL

Ministry of Finance

The Ministry of Finance (MOF) was established in 1869, a year after the **Meiji restoration**, as one of Japan's central government organs. The ministry's roles and functions have undergone numerous changes in the years since. For most of the postwar period, the MOF's operations were based on the Ministry of Finance Establishment Law, promulgated in May 1949. After the Second World War, Allied Occupation officials dismantled other powerful government agencies, such as the Home Affairs Ministry, but kept the MOF intact as a means of facilitating financial system stability and the development of a strong banking system. As a result, the ministry emerged from the Second World War largely unscathed and clearly at the top of the bureaucratic hierarchy.

The ministry has a long history of recruiting the best and the brightest in Japan to join its ranks. In the initial postwar decades, many of the economics departments in top universities were dominated by socialist thinking. As a result, the majority of officials on the elite career track within the ministry held law rather than economics degrees. In more recent years, the number of officials holding economics degrees has risen substantially, although law graduates remain the majority.

Implications of a wide scope of authority

Until 1998, the ministry's tasks spanned from the compilation of the national budget, tax collection, and oversight of monetary policy to the regulation and supervision of private sector finance, the management of national assets, and the regulation of the liquor and tobacco industries. This enormous breadth of authority made Japan's Finance Ministry distinctive when compared to its counterpart finance ministries and treasuries in other countries. The ministry's simultaneous responsibility for fiscal and monetary policy as well as financial regulation and supervision also gave rise to particularly strong links between the ministry and the governing party, private sector corporations (financial institutions, in particular), and other government and quasi-government agencies.

More specifically, the number of former MOF officials occupying seats in the Diet has typically exceeded numbers of ex-bureaucrats from other ministries. At the same time, former MOF officials have assumed larger numbers and more lucrative private sector positions upon retiring from the public service than have former officials from any other ministry. Furthermore, MOF officials on secondment have staffed a distinctively large number of positions within other ministries and agencies.

Even while the ministry has been noted for its strength, however, it has been infamous for its compartmentalization and lack of organizational coherence. It has long been described within Japan as a "bureaucracy within a bureaucracy" (*kancho no naka no kancho*) and as "a collection of bureaux rather than a ministry" (*kyoku atte, sho nashi*). Although MOF officials in the fiscal policy bureaux of Budget and Tax engage in constant interaction with officials in the governing party as part of the annual budget process and review of tax legislation, officials in the financial bureaux of Banking, Securities, and International Finance long enjoyed relative decision-making autonomy. This different pattern of interaction with the Diet across bureaux reflected the relative electoral salience of the respective issue areas.

Fiscal functions

The ministry's fiscal functions involve the administration of public finance. More specifically, the ministry formulates the national budget, oversees the execution of this budget and the collection of tax revenue, manages funds so as to coordinate spending and revenue generation, and manages national property.

The budget formulation process begins in June when government ministries and agencies begin to draw up estimated budgets. These are then typically submitted to the MOF in August and the ministry compiles a national budget proposal. Following Cabinet and Diet deliberations and any amendments (extremely rare), this proposal becomes law and the ministry then moves to spend or allocate money in accordance with the provisions.

Finance ministries or national treasuries in most countries exhibit conservative tendencies, but in Japan, the MOF's persistent articulation of a "balanced budget" principle has been a particularly prominent feature of ministry rhetoric. This principle was first breached in 1965 with the issuance of government bonds to finance public works projects and was encroached upon more severely in the late 1970s and early 1980s when government bonds were also issued to cover revenue shortfalls. As Japan's massive levels of public debt today suggest, the ministry was also unable to adhere to the principle in the 1990s. Nonetheless, the balanced budget principle has remained a strong undercurrent in all of the MOF's policy discussions.

Efforts to suppress excessive public spending have been evidenced in the guidelines for budget requests issued by the MOF each year as part of the annual budget process. Although any ministry or agency may, in theory, request budget appropriations in any amount, the Budget Bureau – with the Cabinet's consent – normally set "ceilings" that indicated the highest levels permissible. These ceilings have ranged from a 10 percent increase on the previous year to a 10 percent decrease on the previous year.

Monetary functions

The MOF is also responsible for the management of Japan's monetary affairs, both domestically and abroad. Carrying out the government's financing operations involves the administration of funds in the ministry's Trust Fund Bureau. Of particular importance is the ministry's management of the Fiscal Investment and Loan Program (FILP). The FILP is a kind of "second budget" that funnels money from postal savings, postal life insurance, welfare, and national pension funds into the government's special accounts, various government organs, quasi-governmental corporations, and local public authorities, in order to implement policy objectives. In April 2001, major reform of the FILP will significantly alter this traditional flow of funds, however, and require traditional fund recipients to turn to other means to procure resources, including the bond market.

The MOF's monetary functions also include the regulation and supervision of private sector financial institutions including banks, insurance companies and brokerages. A so-called "convoy approach" (*goso sendan hoshiki*) to financial regulation characterized the ministry's supervision of private sector finance over the postwar period. This approach ensured that no financial sector actor was left behind and that no actor moved forward so fast as to endanger the viability of others.

The convoy approach also served a multiplicity of interests. The stability it facilitated in the financial sector ensured constant flows of credit to industry as the nation focused on economic reconstruction in the immediate postwar period. Through its support of the banks in this way, the government also cushioned the impact of economic shocks on borrowers. Importantly, the convoy approach also served the interests of banks, for it gave rise to a cartel-like arrangement that benefited all members. Furthermore, the practice of **amakudari** meant that this principle was a reflection of self-interested ministry behavior as well. Any bank that went under would be one fewer potential depository for officials retiring from the ministry. Until the mid-1990s, the ministry successfully upheld this principle.

Finally, the ministry's monetary functions have an international dimension. The ministry formulates, executes and coordinates exchange rate policies, while also supervising the government's external loans and investments. In the wake of the 1997–8 Asian financial crisis, the ministry was particularly active in coordinating and providing aid to countries hit by crisis.

Organizational adjustments to changing needs

Organizational changes have been carried out in the MOF over the postwar period to accommodate changes in the policymaking environment. In response to the growth in Japan's external trade and the liberalization of foreign exchange transactions, for example, a Customs and Tariff Bureau was established in 1961. By 1964, as Japan's economic system became more liberal and the nation became a member of the Organization for Economic Cooperation and Development (OECD), the need to place greater priority on the development of the **capital markets** and foreign exchange transactions was evident. In this year, therefore, a Securities Bureau and an International Finance Bureau were established within the ministry. Then, in 1992, in response to the growing inter-relationship between financial services and the emergence of financial scandals, the ministry established the Financial Inspections Department within the Minister's Secretariat.

Policy breakdown and reorganization of the ministry

The ministry, however, did not always adjust adeptly to changing policy needs. In the 1990s,

the ministry's failure to aggressively tackle the non-performing loan problem in the nation's banking sector led to an unprecedented level of criticism of the ministry, as well as to dire consequences for the economy as a whole.

Public criticism of the MOF in the 1990s was in itself nothing new. The ministry became the target of public criticism on a number of occasions over the postwar period. Prior to the 1990s, however, this criticism bore little connection to policy breakdown per se. Occasional scandals emerged over such things as ministry officials in the Budget Bureau being wined and dined by representatives of quasi-government agencies seeking subsidies from the budget. The introduction of the consumption tax in 1989 led to some public anger directed at the ministry. Criticism of the MOF in the 1990s was distinct, however, in that it depicted the ministry's lax financial supervision and influence on monetary policy in the bubble period as a central reason behind the **bad debt** that plagued the financial system after the bubble's collapse. The bad debt problem, in turn, was perceived as also contributing to the economic downturn.

The political context of MOF criticism in the 1990s also differed from the past, occurring against the backdrop of unprecedented upheaval in the political party system. Criticism intensified from 1995–6 in particular, after the ministry requested public funds to dispose of failed housing and loan corporations called *jusen*. In the wake of this development, the **Liberal Democratic Party**'s coalition partners – and some members of the LDP itself – began calling for the ministry to be "dismantled."

In 1997, legislation was passed in the Diet to reorganize the MOF. In April 1998, responsibility for monetary policy was devolved from the ministry to the **Bank of Japan** with the implementation of the new Bank of Japan Law. Then, in June 1998, responsibility for the regulation and supervision of private financial institutions was transferred from the MOF to a new and independent Financial Supervisory Agency. In July 2000, responsibility for financial system planning was also transferred to the Financial Services Agency (the successor to the Financial Supervisory Agency). As a result of these changes, the scope of authority enjoyed by Japan's Finance Ministry today more closely resembles that of its counterpart agencies elsewhere in the world.

As Japan enters the twenty-first century, the MOF must play a critical role in addressing some of the most difficult challenges faced by Japan in the postwar period. These include restarting the economy after a decade of prolonged economic stagnation and addressing the dire state of public finance. As of 2001, Japan's ratio of government deficit to GDP ranked as the worst among the advanced industrial nations.

With the reorganization of Japan's central government ministries and agencies in January 2001, the Japanese name of the MOF was changed from Okurasho to Zaimusho (literally, "Treasury Ministry"). The official English translation, however, remains "Ministry of Finance."

Further reading

Brown, J.R. (1999) *The Ministry of Finance: Bureaucratic Practices and the Transformation of the Japanese Economy*, Westport, CT: Quorum Books.

Hartcher, P. (1998) *The Ministry: How Japan's Most Powerful Institution Endangers World Markets*, Boston: Harvard Business School Press.

Kato, J. (1994) *The Problem of Bureaucratic Rationality: Tax Politics in Japan*, Princeton, NJ: Princeton University Press.

Mabuchi, M. (1994) *Okurasho Tosei no Seiji Keizaigaku* (The Political Economy of the Finance Ministry's Control), Tokyo: Chuo Koron-sha.

Rosenbluth, F.M. (1989) *Financial Politics in Contemporary Japan*, Ithaca, NY: Cornell University Press.

Vogel, S.K. (1994) "The Bureaucratic Approach to the Financial Revolution: Japan's Ministry of Finance and Financial System Reform," *Governance: An International Journal of Policy and Administration* 7(3): 219–43.

JENNIFER AMYX

Ministry of International Trade and Industry

The Ministry of International Trade and Industry (MITI) is in charge of administering Japan's policies covering international trade and industries other than agriculture. It was established in 1949, taking over from the Ministry of Commerce and Industry. As of 2000, MITI had a staff of 12,346 and annual budget of ¥2.03 trillion. It was restructured as the Ministry of Trade, Economy and Industry (METI) in the context of the complete revision of national administration organization of Japan in January 2001.

The administrative area and organization of MITI

The administrative area of MITI covers most of the private sector (most manufacturing industries, wholesale, retail and service industries) other than agriculture, the transportation business, construction industries, and telecommunication business. MITI is responsible for government policy toward industry and trade covering such matters as the healthy development of industrial sectors, which it supports through advisory and technical support of private sector initiatives; environmental protection as it relates to industrial activity; and the management and resolution of trade conflicts and disputes involving Japanese firms and industry, both domestic and international. While much of MITI's activities seem directed at large companies, it is also responsible for industrial policies affecting small and medium enterprises, as well as patent policy.

The extensive administrative area of MITI is better understood by considering the ministry's organization. The organization of MITI has changed corresponding to the challenges confronting the Japanese economy. In 1973, following a major organizational reform, the ministry consisted of *genkyoku* (original bureaux) which are in charge of policies for each industry and *yokowarukyoku* (inter-industry bureaux) which are in charge of the policies for specialized issue areas such as environmental policy, trade policy and so forth. There are three *genkyoku*: the Machinery and Information Industries Bureau, which is in charge of policy for the machine and information industries; the Basic Industries Bureau, which develops policies for the chemical industry, the steel industry and so forth; and the Consumer Goods and Service Industries Bureau, which oversees policy for the textile and apparel industries, miscellaneous goods, the pottery industry, and so forth.

There are four *yokowarukyoku*. The Industrial Policy Bureau is in charge of industrial policy overall, such as the policy for industrial structure conversion, industrial finance and industrial technology. The International Trade Policy Bureau is in charge of multilateral and bilateral trade negotiation. This bureau is also in charge of policy for the promotion of international trade, such as trade insurance policy. The Industrial Location and Environmental Protection Bureau is in charge of policy for industrial location, preserving the environment and safety. Also, there are three *gaikyoku* (agencies). The Small and Medium Enterprise Agency develops and coordinates small and medium enterprise policy. The Japan Patent Office is responsible for patent administration. The Agency for Natural Resources and Energy is in charge of policies to ensure stability and security of energy and natural resources as well as policies that relate to the energy and mining industry. The Minister's Secretariat has the role of adjusting and coordinating the opinions on industrial policy from the related bureaux and to form the budget and draft laws submitted to the Diet.

The history of MITI

MITI was formally established in 1951. From that date to the present, it has held the primary responsibility for the development of policies affecting the Japan's economy and industrial development. In the 1950s, MITI's primary charge was to strengthen the independent base of the Japanese economy, which had been devastated by the war. In 1951, the **Japan Development Bank** was established as a policy financing bank. The Enterprise Rationalization Promotion Law was promulgated in 1952 to give favorable treatment such as tax credits to encourage enterprise rationalization. Thereafter many other laws were introduced to promote targeted industries such as electronics and various machinery industries. The ultimate objective of these policies and their supporting legislation was the achievement of economic equality with other developed countries. As Japan must rely on the importation of raw materials and food, the acquisition of foreign

currency was a subject of special concern and, in order to address this concern, an export promotion policy was adopted. As a consequence, an export insurance system was carried out beginning in 1950 and from 1953 favorable tax treatment extended to export activities. Also, the **Japan External Trade Organization** (JETRO) was established in 1958 to accumulate and disseminate information on foreign economies. In 1956 Japan joined the General Agreement on Tariffs and Trade (GATT).

In the 1960s Japan became a vital member of the world economy through the liberalization of trade and capital. In 1960, the Japanese government adopted a plan to liberalize trade and currency that raised the rate of trade liberalization from 40 percent to 80 percent within three years. Further, in 1964 Japan accepted the Article 8 obligation of the International Monetary Fund, and carried out its first capital liberalization in 1968. The primary focus of MITI in the 1960s was to cultivate new industries such as automobiles, petrochemical products and synthetic fibers under the difficult circumstance of trade and capital liberalization. MITI put forward a policy of "heavy and chemical industrialization," which it outlined in a document entitlted *Vision of MITI Policy in the 1960s*. At the time, the ministry believed that key industries were suffering from a lack of funds, excessive competition and inability to achieve scale economies. MITI dealt with this problem by means of market-intervening measures such as the use of administrative guidance to carry out advance adjustment of enterprise investment plans, based on its own survey of these plans. (Such measures were discontinued in the 1970s.) A typical example of MITI's efforts to advance improvements in industrial structure through government leadership was the submission to the Diet in 1963 of the Draft Law on Temporary Measures for Promotion of Specified Manufacturing Industries. This Draft Law designated the specialty steel, automobile and petrochemical industries as "specified industries." It ruled that representatives of the industry in question, along with representatives from financial circles and competent ministers should deliberate on "promotion standards" for these target industries in order to cultivate their development in a coordinated fashion. MITI argued that the government needed to carry out a policy of favorable treatment in taxation and funding toward these industries, and also to give them an exclusion from the Anti-Monopoly Law (the Law Concerning the Prohibition of Private Monopoly and the Preservation Fair Trade) if necessary. However the Draft Law was tabled twice and finally abandoned without a vote being taken. Reports at that time indicate that, with the exception of MITI, members of financial and industrial circles and other ministries were opposed to the Draft Law because the bill was seen as strengthening the power of MITI. As a result, MITI's policy gradually shifted to one that was more informational in nature, providing information and advice to complement, rather than control, market mechanisms.

The distortions of high economic growth began to appear in the Japanese economy in the latter half of the 1960s. The first was serious environmental destruction, as reflected in several highly visible water and air pollution disasters. In response, the government promulgated the Basic Law for Environmental Pollution Control in 1967, and MITI formulated new initiatives in support of the measure, such as the development of technology for pollution prevention, promotion of pollution prevention investment, and promotion of positioning technical experts in manufacturing facilities.

The second distortion was the appearance of depopulated areas and the concentration of population in cities. The government tried hard to construct industrial infrastructures of rural districts in response to this problem, and MITI advanced policies to address the adjustment of industrial location by means of the Industrial Relocation Promotion Law (1973).

Trade friction also emerged as a significant issue during this period, as Japan's economic rise led to it becoming a competitive force within the world economy. The US–Japan textile negotiations begun in 1969 became a major political problem for the first time. The negotiations continued until the US–Japan Textile Agreement of 1972, which contained provisions to restrain textile exports from Japan to the USA. Corresponding to this, MITI implemented a policy to promote the abandonment of excessive looms, in order to reduce production capacity and lessen the shock to the domestic textile industry of export reductions.

In 1970 MITI announced its *Vision of MITI Policy in the 1970s*. It identified the knowledge intensification of the industrial structure as the primary focus of its efforts. It specifically targeted the computer and numerically controlled (NC) machine tool industries as well as the fashion industry as representative examples of knowledge-intensive industries. In response to the socio-economic problems that emanated from rapid economic development, it also proclaimed the importance of industry's role in, and responsibility to, society. This represented an important shift in the ministry's orientation. It was at this point that industrial policy at MITI gradually shifted its emphasis toward achieving a sound economic development while taking values other than growth into account.

In 1973 MITI restructured itself and established the Agency for Natural Resources and Energy. Shortly thereafter, the worldwide oil crisis occurred and the Japanese economy experienced a sharp jolt. Quickly the newly formed agency found itself at the center of attention as it worked to develop a plan for enhancing energy efficiency and reducing petroleum consumption. MITI followed through with regulations and policies based on the Petroleum Supply and Demand Optimization Law on Emergency Measures for National Life Stabilization.

As a result of the oil crisis and the end high economic growth, the 1970s was a time when several major industries fell into a serious chronic business slump. In 1978 the Law on Temporary Measures for Stabilizing Specified Depressed Industries was promulgated, and MITI targeted the restructuring of these industries with an aim of reducing excessive capacity and improving operating efficiency thereby enhancing competitiveness.

In the 1980s, trade friction intensified as the trade imbalance between Japan and the USA continued to grow. The areas of trade friction expanded to include automobiles, semiconductors and NC machine tools. As for automobiles, after intense negotiations, Japan agreed to restrain the export beginning in 1981. In the area of NC machine tools, self-restraint was also accepted. In semiconductor negotiations, Japan agreed to introduce an export monitoring system and make efforts to assist US makers' entry into the Japanese market. There was concern within MITI that this series of bilateral negotiations would threaten the world free trade system, with its emphasis on broader, multilateral agreements. In the 1990s much of the trade friction problem was resolved through the development of new international trade rules such as the Marrakesh Agreement establishing the World Trade Organization.

In 1985, the rapid appreciation of the yen following the Plaza Accord brought about a difficult situation for export-led **small and medium-sized firms**. MITI took measures to lessen the shock by promulgating the Law on Temporary Measures for Small and Medium Enterprises in Specified Regions.

In the 1990s, the situation surrounding MITI changed drastically. First, deregulation became an urgent issue and was seen as critical to further economic development in Japan. MITI abandoned its regulation in many fields. The abolition of the Large Retail Stores Law and the liberalization of electric power prices are two examples of MITI's shift. Second, both at home and abroad, the preservation of the environment came to take on greater importance. In this area, MITI began promoting recycling of electrical equipment and other energy and resource conservation activities. Furthermore, MITI pushed policies that sought to reduce industry and consumer demand for energy through research and development on energy efficient and energy conserving technologies. The 1990s was also the decade in which MITI actively worked toward the further construction of international rules of trade, investment, and the protection of intellectual property. In each of these areas, MITI was put in the position of coordinating Japan's domestic system with the larger international system.

Summary

Within the government administration, MITI has been responsible for the oversight of a large portion of the Japanese of economy. MITI carries out its wide and varied duties through a structure of bureaus that have either industry or topic-specific responsibilities. At the ministry level, it coordinates and adjusts policies put forward by individual bureaux. MITI's objectives and the means by which it accomplishes those objectives have evolved over time in concert with the development and evolution of the Japanese economy. The fundamental thrust of that evolution has been in the direction of increasing reliance on approaches that complement market mechanisms. In recognition of further changes in the Japanese economy, MITI has evolved once again. It restructured itself and was reborn as the Ministry of Trade, Economy and Industry (METI) in January 2001 with the complete revision of the national administration organization in Japan.

Further reading

Sumiya, M. (2001) *A History of Japanese Trade and Industry Policy*, Oxford: Oxford University Press.

TAKEHIKO YASUDA

Ministry of Labor

Recently combined in 2001 with the Ministry of Health and Welfare to become the Ministry of Health, Labor and Welfare, the Ministry of Labor (MOL) was originally established in September of 1947. Its charge, according to the Ministry of Labor itself, is to secure stable employment, promote worker welfare, and contribute to economic expansion and stability of national life. Similar to the Department of Labor in the USA with its Bureau of Labor Statistics, the Ministry and affiliated institutions such as the Japan Institute of Labor collect extensive data on the workplace constantly throughout the year, and act as a central clearinghouse for labor-related information. The Ministry is also deeply engaged in labor policy, and is involved in many decisions that bear directly on the economic welfare of employees. The Ministry enforces the nation's labor laws and is also partly responsible for legal revision. Known for its strong support of job security and other characteristics of the stylized view of Japanese labor markets (see **internal labor markets**; **lifetime employment**; seniority wages; **enterprise unions**), the

Ministry has struggled in recent years to adapt labor policy to rapidly changing labor conditions. This includes rising unemployment and a rapidly aging population.

More than twenty statistical surveys per year are performed by the MOL and affiliated institutions. Two well-known surveys are the Monthly Labor Survey and the Basic Survey of Wage Structure. The general purpose of surveying is to identify trends and problems in the labor statistics. Possible problems might revolve around wages, working hours, employment, and personnel and labor management. Additional qualitative data is gleaned through management conferences in each industry and Ministry of Labor research meetings on topics such as personnel and labor management. The level of detail the ministry is able to gather on separate industries and businesses is extensive. Each year, a White Paper on Labor is published by the Ministry based on data collection. The White Paper tends to focus on the issues identified over the course of the year and proposes medium and long-term solutions to these problems. For example, in the midst of continued stagnation in the Japanese economy, rising structural unemployment, and an aging workforce, the 1997 White Paper focused on employment and wages in structural transformation, as well as possible solutions to the inevitable problems that will arise from an aging workforce.

The Ministry remains a large institution broken into many different bureaux and divisions covering the areas of labor administration. Major bureaus include the Labor Relations Bureau, the Labor Standards Bureau, The Women's Bureau, the Employment Security Bureau, and the Human Resources Development Bureau. These bureaux in turn are broken up into divisions. Typical divisions include the Labor Legislation Division within the Labor Relations Bureau, the working hours and working compensation divisions within the Labor Standards Bureau, and the Employment Insurance Division within the Employment Security Bureau. Important affiliated organizations include the Japan Institute of Labor, founded in 1958, which disseminates information to the public through the Employment Information Center within the Institute.

History and description of selected policies

The MOL was founded in the context of a profound period of change for labor policy in Japan. Just after the Second World War, three very important laws – sometimes known as "the three fundamental labor laws" – were passed that were to frame policy for the postwar period. The Labor Union Law (1945) established the right of workers to organize and bargain collectively, and defined unfair labor practices. The Labor Relations Adjustment Law (1946) defined the limits of strike behavior and established procedures for settlement of labor disputes. The Labor Standards Law (1947) legislated, among other things, better working conditions, minimum wage standards, an eight-hour working day, compensation for work related injuries, and lastly, restrictions on female and minor employment. The main thrust of these three laws lasted through the postwar period to the present. Perhaps the most important law for Ministry of Labor jurisdiction was the Labor Standards Law, which was only fundamentally overhauled after fifty years. The terms of the law covered all employees in Japan, unionized and non-unionized alike.

Although many of these terms remain in effect, there have been some changes recently. Restrictions on female employment originally intended as protection – including restrictions on overtime, nighttime, and early morning work – were eventually seen as hindering the move for greater egalitarianism in Japan. These restrictions were recently relaxed, and the Ministry began enforcing more egalitarian work standards. Coupled with the Equal Opportunity Employment Act, women in Japan now have more opportunities and choice than they did before. On this and other issues relating to discrimination, the MOL is combining carrot and stick; companies that conform to new standards tend to get rewarded with penalties levied on firms that violate discrimination legislation. Other recent significant changes to the Labor Standard Law have aimed at making the labor market more flexible by steering workers toward newer industries such as information technology.

Although there are many examples, the minimum wage policy in Japan is a good illustration of the MOL's degree of involvement in everyday labor issues. The Ministry of Labor is in charge of the overall administration of the minimum wage system, and it ensures that minimum wages are revised every year in accordance with changes in overall wages and prices. In sharp contrast to the USA and to many European countries, Japan does not have a uniform national minimum wage. A Minimum Wage Law enacted in 1959 stipulates that individual industries and regions play a major role in determining the level of the wage. On the recommendation of the Minister of Labor or the Chief of the Prefectural Labor Standards Office, a Minimum Wage Council in each prefecture then adjusts the minimum wage accordingly. Contemporary data provided by the Ministry of Labor has the highest minimum wage by prefecture at 5,465 yen per day (in Tokyo, Kanagawa, and Osaka), while the lowest is 4,712 yen (in Miyazaki). Across industries, the highest minimum wage paid in a particular industry per day is 7,280 yen (in general trucking), while the lowest is 4,928 yen (in ceramic ware manufacturing).

Enforcement of the minimum wage law, like enforcement of many of the other labor laws in Japan, is quite difficult. Constrained by a relatively low number of trained monitors and fairly weak punishment, the MOL essentially educates the public with the resources available. Having a many-tiered minimum wage system injects a large degree of complexity into the system, and it is common for employees to be unaware of the level of minimum wage that their employers are legally obligated to pay. As such, the temptation for employers to cheat is high. Every November, the Ministry runs a ten day campaign to educate the public about the year's minimum wage increases and to try to ensure payment of minimum wages.

Despite the inherent complexity of labor markets, the MOL has been strategically involved in shaping their evolution. Throughout the postwar period, for example, the MOL generally has sought to soften the effects of downturns and preserve long term employment - sometimes directly subsidizing firms to ensure that employees will be hired back after a period of layoff. At other points the MOL has brought direct pressure on firms to not fire employees in times of stress. In 1993, when Pioneer Electric officially laid off a group of employees, the MOL objected strongly and brought about a change of heart. However, in the face of continued stagnation and growing recognition of the need for change in labor markets, the stance on preserving employment security has softened.

The private sector plays a major role in shaping change as well. Typical of most diffusion of new organizational forms in Japanese business, private sector companies and bureaucrats work together to legitimate new practices. An example of collaboration between the Ministry of Labor and the private sector was in a 1994 report published by the Employment Information Center. Based on Ministry research on "best practice" already beginning to occur, it urged companies to create three new promotion tracks for a new wage system: true managers leading subordinates, researchers and planners, and skilled workers and technicians. Within categories, the recommendation was to promote according to ability. Hitachi, Matsushita, NTT, Sanyo and other leading companies had all implemented systems like this by the mid-1990s.

The latter half of the 1990s and early 2000s is presenting unique challenges for the MOL, and the situation has remained troublesome for several years running. **Unemployment** overall is at a postwar peak of around 4.9 percent, with involuntary unemployment surging from 320,00 in 1992 to 1 million by 2001. An increasing percentage of this unemployment may be structural, rather than cyclical. Discouraged workers – those who are not even searching for a job – have risen from 1 percent of the workforce to around 2.2 percent. Temporary, part-time, and **contract employees** have risen from 4.7 percent of the labor force to 27.5 percent of the labor force. A slow shift to the service sector remains underway, with the latter rising from 50 percent of the workforce to 55 percent; according to most theory on economic development, this last trend is a good thing. In short, change in labor markets already underway has accelerated dramatically and is causing dislocation of a sort not seen in Japan since the Second World War.

Faced with these realities, the MOL has begun to shift away from employment preservation towards a focus on new job creation, especially in small and medium sized businesses. In 1999 and 2000, subsidies were being granted to employers who hired workers laid off from other firms; this is a practice many Japanese firms still find difficult to do. Extra unemployment measures were built in to automatically kick in should unemployment go above 4.9 percent. Growth sectors of the economy – such as information technology and health services – were provided other employment subsidies. Despite measures such as these, unemployment has persisted. Generally these and other policies have favored older workers and former "insiders" (those employees who worked inside the firm for a long duration), rather than younger workers. Thus, the high unemployment rate for young workers will remain an issue. This also preserves high costs to employers, as older workers are more expensive. In response to this problem, the MOL has begun to focus on training unemployed young employees in hopes of maintaining and improving their skills for a time when employment conditions improve. One thing is clear from recent activity: Japan's labor policy is evolving, but the Ministry of Labor is still very much engaged in the current problems of the day.

Further reading

Lincoln, J. and Nakata, Y. (1997) "The Transformation of the Japanese Employment System: Nature, Depth, and Origins," *Work and Occupations* 33–55.

OECD Economic Surveys (2000) *Structural Policies to Enhance Growth and Secure Recovery: A Review of Progress.*

WILLIAM BARNES

Minomura, Rizaemon

Born in Edo (now Tokyo) on November 25, 1821, Minomura Rizaemon was orphaned early in life. After the death of his *ronin* father, he traveled from Kyushu up to Kyoto at fourteen years of age, then traveled the country eventually settling back in Edo. At nineteen he took a position as a merchant's apprentice. In the markets of Edo he worked hard, and eventually found his way into the merchant house of **Mitsui**. During his tenure Mitsui grew into a financial giant, one of the few to evolve during the **Tokugawa period** (1603–1857) and make a

successful transition in the modern industrialized era, and became the dominant *zaibatsu* of the late nineteenth and early twentieth centuries.

After joining Mitsui, Minomura quickly rose to the top. Through his skill and the development of close ties to the government he was able to steer it through a difficult period. At one point, when Mitsui's financial position was extremely weak, the government imposed a forced loan on Mitsui and other wealthy merchant houses. Because of his government connections, he was able to arrange a remittance, thereby alleviating Mitsui's difficulties. Shortly thereafter he was promoted to the position of head clerk, a position of nearly unassailable power within the firm. Though the Mitsui clan controlled the firm, company custom dictated that a non-family member occupy the position of head clerk and hold operational power.

Through his close ties with the government of the **Meiji restoration**, Minomura was able to receive special privileges for Mitsui. Only two other merchant houses, Shimada and Ono, were able to acquire similar arrangements. It was this access to government contracts, subsidies and monopoly privileges that enabled Minomura to steer Mitsui into the most profitable areas of the newly industrializing economy. For example, roughly two-thirds of the Japanese army's provisions were managed through Mitsui contracts. Recognizing the importance of being physically close to government, Minomura waged a determined campaign with the Mitsui family to move the headquarters from Kyoto, where it had been based for several centuries, to Tokyo. Though the campaign even stirred up the population of Kyoto against him, he eventually succeeded, and moved the headquarters in 1873.

However, in addition to understanding the benefit of close ties to the central government, Minomura also introduced modern banking methods to Japan. He became the first president of Mitsui Bank, the first modern private bank in Japan. Moreover, he was aggressive in steering the Mitsui conglomerate into other key sectors, such as mining, thereby securing a stable foundation for the future.

Minomura was equally capable of divesting Mitsui of unprofitable ventures. When Echigo-ya, one of the oldest and most famous retail stores in

Tokyo, suffered sustained losses, he severed its long-standing connection to other Mitsui enterprises. The move proved beneficial to Mitsui and to Echigoya, as the latter recovered and went on to establish itself as **Mitsukoshi**, the most prestigious department store in Japan. Although he died in Tokyo on February 21, 1877 at the relatively young age of fifty-six, by the time of his death Mitsui's foundation and future developmental path had become firmly established.

Further reading

Amakawa, J. (1968)"The Spirit of Capitalism in Meiji Japan," *Kwansei Gakuin University Annual Studies.*

Hirschmeier, J. and Yui, T. (1975) *The Development of Japanese Business*, London: George Allen.

Lockwood, W.W. (1954) *The Economic Development of Japan, Growth and Structural Change 1868–1938*, Princeton, NJ: Princeton University Press.

ALLAN BIRD

Mitsubishi

Mitsubishi Corporation is the general trading company of the Mitsubishi *keiretsu* founded by **Iwasaki** Yataro in the 1870s. It imports and exports a wide variety of products, as well as financing and investing in various projects around the world. Its 12,000 employees are spread around a network of forty-two offices in Japan and 118 offices and subsidiaries in seventy-three locations overseas.

Mitsubishi Shoji, as it is known in Japanese, first became a separate entity in 1918, formed from the sales division of Mitsubishi Goshi. Mitsubishi Goshi's president, Iwasaki Koyata, had a policy of spinning off parts of Mitsubishi Goshi into separate businesses, including the predecessors of Mitsubishi Corporation's present day sister companies (and major customers) such as Mitsubishi Electric Corporation and Mitsubishi Heavy Industries.

Iwasaki Koyata had a strong liberal and international outlook and his values shaped the Mitsubishi Corporation culture. This is encapsulated by his address to the general managers of Mitsubishi Shoji in 1920, where he outlined the three fundamental principles of Mitsubishi's business ethos as being: corporate responsibility to society, integrity and fairness and international understanding through trade. To this day Mitsubishi Corporation retains a reputation for being "gentlemanly," cautious and having a strong organizational structure.

Up until the mid-1930s Mitsubishi Shoji had limited operations and low profitability compared to its main rival, Mitsui Bussan. In the 1930s it became more profitable through focusing on metals, machinery and exporting from Asia. Although these businesses bolstered the militarist government's ambitions, Mitsubishi was regularly attacked throughout the decade for lacking patriotism.

Mitsubishi Shoji was dissolved by the Allied Occupation into 139 separate companies and forbidden to re-form or use the Mitsubishi name or logo. Due to the pressures of the Korean War, *zaibatsu* were allowed to regroup in the 1950s and eventually Mitsubishi Shoji was re-established in 1954, immediately opening offices in major trading centers around the world.

In the 1960s it became heavily involved in the rebuilding of Japan's industries and a substantial part of its business was purely domestic. Even in 1999 over 40 percent of its trading transactions took place within Japan only. This is despite the fact that throughout the 1970s Mitsubishi Corporation became a major participant in Japanese Overseas Development Assistance projects, opening offices in Africa, the Middle East and Latin America.

More recently, Mitsubishi Corporation has developed various "merchant banking style" functions, including investment funds and mergers and acquisitions, although, like other trading companies, it had to write off substantial bad debts from its *zaiteku* activities in the 1980s.

In the 1980s and early 1990s Mitsubishi Corporation was regularly listed by Fortune as the largest company in the world, in terms of trading transactions ($116bn in 1999) but is currently undergoing a period of retrenchment and **restructuring**, due to the strong impact of the depressed Japanese economy on its performance.

Further reading

Kankokai (ed.) (1981) *Mitsubishi Shashi*, Tokyo: University of Tokyo Press.

Mishima, Y. (1989) *The Mitsubishi: Its Challenge and Strategy*, Greenwich: JAI Press.

Rudlin, P. (2000) *The History of Mitsubishi Corporation in London: 1915 to Present Day*, London: Routledge.

PERNILLE RUDLIN

Mitsui

Mitsui was established in the Meiji era, a period of extraordinary development of Japanese society, especially toward the outside world. As a general trading company, Mitsui established itself as a main source for trading goods, both overseas and domestic. In addition to trading, Mitsui offered a wide range of business support services including: information support for businesses, networking, personnel recruiting, finance and support for new enterprise development.

The modern Mitsui & Co., Ltd. was established on July 25, 1947, forming the nucleus of the so-called Mitsui *keiretsu*. The former Mitsui & Co., Ltd. was officially dissolved after the Second World War because of its **zaibatsu**, a dissolution commanded by the United States in 1947. After the reconstruction, an amalgamation with Daiichi Co. in 1959 shaped today's Mitsui.

Mitsui has a reputation for hiring bright and promising students. In fact, the company attributes its long-term success directly to its talented personnel. Including Tokyo Head Office, Mitsui has thirty-four offices in Japan and eighty-nine offices overseas. Globally, it has forty-two overseas subsidiaries with ninety-one offices, in a total of ninety-three countries. Mitsui holds a large market share in many fields and is one of the largest general trading companies in Japan.

During the high-growth period from the 1960s through the 1980s, Mitsui contributed to the growth of the Japanese economy by diversifying its range of business activities, exploiting foreign resources, and opening up new domestic and foreign markets. Although its core business is in commercial transactions – mainly trading by making good use of substantial information, people and their long experiences. Mitsui has developed many business fields, including: Iron and Steel, Non-Ferrous Metals, Property, Service, Construction & Housing Business Development, Machinery, Chemicals, Energy, Food, Textiles, General Merchandise, Transportation and Distribution, and the Information Industry.

Currently, Mitsui is emphasizing its information technology (IT) business. On February 1, 2000 a company called 7dream.com was established. It is a joint venture with eight companies including Mitsui, 7-11 Japan Co., **Sony** and **NEC**. This company was established to provide total **e-commerce** services. Using multimedia terminals that are set up at every 7-11 store the following services are available: hotel reservation, purchases of airline tickets and books, online distribution of music and so on. It is anticipated that success or failure in information technology business ventures will significantly affect the long-term prospects of the Mitsui company.

Further reading

Fukuyama, F. (1995) *Trust: The Social Virtues and the Creation of Prosperity*, New York: Free Press.

Miyashita, K. and Russel, D. (1994) *Keiretsu Inside The Hidden Japanese Conglomerates*, New York: McGraw-Hill.

Okimoto, I.D. (1989) *Between MITI and the Market: Japanese Industrial Policy for High Technology*, Stanford, CA: Stanford University Press.

MARGARET TAKEDA
MEGUMI KATSUTA

Mitsukoshi

Mitsukoshi was Japan's first department store. Founded in the seventeenth century, Mitsukoshi initiated a number of innovative sales methods through its long history, and the company remains one of the leading retail operators in present-day Japan.

Mitsukoshi's foundation was laid by Takatoshi Mitsui, who opened a *kimono* store named Echigoya in the Honmachi quarter of Edo (now Tokyo) in 1673. Ten years later, the store moved to Surugacho where Mitsui introduced, for the first time in the modern world, the sale by price ticket and cash-and-carry. He also established a money exchange alongside his garment retail business, which would later become Mitsui Bank (now Sakura Bank).

At the beginning of the twentieth century, the house of Mitsui launched a project to establish the first Western-style department store in Japan. The famous six-story building in Renaissance style in Nihonbashi, in central Tokyo, was completed in 1914. Its underground floor, escalator (the first in Japan), a roof garden, and annex theatre (added in 1927) set the precedent for Japanese department store designs. After opening branch stores in Osaka, Seoul (Korea) and Dairen (China), the company changed its registered name from Mitsui-Echigoya to Mitsukoshi in 1928. Mitsukoshi embarked on an ambitious chain-store strategy and built stores in such retail centers as Shinjuku, Ginza, Kobe, Takamatsu, Kanazawa, Sapporo, and Sendai.

After the Second World War, the growth of consumer needs further enlarged its scope of business. The company sought to be a provider of affluent and cultured lifestyle, and diversified into areas of cultural fairs, sale of artworks, the housing business and travel agency. In 1971, it opened its first European branch store in Paris, aiming primarily at Japanese tourists looking for local products. The Paris store was followed by store openings in Rome, London, New York, Dusseldorf, Hong Kong, Frankfurt, Munich, Madrid, and Hawaii. In Japan, Mitsukoshi has eighteen stores as of 2000.

One stronghold of the present Mitsukoshi is its outward sales division, which sells gift items in bulk to corporate clients and high-income customers. Another important division is the building service division, which is specialized in interior designing and furnishing. For example, the Tokyo Dome Hotel, opened in 2000, was provided with banquet rooms and room interiors designed and furnished by this division.

Mitsukoshi's unconsolidated sales in fiscal 1999 was ¥676 billion, with operating profit of ¥9 billion, and recurring profit of ¥6 billion. The company has slightly more than 8,000 employees, and the surface of its retail floors, including tenant shops, is 361,000 square meters.

See also: industrial groups; retail industry

Further reading

Hirschmeier, J. and Yui, T. (1975) *The Development of Japanese Business, 1600-1973*, New York: Allen & Unwin.

—— (1977) *Nnihonno Keiei Hatten: Kindaika to Kigyou Keiei* (The Development of Japanese Business: Modernization and Management), Tokyo: Toyokeizaishinposha.

SHINTARO MOGI

mochiai

Many Japanese companies hold equity shares in trading partners that pass some threshold of public awareness but that are insufficient to confer effective control. The Japanese terms used to describe this practice vary, but one of the most common is *mochiai*. *Mochiai* literally means to balance or remain steady. This meaning provides insight into the practice of cross-shareholding. That is, the **cross-shareholdings** represents a silent financial interest only. Often, but not always, the shareholding is reciprocal. Common examples of cross-shareholding are the share interests that banks in Japan typically hold in their loan clients. The banks hold these share interests to improve their incentives in monitoring the real investments of the loan clients, and to gain access to privileged information. Antimonopoly law limits shareholding by banks and insurance companies to 5 percent and 7 percent of outstanding shares respectively, but the shareholding seldom approaches these limits. Cross-shareholding is most prominent within the financial *keiretsu*. About half of the cross-held shares within *keiretsu* presidents' clubs are held by financial institutions. One-third of the non-ordered pairs of non-financial members of same presidents' clubs are linked by cross-held shares and in about half of these instances the cross-shareholding is reciprocal. Cross-shareholding by non-financial firms has a different rationale from the cross-shareholding of banks. By holding stock in a trading partner a firm weakens its own bargaining position, for its own gain from trade then includes a share interest in the other party's gain from trade. Precisely for this reason the credible threat of divesting cross-held shares bonds the other party to attend to the shareholder's wishes. Cross-shareholding in Japan is often erroneously identified as a takeover defense. The threat of hostile takeover has never been a serious one in Japan, and cross-shareholding is not the most effective defense against a takeover. The other explanations for cross-shareholding are therefore more convincing.

Further reading

Flath, D. (1993) "Shareholding in the Keiretsu, Japan's Financial Groups," *Review of Economics and Statistics* 75: 249–57.
—— (1996) "The Keiretsu Puzzle," *Journal of the Japanese and International Economies* 10: 101–21.

DAVID FLATH

Morita, Akio

Morita is a post-Second World War entrepreneur and innovative business leader, a founding member of **Sony** Corporation who helped turn it into a leading technology company. Ultimately, he became chairman of Sony. Long recognized as a maverick in Japanese business circles, he finally gained acceptability in Japan with his selection as chairman-elect of the Keidanren, the association of Japanese businesses. Unfortunately, a stroke prevented him from taking over the chairmanship.

Morita came from a very successful business family that owned a *sake* brewing company and had created a baking company now called Pasco. He had attended business meetings with his father from an early age in anticipation of his taking over the family business. One of the first signs of Morita's independence was when he declined to do so. As a first son, he broke a tradition that had existed in the family for fifteen generations.

On May 7, 1946, approximately twenty people gathered on the third floor of a burned-out department store building in downtown Tokyo.

At the meeting, they agreed to establish a new company, Tokyo Telecommunications Engineering Corporation. That company later became Sony Corporation. The founders were Masaru Ibuka, a thirty-eight-year-old engineer, and Akio Morita, a twenty-five-year physicist. They started with initial capital of $500.

From the beginning, the company's philosophy was based on its being an innovator, in Morita's words, a clever company that would make new high technology products in ingenious ways. Initially, Ibuka and Morita assumed that all they had to do was make good products. When orders did not come in, Morita shifted to focus on merchandising, while Ibuka remained focused on engineering.

By 1953 the company was struggling to make a profit, surviving in part from family contributions and deferred salaries for seven years. Recognizing the limitations of the Japanese market, Morita made his first trip overseas to develop opportunities there. His first trip was to the USA, a market that would remain a primary focus for Sony.

From the beginning, another focus of Sony was miniaturization and compactness, a focus that also continues today. Unlike many other Japanese companies following the war, Sony was not dependent on assistance from the **Ministry of International Trade and Industry** (MITI). For most of this period, Sony had to battle the bureaucrats at MITI, many of whom did not recognize the potential of Sony's intended technology markets. For instance, it had great difficulty in obtaining a foreign exchange license from MITI to pay $25,000 to Western Electric for the right to use its transistor technology.

Over the next forty years, through perseverance and hundreds of trans-Pacific trips, Morita helped expand a company that is recognized around the world not only as a high-tech company, but the company which usually leads others in developing new technology. His reputation for innovation among his competitors was such that initially Sony could produce a particular model for a year or two before competitors entered the market. Eventually, competitors began to follow Sony's innovations in just six months, and often sooner.

Morita not only led his competitors, but also led consumers. Sony's goal was to lead the public with new products rather than ask them what kind of product they wanted. Since it was so far ahead of the rest of the market, Morita felt the public did not necessarily know what was possible. Some of the products created and introduced by Sony were transistor radios, tape recorders, Betamax video recorders (which was supplanted by the later-introduced VHS of **Matsushita**), and Walkman.

Personally, Morita never stopped his search for change and development. During his first trip to the United States, he made certain he rode the roller coaster at Coney Island. Later in his career, he rode with a stunt pilot as he flew upside down fifty feet above ground level. At the age of fifty-five, he took up the game of tennis; at sixty, he learned to ski, and at sixty-four he learned water-skiing.

Morita's business management policies became famous around the world. He believed that investors and employees are in equal positions, but that sometimes employees are more important because they will be there a long time whereas investors will often get in and out on a whim in order to make a profit. Throughout Sony, management has been dedicated to the principle of upgrading workers. Morita believed that people need money, but that they also want to be happy in their work and proud of it. He measured managers by how well they organized a large number of people, and how effectively they got the best performance from their employees and blended them into a coordinated group. He also believed that when Japanese talk about cooperation or consensus building, it usually means the elimination of individualism. At Sony, his challenge was to bring ideas out into the open.

Morita also felt that an enemy of innovation, which was a key element of Sony's operating policy, could be its own sales organization. If the sales force had too much power, it often discouraged innovation. Morita, on the other hand, was committed to three creativities: creativity in technology, product planning and marketing. His solution to the problem of unleashing this creativity was to set targets instead of giving undefined goals.

Morita's wife, Yoshiko, also had an important impact on Japanese business. She came from a prominent business family. Originally her *samurai* family went into the bookselling and publishing business at the end of the **Tokugawa period** and

expanded the business into a large chain of bookstores. Sanseido, her family's company, publishes the popular Concise line of foreign language dictionaries, an idea that originated with her father. Although she grew up without any real interest in foreign countries and when she was young had no great desire to travel, she became prominent in international business circles and a symbol for Japanese women. She became very involved in helping to educate Japanese women going abroad and wrote a book to help them understand living in foreign countries. It is still used today as a guide. She also did a television show in Japan for ten years, traveling to new fashion centers, bringing back interviews and introducing new ideas to Japan, which was then behind the times in fashion awareness. Her influence may have helped turn Tokyo into an international fashion center.

ROBERT BROWN

motorcycle industry

The motorcycle industry in Japan is a significant industry in that, for several reasons, its impact extends far beyond its current economic size for. First, it gives us an indication of the nature of **competition** in Japan when there is little government intervention in an industry. Second, the world first discovered here that scale alone is not the key to competitiveness, but that experience also matters. Third, this industry experienced some of the earliest areas of successful Japanese foreign investment as **trade barriers** increased.

Japanese firms remain major players in the world motorcycle market. **Honda**, Yamaha, Suzuki and Kawasaki are the four players. While each firm initially had a large commitment to motorcycles, none of these firms currently has greater than half of its sales in this product segment. Only Yamaha, at 42 percent of sales, has more than 10 percent of its sales in this industry segment. Yet Honda builds more motorcycles, even with only 10 percent of its sales volume in this sector. For Kawasaki, a large, diversified heavy equipment manufacturer, its business in motorcycles never was a major share in its total sales. Yet even as the firms have built on their base of motorcycle technology to enter autos (Honda), minicars (Suzuki) and recreational vehicles (Yamaha), the legacy of their motorcycle business is still important.

The nature of competition

When government does not dictate the rules of competition in Japan, new players can enter, and there are frequent pressures for both product improvement and price reduction. The motorcycle industry is a good example of both these phenomena. The motorcycle was never seen by the government as a strategic industry, and thus had little industry-specific government support.

In the early postwar period, we can observe the entry phenomenon. Tohatsu, a reliable, well-run company, had the major share of the industry. Soichiro **Honda** was an inventor whose only earlier experience was in supplying parts to **Toyota**. Yet he was able to identify new markets and utilize new technology in engines to redefine the industry, dethrone the existing leader Tohatsu, and send it into bankruptcy. Thinking unconventionally, Honda realized that people in the immediate postwar economy needed inexpensive ways to get products into the devastated cities from the countryside. He mounted an engine built to run on a noxious mixture based on coal tar to a bike, and sold this to the many people who were profiting from the trade in food. Later, having upgraded engine and machine, he observed a potential market for the motorcycle in the various delivery services that were common in Japan at that time. Designing a carrier that could stay level while a cycle careened through the narrow streets of Japanese cities, he enabled firms and even the neighborhood noodle shop to deliver their wares efficiently. Again, the market expanded.

Pricing was also an important strategy for Honda. The company calculated that it could increase sales and reduce cost by identifying a large market and then designing a new product for that wider market. An easy-to-shift motorcycle, he observed, would enable many more people to be comfortable on a motorcycle, and would increase the market substantially. His design of the Super Cub provided that expanded market and the associated cost reduction.

Experience curve

The Super Cub was a transition to the second area where the motorcycle industry is important for Japanese business, the experience curve. Most analyses of competition had emphasized the importance of the size of the production facility, so-called economies of scale. With this approach, there was no easy way for a new competitor to enter the market because the size of the existing competitors would block the newcomer from profitable operation. The newcomer could not compete on production cost. The successful entry of Honda and the other Japanese firms into the world market demanded an explanation, since their initial size was much less than that of the established players in the UK and the USA. The usual explanation of government subsidies did not provide a convenient explanation for the Japanese success, since the government provided no special support to this industry. Studies by the Boston Consulting Group showed that the companies could indeed succeed even if their initial costs were much higher than that of the foreign players. Given the strategies mentioned above to expand the markets, Japanese firms could increase the volume of production rapidly. As they did so, they learned to produce motorcycles less expensively. A large domestic market provided the opportunity to expand volume quickly for the smaller bikes that were not at that time on offer from foreign manufacturers. As the cumulative volume built up, the firms were able to pass along the savings to their new customers. This led to a virtuous cycle that in turn led to substantial changes in competitive position. Instead of a strategy of simply basing decisions on high volume alone, this approach showed that the growth strategy of Japanese firms could be profitable. Fast growth, if based on these learning efficiencies, could be the basis for sustainable, profitable competition. Pricing based on the experience curve economies gave Honda and the other Japanese companies a sustainable advantage both in domestic and international markets.

When Japanese motorcycle companies tried to compete only on price, however, and hoped that the increased volume would lead to profits, the industry found itself in an unsustainable condition often found in Japanese markets. This is what

Japanese call "excess competition." We can use this industry to learn about the dangers of this type of price competition in Japanese markets. The obsession with share so often found in Japanese markets led the motorcycle industry into a period of chaos in the 1970s. Concerned with its perpetual "number two" status in the industry, the president of Yamaha threw down the gauntlet to Honda, saying that it would take over the top position within a short period of time. Unfortunately, the desire for increased volume was not based on any significant cost advantage at Yamaha. Nor was it based on any ability to design new products at a faster pace than Honda. At that point, Honda was moving into the automobile market, and Yamaha thought it might be distracted, and that Honda would not respond. Honda's response provides an important lesson on the nature of competition in the Japanese market: no firm lets a new player into the market without a significant fight. Images of shared markets and cartelized industries give foreigners the impression that Japanese generally agree to share markets. But if the government is not involved in coordinating the market, this is far from the norm. In this case, Honda responded by reallocating a large number of engineers from the automotive division. It designed a significant number of new models, and matched the decreases in price that Yamaha had initiated. With no significant production advantages and an engineering staff that was not equal to that of Honda, Yamaha had to beat an ignominious retreat. Honda's dominant position in the industry was maintained due to its cost and product design capabilities.

The industry gives one additional example of the importance of experience curve effects, though this example comes from a US company, Harley Davidson, rather than the Japanese firms. Harley Davidson had understood the importance of experience curve economies and had begun to digest many of the lessons of Japanese manufacturing process efficiencies. It also knew that it could be competitive with the Japanese firms at the high end of the market if only it could generate enough sales to internalize that experience in a reasonable period of time. In the Harley Davidson case, the company chose to appeal to the US government to give it a period of protection to achieve that experience level. The government and the firm agreed to an unusual structure for the period of protection that reflected the economies to be expected from the experience curve. An initial high tariff on large Japanese bikes was decreased each year, disappearing in seven years. If Harley Davidson could not reduce its costs and expand the market for its bikes, the reduced tariff protection would doom their strategy. This incentive to improve productivity and develop new products worked well for the company, and it is now competitive in the high end of the market. The company needed less than the seven years to complete its program to increase competitiveness, and the tariffs were abolished ahead of schedule. Harley Davidson, in a move that Honda surely would have grudgingly respected, took out advertisements saying that the firm was now competitive, and no longer needed protection.

Entering international markets

The strategy of new market segments, mentioned earlier, also helped Honda develop new markets overseas. At the time that Honda started to develop the US market, the image of the motorcycle user was not of a mass market of typical people, rather the image was of someone who was rebellious and slightly "off color." To get more people to use the motorcycle, Honda had to create a respectable image. Using an innovative advertising campaign, "You meet the nicest people on a Honda," the company persuaded Americans to accept the fact that everyday people could use this means of transportation. The most memorable ad was of a nun riding over a pristine mountain path.

The challenge of the Japanese motorcycle firms soon generated calls from both Europe and the United States for restrictions on imports. This led both Kawasaki and Honda to set up manufacturing plants abroad. Both firms located in rural US communities where they felt their team-based manufacturing techniques would be more consistent with the culture. These very visible manufacturing operations brought home to Americans many of the Japanese management techniques. The plants arguably stimulated changes in the wider transportation equipment industry as American suppliers learned that they could utilize the techniques to improve productivity within the US environment.

In Honda's case, the investment in motorcycle plants had another benefit. Since the company also competed in the **automotive industry**, it knew that it would soon face similar restrictions on autos. Its early investment in motorcycles, first in Europe and then in Columbus, Ohio, allowed it to generate experience in managing foreign operations and in developing local parts suppliers. This was invaluable in the more complex automobile plant investments that were to follow. Honda's plants in the USA generally have a higher reputation for good management and supplier relations than some other Japanese firms. This is in no small part due to this early experimentation in motorcycles. Just as in the earlier case of experience curve benefits in production, Honda sought out early experience and learning in overseas operations.

The Japanese motorcycle industry is now competing globally. In the late 1990s, there have been increases in production facilities by all four Japanese manufacturers in China. While the industry is no longer the important contributor to the Japanese economy that it was at one time, it remains important for its contribution to the firms. Honda used its engine technology to enter the auto industry. The company used its customer base in the United States, built from its motorcycle bridgehead, to generate the scale needed to compensate for its weakness in distribution in the Japanese market. The industry has also contributed to the understanding by non-Japanese of the Japanese production system and competition.

THOMAS ROEHL

Nakauchi, Isao

Isao Nakauchi was born in Osaka prefecture in August 1922. He graduated from Kobe Commercial High School (now Kobe Commercial University) in 1941, then entered and dropped out of Kobe Economic University (now Kobe University, Faculty of Economics) in 1950, and started to work for Nichimen Corporation. In 1943 he was drafted into the military, and was assigned to service in Manchuria. After the war, he returned to Japan in 1945 and joined his family's business, Daiei Yakuhin Kogyo (Daiei Medicinal Manufacturing).

Nakauchi opened the first supermarket in Japan, Shufu-no-Mise (A Store for Housewives) in the city of Osaka in 1957. In 1963, he opened another store in Fukuoka Prefecture, thus beginning expansion of a chain of stores nationwide. He became the chairman of the Japan Chain Store Association in 1967. In 1970, the name of the stores was changed to Daiei, and Isao Nakauchi became president (he also held the post of chairman starting from 1982). Since then, Daiei has expanded all over Japan using the chain store method and has become a market leader in the supermarket industry with 300 affiliated companies. In 1977, Nakauchi received the Medal with Blue Ribbon (a national award designated for philanthropy and inventions).

Nakauchi received the Sixth Keizai-kai Taisho (the Sixth Economic World Grand Prize) in 1980, and the Pegasus-Club Diamond Award and the Business Excellence International Award in 1987. In 1989, he became the owner of the professional baseball team the Daiei Hawks.

In 1990, Nakauchi became vice-chairman of the Federation of Economic Organizations. He acquired the Recruit Company Ltd. (a recruitment, publishing and services giant) in 1992. In 1993, he received the Grand Cordon of the Order of the Sacred Treasure. Daiei acquired rival supermarkets, Chujitu-ya, Yunid Daiei, and Daihana, in 1994, and launched the first "national chain store" in Japan, with stores covering all of Japan from Hokkaido to Okinawa. Daiei also received the Tenth Corporate PR Award (Special Award) that year. In 1995, Nakauchi resigned as vice-chairman of the Federation of Economic Organizations. In 1996, he received the Comandoll Badge of Leopard Medal.

At present, Isao Nakauchi serves on the board of directors and as a top-advisor of Daiei Incorporated, chairman of the board of directors of Recruit Company Limited, owner of the professional baseball team Fukuoka Daiei Hawks, and on the board of directors and as president of Nakauchi Educational Institution. He was the model used in the national best-selling novel *Kakaku Hakai* (Price Destruction), written by Saburo Jyoyama. His own book, *Waga Yasu-Uri Tetsugaku* (My Philosophy of Bargaining), is about his commercial philosophy and strategy.

Further reading

Nakauchi, I. (1969) *Waga Yasu-Uri Tetsugaku* (My Philosophy of Bargaining), Tokyo: Nihon Keizai Shinbun-sha.

AKI MATSUNAGA
MARGARET TAKEDA

Naniwa bushi

Literally "Naniwa melodies," the term refers to a business negotiation or management style that appeals to intuition, emotion and "gut instinct" rather than reason or fact-based business sense. Naniwa is the former name for Osaka, and the term refers to songs from that area that recount romantic tales of love and daring, often involving Robin Hood-type heroes who lived on the fringes of respectable society and treated those around them with generosity and flair.

In a business context, *naniwa bushi* is used to describe two types of related, but somewhat different behaviors. In negotiating and managerial contexts, it is used to refer to appeals to one's romantic nature (in the sense of chivalry and grand gesture) or to one's emotional side. It can also refer to blatant attempts to appeal to one's sympathy, rather than business judgment.

A second type of behavior characterized as *naniwa bushi* involves acts of hospitality and generosity that exceed what one might normally expect. Showering guests with gifts, extravagant meals and gestures of largesse can serve as a means for achieving cooperation by weakening resolve and lowering defenses so that objective considerations are overwhelmed by good feelings and a sense of indebtedness.

ALLAN BIRD

NEC

NEC, formally registered as NEC Corporation, is a company offering service-related computer and Internet solutions. NEC corporate headquarters is located in Tokyo, Japan. It boasts six production facilities near Tokyo, as well as fifty-six subsidiaries and twenty affiliate firms throughout Japan. NEC's marketing network consists of nearly 400 sales offices and 150 marketing and service subsidiaries and affiliates in thirty-four countries. In addition, as of 2000 NEC has seven R&D facilities in Japan, two in the United States and one in Germany.

NEC was established on July 17, 1899 and has had a long and varied history which can be divided into distinct stages. From 1899 to 1923, NEC was founded as the result of a joint venture with Western Electronic Company of the United States, now Lucent Technologies. During stage two, from 1924–45, NEC expanded into the radio market with both production and research and development facilities. From 1946–64, NEC expanded into computers and electronic switching systems. Its research into transistor technology led the company to apply for numerous patents in Japan and the USA, plunging it into the US market for the first time in 1964. The period from 1964–78 focused on worldwide expansion and diversification for NEC. The company began producing advanced satellite systems, at the same time ushering in their well known "C&C" strategy, combining computer and communications technologies. Also during this period, NEC listed stocks on the London Stock Exchange, the Swiss Exchange, and the Netherlands Exchange.

In 1979, NEC announced the introduction of their first computers, including the supercomputer. By 1986, NEC had developed the dynamic random access memory (DRAM) and by 1986 had developed information-processing systems application architecture. NEC entered the semiconductor market in the early 1990s.

Currently, NEC is divided into three distinct operating divisions, broadly known as NEC Solutions, NEC Networks, and NEC Electronic Devices. NEC Solutions provides Internet-related solutions through the development of applications derived from supercomputers, computers, PCs, printers, and Internet-related services, including Internet access services such as Biglobe. NEC was the first Japanese computer manufacturer to provide integrated Internet services.

NEC Networks is responsible for supplying and supporting network systems. Network systems are best described as equipment which supports photonic IP solutions, ATM solutions, mobile communications, and digital broadcasting. NEC Electronic Devices focuses on advanced electronic equipment such as semiconductors, modules, and ion rechargeable batteries.

Known for charting its own course, NEC pioneered the concept of the "value chain" management in Japan, which seeks to connect and optimize the products and services offered among the three NEC divisions. NEC continues to

experience strong worldwide growth and technological diversification largely due to its relentless
focus on R&D and customer service.

Further reading

MacLellan, A. (2000) "NEC's Divestiture Talk Sets
  Wheels in Motion," *Manhasset: Electronic Buyers'
  News*.
Miyashita, K. and Russell, D. (1994) *Keiretsu: Inside
  the Hidden Japanese Conglomerates*, New York:
  McGraw-Hill.
Okimoto, D. (1989) *Between MITI and the Market:
  Japanese Industrial Policy for High Technology*, Stan-
  ford, CA: Stanford University Press.
Robertson, J. (1999) "NEC Sets Massive Restruc-
  turing Plan," *Manhasset: Electronic Buyers' News*.

MARGARET TAKEDA
SOYEON PARK

negotiations

The way in which Japanese negotiations unfold is
distinctly different from negotiations that take place
within other cultures. These differences can
hamper the success of both sides in cross-cultural
negotiations. It has been shown for example, that
the joint outcomes of Japanese–US negotiations
are worse than if the negotiations had been
conducted within the same culture (Brett and
Okumura 1998). With negotiating experience and
increased cultural understanding, the outcomes of
cross-cultural negotiations generally improve.

Conflict resolution

Negotiations can be used both in resolving conflicts
and in negotiating more general business relationships (for example, buyer/seller agreements, joint
ventures or partnerships). Some of the concepts
that are most relevant to conflict resolution in
Japan are: (1) harmony as a societal goal; (2) the
importance of face-saving and; (3) the use of third
parties to assist in resolving conflicts.

Maintaining harmony is an important part of
Japanese society. Respected Confucian proverbs
emphasize that disharmony is the fault of and an
embarrassment to all of the participants. Each
individual bears some responsibility for having
interpersonal tolerance of others to prevent
disputes from arising. A well-known Japanese
proverb states: "In a quarrel, both parties are to
blame." At least partially because of this, the court
system in Japan is typically not used to litigate
disagreements. Litigation is viewed as a method of
resolving disputes between immoral individuals
when the moral manner of settling disputes by
tolerance and mediation have failed.

Another important concept in Japanese society
and in dispute resolution is the concept of face.
Face refers to the self-image one projects to others.
Respect is the way in which face is maintained.
Maintaining face confirms a person's acceptance in
a society and that person's status. When tensions in
a dispute escalate with either party becoming
emotional, the display of these negative emotions is
disrespectful and result in the loss of face.

When disputes arise in Japan, which is a
hierarchical culture with harmony as a strong value
and a preference for indirect confrontation, there is
a tendency toward early involvement of third
parties. Involving a third party is viewed as a face-
saving, harmony-preserving way to resolve a
dispute. Having the assistance of a third party
who acts as a go-between or mediator can prevent
the loss of face that would occur if one of the
parties expressed their negative emotions in front
of the other party. The Confucian philosophy
embedded in Japanese culture holds that it is a
society's communal responsibility to maintain
harmony. Therefore, people feel personal responsibility to assist with conflicts. The most effective
third party is someone with equal or higher status
relative to each of the parties involved and
someone who knows each party well enough that
they can remain a neutral and unbiased mediator.
The mediator will then typically listen to each side
separately, gathering information and clarifying
their positions. The mediator then conveys information to the other party often removing any
emotional or negative statements from the information passed to the other side. The mediator
may also suggest some possible courses of action
and may, if the conflict is close to reconciliation, try
to bring the two sides together to speak directly to
each other. It is not without personal risk that a

third party undertakes mediation. Should the situation worsen following the mediator's intervention, the mediator may be negatively viewed by one or both parties as *aossekai* (nosey or meddlesome).

General business

Business negotiations are conducted with the hope of mutually beneficial outcomes and are often viewed as having several distinct phases: relationship building; exchanging information; persuasion and compromise; and concessions and agreement. These stages are approached differently by Japanese negotiators and those from other cultures.

Relationship building

In comparison to those in the USA and the UK, Japanese negotiators spend longer periods of time in developing relationships prior to negotiating the specifics of a business deal. The Japanese put significant effort into establishing a harmonious and trusting relationship. It appears that this strategy may help the Japanese to avoid litigation later. USA and UK negotiators appear much more conscious of time pressures and deadlines and often become uncomfortable and impatient with the amount of time the Japanese spend entertaining and socializing in order to evaluate and build a potential long-term relationship.

Japanese negotiators pay close attention to the power of the parties involved. The most important aspect of power is the social status of the negotiators. Exchanging business cards is an important initial ritual to help all involved determine the social status of each person in the negotiations. Often the highest status member of a Japanese negotiating team will be the most quiet during the negotiation, observing closely what is being said by both parties. In the USA and UK, the relative power of the negotiators is more likely to be assessed by determining which side has the best alternative, if the negotiation fails. The Japanese are much less likely to view alternatives as a source of power (Brett and Okumura 1998).

In Japan the buyer is accorded much more status than the seller. In Japan the adage "the buyer is king" is a realistic description of the relationship.

Buyers would typically expect deference and respect from sellers. In return the buyers often exhibit a type of paternalistic or fatherly protection toward the seller. It has been difficult for other cultures to penetrate the Japanese market partially because outsiders trying to sell products or services often have difficulty showing sufficient deference to buyers and developing an adequate level of trust with their Japanese counterparts. Normally in intra-cultural negotiations, Japanese sellers would begin first by explaining characteristics of the product and background factors, but not initially discussing price. Then the Japanese buyer would ask clarifying questions. One study found that when price is eventually discussed, Japanese sellers often suggest a more extreme initial price than would a US negotiator (Graham 1993).

Exchanging information

In Japanese negotiations the exchange of information is a primary part of the negotiation. Negotiators may ask many questions so that they are confident of their understanding. It is common for the Japanese to want more written documentation than is typical in the USA or UK. Published information is viewed as more credible and valuable than oral assurances. When an opponent makes an offer, the Japanese are likely to respond initially with silence or by asking more questions. They are less likely than most opponents to respond to an offer with a counteroffer. During the information exchange, Japanese view US and UK negotiators as honest to the point of discomfort as they communicate even negative information very directly. Japanese negotiators may share less information and are more likely to communicate information subtly and indirectly. This can result in information being lost because negotiators from the US and UK may not realize or fully understand that information is being communicated by Japanese negotiators. The Japanese try to be truthful, but also polite. As a result, they do not share much negative information, and when they do share negative information, it is shared indirectly so as to be less offensive. In comparison to other cultures including the UK, Taiwan, Korea, France, China, Russia, Germany, Brazil and the USA, Japanese negotiators are much less likely to use the word "no" (Graham 1993). For example, "That will be very difficult" is a common, more indirect and polite way for the Japanese to communicate "No, we can't do that."

Persuasion and compromise

US and UK negotiators are most likely to view the persuasion portion of the negotiation as the actual negotiation because they are finally "getting down to the real meat of the issues." They will plan to spend the majority of their time trying to persuade. As a result, they try to move quickly to this phase and try to start bargaining before they have gathered information from the other side. If English is used to conduct the negotiation, then language difficulties may lead the Japanese negotiators to spend more time focused on the numbers and the carefully constructed arguments and persuasions commonly used by US and UK negotiators are likely to be lost.

In contrast, the Japanese believe that if a trusting relationship has been built and they have carefully gathered information and gained an understanding of each side, then little persuasion is necessary. Once the Japanese feel confident that a beneficial long-term relationship can be established and all of their questions have been answered satisfactorily, an agreement can come together fairly quickly. Japanese negotiators may suggest an agreement that addresses the negotiation as one overall package and may view this stage as just working out minor details. This is different from the tendency in the USA and UK to break a negotiation into smaller pieces and try to use persuasive tactics to come to an agreement on each point before proceeding.

The Japanese tend to be less aggressive and more polite negotiators when compared to negotiators from other cultures. They are unlikely to threaten, command or warn and more likely to make recommendations and positive promises. They are therefore, likely to be uncomfortable with aggressive tactics and displays of negative emotions. The Japanese have a proverb, *Tanki wa sonki* which translates, "if you lose your temper, you will lose your case." In negotiating with Japanese, it is best not to show negative emotions or even impatience, the result may be loss of respect. The Japanese are unlikely to enter into arguments. If they think they are right they may just remain silent. Entering into an argument might risk displaying anger or impatience creating a loss of face.

Concessions and agreement

Japanese companies prefer to conduct business negotiations with a team of people. In such as case, concessions are unlikely to be made by the Japanese until they have a chance to confer privately and reach a consensus on their response. They also typically need to consult with their home office. Once a decision has been made, Japanese negotiators tend to make all concessions at the end of the negotiation and expect that these will immediately lead to a final agreement. In contrast, US and UK negotiators tend to make concessions throughout the process and expect their opponents to reciprocate with concessions as well. US and UK negotiators are also likely to characterize the decision-making style of the Japanese team as very slow and unhurried and express discomfort at the lack of decision-making authority a Japanese team typically has. Negotiations are sometimes terminated prematurely because of the occasionally mistaken belief that the negotiations are not progressing.

Japanese are more likely than those from other cultures to respond to an offer or concession with a period of silence. While this silence is usually a common part of Japanese communication style, occasionally this silence is an intentional strategy to communicate displeasure with the offer (Graham 1993). The resulting silence can create discomfort and result in concessions from opponents.

Other differences between Japanese and other negotiators include the Japanese preference for formality, for written agreements that are brief and cover basic principles, and their longer term perspectives. This contrasts with the informality, detailed legalistic contracts and generally shorter term perspectives of US and UK negotiators. In conclusion, while negotiations can easily break down because of a lack of understanding of cultural differences, continuing efforts to understand the cultural differences can be beneficial to both sides.

Further reading

Brett, J.M. (in press) *Negotiating Globally: How to*

Negotiate Deals, Resolve Disputes and Make Decisions Across Cultural Boundaries, San Francisco: Jossey-Bass.

Brett, J.M. and Okumura, T. (1998) "Inter- and Intra-Cultural Negotiations: U.S. and Japanese Negotiators," *Academy of Management Journal* 41: 495–510.

Callister, R.R. and Wall, J.A. (1997) "Japanese Community and Organizational Mediation," *The Journal of Conflict Resolution* 41: 311–28.

Graham, J.L. (1993) "The Japanese Negotiation Style: Characteristics of a Distinct Approach," *Negotiation Journal* 9: 123–40.

Martin, D., Herbig, P., Howard, C. and Borstoff, P. (1999) "At the Table: Observations on Japanese Negotiation Style," *American Business Review* 17(1): 65–71.

RHONDA ROBERTS CALLISTER

nemawashi

The original meaning of *nemawashi* refers to the method by which a tree, especially an old tree, is transplanted from one place to another. According to the method, the root of an uprooted tree is covered with a straw mat and left alone for months; then it is transplanted, so that the tree may not die.

The term is used metaphorically in modern Japanese society to mean laying the groundwork for achieving one's goal, especially agreement in decision making. The nature of *nemawashi* is its informality and off-the-record, if not necessarily secret, communication. Before 1970, very few Japanese language dictionaries listed the metaphorical use of the term, but after 1970 all major dictionaries did. It is also true, however, that in the late 1960s newspapers were already using the term in its later meaning.

The term has been used in all kinds of Japanese organizations besides business. The reason it has had such wide use is because the action of *nemawashi* is closely associated with the traditional Japanese decision-making process, known as **ringi seido**, or the referral and clearance system. According to this system, a plan is initiated by middle management in an organization through examination of its feasibility. Then it is proposed upward for official agreement. The term *ringi*, means offering a proposal from below to above. One critical characteristic of the system is that a unanimous decision at the top level meeting is preferred over a decision by majority. The unanimous decision symbolizes that the plan has been examined from all possible perspectives and that everyone shares responsibility for the execution of it.

Thus, *nemawashi* is an institution, integral to the *ringi-seido*. There are two aspects of *nemawashi* in action, both of which are characterized by informal person-to-person, off-the-record communication. First, when a plan is in the making, the initiator of the plan needs to modify or polish it by contacting all the people the plan would involve after it is officially approved. Those who are contacted are expected to give advice from their own standpoint. In the process, the original plan may be more refined, and, what is equally important, the plan becomes a creation of everyone involved, who all become its supporters.

The second aspect is that in order for the plan to be approved unanimously, all the major decision makers have to be fully informed informally of it. Among these important people, there may be influential people that are only partially affected by the plan. *Nemawashi* is likely to be used with them to smooth the discussion in the meeting.

Thus, *nemawashi* includes explanation, persuasion, request, and asking a favor on a personal basis. *Nemawashi* can be done anywhere, even outside as well as inside the organization. *Nemawashi* is sometimes used in secretive, behind-the-scenes manoeuvering, but its positive aspect has also been pointed out. Compared with a plan that has not been examined thoroughly, a plan that has been screened through examination by way of *nemawashi* in many sections of the organization will usually be a better plan. Additionally, since all possible hurdles have already been cleared before the plan is officially approved, it can be put smoothly into practice. In the same vein, as all the relevant members of the organization are fully aware of the plan, they are quick to cooperate when the plan is executed. Moreover, a unique plan which might be disapproved if it were directly proposed in a meeting has a better chance to be approved if *nemawashi* is properly done.

Some shortcomings of *nemawashi* have also been

pointed out. Since *nemawashi* is done informally on a person-to-person basis, it is hard for a person to respond in the negative. It is also argued that in rapidly changing times, *nemawashi* takes so much time that the organization may lose an opportunity to move in a new direction. Also, a unique, potentially good plan may be turned down in the complex *nemawashi* process if only the negative aspects are examined. The strengths of *nemawashi* contain its weaknesses as well.

Finally, *nemawashi* has been widely practiced in Japan because it is rooted in Japanese culture. Japanese want to avoid harsh face-to-face argument and conflict in meetings, where they know one another well. *Nemawashi* provides a means to avoid the possibility of such conflict.

As Japanese multinationals have introduced *nemawashi* in their overseas operations, it has not been well received. In North America, where *nemawashi* was widely practiced, it was one of the least favored aspects of Japanese management among American employees. Although many American employees, especially middle managers and above, learned how to conduct *nemawashi*, only a few thought the practice had merit.

Despite complaints from American workers, Japanese managers have not tried to change their decision-making style. Due to their close connections with parent companies in Japan, most subsidiaries cannot be that independent. *Nemawashi* remains deeply rooted in the Japanese decision-making process.

Further readings

Sullivan, J.J. (1992) *Invasion of the Salarymen: The Japanese Business Presence in America*, London: Praeger.

Sumihara, N. (1993) "A Case Study of Cross-Cultural Interaction in a Japanese Multinational Corporation Operating in the United States: Decision-Making Processes and Practices," in R.R. Sims and R.F. Dennehy, *Diversity and Differences in Organizations*, Westport, CT: Quorum Books, 135–48.

NORIYA SUMIHARA

New United Motor Manufacturing Incorporated

In 1984, **Toyota** and General Motors (GM) formed the New United Motor Manufacturing Inc. (NUMMI) joint venture to produce subcompact cars in California. Toyota's objectives included beginning production in the United States and gaining experience in working with American unionized labor. GM's objectives were to learn about the efficient Toyota production system and to produce high-quality cars.

The production facility used for NUMMI was a former General Motors plant that had been closed due to labor problems, quality problems, and low productivity. Under the new Toyota management, the plant quickly became the most productive of all GM facilities and the automobiles produced received very high-quality ratings. Grievance rates and absenteeism were exceptionally low, and remain so. Quality and productivity have continued to improve.

Before operations began, Toyota management worked with the United Automobile Workers union to establish a cooperative relationship. The resulting labor agreement provided the strongest job security clause in the industry, included a "no strike" provision with respect to production and safety standards, and emphasized non-confrontational problem resolution. A great deal of time and care were taken in the selection of workers, including interviews to determine the applicant's potential for teamwork. Extensive training was provided for new employees, with more than 11 percent of the workforce being sent to Japan for three weeks of training. The company continues to regularly send employees to Japan for additional training.

The production workforce was organized in teams with team responsibility for quality, productivity, and continuous improvement. Along with the responsibility, each worker had the authority to stop the production line for safety or quality reasons. Team members were given training in problem-solving techniques, were required by the union contract to participate in quality/productivity improvement programs, and were cross-trained to do every job in the team. In addition to the features of the system described above, NUMMI developed relationships with suppliers to support a just-in-time inventory system.

Both Toyota and General Motors met their objectives in forming NUMMI. Toyota sent a group of its managers from NUMMI to apply what they had learned in their new, wholly-owned plant in Kentucky. Executives with experience at NUMMI were subsequently assigned to key positions at Toyota headquarters. GM sent a number of managers to NUMMI for training, and thousands of others on visits. It applied what it learned in NUMMI in the development of its Saturn plant, and is now in a long-term effort to make its other plants more like Saturn. NUMMI continues to produce high quality vehicles, cars for GM and both cars and light trucks for Toyota.

See also: automotive industry; *kaizen*

Further reading

Adler, P., Goldoftas, B. and Levin, D. (1999) "Flexibility Versus Efficiency? A Case Study of Model Changeovers in the Toyota Production System," *Organization Science* 10(1): 43–68.

Duerr, M. (1992) "New United Motor Manufacturing Inc. at Midlife: Experience of the Joint Venture," in A. Negandhi and M. Serapio (eds), *Research in International Business and International Relations, Volume 5, Japanese Direct Investment in the United States: Trends, Developments, and Issues,* Greenwood, CT: JAI Press.

EDWIN C. DUERR
MITSUKO S. DUERR

Nihon Keizai Shimbun

Founded in 1876 as the *Chugai Bukka Shimpo* (Domestic and Foreign Price News), the newspaper adopted the name *Chugai Shogyo Shimpo* (Domestic and Foreign Commercial News) in 1889, and then changed to its current name *Nihon Keizai Shimbun* (meaning Japanese Economic Newspaper) in 1946. It is widely respected in Japan and throughout the world as Japan's foremost business-oriented newspaper, on a par with the *Wall Street Journal* in the USA and the *Financial Times* in the UK. It is the world's largest selling daily business newspaper and, like the *Wall Street Journal* and the *Financial Times*, it includes articles on social trends, culture and the arts, sports and some general news. In the latter part of the twentieth century the newspaper has expanded into other business information-related and business data services. In both English and Japanese, the newspaper's name is often abbreviated to *Nikkei*, a combination of the first syllables of the first two words in its name.

Nihon Keizai Shimbun, Inc. (Nikkei) actually publishes four newspapers as well as thirty-four other magazines. In addition, it also publishes business and economic books, averaging about 300 new volumes annually in the 1990s. In addition to the daily *Nihon Keizai Shimbun*, two of the papers cover specialized areas of business, and the fourth is an English-language publication. The *Nikkei Sangyo Shimbun* (Nikkei Industrial Newspaper) covers economic and business developments in Japan's manufacturing sector. The *Nikkei Ryuutsuu Shimbun* (Nikkei Marketing Newspaper) focuses on developments in the marketing and distribution sectors. Finally, the *Nikkei Weekly* is an English-language newspaper that is a combination of news stories translated from the three Japanese-language papers as well as some features prepared specifically for its English-speaking readership. Also in English, its *Japan Economic Almanac* is a standard reference volume.

Nihon Keizai Shimbun is published daily in both morning and evening editions. Its four main publication sites are Osaka, Sapporo, Seibu and Tokyo. Daily circulation in 2001 exceeded 2,800,000. Outside of Japan, it has news offices in major national capitals and world financial centers.

Nikkei's electronic data services include the English-language News Telecom/Japan News and Retrieval, a counterpart to its Japanese-language Nikkei Needs database. Both services have experienced rapid growth in recent years. Nikkei also supports and produces a wide variety of broadcasting initiatives, and industrial and cultural events.

ALLAN BIRD

NIHON SHOKO KAIGISHO *see* Japan
Chamber of Commerce and Industry

Nihonteki keiei

Nihonteki keiei, "Japanese-style management," refers to a set of management systems and practices that are unique to or characteristic of Japanese companies and which differ from those typically found in non-Japanese, and particularly Western, companies. *Nihonteki keiei* includes **lifetime employment**, **seniority promotion**, **enterprise unions**, **bottom-up decision-making processes**, and other related management practices. Together, these form a unified approach to management that provides benefits such as rich intra-company information flows, low rates of absenteeism and employee turnover, and a high level of employee training and commitment. In the hard economic times following the collapse of Japan's **bubble economy**, the costs of *nihonteki keiei* became more difficult for companies to bear, causing some of its features to be re-examined, modified, or eliminated.

In Japan, as in any country, there is considerable variation in management practice from firm to firm; consequently, the description that follows is a generalization. It should also be noted that *nihonteki keiei* management practices are found more prominently in Japan's large companies than in its **small and medium-sized firms**.

The "three pillars" of Japanese-style management

The so-called "three pillars" of *nihonteki keiei* are lifetime employment, seniority-based wages and promotion, and the enterprise union. Under lifetime employment (*shushin koyo*), employees join a company upon graduation from high school or university with the expectation, on the part of both employee and company, that the employee will remain with the company for his or her entire working career. Employees tend to be hired more for their general characteristics and abilities than for specific skills. The best companies hire from the best schools, so the competition to enter a good university is intense, producing the infamous

"examination hell" that Japanese students experience as they prepare to take university entrance examinations during their final year of high school. The first years of work are an initiation process during which new employees receive general training, learn their firm's history and culture, and experience work in several different departments. They are then given longer term assignments, but will continue to be transferred to other jobs and departments until they reach retirement age, usually 55–60. Only in extreme circumstances, such as near bankruptcy on the part of the firm or criminal behavior on the part of an individual, are lifetime employees laid off or fired.

The commitment to lifetime employment produces a strong bond between company and employee. Employees know that their earnings and benefits depend on the performance of the company, so they work hard to help make their company successful. Companies know that it is unlikely that their employees will move to another firm, so they can invest in employee education and training with little fear of losing the benefits of that investment. Another benefit of the system is efficient information flow within the company. The combination of lifetime employment, frequent transfer, and the after-hours socializing that is a part of Japanese business life means that employees develop extensive people networks throughout the organization. These enable them to keep up to date on what is happening in other parts of the company and to get needed information, answers to questions, and introductions to people whose assistance or cooperation they may need. Lifetime employment also has an important strategic implication: the imperative of providing continued employment for all their regular workers causes Japanese firms to aggressively pursue growth and market share, often at the expense of profitability.

The lifetime employment system applies to only around 30 percent of the Japanese workforce, mostly the regular male employees of larger firms. The majority of Japan's workers, including day laborers, part-time employees, and most female workers (who typically work for a few years after graduation and then get married and "retire" to raise a family), do not enjoy lifetime employment and the benefits associated with it.

In nearly all companies, wage increases and

promotion are based on a combination of seniority and merit, but under *nihonteki keiei*, seniority typically carries greater weight (*nenko joretsu*). This is especially true with wages, which start at low levels and increase as employees reach the age where they need greater income to support their families and pay for their children's education. Promotion is slow, and increasingly merit-based as a person advances to higher ranks; the more-talented employees are promoted more frequently and to higher positions than those with less talent. The average wage gap between top management and ordinary worker is significantly smaller in Japanese companies than in Western ones.

Japanese unions differ from Western unions in that they are organized by enterprise (company) rather than by trade. Each company has just one union and each union negotiates with only one company. All company employees (except for part-time workers and management at the rank of section chief and above) are members, regardless of their job category. Labor–management relations are more cooperative than adversarial, with unions exerting moderate pressure for wage and benefit increases but rarely striking or making demands that would hurt the company's economic health. Unlike trade unions in other countries, Japanese enterprise unions do not present a barrier to employee movement among jobs.

Bottom-up decision making

Decision-making in *nihonteki keiei* is generally described as bottom-up or consensus-based, in contrast to the top-down style that is more characteristic of Western companies. Problems may be identified at any level of the organization, but lower-level managers or task forces are usually given the job of generating solutions in the form of proposals which are then circulated upward to successively higher levels of management through what is known as the **ringi seido**, or memo circulation system. During this process, proposals may be modified and refined. Once a proposal has been approved by all levels in the originating unit, it is circulated laterally to other concerned managers and departments for their review and routine approval. The implementation stage comes only after a proposal has been approved at all levels. Parallel to the formal *ringi seido* is another form of consensus-building known as **nemawa-shi**, informally consulting with others and sharing information about a proposal or decision before a formal decision is made.

While this decision-making process is time-consuming, implementation can be carried out smoothly and quickly as all concerned parties are informed and on board. This is in contrast to top-down decision making, where decisions are made quickly but implementation takes longer because the broader organization has had less input and been given little chance to become familiar with a proposal and convinced of its benefits.

Quality control circles, **just-in-time** production, and **kaizen** are other elements of *nihonteki keiei* that empower and tap the ideas and knowledge of employees in the lower levels of the organization. Quality control circles are groups of workers that meet outside work hours to develop ways to improve product quality or the efficiency or safety of operations. With just-in-time production systems, line workers are responsible for a range of tasks, including stopping the assembly line when there is a problem and taking the initiative to find ways to improve quality and efficiency. *Kaizen*, continuous improvement, enlists the entire work-force in a systematic effort to find better ways of doing things, large and small.

The origins and overseas application of *nihonteki keiei*

Although many of the roots of Japanese-style management are cultural, social, or historical, the lifetime employment system and other key elements of *nihonteki keiei* are in fact of relatively recent origin. Japan's union movement, which had been weak prior to the Second World War, grew into a powerful force following the war, supported by the Occupation authorities and spurred by high unemployment in the early postwar years. Conflict between labor unions and company management became common, and even as economic growth took off in the 1950s, the nation's factories continued to be the scene of frequent and some-times violent strikes, employment and wage insecurity, and fierce battles for worker loyalty between militant leftist labor unions and more moderate, company-sponsored unions. Management-friendly enterprise unions gradually won out over the more militant ones and finally, realizing that continued strife would threaten the nation's economic future, labor and management came to an agreement: companies would ensure rising wages and employment security for all union members by providing seniority-based pay and lifetime employment, while unions and workers would adopt more cooperative and supportive policies toward their companies. This happened around 1960, the same time that Prime Minister Hayato Ikeda announced the **income doubling plan**, and the nation turned its attention more fully to the achievement and enjoyment of economic prosperity.

As Japanese companies expanded overseas in the 1970s and 1980s, they took *nihonteki keiei* with them, experimenting to find out which of its elements would work with and be accepted by non-Japanese workers. In general, Japanese-style management was successful with blue-collar employees. Product quality and production efficiency at Japanese-run foreign plants approached levels achieved in Japan, and blue-collar workers tended to feel more appreciated and empowered under Japanese management, with its greater reliance on initiative and input from line workers, than they had under Western management. Foreign white-collar employees tended to be less happy, complaining that management decisions were made in Tokyo and that a "glass ceiling" limited promotion opportunities for non-Japanese. Japanese companies were able to build relatively cooperative relationships with overseas labor unions, or avoid unionization of the workforce altogether, but lifetime employment was not offered to foreign employees to the extent that it was to regular employees in Japan.

Post-bubble developments

Nihonteki keiei has continued to evolve and adjust to changing external conditions. Change was particularly noticeable during the 1990s, when the economic downturn following the collapse of the bubble economy put heavy pressure on firms to cut costs and increase efficiency. This made certain costs of *nihonteki keiei*, such as the inability to

downsize or shed inefficient workers under lifetime employment and the high salaries paid to older workers under the seniority-based wage schemes, more difficult to bear than they had been in more prosperous, higher growth periods. *Risutora*, or **restructuring**, became one of the strongest, and most feared, trends in Japanese business in the 1990s, as major companies began moving more of their operations overseas and slimming down their Japanese workforces through plant closures and layoffs. For as long as possible, companies avoided outright layoffs, instead downsizing through attrition and by letting part-time workers go. But as recessionary conditions continued, companies' commitment to lifetime employment weakened, and more and more regular lifetime employees, particularly older employees, were pressured to retire or were discharged. The seniority system weakened as well, with wages and promotion becoming increasingly based on merit rather than years of employment.

Social trends also contributed to change. The generation of young people who joined companies in the 1980s and 1990s differed from earlier generations. Dubbed *shinjinrui*, or "new human species," these people seemed to lack the work ethic and company loyalty of their seniors, whose values had been shaped by growing up in less affluent times. Older managers complained that the new generation preferred to go home at five o'clock to enjoy their private lives and interests rather than work overtime or go drinking with work colleagues after hours. There were also an increasing number of young people who felt little attraction to the idea of lifetime employment and slow, seniority-based promotion, preferring instead a chance to prove themselves and be rewarded for their achievements at an early age.

Further reading

Abegglen, J.C. (1958) *The Japanese Factory: Aspects of its Social Organization*, Glencoe, IL: The Free Press.

Abegglen, J.C. and Stalk, G. (1985) *Kaisha: The Japanese Corporation*, New York: HarperCollins.

Clark, R. (1979) *The Japanese Company*, New Haven, CT: Yale University Press.

Marsland, S.E. (1980) *Note on Japanese Management*

and Employment Systems, Boston: Harvard Business School.

TIM CRAIG

Nikkei jin

Nikkei jin literally means people of Japanese descent. The term generally refers to those who are Japanese or of Japanese descent that live outside Japan and possess the nationality of the country where they reside.

Japanese emigration was noted as early as the sixteenth century. However, it was not until after the **Meiji restoration** that large-scale emigration began. Emigrants worked primarily as agricultural and mining laborers; their destinations were South Asia, East Asia, Hawaii, California, the west coast of Canada, and Latin American countries including Brazil, Peru, Argentina, and Bolivia. São Paulo, Brazil has more people of Japanese descent than anywhere else in the world outside Japan.

Beginning in the late 1980s, a significant number of Japanese descendants from Latin American countries, primarily from Brazil, have been returning to Japan to work as foreign laborers. Recent usage of the term *Nikkei jin* by the media in Japan generally refers to these **foreign workers** from South America. Japanese officials maintain a position of not allowing in any unskilled foreign laborers. However, faced with the nation's acute labor shortage in the late 1980s and 1990s, the Japanese government revised their immigration policies and allowed these descendants of Japanese immigrants to South American countries to work and live in Japan for up to three years with a domicile visa. The Japanese authorities hoped that foreigners of Japanese descent would be more likely to blend in with Japanese society, thereby minimizing the effect on the nation's ethnic and cultural homogeneity.

Further reading

Clucas, M. (1995) "Race, Ethnicity, and Life Satisfaction: A Study of Nikkei Workers in Japan," Ph.D. dissertation, Department of Sociology, University of Southern California.

Kitano, H.H.L. (1969) *Japanese Americans*, Engelwood Cliffs, NJ: Prentice-Hall.

Takahashi, Y. (1993) *Nikkei Brajiru Imin Shi* (The History of Japanese Brazilian Immigration), Tokyo: San Ichi Shobo.

MEIKA CLUCAS

NIKKEIREN *see* Japan Federation of Employers' Associations

Nintendo

Founded by Fusajiro Yamauchi in Kyoto, Japan, Nintendo is the oldest company to be involved in the manufacture of video games. Founded in 1889 as the Marufuku Company, it produced elaborately decorated Hanafuda playing cards. The name was changed to Nintendo Koppai in 1907. In the 1970s, Gunpei Yokoi, a Nintendo designer, began creating toys such as the Ultra Hand and the Beam Gun. These toys led to substantial profits for Nintendo and moved it into the first tier of the Osaka Stock Exchange.

In 1975 Nintendo obtained the rights to sell the Magnavox Odyssey game system in Japan and in 1977, working together with **Mitsubishi**, Nintendo developed the TV-Game 6, with 6 variations of Pong; this was later followed by the TV-Game 15. By the end of the 1970s Nintendo had developed a department devoted solely to producing arcade games.

In the early 1980s Nintendo began marketing and distributing its arcade games in the United States, and after some unsuccessful attempts at designing new products, introduced Donkey Kong in 1981. Americans initially mocked this coin-operated arcade game, but then quickly became fascinated by the hero, a carpenter named Mario, who rescued a kidnapped girl from a gorilla. So strong was the demand expressed for Donkey Kong that numerous bootleg copies were produced.

After Donkey Kong's success became apparent, Nintendo was threatened with a lawsuit from Universal for infringing on the 1929 film King Kong. Nintendo refused to settle and countersued instead, claiming that Universal had no rights to

King Kong and that the company was well aware of that fact when suing Nintendo. A judgment of $1.8 million was made in favor of Nintendo.

In 1983 the Famicom was introduced in Japan, an 8-bit game system which was introduced to the US market two years later as the Nintendo Entertainment System (NES.) By this time Nintendo controlled 90 percent of the Japanese game market and in the following year outsold its competitors in the US by a margin of 10:1. In the early 1990s Nintendo introduced the Game Boy, a portable game system which used interchangeable game cartridges. With more than 500 game titles available at the end of 1999, the Game Boy is the best-selling game system to date.

Nintendo faced serious competition in the 1990s. In 1991 the Sega Genesis, a faster system than the improved Super NES, was launched. Although Nintendo had made plans to work together with **Sony** on a CD-ROM project, named the PlayStation, the plans fell through and Sony continued on its own, creating yet another competitor in the video-game market. In 1995 Nintendo showed further signs of distress when Square and Enix, two of Nintendo's main developers, went over to Sony. However, when Nintendo's system was improved again in 1996 and the Nintendo 64 became available in the United States, it outsold both the Saturn and the PlayStation.

In September 1998 Nintendo introduced the Pokémon game. The Pokémon franchise has become a worldwide phenomenon, and ironically has returned Nintendo to the sale of playing cards and toys, which had been responsible for the company's initial success.

Further reading

Sheff, D. (1993) *Game Over*, New York: Random House.

ALEXANDRA COHEN

Nippon Telegraph and Telephone

The telephone company Nippon Telegraph and Telephone Corporation (NTT) was established on April 1, 1885. It currently has 195,000 employees, and a capital of ¥796 billion.

Since 1885, NTT has operated as a public telephone monopoly under the authority of the Ministry of Post and Telecommunications and one of the few public corporations with substantial demand-generating power for information industries. All foreign carriers connect to NTT to do business in Japan. In early 1997, restructuring into three affiliated companies and several subsidiaries combined with market deregulation thrust change upon NTT. In 1997, British Telecom (BT) officials publicly declared that they would seek a preferred partnership with NTT. These overtures had begun in late 1996 when Japan's Ministry of Posts and Telecommunications said it would break up NTT and do away with the regulations that segregated Japan's carriers by international and domestic markets. The Ministry also began easing laws on foreign participation in Japan's market.

The biggest turning point for NTT started in early 1999 when market deregulation pushed NTT into the international telecommunications stage for the first time in its history. Due to Japan's market segregation, NTT's revenues currently come solely from its home market. Despite its size, the company remains uncommitted to the kind of global telecommunications alliance or major merger that the world's other big carriers including AT&T, BT, Sprint, and MCI have sought.

Though less concerned with global markets, NTT has developed new domestic services. In 1999, I-mode services were introduced by NTT DoCoMo and IC public card telephones have also been introduced. Some international telephone services have been established by NTT Communications and ADSL trial services have been initiated by NTT East and NTT West. NTT is currently investing in the next-generation of network operators. NTT said it will commit as much as $100 million to Denver-based Verio, an ISP that has grown rapidly merging small US ISPs. Recently, NTT sought and received telecommunications licenses in major markets including the United States, and it is an investor in a project to connect the United States and China with 30,000 kilometers of fiber-optic cable.

The future goal of NTT is to work toward creating new opportunities for its "information distribution" business in a variety of forms, not limited to the traditional telecommunications field but also including such efforts as construction of platforms to safely and efficiently distribute videos and other types of content. To accomplish this, NTT will seek to apply the R&D capabilities of the NTT Group, whose high standards are recognized on a global scale, and mobilize the group's full range of management resources to provide cutting-edge services at lower prices.

MARGARET TAKEDA

Nissan

Nissan Motor Co. began in a series of mergers and acquisitions during the period 1925–34. Later alliances included producing British Austin cars under license in the 1950s, and the purchase of Prince Motors in Japan in 1966. Nissan likewise invested in a range of specialty assemblers in the 1950s and early 1960s, such as Nissan Auto Body (light trucks), Nissan Diesel (heavy trucks), and parts firms such as Tokyo Radiator. Finally, it came to control a number of its large dealers, often unwillingly when the latter ran into management problems. The largest domestic auto producer from 1937 through 1962, it was then surpassed by **Toyota**, and while it did very well during 1970–6, both domestically and as Japan's leading exporter, it lost market share almost continuously thereafter.

Some of Nissan's long-term problems date to a five-month labor dispute in 1953, resolved only through the formation of a new union. That maneuver was supported by Kawamata Katsuji, who later dominated the firm as president (1957–73) and chairman (1973–85). The conflict produced factions, with the union supporting Kawamata but undermining his successors, such as Ishihara Takashi, who pioneered Nissan's sales in the USA as well as the development of the highly successful Datsun Sunny launched in 1966. The end result was poor coordination among departments – development and engineering did not work with marketing – and a sales force that once refused to work Saturdays as a way to stress union prerogatives. Nissan's domestic output peaked in 1980, and it entered the 1990s with a weak dealership network and a poor presence in the newly developed, more car-oriented suburbs of major cities.

Marketing ineptitude also played a role. The original Datsun logo was dropped in overseas markets in the mid-1980s, and a quirky advertising campaign hurt the launch of the luxury Infiniti in the crucial US market. The firm had long been involved in overseas production, in Mexico from 1960, in the US (Smyrna, Tennessee) from 1984 and in Sunderland, England from 1986. However, its cars were often out of touch with local markets; it reacted slowly to the collapse of the US subcompact car market after 1985. Its Smyrna factory ranked number one in several US production efficiency surveys, and a major new production center in Kyushu, Japan, leaves it with relatively new plants. Such strengths have been offset by poor sales and overcapacity in all major markets since 1992. Large losses led it to close its Zama plant outside of Tokyo in 1995, the first Japanese producer to take such a step, and withdraw from assembly in Australia. Even though it lost money in every year but one during 1992–2000, it delayed restructuring. Renault's takeover in 1999 and the installation of the Brazilian-born Carlos Ghosn as president changed that: revamped marketing, additional plant closures, and the sale of stakes in affiliate companies followed. With 2.5 million units worldwide output, Nissan remains a major producer, but restructuring will likely drive it from its current second place in the Japanese domestic market.

MICHAEL SMITKA

Nomura Securities

Nomura Securities is one of Japan's "Big Three" domestic financial securities companies, which also includes Nikko Securities and Daiwa Securities. It was established in 1925 as a spin-off from the Securities Department of Osaka Nomura Bank Co., Ltd, which was founded by Tokushichi Nomura. Since the 1960s, Nomura has been the largest of all Japanese financial securities companies, and is the leader in almost all domestic securities business fields, including stock trading, bond sales, corporate bond underwriting, and initial public offerings.

For the fiscal year ending March 2000, Nomura's revenues were over a trillion yen, nearly double that of Nikko Securities (approximately 650 billion yen) and Daiwa Securities (approximately 530 billion yen). Because of its overwhelming size and power in Japan, Nomura is occasionally nicknamed "Gulliver Nomura", after the "giant" in Swift's satirical novel. In addition to 124 branch offices in Japan, it also has 105 group companies engaged in activities related to the securities business, such as banking, trusts, information services, consulting, real estate, lease and rental. Group member companies of particular note include Nomura Research Institute (the world's largest commercially-owned think tank), Nomura Asset Management Co., Ltd. (Japan's largest asset management firm), and Nomura Securities International (NSI).

Born in 1878, Tokushichi Nomura was the son of an Osaka moneychanger. In 1908, he left on a five-month trip to the United States and Europe to understand the Western dealing system. After this visit, he established his own clique of financial companies called Nomura *zaibatsu*. In 1925, Nomura Securities was spun off from the Osaka Nomura bank, which was the main bank of the Nomura *zaibatsu* (see **main bank system**). By the early 1960s, Nomura had outstripped Yamaichi Securities, the leading company at that time, to reach the top of the Japanese financial securities industry. (Yamaichi Securities would later file for bankruptcy in 1997). Nomura employees were put under heavy pressures to achieve sales targets. Moreover, performance appraisals for promotions and pay raises were carried out on the basis of an extensive merit system. In those days, the work environment in a Nomura office was often expressed as *suuji wa jinkaku*, meaning that a person was known by his numbers or results. Due to their long work hours, Nomura's employees were described as "Seven-Eleven". In those days, it was often said that a stock pushed by Nomura was sure to go up. By these means, Nomura gradually established itself as a giant among Japanese financial securities companies. At the height of the 1980s **bubble economy**, the number of Nomura customers reached upwards of five million.

After the Tokyo market passed its unsustainable peak in the late 1980s, Nomura was involved in several major scandals. In 1991, Nomura was implicated in illegal loss compensation of over ¥26 billion to favored large customers but not to small individual customers. Also, at that time, financial loans to *yakuza*, or Japanese organized crime gangs, came to light. In particular, the scandal in 1997 had a huge impact on Nomura and other major Japanese securities companies. In that year, illegal payoffs to **sokaiya**, or corporate racketeers, were uncovered. The Securities and Exchange Surveillance Commission of Japan indicted Nomura Securities and its executives. Former managing directors, as well as people at banks who provided financing to the sokaiya for the purchase of Nomura Securities shares, were arrested on suspicion of violating the Securities and Exchange Law for illegal compensation of losses and the Commercial Law for illegal payoffs to *sokaiya*. Afterwards, executives of several major securities companies and banks, including the former Nomura president Hideo Sakamaki, were arrested. This series of events developed into the scandal that shook the financial and securities industry in Japan, with payoff amounts reaching ¥700 million in total. A different sort of challenge faced by Nomura in 1998 was the enormous business loss incurred by its US subsidiary, NSI. A sudden fall in the market prices of real estate bonds along with holdings of problematic Russian national loan bonds led to staggering losses of ¥160 billion by the subsidiary.

Following Nomura Securities International's (NSI) registration as a member of the Boston Stock Exchange in 1969, Nomura has been actively expanding abroad. By 2000, the number of Nomura group companies located in North and South America was twenty-six, with thirty-seven group companies in Europe, and twenty-three group companies in Asia/Oceania. Within the Japanese securities industry, Nomura is the recognized leader in international business. As an example of its international activity, it is known in Vietnam for helping to establish a securities market as well as commercial corporations. Because of its size and extensive overseas presence, Nomura has become one of the more well known Japanese business names to people of other countries.

More recently, according to a business plan announced in October 1998, Nomura has been trying to establish its identity as the top investment bank in Japan. The plan identified the following four areas as cores of its business: global bonds, global stocks, global investment banking, and domestic retail financial services. Nomura has intensively invested its management resources in these fields. Building on its domestic base and aiming at becoming an important global player, Nomura also has been working to reorganize its international business and to improve the efficiency of all its business operations.

Further reading

Alletzhauser, A.J. (1990) *The House of Nomura: The Inside Story of the Legendary Japanese Financial Dynasty*, New York: Arcade/Little, Brown & Co.

Arora, D. (1995) *Japanese Financial Institutions in Europe: International Competitiveness of Japanese Banks and Securities Companies*, Amsterdam: Elsevier.

Fitzgibbon, J.E., Jr. (1991) *Deceitful Practices: Nomura Securities and the Japanese Invasion of Wall Street*, New York: Carol Publishing Group.

Kimura, Y. and Pugel, T.A. (1993) "The Structure and Performance of the Japanese Securities Industry," in I. Walter and T. Hiraki (eds), *Restructuring Japan's Financial Markets*, Homewood, IL: Irwin.

Nomura Securities Company (1986) *Beyond the Ivied Mountain*, Tokyo: Nomura Securities.

HIROTAKA AOKI

Nonaka, Ikujiro

A leading scholar in the field of knowledge creation within organizations, Nonaka obtained a B.A. in political science from Waseda University in 1958 and a Ph.D. in business administration from the University of California, Berkeley in 1972. On the Faculty of Social Science at the National Defense Academy from 1977–9, he then joined the Institute of Business Research, Hitotsubashi in 1979, serving as director of the institute from 1982 to 1995. In

1997 he became the first Xerox Distinguished Professor of Knowledge at the Haas School of Business, University of California, Berkeley. In the same year he founded and became dean of the Graduate School of Knowledge Science. His book with Hirotaka Takeuchi, *The Knowledge-Creating Company: How Japanese Companies Create the Dynamics of Innovation*, won numerous book-of-the-year awards in 1997 and 1998.

Nonaka's theoretical and empirical work on how knowledge is created within organization had a profound effect on theories of organizational learning. In major departure from the dominant view, first propounded by Nobel laureate Herbert Simon, of organizations as "information processors," Nonaka argued the organizations didn't simply process knowledge, but rather they created knowledge. Moreover, it was the knowledge creating activities of organizations that gave them a competitive edge in the market. Though he argues for the universality of his theories of knowledge creation and management, Nonaka's thinking is firmly rooted in an understanding of the **product development** processes common to Japanese organizations.

See also: firm strategies for technology

Further reading

Nonaka, I. and Takeuchi, H. (1997) *The Knowledge-Creating Company: How Japanese Companies Create the Dynamics of Innovation*, New York: Oxford University Press.

ALLAN BIRD

Norin Chukin Bank

Japanese cooperatives, after the enactment of the Industrial Cooperative Society Law in 1900, developed mainly in rural areas as societies undertaking credit, marketing, purchasing and utilization activities in parallel. In 1923, the Central bank for Industrial Cooperatives, the predecessor of the Norin Chukin Bank, was founded for the purpose of expanding credit operations. Its name was officially changed to the Norin Chukin Bank in 1943 when forestry cooperatives joined the Bank.

After the end of the the Second World War, functional associations such as agricultural cooperatives (*nokyo*), fishery cooperatives (*gyokyo*), forestry cooperatives (*shinrinkumiai*), consumer cooperatives (*seikyo*) and credit unions replaced cooperative societies. *Nokyo*, *gyokyo* and *shinrinkumiai*, which support the primary industry, and their respective federations at the prefectural level, engaging in credit-extension business, made capital contributions to the Norin Chukin Bank, and the Bank made a fresh start as the financial institution for the cooperative organizations that operate credit-extension business.

The core of the Bank's business consists of financial services to *nokyo*, *gyokyo*, *shinrinkumiai* and their respective federations. The Bank's primary sources of funds are deposits, the majority of which come from the cooperative system, or deposits obtained from members of Nokyo and other cooperatives. The Bank is also authorized to issue bank debentures under the Law of Central Cooperative Bank for Agriculture, Forestry and Fisheries, and raise funds by selling those bank debentures to individuals and institutional investors.

Loans relating to agriculture, fisheries and forestry constitute an important part of the Bank's business which, consist mainly of loans for procuring fertilizers, feedstuff, agricultural chemicals and machinery as well as for the food processing industry. Other operations include inland exchange, international business, and securities transaction. For international operations, the Bank engages mainly in loan extension and money market transactions from its branches in New York, London, and Singapore. Its locally established subsidiaries engaging in securities business in London and Switzerland operate with central focus on bond issuance and debt securities flotation.

The Bank has fourteen subsidiaries and two affiliated companies, which together form the Norin Chukin Group, and provide securities business, trust services, lease operations and other financial services.

Finding ways to wage competition against large private-sector city banks in the likelihood of further progress in financial liberalization represents the major challenge that lies ahead in the future for the Bank. Elimination of high cost structure associated with the nature of cooperative bank's activities centering on retail business characterized by time deposits and long-term loans is another challenge for the future.

KENJI ISHIHARA

O

office ladies

"Office ladies" (OL) refers to young unmarried women who work full time in assistant clerical occupations. The term emerged during the rapid expansion of a tertiary sector (service and trade) in the 1960s and connotes glamour and freedom for unmarried young women whose life course is in a transition from youth (school graduation) to adulthood (marriage). Working as an OL means a time of "waiting" and preparation for the "real life" that comes after marriage. It is a time to see the world, and to earn and save money for marriage. For this reason, the position is described as *koshikake*, temporary bench. The primary goal of working as an OL is to meet prospective husbands who can bring a comfortable middle-class lifestyle, or alternatively, to return to their home towns to make a better marriage match.

The contribution of office ladies to Japan's GNP is small, especially when compared to that of married women. Young unmarried women constitute less than one-third of the total female workforce, but they make up nearly 50 percent of female clerical workers. Women's representation in clerical occupations declines sharply with age and marriage. Married women, whose jobs are more intermittent, are likely to work in production, both skilled and unskilled, and sales jobs. They provide a vital supply of substantial but cheap labor and act as a buffer in the overall economy.

In contrast to the type of work performed by married women, the position of OL provides a social veneer, embodying the traditional feminine roles. Jobs are more ornamental than substantial.

They remain "ladies" and have decorative value as receptionists or office assistants. They answer telephones, operate photocopy machines, serve tea, and clean the office desks. Office ladies are recruited immediately after high school or junior college. They typically resign from work either upon marriage or the birth of the first child. Pressure for resignation comes from strong social expectations that women are supposed to put their family first. Such pressure is sometimes made through employer suggestions that they retire, a practice known as *kata-tataki* (tap on the shoulder). With the passage of the Equal Employment Opportunity Law (EEOL) in April 1986, however, the suggestion that women retire at marriage is no longer legal.

There is no career mobility, but the lack of a job ladder is for the most part irrelevant. The clearer understanding of the significance of OL requires a larger structural and historical picture. During the rapid economic development of the 1960s, the (new) middle class expanded, and along with it an image of the ideal housewife who is fully committed to the family. Marriage was seen as a ticket out of labor-intensive agricultural or textile mill work or unrewarding office work, as well as an entry into the security of a middle-class lifestyle. The new ideology situated women as nurturers of children, supporters of husband's career (or the family business), and caregivers of aging parents.

Currently, Japan faces an uncertain trend. The strong normative and behavioral consensus that existed about women's roles is crumbling. There is greater awareness among women that employers continue to discriminate against women who do not intend to leave work upon marriage and those with career ambitions. During the 1980s and 1990s, women began to postpone marriage. As the economy opened up more job opportunities, women's life options widened, and the need for rushing into marriage for economic security decreased. Marriage that only increases their family responsibilities and puts an end to their freedom is no longer attractive. The average age of marriage for women rose from twenty-five in 1975 to twenty-eight in 1995, and in the Tokyo area, it is thirty-one. Women on average are having 1.6 children, one of the lowest birth rates in the world. The celebration of single lifestyle among office ladies gave rise to a popular phrase, "office lady syndrome." It describes the orientation of office ladies geared to dining out, fashion, leisure, and travel.

Studies are divided in the interpretation of the "office lady syndrome." Some observers consider it a product of the **bubble economy** of the 1980s. According to this view, women who were pampered by their parents during the bubble era developed a strong sense of money and consumption orientation without long-range life plans or a career orientation. This position suggests the pursuit of conspicuous consumption is more consistent with existing patterns of gender differentiation than it is with the advancement of new roles for women. Alternatively, some suggest that a "quiet revolution" is taking place in this group of women involving the postponement of marriage. According to this view, young women are disillusioned with Japanese men and marriage, question the wisdom of "traditional" women's roles, and are more selective in their life course options. This perspective views women as quiet initiators of social change, including the re-negotiation of gender roles.

See also: salaryman

Further reading

Awaya, N. and Phillips, D. (1996) "Popular Reading: The Literary World of the Japanese Working Women," in A. Iwamura (ed.), *Re-imaging Japanese Women*, Berkeley, CA: University of California Press, 244–70.

Carter, R. and Dilatusb, L. (1976) "Office Ladies," in J. Lebra, J. Paulson and E. Powers (eds), *Women in Changing Japan*, Stanford, CA: Stanford University Press, 75–88.

Clammer, J. (1997) *Contemporary Urban Japan*, Oxford: Blackwell.

Fujimoto, T. (1994) "Office Lady Syndrome: A Gender Comparison of Job Attitudes Among Japanese Clerical Workers," in *Best Papers Proceedings*, Association of Japanese Business Studies, 7th Annual Meeting, Vancouver, British Columbia, Canada, 183–207.

Inoue, T. and Ehara, Y. (eds) (1995) *Women's Data Book*, Tokyo: Yuhikaku.

Lo, J. (1990) *Office Ladies/Factory Women: Life and Work at a Japanese Company*, New York: M.E. Sharpe.

Ogasawara, Y. (1998) *Office Ladies and Salaried Men: Power, Gender, and Work in Japanese Companies*, Berkeley, CA: University of California Press.

Saso, M. (1990) *Women in the Japanese Workplace*, London: Hilary Shipman.

Usui, C. (1994) "Do American Models of Female Career Attainment Apply to Japanese?" Occasional Paper Series No. 9408, Center for International Studies, University of Missouri-St. Louis.

White, M.I. and Barnet, S. (1995) *Comparing Cultures*, Boston: Bedford Books of St. Martin's Press.

CHIKAKO USUI

Ohmae, Kenichi

Kenichi Ohmae was born in the Fukuoka prefecture in 1943. He received his bachelor's degree at Waseda University, his master's degree at Tokyo Institute of Technology, and his doctorate degree at Massachusetts Institute of Technology. After working for Hitachi Limited for two years (1970–2) as an engineer on nuclear development, Ohmae joined McKinsey & Company Incorporated in 1972. He received the Twelfth Keizai-kai Taisho Tokubetsu-sho (Special Prize at the Economic-World Grand Prize) in 1986, and became the chairman of McKinsey & Company Incorporated

Japan in 1989. He resigned from the company in 1994.

Ohmae is well known as a theorist of the opening of the Japanese market. His books include *The Evolving Global Economy: Making Sense of the New World Order, The Invisible Continent: Four Strategic Imperatives of the New Economy,* and *The Borderless World: Power and Strategy in the Interlinked Economy.*

MARGARET TAKEDA

AKI MATSUNAGA

one-to-one marketing

One-to-one marketing relates to the pinpointing of specific needs of individual customers, and it is best understood as the opposite of mass marketing. The concept of marketing was first introduced in Japan in the 1950s, at the initial stage of **economic growth**, and deemed particularly relevant to the buoyant consumer goods industry, which applied methods of mass merchandising during the 1960s.

In the 1970s, however, economic growth came to an end, especially after the oil shock. In the face of a slowdown of the Japanese economy, the traditional policy of swamping the market with a uniform product, which was based on the notion that the market was composed of unspecific customers with homogenous needs, no longer applied. It was thought, instead, that the market had become heterogeneous, requiring differentiated products corresponding to the needs and characteristics of customers forming sub-sets of the entire market (segment marketing).

Segment marketing had three variations. Firstly, target marketing related to methods for approaching and exploiting a particular segment. Secondly, differentiation marketing aimed at several segments simultaneously, which Japanese automotive producers and leading publishing companies typically adopted for their product lineups. Thirdly, focus marketing was specifically employed in regard to a narrowly defined segment.

As the consumer market in Japan was thought to have matured, segment marketing became irrelevant, as it was believed that the entire market was composed of segments within which customer needs were still homogeneous. It was subsequently argued that sorting out the specific needs of individual customers and responding to them could expand sales. In parallel, the growth of the service industry prompted a wide range of business activities to become ever more customer-oriented. In the late 1980s, the notion of customer satisfaction (CS) gained popularity, and a number of CS surveys were conducted so as to gauge a company's overall performance from a broader point of view.

In 1995, the translation of Peppers and Rogers' book *The One to One Future* (1993), was published. The new term "one-to-one marketing" was then interpreted as a long-awaited solution to the above-noted agendas. Peppers and Rogers foresee the possibility of maximizing each customer's satisfaction through the use of computers, from which the sales force can retrieve a large amount of past and new information, previously unavailable and not possible to accumulate, such as requests from various customers, data on past purchases, inclinations, etc. With a continuous renewal of the database on a customer-by-customer basis, companies will, argue the authors, be able to increase their opportunities for contact with the customers over a lifetime than would competitors. Companies would thus retain customers for a long period, which, in turn, would contribute to higher market shares. One-to-one marketing, therefore, is made possible by computer technologies that provide databases, at lower cost than before, for developing new methods to contribute to the customer satisfaction. Its aim is to maximize the time and opportunity share of individual customers.

However, database marketing with the use of computer has been developed in the direct mail industry, and the **retail industry** through the issuance of point cards and credit cards, which can be regarded as one-to-one marketing tools. With the advent of the information society, however, the Internet has become a powerful transaction channel of business to consumer (B to C) marketing, as exemplified by the popularity of Amazon.com.

The term "one-to-one marketing" in Japan tends to be used in a broader context, and also applied to approaching specific customers for a relatively long period of time. For example, a housing company that approaches its customers on the occasions of periodic maintenance and then proposes rebuilding or additions is sometimes referred to as using one-to-one marketing. The term is also used within the automotive retail industry to designate sales efforts to induce current users to choose the same manufacturer's car for replacement.

Sales promotions (SP) with a view to capturing high yield customers are commonly used by door-to-door sales and the department store industry (see **department stores**), and they are also viewed as a form of one-to-one marketing. A uniquely Japanese example of one-to-one marketing are Buddhist temples that apply the notion to the management of their relations with families and persons affiliated with the sect.

See also: marketing in Japan

Further readings

Peppers, D. and Rogers, M. (1993) *The One to One Future*, New York: Doubleday; trans. T. Iseki, *ONE to ONE Maaketingu: Kokyaku Rireishon Senryaku*. Tokyo: Daiyamondosha, 1995.

SHINTARO MOGI

Ono, Taiichi

Taiichi Ono (Ohno) is an engineer and executive who guided the development of the **Toyota production system**. A graduate of Nagoya Higher Industrial School, Ono worked for Toyoda Spinning before joining **Toyota** Motors in 1943. Influenced strongly by Fordist mass production and Frederick Winslow Taylor's theories of scientific management, Ono was dedicated to eliminating waste, increasing labor productivity and cutting costs on Toyota's production lines. Through a process of constant analysis and experimentation on the shop floor, Ono adapted American manufacturing models to Japanese realities, introducing a series of production management innovations between the late 1940s and the mid-1960s. These highly successful methods, including multi-machine handling, small-lot production, the **just-in-time** concept, and the *kanban* system, revolutionized traditional manufacturing practices and were widely emulated both in Japan and abroad.

Further reading

Cusumano, M.A. (1985) *The Japanese Automobile Industry: Technology and Management at Nissan and Toyota*, Cambridge, MA: Council on East Asian Studies, Harvard University.

WILLIAM M. TSUTSUI

organizational learning

When organizations and its members acquire new knowledge and new insights, organizational learning occurs. To sustain competitive advantage in the global market, organizations should maintain effective organizational learning and continuously overcome any obstacles to learning. Although the processes of the organizational learning cycle itself do not differ much, the learning methods of Japanese firms differs from those of US firms in a few essential points, and this in turn leads to other differences.

Historically, theories of organizational learning appeared around the early 1960s. These early theories were based on studies of organizational adaptation. Organizational adaptation simply means defensive adjustment to gaps, for example, the gap between the aspiration level and the real performance of an organization. On the other hand, the more recent definition of organizational learning includes new understanding of causal chains and changing shared beliefs and values of organizational members. Firms that want to succeed in their business need continuous change in existing and obsolescing values. In other words, they need organizational learning. As a result of this change in perspective, the study of organizational learning has become more popular.

It was around the year 1990 that the term "organizational learning" became a subject of great interest among both academic people and businesspeople. The prominent work of Peter Senge's *The Fifth Discipline* played an important role in popularization of this term. He focused on a "learning organization" and the applied theories of organizational learning. Because his discussion on it attached importance to implementation and was perceived as useful, the concept was welcomed by businesspeople. Another reason for the rapid diffusion of this term was that executives of US firms noticed the strong power of effective organizational learning for gaining competitive advantage. They regarded the overwhelming victory of many Japanese manufacturing firms in the 1980s as due to a learning-oriented corporate culture and to daily learning activities on the shop floor.

Many Japanese manufacturing firms had long made efforts towards **quality management** and the development of education systems for their employees. A typical example can be found in the activities of **quality control circles** formed by blue-collar workers, which became very popular from the late 1960s to the mid-1970s. Members of QC circles decided upon a common theme by themselves. Themes aimed at the improvement of the performance of both the team and the corporation. Because QC circles were not activities maintained by compulsion of managers but by means of individual pursuit of self-fulfillment, motivation for learning through circle activities was high. The learning-supportive atmosphere of Japanese firms also helped employees to participate in the activities positively. For example, executives and managers were ready and quick to adopt many new ideas proposed by circle members. Their attitude was useful in enhancing employees' perceptions that each was an active member of the firm and that members' ideas could directly improve corporate performance. As whole, these activities enabled Japanese firms to have continuous and effective organizational learning.

It is difficult, however, for any firm to maintain effective organizational learning practices. The capability that firms need is always changing in concert with changes in a firm's environment. Some Japanese firms that were successful in the 1980s now confront many difficulties, which hinder desirable organizational learning. Some of these obstacles are common to all firms, and some are specific to Japanese firms.

The process of organizational learning

The cycle of organizational learning generally consists of four phases. The first phase is "planning," in which people clarify what they learn or must learn in the organization. At the second phase "action," people attempt to carry out the plan developed in the previous phase. The third phase is "reflection." People conduct feedback, examining their action and inquiring as to whether or not it is consistent with organizational values and vision, and if it has been carried out correctly. The forth is "memory," during which the learning acquired from the three previous phases is shared with other organizational members. Memory is also the starting point of the next learning cycle. Effective organizational learning can be maintained when this learning cycle continues in iterative fashion without interruption. The so-called PDCA (Plan-Do-Check-Action) cycle is another way of understanding the learning cycle.

Argyris and Schön (1978) note that there are two levels of organizational learning. The first level is single-loop learning, which occurs when organizational members do not question organizational values or approaches, but simply detect and correct errors. *Kaizen* is an example of single-loop learning. The second level of organizational learning is double-loop learning. Members engage in double-loop learning when they question or explore organization values and perspectives, replacing obsolete value with new, more appropriate ones. The difference between the two ways of learning is in the method of reflection that occurs during the third phase of the organizational learning cycle. When members regard the cause of a problem as not embedded in organizational values, but rather as a behavioral error, they engage in single-loop learning. When reflection leads to a replacement of existing organizational values with a new one, then double-loop learning occurs. Both types of learning are important for organizations. Effective single-loop learning is useful to improve the daily task performance, while effective double-loop learning enables organizations to adopt innovative ideas thereby transforming themselves.

Though the same learning cycle can be applied to both, there are several intrinsic differences between Japanese and US firms. The first difference is found in the main entity of organizational learning. In US firms, top management tends to engage in double-loop learning much more than other layers of the organization because of a top-down management style. Conversely, middle and lower level personnel tend to be more involved in single-loop learning.

The merit of this style is rapid execution and diffusion of the learning results acquired by top management. The downside is that the firm's fortunes are directly affected by the top level's ability or inability to realize double-loop learning.

In contrast to US firms, most Japanese firms have **bottom-up decision-making processes**. Based on their daily experiences, employees at the front-line make proposals to those above them. When proposals are good, managers are ready to receive them as the result of organizational learning and diffuse the new knowledge throughout the organization. In addition, the role of middle management in learning is quite important for Japanese firms. They pull critical information out of lower employees and translate this information into a form accessible to the top management of the organization. They also communicate upper management's requests to lower levels, again after transforming such requests into an accessible form. In this sense, the middle manager's function is to act as a catalyst of effective organizational learning. If middle managers function well, both single-loop and double-loop learning will effectively appear at any place within the organization. The merit of this style of organizational learning is that the organization is strongly supported by every employee who is highly learning-oriented. The demerit is that an organization can be severely damaged by the failure of middle management to adequately carry out this function.

The second difference between Japanese firms and US firms is the way they transfer new values and knowledge. In US firms, employees record most of their new knowledge in a formal document, which is so-called explicit knowledge. Because of this, anybody who reads the document can imitate and utilize it at once. In the case that organizational members transfer their knowledge and values as explicit knowledge, it is also difficult to realize double-loop learning because there is less chance to add new values to existing values. At the same time, the possibility of effective single-loop learning is high because the loss of knowledge through transfer is a minimized.

In contrast, the really important knowledge – values and orientations – for Japanese firms tend not to be explicit. Just like the relationship between an apprentice and a master craftsman, employees must carefully observe their bosses or other skilled persons and develop through observation and "intuition" the ability to do their work. In other words, most of the important knowledge is reserved and transferred as tacit knowledge in Japanese firms. The success of transferring tacit knowledge greatly depends on the capability of the receiver, that is, the user of organizational shared knowledge. If the receiver acquires as much learning through accessing the tacit knowledge of their boss and organization and adds new insights of their own, the receiver can experience both single-loop and double-loop learning. However, in the case of a poor or ineffective receiver, even single-loop learning can be difficult to achieve, resulting in significant loss in potential organizational knowledge, and at a high cost in resource investment.

Obstacles to effective organizational learning

There are several obstacles to effective organizational learning. Some are common to every organization, while others are unique to US firms or Japanese firms. The types of obstacles firms confront depend on differences in their approach to learning, as noted above. An example of a common obstacle is that, as a result of organizational culture, most organizational members are reluctant to change present conditions or to accept new ways of doing things. In such a culture, members lose opportunities to learn, because people only notice a problem in existing practices or values when confronted with a different perspective or way of doing things. In addition, organizations which have such a culture produce members who dislike change or non-routine events, thereby limiting the effectiveness of employee training and socialization systems. Because they take existing values and practices for granted, new approaches and proposals are often rejected and the person proposing the change is gradually discouraged by repeated refusal. When people hesitate about doing challenging things, there are fewer and fewer chances to learn new things. Under this condition, the organizational learning cycle does not function, so neither single-loop nor double-loop learning can occur. When there is a communication block between departments of the firm, each department tends to develop a defensive mindset, leading departmental members to reject ideas from outside their own department. In order to solve this problem, firms need to change organizational culture through the development and use of cross-functional teams.

The absence of a clear corporate vision can also be a critical factor in obstructing organizational learning for both Japanese and US firms. However, the reasons are different for the two types of firms. In the case of US firms, the absence of vision prevents executives from attracting employee acceptance and enthusiasm, thereby reducing employee contributions to the organization. Because they lack the power to motivate organizational members, they cannot achieve effective organizational learning. On the other hand, the absence of vision in Japanese firms exerts a bad influence mainly on middle managers in Japanese firms, because it makes it difficult for them to understand the future orientation of the organization or what they should do to convey a motivating vision to lower level employees. When middle managers do not function well as catalysts of organizational learning, neither the top management nor the lower level achieves adequate learning. Generally, Japanese executives, in comparison with US executives, do not explicitly express corporate vision and beliefs. This lack of explicitness needs to change if Japanese firms are to promote enhanced learning activities.

One of the obstacles specific to Japanese firms is the possible deterioration of employees' learning capabilities. Recently, it has become important for Japanese firms to try to improve the quality of white-collar workers. If their capability of receiving tacit knowledge or of translating frontline employees' requests into adequate information is low, most of the tacit knowledge will be gradually lost and the organization will lose its competitive edge in international markets. To avoid this, Japanese firms must upgrade the quality of their employee training activities. At the same time, they need to transform tacit knowledge into explicit knowledge that all members can use.

Further reading

Ando, F. (2001) *Soshiki gakusyu to soshiki-nai tizu* (Organizational Learning and Navigation Maps in the Organization), Tokyo: Hakuto Shobo.

Argyris, C. and Schön, D.A. (1978) *Organizational Learning: A Theory of Action Perspective*, Reading, MA: Addison-Wesley.

Hisamoto, N. (1998) *Kigyo-nai roshi kankei to jinzai keisei* (The Labor-Management Relations in the Organization and Human Development), Tokyo: Yohikaku.

Nonaka, I. and Takeuchi, H. (1995) *The Knowledge-Creating Company*, Oxford: Oxford University Press.

Senge, P. (1990) *The Fifth Discipline*, New York: Doubleday.

FUMIE ANDO

outplacement

Outplacement is a way to adjust a company's human resources by encouraging employees to transfer their jobs through use of outside placement corporations. It has been firmly established in Japanese economy and society from the 1990s. Outplacement requires employees to find and transfer to jobs beyond those that might be possible in subsidiaries and affiliated firms. It is very different from the manner in which large Japanese companies had traditionally managed human resource adjustments. The primary difference is that outside personnel service companies mainly help employees find a job.

The conventional approach to human resource adjustments

The conventional characteristics of the Japanese employment system are permanent employment and the seniority system. Although large enterprises adopted these systems, the adjustment of human resources was still carried out for middle-aged and older employees. Older employees not critical to the firm were required to permanently leave their positions and work for subsidiary or affiliated companies (*tenseki*) or to temporarily transfer to subsidiary or affiliated companies (*syukkou*). *Tenseki* means employees resign their position, and work for the subsidiary or affiliated companies, so it is essentially a job change. *Syukkou* refers to when employees work for subsidiary or affiliated companies, and receive a salary from them, but employees continue to belong to the original company. Middle-aged and older employees tend to be transferred to subsidiary or affiliated companies for *syukkou*. However, after a few years of *syukkou*, this usually turns into *tenseki*. In these situations, the Japanese company secures employees' positions without the aid of personnel service companies.

The influence of economic and social change

The employment system in Japanese companies began to change in the 1990s because of changes in the economic structure and the aging of society. With the collapse of the **bubble economy**, the Japanese economy entered a period of maturity. Under economic stagnation, the need for companies to achieve enhanced efficiencies increased, which made it difficult for companies to maintain the long-term employment and seniority system. Though some sectors of the economy, such as computer manufacture and information services, were experiencing labor shortages, most other industries had a labor surplus. Consequently, there was a severe need to redistribute human resources out of some firms and industries and into others. At the same time, with the aging of society, it was difficult for older workers to secure employment opportunities. In response personnel service companies began to emerge to help struggling firms find positions for redundant employees.

Legal issues and obstacles

Historically, labor restructuring and mobility has been handled mainly buy public agencies under the jurisdiction of the Minister of Labor. This was codified in the Syokugyou Antei Hou (Occupational Security Law). These agencies focus on blue-collar workers, so that when labor restructuring and redistribution began to occur among white-collar workers, they lacked sufficient knowledge or skill to adequately respond. They had difficulty addressing the variety of industries involved and the overall volume of white-collar workers in need of new positions. As a consequence, private personnel services began to appear. Personnel services had initially been granted permission to work with white-collar workers after a revision to the law in 1967. However, at that time, such firms provided services

primarily for temporary or part-time workers such as housewives returning to work. Until 1997, when the law was again revised, white collar placements totaled less than 5 percent of all placements. In the aftermath of the 1997 revisions there was immediate and rapid growth in the number of personnel services companies operating in Japan.

With structural changes in the Japanese economy and society demand for outplacement services has increased significantly. Because outplacement is often part of a company's larger human resources management strategy, it is sometimes described as restructuring (*jinin sakugen*). The emergence of outplacement as a more widely accepted practice and the emergence of personnel services companies signify an important shift in the human resource practices of Japanese firms. The extent and permanence of this shift and its ultimate impact on traditional personnel practices remains to be seen.

Further reading

Abegglen, J.C. and Stalk, G. (1985) *Kaisha: The Japanese Corporation: The New Competition in World Business*, New York: Basic Books.

Cole, R.E. (1979) *Work, Mobility and Participation: A Comparative Study of American and Japanese Industry*, Berkeley, CA: University of California Press.

Dore, R.P. (1973) *British Factory Japanese Factory: The Origins of National Diversity in Industrial Relations*, Berkeley, CA: University of California Press.

Takanashi, A. (ed.) (1994) *Kawaru Nihongata koyou* (The Change of the Japanese Employment Style), Tokyo: Nihon Keizai Shinbunsya.

Yashiro, N. (1997) *Nihonteki Koyou-Kankou no Keizai-gaku:Roudou-Shijou no Ryudouka to Nihon-Keizai* (Economics of Japanese Employment Custom: Labor Market Mobilization and Japanese Economy), Tokyo: Nihon Keizai Shinbunsya.

MASANORI YASUMOTO

overseas business of small and medium-sized enterprises

Japanese small and medium-sized enterprises (SMEs), especially manufacturing firms, have been moving production offshore due to the strength of the yen, low-priced imports, and the abundance of inexpensive labor overseas, especially in Asia. Among manufacturers with fewer than fifty employees, only a small number were operating abroad in the 1970s. However, the numbers of SMEs operating overseas has been climbing steadily since the 1980s.

Pressure from large businesses for SMEs to lower prices has also caused medium and small sized companies that supply the **electronics industry** and **automotive industry** in Japan to look overseas for sourcing parts and manufacturing. The need for these SMEs to find foreign partners is greater than ever. SMEs, however, face hurdles of language barriers and concern about red tape when expanding their businesses overseas. Private and public-sector organization programs are helping Japanese SMEs stake a more global approach to their businesses. For example, since 1994, JETRO (**Japan External Trade Organization**) has an advisory program to help SMEs in Japan find import and export partners. The purpose is to encourage grass-roots level operations.

The major destinations for Japanese SMEs have been China and the United States. In 1995 SME foreign direct investment (FDI) was 783 projects. FDI by region included 434 projects in China, 109 in ASEAN (Association of Southeast Nations), 55 in Asian NIEs (Newly Industrialized Economies), 15 in other Asian countries, 30 in Europe, 103 in North America and 37 in other countries. Most of the FDI has been in manufacturing (573 projects in 1995), followed by commerce (59) and service (31). Sixty percent of these overseas manufacturing operations have been **joint ventures**. In China most ventures have been production operations, while in ASEAN countries Japanese SMEs are involved primarily in processing and assembly. To assist SMEs with overseas business, JETRO has established Local to Local Initiatives for Mutual Industrial Development. This program brings together regional level groups and SMEs in Japan and overseas. Since 1993, JASMEC (Japan Small and Medium Enterprise Corporation) has been expanding ways it can assist SMEs in internationalization. International advisors who have extensive international business experience provide advice to SMEs interested in business tie-ups with

foreign firms. JASMEC also provides guidance and support for overseas expansion and procurement of parts and materials in the international market. They conduct overseas training services for personnel and management as well as provide loans to SMEs.

A 1997 JETRO survey found 57 percent of SME respondents already had, or were planning, overseas operations. Of those planning to go overseas, 57 percent said they are looking to enter an ASEAN country because of political and social stability. In contrast, the potential domestic market attracted Japanese SMEs to China (56 percent) and India (59 percent), while in Hong Kong it was the infrastructure that was most attractive (40 percent). As mentioned earlier, one reason SMEs go overseas is for the inexpensive labor. Japanese SMEs in Asians countries have found that China and India have lower wages than ASEAN countries, while Hong Kong and Singapore have the highest wages. One of the difficulties SMEs face overseas is procuring enough materials and supplies. One-third of Japanese SMEs in ASEAN countries report that 50 percent of raw materials and supplies are sourced locally. This compares with only 16.4 percent in China, but is below the 67.9 percent reported by firms in India. Overseas business was seen as a good investment strategy in ASEAN (50.4 percent), Hong Kong (65.8 percent), and Singapore (61.6 percent). Only 19.9 percent of the respondents planned to increase research and development overseas, but they were planning to increase production in the Philippines (76.2 percent), India (75 percent), and Indonesia (71.6 percent). Many of these firms are also exporting in ASEAN (94.1 percent). Thirty-one percent of respondents stated that at least 50 percent of their exports went to other ASEAN countries. The findings of this survey found that 62.7 percent of the respondents were profitable in 1997, down from 68 percent in 1995.

The major problems cited by these firms were rising local wages and labor relations. Country-specific problems include a complicated tax system in China, and difficulties in accessing capital in India.

Compared to large firms, it is more difficult for SMEs to expand into foreign markets. To offset these difficulties, groups such as the Osaka Global

Business Opportunities Convention (G-BOC) assist Japanese and foreign firms in finding partners. The G-BOC, held under the auspices of JETRO, MITI (**Ministry of International Trade and Industry**) and the Osaka Chamber of Commerce and Industry, has been held in Osaka every year since 1990. Its purpose is twofold: to help foreign SMEs to gain a foothold in the Japanese market and to help connect Japanese SMEs with foreign partners.

Japanese SMEs have used a variety of approaches in their businesses. These include overseas expansion and offshore operations such as foreign direct investment project, wholly-owned subsidiaries and joint ventures; import and export partnerships, exploring the world market for new ideas and new customers, and other cooperation with foreign counterparts.

The high yen and the growing overseas presence of large Japanese firms continue to provide strong incentives for SMEs to pursue overseas expansion. However, with overseas expansion, many SMEs now confront important challenges in developing overseas research and development capabilities, establishing extensive after-sales service capabilities in overseas locations and responding to calls for greater environmental protection in their Asian and Southeast Asian manufacturing operations. In short, Japanese SMEs now confront all of the major issues encountered by the large Japanese multinational corporations.

See also: economic crisis in Asia; Japanese business in China; Japanese business in Southeast Asia; overseas research and development; small and medium-sized firms

Further reading

JASMEC (Japan Small and Medium Enterprise Corporation) Home Page, http://www.jsbc.go.jp/english.

TERRI R. LITUCHY

overseas education

Many Japanese students spend a high school or college semester or a year abroad to learn about another country. The Japanese usually look on this experience favorably, as long as the student is able to fit back into the Japanese education system upon return to Japan, something that can be difficult given strong social pressures for conformity to peer norms in areas of speech, appearance and behavior.

More and more Japanese are being sent to work overseas, and many of them bring their families with them. A real concern is whether or not their children will fall behind their peers in schools back in Japan. Consequently, there has been a demand for Japanese schools overseas. **Keio University** and several other educational institutions in Japan have opened "branch" campuses in the USA and elsewhere in the world to address this need. Where Japanese children are unable to attend a Japanese school, they will attend local American schools, and then attend Japanese schools in the evenings or weekends to keep up in Japanese language and mathematics, the latter of which is more advanced in Japan than in the United States.

One of the major concerns for most Japanese expatriates is what will happen to their children upon return to Japan. Beginning in the early 1980s, Japanese educators identified a problem with *ijime* (bullying) of returning Japanese children. Known as *kikokushijo* (literally "returning home children"), these children were often singled out by classmates because they dressed differently, spoke differently or had different interest and hobbies. In response, the Ministry of Education established "magnet" schools where *kikoushijo* could be grouped and received special educational support and counseling.

There are several other types of Japanese overseas education. The National Association of Japan-America Societies is a private, nonprofit network of thirty-five Japan-America societies across the United States. Its mission is education about Japan and US–Japan relations. Most societies have speakers that address business, political and cultural issues. They also offer Japanese language classes. The society has over 30,000 members (mostly in the 25–50 age group) across the United States including over 30 percent of Japanese who are residents in the United States.

The Japan Business Information Center (JBIC) is a privately funded non-profit business association. Its mission is to improve bilateral understanding between Japan and the USA. The JBIC established its first overseas office of the Keizai Koho Center in 1992. The Center's mission is to promote understanding through communication, dialogue and cooperation of Japanese and American business leaders and educators. The JBIC sponsors seminars and lectures, social studies programs, and business school programs.

TERRI R. LITUCHY

overseas production

Overseas production on the part of the Japanese manufacturing industry entered a period of rapid expansion in the latter part of the 1980s. While the ratio of overseas production, as measured in terms of sales by overseas manufacturing subsidiaries compared with sales by all manufacturing corporations in Japan, stood at only 3 percent in 1985, it had jumped to 13.1 percent by 1998. The same ratio for only those corporations that had undertaken some overseas production was 32.2 percent in 1998.

The Japanese manufacturing industry first ventured overseas in the beginning of the twentieth century when Japanese companies in the cotton spinning industry first established overseas production operations in China. Later, as Japan's sphere of influence gradually expanded, more such overseas manufacturing facilities sprang up in China, as well as on the Korean peninsula and Taiwan. However, when the Second World War ended in defeat for Japan, such holdings were seized, and Japan lost all of its overseas assets.

In 1950, a few years after the end of the war, overseas production resumed on a very limited basis. Most of these efforts targeted locations within Asia, although a certain number also included the industrially advanced nations. In 1970, the Japanese government promoted the liberalization of foreign direct investment (FDI), and in accordance with the third phase of this liberalization, which was implemented in 1971, the government removed restrictions on the value of investment that would qualify for automatic approval. Nevertheless, at this time the Japanese manufacturing industry continued to pursue its fundamental

post-war strategy of developing overseas markets through exports from Japan. As far as manufacturing industries were concerned, "internationalization" remained primarily a matter of promoting exports.

Eventually, there occurred changes in the international business environment that began to exert pressure on this export-driven strategy for internationalization. These changes were the development of trade friction and the **appreciating yen** that followed in the wake of the Plaza Accord. The Japanese manufacturing industry, which needed to find some way of responding to trade friction and yen appreciation, had no alternative but to begin to undertake overseas production in the industrially advanced nations, first in the United States, and then later in Europe. By the 1990s, Japanese manufacturing industries had achieved a truly globalized stage of development with production footholds in Asia, Europe, and North America.

It is worthwhile to consider the differences in amount of FDI as well as in the volume of sales posted by overseas subsidiaries according to the type of industry. In terms of FDI, the **electronics industry** accounted for the largest proportion of such investment at 27 percent, followed by vehicle and chemical manufacturing industries at 13 percent each. These three industries taken together thus comprised approximately one-half of all investment by Japanese manufacturing industries in overseas production. Metals manufacturing (ferrous and non-ferrous), foods, general equipment, and precision tools manufacturing industries followed, in that order. The strongly export-competitive electronics, automobiles and chemical manufacturing industries were, not surprisingly, the top three industries to engage in FDI. Furthermore, electronics and automotive manufacturing showed the highest ratios of overseas to domestic production within their own industries.

In 1998, the ratio of overseas sales registered by each industry against the total overseas sales by all overseas production operations revealed that the electronics, auto, and chemical manufacturing industries accounted for more than 70 percent of all overseas production sales, at 32.5 percent, 31.9 percent and 8.2 percent respectively. In terms of the regions in which these sales occurred for each of these industries, it is clear that the electronics industry achieved most of its sales in Asia, followed by North America and then Europe. The vehicle manufacturing industry had its largest volume of sales in North America, followed by Europe and then Asia; the chemicals industry was biggest in North America, then Asia and finally Europe.

Next, let us examine the amount of FDI, the volume of sales, and the number of employees at these overseas production operations on a region-by-region basis. North America ranks number one in terms of amount of FDI as well as volume of sales, while Asia is first in terms of number of employees. The cumulative figure for amount of FDI in the years 1951 to 1999 is approximately $288.7 billion. As much as 85 percent of this activity is concentrated in the three regions of North America, Europe and Asia. Of this, $125.8 billion (43.6 percent) is invested in North America, ($116.6 billion or 40.4 percent of the total in the United States), $76.3 billion (26.4 percent) is spent in Asia, and $52.8 billion (18.3 percent) in Europe. Other regions include Central and South America where FDI amounted to $20.3 billion (7.0 percent), Oceania with $8.5 billion (2.9 percent), the Middle East with $3.8 billion (1.3 percent), and Africa with $1.2 billion (0.4 percent).

Turning to the volume of sales by overseas production operations, North America is the highest with Asia and then Europe following in that order. Finally, persons employed at Japanese overseas manufacturing facilities in 1998 number approximately 2.2 million in total, of which 1.4 million (61.1 percent) are in Asia, 473,000 (21.3 percent) are in the North America, and 241,000 (10.9 percent) are in Europe.

The reason that Japanese manufacturing industries chose to pursue an export-led strategy for such a long period after the Second World War and that they eschewed a policy of venturing abroad with production operations lay in the characteristics of the Japanese-style management system. The leaders of Japanese manufacturing industries had no confidence that their management system, created and cultivated in Japan, was capable of being applied in the midst of a different managerial environment, particularly as obtained among the industrially advanced nations. The export strategy, therefore, came to be viewed as the best means for

promoting the internationalization of Japanese business *vis-à-vis* those nations. However, after the Second World War, the Asian countries adopted policies to promote their own industrialization through import substitution. Manufacturing corporations from the industrially advanced nations expected Asian countries to pursue a policy of local production of goods that they would otherwise have had to import. Therefore, in order to promote industrialization and to nurture and protect their own fledgling manufacturing industries, these developing nations applied high tariff rates on the import of finished products. These policies also facilitated efforts by the Japanese manufacturing industries to locate production facilities in those countries.

Local overseas production on the part of Japanese manufacturing industries in the industrially advanced nations raised the question of whether it would be possible to successfully transfer the Japanese-style management and production system overseas. Broadly speaking, this concerned the problems of the transferability of work organization and of technology. The Japanese-style management and production system, otherwise known as the **Toyota production system**, was characterized by features such as a highly skilled workforce, a wage system identical to that for white collar personnel, **quality management** on the production line, a parts procurement system that minimized parts inventory (just-in-time), *kaizen*, consensus-style decision making, and participatory labor relations.

The problem was whether Japanese manufacturers would be able to maintain its large competitive advantage and apply its homegrown management and production system in its overseas manufacturing operations. Among the industrially advanced nations, the managerial environment differed significantly from that of Japan and there was also a well-established production system already in existence. If the Japanese manufacturers were going to hire local managers and local production workers, and if they were going to procure products from local materials and parts manufacturers, then it was clear that they were going to be influenced by the existing local manufacturing system. Ultimately, the overseas manufacturing operations were able to succeed in transferring the Japanese system. However, although it was difficult to transfer the system in its purest form, it was possible to implement a management and production system that combined elements from the local and the Japanese systems. The answer lay in the hybridization or transformation of the Japanese system. As a result, overseas production by Japanese manufacturing industries promoted the international spread and acceptance of the Japanese manufacturing system.

The transfer of Japanese manufacturing operations to North America, and particularly to the United States, began to accelerate in the 1970s, and was especially pronounced through the 1980s. This was largely the result of measures to cope with trade friction as well as the yen appreciation that followed in the wake of the Plaza Accord. Most Japanese FDI in the United States was in the electronics, vehicle, chemicals, and general equipment manufacturing industries. The regions that benefited from this investment were firstly the western United States followed by other parts of the country. By industry, although many electronics manufacturing plants were in California, these plants also spread to other parts of the country. In contrast, a characteristic of the auto parts makers and assemblers was that their plants were concentrated in the region extending from Michigan to a region just south of the Midwestern United States. Since the manufacturing industry in North America achieves about 90 percent of its sales within North America, there is a strong tendency for most of its activities to be confined within a given region.

Although the expansion by Japanese industry to Europe also began to increase in the 1970s, the same as in North America, it was concentrated mainly in the period leading up to the integration of the European markets in 1992. The trends for FDI by industry were the same as in North America, favoring the electronics, vehicle and chemicals manufacturing industries, respectively. The United Kingdom received the largest proportion of Japanese FDI, or approximately 30 percent, followed by France and then Germany. Together, these three countries accounted for more than half of all Japanese manufacturing FDI in Europe. Spain, the Netherlands and Italy followed, in that order. The European manufacturing industry was also similar to the North American industry in that most of its sales were from within its own region, and exports outside of the region were very limited.

The roots of the expansion of Japanese industry into Asian countries can be found in Japanese direct investment in China in the beginning of the twentieth century. Asia was also the first region to receive Japanese FDI after the Second World War. In the 1960s, investment targeted the Asian NIEs such as Taiwan and Korea. In the 1980s, ASEAN countries and in the 1990s China, India and Vietnam became the focus of investment. Additional investment ground to a halt with the 1997 Asian currency crisis.

By industry, while the cotton spinning industry was historically the most important focus for investment, in modern times the electronics and then the chemicals industries carry out most of the investment. Two characteristic features of Japanese investment in the Asian countries is the overwhelming prevalence of **joint ventures** as a form of investment, and the large number of employees. Manufacturing in the Asian countries serves not only to produce goods for sale in those countries but also to produce goods for export to Japan and the other industrially advanced nations. Approximately 60 percent of the products are sold in Asia and the rest is exported, mainly to Japan, the United States, and Europe.

Further reading

Abo, T. (ed.) (1994) *Hybrid Factory: The Japanese Production System in the United States*, New York: Oxford University Press.

Itagaki, H. (ed.) (1997) *The Japanese Production System: Hybrid Factories in East Asia*, London: Macmillan.

Liker, J.K., Fruin, W.M. and Adler, P.S. (eds) (1999) *Remade in America: Transplanting and Transforming Japanese Management Systems*, New York: Oxford University Press.

MITI (2000) *Dai 29-kai, 1999-nen Kaigai Jigyo Katsudo Kihon-Chosa Gaiyo* (Research Outline on the Oveaseas Business Activities of the Japanese Companies in 1999, No. 29), Tokyo: MITI.

MOF (2000) *Zaisei-Kinyo Tokei-Geppo: Tai Nai-Gai Minkan Toshi-Tokushu* (Ministry of Finance Statistics Monthly: Special Issue for the Foreign Direct

Investment and Inward Investment), No. 584, December, Tokyo: MOF.

Oliver, N. and Wilkinson, B. (1992) *The Japanization of British Industry: New Developments in the 1990s*, Oxford: Blackwell.

HIROSHI KUMON

overseas research and development

In its narrowest sense, "overseas research and development" refers to the off-shore research and development activities of Japanese corporations. However, the term can also be applied more broadly to encompass the acquisition in Japan of research and development capabilities, as well as joint activities involving Japanese and non-Japanese researchers, either in Japan or overseas.

Japanese are not known for the type of "breakthrough" creative or innovation that is revered in the west. Among Nobel laureates in the physical sciences, only one is Japanese. The reasons for Japan's shortcomings in this area have been widely debated within the Japanese business community and the wider society at large. Some blame the educational system, which emphasizes rote memorization over creative problem solving. Others blame the nature of Japanese society with its tight strictures on roles and responsibilities and its avoidance of risk-taking or failure. Whatever the reasons, real or imagined, many Japanese companies have opened or moved their research and development operations overseas to countries perceived as having more creative workforces. Japanese firms and government agencies are also hiring foreigners to work in Japan or moving their R&D operations overseas to overcome these difficulties.

Overseas research and development takes place through the formation of research agreements between Japanese companies and American universities. Such agreements may cover the establishment and operation of R&D facilities as well as licensing agreements. In 1990, for example, Hitachi Chemicals and the University of California at Irvine signed a $16.5 million agreement in biotechnology. In exchange for a new university building, Hitachi employees have unrestricted access to the university researchers' laboratories and research notes. Also in 1990, Shiseido, the cosmetics company, pledged $85 million over ten years to develop a research center at a hospital affiliated with Harvard University in exchange for licensing rights to all technology developed there.

Hiring foreigners for research and development positions in their Japan operations is another strategy that Japanese firms adopted beginning in the early 1980s. Prior to that time, labor laws and restrictions on immigration made it extremely difficult to bring in foreign workers, even in research positions, for anything other than short-term stays. By the late 1990s changes in labor and immigration laws have effectively removed most obstacles. The result has been a significant increase in foreign hires. For instance, at the Advanced Telecommunications Research Institute, more than 25 percent of the 230 researchers are foreigners. There appears to be little resistance to this recent development. Research chiefs are allowed to hire foreign researchers at their own discretion.

Japanese firms are not only hiring foreign researchers for their R&D efforts in Japan, they are also hiring scientists, many of whom teach at US universities. These scientists now work for private Japanese firms with R&D operations in the United States. Another approach to enhancing R&D capabilities is the acquisition of "boutiques," small start-up firms often headed by scientists with a marketable specialized technology, patentable process or product. Much of this activity began in the late 1980s when many firms were flush with money. At the same time that Japanese firms were looking to acquire R&D capabilities overseas, many high-tech and biotech firms in the US were looking for infusions of capital to cover their start up costs. In return for their financial investments, Japanese firms got innovative technologies that they could not develop at home in a cost effective manner.

The Japanese government also provides substantial assistance in research and development. Government organizations such as MITI fund research in a variety of fields. They currently support fifteen research laboratories in Japan, some of which involve US companies or US researchers. The Japanese government is also funding a multimillion dollar semiconductor research project. MITI has committed $160 million on a R&D project with a super-clean room facility to begin in 2002. As a result of opposition to the project voiced by US semiconductor firms the Japanese have decided to open up this project to foreign firms such as Motorola, Texan Instruments, and IBM.

Smaller overseas R&D activities are sponsored by prefectural and city governments. The Osaka government, for example, encourages R&D at home and overseas by organizing events for Japanese firms to find overseas partners. For example, the Global Venture Forum brings companies in new, high-tech and emerging fields of business together with potential Japanese partners.

The Japan Society for the Promotion of Science (JSPS) brings Japanese and foreign researchers together. JSPS provides funding for research collaboration. In 1996, 315 foreign fellowships (from over eleven countries) and seventy-nine foreign postdoctoral fellowships (from over twenty-five countries) were funded. The Society also sends Japanese researchers overseas through bilateral exchanges (129 Japanese to twenty-six countries), fellowships to visit Southeast Asia (fifty-one Japanese fellows to five countries), and postdoctoral fellowships (fifty-five in 1996). Finally, the JSPS funds and hosts joint research and seminars in Japan as well as bilateral programs in France, Germany, the UK and the USA. JSPS has offices in the USA, Egypt, Germany, Brazil, Thailand, and Kenya.

See also: Japanese business in the USA; small and medium-sized firms

TERRI R. LITUCHY

P

patent system

Copyright

Copyright protection arises automatically on creation of an object in the literary, scientific, artistic or musical field. It is not dependent on application and registration; nor is it dependent on publication. Based on the European principle of *droit moral*, authors have moral rights to their works to protect from unauthorized use even if not released to the public. Such moral rights also include the right to be identified as the author and the right to prevent unauthorized alteration.

Protection is available for architectural works, choreography, compilations and database works, computer programs, maps, motion pictures, pantomimes, and photographs. Excluded are materials whose republication is in the public interest, such as statutes, orders, ordinances, court decisions, and official government publications.

Authors have the right to adapt, broadcast, copy, exhibit, lease, perform, recite, screen, and translate their work, as well as request payment for private use – including digital audio or visual display. Transfers of copyrights are permitted, but must be registered with the Ministry of Education to be enforceable. Neighboring rights exist for performers, phonograph record producers and broadcasters. Performers' rights include the exclusive right to audio and video recording, broadcasting, leasing, and request payment for lease to public. Phonograph record producers' rights include rights to reproduce, leases to public commercial records, and to request payment. Broadcasters' rights include rights to reproduce, rebroadcast, transmit, communicate and enlarge images.

The term of copyrights is lifetime of author plus fifty years. The fifty-year period is from death, publication if published under an assumed name, or from publication for works of an organization. Moral rights, however, can only be exercised by an author – meaning they are valid only during the author's lifetime. In some cases, immediate family members of a deceased author may seek an injunction or damages to the author's honor. Neighboring rights are valid for fifty years from the first performance, recording or broadcast. All duration periods are counted from January 1 following death, creation or publication.

Copyright holders may grant exclusive publication rights to third parties. To be effective against third parties, the grant must be registered with the Agency for Cultural Affairs. Unless otherwise agreed, the recipient must publish within six months after receipt of the manuscript and keep it in print (if normal in the publishing business). If the recipient breaches these requirements, the holder can cancel the publication rights. Unless otherwise agreed, publication rights expire three years from first publication. Limited assignments of copyrights are possible. For instance, authors can split translation, publication and performance rights among different parties. Infringers are subject to injunction, civil damages and criminal liabilities. Infringers of moral rights can also be forced to take appropriate measures to restore the author's lost honor.

Japan is a party to many international copyright agreements, including the Berne Convention,

UNESCO Treaty, Convention for Protection of Producers of Phonograms against Unauthorized Duplication of Their Phonograms, and International Convention for the Protection of Performers, Producers of Phonograms and Broadcasting Organizations.

Patents

Patent rights are created by application and registration with the Patent Office. The same rules apply to Japanese registrants and foreigners residing or doing business in Japan. The patent rights of foreigners living abroad and not doing business in Japan, however, are governed by any applicable treaty between Japan and the foreigner's nation, and by the one year rule of the International Convention. The Convention gives parties one year to apply for a patent in any country that has signed the convention, with the year measured from first filing in another signatory country. Nonresident foreigners must apply for patent rights through a local attorney or patent agent.

Applications must be in Japanese. Since July 1, 1995, applicants may file specifications, drawings and abstracts in English as long as a Japanese translation is submitted within two months. If requested by the applicant or an interested third party, examiners of the Patent Office will review the patent application. The request must be made within seven years of the date that the patent application is filed. Examiners must review the patent based on patentability.

On January 1, 1996, the post-grant opposition system was introduced, under which third parties can object to patents after issuance but within six months of public notice of patent issuance. For patents filed before January 1, 1996, third parties must object within three months after publication of the examined application.

Patent applications are made public in the *Patent Gazette* 18 months after patent application is made. From public disclosure, applicants can claim infringement and seek compensation against infringers. Compensation is based on normal royalty rates. Collection under the claim, however, cannot be made until publication following examination.

To receive a patent, an article or process must be patentable. Patentability is only available to high-grade inventions of articles or industrial processes. Patentability is not available to items that could potentially injure public order, morals or health. Patentability also requires the article or process be new. This means it could not have been described in written publications distributed in Japan or any foreign country, or in any other prior patent application. The scope of the patent is based on the description of scope in the patent application. Third parties can apply to the Patent Office for a non-binding, advisory opinion on scope.

Japan is a first-to-file nation. This means a patent will be issued to the first to file, not the first to invent. If several applications covering the same article or process are filed on the same day, no patent will be issued until the applicants resolve who has priority. In addition to examining applications, the Patent Office has jurisdiction over invalidity of patents, appeals from decisions of examiners refusing to issue patents, and amendments to issued patents. Appeals from the Patent Office are taken to the Tokyo High Court.

Since July 1, 1995, a patent term is twenty years from date of application. On application, the term may be extended for a maximum of five years if the invention could not have been used for two years or more due to data accumulation required under the Agricultural Chemicals Control Law or Pharmaceutical Affairs Law. Patents cease on expiration of the term, abandonment or invalidation by the Patent Office.

Patents are property rights and can be transferred voluntarily (license, pledge) or involuntarily (on death or by claim of creditors). To be effective, such transfers (other than inheritance) must be registered with the Patent Office. In case of co-owned patents, the approval of all owners is required. Applications are also transferable.

There are two types of patent licenses. Exclusive licenses giving another party exclusive rights to a patent must be in writing and registered with the Patent Office. Such licenses grant the licensee exclusivity even against the original owner. As such, the exclusive licensee can seek injunctive relief and civil damages for its injuries.

Under ordinary licenses, the licensee has the right to use a patent, but not exclusively. The owners (and possibly third parties) have the right to use the patented article or process. Such licenses arise by contract, compulsory order of the Patent Office or the Ministry of Economics, Trade and Industry (formerly MITI), or under law (such as an employer's right to use its employees' inventions, as discussed below). The remedies of ordinary licensees are limited. They usually cannot obtain an injunction, although they can seek damages. Although not required by law, registration with the Patent Office has the advantage of confirming licensee's rights against third parties.

Patent owners can be required to grant a license in three instances. First, the Director General of the Patent Office may grant such compulsory licenses if the patented invention has not been worked in Japan for more than three consecutive years. Second, the Minister of Economics, Trade and Industry may also grant them if in the public interest. Third, the owner of an improvement patent can request a license from the owner of the underlying patent.

Employees have rights to inventions not in the scope of their work. In Japan, such inventions are called not in service. In such cases, any exclusive license from the employee to its employer prior to invention is unenforceable. Employees are entitled to reasonable compensation for not-in-service inventions.

Utility models

Although related to patents, a separate statute, the Utility Model Law, covers utility model rights. Inventions entitled to protection as utility models do not need to be as high grade as those seeking patent protection. They must, however, have a practical utility in terms of form, composition or assembly. Covered models are entitled to the same protection as patents. The term of protection is six years from application date. The Patent Office does not examine utility model applications. Instead, an applicant applies to the Patent Office for a search report on prior applications. If none exists, it can give a warning to the alleged infringer along with a copy of the search report. A third party can challenge a utility model by an interested third party filing an invalidation action with the Patent Office. Infringement actions involving the same parties will be stayed pending the result of any invalidation action.

Designs

Designs can be protected under a process similar to that for patents. There are three requirements for protection: the designs must be of a new variety, have an industrial nature, and relate to form, pattern, coloring or a combination. Designs are different from patents and utility models in that they need not have a practical use, they can simply relate to ornamentation.

To register a design, an application is filed with the Patent Office. The application is checked for compliance with statutory requirements and examined on the merits. No publication, however, is made. If the application is approved, the design is registered. After registration, a design can be challenged for noncompliance with statutory requirements. The term of protection is fifteen years from registration.

Plant species and semiconductor integrated circuits

Some protection exists in Japan for improvements in plant species and circuitry of semiconductor integrated circuits. Japan is a party to the Patent Cooperation Treaty and the Agreement on Trade-Related Aspects of Intellectual Property Rights.

Trademarks

A trademark is any written character, sign, design, solid body or combination, whether or not with a color, which is used to distinguish a product or service as coming from a particular source. The source may be a manufacturer, producer, wholesaler, or retailer.

Only trademarks registered with the Patent Office are entitled to protection. To register, an application covering the trademark must be filed with the office. The proposed trademark must be distinctive. Additionally, it must not resemble marks of international organizations, governments, and registered or widely-known trademarks for the same or similar goods or services; nor may it be a red cross, or injurious to public morals. Since April 1, 1992, service marks can be registered. The term of trademark rights is ten years from date of registration. Additional ten-year renewals are possible.

Foreign trademarks can be registered in Japan. Japan is a party to the Trademark Law Treaty.

Trademarks are transferable. They can be transferred separate from the underlying business. In case of a trademark covering two or more products, the trademark may be split. Trademark licenses are also permitted. To be effective, transfers must be registered with the Patent Office. In case of co-ownership, all owners must consent to the transfer or license.

Trademarks can infringe previously registered patents, utility rights, designs or copyrights. In such case, they cannot be used without the consent of the prior, conflicting owner. An infringer is subject to an injunction, civil damages or criminal action. Any interested party can seek to invalidate a registered trademark. The grounds can be failure to satisfy registration requirements, improper use, or non-use for more than three years.

Trade Names

Trade names can be registered. Once registered, a third party in the same municipal area cannot use the same or similar name for the same type of business. Infringers are subject to injunction and civil damages. Company trade names must indicate the type of company (e.g., partnership or corporation). Personal trade names can be transferred or inherited, but to be enforceable must be recorded. Trade names are valid until cancelled by the holder, or by petition of a third party showing that it has not been used for two years.

ROBERT BROWN

permanent employee

Also known as regular employees (*seishain* or *hirashain*), workers in this category occupy a position roughly equivalent to exempt employees in the USA. Permanent employees accept ove-time work, flexible job assignments, job rotations, job transfers, job retraining, temporary or permanent assignment to affiliated firms in exchange for employment security; that is, they will not be laid off except under extreme economic conditions. Permanent employees are also known as salarymen (see **salaryman**), however, that denotation applies only to white-collar workers. Permanent employees may also occupy blue-collar or production floor positions. **Contract employees** or temporary employees represent the alternative to permanent employees, having less expected of them by the enterprise and receiving less in return.

Permanent employees are found primarily in larger enterprises, although medium-size enterprises may also offer some employees permanent status. Historically, the percentage of permanent employees has probably never exceeded 30 percent of the labor force. One study of companies listed on the first rank of the Tokyo Stock Exchange calculated the percentage of permanent employees in those companies at 25 percent in 1974. By 1993, just 17 percent of the employees were so classed. However, observers disagree on both the definition and the proper calculation of what constitutes a permanent, or regular, employee. In 1997, Brown *et al.* (1997), using a different method of calculation, concluded that the number of permanent employees was significantly higher, upwards of 75 percent in some sectors.

Differences in definitions of what constitutes a permanent or regular work address a more fundamental issue: the widespread disparity in work hours and conditions, and in compensation and benefits across employees designated as permanent. The prolonged recession of the 1990s has further clouded the situation by eroding the implicit agreement underpinning the permanent employment agreement. Even very large companies are no longer able to make implicit, but firm guarantees that permanent employees will not be let go.

See also: lifetime employment; outplacement

Further reading

Brown, C., Nakata, Y., Reich, M. and Ulman, L. (1997) *Work and Pay in the United States and Japan*, New York: Oxford University Press.

Tachibanaki, T. (1996) *Wage Determination and Distribution in Japan*, New York: Oxford University Press.

ALLAN BIRD

pharmaceuticals industry

The Japanese pharmaceuticals industry is comprised of firms that primarily serve the Japanese internal market. Japan has a universal coverage health care system. Therefore, a discussion of the industry must include an explanation of those aspects of the health care system that impact the strategies of the pharmaceutical firms in Japan. The domestic market focus of the firms in the Japanese pharmaceuticals industry has put these firms at a competitive disadvantage as the industry evolves worldwide. Japanese firms are increasing their research and development efforts and expanding their international activities, but they remain behind the competitive levels of their American and European counterparts.

The Japanese demand for pharmaceuticals is the second largest, after the United States. Japanese consume about 13 percent of the developed world's pharmaceuticals, compared to 42 percent for the United States. Sales in the industry have been flat over the period from 1995–2000. Takeda Chemical Industries and Sankyo are the largest Japanese firms, but their pharmaceuticals sales are much less than half of the sales of the large North American firms. No Japanese firm ranks in the top ten of the pharmaceutical industry worldwide, in contrast to many other Japanese industries where Japanese firms are more likely to appear as world leaders. The other top domestic firms are as follows, in order of sales in 1999, Yamanouchi, Daiichi, Eisai, Shionogi, Taisho, Fujisawa, and Banyu. Only at the tenth ranking do we observe any firm with foreign control, with Merck having substantial ownership in Banyu. New entrants in the industry have come from increased foreign firm activity and from firms that diversify out of related technologies. Kirin (beer fermentation technology) and Kyowa Hakko (fermentation) and Asahi Kasei (chemicals) are examples of some of the new players.

The Japanese government, via the Ministry of Health and Welfare, shielded the industry during the immediate postwar period. The government set high prices for drugs. The firms were allowed, under Japanese laws, to copy drugs developed overseas merely by altering the process in making the pharmaceuticals. This obviously reduced the requirement for R&D for the local firms. To make this environment even more comfortable, foreign firms were encouraged to license their pharmaceuticals to local firms, filling out the portfolio of the local pharmaceutical. Moreover, foreign firms were restricted from registering drugs in their own name in Japan. Restrictions on foreign firms generally applied to pharmaceuticals firms as well. Thus, most foreign firms decided to let Japanese firms market their products under contract.

The Japanese pharmaceutical firms were obliged to share this wealth in the protected market, however. In the West, the prescribing of drugs is kept separate from the actual sale of these products. In Japan, however, the doctor who prescribes the drug also profits from the sale of these products. Since the doctor can choose the drugs to prescribe, the system has evolved into a bilateral monopoly that requires the pharmaceutical firms to bid for the business of the doctors. The doctors, having received the drugs at a discount from the pharmaceutical firms, can sell the drugs to patients at the government-regulated fixed price, pocketing the difference. This revenue was a major part of the income of many doctors in private practice. To keep the business of the doctors, the firms not only provide discounts, but also provide services and information to the doctors. To keep the business of the doctors, the firms feel pressure to have a full line of pharmaceuticals products. This has led to a licensing of drugs from abroad, but it also has led to a desire to copy any drug developed by another domestic rival. This excessive variety of drugs has become most significant in the antibiotics area, where the profusion of "me-too" drugs has led to increasingly resistant strains of bacteria in Japan.

The Japanese health care system thus introduced substantially different incentives for Japanese pharmaceutical firms. These health care system elements led the Japanese firms to develop differently from those in other markets, and made it hard to transplant any strategy to other markets.

Starting in 1975, three changes impacted the industry, putting pressure on the industry to change its ways of doing business. First, Japanese laws on intellectual property changed. Second, Japanese health care cost increases forced the government to become more concerned about cost controls. Third, Japanese government rules on foreign firm participation in the market were loosened, allowing foreign firms to more easily set up their own operations in Japan. More detail on the impact of each of these changes follows.

Changing laws on intellectual property

In 1975, Japan adjusted its laws on intellectual property to be consistent with those of developed countries. Japan by that time had developed sufficient technology of its own that required similar protection. Thus the combination of domestic and foreign pressure for change increased. Japanese pharmaceutical firms could no longer use a different production process to produce the same drug. For the Japanese pharmaceuticals firms, this change required them to increase their expenditures on technology, either via licensing of the foreign drugs, or via an increase in the domestic R&D that they performed.

Pricing pressures

As the costs of medical care continued to increase, Japan in the 1970s was faced with major budget pressures as the rate of growth in the economy slowed. This put increased pressure on a system that had allowed the firms in the industry to earn high profits. Around a third of Japanese health care costs came from expenditure on pharmaceuticals. The government made several changes that forced the firms to become more innovative. The prices for new products were set at a lower level unless the drug was a significant improvement in efficacy compared to existing drugs on the market. A "me-too" drug to match the portfolio of another firm would not be very profitable under these rules. In addition, the prices allowed for a drug were decreased each year. Thus, even a blockbuster drug would gradually lose its profitability as the government lowered the prices of the drug over time. Note the difference in pricing strategy that this implies compared to the system in the United States. The US pattern of high prices until the patent expires is not found in Japan. The gradual reduction in prices makes the price of a drug at the end of its patent life relatively low. Thus, there is much less activity in the generic drug market. If the brand name drug is relatively inexpensive by that

time in its economic life, then it is hard to market a generic alternative. Note also that the price of the drug is no longer based on the cost of development, but on its efficacy. Unless the firm can spend its research and development resources effectively, and generate products that have significant medical value, it is unlikely to be handsomely rewarded for its innovative activity.

The investment climate for foreign firms

The change in the environment for foreign firms came somewhat later, but by the middle of the 1980s, foreign firms could develop their own operations in Japan rather freely. They could take advantage of the change in the patent laws to protect their position in the Japanese market. They could register their own products in Japan. Restrictions on investment had been generally liberalized starting in the early 1970s. The new Foreign Exchange Control Law in 1980 allowed them to move funds freely across the border. The result was an increase in marketing by the foreign firms and a gradual development of their R&D facilities in the Japanese market as well. By the late 1990s, this resulted in a market share for directly marketed foreign pharmaceuticals of about a quarter of the Japanese market. With the option to operate in Japan now open to them, foreign firms were much less likely to license their attractive products to Japanese competitors.

The changing nature of competition in the pharmaceuticals industry

The result of these changes is an industry that is trying to change to become more focused on the research and development function. This has led to a substantial increase in R&D effort on the part of Japanese firms, both internally and via alliances. The strongest firms in the older system were those firms with the widest network of doctors, and the best system of marketing. Under the changed environment, firms that had developed a less conventional, domestically focused program of research could be successful as well in the industry. This was the approach used by many of the "outsider" firms such as Kyowa Hakko and Asahi Kasei. In their other industries, these firms had faced more competition. They had seen less incremental innovation and more radical changes in technology and competitive position. Market shares became less stable in this period, and strategies of firms tended to change more over time as the innovative results allowed for changes in the path of pharmaceuticals development.

The firms in the industry also changed their attitude toward international cooperation. Previously, firms were content to contract for available drugs with the established firms. After the changes in the 1980s, we observe a variety of alliances with overseas firms, both to develop and take advantage of domestically produced drugs. It should be noted that we have not yet observed another type of cooperation, mergers of Japanese firms. Except in the case of Green Cross, a company tainted by scandal, no major firm has been involved in merger, in sharp contrast to the situation in Europe and North America.

This move toward more research and development has introduced much more variety into the strategies of the firms in the industry. Some firms have deepened their established relationships with domestic research institutes and individual doctors. If that network was strong, like it was with the largest firms, then international activities can mainly focus on getting the greatest and fastest return on the increasingly capable domestic innovative organization. The role of overseas labs in this type of company is to assure fast approval, and to assure that the appropriate uses of the drugs are identified in the various markets.

If a firm is not as confident in its domestic network of research, it is possible to use the international markets to develop the truly innovative products that will allow these firms to compete more effectively in the domestic market. For this type of firm, the organizational requirements for a strong international commitment are much higher. They must identify a good source of innovation, either at a university or via a researcher who can lead their own laboratory. They must then be sure that their organization can work with these outsiders to take full advantage of the innovation. Note that this type of firm is more likely to be smaller, and needs to find a way to get the attention of marketers and doctors in the domestic market. The foreign-bred innovation can provide that entry.

New players in the industry often find that they do not have within their own organization the full complement of skills necessary to be competitive in the industry. For these firms, foreign partners allow them to acquire access to the mix of skills they need to be competitive in the market. These Japanese firms often have skills in the bulk processing of drugs, a result of the fermentation technology that bought them access to the industry. Foreign biotech firms are natural allies of these players, as scaling up the volume of product for clinical testing and later for actual commercial sales is essential for a biotech firm's success in the marketplace.

The changes faced by the Japanese pharmaceuticals industry have led to substantially greater variety in the strategies within this industry. In the less regulated industry, firms have chosen a variety of paths to deal with the changed environment. The Japanese industry continues to struggle against the major players in the world marketplace and in Japan. Individual products are successfully sold internationally, such as Yamanouchi's Pepcid. Yet even here, Yamanouchi felt that it did not have the worldwide marketing to take advantage of the discovery. Merck thus could share in the profits for this revolutionary discovery. The limited scale of the domestically focused industry limits competitiveness, even as the R&D expenditures of companies as a percentage of sales approach Western company levels. While foreign firms have continued to increase their presence in Japan, there is evidence that the above changes in strategy have allowed Japanese firms to maintain their competitive position in the Japanese marketplace and at times to be competitive in world markets as well. This type of fast-changing environment is going to be faced by an increasing number of domestically oriented industries in the Japan of the twenty-first century. Thus, the behavior of firms in the pharmaceuticals industry, and the experience of the industry as a whole, provide possible insights into how similarly domestic-oriented industries may evolve in the future.

THOMAS W. ROEHL

post-Second World War recovery

Japan's recovery from the Second World War during the first decade of the postwar period lay the foundation for the nation's "economic miracle," the period of rapid economic growth (*kodo seicho*) that would continue until 1973. While many of the factors that underlay Japan's postwar economic success existed prior to the war, occupation-period social and economic reforms, the taming of inflation under the "Dodge Plan," and the demand for Japanese goods created by the Korean War were critical in getting the economy back on its feet and setting the stage for sustained economic expansion in the decades to follow.

The situation at the end of the war

When the Second World War ended with Japan's official surrender aboard the US battleship *Missouri* on September 2, 1945, the Japanese economy had been shattered. The war had destroyed a fourth of Japan's national wealth and assets, a fourth of its buildings, and 82 percent of its shipping. The nation's economic output had dropped to pre-First World War levels. Tokyo and other large cites had been reduced to rubble by the Allied bombing campaign. Inflation was high, unemployment was widespread, and there were severe food shortages. Over 6 million Japanese civilians and soldiers returned home from overseas to find a country that could not support them. On top of this, a generation of Japanese business leaders were being purged by the Allied Occupation force in an effort to break up the **zaibatsu**, Japan's large corporate groups, which had cooperated closely with the military in building up the country's war capabilities.

Not all was bleak, however, as Japan also possessed some important economic assets. From the **Tokugawa period** (1603–1867), Japan had inherited a relatively well-educated population, high levels of savings for investment, advanced agricultural technology, and a strong infrastructure of roads and irrigation. From the beginning of the Meiji period (1868–1912) through the 1930s, the foundations of economic strength had continued to

be built: compulsory education was introduced, Western technology was imported, the **Bank of Japan** was established, the transportation and communications infrastructure was enhanced, and there was high labor mobility across regions and economic classes. These conditions produced levels of prewar economic growth that compared favorably with those of other countries and helped transform the Japanese economy from a primarily agricultural state to an industrial state capable of creating a formidable war machine. Nevertheless, few observers in the early postwar period foresaw a particularly bright economic future for Japan. The country's chief competitive advantage was seen to be its cheap labor. When asked in 1950 about future trade possibilities with the United States, John Foster Dulles, a key US policy maker on Japan, suggested that Japan might focus on shirts, pajamas, or cocktail napkins.

Occupation-era economic reforms

Allied military occupation of Japan began in August 1945 and lasted until April 28, 1952, when the San Francisco Peace Treaty signed by Japan and forty-eight other nations in September 1951 went into effect. Nominally, it was the Allies who occupied Japan, but in reality the occupation forces were overwhelmingly American. They were headed by General Douglas MacArthur, who was appointed Supreme Commander of the Allied Powers (SCAP) and whose ideas and personality dominated the occupation era.

A primary goal of the occupation was to rid Japan of militarism, and the Americans believed that the best way to do this was to create a democratic society. In 1946, MacArthur and his advisors drafted a new Japanese Constitution, which went into effect on May 3, 1947. The new Constitution made the Emperor a "symbol" of the nation rather than its political head, abolished the army and navy, gave women the right to vote, and renounced war as a sovereign right of the nation. The occupation also sought to democratize the economy in order to achieve a broader and more even distribution of wealth and of ownership of the means of production. To achieve this, occupation leaders introduced anti-trust measures, land reform, and labor reform.

In 1946–47, occupation authorities technically dissolved the *zaibatsu*, which had cooperated closely with the military before and during the war, by requiring them to auction off shares held by their family-owned holding companies. Ten holding companies, Japan's two largest trading companies, and twenty-six of the nation's largest industrial corporations were dissolved. Over a two-year period, 1.4 million company shares were sold to the public. In 1947, the occupation authorities introduced a new Antimonopoly Law and other legislation, modeled after American anti-trust laws, designed to break up existing monopolistic companies and prevent the formation of new ones. A **Fair Trade Commission** was also established to watch over business and prevent monopolistic practices.

The occupation program with perhaps the most wide-reaching consequences for Japanese society was land reform. The goal of this was to redistribute the land of absentee landowners to the tenant farmers who had been farming it. Landowners were allowed to keep up to 7.5 acres of land to farm themselves, plus an additional 2.5 acres of tenanted land. (Larger plots were allowed in Hokkaido.) The rest was purchased by the government and resold to existing tenants at bargain prices. The result was a drastic redistribution of wealth that contributed to a convergence in the standard of living and helped create a new middle class. It also brought income equity and stability to the agricultural sector, contributing to a rapid increase in agricultural production and ensuring a stable food supply. In creating many small plots of farmland, however, the land reform program prevented farmers from attaining economies of scale. As a result, Japanese agriculture remained inefficient and later came to be heavily subsidized.

Prior to and during the war, wages and union activity were suppressed by the military and the *zaibatsu*. Occupation authorities reversed this by encouraging the formation of labor unions and setting standards for working conditions and compensation. The Japanese government was pushed into enacting the Labor Union Law of 1946, the Labor Relations Adjustment Act of 1946, and the Labor Standards Law of 1947. Unions were quickly formed in every sector of the economy. Four and a half million Japanese workers joined labor unions in the first year of the occupation, and the percentage of unionized workers rose from 3.2 percent in 1945 to 53 percent by 1948.

With unemployment high – 13 million Japanese workers were without jobs in 1946 – and inflation running out of control, many union leaders pushed for radical action. There were widespread strikes. On May Day in 1946, in the largest demonstration in the nation's history, more than 2 million people took to the streets to demand wage increases, political power, and worker control of factories. A turning point came when a general strike, which all of Japan's unions planned to participate in and which threatened to shut down the country, was called for February 1, 1947. MacArthur, uncomfortable with the socialist direction in which Japan's labor movement was moving, banned the strike and began a purge of radical union leaders, including many communists. However, even with occupation authorities withdrawing their active support of labor unions, strikes and labor-management conflict continued to increase. (It was not until the 1960s that labor–management cooperation emerged in Japan.)

The change in attitude toward labor unions was part of a more general shift in occupation policy that resulted from the onset of the Cold War. This shift later became known as "the reverse course." By 1948, tensions between the United States and the Soviet Union were rising over the spread of communism, causing American policy makers to revise their thinking about Japan's place in the postwar world. The new view was that the USA could not afford to have a weak Japan; rather, Japan was to be a strong Pacific ally in the fight against communism. George Kennan, a major architect of early Cold War US foreign policy, recommended after a visit to Japan that "no more reform legislation should be pressed. The emphasis should shift from reform to economic recovery" (Kennan 1967). This policy shift became more pronounced with the victory of communists in China in 1949 and the outbreak of the Korean War the following year. One change it brought about was a suspension of the policy of breaking up large companies; emphasis was instead shifted to encouraging increased production by existing companies to strengthen Japan's productive capacity. Another effect was that the US began to pressure Japan to rearm and side with America in the Cold War. Although a police reserve force – the forerunner of Japan's Self-Defence Force – was established in 1950, pressure to rearm further was resisted by Prime Minister Shigeru Yoshida, who feared that the military expenditures rearming would entail would damage Japan's fragile economic recovery. In the San Francisco Peace Treaty a deal was struck: Japan would regain its independence in exchange for allowing the US to keep its military bases on Japan soil.

Taming inflation

One of the most difficult postwar problems Japan faced was inflation. In the first three years after the war, as the Japanese government printed money at a high rate to pay off war bonds and finance government spending, inflation ran rampant: prices rose by 364.5 percent in 1946, 195.9 percent in 1947, and 165.6 percent in 1948. The government attempted to control inflation through price controls and by freezing assets, but these policies were not effective. Finally, in February 1949, the USA sent Joseph **Dodge** to Japan as economic and financial advisor. Dodge was a Detroit banker who had been credited with stopping runaway inflation in postwar Germany, and his policies in Japan, which became known as the "Dodge Plan," consisted basically of balancing the budget, so that the government would not need to print money to finance its spending. An official exchange rate was also established, at 360 yen to the US dollar.

The Dodge Plan was successful in controlling inflation; as the fiscal budget was tightened, prices stabilized, enabling price controls to be lifted. However, the tight fiscal policy also pushed the economy toward recession. A major user of government funds had been the Reconstruction Bank, which was established in January of 1947 for the purpose of accelerating the recovery of Japanese industry. The Reconstruction Bank made loans to public corporations and issued bonds, using the proceeds to subsidize key industries such as coal, fertilizers, electric power, iron, and machinery. Most of these bonds were purchased by the Bank of Japan. Forced to balance the budget, the government had no choice but to cut subsidies. Without government funds, thousands of firms went bankrupt. Public and private companies laid off over 2 million workers in 1949, and national production, which had been on the rise, stalled. At this point, Japan's economy was rescued from what might have been a severe recession by an event that some called a "divine gift:" an unexpected demand for Japanese goods brought about by the Korean War.

The Korean War and the beginning of sustained rapid growth

In June 1950, war broke out on the Korean Peninsula between North Korea, backed by the Soviet Union, and South Korea, backed by the United States. Japan was used as a supply base for American and United Nations forces, creating a sudden and large demand for Japanese-made goods. The result was a "procurement boom:" between 1950 and 1954, the US spent almost $3 billion in Japan for military supplies, and the Japanese economy grew quickly. Although inflation resumed for a time during this period, the economic benefits were far greater: production expanded, jobs were created, and the exports brought in much-needed foreign reserves, which could be used to import technology.

By the mid-1950s, Japan's economic miracle was underway, and postwar pessimists were about to be proven wrong. In 1955, the Japanese economy surpassed its former peak size, and over the next two decades a remarkable record of economic expansion was achieved, with annual GNP growth averaging 9.1 percent in 1955–60, 9.8 percent in 1960–5, and 12.1 percent in 1965–70. Equally important, the economy evolved from a reliance on cheap labor – textile firms were Japan's largest companies in the 1950s – to a focus on progressively more capital and technology-intensive industries such as steel, automobiles, and electronics.

See also: American occupation; economic growth

Further reading

Dower, J. (1999) *Embracing Defeat: Japan in the Wake of World War II*, New York: W.W. Norton

Ito, T. (1992) *The Japanese Economy*, Cambridge, MA: MIT Press.

Kawai, K. (1960) *Japan's American Interlude*, Chicago: University of Chicago Press.

Kennan, G.F. (1967) *Memoirs: 1925–1950*, Boston: Little, Brown.

Kosai, Y. (1997) "The Postwar Japanese Economy: 1945–1973," in K. Yamamura, *The Economic Emergence of Japan*, New York: Cambridge University Press.

TIM CRAIG

postal savings

Japan's postal savings system was introduced in the nineteenth century when, according to the prevalent moral attitudes of the late Edo period, saving was not socially condoned. A popular saying admonished that "trying to get one *sen* (cent) to last from one day to the next was shameful." At that time there were no banks or other private institutions in Japan interested in personal savings, either in the cities or the rural areas. Despite such conditions Maejima Hisoka, founder of Japan's national postal system (1871), introduced, a Japanese postal savings system which he based upon first-hand observations of the British postal savings system. Maejima had been greatly impressed with the positive role he perceived the postal saving system to be playing in English society. Through his relentless efforts, in May 1875 post office branches for the first time began accepting deposits at eighteen locations in downtown Tokyo and at one office in Yokohama. The number of post offices rapidly expanded to rural regions soon thereafter. Japan was the fourth country to establish postal savings and the first in a developing economy.

The Japanese postal savings system was instituted at a time when Japan had just left behind centuries of feudalism and isolation. Its leaders had taken note of the foreign indebtedness of the Ottoman and Chinese empires. After its own postal savings system was set up, the Japanese state was able to forswear all foreign borrowings for the next thirty years (until the advent of the Russo-Japanese War). It can be said that the establishment of a postal savings system at such a critical juncture in its history provided Japan with a significant resource in its future economic and social development.

Indeed, the postal savings forms and posters of the late Meiji and Taisho eras (1900–25) document the appeals used by the post office to encourage individuals to save, both for their personal future prosperity and for the prosperity and development of the nation. One of the postal savings system's unique attributes, and the probable basis for its early mass appeal, was the fact that at one time it accepted deposits as small as one-half a *sen* (¥1 = 100 *sen*).

In the mid-1880s, Finance Minister Matsukata brought postal savings funds under the control of the **Ministry of Finance** and directed their use towards national goals. The success of the system grew and postal savings deposit campaigns were initiated at various times to remedy specific problems. For example, during the inflation following the First World War, a campaign was launched to encourage savings to stem spending and absorb the excess liquidity that had resulted from the war.

As the Japanese economy developed, the postal savings system was able to respond to the changing circumstances. Some of the issues besides inflation that the postal savings system helped the government confront included providing pump-priming for private sector support to new and developing industries, development and modernization of infrastructure, non-inflationary funding of government deficits, pumping up the economy during recessions, and at times stabilizing **capital markets**. Historically, however, its foremost goal has been economic development.

Starting in the postwar period and until the end of 2000, postal savings funds were lent to the Fiscal Investment Loan Program (FILP) (*zaisei toyushi* – the so-called "*zaito* system"), managed by the Ministry of Finance. Major recipients of FILP funding included the **Japan Development Bank** (JDB), which allocated funds for industrial development to meet national and regional development goals. Other public policy-based institutions which received FILP funds during this period included the **Export-Import Bank of Japan**; regional development finance institutions, such as the

Hokkaido-Tohoku Development Corporation and the Okinawa Development Finance Corporation; the Japan Finance Corporation for Small Businesses and the People's Finance Corporation, which provide loans for **small and medium-sized firms**; and the Housing Loan Corporation for housing finance.

Whatever the policy intention, political trade-offs were involved in the FILP system. During the 1990s a majority of funds for developmental purposes were not channeled through the JDB or other government-owned banks and policy-based financial institutions, but instead were directly parceled out to designated quasi-governmental companies such as the Japan Highway Company and other politically well-connected recipients of infrastructure development funds tied to construction and real estate industries interests. Political considerations were never far from such an investment/disbursement system favoring rural provincial areas rather than urban industrial centers.

Critics have questioned the continued need for and the efficiency of these types of development-lending practices in the presence of a developed capital market. Others have pointed to the separation between the collection function by the postal savings system and the disbursement function by FILP as an underlying cause of inefficiency. Indeed, for the past several years, the Postal Savings Bureau lobbied to invest the funds it collects in the financial markets on its own, thereby bypassing the policy-based designated-finance FILP system. Beginning April 2001, the reorganized Postal Savings Agency was given discretion over the investment of collected funds thereby opening it to market risk.

Critics from the **banking industry** have also complained of the unfair advantages given the postal savings system by its numerous exemptions, including from national and local taxes of all types and payments to the Deposit Insurance Corporation. It is also exempt from **Bank of Japan** reserve requirements and the payment of dividends that private banks make to their shareholders. On the other hand, banks have been allowed for many years to offer the same products that postal savings offer their clients, but have not done so. Postal savings officials counter criticisms of its supposed

competitive advantage by pointing to the costs they must bear in providing postal, savings and life insurance services in rural areas to fulfill their mandate. A good case can also be made that the postal savings system helps keep the private sector "honest," and that, in the absence of competitive pressures from the postal savings system, the private sector banking has shown little innovation on its own, and in the past made few efforts to provide competitively priced retail banking services and products for the general public.

The success of the postal savings system, however, can be chiefly attributed to the fact that Japan's 24,537 post offices function as collection points for its savings system, far outstripping the 16,000 branches of all 110 banks, savings and loans, and other financial institutions in Japan. In fact, Japanese people are on average within 1.1 kilometers from a post office, while bank branches are typically found clustered in business districts. Of the 3,235 cities and municipalities that have post offices, some 567 are without banks. This widely based infrastructure of post offices offers tremendous economies of scale, especially in reaching out to rural areas where there would be little profit margin for a stand-alone institution such as a bank.

For many years now, Japan's private banking sector has called for the break-up and privatization of the postal savings system, envying the huge amount of individuals' deposit the postal savings system continues to garner. At the end of March 2000, there was ¥260 trillion in personal savings on deposit in the system, representing 36 percent of all personal savings on deposit in Japan, and nearly equal to the combined personal savings deposited among all private sector commercial institutions – that is, all city, regional, and second-tier regional banks – making Japan's postal savings system the largest financial institution in the world. Since 1990, there has been a steady flight to safety with banking deposits contracting and with marked increases annually in the size and number of depositors in postal savings accounts as public confidence in Japan's banking system increasingly erodes.

When Maejima first established the Japanese postal service, he appointed prominent individuals in rural areas as local postmasters who, in turn, provided postal station facilities at little or no cost. Even today, some 80 per cent of Japan's post office buildings are privately owned by their postmasters, most having inherited their positions for many generations. Needless to say, these postmasters are a powerful force in regional and national politics. Together with the postal workers union, they have been able to foil banking industry efforts to marginalize or abolish Japan's postal savings system.

The postal service has materially improved the quality of financial services available to the general public, offering products such as life insurance and pension plans (both managed separately from postal savings), as well as a nationwide network of 21,796 automatic teller machines that can be used to make deposits, withdrawals, credit card payments, or to pay utility bills or transfer payments to anywhere in Japan without the fees exacted by banks. Banks are just now beginning to compete in response to consumer pressures.

Although some critics have argued that the entire infrastructure of the postal savings system is subsidized by revenues from postal operations, cost analysis shows there is no such subsidy. In fact, without the multiple use of the existing infrastructure, the postal system would find it difficult to sustain mail delivery operations in many rural areas on its own.

Further reading

Scher, M.J. and Yoshino N. (2002) *Postal Savings Systems in Asia*, Tokyo: United Nations University Press.

MARK J. SCHER

pricing practices

The Japanese wholesale and distribution system is characterized by three predominant pricing practices that serve to (a) link wholesalers and retailers exclusively to one producer, or suppliers to one assembler; (b) to maintain product prices at desired levels; and possibly (c) to create entry barriers by tying up retailers or suppliers. Pricing practices are directly linked to other "customary trade prac-tices" (*shokanko*) such as rebates (discounts to the retailer depending on sales volume etc.) and returns of unsold goods (whereby producers promise to accept returns of goods on the condition that the retailer follow its guidance on price or other matters). These *shokanko* practices reinforce the bargaining power of the producer/assembler over the retailer/supplier.

After-sales price adjustment

After-sales price adjustment (*ato-gime*) has long been the dominant practice in intermediate products, such as steel, lumber, auto parts, and glass. The producer indicates a "standard price" (*tatene*) to a general wholesaler, who then indicates a standard price to a regional wholesaler, etc., but the final transaction price is determined only after the product has been sold to the end user and the actual market price been established. Based on this market price, the producer determines the margins of its wholesalers that are often specialized and exclusive. Combined with an intricate rebate structure, this creates a system under which the profit structure within the entire chain of whole-salers and retailers can become dependent on the producer. Yet, the producer's powers to squeeze the suppliers' or distributors' profits are counterba-lanced by the producers' dependency on the specialized wholesalers: if all producers have exclusive wholesalers, switching is impossible.

Through the *ato-gime* system, most intermediate product prices are negotiated *post hoc*. The system is extremely opaque, and it is unclear to what extent intermediate product prices may be fixed, since the actual end prices are unknown. Yet, no anti-trust case has been brought against after-sales price adjustment, mostly because establishing evidence of coercion is impossible. While some industries moved away from *ato-gime* in the 1990s, it remains the predominant pricing mechanism in many intermediate product markets.

Suggested retail price

The dominant pricing practice for consumer products is that of suggesting a retail price (*kibo kakaku*), especially for end-products in industries dominated by specialized retail outlets (such as cars, electric appliances, or cosmetics). In theory, the manufacturer indicates a retail price but the retailer is free to determine the eventual price. While widely practiced in the USA and Europe, suggesting a retail price is even more common in Japan. According to a poll in the early 1990s, 85.5 percent of all manufacturers indicated a resale price for their product. A problem with anti-trust legislation occurs when the producer entices or coerces the retailer to stick to the suggested price.

One example of effective price suggestions is the stationery industry. Pens and pencils typically have a price printed on the product and sell for this price at most stores. Yet, while this is *de facto* price maintenance, Japan's **Fair Trade Commission** (JFTC) has allowed the practice to continue, maintaining that it is unaware that retailers are forced to follow the recommendation.

Retail price maintenance

A stronger version of "suggested retail prices," retail price maintenance (*saihanbai kakaku iji koi*) is an anti-trust violation, except in a few specified industries. Under this system, the producer determines the final retail price (sometimes printed on the container) and enforces this price by monitoring the retail system and punishing violators through measures such as penalty payments or interruption of shipments. Producers may pursue pro-competitive goals with this practice, such as ensuring good after-service or regional product availability. However, maintaining retail prices can also be used to prevent discounts and competition, or to enforce price cartels among producers (because any price deviation is attributable to the producer). In the USA, retail price maintenance is considered *per se* illegal; it is illegal even without proof of restricted prices or competition. In Japan, it is in principle illegal for a manufacturer to restrict the sales price.

Yet retail price maintenance remains widespread in Japan for two primary reasons. First, it is rarely used such that the anti-trust authority could easily prove a violation, because suggesting a retail price is permitted. Even if the JFTC can prove that retailers were coerced, the law does not prescribe more stringent measures than a cease-and-desist order without penalties. Second, in the

past the law has allowed for exemptions from the general rule of (a) daily use consumer products, allegedly so that the price can indicate quality (until the 1970s); (b) pharmaceuticals and cosmetics; and (c) copyrighted materials such as books and records. In the 1950s, the first of these three categories was used not only for toothpaste, soap, men's white shirts, or caramel candy, but also in designated strategic export products such as cameras. In several subsequent reviews of the system, the list of exempted products was progressively shortened: by the 1970s, only consumer products under ¥1000 could be exempted, and by the 1990s, only pharmaceuticals and copyrighted works (such as books) were legally allowed to uphold retail price maintenance.

Further reading

Flath, D. (1989) "Vertical Restraints in Japan," *Japan and the World Economy* 1: 187–203.

Kawagoe, K. (1997) *Dokusen kinshi-ho – kyoso shakai no feanesu* (The Antimonopoly Law – The Fairness of a Competitive Society), Tokyo: Kinzai.

Ramseyer, M. (1985) "The Costs of the Consensual Myth: Antitrust Enforcement and Institutional Barriers to Litigation in Japan," *Yale Law Journal* 94(3): 604–45.

Schaede, U. (2000) *Cooperative Capitalism: Self-Regulation, Trade Associations, and the Antimonopoly Law in Japan*, Oxford: Oxford University Press.

ULRIKE SCHAEDE

Prince Shotoku's Seventeen-Article Constitution

Issued by Prince Shotoku (Shototku Taishi, 573–621) in 604, the seventeen articles were Japan's first constitution. The articles present a code of morals by which the ruling class should live, rather than a set of rules by which a government could be maintained. The articles are firmly rooted in Buddhist and Confucian ideals. The central thesis of the articles is the divine nature of authority and the responsibility of both superior and subordinate to respect one another.

The first article lays out the basic notions of superior and subordinate responsibilities and emphasizes the importance of respect, temperance and harmony:

Harmony is to be valued, and an avoidance of wanton opposition to be honoured. All persons are influenced by class-feelings, and there are few who are intelligent. Hence there are some who disobey their lords and fathers or who maintain feuds with the neighbouring villages. But when those above are harmonious and those below are friendly, and there is concord in the discussion of business, right views of things gain spontaneous acceptance. Then what is there that cannot be accomplished?

The ideals of the Seventeen-Article Constitution exerted a profound influence within Japanese culture and society. While directed toward the ruling class, the ideals can easily be applied to other relationships where there are superiors and sub-ordinates. For this reason, they were often espoused in business organizations in the pre-Meiji era. The **Meiji restoration** brought about a renewed interest in, and respect for, the imperial family and of imperial guidance. Under these circum-stances, it was only natural the Seventeen-Article Constitution would again be brought forward as foundation for moral leadership.

In the second half of the twentieth century, Japanese business leaders still invoke the articles and promote their acceptance as a foundation for management philosophy. Yoshio Maruta, a former president of **Kao**, was typical of such leaders, actively circulating copies of the articles to employ-ees and colleagues as well as developing his own management philosophy based on the articles.

ALLAN BIRD

product development

Product development is the process by which, through a combination of technological knowledge ("seeds") and information about marketplace opportunities ("needs"), an idea is embodied in a usable product and is sold to customers. Product development refers both to the development of new products and to changes in existing products. It involves interactions across functions, such as research, product engineering, process engineering, manufacturing, and marketing, usually (though not necessarily) within a single company. Since the early 1980s, product development has been a focus of research not only in the field of technology management but also in strategy (as a critical element of competitive advantage) and the study of organizations (as a venue of interactions across groups with different professional specializations). From the mid-1980s to the mid-1990s, Japanese "best practice" in product development had a significant impact both on academic paradigms and on companies around the world. However, like so many other features of Japan's business system, the potential weaknesses of Japanese product development became increasingly evident after the collapse of the **bubble economy** in the early 1990s.

Research on product development processes in Japanese firms began in the mid-1980s, pioneered by a group of researchers at Hitotsubashi University in Tokyo (Imai *et al.* 1985; Takeuchi and Nonaka 1986). Interest among Western scholars and managers grew quickly, driven by the widespread recognition that Japan's leading companies excelled not only in manufacturing but also in developing products that were well-received by customers around the world. In a range of industries, including consumer electronics, autos, cameras, copiers, and computers, product development exhibited several strengths:

- *speed* (relatively short development cycles from initial product concept to product launch);
- *high productivity* (fewer engineering hours required for product development);
- *design for manufacturability* (product designs that facilitated a smooth transfer into production, with few quality problems);
- *rapid incremental improvement* (each new product quickly followed by sequences of new and improved generations);
- *effective use of external technology* (a willingness among engineers to draw on technologies and componentry generated outside their firm, a trait envied by many American R&D managers, who complained of their engineers' NIH –

"Not-Invented-Here" – resistance to technology that their organizations did not generate themselves).

Understanding how Japanese companies generated and sustained these features of product development involved research at three interrelated levels of analysis: the product development project, the firm itself, and the firm's external networks, with the greatest attention focused on the first level, the project. Some of the most detailed research at all three levels has been carried out in the context of the automobile industry (Clark and Fujimoto 1991; Cusumano and Nobeoka 1996). Fundamental patterns seemed to hold, however, across industries, especially at the project level. The key feature of project-level processes in Japanese firms has been dense and rapid cross-functional communications, based on the following practices:

- overlapping phases, where the next phase of a project begins while the preceding one is still in progress, with dense interactions across the team members involved in each phase, and at least some members are involved in multiple phases;
- cross-functional project membership, with project team members from production and from marketing involved from the beginning stages of the project;
- "heavyweight project manager," meaning a single project leader with authority and responsibility for the entire product development process, from concept creation and the interface with marketing through process engineering.

Takeuchi and Nonaka (1986) compared these practices to the US standard practice in the mid-1980s with a sports metaphor: the US model resembled a relay race, in which the "baton" of the product design was passed from one specialized group to another, whereas the Japanese model resembled a rugby game, in which team members interacted intensively to move the ball down the field. US firms tended to use another metaphor to describe the interaction between engineering and manufacturing: "throwing it over the wall." Although Japanese project-level practices differed significantly from US practices in the mid-1980s, they were picked up and emulated by US

companies over the succeeding decade, particularly in the auto industry.

Practices at the organizational level, however, were more deeply rooted in the Japanese business system, and proved less easy for foreign competitors to emulate. These centered on human resource management practices and on the organization of R&D. Japan's human resource management practices included the systematic transfer of engineers across functions, to carry technological and organizational knowledge and to facilitate effective and rapid communication in product development (Kusunoki and Numagami 1997). Even within the R&D function, engineers were often transferred within a product family, either to work on subsequent generations of a particular product, or to participate in new product development in a closely related area. Cross-functional transfers were eased by the shared socialization of personnel in standardized entry-level training programs, in which all new employees who had graduated from university, including engineers, went through a common orientation to the company, including some first-hand exposure to production and sales. The locus of responsibility for the engineers' careers was clearly assigned to the company, not the individual engineer. This also enabled companies to send their engineers on assignments to outside sources of technology (universities, government laboratories, other companies) to bring new technologies back to the company.

The organizational structure of Japanese companies also played a role in product development processes: companies tended to co-locate process engineering and incremental product development with manufacturing, in engineering centers or divisional laboratories built in or close to factories (see Fruin 1997). This facilitated the speedy transfer of technology from development into manufacturing and also encouraged rapid incremental product and process improvement, since design improvements rarely needed to be sent back to the central facility for technical inputs. Especially in electronics, the divisional laboratories in the development factories were entrusted with incremental improvement of products and variations on product platforms, while corporate laboratories focused on fundamental technology development and the development of significantly new products.

Finally, product development in Japanese companies involved close cooperation with an external network of key suppliers. Clark and Fujimoto (1991) identified the importance of "black box" suppliers in the Japanese auto industry, where the auto firm provides suppliers with general specifications and entrusts them with the completion of the designs. These key suppliers were involved in the product development process at an early stage, resulting in "parallel engineering" where suppliers were designing components in parallel with (and in close cooperation with) the product design process. This shortened the development process, especially since Japanese firms have traditionally relied on their suppliers for significantly more of the final value added of the product.

As the strengthening yen eroded Japan's manufacturing competitiveness and as both US and Asian competitors learned from the Japanese production system, many Japanese companies resorted increasingly to their product development capabilities to maintain their competitive advantage. Steady streams of new products and new models of existing products came out of their R&D organizations, encouraged during the bubble economy of the late 1980s and early 1990s by the seemingly insatiable appetite of Japanese consumers for novelty and by the flow of resources into R&D. The collapse of the bubble economy left many Japanese firms with a proliferation of closely related and marginally differentiated products. As Fujimoto (1997) put it, Japanese firms may have developed lean production, but they had fallen into "fat design," or excessive product complexity and proliferation. In the 1990s, many firms engaged in pruning and rationalizing their product lines, trying to re-focus their product development by applying stricter business-based criteria for R&D investments.

See also: electronics industry; export and import of technology; firm strategies for technology; industrial policy; Nonaka Ikujiro; overseas research and development; patent system; research cooperatives; science and technology policy; software industry; VLSI Research Cooperative

Further reading

Clark, K.B. and Fujimoto, T. (1991) *Product Development Performance: Strategy, Organization, and Management in the World Auto Industry*, Boston: Harvard Business School Press.

Cusumano, M.A. and Nobeoka, K. (1996) "Strategy, Structure, and Performance in Product Development: Observations from the Auto Industry," in T. Nishiguchi (ed.), *Managing Product Development*, New York: Oxford University Press, 75–120.

Fruin, W.M. (1997) *Knowledge Works: Managing Intellectual Capital at Toshiba*, New York: Oxford University Press.

Fujimoto, T. (1997) "The Dynamic Aspect of Product Development Capabilities: An International Comparison in the Automobile Industry," in A. Goto and H. Odagiri (eds), *Innovation in Japan*, New York: Oxford University Press, 56–99.

Imai, K., Nonaka, I. and Takeuchi, H. (1985) "Managing the Product Development Process: How Japanese Companies Learn and Unlearn," in K. Clark, R. Hayes, and C. Lorenz (eds), *The Uneasy Alliance: Managing the Productivity-Technology Dilemma*, Boston: Harvard Business School Press, 330–81.

Kusunoki, K. and Numagami, T. (1997) "Intrafirm Transfers of Engineers in Japan," in A. Goto and H. Odagiri (eds), *Innovation in Japan*, New York: Oxford University Press, 173–203.

Liker, J.K., Ettlie, J. and Campbell, J.C. (eds) (1995) *Engineered in Japan: Japanese Technology Management Practices*, New York: Oxford University Press.

Nonaka, I. and Takeuchi, H. (1995) *The Knowledge-Creating Company: How Japanese Companies Create the Dynamics of Innovation*, New York: Oxford University Press.

Takeuchi, H. and Nonaka, I. (1986) "The New Product Development Game," *Harvard Business Review* 64(1): 137–46.

ELEANOR D. WESTNEY

promissory notes

A promissory note is a legal paper by which the maker promises to pay a sum certain to the payee or due holder (holder in due course) at a definite time, that is the date of maturity. By issuing a promissory note, therefore, the maker is obliged to pay to payee or due holder. Apart from exercising the right, the payee may endorse the note and negotiate it with others. The issue of a promissory note is subject to a stamp tax.

Promissory notes have been extensively used as a means of payment (item) and of extending credit. At present in Japan, most promissory notes take the form of a uniform instrument defined by the Japanese Bankers Association (Zenkoku Ginko Kyokai, or Zenginkyo) and delivered by financial institutions to their current account holders. Financial institutions do not clear promissory notes using any other form, and can refuse to deal with the issuer in cases where they elect not to honor the bill, which may often lead to bankruptcy of the issuer.

The payment of promissory notes is made possible by a clearing system, in which all financial institutions in a designated area gather in the clearing house every business day and present notes to be collected from each other. Clearing houses are designated by the Minister of Justice, and currently number 185 throughout Japan. But most clearing takes place in that of Tokyo. The total value cleared in 1997 was ¥1,516 trillion, of which the Tokyo Clearing House handled ¥1,112 trillion. The use of promissory notes, however, is in decline due to tax evasion and diversification in the means of payment. In 1997 the Tokyo Clearing House cleared 100 million items including checks, bills, and others, compared with 141 million items for ¥4,033 trillion in 1990.

Further reading

Maeda, H. (1999) *Tegata Kogitte Ho* (Bills and Notes Law), Tokyo: Yuuhikaku.

Oda, H. (1997) *Basic Japanese Laws*, Oxford: Oxford University Press.

Seki, T. (1996) *Kin-yu Tegata Kogitte Ho* (Financial Bills and Notes Law), Tokyo: Shadanhojin Shoji Houmu Kenkyukai.

Yoshihara, S., Kaizuka, K., Rouyama, S. and Kanda, H. (2000) *Kin-yu Jitsumu Daijiten* (Dictionary of Professional Financing), Tokyo: Kabushiki Gaisha Kinzai.

KAZUHARU NAGASE

Q

quality control circles

Quality control circles (usually referred to in Japan as QC circles or QCC) are small groups consisting of front-line employees who control and improve the quality of their work processes, products and services on an ongoing basis. These small groups operate autonomously, utilize quality control concepts and techniques, draw upon their members' creativity and promote self- and mutual-development. Their aim is to develop members' capabilities, make the workplace more vital and satisfying, improve customer satisfaction and contribute to their company and society.

QC circles originated in post-Second World War Japan as one of the important elements of company-wide quality control, along with the utilization of statistical techniques by engineers and technical staff, and the implementation by top and middle management of systematic organizational improvement activities such as policy management. With the increasing recognition of the importance of quality control in the workplace, the magazine *Genba to QC: Quality Control for the Foreman* was first published in April 1962 with a targeted readership of supervisors and workers. (The magazine was later to be retitled *FQC* in 1973 and *QC Circles* in 1988). In its first issue, the magazine called for the formation of QC circles in the workplace. Also at that time, the QC Circle Headquarters was founded within the Japanese Union of Scientists and Engineers. The first circle to be registered with the QCC Headquarters was from **Nippon Telegraph and Telephone**. By March 1963, there were thirty-six registered QCC

representing many different companies. The first QC circle conference was held in 1963, and regional chapters of QC circles were organized in 1964. The number of registered circles increased to 10,000 by 1970 and experienced another period of rapid increase in the early 1980s, reaching an all-time high of nearly 30,000 circles in 1984. As of 2000, the number of registered circles was 4,594. It should be noted, however, that QCCs have evolved into various forms within individual Japanese companies, and most of these small groups do not formally register with the QCC headquarters.

Worldwide attention to Japan's QC circle phenomenon was initiated by J.M. **Juran**'s presentation on the subject at the European Organization for Quality Control conference held in Stockholm in 1966. Lockheed Missiles and Space Company is generally recognized as being the first Western company to introduce QCCs, which it did after a study mission to Japan in 1973. By the late 1970s, countries in Asia, America, and Europe had introduced QCCs or similar small group activities, with the first international QC circle convention held in 1978. By the mid-1980s, the quality circle boom in many Western countries was beginning to pass, though many companies continued to involve employees in quality improvement activities under different formats and names such as process action teams. Today, QC circle activities are found in more than seventy countries or regions, with Japan and other Asian countries being the most active practitioners.

A QC circle is usually comprised of from five to seven members who work together in a single unit work area. Typically, the foreman directly overseeing QC activities or one of the members with seniority serves as the leader of the circle. In some cases, front-line employees with the same duties at different workplaces also join together to form a circle. Most circles hold meetings once or twice a month, though frequency varies depending on the theme or subject a particular circle is working on. The themes taken up by QCCs are diverse, including quality, cost, or safety issues at the workplace, operational efficiency and improvement, problems related to internal or external customers, or how to create a bright and satisfying workplace.

QC circle activities have several distinguishing features. They provide a mechanism which mutually supports employees in: (1) learning a rational way of thinking and scientific/problem solving methods through the study of quality control principles and techniques, (2) building teamwork and fostering discussion among employees with shared work knowledge and experience, and (3) contributing to the company by solving problems in the workplace. In carrying out these activities, QC circles typically employ a common set of improvement tools, such as the seven tools of QC. Other distinguishing features include the use of the eight-step QC story as a guide for problem solving, as well as the characteristic way in which QCCs are organized and operate.

Benefits typically enjoyed by companies with QC circle activities include: (1) the development of employees that are highly motivated and have the capability necessary to tackle problems which the company faces; (2) improvement in quality and productivity that, in turn leads to an increase in customer satisfaction; and (3) the achievement of broader company goals including contributing to the improvement of society.

Some challenges faced by companies when carrying out QC circle activities include sustaining enthusiasm and activity levels of QCCs as well as adapting to changing values regarding lifetime employment, work and private life. Larger organizations usually establish a position or department with responsibilities for administration and promotion of QCC activities.

Though originating in manufacturing departments, QC circles are now found in sales, engineering, and other departments and have spread to service industries such as hospitals, banks, hotels and retailing. Accompanying these changes, variant forms of QC circle activities have emerged, including "joint QC circles" which undertake problems that cross workplace boundaries, "theme-oriented QC circles" which involve people facing similar problems within different workplaces, and "sub-circles" and "theme leader" structures. The range of techniques and methods used by QCCs also has expanded, and QCCs often have become involved in other company initiatives such as occupational safety management, value analysis/engineering, and total productive maintenance (TPM).

See also: quality management; total productive management

Further reading

Cole, R. (1989) *Strategies for Learning: Small Group Activities in American, Japanese, and Swedish Industry*, Berkeley, CA: University of California Press

Ishikawa, K. (ed.) (1984) *Quality Control Circles at Work: Cases from Japan's Manufacturing and Service Sectors*, Portland OR: Productivity Press.

Lillrank, P. and Kano, N. (1989) *Continuous Improvement: Quality Control Circles in Japanese Industry*, Ann Arbor, MI: Center for Japanese Studies, University of Michigan.

QC Circle Headquarters, JUSE (1996) *QC Circle Koryo: General Principles of the QC Circle*, Tokyo: JUSE Press.

—— (1997) *How to Operate QC Circle Activities*, Tokyo: JUSE Press.

TAKESHI NAKAJO

quality management

Quality management is defined as a system of means for economically producing goods or services to satisfy the needs of the customer. Leading Japanese companies have come to be known for a variety of best practices in quality management that have greatly influenced the development of quality management worldwide, particularly during the 1980s. The cheap and shoddy image held by "Made in Japan" goods after the Second World War was replaced by a reputation for high quality and reliability. The history and major players behind this transformation will be outlined first, followed by a discussion of the conceptual, methodological and organizational features of Japanese quality management.

History and development

Though there was a very limited awareness and practice of quality control methods before the Second World War, the major origins of Japanese quality management can be traced to the post-Second World War occupation era. Troubled by frequent problems with the telephone system, the occupation's General Headquarters had American experts give extended seminars on management, including quality control, to managers in the telecommunications industry in 1949. Also, during the early postwar years, two non-profit organizations were established that were to become influential leaders in the development and promotion of Japan's quality movement: the Union of Japanese Scientists and Engineers (JUSE) and the Japanese Standards Association (JSA). These organizations also began to offer educational programs on quality control in 1949, and in that same year JUSE established its first Quality Control Research Group.

It was to this receptive environment that JUSE invited W. Edwards **Deming**, an American expert, to lecture on statistical quality control in Japan in 1950 and again in 1951. The lecture notes were published and Deming donated the royalties to JUSE. Using these funds, in 1951 JUSE established the Deming Prize to honor individuals and to recognize companies excelling in the implementation of quality management. Over time, the Deming Prize was to prove itself as a powerful vehicle for advancing the Japanese quality movement. In 1954, another American quality expert, J.M. **Juran**, was invited by JUSE to lecture in Japan. In that and later visits, Juran presented a more managerial approach to quality. It should be noted that senior executives formed the audience for several of Deming's and Juran's lecture series, symbolic of the high degree of awareness and support that Japanese top managers were to give to their companies' quality efforts.

During the 1950s, quality management gained increasing acceptance among Japanese manufacturers, though the emphasis originally was on applying statistical methods in manufacturing activities. By the late 1950s to early 1960s, leading companies were extending quality management to include marketing, design, manufacturing, sales and other functional areas. At the same time, employees at all levels of the organization were becoming involved in quality control and improvement. A major vehicle for the involvement of front-line employees was through **quality control circles** beginning in the early 1960s. In this way, Japanese quality management was broadening to become a truly company-wide activity, unlike in the USA and other countries where quality typically was in the hands of quality specialists and was not a management priority.

From the 1960s through the 1980s, Japan experienced a quality management boom. During this time, quality management matured as a company-wide activity and was extended to a corporate group-wide level. Also, beginning in the 1970s, some Japanese service industries began formal quality management efforts. By the mid-1970s, J.M. Juran estimates that Japanese industry had caught up with and begun to surpass Western industry in its ability to create quality products. Evidence from a number of industries emerged to substantiate the Japanese quality advantage. One particularly detailed study on the room air conditioner manufacturing industry showed startlingly large gaps in quality performance in the early 1980s (see Garvin 1988). For example, while Japanese manufacturers had defective rates of 0.0 to 0.3 percent for incoming parts and materials, American manufacturers experienced defective rates of 0.8 to 16.0 percent. In other words, even the worst performing Japanese manufacturer was still nearly three times better than the best performing American manufacturer. Similarly large gaps were found for assembly-line defect rates and service call rates. Other studies on televisions, memory chips, and automobiles, likewise showed higher quality levels for Japanese-made products.

Spurred by these dramatic quality differences, Western companies showed an immense interest throughout the 1980s in learning and adopting

Japanese-style quality management. Other turning points included the 1980 broadcast in the USA of the NBC television documentary *If Japan Can...- Why Can't We?*, which introduced Deming's past activity in Japan to a wide audience. Also attracting attention was the awarding of the Deming Prize in 1981 to Yokogawa Hewlett-Packard, which in the process had transformed itself from H-P's worst to best-performing division. Though a great number and variety of organizations and individuals contributed to the dissemination of Japanese quality management abroad, the role of Japanese joint venture and affiliated companies merits special note. Several such companies, including Yokogawa Hewlett-Packard, Fuji Xerox, Texas Instruments Japan, IBM Japan, Aisin Warner, and Mazda, served as models and information conduits for interpreting and transferring Japanese best practices to overseas counterparts. The profound effect of Japanese quality management on world-wide practice was readily seen in many quality-related articles and training manuals of the early 1980s which often contained direct translations of the original Japanese concepts and approaches. Also during this time, the Deming Application Prize was opened up to overseas applicants, with Florida Power and Light becoming the first overseas recipient in 1989 followed by Taiwan Phillips (1991) and AT&T Power Systems (1994).

Since the 1990s, quality management has received less prominence in Japan. In part, this is due to the fact that its major concepts and practices have become ingrained into corporate routine. At the same time, some criticism has emerged regarding the tendency for certain practices to become ritualistic or bureaucratic, and others have pointed out the need for fresh, new ideas and approaches. A spate of quality and safety problems in 1999 and 2000 also raised questions about a seeming quality malaise in segments of Japanese industry. Companies whose quality reputations were tarnished include a Sumitomo subsidiary that used unsafe processes leading to the Tokaimura nuclear accident, Snow Brand whose contaminated milk products caused illness in 15,000 people and Mitsubishi Motors which was implicated in the long-term cover-up of defects to avoid product recalls.

Some areas of notable activity in the 1990s, however, included the push by Japanese companies

for certification to ISO 9000, the international standard for quality management systems. At first, Japanese firms showed little interest in the standard due to the perception that their own quality performance levels were high and would not benefit from ISO 9000's rudimentary, conformance-based approach. When it became clear that ISO 9000 was becoming a market requirement, however, Japanese firms earnestly began certification efforts on a wide scale. Other developments included the introduction of alternative awards to the Deming Prize. Affiliated with the **Japan Productivity Center for Socio-Economic Development**, the Japan Quality Award was launched with an award system and criteria similar to the Baldridge Award in the USA. Also, in 2000 JUSE established a new category of awards, Japan Quality Recognition Awards, to complement the Deming Prize. One award recognizes achievement in TQM and is positioned as a stepping-stone to the Deming Prize, while another award recognizes the development of innovative quality methods or systems.

Concepts and methods

Over the course of its development, Japanese quality management has come to be characterized by a number of concepts, tools, and methods. In some cases, these are new contributions to the practice of quality management, while in other cases they are conventional ideas cast in a different light or with a new emphasis.

Kaizen, or the continual pursuit of improvement, forms the philosophical basis for quality management and other Japanese approaches such as **just-in-time** and total productive maintenance. Japanese quality leaders speak of quality management as being a "revolution in thought" wherein one attains a problem-consciousness and seeks to prevent rather than fix problems after they have occurred. Through the repeated cycle of Plan-Do-Check-Act (PDCA), all aspects of business activity are to be evaluated and acted upon for improvement. To carry out *kaizen*, Japanese companies emphasize the need for the participation of all employees, at all levels, and in all departments. This is accomplished through quality control circles, quality audits by top management, *hoshin kanri* and other activities described below. Also essential is a customer-orientation. An axiom of Japanese quality management is "market-in – not product-out". In another saying, "the next process(es) is your customer," Japan taught the important concept of recognizing internal customers as well as external customers. Japan was also the origin of the well-known classification of customer expectations for product quality into delighters, satisfiers, and must-be/dissatisfiers.

Japanese quality management also has emphasized the scientific method through the use of data to make decisions, analyze problems and implement improvements. This notion is symbolized by sayings such as "speak with data" and "manage by the facts." Along with this, Japanese companies stress the *3-gen* principle of observing the actual object in question (*genbutsu*) and actual situation (*genjitsu*) at the actual location (*genba*) (see **genba-shugi**). To support this emphasis on data and the involvement of all employees, Japanese industry promoted the widespread use of a problem-solving toolkit called the seven tools of QC: Pareto diagram, cause-and-effect diagram, stratification, checksheet, histogram, graphs and control charts, and scatter diagram. Made famous in Japan and abroad through Kaoru **Ishikawa**'s book, *Guide to Quality Control*, this package of basic tools became an important feature of Japanese quality management as employees at all levels in the organization are able to learn and apply these tools. Ishikawa contended that the majority of quality problems could be solved with their use alone. Prompted by the popularity of the seven tools, JUSE later coordinated the development of another set of tools called the "new seven tools," or seven management tools, which are used for planning and for organizing and understanding complex information.

Another important aspect of Japanese quality management has been its emphasis on system design and the upstream activities of process and product design. Shigeo **Shingo** and others emphasized the use of *poka-yoke*, or error-proofing techniques, to design out the possibility of mistakes in work processes. A widely used technique for **product development** called quality function development (QFD) was also developed in Japan. Through a series of matrices, QFD translates customer requirements into technical requirements and product specifications. In addition, the Japanese practice of concurrent engineering, wherein the product is designed in parallel with its related production processes, has become an accepted best practice. Also receiving worldwide attention have been the ideas and methods of Genichi **Taguchi**. He advocates a quality engineering approach that emphasizes the reduction of variation, the importance of making products and processes robust to variability in operating and usage conditions, and the use of designed experiments.

Organizational framework

The organizational implementation of Japanese style quality management can be conceptualized as a framework of top-down, lateral, and bottom-up activities (see Akiba *et al.* 1992). Just as a cloth is made strong by its cross-woven threads, quality management requires a coordinated combination of vertical and horizontal activities.

Top-down activities include *hoshin kanri* and internal quality audits by top management. Variously translated as policy deployment or management by policy, *hoshin kanri* refers to a management process for identifying goals (usually annual) and deploying them throughout all levels of business planning and activity. The aim is to focus effort and resources on a few priority issues for breakthrough improvement. Essential to *hoshin kanri* is a back-and-forth dialogue (called "catch ball") between all levels and departments of the organization about not only the goals, but also the concrete means for their achievement. Another way that top management is involved in quality management is through regular reviews of the quality system called quality audits (*QC shindan*). Their purpose is not inspection, but rather to evaluate management processes and provide and opportunity for discussion. Typical items covered include the progress of *hoshin kanri* activities, the implementation status of routine control and improvement activities, and the status of QC circle activities. Quality audits are usually conducted at multiple levels in an organization. In a presidential audit, the company president reviews quality activities company-wide. Division and section managers may also conduct audits within their own areas.

Lateral activities include cross-functional management and management of daily work. Cross-functional management (*kinoubetsu kanri*) is the organizational tool for interdepartmental coordination. To implement cross-functional management, permanent steering committees are typically formed to coordinate and review progress with regard to quality, cost, and delivery performance. For each committee, the senior managing director of the relevant functional area, such as quality, is installed as committee chair and directors of other functional areas are included as committee members. Management of daily work (*nichijo kanri*) refers to the application of the plan-do-check-act (PDCA) cycle in each individual's routine work activities. The idea is to evaluate, define, and standardize all work activities and where possible to extend best practices to other workers and departments.

The principal means of bottom-up involvement in quality management activities is through **quality control circles** (QCC). Typically, QC circles are small groups of front-line employees from the same workplace who meet regularly on a voluntary basis to carry out quality control and improvement activities. Education and training are important aspects of QCC activity, and all circle members are expected to master and apply the seven tools of QC. Many companies and other organizations sponsor QC circle conferences where employees present their improvement projects and often compete for awards.

Terminology

Several different Japanese terms, as well as English acronyms, are commonly used when referring to quality management in Japan. The most basic term is *hinshitsu kanri*, which can be narrowly translated as "quality control," though the Japanese use the term in a broader sense that may be equated with "quality management." The acronym "QC" also is commonly used in Japan with this same generic meaning. Beginning in the 1960s and 1970s, as Japanese companies broadened the scope of quality management activities to include more functional areas and organizational levels, the term *zenshateki hinshitsu kanri* came into common usage to emphasize the "company-wide" nature of quality management. Also, the acronym "TQC" (from Total

Quality Control) was borrowed from the US and used interchangeably with *zenshateki hinshitsu kanri*. However, to distinguish the progressive Japanese-style TQC from the Western-style TQC which had relied more heavily on quality specialists, Japanese companies and authors coined the English term Company-Wide Quality Control (CWQC) to use when explaining Japanese-style quality management to overseas audiences. Thus, the term CWQC is found in many English language sources, while the equivalent term "TQC" is found throughout Japanese language sources. To confuse matters further, the term "total quality management" (TQM) came into popular usage in Western companies during the 1980s and 1990s to denote their newly adopted approach to quality management which was largely modeled after Japanese practices. Despite this change in terminology overseas, Japanese companies continued to use the English acronym TQC domestically up until 1996 when the Union of Japanese Scientists and Engineers (JUSE) made an official change to TQM (*sogoteki hinshitsu kanri*).

Further reading

Akiba, M., Schvaneveldt, S.J. and Enkawa, T. (1992) "Service Quality and Japanese Perspectives," in G. Salvendy (ed.), *Handbook of Industrial Engineering*, 2nd edn, New York: Wiley, 2349–71.

Garvin, D. (1988) *Managing Quality*, New York: The Free Press.

Ishikawa, K. (1985) *What Is Total Quality Control? The Japanese Way*, trans. D. Lu, Englewood Cliffs NJ: Prentice-Hall.

Nemoto, M. (1987) *Total Quality Control for Management: Strategies and Techniques from Toyota and Toyota Gosei*, trans. D. Lu, Englewood Cliffs NJ: Prentice-Hall.

Nonaka, I. (1995) "The Recent History of Managing for Quality in Japan," in J.M. Juran (ed.), *A History of Managing for Quality*, Milwaukee, WI: ASQC Quality Press, 517–52.

Shiba, S., Graham, A. and Walden, D. (1993) *A New American TQM: Four Practical Revolutions in Management*, Portland, OR: Productivity Press.

SHANE J. SCHVANEVELDT

R

Rengo

Rengo is the acronym for Nihon Rodo Kumiai Sorengokai, translated as the Japanese Trade Union Confederation. Comprising unions in both the private sector and in the public sector, with total membership of approximately 8,000,000 (about 68 percent of organized labor), it is by far the largest, the most representative, and the politically most significant national center of labor organizations in Japan. However, Rengo's authority over its constituent organizations (industrial unions), let alone over the **enterprise unions**, the basic and most powerful level of union organization, is limited. Likewise, in the labor market, it is a junior partner of the government and of Nikkeiren, the **Japan Federation of Employers' Associations**.

History

From the mid-1950s until Rengo's establishment in 1989, Japanese unions lacked one, overarching national center. Throughout most of this period, unions were affiliated either with one of several rival national centers (**Sohyo**, Domei, Churitsu Roren, and Shinsanbetsu), or with none. Divisions were largely along Cold War-related ideological lines reinforced by sectoral interests (public vs. private), and partly along diverging perceptions of the role of unions in the place of employment, society, and the polity.

The main driving force for unification came from pragmatic, non-doctrinaire leaders of unions in the private sector. Major milestones were the formation in 1982 of Zenmin Rokyo (All-Japan Council of Trade Unions in Private Industries); and the reorganization in 1987 of Zenmin Rokyo as Rengo, following the dissolution of Domei, Churitsu Roren, and Shinsanbetsu. In 1989, Sohyo, formerly the largest and ideologically most "militant" national center, consisting primarily of public sector unions, dissolved, and most of its affiliates joined Rengo.

Unification was enhanced by union leaders' sense of vulnerability in view of domestic socio-economic and demographic changes, especially following the oil crisis, and of mounting external pressures to open the Japanese economy to foreign competitors. Considerable gains previously achieved through labor–management consultation and cooperation at the enterprise became insufficient, and had to be supplemented by state intervention. To become credible partners in public policy making, unions at all levels had not only to close ranks, but also soften their ideological tone and adopt a more cooperative posture toward the then ruling **Liberal Democratic Party** (LDP) and the national bureaucracy. The LDP and the bureaucracy reciprocated by incorporating increasing numbers of leaders of industrial unions and national centers into policy processes. This opening toward labor was facilitated by the phase out of the Cold War and its rendering long-standing ideological rifts largely irrelevant.

Under the assertive leadership of Yamaghishi Akira, its first president, Rengo played a notable role in exacerbating fission within the LDP, forming the anti-LDP coalition in 1993, and instituting political reforms in 1994. Moreover, in addition to fielding its own candidates in elections, it sought to reunify the socialist parties into a new moderate, social democratic party that would play a major role in a realigning multi-party system, but without success.

Structure and functions

Among Rengo constituents, the legacy of past affiliation with rival national centers, especially Sohyo and Domei, persists, albeit in different organizational forms and on a more moderate scale and intensity. The unification of formerly rival unions at the level of respective industries is progressing, but at a snail's pace.

Rengo's top leaders hail from its affiliate unions; and upon completing their term, they return to their firm/government ministry, enter politics, or land a managerial or advisory position in union-related organizations in such areas as education and welfare. The administrative officials at headquarters are largely from affiliated unions; a few "professionals" (*propa* in Japanese) have been recruited directly, mostly after graduation from university.

For its rather limited finances, Rengo depends on its affiliates, which in turn are financed by their affiliate enterprise unions. The latter retain the lion's share of individual members' dues. *Vis-à-vis* its affiliates, Rengo is largely supportive, advisory, and coordinating, rather than authoritative; it is not a "peak association" in the terminology of the literature on "neo-corporatism." It disseminates information and research results from government and other sources, including its own Research Institute for the Advancement of Living Standards (Rengo Sogo Seikatsu Kaihatsu Kenkyu jo; Rengo Soken, in short). It adopts guidelines for the annual spring labor offensive and for union support of parties in elections. It encourages unification of affiliates in the same industry. It seeks to adjust divergent interests of unions in different sectors and in industries differently affected by globalization and deregulation. And, in view of declining union organization rates, it urges reluctant affiliates and their enterprise unions to organize irregular employees and the unemployed, and launches organization drives on its own.

More widely, Rengo leaders make statements on public issues directly and indirectly relating to employees. They meet Nikkeiren leaders to iron out differences, launch joint research projects, and jointly issue policy demands and proposals regarding such issues as employment security and taxation. They also participate in government-appointed formal **shingikai**, semi-formal *shiteki shimon kikan*, and informal forums of policy consultation, as well as in private-sector policy study and advocacy forums.

Internationally, Rengo offers aid through its Japan International Labor Foundation (JILAF); cooperates with international NGOs; plays a leading role in the Asian branch of the ICFTU; represents labor in the Japanese tripartite delegation to the International Labor Organization; and participates, together with the **Ministry of Labor** and Nikkeiren, in periodic dialogues on labor issues with counterparts in other countries, notably Germany.

Rengo has achieved only part of its initial goals. But though ideologically conservative, it has not presided over the demise of labor unionism in Japan, as some observers had predicted. Rather, it is considering new roles, defining new missions, and launching new programs to invigorate all three levels of union organization.

See also: history of the labour movement; lifetime employment

Further reading

Koshiro, K. (ed.) (1998) *Sengo gojunen: sangyo, koyo, rodo shi* (Postwar 50 Years: Industry, Employment and Labor History), Tokyo: Nihon Rodo Kenkyu Kiko.

Kume, I. (1998) *Disparaged Success: Labor Politics in Japan*, Ithaca, NY: Cornell University Press.

—— (2000) "Rodo seisaku kettei katei no seijuku to henyo" (Maturity and Transformation of Labor Policymaking Processes), *Nihon rodo kenkyu zasshii* (Japan Institute of Labor Journal) 475: 2–13.

Rengo (annual) *Seisaku seido shu: seisak seido yokyu to teigen* (Policy and Institutional Demands and Proposals), Tokyo: Rengo Headquarters.

Shinoda, T. (1997) "Rengo and Policy Participation: Japanese-Style Neo-Corporatism?" in M. Sako and H. Sato (eds), *Japanese Labour and*

Management in Transition, London: Routledge, 187–214.

EHUD HARARI

research cooperatives

Research cooperatives, also known as research consortia, are temporary alliances of potential competitors in the same industry for the purpose of joint research and development. Research cooperatives in Japan come in private and public forms. They first appeared in 1956 and soon became part of the government **industrial policy** tool set. While the early cooperatives aimed at catching up with the West, projects after 1980 have focused on basic research. Throughout, the role of public funding has remained small as compared to the United States. While organizing research in cooperatives has numerous theoretical advantages, empirical evidence has shown no clear link between the presence of cooperatives and industry competitiveness.

Forms and actors

There are private and public research cooperatives in Japan. In a private cooperative, the participant firms often found a jointly-held corporation (*kabushiki kaisha*) to coordinate research activities. An example of this type is the Semiconductor Leading Edge Technologies (SELETE) cooperative, Japan's counterpart to the Semiconductor Manufacturing Technology (SEMATECH) cooperative in the United States.

Public cooperatives involve not only firms, but also sponsoring government bureaucracies, **industry and trade associations**, public research laboratories, and universities. Prominent examples include the VLSI, Supercomputer, and Fifth Generation research cooperatives.

Since public cooperatives are at least in part publicly funded, the sponsoring government bureaucracy, such as the **Ministry of International Trade and Industry** (MITI) for manufacturing industries, plays an important role in creating them. After an initial proposal to undertake a public research project, often from firms or academics, the ministry in charge of the project industry has a deliberation council (**shingikai**) evaluate the proposal. Once the council decides in favor of a project, the ministry proceeds in several directions. First, it secures funding for the project, either from the **Ministry of Finance** or from other sources of income such as the proceeds from publicly licensed betting at bicycle races. Second, it selects firms and public research laboratories to participate in the project. Central criterion for firm selection is the likelihood of becoming a leader in the new technology, and in most cases, the number of participant firms is less than 20. Third, if the project creates a new industry for which no industry association exists that could coordinate research activities, the ministry founds a new industry association together with the participant firms.

The implementation of the project is in the hands of the respective industry association. It serves as a coordinator for, and forum for information exchange between, the participant firms and laboratories, which often split up into groups to work on a small number of smaller projects. It acts as a conduit to government by disbursing government research funds to cooperative members and reporting to the government on behalf of the cooperative. Finally, association councils provide a forum for feedback from university researchers, who seldom participate directly in public cooperatives.

Historical development and government funding

Research cooperatives are roughly modeled on the British Research Associations of the First World War. The first research cooperative in Japan dates to 1956, when a number of automotive air filter manufacturers formed a collaborative venture. The first government-sponsored cooperative appeared in 1959, and in 1961, the Engineering Research Association Act officially recognized research cooperatives and bestowed a number of tax benefits on them. A total of about 150 cooperatives have since been registered under the Act; however, the actual number of research cooperatives is considerably higher and not precisely known, as not all cooperatives are registered.

The characteristics of public cooperatives changed fundamentally around 1980. Projects before then focused on catching up technologically with Western competitors. They aimed to produce commercializable products and lasted on average about five years. Public funding covered only part of the total research expenses and came in the form of conditional loans (*hojokin*), which firms were to pay back if the cooperative was successful (which they did for about half of all loans). Cooperatives financed through *hojokin* retained the patent rights to all technologies developed.

As Japan caught up with the technology frontier around 1980, the focus shifted toward basic research. Cooperative lifetimes lengthened to an average of about ten years, as basic research requires more time, and public funding began to cover all research expenses to make the risk associated with basic research more palatable to firms. The funding scheme changed to reimbursements for commissioned research (*itakuhi*), which firms need not repay; however, all patents remain with the government, which licenses out the technology on a non-discriminatory basis. Most government funding for research cooperatives has gone to three areas: semiconductors and computers, petroleum and chemicals, and power generation and distribution.

Overall, the role of public funding in Japanese research cooperatives has been modest. Between 1960 and 1991, such funding amounted to about 0.47 percent of GDP in Japan, compared with about 1.32 percent over the same period in the United States. The average government budget per project has been about ¥8.4 billion ($76 million), while SEMATECH alone had received US$850 million from the US government by 1996 (Sakakibara 1997).

A success?

Whether research cooperatives have been a successful vehicle for promoting research is subject to debate. Theoretically, cooperatives should be advantageous for participating firms in a number of ways. Among others, the literature suggests that the pooling of research resources helps avoid wasteful duplication of research efforts and speeds the diffusion of technology; the contribution of public funds to cooperatives alleviates the financial risk for firms of undertaking basic research with unclear benefits; and the public commitment of government money to a given project after extensive expert consultations signals to firms that the target technology may be viable. However, empirical research has unearthed no clear link between the presence of research cooperatives and industry competitiveness, and where cooperatives have been successful, it is not apparent that firms would not have developed the technology on their own.

Further reading

Aldrich, H.E. and Sasaki, T. (1995) "R&D Cooperatives in the United States and Japan," *Research Policy* 24: 301–16.

Callon, S. (1995) *Divided Sun: MITI and the Breakdown of Japanese High-Tech Industrial Policy, 1975–1993*, Stanford, CA: Stanford University Press.

Okimoto, D.I. (1989) *Between MITI and the Market: Japanese Industrial Policy for High Technology*, Stanford, CA: Stanford University Press.

Sakakibara, M. (1997) "Evaluating Government-Sponsored R&D Cooperatives in Japan: Who Benefits and How?" *Research Policy* 26: 447–73.

MICHAEL A. WITT

restructuring

The term, restructuring, or *risutora*, began to appear in the Japanese vocabulary in the late 1980s, as exporting firms took measures to respond to the *endaka*, or abrupt increase in the yen after the Plaza Accord in 1985. Restructuring gained momentum in the 1990s, after the bursting of the **bubble economy**. Mentions of *risutora* in the **Nihon Keizai Shimbun**, Japan's leading business daily, increased from 505 in 1990 to 5,324 in 1994, and it was difficult to find a firm not talking of restructuring. By the end of the 1990s, however, "restructuring" appeared less frequently in the Japanese business press, in part because it had become associated with downsizing. While there were very few outright layoffs during the restructuring movement, firms used other methods to reduce their workforces, and employees and the general public correctly associated *risutora* with job losses.

Even during the restructuring movement in the 1990s, Japanese firms were extremely hesitant to lay off employees. Several factors made outright layoffs difficult. First, courts tended to favor employees in lawsuits over severance. Employers had to demonstrate pressing economic hardship (such as looming bankrucpty) to conduct layoffs without legal repercussions. **Enterprise unions** also opposed layoffs, preferring instead to negotiate gradual programs of labor force reduction. Layoffs and other forms of downsizing also invited bad publicity. Pioneer discovered this in 1993, when it gave thirty-five senior employees a choice between retirement and dismissal. This announcement was featured prominently in the mass media as a harbinger of the end of permanent employment. Several weeks later, Pioneer retracted its decision, allegedly due to concern about unfavorable publicity and pressure from its labor union.

In restructuring, Japanese firms tended to adopt several measures that stopped short of outright layoffs. The first was *shukko*, or dispatch of employees either temporarily or permanently to related companies. When firms exhausted their options for *shukko*, as receiving firms became less willing and able to accept redundant employees, they turned to other methods of downsizing. Many women in secretarial or clerical positions were encouraged to retire and were subsequently replaced by soft-drink machines and temporary employees. Firms also offered early retirement packages to increasingly younger cohorts of male employees. The mass media reported cases of "bullying," in which firms harassed employees into resigning, though this kind of activity has been difficult to verify. Many firms also eliminated or reduced hiring of new cohorts of graduates for one or more years. Though this reduced headcount without layoffs, it also had implications for the *nenko joretsu* system, in which successive cohorts of employees moved up a fixed promotion hierarchy. Hiring reductions left gaps in this hierarchy, and increased the average age of a company's labor force.

The magnitude of restructuring among Japanese companies during the 1990s did not reach the levels of US companies during a similar period.

Sweeping and immediate reductions of 10 percent of a firm's labor force – not uncommon in the USA – remained rare. Nevertheless, restructuring had a real impact. According to **Ministry of Labor** statistics, the percentage of job separations among firms with over 1,000 employees due to management circumstances (as opposed to retirement and other individual circumstances) increased from 2.3 percent in 1980 to 9.3 percent in 1998. The **unemployment** rate grew to historically high levels (though still relatively low by US standards).

Changes in organization structure often accompanied workforce reductions. Many firms attempted to move towards flatter hierarchies and reduction of job titles. There was also a move in many large companies to reorganize along business units rather than functional groups or factories. These reorganizations occurred under the rubric of the "company system," a term that reflected the objective of encouraging business units to act as independent companies, with profit and loss responsibility. It is not clear how deep these changes were, and how much they went beyond newspaper headlines and organizational charts. They did, however, suggest a change in managerial thinking from a company as a cohesive community, to company as a set of discrete, though related, operating units.

Another aspect of restructuring involved renegotiation of long-term relationships with business partners, in particular with parts suppliers and distribution channels. Though accounts of large manufacturers cutting ties to small suppliers attracted media attention, more common were cases in which buyers reduced purchases over several years, and provided encouragement and active assistance for its suppliers to diversify their business opportunities.

Foreign investors, who after the bursting of the bubble were increasingly active and vocal investors in the Japanese stock market, welcomed restructuring. Stock analysts at foreign firms touted companies that had announced restructuring programs as good investments. The Japanese public saw restructuring in a less positive light. The unwillingness of the Japanese consumer to spend money, a tendency that prolonged the post-bubble recession, was in part due to uncertainty over future employment prospects under continued restructuring.

Perhaps the best-known case of restructuring during this period occurred after Renault took a controlling stake in Nissan in 1999. Renault dispatched Carlos Ghosn to serve as COO and later president. Ghosn embarked on an intense restructuring program, featuring deep cuts in employment and severance of long-term supplier relationships. Even so, employment reductions were carried out through early retirement, reduced hiring, and attrition rather than outright cuts. Ghosn at first attracted heavy criticism for unfeeling and un-Japanese behavior towards employees and long-term stakeholders, though as Nissan's operating performance improved, this criticism became increasingly subdued.

See also: lifetime employment

Further reading

Lincoln, J.R. and Nakata, Y. (1997) "The Transformation of the Japanese Employment System: Nature, Depth, and Origins," *Work and Occupations* 24: 33–55.

Mroczkowski, T. and Hanaoka, M. (1997) "Effective Rightsizing Strategies in Japan and America: Is There a Convergence of Employment Practices?" *Academy of Management Executive* 11: 57–67.

Usui, C. and Colignon, R. (1996) "Corporate Restructuring: Converging World Pattern or Societally Specific Embeddedness?" *Sociological Quarterly* 4: 551–78.

CHRISTINE L. AHMADJIAN

retail industry

The huge retail industry in Japan embodies a very complex scheme of cultural categories. Japanese retail analysts have classified the industry into two sections: one selling without stores and the other selling through stores. The former consists of mail-order houses, telephone sales, television shopping services and so on; the latter includes shopping centers, middle- to small-scale retailers (discount stores, convenience stores, and specialty stores), and large-scale retailers (primarily, **department stores** and supermarkets; see **superstores**).

Brief history of the modern retail industry

The development of the modern retail industry in Japan was marked by the opening of **Mitsukoshi** in 1904. The establishment of Mitsukoshi also symbolized a retailing "revolution" at that time. The company introduced a set of new retail techniques and management, including "cash payments and no haggling" policy, direct sourcing of merchandise from manufacturers, selling by display rather than *za-uri* sales, and so on. Other traditional drapery stores followed Mitsukoshi, developing their stores into modern department stores between the end of the Taisho period and the beginning of Showa. At that time, the major clienteles for department stores was confined to members of high society.

In 1929, Ichizou Kobayashi of Hankyuu Railways founded the world's first railway store in its Osaka Umeda station. Many railway companies followed Kobayashi's lead after the war. The major reason for the prosperity of railway department stores was the rapid growth of population in major cities. The emergence of railway department stores also widened the clienteles of department stores to include the lower-middle class urban masses.

Department stores expanded rapidly to exploit the high-speed economic growth of Japan in the 1960s. At the same time, supermarkets, a new retail format, emerged. In 1953, Kinokuniya built Japan's first self-service supermarket. The rapid growth of the supermarket business coincided with the emergence of a standardized consumer market in which everyone with the wherewithal sought the same material goods. Supermarkets successfully capitalized on this market because they could offer the high-volume and low-profit sales for a limited range of products that best matched this market. Another reason for the rapid growth of the supermarket business in the 1960s was that the expansion of supermarket companies was not limited by the Department Store Law. **Daiei** outperformed Mitsukoshi and became the sales leader of all individual retailing companies in 1972.

Threats also came from another new retail format: specialty shops. From the mid-1960s, a group of customers seeking fashionable merchandise emerged. Companies specializing in different merchandise started to build their specialty shop chains all over Japan to exploit this market.

Department stores responded to these threats in two ways. Firstly, large city department stores started developing shopping malls in suburban areas to cater to the ever-expanding market there, which further facilitated the growth of specialty shops. Secondly, some local department stores joined the merchandise network of large-scale stores and even merged with them.

In the 1970s, large-scale retailers suffered a double blow. The first was the economic downturn after the oil shock. The second was the introduction of the new **Large Retail Store Law** that was extended to also cover general merchandise stores (GMS). Large department stores responded by slowing down new investment and laying off staff. In contrast, the large GMS adopted a diversification strategy.

After the Plaza Accord in 1985, the Japanese yen appreciated rapidly, resulting in the stabilization of the price of consumer goods. At the same time, interest rates were very low but stock prices and property prices were high. The average salary increased rapidly because of a general manpower shortage. These forces allowed the retail market to prosper. The sales of department stores, especially the sales of luxury goods such as jewelry, rebounded very quickly. Department stores invested substantially in building large new stores and creating elegant sales floors for luxury goods. Daiei also continued its diversification strategy in the 1980s, aggressively branching into other non-retail businesses, while **Ito-Yokado** was determined to reform its retail business by building a scientific retail management system to improve its profitability.

However, the sales of department stores in the 1990s declined rapidly following the collapse of the **bubble economy**, while the cost, including new land tax, salary and so forth increased substantially. Consequently, the profits of most department stores continuously decreased from 1992. Some retail analysts even argued that department stores were going to disappear. Large GMS experienced difficult times as well. Even Ito-Yokado, the most profitable, started recording a negative profit growth in 1994. Some companies like Daiei chose to reform the organization of its business. Ito-Yokado did not change its organization, but enhanced the autonomy of each individual store manager.

Large-scale stores

Department stores can be classified according to their origins: those originating from the "kimono tradition" and those from the "railroad tradition." The former have a longer history and have thus generally more prestige than those from the latter. Major kimono stores included Mitsukoshi, Matsuzakaya, Isetan, Takashimaya, Sogou, and Daimaru. The railroad tradition started with Ichizo Kobayashi of Hankyuu Railways in 1929. The idea was simple: railroad companies built their stores in terminals instead of in central business locations, designing them as full-blown department stores from the beginning. Their railroad connections enabled them to go to the customers and to create their own markets. Odakyuu, Keiou, and Tobu were major railway stores in Tokyo. In addition, there was Sotetsu in Yokohama, Meitetsu in Nagoya, and Kintetsu, Hanshin, Hankyuu and Sanyo in the Kansai area.

Suupaa is a truncated loanword and is referred to three forms of supermarkets. The first is called *shokuhin suupaa* (food supermarkets), itself modeled on the supermarkets in the USA. *Shokuhin suupaa*, by definition, must generate no less than 70 percent of their income from food alone. The second is referred to specialty *suupaa* including apparel and household goods *suupaa*. A specialty *suupaa* must have a sales floor of no smaller than 500 square meters and generate no less than 70 percent of its sales from the merchandise it specializes in. The final form is the *sougou suupaa* (general supermarkets) that devote themselves not only to food sales but also to the sale of a wide range of merchandise including textiles, household goods, furniture and electrical appliances. Therefore, the term *sougou suupaa* refers to a sort of combined supermarket and mini-department store which is similar to a department store in form and should be thought of as a GMS.

*Sougou suupaa*s are different from department stores in three major ways: the organization of operations, the number of outlets, and the social prestige attached to them. Generally, most department stores are located in a city's earliest established central business district to emphasize high quality goods, comprehensive customer service, and target high-income customers. *Sougou suupaas* are located close to residential areas, in order to be more easily accessible, focus mainly on daily necessities, and target ordinary housewives.

Shopping centers

Shopping centers in Japan can be classified into two types: general and specialty shopping centers. The general shopping center is a multi-functional retail format that usually includes one or two large-scale retailers as its core stores, supplemented by various retail formats such as specialty shops and local retailers. It also houses restaurants, sport and leisure centers, cinemas, churches, and other public facilities. All these establishments are integrated into a single retail space, catering to different needs of the community in which the shopping center is located. General shopping centers are not just a shopping complex but also a community center.

General shopping centers require large land areas. They are usually located in suburban areas where land is much cheaper than city centers but less accessible by trains. General shopping centers are also located at the nodes of highway networks and provide extensive car parking facilities so that customers can go there by car. This is why general shopping centers did not emerge until cars had become popular and the population of suburban area had grown rapidly in the 1960s. The first shopping center in Japan was the Tamagawa Takashimaya Shopping Center developed by Takashimaya in Tokyo in 1969. Since then, developers have gradually established large general shopping centers all over Japan. Famous large general shopping centers include MYCAL Honmoku, Hikarigaoka, Rarapouto, and Harborland.

Specialty shopping centers do not have core stores. They can be further divided into two types: extensive underground shopping centers and multi-story shopping buildings. The former usually connect with public transport stations and large department stores within city centers. Central Park of Nagoya is one of the most famous underground shopping malls in Japan. Most of the latter are "fashion buildings," which usually have at least four floors, with food stores at the first floor, followed by fashion and variety shops, and finally restaurants at the top floor. These fashion buildings are always located in city centers, close to department stores or main railway stations. Parco of the Saison Group, 109 of Toukyuu Group, and Forus of the Jusco Group are famous fashion buildings in Japan.

Mid-sized and small retailers

Specialty shops refer to any store that generates more than 90 percent of its sales from a single type of merchandise. The strength of specialty shops lies in its expertise in their merchandise, back-up service, and flexible customer service. Specialty shops started to establish chain stores in fashion buildings, underground shopping malls, and shopping centers from the 1960s rather than operating solely through their freestanding outlets because the former was much cheaper than the latter. The development of shopping centers accelerated the expansion of chains of specialty shops. Additionally, during this period newly established families became individualized in taste and fashion conscious, and the merchandise displayed in department stores no longer appealed to them. This explains why many chain stores specializing in electrical appliances, shoes, men's suits, books, furniture, cameras, and so on emerged and prospered after the 1960s. Famous specialty chain stores include Best Denki (electrical), Chiyoda (shoes), Aoyama (men's), Kinokuniya (books), Bic Camera (cameras), and Shimashi (furniture).

Konbini (convenience stores) are defined in Japan as a self-service store, having a sales area of less than 200 square meters, operating no less than sixteen hours a day with no more than two closing days a month, and generating less than 30 percent of total sales from fresh foods. The major merchandise offered by convenience stores are processed food, daily foods, fast foods, and non-food items. It is very obvious that the strength of convenience stores lies in the "convenience" demanded by the urban consumer lifestyle in Japan. **7-11 Japan**, a subsidiary of Ito-Yokado, started Japan's first convenience store in 1973. Other large GMS subsequently established their own convenience stores such as Daiei's Lawson and Seiyu's Family Mart.

The key issues of operating a convenience store are efficient use of space and rapid stock turnover, which are further dependent on accurate estimation of customers' needs thereby avoiding stock-outs or excess inventory. Running a convenience store successfully thus requires advanced information technology and efficient physical distribution systems. Most convenience stores had already equipped themselves with electronic ordering and point-of-sale systems by the 1980s.

Discount stores have no clear definition but generally refer to stores which sell merchandise at 20 to 30 percent discount of the price recommended by manufacturers. Discount stores date back to the 1970s when large GMS branched into other retail businesses including discount stores. These large GMS originally were discount stores at the beginning and they later developed themselves into large GMS, no longer appealing to the customers with low price but through offering a wide range of merchandise. In the 1970s, the large GMS started to develop new discount stores that reduced price by strictly controlling operation costs, rather than by selling low-quality goods. These new discount stores successfully overcame of the image of selling cheap but low-quality goods. Discount stores grew rapidly in the 1980s and reached their peak in the early 1990s when Japan's economic bubble burst. Economic recession led Japanese consumers to seek value for money. Discount stores have been particularly successful in the field of cosmetics, liquor, and imported foreign goods.

Further reading

Larke, R. (1994) *Japanese Retailing*, London: Routledge.

Niikei Ryuutsuu Shinbun (ed.) (1993) *Ryuutsuu gendaishi* (The Modern History of Distribution), Tokyo: Nihon Keizai Shinbun, Inc.

HEUNG-WAH WONG

ringi seido

Ringi seido is a distinguishing characteristic of Japanese management and refers to the proposal discussion system that relies on horizontal and vertical employee participation in reaching a consensus on important organizational decisions. Two key features of this system are the bottom-up nature of employee participation and the circulation of the *ringi-sho*, a proposal document, throughout the sectional, divisional, and corporate levels of the organization to build consensus and commitment to company goals. However, at each level, the formal circulation of a proposal is usually preceded by a thorough discussion of the details and alternative solutions. This process captured the attention of Western managers, researchers, and consultants during the mid and late 1980s when interest in Japanese management peaked.

The *ringi* system can have a significant impact on the effectiveness of organizational structure, strategic planning, **negotiations**, participation, commitment, and **organizational learning**. This is because *ringi seido* is more than just employees signing off on proposals, it is also a significant organizational process driven by information gathering and consensus building objectives. Some of the key activities in this process include:

- problem identification
- information gathering/analysis
- informal discussion/consensus building
- formal meetings and deliberations
- proposals circulated/revised
- final decision and implementation

The range of these activities indicate that *ringi seido* is a multi-step procedure that involves all levels of the organization in the attempt to decide an appropriate course of action. In giving structure to the decision-making environment of Japanese firms, this system impacts many key organizational functions and business strategies.

Japanese organizational structure places great emphasis on intra-firm communication. *Ringi seido* therefore plays a key role in company-wide communication and business strategies. From the open layout of offices to the active rotation of employees throughout the Japanese firm, the focus is on building intra-firm relationships and avenues of communication. Once these are in place, it is then possible to more easily manage firm-specific information, skills, and knowledge. Moreover, the group orientation of Japanese corporate culture provides the mutual monitoring and information sharing that gives direction to many organizational activities. The *ringi* system is clearly an important aspect of the communications network that helps to structure organizational activity in Japanese firms.

Ringi also has an impact on the strategic planning process in Japanese firms. The literature on *ringi* generally highlights the bottom-up aspect of the process. However, it is often the executives at the top that identify a particular problem and indirectly challenge lower and middle managers and their staff to find a solution. By carefully identifying a set of key problems which the organization faces, management lays the groundwork for long-term strategic plans. Lower-level employees' generation of alternative solutions sets the stage for the effective implementation of consensus driven strategies. Many scholars thus point out that Japanese management cleverly combines the decentralization of employee participation with a high concentration of formal authority.

Formal and informal negotiations are key elements of the *ringi* system. The informal process of **nemawashi** (root binding or sounding out) helps to build consensus. This process is extremely important in generating alternative solutions to problems as well as in resolving inter-group or interdivision differences. The literature on intra-firm negotiations point out that Japanese employees and managers often employ informal meetings on the job and after work to suggest solutions and arrive at compromises. It is due to this type of extensive preparation and these behind-the-scenes informal negotiations that the formal circulation of the *ringi-sho* generally becomes a simple process of signing off on accepted proposals.

Since the bottom-up approach of the *ringi* system involves employees in problem solving, it requires the delegation of responsibility and active participation to be successful. In Japanese organizations, the *ringi seido* helps to create a high participation environment. By spreading market information and organizational problems throughout the firm, a sense of crisis can often be created. The goal of management is clearly to mobilize employees to find alternative solutions and share responsibility for the execution of new strategies. In continually sharing information and delegating responsibility, Japanese firms are able to foster a sense of community and enhance organizational commitment. This approach may explain the extensive use of company-wide campaigns in Japanese firms.

Finally, some researchers have linked high participation systems such as *ringi seido* to the organizational learning capabilities of Japanese firms (see **Cole**; **Nonaka**). Organizational learning relies on a firm's ability to harness the information-gathering and problem-solving abilities of individuals and groups, with the goal of converting this knowledge into sustainable company adaptation routines. The development of problem-solving routines and procedural knowledge has been shown to be crucial for effective **quality management**, **product development** and process innovation (see **kaizen**). The *ringi* system can thus be considered as one of the reliable problem-solving and implementation processes that aid organizational learning.

As a group-oriented and consensus-driven decision-making system, *ringi seido* can help to create a sense of community. Although Japanese managers use the system to share responsibility and mobilize employee efforts, it also means that lower ranking employees can have a significant impact on company strategy. Aside from the intra-firm factors mentioned above, the ringi system can impact inter-firm dynamics. Contract negotiations, alliances, affiliate management and new business establishments can all be influenced by *ringi seido*. The process sometimes appears to be slow and frustrating for foreigners doing business with Japanese firms. Moreover, the slower pace and less drastic decisions which result from *ringi seido* can be a disadvantage in rapidly changing environments. However, since there is generally less dissension once a decision is reached, there tends to be faster implementation of the objectives. As with other aspects of Japanese management, this approach to decision making is embedded in complex social relations that depend on trust and a commitment to organizational objectives.

ROBLYN SIMEON

S

salaryman

"Salaryman" is both an image and an occupational category that has come to represent the Japanese middle class. Salaryman refers to white-collar male workers employed by large modern private sector corporations. The term embodies all the stereotypical images associated with Japanese corporate employees: loyalty, commitment and obedience to the firm in exchange for security, protection and rewards from the firm. Although white-collar male employees constitute about a third of the labor force, those working in large private corporations account for less than 15 percent of the labor force. Thus, the class of salaryman is small numerically, but serves as an "ideological reference group" for the working population.

The meaning or image of a salaryman and his relation to his firm can be compared to the *samurai* warrior's relation to his lord. During the Tokugawa period (1603–1867), *samurai* devoted themselves to feudal lords and to the expansion of the privilege and prestige of the lord's house and fief. Notions of loyalty and personal sacrifice have clear parallels with the symbolic conception of the salaryman. Thus, the salaryman is sometimes called the modern *samurai* or corporate warrior.

The metaphorical comparison is powerful, but locating the job category of salaryman within the larger social structure may draw a clearer understanding. The Japanese word *salari man* (salary man) can be traced back to the 1930s. It became popular with the rise of the (new) middle class after 1955. After the Second World War, the farming population declined drastically and the working class

(skilled and unskilled workers) and the middle class (white-collar workers) expanded. Today, the working class and the middle class each constitute slightly over one-third of the working population. Independent small proprietors and their family workers make up about a quarter of the labor force. (Remaining percentages are public sector workers and those unemployed.)

Precarious working conditions that characterize small business sectors are in sharp contrast to working conditions of white-collar employees of large firms. The salaryman's life is more stable and less affected by economic cycles. It provides secure employment and a lifestyle that is bright and glamorous. The stability of the income, job security, career outlook, and the lifestyle constitute the essence of the salaryman and salaryman family.

The salaryman class is generally well-educated. Salarymen are recruited right after graduation from a university, accorded with apparent lifetime employment and pursue careers through the firm-based internal labor market. Large corporations provide the salaryman with housing benefits, family allowances, pensions, housing loans, and recreational benefits. In return for job stability, economic security, and corporate benefits, a salaryman pledges his allegiance to the firm. He is expected to devote himself to the needs and commands of the company at the expense of his personal rights and choices.

The salaryman's career path, which centers on the same company for his entire life, is not a typical career path for Japanese. Given the heavy concentration of small and medium-sized firms in the Japanese economy, job changes are higher than might be expected, especially from medium-sized firms to small firms or from one small firm to another. Overall job mobility rates in Japan are quite comparable to those in Europe. Thus, the concept of salaryman may overlook the high degree of labor mobility among workers in the large number of small enterprises.

The bright image of salaryman as a high-status career changed in the 1980s and 1990s. Lifetime employment, seniority-based promotion, and in-house training have locked salarymen into a rigid system of career attainment. A salaryman's career is shaped and re-shaped depending on the company's goals, allowing little autonomy over his career development. For example, rotations of jobs are a standard part of corporate career development and salarymen are dispatched from one geographical location to another. These company assignments increased the number of *tanshin funin*, temporary family separation. In 1985 there were 200,000 married men who were classified as *tanshin funin* and more than half of these men were in their forties. *Tanshin funin* is often triggered by children's education or family's needs to care for elderly parents. At the age of fifteen, Japanese children take the single most important examination of their lives: high school entrance exams that may well determine their future. Once children enter a good high school, they will have better chances of getting into good universities. Parents attempt to avoid any disruption at this point in their children's education. And so, salary-men take *tanshin funin*.

Salaryman's dedication to a company limits his position in family life to not much more than a bread winner role. Long hours of daily commuting, overtime work, and evening socializing with co-workers leave very little time for personal or family leisure. Young women have begun to expect more family participation from the men. Divorce rates are rising among middle-aged couples, with women claiming it difficult to live with men who have such a single-minded pursuit of work and little usefulness around the home. ***Karoshi***, death from overwork, is also rising and a number of lawsuits have been brought against companies. The courts have upheld a number of wives' claims that their husbands' deaths were caused by the overwork demanded by their companies, ordering the companies to pay compensation.

The celebration of Japan's labor management practices ended abruptly in the 1990s with the steepest slump in Japan's postwar economy. Suddenly companies rushed into restructuring and downsizing, threatening a social contract that has stood at the core of Japan's success. Corporate life that was rigid but secure suddenly became insecure. Employee expectation that loyalty to the company would be returned has been broken.

Further reading

Powell, B., Takayama, H. and McCormick, J. (1995) "Who's Better Off?" in M.I. White and S. Barnet (eds), *Comparing Cultures*, Boston: Bedford Books of St. Martin's Press, 274–83.

Rosen, D. and Usui, C. (1994) "The Social Structure of Japanese Intellectual Property Law," *UCLA Pacific Basin Law Journal* 13(1): 32–69.

Sugimoto, Y. (1997) *An Introduction to Japanese Society*, Cambridge: Cambridge University Press.

Vogel, E.F. (1963) *Japan's New Middle Class*, Berkeley, CA: University of California Press.

CHIKAKO USUI

samurai, role of

Originally a kind of warrior-bodyguard, the role of the *samurai* was completely transformed during the **Tokugawa period** to constitute a portion of a hereditary elite which stood above and ruled over the bulk of the population. *Samurai* were distinguished by their appearance, by the fact that only they could carry weapons, and by language usage. That segment of Japanese society developed its own style of religion, lifestyle and entertainment, and exerted a strong influence on the values of modern Japan.

The word *samurai* brings to mind dramatic images of bravery, dedication to duty, extremely developed fighting skill, a highly idealized vision of masculinity. Originally part of Japanese folklore, those images are now shared by people all over the world. Hollywood has in several instances chosen to use themes and artifacts from the *samurai* tradition in making movies designed to reach the imaginations of young people, even when the setting has nothing to do with Japan. In Japan itself the *samurai* image is introduced to each new generation through relatively accurate historical documentation, and through liberal amounts of entertainment fantasy. When a Japanese boy is born, he is typically provided with a decorative *samurai* helmet and sword for display on Children's Day, a symbol of the new masculine unit of the home. When thought of in a positive light (which is definitely not always the case today), the self-sacrificing salaried employee of a large corporation is sometimes referred to as a modern-day *samurai*.

The word *samurai*, closely associated and often used interchangeably with another word, *bushi*, both denoting warrior, had its initial widespread application in the thirteenth century, and continued to be used to refer to a specific and official category of Japanese men until the end of the nineteenth century. However, glamour associated with the samurai image is actually drawn from only a part of that time, roughly from the early thirteenth to the beginning of the seventeenth centuries. For the final two and three-quarter centuries of its existence during the Tokugawa period and its immediate aftermath, the role of *samurai* was fundamentally altered.

The Tokugawa regime transformed Japan into a system of fiefs or feudal estates tightly controlled and carefully watched over by a central government. The crowning accomplishment of the Tokugawa rulers was the peace the regime was able to enforce for a very long time. Ironically, in a society ruled by warriors, all military activity disappeared under the Tokugawa, and was not to appear anywhere in the land again for more than ten generations.

During Japan's long period of civil wars, wars fought until the mid-1500s almost exclusively by *samurai*, a great many of those warriors did not live past the age of twenty-five. Most *samurai* were sons of *samurai*, but a promising peasant lad could be trained as a *samurai* if he caught the attention of the rulers of his estate, and stories of farm boys who became famous *samurai* are not uncommon. All that changed under the Tokugawa. *Samurai* were made an hereditary caste; for most of the period of Tokugawa rule, the *samurai*, the warrior caste, were

not warriors at all, but rather a category at the bottom rung of a ruling aristocracy.

Samurai was a term used in some cases to refer to all of the ruling aristocracy outside the court nobility surrounding the Emperor in Kyoto. However there were other more specific titles which applied to those of the highest status in feudal Japan, and *samurai*, then and now, most often identified the men at the large bottom level of the Japanese ruling caste. In the eyes of ordinary people, they were a kind of elite police. It is only a slight exaggeration to state that *samurai* lived lives almost completely shut off from ordinary Japanese society.

The *samurai* caste was not a single status; some *samurai* had retainers of their own, and the amount of pay in the form of rice made to each *samurai* family varied considerably. Most were at the bottom of the caste however, and although we can call *samurai* aristocrats due to their elevated status and power over commoners, ordinary *samurai* themselves were not usually wealthy people. Until the very end of the regime, it was shameful for those with real power if *samurai* under their command did not dress well and have the best equipment. However, these things were issued to most *samurai* in the same way that slaves or prisoners are provided for.

During the civil war period, most *samurai* spent most of their waking hours preparing for the inevitable battles. They never constituted a large segment of the people as a whole, probably no more than 1 percent. Soon after 1600, as an official caste in the Tokugawa social system, and with no more fighting to do, *samurai* men began to live as long as other men; together with their families, they came in time to constitute from 7 to 8 percent of the total Japanese population. *Samurai* were normally quartered on the castle grounds of their master, either the *daimyo* of a feudal estate or the head of one of the several branches of the Tokugawa clan. Young *samurai* continued to be trained in the martial arts, but after 1600 there was plenty of time for other pursuits, and over time *samurai* became a highly educated cadre, universally not only literate but well schooled in history and philosophy. Only *samurai* were allowed to carry weapons, and although they swaggered through the streets of Tokugawa Japan with their two swords in evidence, the real job for most *samurai* was as bureaucrats.

See also: giri

Further reading

Shinoda, M. (1960) *The Founding of the Kamakura Shogunate*, New York: Columbia University Press.
Totman, C.D.(1967) *Politics in the Tokugawa Bakufu*, Cambridge, MA: Harvard University Press.
Varley, P.H. (1970) *The Samurai*, London: The Trinity Press.

JOHN A. McKINSTRY

sarakin

A contraction of the Japanese term "salaryman financing," the term *sarakin* refers to finance companies with notoriously high interest rates or involved in loan sharking operations, often with close ties to *yakuza*, the Japanese mafia. *Sarakin* emerged in the 1970s in response to an unmet demand for consumer credit. Major legislative reforms in the early 1980s served to rein in *sarakin* practices. Legislation, however, has not helped *sarakin* overcome the historically negative image of moneylenders. This stands in contrast to their US counterparts who were able to make the transition to becoming financial firms offering a wider array of services. Instead, the gap for consumer credit once filled by *sarakin* has been taken over by banks and *shinpan* (sales finance corporations).

Historical development

In the early 1970s, individuals seeking loans for purposes other than to buy a house confronted social stigma and practical challenges. Social stigma generally attached to people who found themselves in circumstances necessitating the borrowing of funds. In addition to social disapprobation, the market for consumer lending through established banks and other lending institutions was not well developed. There were numerous regulatory barriers besides which industrial demand for investment funds was swallowing up most of the available capital. *Sarakin* stepped in to fill the niche.

Located near virtually every train station and neighborhood, most *sarakin* were small operations, usually with only a single office. The attractiveness of *sarakin* was obvious: they provided small, for the most part unsecured, loans and required little more than a signature. Annual interest rates, however, were exorbitant, often exceeding 100 percent. Indeed, the legal limit at that time was 109.5 percent. For delinquent payers, collection methods were aggressive, and included such things as personal visits to one's residence, intimidating calls to one's employer and threats of physical violence. One estimate of *sarakin* with *yakuza* ties placed the number at over 3,000. Despite their overall unsavory image, by 1975 *sarakin* held 4 percent of Japan's total consumer credit.

The second half of the 1970s and early 1980s saw explosive growth among the *sarakin*. Their share of consumer credit grew to nearly 14 percent in 1982 from its 4 percent level in 1975. The number of *sarakin* also grew dramatically, with some estimates placing the number of *sarakin* at roughly 220,000. Though most of these were still of the one-office variety, four of the largest operated nationwide, with hundreds of offices, and holding individuals' accounts numbering in the hundreds of thousands.

In 1983, the Diet passed the Loan Shark Control Bill, reining in the growth of *sarakin* and significantly reducing the maximum annual interest rate allowed. The top rate was lowered in phases from 109.5 percent to 73 percent in 1983, then to 54.75 percent in 1986, and then to a final position of 40 percent in 1991. The legislation came about in response to widespread social concern over *sarakin*-related suicides and disappearances. A study by the National Police Academy identified over 1,000 suicides which it classified as *sarakin*-related. It also classified 10,000 disappearances as *sarakin*-related, suspecting these people of fleeing creditors. In a separate analysis, fifteen murders in the first four months of 1984 were also classed as *sarakin*-related.

Despite the 1983 legislation, numerous *sarakin* continued to operate as usual. In one instance, the Saitama police arrested three loan sharks for charging ¥40,000 interest on a three-day loan of

¥60,000, fifteen times the allowable rate of ¥3,700. Such incidents prompted an investigation by the National Tax Agency, which concluded that 80 percent of *sarakin* were evading taxes and generating incomes three times the reported average.

Over time the Loan Shark Act took its toll. The phased-in interest rates, coupled with the growth of consumer lending practices among banks and *shinpan* led to a shakeout. From a peak of 220,000 in 1980, *sarakin* numbers dropped to 37,000 by the early 1990s. Some observers speculate that bad practices winnowed out many of the small *sarakin*. Poor screening processes, unsophisticated collection methods and high levels of unrecovered loans drove out many. Those who remained pursued cooperative efforts in terms of sharing credit information and sought scale economies in transaction processing.

Large *sarakin* who survived the shakeout of the early 1990s are thriving at the turn of the century. Takeufuji reported 1999 earnings at nearly ¥53 billion, a 27.8 percent improvement over 1998. Acom and Promise, two others, reported similar earnings levels. At the same time, leading *sarakin* have dropped their top annual rates down to a range of 25.55 to 29.2 percent. Finally, consumer behavior suggests that the position of *sarakin* will remain prominent. The average level of consumer debt (using the ratio of debt:disposable income) for Japanese now exceeds that of the USA.

ALLAN BIRD

science and technology policy

Japan's science and technology policy historically emphasized the importation and adaptation of foreign technology. This was considered essential to Japan's military and economic security. After the Second World War, the focus on foreign technology continued, though the emphasis shifted almost exclusively to commercially important technologies. As Japan moved to a leadership position economically and closed its technological gaps with the West in the 1960s and 1970s, new concerns emerged. These included the development of a stronger ability to perform basic research and to contribute to the world stock of technology.

Although Japanese policy makers have tended to craft more coherent statements of national science and technology policy than their US counterparts over the years, the Japanese government has always spent far less as a percentage of overall national R&D spending than the US government.

Through the Second World War

Although the Tokugawa government (1603–1868) severely restricted Japan's contacts with the outside world from the early seventeenth century until the mid-nineteenth century, it did allow the import of foreign books on science and technology and supported the translation of many of them. After Japan was opened to contact with the Western world, its government hoped to combine Western technology with Japanese values, thereby building a strong nation able to maintain its independence. In the late nineteenth century, foreign engineers were hired to help build a technological infrastructure and to teach technology to the Japanese. Young Japanese were also sent abroad to learn about technology. By 1873, more than 500 foreigners were working for the Japanese government and some 250 Japanese were studying abroad at government expense.

The Japanese government also began structuring itself to import and adapt foreign technology. The Ministry of Engineering (also called Ministry of Industry) was established in 1870 with the major mission of bringing in mining and manufacturing technology. In 1886 the Patent Office was established. Government involvement in technology accelerated during the First World War. Around this time the Ministry of Education began offering research grants for natural science research. National Research Institutes in such fields as electrical engineering and metallurgy were also set up. The military established R&D centers: the Naval Research Institute, in particular, became quite strong in the electronics area, and wartime researchers at the institute, including **Morita** Akio (a co-founder of **Sony**), went on to become leaders in the consumer electronics industry.

As international tensions escalated in the 1930s, the Japanese government sought to mobilize its technological resources. In general, these efforts were unsuccessful. Rivalries between the military services, shortages of materials, and the induction of many researchers into the military, all weakened the development of Japanese technology. The severance of ties with foreign sources of technology in the United States and Europe also hurt.

Postwar period

With the end of the Second World War, US occupation authorities dismantled the Japanese wartime technology policy apparatus and prohibited research in areas such as aviation and radar. Many aviation researchers moved to the automobile industry and many of the radar researchers moved to the consumer electronics (and later the semiconductor) industry.

In the early postwar era, Japan desperately needed to import new technologies. At the time Japan was chronically short of foreign exchange, which was rigidly rationed by the government. A major challenge was to establish mechanisms for Japanese firms to pay foreigners for technology. A framework for doing this was established with the passage of the Foreign Exchange and Foreign Trade Control Law (1949) and the Foreign Investment Law (1950). Under these laws, Japanese firms applied to the government, most often the **Ministry of International Trade and Industry** (MITI), for approval of technology import agreements. If approval was granted the firm was allowed the foreign currency to pay for the technology. In the 1950s and 1960s some 13,000 agreements were screened and approved by the government. While government involvement may have slowed the flow of technology into Japan, it apparently also resulted in Japanese firms getting better terms than they might have otherwise. MITI could refuse to approve agreements if the terms seemed too generous to foreigners. It could also keep Japanese firms from bidding against each other to raise the price of a technology.

The emergence of modern science and technology policy

While MITI, the **Ministry of Finance**, and other ministries concerned themselves with Japan's technology import policies, other initiatives in the area of science and technology and policy were

begun in the 1950s. In 1956 the Science and Technology Agency (STA) was established as a cabinet-level body reporting to the prime minister. This signified that science and technology policy was formally recognized as having an important role within the national government. In 1959 the Council for Science and Technology (CST) was established with STA staff to make recommendations to the prime minister on the overall directions of Japanese science and technology policy.

In 1960 the CST proposed a comprehensive plan for the development of science and technology in Japan over the coming decade. This was part of the government's **income doubling plan**. The comprehensive plan called for the elimination of the technological gaps between Japan and the West. It recommended increasing the number of science and engineering universities and increasing spending on R&D to 2 percent of GDP, double the 1959 level. This would have been comparable to the percentage in the UK, though still below the 2.7 percent being spent at the time by the USA.

While the STA concentrated on general policies and on certain national projects, such as those related to nuclear energy and space exploration, MITI shifted its interest from technology import controls (which were being phased out as Japan joined the OECD) to policies that would promote the development and use of industrial technology. In its "vision" for the 1960s, MITI proposed a variety of policies for the promotion of industrial technology, including the use of subsidies and tax relief. At this time the decision was also made to build Tsukuba Science City.

In 1966, the CST issued new recommendations on science and technology policy designed to help Japan cope with the opening of its economy. Now the target was for R&D spending to reach 2.5 percent of GDP, near the US level. The CST wanted to see a new emphasis on long-term planning. CST's proposed Basic Law for Science and Technology, however, was not passed.

Changes in the 1970s

As Japan entered the 1970s it was no longer a poor country, and policy concerns shifted from economic growth to environmental protection. The energy crises of the 1970s brought new interest in energy conservation and finding alternative sources of energy. Japanese policy makers also believed Japan had to become competitive in emergent new industries. In its recommendations for the 1970s, the CST gave new attention to technology assessment and soft science. It set a long-term goal of increasing Japan's investment in R&D to 3 percent of GDP. As Japan became embroiled in conflicts with its trade partners, and the Japanese became concerned about their image as a nation of copiers, there was new interest in international cooperation in the development of technology.

MITI also issued a new vision for the 1970s that called for the development of pollution control technology, energy-saving technology and alternative sources of energy. In a 1975 interim report, MITI called for research on nuclear fusion and computers. One MITI policy device was the use of **research cooperatives**, made up of industrial firms and government laboratories supported by government subsidies and tax benefits. Perhaps the most publicized of these was the **VLSI Research Cooperative** which targeted the development of semiconductor technologies for use in computers. Although the VLSI consortium is generally portrayed as having been successful in accelerating Japan's technology progress, the record of the research cooperatives in general is controversial. In the 1980s MITI established new R&D programs to promote "future" industries, including new materials and biotechnology. Another new area of policy was the creation of regional technology centers.

CST believed Japan's major priorities for the 1980s should include a strengthening of its ability in basic research. Throughout the 1980s the CST worked on the development of basic guidelines for a new science and technology policy for Japan. In a report approved by the cabinet in 1986 two main pillars of science and technology policy were identified, basic research and internationalization. Now the goal was to increase R&D spending to 3.5 percent of GDP.

After the bubble

After the bursting of the **bubble economy** of the 1980s, new problems emerged for Japan's science and technology policymakers. Corporate spending on R&D declined for the first time since the Second World War in 1992 and again in 1993. Enrollments in science and engineering departments started declining in 1988. Younger Japanese seemed to be turning away from an interest in science and technology.

The CST revised the general guidelines for science and technology policy. A new Science and Technology Basic Law, based on the revisions, was passed by the Japanese Diet in 1995. The new law called for government to prepare and implement two successive five-year basic plans. The goals of the plans were to make the Japanese science and technology system more innovative and cost efficient by addressing such problems as the decline in private R&D spending, the generally poor Japanese R&D infrastructure, and the obsolescence of facilities at national universities and national laboratories.

The guidelines pointed to other problems and suggested remedies. It noted, for example, the relative lack of mobility of Japanese researchers between the government, private and university sectors. Under the new law, professors at national universities would be freer to work as consultants or in joint research with the private firms. The new law also introduced more competition amongst those applying for government research support and sought to standardize the review process. It increased the number of postdoctoral fellowships and sought to encourage more foreign researchers to work in Japan. New tax deductions and subsidies were offered to encourage small and medium sized firms to spend more on research. The new law also supported the development of regional science and technology centers.

Major changes in Japan's administrative structure are scheduled for 2001. The STA is to be merged with the Ministry of Education, Science and Culture. STA's Atomic Energy and Nuclear Safety Bureaus are to be moved to MITI. MITI's research institutes are to be merged into a new Industrial Science and Technology Institute. The Institute will be an independent administrative agency partially funded by the government, but not considered to be part of the government.

Distinctive features of Japan's science and technology policy

Japan's science and technology policies have

differed somewhat from those of the USA and Western Europe. There was a much greater emphasis on the acquisition of foreign technology, particularly in the first few decades after the Second World War. There was little emphasis on defense spending and, partly as a consequence of that, the share of R&D spending supported by the government was typically lower (20 percent in the late 1990s, compared to more than 30 percent for the USA). Another consequence of the lack of emphasis on defense spending was that the Japanese government was far less able to offer the lure of government procurements to encourage the development of specific technologies.

Further reading

Callon, S. (1995) *Divided Sun: MITI and the Break-down of Japanese High-Tech Industrial Policy, 1975–1993*, Stanford, CA: Stanford University Press.

Goto, A. and Odagiri, H. (eds) (1997) *Innovation in Japan*, New York: Oxford University Press.

Lynn, L. (1982) *How Japan Innovates: A Comparison with the U.S. in the Case of Oxygen Steelmaking*, Boulder, CO: Westview.

Morris-Suzuki, T. (1994) *The Technological Transformation of Japan*, New York: Cambridge University Press.

Science and Technology Agency, Japan (annual) *Indicators of Science and Technology*. Tokyo: Ministry of Finance Printing.

—— (annual) *Kagaku gijutsu hakusho* (Science and Technology White Paper), Tokyo: Ministry of Finance Printing.

LEONARD H. LYNN

seniority promotion

Known as *nenko joretsu* in Japanese, along with **lifetime employment** and **enterprise unions**, seniority promotion is considered one of the **three sacred treasures** of the Japanese management system. It refers to the practice of promoting employees on the basis of seniority in the firm rather on the basis of merit. This type of promotion system is sometimes described as an "escalator," suggesting that one steps on at the bottom and then automatically rises within the organization. It is often portrayed as reflecting the collective, egalitarian nature of Japanese organizations and as being rooted in the deeper values of Japanese society. However, it applies only to permanent, or regular, employees of the firm, whose numbers comprise a minority within the total labor force and even within the company. Moreover, the evidence for seniority promotion suggests that the practice is more textured than is commonly thought. In the face of a prolonged recession, heightened competition with non-Japanese firms both at home and abroad and a tight labor market for college graduates, firms are moving away from their emphasis on seniority as a key criterion in promotion decisions.

Cultural foundations

Harking back to pre-Meiji era *ie*, Japanese work organizations have had a long history of respect for seniority. At a more fundamental level, the foundation for seniority promotion is sociocultural norms rooted in the Confucian-based values of respect and deference toward seniors. The assumption embedded in this value is that as a consequence of age and experience, seniors have more knowledge and wisdom. Within a workplace context, this same assumption is held. Longer tenure implies a greater knowledge of the firm and its competitive environment that translates into better judgment. Within the merchant houses and **guilds** of the pre-Meiji era, there was good reason to accept this assumption, as individuals worked their way up through apprenticing to someone more skilled and more knowledgeable. The correlation between age, experience and knowledge/skill was more clearly discernible.

A related rationale for the logic of seniority promotion is that given the norms in the larger social context, employees of an organization would feel uncomfortable working for someone younger than themselves or supervising someone older than themselves. In short, seniority promotion was deemed necessary to maintenance of good company morale and harmony.

Seniority promotion is also predicated on the notion of rewarding loyalty. Advancement in rank is recompense for working hard on the company's behalf. A refinement of this argument is that promotion is a form of "serial equity" in which the employee works hard in the early years in exchange for the promise of greater reward and promotion later in the career.

The reality of seniority promotion

Western discussion of seniority promotion has often been simplistic. A superficial case for seniority promotion is easily found in the behavior of **torishimaryakukai** (board of directors) at the time that a new president is selected. The traditional practice, still common, is for members of the *torishimariyakukai* (board of directors) who are younger than the incoming president to resign their positions, either immediately or at the end of their two-year appointment. Though this phenomenon appears to support the notion of seniority promotion, it does not withstand close scrutiny. Under a pure seniority system, there would be no one older than the incoming president (though there might be some who were the same age). There are other equally compelling explanations for what transpires with the succession of presidents. As the new president will have a tenure of six to eight years, directors who are older have little prospect of further advancement. New presidents also prefer to have their own people in place, so it is natural to leave and make room for them. Elements of the values underlying seniority promotion may contribute to exit phenomena surrounding CEO succession, but alone do not provide a compelling explanation.

The evidence for seniority promotion at lower levels of the organization is equally complex, due to the length of time between promotions and the nature of cohort recruitment. In large firms, employees enter directly from university in large cohorts. Japanese firms tend to hire annually in large cohorts and employ an internal labor market system (see **internal labor markets**) in which job vacancies are filled from below rather than from an external labor pool. Large, particularly traditional, firms tend to prolong the period before one's initial promotion as compared to Western firms, where promotions can occur early in one's career. As a result, these cohorts tend to move up and through the organization as a group. However, over time they will begin to separate based on performance. For high performers, the first promotion to a managerial position (most likely *kakaricho*, sub-section head) will come as early as the fifth year. For average performers, promotion to *kakaricho* may not come until year seven or eight. If subsequent promotion opportunities present themselves on a four-year basis, and differences in rates of promotion persist, then over a sixteen-year period high-performing and average-performing members of the same cohort will find themselves several levels apart. When one factors in the presence of new cohorts entering annually and the recognition that firms have a pyramidal structure, it is difficult to countenance a pure seniority promotion system

The metaphor of promotion as an "escalator" requires some modification. First, access to the escalator is highly restricted, applying only to permanent employees. Second, there are multiple escalators – at least one for each cohort. Third, based on performance, managers end up on escalators that move at different rates. Finally, through **shukko** and related practices, voluntary exit and **outplacement**, workers are moved off the escalator in order to make room for those below them.

Age versus ability

The conception of seniority promotion derives from a much larger distinction between Japanese and Western firms, the relative importance of age and ability as criteria on which to base not only promotion decisions, but also decisions on compensation. The traditional Japanese system has tended to place a greater emphasis on age as a criterion for both pay and promotion than is found in Western firms. Japanese have tended to give age more importance. It is important to note that even in Western countries, seniority carries weight and contributes both to pay and promotion decisions. However, its relative weight has been much greater in Japan.

There is evidence that the relative weight of age has been shifting, particularly from the 1980s onward. A tightening labor market has left new recruits with more options, to which they have responded with higher levels of mobility. In order to retain them, firms have been moving up promotion timetables and increasing the weight of performance criteria in making promotion decisions. The presence of Western firms, which no longer suffer a stigma as unstable employers, has served to amplify the different options open to new recruits: fast versus slow promotion, performance versus tenure.

The internationalization of Japanese firms has also forced many to confront conflicting pay and promotion policies between Japan-based operations and overseas subsidiaries. The pressure to standardize, or at least bring into greater conformity, human resource management policies and practices has led many to opt for increasing the weight of performance over age. Internationalization has also created a competitive environment in which seniority promotion policies placed Japanese firms at a competitive labor disadvantage.

Finally, many of the most dynamic industries in twenty-first century Japan – high tech, **e-commerce**, financial services, telecommunications, biotech – are industries without strong ties to the traditional Japanese management system and led by younger business leaders, often operating on the periphery of the established, conservative business community. Consequently, firms in these industries have demonstrated a greater willingness to break with business norms and sociocultural values.

Further reading

Brown, C., Nakata, Y., Reich, M. and Ulman, L. (1997) *Work and Pay in the United States and Japan*, New York: Oxford University Press.

Clark, R. (1979) *The Japanese Company*, Berkeley, CA: University of California Press.

Tachibanaki, T. (1996) *Wage Determination and Distribution in Japan*, New York: Oxford University Press.

Rohlen, T. (1974) *For Harmony and Strength*, Berkeley, CA: University of California Press.

ALLAN BIRD

7-11 Japan

7-11 Japan is Japan's largest chain of convenience stores, with 8,200 outlets nationwide. The company helped revolutionize retailing in Japan in the 1970s and 1980s, pioneering the development of the convenience store industry and introducing computerized point-of-sale (POS) systems to improve inventory and shelf space management and enhance profitability.

Prior to the 1970s, Japanese retailing was dominated by small mom-and-pop stores and a few large department stores. During the 1960s and 1970s, the retail chain Ito-Yokado built a growing chain of **superstores** – multi-story stores containing several types of retail outlets – in suburban areas of Japan. The success of **Ito-Yokado** and other superstores hurt the business of mom-and-pop operations, prompting the Japanese government to establish the **Large Retail Store Law** to protect small shop owners. Enacted in 1974 and strengthened in 1979, the Large Retail Store Law restricted the opening of new stores with sales floors above a certain size and limited the operating hours of new and existing large stores.

In 1974, Ito-Yokado secured a license from Dallas-based Southland Corporation to operate 7-11 stores in Japan. Fifteen 7-11s were opened in Japan in that year, and over the next twenty-five years the chain expanded at a rate of over 300 new outlets per year. With an average floor space of only 1,000 square feet, the stores avoided regulation under the Large Retail Store Law and competed successfully with the mom-and-pop stores on basis of long operating hours and lower prices. 7-11 Japan followed a policy of franchising stores rather than owning them, and many small retailers became 7-11 franchises. In 1991, Ito-Yokado bought out Southland, the owner and operator of the 7-11 chain in North America. In the 1990s, 7-11 was Japan's most profitable retailer. Total sales in 2000 were $20 billion.

7-11 Japan owes much of its success to innovative management, particularly the introduction and development of point-of-sale (POS) systems that monitor the flow of every item of merchandise through purchase, inventory, sale, and restocking. First introduced in 1982, 7-11 Japan's POS systems allowed two-way information flow between individual stores and company headquarters, and revealed clearly and immediately which products sold well and which did not. The profit performance of individual items replaced supplier power as the determinant of which products were given shelf space. Centralized ordering also gave 7-11 increased bargaining power with distributors, resulting in more frequent and smaller deliveries.

7-11 Japan has also steadily increased the number of products and services offered in its stores; consumers can purchase an astounding variety of items, as well as make color copies, send faxes, order tickets, and pay electric, gas, water, telephone, insurance, and NHK television bills. In 2000, with further land-based growth becoming difficult and online shopping taking off in Japan, 7-11 Japan joined with **NEC**, **Sony**, **Mitsui** & Co, Japan Travel Bureau and other leading Japanese firms to set up an e-commerce market which integrated the convenience of online shopping with in-store payments and merchandise pick-up capabilities.

TIM CRAIG

shareholder weakness

Japanese managers have not had much pressure from shareholders. One of the main reasons for this is that the majority of shares in Japanese firms have been held by so-called stable shareholders such as affiliated or *keiretsu* firms, banks, and insurance companies. These shareholders, who are called *antei kabunushi* or *seisaku toshika'* in Japanese ("stable shareholders" or "strategic investors") often have other relationships, such as lending, insurance sales and other commercial trades with the firm in which they own shares. In many cases, these equity holdings are reciprocated among affiliated firms through cross-shareholding arrangements (see **cross-shareholdings**). It is suggested that 70–75 percent of listed shares of Japanese firms are owned by stable shareholders and 15–20 percent of listed shares are cross-held, although these numbers have been declining in recent years.

It is commonly argued that stable shareholders own shares primarily to cement and grow stable business relationships rather than to earn returns on their equity investments and thus, shares held by stable shareholders are rarely if ever sold. Because of these motives in shareholdings, stable sharcholders' main concern has not been stock price appreciation or dividend incomes. Thus, stable shareholders have not been exerting much pressure on management of the company in which they hold shares to improve investment return to shareholders. Also, because of cross-shareholding relationships, some stable shareholders have a strong incentive not to meddle with other companies' management because such action may be reciprocated. These arrangements, therefore, allow management to maintain strong control over the company.

In addition to large shareholdings by stable shareholders, the role of the board of directors of Japanese firms functions to allow managers to pay only minimum attention to the shareholders' interests. Although the directors of the board are assumed to represent shareholders, they are not motivated to do so because they are usually chosen by the president and are thus in effect junior officers of the company. Further, very few directors own stock in the company or are compensated through stock price-linked packages, although such compensation plans are increasing in recent years. Thus, there is no internal mechanism that can promote the interests of shareholders who seek investment returns.

While shareholders of Japanese firms have had only limited influence over management, this situation shows some sign of change due primarily to the changing ownership structure. In recent years, Japanese firms and banks have been gradually selling their shareholdings in other companies and unwinding part of their cross-shareholdings, and share-ownership by foreign institutional investors has been increasing. Although it is far from the situation in the USA, the number of investors who are sensitive to investment returns is increasing.

See also: corporate governance; torishimariyakukai

Further reading

Abegglen, J. and Stalk, G. (1985) *Kaisha: The Japanese Corporation*, New York: Basic Books.

Charkham, J. (1994) *Keeping Good Companies: A Study of Corporate Governance in Five Countries*, Oxford: Clarendon Press.

Gerlach, M.L. (1992) *Alliance Capitalism: The Social Organization of Japanese Business*, Berkeley, CA: University of California Press.

Kester, W.C. (1991) *Japanese Takeovers: The Global Contest for Corporate Control*, Boston: Harvard Business School Press.

TORU YOSHIKAWA

Sharp

Sharp Corporation is a major Japanese electronics company known as a pioneer in developing and introducing new products, including Japan's first commercial radio and television sets, and the world's first electronic calculator and liquid crystal display (LCD). Sharp was founded in 1912 by Tokuji **Hayakawa**, an inventor whose first patent was for a snap buckle called the Tokubijo. In 1915, Hayakawa invented the Ever-Sharp mechanical pencil, from which his young company later took its name. In the 1920s Sharp moved into the field of electronics, starting with the assembly of crystal radio sets in 1925 and the development of Japan's first AC vacuum tube radio (the Sharp Dyne) in 1929. The company developed and began mass producing televisions in 1953 and microwave ovens in 1962, and electronic desktop calculators in 1966.

Since the 1970s, Sharp has become especially well-known as a leader in LCD and optoelectronic technology. In 1973, Sharp introduced the world's first practical liquid crystal display, in the form of the EL-805 LCD pocket calculator. Until that time, calculators had used fluorescent character display tubes or light-emitting diodes for the number display. These consumed a large amount of energy, severely limiting the length of time a calculator could operate on batteries. Using an LCD for the number display meant that much less power was required; the EL-805 could run for 100 hours on a single AA battery, about 1 percent of the energy consumption of previous calculators. Although priced higher than other calculators, the EL-805 sold well, starting a trend toward smaller and thinner machines. By 1979, Sharp was producing a calculator that was only 1.6 mm thick.

Sharp has continued to push LCD and optoelectronics technologies forward, and to apply these to a broad range of products, including electronic translators, video cameras and projectors, wall-mounted televisions, fax machines, copiers, and notebook PCs (personal computers).

In 2000, Sharp had 60,000 employees worldwide. Almost half were working in its sixty-six overseas operations, which included representative offices, sales subsidiaries, manufacturing plants, and research and development centers in thirty different countries.

See also: electronics industry

TIM CRAIG

Shibusawa, Eiichi

Eiichi Shibusawa (1840–1931) was a prominent businessman who lived during the most extraordinary changes in Japanese history. Often called the father of modern Japanese capitalism, he was one of the most crucial agents of change during the Meiji and Taisho periods. His contribution may be categorized into four areas. First, Shibusawa is known as a banker-entrepreneur who helped build more than 500 companies, covering the entire spectrum of the new economy. Second, he is known as the founder of *zaikai*. He advocated a new style of business policy leadership through the organization of business and commerce associations that stand as a counterbalance to the government. Third, Shibusawa pursued active roles for business associations and leaders in international economic diplomacy, especially in improving US–Japan relations. Fourth, he advocated the moral obligations of business leaders to the community and stood at the forefront of philanthropy in education and social reform.

Shibusawa was born in 1840 to a wealthy farmer-merchant family in Chiaraijima, Saitama prefecture, a village some fifty miles northwest of Tokyo. The family had substantial land holdings, where rice, barley, indigo, and silkworms were cultivated. At the age of fourteen, the young Shibusawa was brought into the family business. Under the stratified class system of the Tokugawa era, business and commerce were looked down upon and merchants were kept in the lowest class. Wealthy merchant families did not escape from the arbitrary use of power by the ruling *samurai* class. Shibusawa's family's experience was no exception. The family was often obliged to make substantial donations to their local *daimyo*. In recognition of family "services" Shibusawa's father was given official permission to use a surname and wear a pair of *samurai* swords. Though this was a standard means for rewarding rich farmers and merchants who contributed to *daimyo*'s finances, it did not mean the family received respect from the authority.

In 1861, at the age of twenty-two, Shibusawa went to Tokyo. This was a time when Japan was swept with violent confrontations between the Tokugawa Bakufu and several powerful domains (Satsuma, Choshu, Tosa). A struggle, triggered by the Bakufu's signing of a Treaty of Commerce with the USA in 1858, ensued between these groups. Shibusawa himself attempted to organize a local uprising against the Bakufu. However, by an ironic twist of fate, instead of carrying out his original intention of overthrowing the Bakufu, he became a Bakufu retainer at Hitotsubashi House in Kyoto, a high-ranking branch of the ruling Tokugawa family. Starting as a doorkeeper, Shibusawa moved up the ranks quickly as he successfully carried out tax reform for the Hitotsubashi domain. When the Tokugawa Shogun decided to send his younger brother to the World's Fair in Paris, Shibusawa was given the opportunity to accompany the young lord. The delegation departed in February 1867 but was abruptly ordered to return to Japan after the Tokugawa Bakufu collapsed and the Meiji Emperor was restored. The group returned from a nearly two-year study of Paris in late 1868.

In 1870 Shibusawa was unexpectedly recruited into the Meiji government's Ministry of Finance to modernize Japan's tax and monetary systems. He helped create the Daiichi Kokuritsu Ginko, the first national, Western-style banking institution in 1873. However, he resigned from the ministry soon after and became chief executive officer (*todori*) of Daiichi. He was then thirty-four years of age. From his position at Daiichi until his retirement in 1916, Shibusawa built Western forms of organizations (*kabushiki kaisha*) ranging from paper mills and cotton spinning to railroad and shipping, public utilities, life insurance, hotels and theaters, and resort development. Some of the high-profile companies he built include Oji Paper, Osaka Cotton Spinning, Tokyo Chemical Fertilizer, Shinagawa Glass, Ishikawajima Shipyard, Tokyo Gas, Tokyo Electric Light, Tokyo Marine Insurance, and Tokyo Imperial Hotel.

Shibusawa advocated a "group-oriented" capitalism, with emphasis on business involvement in government policy. There were two contrasting styles of thought on capitalist development at the beginning of Meiji. One style is represented by Shibusawa, and the other by Iwasaki, who founded the Mitsubishi **zaibatsu**. Iwasaki's ideas were closer to a Western style of monopoly capitalism with ownership control. In contrast, Shibusawa believed that a society prospers when business organizations pool resources and form groups (*zaikai*). Top business managers would be *zaikai jin*, or the people who think about the future of the industry as a whole and lead the industry. In addition, Shibusawa wanted *zaikai* to stand as a counterbalance to the government, opposing the heavy-handed government control of business and the stratified class system that kept merchants in the lowest class. He emphasized the importance of business leading the government. To nurture talent in business and to foster high status and respect for the business world, Shibusawa organized business associations, beginning with the Tokyo Chamber of Commerce (Tokyo Shoko Kaigisho) in 1891 and the Japan Federation of the Chamber of Commerce involving some fifteen local associations in 1892.

Shibusawa's vision was not limited to domestic economic development. He advocated that US–Japan relations be based on a multilateral framework that included China. Furthermore, he initiated business/economic diplomacy (*minkan keizai gaiko*) as a distinct non-government track of diplomacy operating at the level of business and industrial associations. Shibusawa emphasized the importance of exchanging economic/business missions composed of corporate leaders and representatives of business associations between countries. He believed that these activities are a part of corporate leaders' responsibilities and should not be limited to government level diplomacy or individual businessmen's negotiations.

From the early stage of his career, Shibusawa initiated philanthropic activities in education and social welfare (for example, Tokyo Yoikuin). As a dedicated student of the Chu Tzu school of Confucianism, he emphasized "Rongo to Soroban," expressing through his business principles that the pursuit of profit must be guided by moral obligations to the society and community. Inspired by his observations during his tour of Europe and the USA, he considered philanthropic activities a necessity for good business leadership and demonstration of corporate responsibility to the local community.

Further reading

Kimura, M. (1991) *Shibusawa Eiichi*, Tokyo: Chuo koronsha.

Obata, K. (1938) *An Interpretation of the Life of Viscount Shibusawa*, Tokyo: Tokyo Printing Company.

Sakaiya, T. (1997) *Twelve People Who Made Japan*, Tokyo: PHP.

Shibusawa Kenkyukai (ed.) (1999) *Koeki no Tsuikyusha: Shibusawa Eiichi*, Tokyo: Yamakawa Shuppansha.

CHIKAKO USUI

shingikai

Translated as "deliberation councils," *shingikai* is the general designation of more than 200 government-appointed public advisory bodies, also variously named *chousakai, shinsakai, kyougikai, kaigi*, and *iinkai*. Established by legislation or government ordinance, they form a highly salient tip of an iceberg of formal, semiformal, and informal networks of government–private sector consultation in practically all areas of public policy.

Shingikai are appointed, assisted, and steered mostly by government ministries. Several, including some of the most famous ones, have been appointed by prime ministers. Their membership is partly or wholly composed of persons from outside government, notably representatives of special interest groups, scholars, and even senior members of the major mass media. They are formally requested to study and deliberate new policies, to consider complaints, standards, qualifications, authorizations, and administrative punishments, and, very rarely, to mediate conflicts of interests.

Most government bills are being considered in *shingikai* prior their submission to the National Diet (parliament).

Historically, the roots of Japanese public advisory bodies go back to the Meiji era. But it was the **American occupation** which, as part of a series of democratic reforms, called for *shingikai*'s statutory foundation and, for the first time, specified guidelines regarding their structure and operation. Initially, the occupation authorities intended all advisory bodies to be formed on an ad hoc basis and to be of the formal, *shingikai* variety. In fact, however, most of them have become "permanent," and their members are appointed for fixed, but renewable, terms. And in due course, alongside *shingikai*, numerous semiformal bodies, misleadingly known as *shiteki shimon kikan* ("private" advisory bodies), have been formed by government. Some of these bodies have been similar to *shingikai* in salience, membership composition, tasks, and functions.

The occupation, and ostensibly Japanese authorities, have three major goals for *shingikai*: injecting new ideas into government, promoting equitable public participation in policy processes, and safeguarding fairness in administration. In fact, it has widely been argued, *shingikai* have failed to achieve these goals for lack of autonomy, competence, and representativeness. Allegedly, they are controlled and/or manipulated by bureaucrats who appoint their members and "service" them; they lack pertinent information and data, other than that provided by bureaucrats; and their membership is skewed in favor of business and finance, such as *zaikai* and **industry and trade associations**. While justified in some cases, this view is somewhat outdated, especially in the case of labor policy processes, and fails to fully grasp *shingikai*'s roles in the complex and subtle context of policy consultation in Japan.

See also: industrial policy; nemawashi

Further reading

Harari, E. (1997) "The Government-Media Connection in Japan: The Case of Public Advisory Bodies," *Japan Forum* 9: 17–38.

Kume, I. (2000) "Roudou seisaku katei no seijuku

to henyou" (Maturity and Transfiguration of
Labor Policy Process), *Nihon roudou kenkyuu kikou*
42: 2–13.

Schwartz, F.J. (1998) *Advice and Consent: The Politics of
Consultation in Japan*, Cambridge: Cambridge
University Press.

Sone Kenkyuukai (1995) *Rinchou gata shingikai*
(Temporary Investigative Council Type *Shingikai*), Tokyo: Keio Daigaku Hougakubu.

Sone, Y. (1998) "'Zoku gakusha' ga habiru
shingikai wa haishi yori kyousou wo" (Instead
of Abolishing Shingikai Strewn With "Tribal
Scholars," Make Them Competitive), *Ronza* 43:
106–13.

EHUD HARARI

Shingo, Shigeo

An industrial engineer at **Toyota**, Shigeo Shingo
(1909–90) developed Zero Quality Control (ZQC),
which is based on preventing errors in manufacturing processes, or detecting them simply and
immediately. Key to ZQC are *poka-yoke*, mistake-
proofing, devices. These are simple checks built
into the process, to prevent a faulty component
from proceeding down the line (e.g., physical
blocking of an oversized piece) or to provide
immediate feedback to workers regarding a
problem (e.g., a buzzer). Noticed quickly, the faulty
component can be repaired or removed before it
creates more difficult and expensive problems later
in the process. Shingo also developed single-minute
exchange of die (SMED) techniques for faster
changing of tools on production lines, providing
efficiencies from the use of smaller lot sizes.

See also: quality management; Toyota
production system

Further reading

Shingo, S. (1986) *Zero Quality Control: Source Inspection
and the Poka-Yoke System*, Cambridge: Productivity
Press.

ELIZABETH L. ROSE

shukko

Shukko refers to the practice of employee transfers
between firms. There are two types of *shukko*. In the
first, an employee retains his or her original
company affiliation while transferred temporarily
to another firm (*zaiseki shukko*). In the second, the
employee is transferred permanently (*tenseki shukko*).
Shukko exists at all levels: from junior engineers
transferred temporarily for on-the-job training, to
redundant factory workers reassigned to new
businesses, to retiring managers dispatched to run
affiliates, to bankers sent to reorganize a troubled
firm. *Shukko* has three principal roles: to reduce
labor costs by reallocating redundant employees, to
promote inter-organizational knowledge exchange,
and as a monitoring and governance device
wielded by external stakeholders such as main
banks or trading partners.

Firms frequently use *shukko* to reduce costs.
Large Japanese industrial firms transfer redundant
employees to businesses ranging from suppliers and
sales organizations, to affiliates in businesses
ranging from landscape maintenance to real estate
management. From a labor cost standpoint, *shukko*
is not costless. Firms often pay the difference
between an employee's previous wages and those in
the new job.

Shukko also occurs routinely when an employee
reaches retirement age of 55–60. Those employees
who do not make it to the ultimate status of board
member (**torishimariyakukai**) are commonly
transferred to smaller affiliates, often as senior
managers. For the receiving firm, these managers
are often valuable repositories of management
skills. For the larger sending firm, *shukko* allows it to
provide opportunities for advancement for younger
managers while assuring jobs to its retirees.

Shukko is also an important vehicle for the
transfer of knowledge between firms and their
buyers and suppliers. Firms often transfer their
own engineers through temporary assignments to
work side by side with employees of suppliers and
buyers of their products. These employees retain
their loyalty to the dispatching firm, and act as a
bridge between it and the receiving firm. In this
way, they are able to transfer information and gain
tacit knowledge. Through direct exposure to the
work rhythms and social networks of another firm,

employees develop a feel for how the partner operates without having to put that knowledge in explicit form (e.g., as a set of specs or memos). The easy exchange of employees between manufacturers and suppliers has been linked to effective product development in many Japanese automotive and electronics firms.

A third form of *shukko* exists at a company's upper echelons. The boards of Japanese companies are heavily interlocked with those of banks and business partners. Manufacturers dispatch their own managers to top executive positions at suppliers while banks place their own executives on boards to monitor and oversee firms to which they have made loans. In this respect, *shukko* plays an important role in **corporate governance**.

While it is very difficult to obtain data on shukko at the firm level, the Japanese **Ministry of Labor** collects and reports aggregate data on *shukko*. Several patterns are apparent in *shukko*. First, large firms tend to dispatch employees to smaller firms. Employees sent to *shukko* from large firms to smaller ones rarely return to their original firm. *Shukko* rates tend to be higher in manufacturing industries, and *shukko* is far more common for men than women. *Shukko* rates also increase during recessionary times, and decrease during periods of growth. Nevertheless, because *shukko* is not only a means of cost reduction, but a means to share knowledge, solidify interfirm relationships, and influence and control business partners, it continues even during good times. Finally, *shukko* occurs between affiliated firms: it is very unlikely that a firm would dispatch employees to a firm with which it has no business relationship, and *shukko* to a competitor is unheard of. More often than not, *shukko* occurs between firms linked by an ownership tie.

Advantages

The institution of *shukko* has allowed large Japanese firms to maintain a considerable degree of labor flexibility while maintaining the **lifetime employment** system. Firms use *shukko* both as an escape valve when faced with redundant workers, and as a regular step in the *nenko joretsu* promotion hierarchy, through which older employees with no more promotion prospects at their own firm are sent to smaller affiliates. *Shukko* is also an important tool for the exchange of knowledge and transfer of organizational culture. Through *shukko*, a company gains access to the knowledge base of the transaction partner. Even when the *shukko* is permanent, the relocated employee still identifies with the dispatching company and stays in regular contact with it. As a method of coordinating goals and operations and exchanging knowledge and skill between affiliated or transacting organizations, the *shukko* mechanism may be without peer. It plays a major role in forging the strong partnerships among banks, customers, suppliers, distributors, and even government ministries that characterize the Japanese business system.

Disadvantages

A major disadvantage of *shukko* is that it is more costly than layoffs. The originating firm usually pays the difference between an employee's wages at his or her new job and the former one. The need to provide new opportunities for redundant workers through *shukko* has encouraged firms to continue costly equity and business relationships with firms that receive *shukko*. *Shukko* may also place an unnecessary burden on the receiving company, since it often has little choice in whether it will accept these employees.

See also: lifetime employment; restructuring

Further reading

Cole, R.E. (1979) *Work, Mobility, and Participation: A Comparative Study of American and Japanese Industry*, Berkeley, CA: University of California Press.

Lincoln, J.R. and Ahmadjian, C.L. (2000) "Shukko (Employee Transfers) and Tacit Knowledge Exchange in Japanese Supply Networks: The Electronics Industry Case," in I. Nonaka and N. Nishiguchi (eds), *Knowledge Emergence: Social, Technical, and Evolutionary Dimensions of Knowledge Creation*, New York: Oxford University Press.

Nishiguchi, T. (1994) *Strategic Industrial Sourcing: The Japanese Advantage*, New York: Oxford University Press.

Nonaka, I. and Takeuchi, H. (1995) *The Knowledge-Creating Company: How Japanese Companies Create the*

Dynamics of Innovation, New York: Oxford University Press.

CHRISTINA L. AHMADJIAN
JAMES R. LINCOLN

small and medium-sized firms

There are over 6.5 million small and medium-sized enterprises (SMEs) in Japan. This figure reprents more than 95 percent of the business organizations in Japan. The definition of SMEs and small-scale enterprises was set by the Small and Medium Enterprise Law. These definitions vary by sector. An SME in manufacturing and mining is not more than 300 employees or 100 million yen, while a wholesale firm is not more 100 employees and 30 million yen, and for retail and services, it is not more than fifty employees or 10 million yen. A small-scale enterprise in manufacturing has not more than twenty employees, while for commercial or service firms it is not more than five employees. The largest concentration of SMEs is in the Osaka area.

SMEs have always had a significant impact on the Japanese economy. Out of 6.5 million private business enterprises (excluding primary industry), SMEs accounted over 99 percent in 1986. Of the 54 million people employed nationwide, 78–80 percent were employed in SMEs. There are two main categories of SMEs in Japan: subcontracting companies and independent companies. SMEs account for 52.9 percent of manufacturing, 61.9 percent of wholesale, and 77 percent of retail. Since the passage of the Small and Medium Enterprise Basic Law (1963), these ratios have remained constant for more than thirty years.

The Basic Law recognizes that SMEs play an important role in the Japanese economy. The objectives of the Law is to promote the growth and development of SMEs and to enhance the economic and social well being of entrepreneurs and employees of SMEs. The Law recognizes the special challenges that SMEs face and stipulates that the government must implement necessary measures in such areas as modernization of equipment, improvement of technology, rationalization of management, preventing excessive competition, stimulating demand, and ensuring fair business opportunities. Prefectural governments, regional bureaux of the **Ministry of International Trade and Industry** (MITI), **Japan External Trade Organization** (JETRO), and Japan Small and Medium Enterprise Corporation (JSMEC) provide various kinds of assistance to SMEs including consulting and advising, finance and training programs, and financing assistance. For example, the Japan Small and Medium Enterprise Corporation (JASMEC) provides: guidance, advice and consulting; collection and dissemination of information; management of mutual relief funds for small-scale enterprises and for preventing chain-reaction bankruptcies of small and medium-sized firms.

Other laws also protect SMEs such as the **Large Retail Store Law**, which places restrictions on the opening of large stores. However, as Japan is working on economic recovery, and therefore restructuring, some of these protections will be lost. Some observers argue that SMEs will survive because of their maneuverability, innovation, advances in information technology, corporate downsizing and outsourcing of in-house operations.

Challenges remain for SMEs. In a commentary published in *Japan Update (1995)*, Takashi Kitaoka, President of Mitsubishi Electric, noted that small businesses do not prosper in Japan because large companies have a monopoly on talented people. Also, history, culture and the **education system** encourage uniform attitudes and discourage differences of opinion or creativity. Of small manufacturing organizations, 56 percent are subcontractors, who are dependent on large parent organizations. Subcontracting companies, compared to independent SMEs, are less likely to have control over their product prices, and introduction of technologies and management interventions. This in turn affects the organizational culture of the SME and the attitudes and behaviors of employees.

SMEs are also not likely to offer the benefits of lifetime employment to even a minority of their employees. They also experience more difficulty in implementing some management techniques such as **quality control circles**. SMEs, on the other hand, are more likely to hire women or to be owned and operated by women. Japanese women, finding discrimination in large firms, especially during the current recession, are starting their own businesses in increasing numbers.

There are several industries in which small firms dominate. SMEs control the multimedia and CD-ROM markets. Originally sparked by SMEs, large rivals have entered the market generating some competition, but SMEs still dominate with over 6,500 titles available in 1996 (vs. 2,500 in 1995).

The **economic crisis in Asia** has had a serious impact on SMEs in Japan. Many have gone bankrupt, lost sales, or experienced heightened competition from large firms with lower-cost, overseas operations or low-cost products. The number of businesses subscribing to JASMEC's mutual relief funds has been increasing since the mid-1980s. JASMEC has provided more funds to small-scale firms: from 1.83 million accounts in 1984 to 3.86 million in 1996. A total of ¥6.1 trillion has been provided to the following sectors: service (21.6 percent), retail (29.3 percent), manufacturing (22.1 percent), construction (13.4 percent), whole-sale (4.7 percent), real estate (3.5 percent), transportation and communication (3.1 percent) and other sectors (2.3 percent).

The failure of a client can trigger chain-reaction bankruptcies among SMEs. To prevent this, JASMEC operates the Mutual Relief System for Prevention of Bankruptcies. As of 1997, there were over 740,000 accounts (150,000 loans) in wholesale and retail (39.8 percent), manufacturing (38.3 percent), construction (15 percent), transportation and communications (1.6 percent), mining (0.2 percent) and other (5.1 percent) with total loans of ¥301 billion.

With the bursting of the **bubble economy** and more large manufacturing firms moving offshore for cheaper production, SMEs have become desperate. They cannot compete with lower-cost overseas SMEs and are receiving fewer subcontracting jobs. However, in some specialized industries SMEs are finding ways to survive. In industries involving precision machining and non-standard projects that require highly skilled labor rather than mass production, SMEs are stable. They are also doing well in semi-conductors, unmanned production lines and non-contact inspection machinery for precision products. The

economy has also encouraged SMEs to become more independent and to become international. Finally, because large corporations in the retail sector have developed low-priced private brands, SMEs have also had to introduce low-cost products and private brands in order to differentiate themselves from the larger companies.

An additional issue that affects SMEs is the increasing concern about the environment. SMEs used to be exempt from recycling laws. Now, medium-sized manufacturers with sales exceeding ¥240 million and wholesalers, retailers and services SMEs with sales over ¥70 million have to pay their share of the recycling. Although no one can deny that environmental regulations are necessary to protect the environment, they cut into the profits of SMEs that are already struggling.

See also: overseas business of small and medium-sized enterprises

Further reading

Japan Small and Medium Enterprise Corporation (JASMEC) Home Page, http://www.jsbc.go.jp/english.

TERRI R. LITUCHY

social marketing

Social marketing is interpreted as applying to two activities. Firstly, the term relates to the application of various concepts and tools of marketing, which have been developed in commercial activities, to the management of such non-profit organizations as universities and hospitals, or to the deployment of social reform activities such as anti-AIDS campaigns.

Secondly, social marketing is understood to call for the recognition of responsibilities that companies bear in regard to their role within society. Marketing should be carried out, and then, in order to check and offset unintentional anti-social activities, such as pollution or the publication of false financial statements, the marketing policy of each company should include some explicit contributions to society. Typically, it calls for building a good relationship between the company and its surrounding communities.

The above notions of social marketing were introduced to Japan primarily through the works of Kotler and Zaltman (1971) and Lazer and Kelly (1973). It is generally understood that their theories were developed in the US in response to critical views of big business and the establishment in the late 1960s, when the US saw a series of protests against the Vietnam War, the civil rights movements, and growing consumerism.

In Japan, the term social marketing began to be used among business people in the 1990s, but some precursor movements can be found. By the end of the 1980s, it was generally recognized that Japan, the second largest economic power after the USA and having deployed overseas networks of corporate activities, should upgrade its international contributions and realize a society that would correspond to its wealth. As a result, such terms as "philanthropy" and "mécénat" (the French word for patronage) gained popularity. The Association for Corporate Support of the Arts (Kigyou Mesena Kyougikai) was founded in 1990.

After the fall of the Berlin Wall in 1989, assistance to the former Socialist countries moving toward the market economies required corporate participation. In 1992, the United Nations Conference on the Environment and Development (Earth Summit) in Rio de Janeiro, Brazil, urged business entities to take environmental concerns into considerations. These international developments also contributed to the dissemination of the term social marketing, in the broader meaning of society-oriented corporate activities. As a consequence, social marketing is often used in Japan as synonymous with society-oriented activities provided by companies, although a distinction is made when experts use this term.

See also: business ethics; environmental and ecological issues; marketing in Japan

Further reading

Kotler, P. and Roberto, E. (1989) *Social Marketing: Strategies for Changing Public Behavior*, New York: The Free Press; trans. T. Izeki, *Soshal Maaketingu:*

Koudou Henkaku no Tameno Senryaku, Tokyo: Daiyamondosha, 1995.

Kotler, P. and Zaltman, G. (1971) "Social Marketing: An Approach to Planned Social Change," *Journal of Marketing* 35(7): 3–12.

Lazer, W. and Kelley, E. (1973) *Social Marketing: Perspectives and Viewpoints*, Homewood, IL: Richard D. Irwin.

SHINTARO MOGI

software industry

Japan's large, vertically integrated hardware/software firms were able to build up their software skills in a relatively protected environment during the 1960s and 1970s. They were able to clone IBM machines and "borrow" IBM's software, changing it enough to make it incompatible with other systems. This allowed the firms to avoid the heavy costs of creating and maintaining their own standards or paying the American giant huge royalty fees. This strategy backfired in the early 1980s when they were caught stealing IBM's secrets and forced to pay for use of IBM's software. During the 1980s they struggled to reduce their dependence on the IBM standard by creating proprietary versions of UNIX-based systems and by developing a new Japanese operating system called TRON. In the early 1990s, software firms and the state realized that clinging to their closed standards was creating a serious lag between Japanese and US software. Thus they started embracing international operating system standards such as Windows and UNIX, though they continue to be interested in free-of-charge, open systems standards such as TRON and LINUX. They still continue to lag significantly behind their US counterparts, but are second only to the USA as a world power in the field of software.

The 1960s and 1970s

Japan's software industry grew out of the state's efforts to promote the computer industry starting in the early 1960s. When IBM announced its new advanced 360 series of computers in 1964, the **Ministry of International Trade and Indus-**

try (MITI) promptly set up its first major computer project involving software, the Super High-performance Computer Project (1966–71). To develop the project's software, MITI helped create the Japan Software Company, a joint venture among the three strongest hardware makers – NEC, Fujitsu, and Hitachi – and the Industrial Bank of Japan, a bank supportive of state policies. The company was to develop an operating system (OS) that could run on all three makers' machines. But the vertically integrated, hardware/software firms had no incentive to follow MITI's plan for a common software standard. They were all losing heavily in their hardware divisions even though they were locking-in users with closed standards. The software budget for the project was only 25 percent of the project's total cost, reflecting the state's lower priority for software than hardware as well as the **Ministry of Finance**'s (MOF) reluctance to fund what it saw as intangible products.

The Japan Software Co. did not meet its ambitious objectives. State and corporate lack of knowledge about software technology, minimal financial support, and contradictory incentives for the firms led to its bankruptcy in 1972. External events also made the company obsolete. In 1969, IBM, under pressure from the US Department of Justice's anti-trust investigations, decided to un-bundle (price and sell as separate products) its hardware and software. This opened up a world of opportunity for Japanese hardware makers. IBM's unbundling allowed Fujitsu and Hitachi, two of Japan's top three hardware makers, to take an IBM-compatible route. Most importantly, while tied up with anti-trust concerns, IBM was not in a position to complain about small, foreign competitors essentially copying its OS and applications software. This allowed MITI and the makers to focus on hardware, which they could legally reverse engineer, and enabled the broader strategy of competing through scale economies and manufacturing expertise.

Fujitsu and Hitachi modified IBM's OS standard enough so that it would not be compatible with other IBM-based machines. And they continued to bundle their hardware and software. By doing so, they locked in users, preventing them from combining different brands of hardware and software without costly adjustments. NEC had technological ties with Honeywell, but created its own closed standard too.

Though the state primarily promoted hardware throughout the 1970s, it did not completely ignore software. MITI was particularly concerned about alleviating the shortage of software engineers. In 1970 it created the Information Processing Promotion Association (IPA) to help small, independent software houses develop standardized, general purpose applications software packages with the goal of increasing the number and productivity of programmers. As part of this effort, the IPA organized several MITI-funded research projects. But the IPA and its projects have not been very effective. Poorly funding and the lack of a strong intellectual property regime to protect software inventions contributed to the IPA's inability to nurture new software programs and firms. Also, since the firms sold their software and hardware as a package incompatible with other systems, there was virtually no demand for IPA-supported software packages.

Even had there been greater funding and better legal protection, it is unlikely the IPA and its projects would have been very effective because they worked at cross-purposes with key pillars of Japan's catch-up system of capitalism. The bank-centered financial system meant capital markets were underdeveloped, which discouraged the emergence of a venture capital market and new firms. The lifetime employment and seniority wage systems obstructed labor mobility. The *keiretsu* **industrial groups** and other loose alliances that permeate Japan's economy also served to create an environment in which users, loyal to their allied computer maker and locked into their closed standards, could not and would not easily switch computer systems or software. In this context, closed standards and customized software thrived. This was not a problem as long as the firms could quickly copy IBM's software and thereby provide their locked-in users with software that met their needs. But as IBM made it more difficult for clone makers to quickly respond to new IBM machines, it meant that users were increasingly stuck with software significantly inferior to software packages based on international standards sold on the open market.

The state and the makers simply did not grasp the long-term negative impact of closed standards. Moreover, a focus on increasing the number and productivity of software engineers was ineffective in an industry where concept, individual creativity, and proprietary but quasi-open standards, not merely productivity of software engineers and manufacturing expertise, were key.

The 1980s

The turning point in the industry was in the summer of 1982 when Japanese computer firms, desperate to get information on IBM machines before they hit the market, were caught stealing IBM software technology. This FBI sting case sent shock waves through the industry. The free ride on IBM was no longer free. The firms now had to pay huge annual licensing fees to IBM. From then on, the firms tried to diversify the standards they relied on, especially their dependence on the IBM mainframe standard. In the 1980s, there was a strong move toward UNIX-based systems through the government-sponsored Sigma Project (1985–90) and a private sector-initiated attempt to create a unique Japanese operating system standard called TRON.

The Sigma Project selected UNIX, an open standard, as its focus. The goal was to encourage makers to unbundle by providing them with an open standard as an alternative to IBM. But the firms, desperate to lock in their customer base in order to maximize profits, made their own closed version of UNIX-based software and bundled it with their hardware. This meant independent software makers still had little incentive to develop new software.

In the Sigma Project, as in earlier IPA projects, the state made the same mistake of seeing efficient production as the software industry's key problem. Again they focused funds and researchers on increasing the productivity of software engineers rather than software concepts and functions that users desired. Some analysts argue that the project pushed the industry toward the UNIX standard much quicker than would have otherwise occurred. But even MITI and IPA officials agree that the move would have happened anyway and that the

jump-start was probably not worth the project's cost (¥22.3 billion yen, or $131.2 million).

The TRON project was aimed at having a uniquely Japanese OS. Announced with great fanfare and media coverage in 1984, the project still continues today. Most agree that TRON was not a great standard, but the fact that the world was largely locked into IBM mainframe and PC (MS-DOS) standards at the time meant that even if TRON was superior, it would have had great difficulty succeeding internationally.

The 1990s

In the early 1990s Japan's computer software industry was at a crossroads: it could continue offering closed, modified versions of foreign standards or unbundle and embrace open, internationally accepted standards such as the Wintel (Windows Intel) standard. It became increasingly clear to the government, users, and makers that the costs of closed standards were mounting and that to become internationally competitive, computer producers needed to unbundle, move toward open standards, and shift their focus from quantity to quality.

The problems were obvious. But the solutions were less clear. The government, viewing software as an industry with critical spillovers onto the rest of the economy, strongly favored convergence with international standards even though it would hurt the hardware/software makers temporarily. MITI was acutely aware that the targeting policies that had worked so well in other industries were not working in software. The firms were afraid to unbundle without assurance that all would do so. But the market was not waiting for Japanese firms to make up their minds. By the early 1990s, Windows, Intel microprocessors and the Internet swept the globe.

The quickest and most politically acceptable way to get the industry to unbundle and move toward open, internationally accepted standards was to have foreign firms force the conversion. Starting in late 1992 MITI started publishing reports openly welcoming foreign software into Japan. MITI did not simply want imports; it wanted foreign firms to participate in the market. This move was not so much an embracing of internationalization. Rather MITI was desperate and felt that even if the firms were foreign, they needed to have cutting-edge software firms in the domestic market to promote the domestic industry and provide all Japanese firms with the software they needed to become more efficient.

As a result, in the 1990s we saw a sharp rise in the market share of foreign software companies. Microsoft currently dominates Japan's packaged software market. US hardware makers, such as Dell, Compaq, and Gateway, have gained only small (1–3 percent) shares of the market. But the sudden entry of foreign hardware and software makers in the early 1990s pressured Japanese makers to converge with internationally accepted standards such as DOS, and more recently, the Wintel and NT standards.

While Japanese software/hardware firms have started offering new machines based on international standards, the economy as a whole has been slow to downsize. Lock-in to proprietary standards means that shifting to a new standard makes a company's current software obsolete, inevitably slowing their conversion.

The government's role in the 1990s and 2000s clearly declined in significance but remains important. There are numerous ongoing national R&D projects related to software, such as for massive parallel processing machines and the Internet. Moreover, the state has tried to revise the copyright law to make it legal to decompile foreign software. And it has tried to institute a voluntary quality certification scheme for software, which foreign makers say would require them to divulge proprietary information to gain approval. These tactics have been unsuccessful, but only due to close vigilance by foreign companies operating in Japan as well as heavy pressure from the US government.

The 2000s

The lag of Japanese firms in software and Internet-related technologies is still growing in the 2000s. They have caught up in most hardware technologies but their industrial system needs to change its emphasis from manufacturing to promoting invention and entrepreneurship. Such change would help industries such as software and biotechnology,

where technological change is rapid and unpredictable and where the idea, not superior manufacturing techniques, is key to competitive success. Unfortunately, the long, deep recession in the 1990s, which started primarily as a bad debt banking crisis, is affecting Japan's industrial base and is slowing efforts to deal quickly with their software problems.

See also: computer industry

Further reading

Anchordoguy, M. (1989) *Computers, Inc.: Japan's Challenge to IBM*, Cambridge, MA: Harvard University Press.
—— (1997) "Japan at a Technological Crossroads: Does Change Support Convergence Theory?" *Journal of Japanese Studies* 23(2): 363–97.
—— (2000) "Japan's Software Industry: A Failure of Institutions?" *Research Policy* 29: 391–408.
Baba, Y., Takai, S. and Mizuta, Y. (1996) "The User-Driven Evolution of the Japanese Software Industry: The Case of Customized Software for Mainframes," in D.C. Mowery (ed.), *The International Computer Software Industry*, Oxford: Oxford University Press, 104–30.
Cusumano, M. (1991) *Japan's Software Factories*, Oxford: Oxford University Press.

MARIE ANCHORDOGUY

Sohyo

The General Council of Trade Unions, or Sohyo in Japanese, was the largest trade union confederation in Japan from 1950 to 1989 and was a stronghold of radical unionism mainly supported by public-sector unions. It laid the foundation for the coordinated wage determination system known as spring labor offensive or *shunto*, which attempted to overcome the limits of **enterprise unions** in Japan. Sohyo's presence, however was more striking in the realm of politics than in economics. It had a huge influence over the direction of the Japan Socialist Party (JSP) by assisting it financially and supplying candidates for public office. It was politically opposed to moderate, private-sector unions affiliated with other labor confederations,

Domei (Japanese Confederation of Labor), and its political representative, the Democratic Socialist Party (DSP). Sohyo's leadership and influence began to erode after the oil crisis, when unions in the big, export-oriented corporations began to ally, which undercut the rivalry between Sohyo and Domei. The cooperation of these unions eventually led to the demise of Sohyo and the birth of a new confederation, Rengo (Japanese Trade Unions Confederation, JTUC in 1989.

The origin of Sohyo

Sohyo was created by anti-communist trade unionists in July 1950, and its foundation was facilitated by the Supreme Commander of Allied Powers (SCAP). At its inauguration, Sohyo declared that it would seek membership in the International Confederation of Free Trade Unions (ICFTU), which had been created in 1949 in opposition to the communist-dominated World Federation of Trade Unions (WFT). However, by 1951, Sohyo had swung left. Minoru Takano took leadership in March 1951 at Sohyo's second congress, which rejected Japan's rearmament. Takano likened Sohyo's transformation to "SCAP's hatching a chicken which turned out to be an ugly duckling." Sohyo's political activities irked moderate unions, which abhorred extra-parliamentary political actions. In 1953 moderate unions dropped out of Sohyo and eventually formed the second largest trade union confederation, Domei.

By 1958, Takano's leadership was contested and he was replaced by Kaoru Ohta and Akira Iwai. The new leaders pushed economic rather than political struggles and pursued a strategy of joint actions for wage increases, which laid the foundation for the spring labor offensive. Even though the new leaders emphasized the importance of economic issues, Sohyo kept its pacifism and anti-monopoly stance, which crystallized in the mass movement against the revision of the US–Japan Security Treaty and the Miike coalminers' strike in 1960. The defeat of Sohyo in both incidents marked a watershed. While Marxist-Leninism had drawn support among young rank-and-file unionists throughout the struggles, demands for cooperative unionism grew among union leaders and employers.

Political radicalism continued to characterize Sohyo because the largely politically radical public sector unions constituted more than 60 percent of Sohyo's membership. In contrast, Domei principally consisted of private sector unions. When it was formed in 1964, it embraced 1,360,000 members as opposed to Sohyo's 4,200,000. Sohyo comprised 2,510,000 members in the public sector and 1,670,000 in the private sector, whereas Domei consisted of 80,000 unionists in the public sector and 1,600,000 in the private sector unions.

From its birth, Sohyo officially supported the Japan Socialist Party, especially its left wing. The tight relationship between Sohyo and the JSP was called the "JSP-Sohyo bloc" which rivaled the "DSP-Domei bloc." Sohyo provided indispensable financial support to the JSP and also supplied candidates. By the mid-1970s 50 percent of the JSP parliament in the lower house and 70 percent of those in the upper house were unionists endorsed and supported by Sohyo. Among the Sohyo-affiliated industrial union federations, the Japan Teachers' Union, National Railways Workers' Union, and Postal Workers' Union sent the largest numbers of representatives to the Diet.

The demise of Sohyo

Sohyo, once a mighty political actor, disappeared in 1989 as a result of the growing antagonism between the public sector unions and unions in the export-oriented big corporations. This new conflict of interest cut across the political and ideological rivalry between Sohyo and Domei, and led to the total reorganization of the labor movement.

In 1975, the Spring Offensive, International Metal Workers Union-Japan Council (IMW-JC) and Domei agreed on wage restraint in exchange for employment security. While IMF-JC came to be a wage setter and dilute the role of Sohyo, Sohyo did not support employment and industrial policies demanded by the private sector, which further widened the gap between the public and private sector unions. Moreover, affiliates of the Public Employees' Union and the Public Enterprise Union Council embarked on a strike to recover the right to strike that they lost in 1948. Sohyo's political activism accelerated the unification process of the private-sector unions and the defeat of the "strike for the right to strike" made Sohyo leaders take a more realistic approach.

A unification process led by big corporation unions became explicit by the mid-1970s. In 1979, Sohyo leaders accepted unification led by those private-sector unions and allowed each member industrial union to decide whether or not to join a unified confederation. Moreover, Sohyo leaders agreed that a new confederation would seek membership in the ICFTU, although the ICFTU affiliation issued remained controversial, separating Domei-affiliated unions and Sohyo's left-wing unionist, until the dissolution of Sohyo. In 1980, five Sohyo-affiliated private-sector unions joined Zenminrokyo (Japanese Private Sector Trade Union Council) which developed into a unified, private sector labor confederation called Minkan Rengo, Domei and the other two confederations were disbanded. By that time, most Sohyo-affiliated private sector unions had joined the new confederation, and so the inclusion of public sector unions in Minkan Rengo came onto the agenda. Acrimonious disputes erupted in all public sector unions. The left-wing unionists, who wanted to defend the traditional tenets of Sohyo radicalism, were eventually left out of the unification negotiations and formed marginal left Socialist or Communist confederations. A new unified labor confederation, Rengo was then formed in 1989 under moderate leadership, and Sohyo ended its thirty-nine year history.

Further reading

Hiwatari, N. (1999) "Employment Practices and Enterprise Unionism in Japan," in M. Blair and M. Roe (eds), *Employees and Corporate Governance*, Washington, DC: The Brooking Institution, 275–313.

Kume, I. (1998) *Disparaged Success: Labor Politics in Postwar Japan*, Ithaca, NY: Cornell University Press.

Miura, M. (2000) "Did the Japan Social Party's Activists Commit Political Suicide: Typology of Activism and Party Strategy," *Shakai Kagaku Kenkyu* (The Journal of Social Science) 51: 5–6, 221–51.

Price, J. (1997) *Japan Works: Power and Paradox in Postwar Industrial Relations*, Ithaca, NY: Cornell University Press.

Shinoda, T. (1997) "Rengo and Policy Participation: Japanese-Style Neo-Corporatism?" in M. Sako and H. Sato (eds), *Japanese Labor and Management in Transition*, London: Routledge, 187–214.

MARI MIURA

sokaiya

A *sokaiya* is a corporate extortionist who purchases a small number of shares in order to gain access to a company's annual stockholders' general assembly meeting (*sokai*) and then attempts to extract money or other benefits from the company in exchange for ensuring that the meeting is short and tranquil. While the distinction is not always clear-cut, there are two main roles played by *sokaiya*. *Yato sokaiya* (opposition party *sokaiya*) threaten that unless they are paid off, they will disrupt the assembly and embarrass top executives by loudly and persistently asking board members questions about real or alleged problems relating to the quality of management (poor investments, low profits and the like) or the personal and family lives of executives (extra-marital affairs, questionable finances, etc.). *Yoto sokaiya* undertake, for a fee, to ensure a smooth meeting by suppressing dissent by other shareholders, including other *sokaiya*. This may be done by shouting them down, buying them off, or using physical intimidation. *Sokaiya* groups typically try to portray themselves as corporate activists acting as watchdogs to protect the small investor. Some groups operate quite openly, with plainly marked offices and even web sites. A common euphemism for *sokaiya* is *tokushu kabunushi* (special shareholder). Similar activities are undertaken in South Korea by hecklers known as *chongheoggun* and in Italy by gadflies known as *disturbatori*.

The emergence of *sokaiya* can be traced back to the early Meiji period, when influential fixers began to assist managers, who were unaccustomed to the intervention of outside investors due to the late introduction of the joint stock corporation. Their numbers exploded during the 1970s after shareholder activism protesting the Vietnam War and the Minamata mercury pollution incident revealed top executives' vulnerability to embarrassment at the shareholders' meeting. They peaked in 1982 when the National Police Agency (NPA) estimated that there were over 6,783 active *sokaiya*, 2,012 of whom were believed to be *yakuza*.

To combat this problem, more and more companies began to hold their annual stockholders' assemblies on the same day in late June to make it difficult for *sokaiya* to attend more than one meeting. By the 1990s, over 2,000 companies were holding their meetings simultaneously. The NPA dispatched over 10,000 officers to guard the meetings held that day, and companies supplemented this with large numbers of private security staff and employee volunteers. The Commercial Code of Japan was also revised in 1982 to make it illegal to pay off *sokaiya*. The offense, known as *rieki kyoyo* (conferring a benefit), prohibited the provision of any benefit to a shareholder in connection with the exercise of that shareholder's rights, such as the right to ask questions or vote. Penalties could include up to six months imprisonment or a fine of 300,000 yen. The revisions also raised the number of shares necessary to vote to a par value of 50,000 yen. Since most Japanese shares have a par value of 50 yen, this amounts to 1,000 shares in most cases.

While the number of *sokaiya* officially reported by the NPA declined to just a few hundred by the late 1990s, many of those who fell off the official list because they no longer owned enough shares to meet the higher ownership threshold did remain active and simply changed their techniques. Instead of demanding cash payments, they used a variety of other mechanisms, including the sale of proprietary publications at exorbitant prices (the most common method), payments for services not used (such as rent for training facilities or beach houses), or inflated payments for miscellaneous services ranging from advertising to the leasing of potted plants. Involvement with *yakuza* (organized crime) groups also increased. Such underworld ties resulted in an implicit threat of physical injury or death in cases of non-payment which is an additional factor motivating executives to cooperate with *sokaiya*.

A series of scandals in 1997–8 which resulted in the resignation of over 100 executive and dozens of arrests prompted further countermeasures. The penalties under the **Commercial Code** were increased to three years and a fine of up to 3 million yen, and it was made illegal for *sokaiya* even to request a payoff (prior to this it had only been illegal to accept one). Those who made threats (as opposed to requests) could receive up to five years and a 5 million yen fine. The NPA pushed both general business associations such as Keidanren (the Federation of Economic Organizations of Japan) and sectoral industry associations to issue declarations that they would not deal with *sokaiya* and to establish task forces to ensure compliance. Some firms opened up their shareholders' meetings or broadcast them live on the Internet to show they had nothing to hide and posted signs indicating they would refuse to deal with *sokaiya*. Nevertheless, repeated surveys in the late 1990s showed many firms still dealing with *sokaiya*.

Traditionally analysts have attributed the longevity of the *sokaiya* phenomenon in Japan to a cultural aversion to embarrassment and loss of face that makes Japanese executives particularly vulnerable to blackmail. It has also been suggested that structural factors such as the lower level of corporate disclosure in Japan may create a demand for secrecy. *Sokaiya* exploit this through blackmail due to the unavailability or inconvenience in Japan of other methods of profiting from negative information, such as short-selling. Both arguments are compatible with the difficulty Japan has experienced in eradicating *sokaiya* activity.

See also: corporate governance; stockholders' general assembly

Further reading

Szymkowiak, K. (1994) "Sokaiya: An Examination of the Social and Legal Development of Japan's Corporate Extortionists," *International Journal of the Sociology of Law* 22: 123–43.

Ursacki, T.J. (2000) "Restoring the Legitimacy of Japanese Business in the Post-Bubble Era: Can Good Economics Make Good Ethics Easier?" in P. Bowles, and L.T. Woods (eds), *Japan After the Economic Miracle: In Search of New Directions*, London: Kluwer Academic, 37–57.

West, M.D. (1999) "Information, Institutions and Extortion in Japan and the United States:

Making Sense of Sokaiya Racketeers," *Northwestern University Law Review* 93: 767–817.

TERRI URSACKI

Sony

Sony Corporation is a diversified consumer electronics manufacturer headquartered in Tokyo. In 1999 its fiscal year sales totaled over $56 billion and it employed 177,000 workers. As of 1999 Sony Group was comprised of over 1,000 consolidated subsidiary companies, some of which are located abroad. The predecessor company to Sony was Tokyo Tsushin Kogyo K.K. (Tokyo Telecommunications Engineering Corporation, also known as Totsuka), founded by Masaru Ibuka in 1945. Masaru Ibuka and Akio Morita incorporated Totsuka on May 7, 1946; the firm had approximately twenty employees and an initial capitalization of 190,000 yen. Its major competitors have been Philips and Matsushita Electric Industrial Corporation.

Totsuka's first product was an adapter to convert medium-wave radios into superheterodyne, or all-wave, receivers. Soon, however, the company branched out to make a variety of other electronic goods. Due to the difficult conditions following the Second World War, most of its sales were to the government and Nippon Hoso Kyokai (Japan Broadcasting Corporation). The company's business connections with the Occupation Forces led to knowledge of magnetic sound recorders and the development of a tape recorder. Totsuka introduced the first Japanese magnetic tape recorder and recording tape in August of 1949. This was the first expression of Sony's engineering-oriented culture and philosophy of innovation.

The invention of the transistor at Bell Laboratories in the United States was known to Ibuka in the late 1940s, but it was not until March 1952 that Ibuka visited the United States for a three-month inspection tour to learn about tape recorder manufacturing by American companies. While in the USA he recognized the potential of the newly invented transistors, and upon returning to Japan Totsuka decided to pay $25,000 to license the transistor technology from Western Electric. Totsuka had to get a permit from the Ministry of International Trade and Industry (MITI) to remit foreign currency abroad, but MITI initially rejected the application because the company was too small. Eventually Totsuka received permission, and in August 1953 Morita signed a licensing agreement with Western Electric. In May 1954 Totsuka introduced the first transistors made in Japan, and in August 1955 the company produced the first Japanese transistor radio. The firm rapidly transistorized various other consumer electronics products, and experienced great success domestically and in export markets.

Wanting to export its products and believing the company's name was too difficult for foreigners to pronounce, in 1955 Totsuka began selling products under the Sony name. "Sony" was an amalgamation of two words: the Latin word *sonus*, which is the root of the such words as "sound" and "sonic," and "sonny," meaning little son. In January 1958 Totsuka's name was officially changed to Sony Corporation.

Sony's most famous product is the trinitron tube, developed in April 1968. Many believe the trinitron has superior picture quality to conventional picture tubes, and it continues to be the signature Sony product. In 1975 Sony introduced the Betamax videocassette recording system; however, it lost the VCR market to the VHS system invented by the Japan Victor Corporation. This was Sony's most serious marketing failure. In 1979 Sony introduced a small portable stereo tape player, the Walkman, which proved to be an enormous success. In October 1982 Sony introduced the first music CD players for the Japanese consumer market. In the late 1990s Sony successfully brought out the Sony Playstation, which challenged Nintendo, the market leader in video games.

By the dawn of the twenty-first century Sony had become a globalized firm that operated major production facilities in Japan, North America, and Asia. It was the first Japanese firm to undertake television manufacturing in the developed countries. In 1960, Sony Corporation of America was established in the United States. Sony broke ground in January 1971 on its San Diego color television factory, its first overseas factory. In 1974 it opened its first European television factory in

Bridgend, Wales. In 1988 Sony acquired CBS Records Inc., and in 1989 Sony acquired the movie company Columbia Pictures Entertainment. It was the first major Japanese company to have non-Japanese members on its board of directors. Sony was also the first Japanese electronics firm to globalize and has continued to be a Japanese leader in this endeavor.

Sony has a reputation for being more Westernized than its Japanese competitors. It prides itself on its ability to innovate and to create attractively designed products. For example, in a break with tradition Sony announced in 1997 that it would no longer consider a graduate's university as a major factor in the hiring process in its subsidiaries in Japan. More than any other Japanese electronics manufacturer, it has earned a reputation for product development and engineering prowess combined with a sophisticated sense of design.

See also: electronics industry; Matsushita Electric Industrial Corporation; Morita, Akio

Further reading

Lyons, N. (1976) *The Sony Vision*, New York: Crown Publishers.
Morita, A. (1986) *Made in Japan: Akio Morita and Sony*, New York: E.P. Dutton.
Nathan, J. (1999) *Sony: The Private Life*, New York: Houghton Mifflin.
Sony Corporation (1999) http://www.world.sony.com/CorporateInfo/huhou-e.html.

MARTIN KENNEY

standard setting

Japan's semi-statist approach to standards has accelerated broad adoption of new technology but also provoked trade friction. In other advanced countries, the national standards organization receives only a minority of its funding from the state, as in Europe, or is entirely member supported, as is ANSI in the USA. Japan's national standards organization, the Japan Industrial Standards Committee (JISC, Nihon Kougyou Hyoujunka Chousakai), is a section of the Standards Department within the Agency for Industrial

Science and Technology (AIST) of the Ministry of Economy, Trade, and Industry (METI, formerly **Ministry of International Trade and Industry**, MITI). METI shares supervision of one-eighth of the 9,000 Japan Industrial Standards (JIS) with another ministry, usually telecommunications or health. The 1949 Industrial Standardization Law (Kougyou Hyoujunka Hou) requires that all environment, health, and safety regulations must conform with JIS. Quite separately, the Ministry of Agriculture supervises several hundred Japan Agricultural Standards (JAS) for medicines, agricultural chemicals, silk yarn, foodstuffs, and forest products. Any JIS or JAS requires final approval from the relevant minister; one-tenth of JIS also require companies to have their factories inspected and earn the right to display a "JIS mark" on their products. JIS certification and other government testing have increased the potential for JIS to serve as **trade barriers**. Non-Japanese firms have also complained about language barriers: 75 percent of JIS lacked an official English translation in 1980, 57 percent in 1986, and 29 percent in 1998.

JISC is less a regulatory office than a small "think tank" that coordinates – partly via a "long-range plan for the promotion of industrial standardization" issued every five years since 1961 – work by outside organizations, most notably the somewhat larger Japan Standards Association (JSA, Zaidan Houjin Nihon Kikaku Kyoukai). Top JISC officials have sometimes served simultaneously at JSA, which functions as publishing house, lead coordinator for some prominent JIS standards, accreditor for the JIS mark, and general "change agent" for standardization and **quality management**. JSA has 11,000 regular members (up dramatically from only 811 members in 1972), a staff of 160, and an annual budget of ¥6 billion. JSA claims that half of all firms take part in its conferences, courses, seminars, and other activities. The agriculture ministry established an analogous "helper" organization, JAS Kyoukai, in 1962.

JISC and JSA work with over 200 industry associations, most of which are ministerially "approved" associations (*shadan houjin*). Early retirees from the ministries preponderate as association executives (*senmu riji*, *joumu riji*) and retain well-institutionalized ties back to their former ministry (see **amakudari**; **industry and trade associa-**

tions); by 1991, industry associations had promulgated over 4,800 non-JIS standards. During the 1990s, a reaction against overly specialized standards from the **bubble economy** led to broader standards foundations (*zaidan houjin*) being established (e.g., Chemical Standardization Center) or strengthened (e.g., Japan Information Processing Development Center). Even apparently independent standards organizations tend to align with METI: the Kyoyohin Foundation, whose E&C Project has sought standards supporting "simple use for everyone" since 1991, became a METI-approved organization in 1999. JSA has increasingly led multi-sector standards projects (e.g., information processing, ISO 9000/JIS 9900 management standards). AIST research labs such as the Electrotechnical Laboratory, specially designated private or quasi-governmental institutes and, more rarely, academic societies all host industrial standards research. The JIS Center (*Kurashi to JIS sentaa*) established at Tsukuba in 1995 with an annual budget of $1 million, investigates pre-competitive standards.

History

Although the establishment of a Japan Engineering Standards Committee (JESC, Kougyouhin Touitsu Chousakai) in 1920 emulated many other countries at that time, Japanese firms devoted more attention to standardizing company-level workplace practices (*hyoujun-ka*) than to developing formal, national standards (*kikaku-ka*). From 1930–7, an "external" bureau of the ministry of commerce and industry, the Temporary Industrial Rationalization Bureau (TIRB, Rinji Sangyou Gouri Kyoku), worked closely with **zaibatsu** groups, journalists, and academics to plan for simplification, rationalization, modern management, and formal standards. To promote these objectives more widely, TIRB established a helper organization (Nihon Kougyou Kyoukai) in 1931 that merged with the Japan Management Association (JMA) in 1942. Only 520 JES standards existed in April 1941, but during the height of the war, JMA oversaw the diffusion of 931 temporary standards (T-JES) based on simplified procedures. The Aircraft Technology Association (Dai Nippon Koukuu Gijutsu Kyoukai) established by the technology

agency (*gijutsuin*) then under the prime minister's office issued 666 aircraft standards (Dai Nippon Koukuuki Kikaku).

After the war, with ministerial approval on 6 December 1945, the Japan Standards Association was detached from JMA and, along with the technology agency, given offices inside the patent and standards office of the ministry of commerce and industry. JESC was re-established as JISC in February 1946, which issued its first postwar standard in September 1946. In May 1948, GHQ ordered the adoption of 766 US standards and 288 Australian standards; Japan undertook relatively intensive exchanges with, and study of, standards organizations from twenty-one countries including Holland, Switzerland, Finland, China, and Chile. The Industrial Standardization Law (Kougyou Hyoujunka Hou), which followed in July 1949 (law no. 185; with relatively minor revisions in 1966, 1980, and 1997), regulates JISC, the issuance of JIS and the "JIS mark," and most other aspects of Japan's formal standards. The first factory to receive the "JIS mark" was Tokyo Steel's Adachi factory in August 1950.

Japan's signal achievement in the first postwar decades was an unusually tight integration of prewar workplace mobilization with a rapidly expanding national system of formal standards. In 1952, there were 2,509 JIS, increasing 82 percent by 1957 and 166 percent by 1967. Many companies and supplier associations based their in-house standards and operation manuals on JIS or related industry association standards. Shopfloor workers – prepared by an education and employee training system that produced broad, rather than specialized, human capital – learned to incrementally revise the standards governing their own work. JSA disseminated these developments to **small and medium-sized firms**, which also helped large firms rationalize their supply chains. Even the broader society participated: thousands of homemakers, for example, for decades regularly reported on consumer products awarded the JIS mark.

Formal standards reduced industry-wide price levels while the involvement of shopfloor workers in standardization encouraged firms to add product features and improve quality (see **kaizen**). Standardization aimed at price *and* quality facilitated massive export drives, for example, in facsimile machines, computer displays, and data storage technology. Occasionally, as with facsimile machines, Japanese firms coordinated not only in the early development of a national standard but also on a shared strategy for international standardization.

Japan signed the GATT Standards Code Agreement on Technical Barriers to Trade (TBT) in 1980. Access slowly broadened; JIS technical committees first permitted non-Japanese firms to attend drafting committees in 1983, to propose drafts and attend technical committees and Division of Council meetings in 1985, and to become registered members in 1987. Yet the locus of standardization also shifted – sometimes aided by ministerial funds and policies – to less conspicuous settings such as industry associations, quality control commissions, company president meetings, **research cooperatives**, ad hoc commissions, and special-purpose foundations (*zaidan houjin*).

Firms on the technological frontier often favored less binding forms of cooperation than the JIS framework; moreover, as products became more networked, control of networking interfaces by a single firm was becoming a more important strategic asset. The number of JIS rose only 8 percent between 1975 and 1989 and declined absolutely during most of the 1990s. The number of companies subscribing to JIS declined 23 percent between 1979 and 1994.

As the JIS framework weakened, ministry intervention tended to reduce the number of competing alternatives without preventing standards races from spilling over into the marketplace. Vigorous last-minute MITI intervention into consumer video standardization in 1976, for example, winnowed the four contending standards down to two but was unable to forestall a decade-long market contest between Betamax and VHS. Similarly bounded competitions broke out in analog camcorders, videodisks, game machines, and cellular telephones. Even collaborative standards research increasingly let companies pursue alternative (rather than complementary) standards; for example, in the Real Internet Consortium's next-generation router project, Hitachi pursued a supercomputer approach, while **NEC** tried parallel processing. Standards competitions were least likely in industries facing organized demands for a single

standard from foreign user firms (for example, in DVD) or dominated domestically by a single firm such as **Nippon Telegraph and Telephone** or NHK (such as satellite broadcasting and cable).

Transnational standards

Moreover, nation-based standard setting was under challenge everywhere. Japanese firms sought to deepen the presence of Japan-centered production networks in other countries, but they faced new approaches to standard setting from the USA and Europe. Anti-trust policy in the US facilitated contests for winner-take-all control of global *de facto* standards anywhere in the IBM or AT&T supply chain (e.g. Microsoft, Intel, Cisco); Japan's *keiretsu* rivalries often hindered similar strategies from developing in Japan. Meanwhile, Europeans invested heavily in the development of European standards that were often seamlessly adopted by international organizations, often rejecting alternative proposals by Japanese firms (e.g., condoms, medical imaging, cellular phones). Japan held relatively few secretariats at ISO and IEC – despite sending large delegations to almost every technical committee and being the leading source of overall financial contributions – and was often confined to the testing and refinement of proposals put forward by others.

JIS influence in Asia (e.g. steel JIS in China) – cultivated by the Japan International Cooperation Agency (JICA) – has the potential to offer some international leverage. Thus, JISC has long played a leading role in the Pacific Area Standards Congress (PASC) and sought to increase the influence of PASC members within ISO and IEC.

With hesitations, Japanese firms have sought to integrate externally generated international standards. Japanese firms initially criticized ISO 9000 standards as a redundant expense, for example, but by the late 1990s Japanese firms had become the leading holders of ISO certifications worldwide: companies such as NEC and Mitsutoyo offered their own ISO certification services, creating new tie-ins and opportunities for their core businesses, especially in Europe. Similarly, NTT resisted international standards in second-generation mobile telephony, but in the third generation allied quite closely with Europe-based international standards; in 1998, an official from the telecommunications ministry became the first Japanese head of the International Telecommunications Union.

After Japan signed the WTO Agreement on Trade-Related Aspects of Intellectual Property Rights, JIS underwent a "zero base" review during 1997–2000: of 8,253 standards, 10 percent were withdrawn (including 15 percent of JIS marks) while 36 percent were already equivalent to international standards. According to changes in the JIS Law made in 1997, standards projects can begin without JISC preliminary assessment, and private and foreign organizations can offer JIS mark certification. Agriculture standards followed: the JAS Law was revised in December 1998, and a five-year review of JAS, omitting pharmaceuticals and alcohol, began in 1999.

Ministerial influence, although trimmed in routine matters, has also gained new strategic outlets. In 1998, MITI began approving standards projects on a five-year provisional basis if conflicts among firms temporarily block creation of a JIS standard. In 2001, METI reorganized JISC to target international standards more favorable to Japan. JISC staffing nominally doubled to 225, and the number of JIS began rising for the first time in two decades.

Further reading

JETRO (1995) *Kokunai dantai kikaku mokuroku* (List of Domestic Industrial Group Standards), Tokyo: JETRO.

Johnson, C. (1982) "The Rise of Industrial Policy," *MITI and the Japanese Miracle: The Growth of Industrial Policy, 1925–1975*, Tokyo: Charles E. Tuttle.

JSA (1995) *Nihon Kikaku Kyoukai 50 nen no ayumi* (Japan Standards Association's Fifty-Year Walk), Tokyo: Nihon Kikaku Kyoukai.

McIntyre, J.R. (ed.) (1997) *Japan's Technical Standards: Implications for Global Trade and Competitiveness*, Westport, CT: Quorum.

Nakamura, S. (1993) *The New Standardization: Keystone of Continuous Improvement in Manufacturing*, trans. B. Talbot, Portland, OR: Productivity Press.

Noble, G.W. (1998) "Standard Setting and R&D Consortia in Japan's Video Industry," in *Collective Action in East Asia: How Ruling Parties Shape Industrial Policy*, Ithaca, NY: Cornell University Press, 93–122.

JAY TATE

stockholders' general assembly

Japan, like most other countries, requires public companies to hold an annual stockholders' general assembly, or shareholders' meeting (*kabunushi sokai*), at which the investors in the firm gather to hear reports about the company's progress and to vote on various proposals for the future. Under the **Commercial Code** the assembly is empowered to make decisions such as the appointment of directors. However, Japanese shareholders' meetings are distinguished by two notable characteristics: most are very short and the vast majority are held on the same day at the same time. As a result, in practice the role of the shareholders' meeting in making decisions about the company's future is quite minor. Such decisions are made elsewhere, with approval at the meeting a mere formality.

In 1997 the average length of a shareholders' meeting for a publicly listed company in Japan was twenty-nine minutes, with less than 5 percent taking more than an hour. Many lasted less than fifteen minutes, and at more than three-quarters of the meetings no questions at all were asked from the floor. This is in sharp contrast to North American practice, where social activists, gadflies and disgruntled ordinary shareholders often drag out meetings for several hours, and some companies purposely hold long meetings to showcase their plans. It is also a marked contrast to the drama which sometimes attends shareholders' meetings in North America, where proposals from the floor and even fights for control of the firm are not uncommon, and where large institutional investors have been known to join together to vote to dismiss managers they felt were underperforming.

There are several reasons for these differences in the length of the shareholders' meeting. Most Japanese stock market-listed companies have several major shareholders such as banks, trust banks, insurance companies and fellow *keiretsu* members, who together own a controlling stake in the company (40–70 percent). These shareholders deal with the company regularly on a long-term basis, and hence are regularly kept up to date on its activities. They hold their shares to solidify long-term business relationships and will have worked out any differences well before the meeting. Thus, management almost always has the votes it needs to ensure passage of its proposals. There are also no outside directors on most Japanese boards, so the directors seldom engage in public power struggles.

Under a revision to the Criminal Code which came into effect in 1982, in order to attend the meeting investors must hold shares with a par value of at least 50,000 yen, which usually means 1,000 shares. This prevents small shareholders from attending. Moreover, managers often pack the meeting with supportive employee shareholders to ensure swift and discussion-free passage of management proposals, and many have also resorted to the use of *sokaiya*, corporate extortionists, who will, for a fee, ensure that no embarrassing matters are raised by verbally or physically intimidating any troublesome attendees.

Only shareholders who have held at least 1 percent of the company's shares for six months prior to the meeting can make proposals, and 3 percent is necessary to see the company's books beyond the published financial statements. Thus, smaller shareholders are precluded from using the meeting as a forum to investigate or attack management.

While the traditional explanation for managers' preference for short, quiet meetings was the aversion to embarrassment and loss of face in Japanese culture, some research has shown that companies which usually have a short shareholders' meeting suffer declines in stock price when a long meeting (over one hour) is reported in the press. Thus, there may be a rational economic element to this preference as well.

Annual general meeting day is a major event with front-page coverage in all the major national daily newspapers in Japan. Companies whose meetings have lasted more than one hour are prominently named. Over 90 percent of Japanese companies listed on the First Section of the Tokyo Stock Exchange hold their annual meeting on the same day in late June. Most Japanese companies have been encouraged to adopt a year end of March 31, which coincides with the end of the

government's fiscal year. These companies then hold their meetings three months later, in June. Over time they have tended to coalesce on the same day in late June as a measure to counteract hostile *sokaiya*, who threatened to drag out and disrupt the meetings if not paid off. By holding all meetings at the same time on the same day under heavy police protection, managers could ensure *sokaiya* were unable to attend more than one company's meeting each. This had the side effect of preventing ordinary shareholders from attending more than one meeting as well. While less than ideal from a corporate governance standpoint, this effect was welcomed by most Japanese executives since it further ensured that the meeting would not raise any embarrassing issues.

A series of scandals during 1997–8 revealed that many companies had been paying off *sokaiya* for years, some even after earlier convictions for doing so. Pressure from the authorities and public opinion pushed these companies to reform their approach to the shareholders' meeting. Beginning in 1999, several started to broadcast their meetings on the Internet or make other arrangements to be more open in order to reassure investors and others that they had indeed cut their ties to the *sokaiya*. These companies have been joined by a number of others that have adopted a more open approach out of a desire to attract international investors, who have often been dismayed by a perceived lack of transparency in Japanese management.

See also: corporate governance; cross-shareholdings

Further reading

Nakane, F. (1995) "The Commercial Code and The Audit Special Exceptions Law of Japan," *EHS Law Bulletin Series*, EHS Vol. II, Tokyo: Eibun Horeisha Inc.

West, M.D. (1999) "Information, Institutions and Extortion in Japan and the United States: Making Sense of Sokaiya Racketeers," *Northwestern University Law Review* 93. An excerpt, "Making Sense of Japan's Sokaiya Racketeers," appeared in 42.2 Law Quadrangle Notes 72 (summer 1999).

TERRI URSACKI

strategic partnering

"Strategic partnerships" – also commonly known as "strategic alliances" – are usually formed to create competitive advantage on a worldwide basis. The term "partnership" is commonly used when two firms are involved, whereas "alliance" may be used when there are two or more firms. The intention of partnerships is a long-term contractual relationship where firms share control over their firms' resources. Firms may selectively share control, costs, capital, access to markets, and information and technology. Partnerships may take many forms. Some more common activities include: joint research projects, technology sharing, use of product facilities, joining forces to manufacture components, assembling finished products together, and marketing the partner's products.

Historically, export-minded firms in industrialized nations sought partnerships with firms in less developed countries to export and market products in that less developed country. Such arrangements were often required to win local government approval for economic activity and marketing in the less developed country. More recently, companies from different parts of the world form strategic partnerships and alliances to strengthen their mutual ability to serve whole continents. Particularly when companies lack particular resources essential for competition on the international stage, they may seek out a partner holding the keys to further expansion. Of course, any help must be reciprocated.

Although the rewards are enticing, maintaining partnerships is not easy. Forming partnerships initially is usually a challenge, but maintaining the partnership for the long run is extremely difficult. Time and money costs of coordination are usually expensive in the short run and can even increase in the long run. Partnerships often break down when one or both of the partners feel that they are not benefiting as planned, and partnerships become especially vulnerable when one partner begins feeling exploited by the other. Collaboration between independent companies can be very difficult because of language and cultural barriers. Finally, depending on another for essential expertise and capabilities is threatening and requires trust. Over the long run, this trust frequently breaks down.

In partnerships and alliances out of Japan, Japanese companies often form strategic alliances with European companies to strengthen their ability to compete in the European Union. They have also been actively forming alliances with Asian firms to capitalize on the opening up of Asian markets. In the USA, Japanese companies have consistently had relatively poor performing alliances, with the exception of the auto and consumer electronic industry. The high costs of serving the highly competitive US market has led to disappointing operating returns for many Japanese firms. Strategic alliances, however, remain an attractive way for Japanese firms to enter US markets due to the fact that Japanese companies have only had about a 30 percent success rate with cross-border acquisition. Cross-border acquisitions have been unsuccessful because they have primarily been done on a "hands off" basis, which prevents the collaboration necessary to two-way learning and minimizes the opportunity to capture value through consolidation.

An example of a company active in forming strategic partnerships is **Toshiba**. Japan's oldest and third-largest electronics company, Toshiba has used strategic alliances as the cornerstone of its corporate strategy. Some of its most prominent strategic alliances are with IBM (to make flat-panel liquid crystal displays in color for portable computers), Motorola (to design and make dynamic random access memory chips) and Apple Computers (to develop CD-ROM based multimedia players that plug into television sets). The company – like many other globalizing corporations – believes that these alliances are necessary because technology has become so advanced and the markets are so complex that no one corporation can be the best at an entire process any longer.

In Japan, more than half of all foreign entries have been accomplished through strategic alliances. Relatively few acquisitions of attractive Japanese companies take place. Alliances in Japan tend to last at least 15–20 years, twice as long as anywhere else. Even if both partners are not satisfied with the alliance, the costs of breaking up are high; it is often difficult to find replacement partners. The alliances usually involve the sharing of personnel, quality control, product development and just-in-time inventory systems. Historically, Western companies have offered innovative products and technology in return for access to Japanese markets. Over time, Japanese firms typically learn the technology themselves and are more likely to terminate the alliance if their partner is no longer contributing what they perceive as a fair share. In these cases Japanese companies often buy out their partners; Japanese partners have been the acquirers in approximately 70 percent of the terminating ventures in Japan. Because Japanese markets can be so different and difficult to penetrate, US companies are still reliant on alliances with Japanese competitors to learn production and marketing processes. Furthermore, Japan's government regulation and policies can make access to Japanese markets very difficult for foreign firms, thereby giving Japanese companies a valuable bargaining chip when forming strategic alliances.

Further reading

Bleeke, J, and Ernst, D. (ed.) (1993) *Collaborating to Compete: Using Strategic Alliances and Acquisitions in the Global Marketplace*, New York: John Wiley and Sons.

WILLIAM BARNES

subcontracting system

The Japanese system of subcontracting, characterized by continuity and stability in supplier-assembler relationships between core firms and tiered medium and small-scale parts providers, is a distinctive feature of the Japanese business system. This unique system of external architecture evolved in response to wartime government mandates, immediate postwar labour surpluses and the high growth and labour short economy of the 1960s.

Shitauke, as subcontracting is known in Japanese, is symbolized by firms such as **Toyota** and **NEC** which are surrounded by their respective *keiretsu* or supplier groups. Relationship contracting as compared to spot trading is the hallmark of the Japanese subcontracting system. In the West,

customized components are generally manufactured in-house or by wholly-owned subsidiaries of the assembler. In Japan, such items are produced by independent members of the *keiretsu* who are willing to take the risk of establishing dedicated production facilities and installing transaction-specific assets.

Japan's subcontracting system comprises long-term relational contracts for parts and components, with first, second and third-tier suppliers stratified according to each supplier's range and level of technical expertise, attitudes to risk and relative bargaining power (Aoki 1988). However, supplier–assembler relations in Japan are not monolithic, with practices differing between two plants in the same industry and between different industries. This distinctive system of continuous trading between manufacturers and suppliers rests on relational contracting that facilitates the sharing of product knowledge and encourages system flexibility. One element in the wider architecture of the Japanese firm, which includes interrelated work and industrial organization practices, the subcontracting system provides Japanese firms with competitive advantages through acquisition of organizational knowledge, establishment of organizational routines and the development of a cooperative ethic.

How buyers set specifications for suppliers, and how suppliers meet those specifications, defines the Japanese subcontracting system (Asanuma 1989). Subcontracting in Japan involves the transfer of codified and tacit know-how, embodied in product specifications, pricing regimes, shipment scheduling, and quality control mechanisms. Such decision making and problem solving facilitates learning, while attenuating informational asymmetries between partners. Suppliers learn to achieve reliability in quality and delivery and meet targeted percentage price reductions, over a specified time through rationalization or productivity improvement (Asanuma 1985b). Buyers learn to commit to suppliers by assessing suppliers' performance and ranking suppliers into tiers. Buyer commitment and supplier reputation allow both parties to invest in specific human capital (design engineers) and physical capital (machines). For both parties, these network specific assets act as an additional incentive device to ensure contract compliance, attenuate opportunistic behaviour and preserve the long-term supply relationship, given low second-best uses and high switching costs when specialized assets are present. Repeat contracting between buyer and supplier furthers learning and creates trust and cooperation, which also acts as an incentive for maintaining the subcontracting system over time.

The term "subcontractor" in Japanese has been sometimes associated with the exploitative use of small businesses as a buffer against business fluctuations by large firms, especially by Marxist scholars. Lower profit rates and wage rates in small firms are often cited as evidence to support this position. According to the Marxist view, large firms are able to protect their own profits by transferring the impact of cyclical downturns to small contractors over whom they hold monopolistic advantage, by either reducing the orders to suppliers by a larger amount than the decrease in demand for the end product or by forcing suppliers to accept less favourable terms through lower prices. The evidence to support such exploitation is mixed. Studies of profit rates in manufacturing in Japan suggest that whilst profit rates are lower in the small firms normally associated with subcontracting than in large firms, they are higher than the average for manufacturing as a whole. This view of subcontracting is essentially similar to any competitive spot transaction, which might take place in any market.

Essential to an understanding of subcontracting in Japan is its quasi-vertical integration, more akin to intra-firm transacting than to spot transacting. Component suppliers also play a major role in the **kanban** or **just-in-time** production system that originated in Toyota and is an example of a structure possible only under relationship contracting. Subcontracting relationships in Japan overlap to some extent with Japan's *keiretsu* business groupings. Many automobile suppliers are organised in this way. Toyota for example has a stable organisation of supplier firms known as *kyohokai*. However, members of Toyota's *kyohokai* generally include only the larger first tier suppliers and represent only a fraction of the many thousands of suppliers. However, in other industries such as electronics, relationships between core firms and suppliers are less well defined and similar associa-

tions that include major plant suppliers have not been organized.

Subcontracting relations in Japan are widespread and pervasive. For example, Asanuma (1985a) found that the cost of purchased parts was as much as 70 percent of the unit production cost for any of the representative carmakers in Japan. According to a survey by the Agency for Small and Medium-Sized Enterprises, an unnamed manufacturer of automobiles had direct relations with 122 first-tier suppliers and indirect relations with 5437 second-tier suppliers and 41,703 third-tier suppliers. After adjusting for double counting this manufacturer was the core firm of a hierarchy of 35,768 suppliers.

Three different types of vendor supplier relationships are clearly discernible within Japan's subcontracting system. The first distinction to be made is between catalogue goods (CG) and ordered goods, that is between those goods which are standardized and ready-made and can be purchased in open markets, and those components that are supplied in accordance with the purchaser's specification. While some suppliers supply both marketed and ordered goods, firms tend to supply either one type or the other.

Ordered goods can be further divided into two types of suppliers: design approved (DA) vendors and design supplied (DS) vendors. DA suppliers manufacture parts from designs made by the suppliers themselves and approved by the assembler. DA suppliers have a relatively unique stock of production knowledge and directly supply essential components to the prime manufacturer. This type of supplier may provide components such as advanced electronic equipment, bearings, brakes and carburettors, which may be patented products or products in which the prime manufacturer (assembler) does not have comparable technological expertise. DS suppliers, on the other hand, manufacture components according to designs and specifications supplied by the assembler. These suppliers generally have less specialized technological expertise and supply less crucial components (such as lamps or plastic mouldings) to the primary manufacturer.

DS suppliers fit most closely with the popular image of the subcontractor referred to as *shitauke* in Japanese. They are considered to have relatively weaker bargaining power *vis-à-vis* the contracting firm because they lack specialized technological expertise (Aoki 1988). As a result, this type of subcontractor in Japan has long been under the protection of Japanese law. The *shitauke* firm is a legal concept defined in Japanese law as a firm with 300 or fewer employees or with a paid-up capital of ¥100 million or less. Notwithstanding the legal and conventionally accepted usage of the term *shitauke*, the subcontracting system in fact involves a continuum of contractual relationships between a prime manufacturer and its subcontracting members, stratified according to the technological capacities of individual supplying firm. The balance between these categories varies between industries according to the extent of standardization of the component being supplied. The more standardized the component, the more likely it will be supplied as a CG while the more customized the component, the more likely it will be supplied as a DS or DA component.

Virtually all automobile components, for example, are either DS or DA, while electric machinery components, which are much more standardized, have a higher proportion of CG components (Asanuma 1989). DA and DS suppliers, because of the high level of customization and asset specificity or their components, are likely to be much more dependent on the prime manufacturer (assembler). Large suppliers and suppliers with technical expertise tend to supply more catalogue goods than ordered goods, and of the ordered goods more DA than DS components. This is partly because greater technological know-how and human resources enable these firms to have substantial design and drawing capabilities and partly because they are in a better position to absorb the economies of scale that come from producing a large quantity of standardized products. Some CG suppliers, as a result, are often large independent firms and include many large corporations such as NEC, **Matsushita** and Hitachi who themselves are major manufacturers of finished goods.

Perhaps the two main features of Japan's subcontracting system which contrasts with assembler–supplier relations in the West are the long-term cooperative relationships between assemblers and suppliers based on repeated interactions and suppliers' willingness to make customized investments. Namely, Japanese manufacturers purchase intermediate products (component parts) repeatedly from a limited number of suppliers, who are willing to make investments specific to their purchaser in order to produce customised investments. For example Dyer and Ouchi (1993) found, based on their study of the Japanese automobile industry, that Japanese suppliers were willing to invest in customized equipment and customer specific human capital and locate their plants close to the manufacturer. This allows Japanese assemblers to reduce the level of capital tied up in inventories. Strong technical interaction between assemblers and suppliers in the Japanese subcontracting system, involving routine exchange in personnel and information, also allows greater efficiency and faster product development. Toyota, for example is able to develop a new model in just fifty months, almost 40 percent faster than automobile US automobile manufacturers (Dyer 1994). Finally, the willingness of Japanese suppliers to invest in customised assets due to the long-term relationship characteristic of the Japanese subcontracting system, also plays an important role in the improvement of both productivity and quality improvement. This factor is often singled out as a major reason for the strong performance of Japan's tightly integrated production system.

From the suppliers' viewpoint, there is a strong incentive to acquire sufficiently high technology to make their own drawings and be promoted from a DS to DA supplier and hopefully to a CG supplier so that they can reduce their dependence on a single purchaser, differentiate themselves from rival suppliers and also increase their profit margins. They are therefore motivated to invest in technological acquisition and engineering capabilities.

The nature of the contract between prime manufacturer and the first-tier supplier has been articulated by Asanuma (1989). Normally, the contract period between the prime contracting firm and its subcontractor corresponds to the duration of a particular model. The prime contracting firm guarantees not to switch suppliers or manufacture in-house the contracted part for the life of the model. In Japan, it is quite unusual for the subcontracting relationship between an assembler and a supplier, once begun, to be terminated. Relationships between assemblers and suppliers continue on a semi-permanent basis even through model changes, although a supplier's rank and bargaining position may change over time.

The Japanese subcontracting system provides competitive advantages that include production and contract flexibility, economies of scope and specialization, and productivity improvement. Contracts between the prime manufacturer and suppliers set both the price and quantity which are determined on the estimated unit cost plus an agreed markup and on production forecasts, but are subject to change depending on fluctuations in demand and changes in input costs. Minor changes in supplier output are driven through daily *kanban* orders from the assembler which, as noted earlier, helps to keep inventory suppliers to a minimum in accordance with the just-in-time system. More significant changes to production schedules occur on a monthly basis, and suppliers are notified in advance of changes in production schedules. Price adjustments also occur when production costs change. Usually, changes in production volumes causing increases in the fixed cost per unit of the supplier are met by the assembler. Changes in variable costs occasioned by increases in material costs are also usually met by the prime manufacturer (assembler). However, increase in labor costs are usually expected to be met by the supplier through productivity improvements. Productivity improvements are generally shared between the assembler and supplier, depending on whether the cost reduction is due to the initiative and investment of the supplier or the assembler.

Strong incentives and competition also exist between suppliers. Suppliers who are evaluated positively in terms of performance may well be promoted to a higher category and allowed higher profit margins, while those who are poorly evaluated may be demoted in rank and have lower mark-ups imposed. Poor performance may result in a refusal by the assembler to place further orders, but this is rare, and suppliers are usually given the opportunity to redeem their position (Asanuma 1989). In this way, both competition and quality improvement are characteristic of the Japanese subcontracting system.

It has been suggested that the rapid advance in information technology may change the basic nature of the Japanese subcontracting system and manufacturer–supplier relations, with manufacturers moving increasingly to the procurement of standardized rather than customized parts which could be sourced through the Internet rather than from a limited number of suppliers within their own corporate groups.

Further reading

Aoki, M. (1988) *Information, Incentives and Bargaining in the Japanese Economy*, Cambridge: Cambridge University Press.

Asanuma, B. (1985a) "The Contractual Framework for Parts Supply in the Japanese Automobile Industry," *Japanese Economic Studies*, Summer: 54–78.

—— (1985b) "The Organization of Parts Purchases in the Japanese Automobile Industry," *Japanese Economic Studies*, Summer: 32–53.

—— (1989) "Manufacturer Supplier Relationships in Japan and the Concept of Relationship-specific Skill," *Journal of the Japanese and International Economies* 3: 1–30.

Dyer, J. (1994) "Dedicated Assets: Japan's Manufacturing Edge," *Harvard Business Review* (November–December): 174–8.

Dyer, J. and Ouchi W.G. (1993) "Japanese Style Partnerships: Giving Companies a Competitive Edge," *Sloan Management Review* 35: 51–63.

Odagiri, H. (1992) *Growth Through Competition, Competition Through Growth: Strategic Management and the Japanese Economy*, Oxford, Clarendon Press.

WILLIAM PURCELL
STEPHEN NICHOLAS

suggestion systems

Japan's first suggestion program was started by Kanebo Company in 1905. Kanebo modeled its program after executives saw similar ones at work in the United States. However, it was not until the 1950s that suggestion systems became commonplace in Japanese companies. To an unforthcoming workforce accustomed to following top-down dictums in a vertically integrated hierarchical society, the idea of offering suggestions to superiors was not quickly accepted. However, in the 1960s companies began to integrate suggestion plans with a variety of small-group activities such as **quality control circles** and *jishu kanri* (autonomous control) teams. This combination proved more successful in generating suggestions.

For example, in 1976, **Matsushita** Electric reported an average of fifty suggestions per production worker in its Ibaraki television plant. In recent years, the company as a whole has been averaging over ten suggestions per worker (factory and office workers combined). The acceptance rate at Matsushita averages about 10 percent. This figure was the norm for most successful companies that depended on such input from employees for idea generation.

By 1982, a survey of 512 organizations conducted by the Japan Human Relations Association and the Japan Suggestion System Association showed an increase in suggestions per employee to 14.74. At Hitachi Ltd. alone, 5.8 million suggestions (102.59 per person) were received. Other firms experienced levels as high as 400 suggestions per employee. According to the 1982 survey, the largest percentage of suggestions (35 percent) address work process improvement. Other types of suggestions (10 percent) addressed machine tools, work environment, and ways to save energy, resources and materials.

There have been continuous improvements in the suggestion system as it has been applied and experienced in the Japanese culture over time. One significant adaptation was going from a passive to active strategy of suggestion accumulation. The former involved providing suggestion boxes for employees and waiting. The latter involved active campaigns educating and rewarding personnel in regards to fulfilling suggestion quotas. These innovations in the system are congruent with the commitment of Japanese management to developing employees skills fully, and understanding that employees can make real contributions to organizational effectiveness.

By the 1990s suggestion systems have permeated through organizational structures into the school system. As early as first grade at school, children are encouraged to make suggestions. Indicators include the ever-present suggestion boxes, in the classrooms, hallways, and outside of the principal's office, suggestion campaign slogans on banners, and audio reminders via the public announcement system.

Further reading

Cole, R.E. (1979) "Made in Japan: A Spur to US Productivity," *Asia* (May–June): 6.

Hattori, I. (1985) "Product Diversification," in Thurow (ed.), *The Management Challenge: Japanese Views*, Cambridge, MA: MIT Press.

JETRO (1982) "Gauging and Comparing Economic Productivity," *Focus Japan*, September: JS-A.

Keizai Koho Center (1990) An International Comparison, Tokyo.

Lillrank, P. and Kano, N. (1989) *Continuous Improvement*, Ann Arbor, MI: Center for Japanese Studies, University of Michigan.

MARY YOKO BRANNEN

Sumitomo

Sumitomo Corporation, one of Japan's largest and most successful trading companies, was established on 24 December, 1919. Currently, it has 192 offices worldwide, including 158 offices in 88 countries and thirty-four offices in Japan. In addition to Sumitomo company offices, there are a vast number of consolidated subsidiaries, 553, of which 346 are overseas and 207 are domestic. The total number of associated companies is 214, of which 132 are overseas and 82 are domestic. Sumitomo is an increasingly global company with stock market listings in Tokyo and Frankfurt. The number of employees in the Sumitomo Corporation is 8,192, and the total number of employees working for consolidated subsidiaries is 33,057. The Sumitomo product lines include metals, machines, media, chemicals, fuel, food, fiber and construction.

The commercial history of the Sumitomo family began when Masatomo Sumitomo, the founder of the Sumitomo family, opened a medicine shop and bookstore in Kyoto in the beginning of the seventeenth century. Later, his heir, Tomomochi Sumitomo, created the first copper trading company in Japan, which was to become the foundation of the future Sumitomo enterprise. At the same time, the company entered into the business of running copper mines, with the Besshi Copper Mine established in 1690. Besshi continued to produce copper and contribute to Sumitomo for more than 280 years until its end in 1973. A new Western technique was introduced to the Besshi Copper Mine in the beginning of the Meiji Era (1868), and copper production increased rapidly. The increase in copper production allowed the company to diversify into a variety of business ventures.

The Sumitomo *zaibatsu* (a monopolistic group of companies run by one family) grew out of this Japanese merchant house to become one of the largest *zaibatsu* in Japan, controlling some 135 companies by 1945. Sumitomo was so successful and influential that it is widely credited with turning the country into a modern, capitalist society as Japan gradually opened up to the rest of the world during the latter part of the nineteenth and first half of the twentieth centuries.

When the Second World War ended in 1945, all *zaibatsu* in Japan were dissolved and holding companies were banned. As a result, affiliated companies had to begin independent business operations. Sumitomo was likewise dissolved, and each company of Sumitomo started out on its own as an independent company. But very soon thereafter, as with all former *zaibatsu*, the companies regrouped into modern day "*keiretsu*" and were back in business as a powerhouse group of companies.

The Sumitomo Corporation has maintained its high status in Japan, being regarded as the "Big 3 and Best 1," indicating that they rank in third place in terms of sales and in first place in terms of employment. Generally, Sumitomo's business management ability has a respected reputation. The Sumitomo Group has a hard-and-fast rule that the sales staff must not manage. So management staff are highly trained and, in turn, are responsible for the training of their sales staff. With the help of their management system, Sumitomo Corporation has reaped vast profits and is a major success story in Japan.

Further reading

Kearns, R.L. (1992) *Zaibatsu America*. New York: The Free Press.

Uchida, Y. (1995) *Shosya*, Tokyo, Japan: Kyouikusya Publishing.

MARGARET TAKEDA
IPPEI ICHIGE

superstores

The superstore is not a native Japanese retail category. The closest category is *suupaa*, a truncated loanword used to refer to three forms of supermarkets. The first is called *shokuhin suupaa* (food supermarkets), itself modeled on supermarkets in the USA. *Shokuhin suupaa*, by definition, must generate not less than 70 percent of their income from food alone. The second refer to specialty *suupaa* including apparel and household goods *suupaa*. A specialty *suupaa* must have a sales floor of no smaller than 500 square meters and generate no less than 70 percent of its sales from the merchandise it specializes in. The final form is *sougou suupaa* (general supermarkets) that devote themselves not only to food sales but also to the sale of a wide range of merchandise, including textiles, household goods, furniture and electrical appliances. Therefore, the term *sougou suupaa* refers to a sort of combined supermarket and mini-department store which is similar to a department store in form and should be thought of as a general merchandise store (GMS).

The category of *suupaa* can be seen as the result of a historical process in which Japanese borrowed the concept of supermarket chains from the USA in the 1950s and domesticated the concept into things Japanese. At that time, some retailers adopted most elements of supermarket operations such as self-service techniques, mass merchandising, and pricing, but widened the range of merchandise to include textile, variety, furniture, electrical appliances, and so forth rather than confine themselves solely to food sales. They also built large stores from the outset to house the wide range of merchandise. In the 1960s, these retailers established chain stores all over Japan. This is how *sougou suupaa* were developed. At the same time, some small grocery shops chose to stick to the American format of supermarkets and became *shokuhin suupaa*. Other retailers applied the concept of supermarkets to sell non-food merchandise such as apparel and household goods. This is the origin of specialty *suupaa*.

Among the above three forms of supermarkets, *sougou suupaa* is closest to the concept of superstores. *Sougou suupaa* can be classified into national, regional, and local. A national *sougou suupaa* must, by definition, operate outlets across more than four prefectures. Secondly, it must also have a network of outlets in two or more of the following cities: Tokyo, Osaka, and Nagoya. The Daiei group, Seiyu group, and Ito-Yokada group are several well-known examples. A regional *sougou suupaa* must run stores across four prefectures. The former Yaohan Japan is a good example. The differences between national and regional *sougou suupaa* in corporate strength and reputation have been significant. Finally, a local *sougou suupaa* is defined as a supermarket that operates outlets across three prefectures such as Marunaka.

Large department stores are sometimes called superstores because of their operation scale. However, department stores and *sougou suupaa* differ in three major ways: the organization of operations, the number of outlets, and the social prestige attached to them. *Sougou suupaas* are self-service operations, with chain-style organization – in other words, with separate merchandising and store operations – while department stores are not differentiated according to these functions. The second characteristic of supermarkets is their large number of outlets. Daiei, for instance, directly operated 317 stores all over Japan in 2000. In contrast, Isetan operates only seven outlets. Department stores and *sougou suupaa* are also different in terms of social prestige: their respective statuses are rooted in their histories and are related to the physical locations of their stores. Department stores, especially those such as Mitsukoshi of the so-called "kimono tradition," can boast longer histories than supermarkets – and, in Japanese business generally, a long corporate history tends to be related positively, in consumers' minds, to quality and prestige. The "goodwill" created and sustained by stores over a long period of time thus leads to a good corporate image.

Looking at differences in their business strategies suggests some meaningful connections between the categorical distinctions of prestige and such elements as merchandising policies, customer services, price, location strategies, clientele, and staffing. Japanese retail experts classify merchandise into two categories according to customers' purchasing behavior. The first is called luxury merchandise (*kaimawari hin*) which refers to such items as high fashion, jewelry, and so on. The purchasing frequency of luxury merchandise is low and customers tend to be choosy. The second category consists of daily necessities (*moyori hin*) such as food, daily items, and household utensils. Unlike luxury merchandise, the purchasing frequency of daily necessities is high. Customers tend to shop in stores convenient to them such as those close to their places of residence.

In order to maintain their high status, most department stores have adopted a merchandising policy that centers on luxury merchandise supplemented by daily necessities. In contrast, *sougou suupaa* focus mainly on daily necessities. Moreover, department stores stress textiles, while *sougou suupaa* focus on food and daily necessities. Generally, sales of textile merchandise alone have constituted 40 to 60 percent of the total sales of department stores.

High-quality goods and comprehensive customer services result in high prices, which themselves contribute to prestige. *Sougou suupaa*, due to their emphasis on daily necessities, are less expensive. In fact, low prices were the *raison d'être* of supermarkets when they started to flourish in the 1960s.

Moreover, in order to be consistent with their high status, most department stores, especially those from the "kimono tradition," have located their stores in the earliest established central business districts, such as the Ginza in Tokyo. Such locations can give department stores an atmosphere of tradition and exclusiveness that attract rich customers. *Sougou suupaa*, on the other hand, have located their stores close to residential areas, in order to be more easily accessible. The key consideration here is convenience, as wealthy customers have never constituted their core clientele.

See also: Daiei; Ito-Yokado; retail industry

Further reading

Larke, R. (1994) *Japanese Retailing*, London: Routledge.

HEUNG-WAH WONG

supply chain management in Japan

In Japan as in other countries, supply chain management (SCM) refers to the integration and management of the business processes that link original suppliers with producers, distributors, and ultimately consumers. The objective is to optimize the responsiveness and cost performance of the entire supply chain, rather than focus narrowly on business activities within any one company. Since the 1990s, SCM has received considerable attention worldwide. Certain Japanese business practices, most notably those of **Toyota** and its *keiretsu* group members, have been recognized by many as providing an early prototype of supply chain management (see **Toyota production system**). Subsequently, Japanese industry has looked to the USA as a leader in innovating SCM, particularly for utilizing information technology and the Internet.

In its development, supply chain management has drawn upon many aspects of Toyota's business practices. In fact, many top managers in Japan use the terms supply chain and "demand chain" interchangeably, borrowing terminology from Toyota's pull-system of production which initiates the production of parts only as they are actually used, or demanded, by downstream stages of the production system or supply chain. The aspect of the Toyota production system most relevant to SCM is its extensive degree of information sharing between supply chain members. For example, Toyota provides information on new car models to first-tier suppliers who then work together with Toyota to design the parts. Toyota also provides a rough production schedule to parts suppliers one-month in advance, and then places the actual purchase order ten days in advance. Consequently, suppliers have adequate time to prepare materials without maintaining perpetual inventories. Toyota's dealer network also provides demand forecasts to Toyota one month in advance, and finalizes purchase orders ten days in advance based on a mix of actual customer orders and forecasted demand. Toyota then sequences its final assembly of automobiles according to the dealer delivery schedule. Aiming to increase the responsiveness of its supply chain, Toyota has set a goal to build 70 percent of cars to customer order by 2010, up from 30 percent in 2000. This will require increased use of information technology and customer relationship management (CRM) systems, together with significant reductions in total manufacturing lead-time.

Many supply chains in Japan are still formed largely along *keiretsu* lines, but are moving increasingly towards an open network model. The bursting of the **bubble economy** and various competitive factors have pushed companies to look for suppliers outside their own *keiretsu* affiliation. The increasing numbers of Internet-based transactions and the emergence of e-markets for the purchase of supplies have also accelerated the move towards network supply chains. At the same time, it should be noted that many companies never had *keiretsu* affiliations or have always been a supplier to more than one *keiretsu* group. Other industries, such as fashion apparel, had never developed close relationships among members in their supply chains. Textile manufacturers, apparel manufacturers, and retailers independently determined their own production and ordering schedules based on their own individual sales forecasts. Due to this lack of information sharing and coordination, retailers routinely experienced 20 percent opportunity costs and apparel manufacturers had 30 percent obsolescence of inventories. To address these problems in the fashion apparel supply chain, the former **Ministry of International Trade and Industry** or MITI (now the Ministry of Economy, Trade and Industry, METI) launched the Quick Response Architecture Initiative (QRAI) in 1998. Through a one and a half year project involving multiple entities, several improved business approaches were proposed including the introduction of quantity flexibility contracts, information sharing, synchronized schedules with small lot sizes for production and delivery, continuous optimization of production and delivery schedules, and other operational techniques of SCM.

Information sharing is widely recognized as the most important issue for supply chain management, whereas the obstacles to efficient SCM are generally recognized to be (1) long lead times, (2) too many stages in the supply chain, and (3) demand uncertainty and independent decision making. Many excellent examples of reducing production lead-time exist in Japanese industry, including Toyota. For eliminating redundant stages in the supply chain, the retailer, **Ito-Yokado**, provides a good example with its introduction of a vendor managed inventory program for daily necessity items. To deal with demand uncertainty, some manufacturers have begun implementing Internet-based design and ordering systems, such as Sharp's system for microwave ovens. To coordinate decision making, some companies have introduced continuous replenishment planning (CRP) systems. For example, Japan's multitude of small stationery shops launched a cooperative logistics system in 1998 and then extended it into an "efficient supply chain management system" in which continuous replenishment planning is the core. Using this system, member companies, including manufacturers such as Pentel, as well as distributors and retailers have targeted to reduce average inventories by up to 50 percent, average shortages to zero, and average delivery cost by 50 percent.

While the term "supply chain" typically refers to inter-firm linkages, many large Japanese companies also speak of managing their own "internal supply chains" (*kigyounai sapurai chien*). As part of efforts to improve their internal supply chains, **Sony** and National/Panasonic (**Matsushita**), for example, have integrated their various manufacturing resources in order to simplify and enhance the efficiency of procurement and manufacturing. Many Japanese companies have eliminated their logistics activities and instead have outsourced the logistics function to third-party logistics providers. Another area of activity for many companies has been to better synchronize their logistics planning with manufacturing planning.

Since the late 1990s, most large Japanese firms have established departments with responsibilities for supply chain management. Furthermore, almost all consulting companies, as well as industry and trade associations, have SCM divisions. Organizations that have actively organized conferences and promoted SCM in Japan include the Japan Institute of Logistic Systems and a Japanese branch of the US-based Supply Chain Council.

See also: distribution system

Further reading

(1998) "Tokushu 1: Sapurai chien senryaku / Tokusyu 2: Baryu chien saikouchiku" ((Special Issue on Supply Chain Strategy and Value Chain Restructuring), *Diamond Harvard Bijinesu* 23(6).

(1999) "Tokushu: Sapurai chien manejimento" (Special Issue on Supply Chain Management) *Opereshonzu Risaachi, Keiei no Kagaku* 44(6).

(1999) "Kaigishiryou No.1, No.2" (Proceedings of Logistics Software Conference, Vols 1–2), *Rojisuteiku Sofuto-uea Zenkoku Kaigi*, Tokyo: Nihon Rojisuteikusu Sisutemu Kyoukai.

DE-BI TSAO

T

Taguchi, Genichi

Taguchi (1924) has made important contributions to technical aspects of **quality management**. He developed the quality loss function, based on the notion that any deviation from a target value creates user dissatisfaction (loss to society). Losses associated with being very close to the target are small, but increase quickly (parabolically) with distance from the goal. This approach is very different from the traditional view of an acceptable range (specification limits), focusing instead on a specific target. Taguchi aims toward uniformity, rather than compliance with specifications. Emphasizing robustness in both design and process, Taguchi also popularized a simplified version of statistical design of experiments. While his approach displeases statisticians by not fully specifying interactions between variables, many engineers find it to be more accessible than traditional experimental design.

Further reading

Phadke, M.S. (1989) *Quality Engineering using Robust Design*, Englewood Cliffs, NJ: Prentice Hall.

ELIZABETH L. ROSE

takeovers

A takeover occurs when one company (individual, or institution) acquires control rights of a target company. Control rights are usually obtained through the buying of more than 51 percent of a firm's shares. In the typical principal–agent view of the corporation developed in US and British economics, the "principal," or owner, then has the right to control the "agents," or managers, who run an organization. It is the manager's duty to maximize profit; by maximizing profit, the manager maximizes share prices for shareholders. Managers who do not do this suffer falling share prices and the eventual threat of unwanted (or hostile) takeovers. Because of this constant pressure, managers fall in line and maximize profits for shareholders. All of this ensures rapid and efficient resource allocation in the economy. This view of **corporate governance** is common in the USA, but has only recently gained ground in Japan and Germany.

The belief in the ultimate efficiency of takeovers may be one reason why they occur in the USA. Another reason is related to the relative ease with which a determined acquirer of shares can obtain a majority stake in the US context. Although many deterrents to takeovers have been invented over the course of the past two decades, US and British capital markets tend to be much more fluid than their Japanese counterparts. Yet a third possible reason, although usually not mentioned by economists, is that the underlying work culture in the USA is permissive of takeovers. US employees may not identify themselves with the fate of one company to the degree that Japanese employees might. With well-developed external labor markets, US employees may also have more opportunity to change jobs if dissatisfied with a current employer.

In contrast to the US corporate governance

environment, many observers in the 1980s and 1990s argued that the managers of large Japanese firms traditionally see themselves not as agents for shareholders, but as agents for the firm's core employees and for other firm stakeholders. Instead of maximizing short-term profit (hence share price), managers focused on other goals such as firm growth and the long-run maximization of employee well being. At least partly because of this, managers and employees may have not been disposed to wanting to grow the firm through external takeovers or mergers. Instead, Japanese firms were inclined to grow internally, including through the creation of subsidies. In contrast to the US model, this view of firm control was also theorized to be efficient. Employees with job security, good pay, and firm specific training are productive employees concerned with quality; higher productivity and quality for the firm translates to greater long-term efficiency and growth.

Takeovers were said to be rare for several reasons. First, the form of ownership was said to be important as a deterrent. The stylized facts for the postwar Japanese financial system are that arm's length, speculative shareholders have traditionally played very little role in corporate decision making. Because a significant percentage (often a majority) of the Japanese firm's capital providers are "patient" and not willing to sell shares, this was said to block out unwanted takeovers and shield the firm from speculation in the capital markets (see **main bank system**; **cross-shareholdings**). As some researchers have also pointed out, firms that do not have shares held by large patient investors were also not taken over in Japan, so the relevant deterrent may be not be related to ownership. Hiroyuki Odagiri and others stressed the importance of firm culture, and labor practices in deterring takeovers. If employees view the firm as a community, they are likely to view an offer of a takeover (whether friendly or hostile) as an intrusion. Also because of the specificity of Japan's **internal labor markets**, it is quite difficult to mesh one firm's labor practices with another's.

Although takeovers are slowly increasing in Japan and the corporate governance model is in flux, the evidence that US-style takeovers will take hold in Japan is not conclusive. Although cross-shareholdings are unraveling and the main bank system is under extreme stress, there are still relatively few takeovers in Japan. Japan just recently witnessed its very first domestic hostile takeover attempt in 2000, when a former top Japanese bureaucrat made headlines with a hostile takeover bid of Shoei, a raw silk maker which now makes batteries. The bid failed, but the bidder went on to reinvent himself as an "activist" shareholder interested in exercising shareholder voice to affect change. Activist shareholders buying large stakes in a company and attempting to persuade recalcitrant managers to change may achieve some influence. However, there are many reasons why employees and managers may resist, including their belief that these shareholders may damage, rather than help, the long-run viability of their firm.

Further reading

Kester, W.C. (1991) *Japanese Takeovers: The Global Quest for Corporate Control*, Boston: Harvard Business School Press.

Odagiri, H. (1992) *Growth through Competition, Competition through Growth*, Oxford: Oxford University Press.

WILLIAM BARNES

Tanaka, Kakuei

Kakuei Tanaka was Prime Minister of Japan from July 6, 1972 to November 26, 1974. Tanaka is best known for creating big money politics and his involvement in the Lockheed scandal. Tanaka, however, represents a transition in the political economy of Japan. He rose to power as one of the first in a long line of "professional politicians," as the Yoshida School of ex-bureaucrat politicians declined. In the heady days of economic expansion, when the flows of money and votes involved enormous public works projects, Tanaka created the "dual power structure" of Japanese politics in which unofficial power brokers, like Tanaka, controlled major political offices.

In April 1947, Tanaka won election as Progressive Party representative from Niigata. From here he began his involvement in massive government spending on infrastructure (roads, bridges, tunnels) to remodel the archipelago. Tanaka's talents were in raising money and organizing people. His money pipeline was rooted in numerous ghost corporations that speculated in stocks and real estate. Tanaka's national power base was a group of conservative Diet members called *gundan* (army unit). He built his *gundan* on patron–client relations, providing money for loyalty and votes.

From 1976 to 1983, the years between his arrest and the trial verdict, he used his *gundan* to convert the **Liberal Democratic Party** (LDP), the bureaucracy, and business into an interconnected system of money and power. He became known as "Shadow Shogun of Mejiro" (the prime minister's residence). For example, by 1980 Tanaka's *gundan* was the largest faction in the LDP. All three prime ministers during Tanaka's trial (Ohira in 1978, Suzuki in 1980, and Nakasone in 1982) owed their positions to Tanaka. In response, Ohira gave the *gundan* four of twenty-one cabinet positions; Suzuki gave six and Nakasone gave eight positions.

Tanaka worked the bureaucracy with flattery, services and payoffs. He raised the salary of executives of public corporations, pleasing bureaucrats intent on retirement to these corporations. Tanaka was so well received by bureaucrats that he was called upon to adjudicate jurisdictional boundaries among the ministries and agencies. Yet his most characteristic form of influence was his flagrant attempts to buy allies among the bureaucrats, particularly in the Ministry of Construction. Tanaka paid their travel expenses and providing expensive gifts along with statements of sympathy for their low salaries.

Tanaka's connection with business was basically a pork-barrel relationship. Tanaka advocated for and protected business, for example, by passing pro-business tax cuts. He lobbied for individual businesses and negotiated mergers. By the 1960s, construction spending was a main pillar of the economy equaling 20 percent of GDP and 10 percent of employment. Tanaka often controlled *dango* bid rigging, because of the opaque process of awarding government contracts, which comprised 30–40 percent of all construction. In return, Tanaka received between a 1–3 percent kickback

on the contracts. In addition, Tanaka systematically used the regional branches of the benefited construction companies as bases for the political campaigns of local *gundan* politicians.

Tanaka's lieutenants (Kanamaru, Takeshita and Ozawa) continued Tanaka-style politics and broadened their base into **foreign aid** and the finance sectors. However, by the mid-1980s scandals rocking the legitimacy of the LDP, a ballooning budget deficit, a 3 percent sales tax, changing US–Japanese relations, and world criticism of Japan during the Gulf War all led to the destablization of the politics of the *gundan*.

Further reading

Junnosuke, M. (1995) *Contemporary Politics in Japan*, Berkeley, CA: University of California Press.
Schlesinger, J. (1997) *Shadow Shoguns*, New York: Simon & Schuster.

RICHARD A. COLIGNON

telecommunications industry

Japan's telecommunications industry is second in size and technological advancement to that of the United States. Government control of the industry in the form of the monopoly firm, the Nippon Telegraph and Telephone Company (NTT), was of critical importance up through the 1970s. State control allowed for heavy investment in the industry and protected it from foreign inroads, leading to a high quality, reliable system by the late 1970s. When NTT was partially privatized in 1985 (the government still owns the majority of the shares), the Ministry of Post and Telecommunications (MPT) gained increased regulatory authority over the industry. MPT's policies, the deep recession in Japan in the 1990s, the politicized environment within which NTT operates, and NTT's sluggishness in moving into new technologies such as those related to the Internet, have weakened NTT and its family of firms. While Japan leads the world in cell phone technology in the early 2000s, it lags in most other telecom technologies.

The 1950s, 1960s, and 1970s

NTT was created as a public corporation in 1952 just as the US Occupation of Japan was ending. Three key factors contributed to NTT's auspicious beginning. First, NTT set sail at a time when the international environment was very favorable and the technological trajectory was clear. Close relations with Bell Laboratories of the USA provided NTT with significant technological assistance during this period, when Japanese companies essentially reverse-engineered AT&T products.

Second, NTT was established at a time when Japan was pouring its efforts into building up the entire economy. No longer interested or able under Article 9 of the constitution to defend itself militarily, Japan turned to a strategy of defense through a strong economy and technological base. The telecom industry and NTT were a key part of this strategy. Indeed, NTT became Japan's Pentagon, a protected safe haven for research to strengthen the nation's technological base.

Third, an innovative system of financing allowed for heavier investment in NTT than otherwise would have been possible. Up until the early 1980s, a system of telephone subscriber bonds, used only in Japan, required that phone users purchase a ¥100,000 government bond ($300–$400 depending on the exchange rate) to get a phone. This money was returned to the subscriber after ten years. This system funneled a huge amount of up-front money into the industry, much more than the government alone could have provided. Phone users also supported NTT through high installation fees (still ¥72,000 or $720 in 2000). NTT did not profit heavily from these large fees. Rather, the money was used to pay high prices to the firms that made equipment for NTT. These firms, members of the so-called NTT family, include NEC, Fujitsu, Oki, and Hitachi. NTT bought equipment from family firms on a cost-plus basis, much like the Pentagon in the USA. In short, money from phone users was used to build up a strong telecom industry and a strong set of telecom firms.

When NTT needed equipment, it met with its family of firms to discuss the product and set specifications based on NTT's proprietary standards. Orders for sophisticated switching equipment went to the big four makers: Fujitsu, NEC, Oki, and Hitachi. The R&D was done collaboratively amongst the firms and NTT's advanced labs. Ties between NTT and the firms were cemented by the practice of ***amakudari***, the retirement of NTT officials onto the boards of NTT family firms. NTT nurtured the firms and in return the firms took care of retiring NTT officials. The NTT family system worked well through the 1970s. By the late 1970s NTT had met its two key goals of providing direct dial service throughout the country and eliminating the backlog of phone orders.

Because of its large budgets and impact on growth rates and employment, politicians did try to influence NTT's investment decisions. To protect its autonomy as well as to assure the political stability and pro-business policies required for its objectives, NTT made indirect campaign contributions to politicians. More specifically, by paying high prices for equipment, NTT provided family firms with the extra funds they needed to make significant campaign contributions. Political interference in NTT's affairs was kept in balance up until the late 1970s. In the 1980s technological change, a shift in the international environment, the nation's deteriorating national debt problem, and the erosion of the consensus among state actors on how to use NTT for the national purpose led to increased politicization of NTT and the erosion of an effective state-guided strategy toward the industry.

The 1980s and 1990s

By the late 1970s NTT had met its key goals. But now that it had caught up with the west in basic phone infrastructure, it needed a new mission in an era when the technological path was no longer clear. Political, economic and technological conditions were changing, leading to a discussion over privatizing and breaking up NTT. This discussion was stimulated in part by the US government's break-up of AT&T and the British government's privatization of British Telecom (BT).

At this same time, various scandals raised questions about NTT's inefficient management and its overall legitimacy as a protected national monopoly. Corporate users started complaining about NTT's low-quality data communications services and its high prices. The USA, facing growing deficits with Japan, started pressuring NTT to procure foreign telecom equipment. Once doubts were raised about NTT's future, state and corporate actors with strong stakes in the outcome realized that NTT would be privatized and possibly divested and decided it may as well be changed to their benefit.

The key actors had different motivations for privatizing and breaking up NTT. The **Ministry of Finance** (MOF) wanted NTT to be privatized so it could sell NTT shares to reduce the nation's rising debt. Big business wanted the debt problem to be solved without tax hikes and thus favored privatization. The **Ministry of International Trade and Industry** (MITI), which oversaw the computer, semiconductor, and other manufacturing industries, wanted to wrestle control over the telecommunications industry, which was in MPT's jurisdiction. MPT bureaucrats believed that if NTT was privatized and broken up, MPT would gain regulatory powers that would make it a powerful policy agency like MITI and MOF. Non-NTT family firms were pressing for the giant's privatization because they wanted a piece of NTT's pie.

In short, the motivation for privatizing and breaking-up NTT was primarily political. While couched in terms of economic efficiency, user benefits, and long-term competitiveness, the debate was really driven by a power struggle. Thus, what had been an effective industrial policy toward NTT and the industry up through the 1970s disintegrated into political squabbling. Various actors tried to manipulate NTT for their own purposes with little attention given to the long-term competitiveness of the industry and user benefits. There was no longer a strong state consensus on how to use NTT for the national interest and the result was serious politicization of NTT and an over twenty-year debate over whether to privatize and break up the telecommunications giant.

NTT was partially privatized in 1985 (the government stated it would hold 30 percent of the stock indefinitely, and held two-thirds of the stock until the late 1990s). MOF and MPT were the big winners in the partial privatization. MOF could sell NTT stock to help shore up national coffers. and MPT gained vast regulatory powers that had formerly been held by NTT.

While MPT professes to be increasing user benefits and nurturing new firms, Japan's telecom charges remain quite high by international standards, and competition is weak. Competition only exists in cell phones and long-distance markets, but even then MPT keeps prices relatively high and tightly controls entrants. NTT's dominance of local calls and the fact that all long-distance carriers have to pay NTT high connection fees to connect to its local lines has become a major trade issue between the US and Japan in the early 2000s. Growing domestic constituencies are also complaining about NTT's dominance. As long as NTT is largely a government-owned firm enmeshed in a political environment in which it is a major provider of public works and cannot fire workers, it is destined to lag in cutting edge technologies and communications services.

The decision to divest NTT was delayed from 1985 to 1990, 1990 to 1995 and again to 1996. The delay was largely due to MOF's concern that divestiture would hurt NTT's stock price as well as NTT's strong opposition to the proposal. In 1996 a compromise was reached to break NTT into three firms: one local company covering eastern Japan, one local company covering western Japan, and a long-distance firm. But these three firms, together with other NTT spin-offs such as the mobile phone giant, NTT DoCoMo, have been put under an umbrella holding company. There is consensus that this "break-up" is having little impact on competition. The "break-up" compromise allows the Japanese government to tell the USA that it has broken up NTT and saves the face of MPT, which has long been pushing for a break-up. It also allows NTT to say it was not broken up but instead strengthened through integration under a holding company.

The 2000s

Japan lags the west in Internet use, high fees and other advanced telecommunications services with the exception of the cellular phone. While mobile phones meet the needs of Japanese citizens, who spend long hours commuting, the high rate of cell phone usage is also the result of the high cost of installing a regular phone line. Indeed, there are now more cell phone subscribers than those for installed lines.

There is a sense of crisis in the industry in the 2000s just as there is in many high tech sectors. Japan has succeeded in manufacturing high quality goods and now it needs to become a more inventor and entrepreneur-friendly nation. Japan's success in mobile phones has only been in Japan because of its closed standards. But NTT DoCoMo is planning to offer an internationally compatible standard in its next generation cell phones. As for the Internet, while use is growing, there are many barriers to its full-fledged use other than high local phone rates. These include close interfirm *keiretsu* ties, lifetime employment and seniority wage practices that make it difficult to restructure firms to gain efficiencies from the Internet, traditional reliance on personal contacts, and the like.

There is a growing debate over whether the state should sell all its NTT shares to allow the giant to restructure itself to compete internationally. But even if the government does sell its shares, the politics of the situation, especially given the deep recession, will most likely work against any dramatic change in NTT in the foreseeable future.

See also: computer industry; software industry

Further reading

Anchordoguy, M. (1989) *Computers, Inc.: Japan's Challenge to IBM*, Cambridge, MA: Harvard University Press.
—— (2000) "Building a Telecommunications Industry: The Developmental State and the Nippon Telegraph and Telephone Company" and "The Politicization and Erosion of the Developmental State: Japan's Telecommunications Industry, 1980–2000," working papers.
Fransman, M. (1995) *Japan's Computer and Communications Industry: The Evolution of Industrial Giants and Global Competitiveness*, Oxford: Oxford University Press.
Ian, G. (1991) "Re-regulation, Competition and New Industries in Japanese Telecommunications," in S. Wilks and M. Wright (eds), *The Promotion and Regulation of Industry in Japan*, New York: St. Martin's Press.

Johnson, C. (1989) "MITI, MPT, and the Telecom Wars," in C. Johnson, L. Tyson, and J. Zysman (eds), *Politics and Productivity*, Cambridge, MA: Ballinger.
Vogel, S. (1996) *Freer Markets, More Rules*, Ithaca, NY: Cornell University Press.

MARIE ANCHORDOGUY

three sacred treasures

The "three treasures" is a culturally-tinged euphemism for the most commonly cited elements of the Japanese management system: **enterprise unions**, **lifetime employment** and **seniority promotion**. These distinctive aspects of the traditional post-Second World War Japanese firm were first identified in James Abegglen's pioneering work, *The Japanese Factory*. Proponents of Japanese-style management argue that these three elements are the key to Japanese success in human resource management.

The "sacred treasures" is a reference to the mirror, sword and jewel, three objects accorded great reverence in Japanese mythological history which are viewed as tokens of the emperor's legitimate authority. The actual mirror, sword and jewel are located, one each, at Japan's three most important Shinto shrines: Izumo, Atsuta, and Ise.

Further reading

Abegglen, J.C. (1958) *The Japanese Factory: Aspects of its Social Organization*, Glencoe, IL: The Free Press.

ALLAN BIRD

Tokugawa period

The period of formal rule by the fifteen Tokugawa shoguns (1600–1868), often called the Edo Period, was a time of tight control of a central government over more than 250 feudal estates. Japan was cut off from the outside world during most of the Tokugawa period. Social ranking was strictly enforced with the warrior and noble caste on top and everyone else beneath. It was a time of peace and relatively strong commercial development in Japan's cities, with the political capital at Edo experiencing spectacular growth in power and size. The Tokugawa period began with the victory of the Tokugawa forces and their allies at the battle of Sekigahara in 1600, enduring until 1868, the year of abdication of the last Tokugawa Shogun and the official start of the Meiji period. The regime was the ultimate power in the land for almost all of that time. What happened during the Tokugawa period both in direct and indirect reaction to policies of the regime, is of overwhelming importance in understanding the character of modern Japan.

In comparison with other regimes over the past few centuries, the central authority established by the Tokugawa clan shortly after 1600 was remarkable in many ways. It lasted for two and one-half centuries, ruling over one of the most populous nations of the world, wielding together and controlling a political system extending more than a thousand miles from northeast to southwest, with areas cut off from each other by mountain ranges difficult to cross even now. The degree of rearrangement of a large society, and the techniques used for tightly controlling such a society, are impressive even by contemporary standards. The regime brought lasting peace to a society which had institutionalized nearly continual civil war for more than a hundred years. Effective central authority was instituted over a nation that had not had more than brief periods of central government for nearly a thousand years. It ruled to a surprising degree by written decree, at a time when mass-production of written materials was limited and difficult to disseminate. Following its initial hundred years or so, the Tokugawa regime was the government of one of the most literate and orderly societies prior to the twentieth century.

Tokugawa Ieyasu, founder of the Tokugawa regime, the first of fifteen men to serve as Shogun, or secular ruler of Japan, during the Tokugawa period, did not simply spring up and put an end to the period of civil wars by himself or with his own military forces. The unification of Japan under a single military leader, bringing an end at least temporarily to the struggle for power among the larger feudal estates, had been accomplished more than thirty years before the beginning of the Tokugawa period by the great warlord Oda

Nobunaga. Unification did not mean the disappearance of feudal estates, but the estates and the *daimyo* who headed them were forced to give up a degree of autonomy, especially military autonomy, and acquiesce to a central political power. Following the assassination of Nobunaga in 1582, the mantel of centralized authority over the feudal estates fell to the flamboyant former peasant, Hideyoshi, who helped pave the way for the Tokugawa regime by moving yet more authority in the direction of central power.

Tokugawa Ieyasu was a man born to a time and to a station in life characterized by armed struggle, intrigue, military alliances both overt and secret, subversion of authority and other aspects of extreme individual and societal insecurity. Perhaps it was natural that his passion in life was to create stability and establish power over the land that would pass on to his heirs indefinitely. He was clever enough to understand that this could not be accomplished merely through military domination. Several radical policies were instigated during the first decade of rule which literally changed the face of Japan. Those *daimyo* whom the regime did not trust because they had opposed Tokugawa's bid for control were relocated, literally ordered to move estates to areas far from the capital, construct new castles, and make a home for themselves where more reliable *daimyo* could keep an eye on them.

The new regime decided not to rule from the Kansai area, around Kyoto and Osaka, which had been the political and commercial center of Japan for most of its history up to then. An enormous castle project was begun by Ieyasu, continued by his son Hidetada, and finally completed by his grandson Iyemitsu in the area close to the mouth of the Edo River. There was a small castle already there, but nothing else. As had happened once before in Japanese history in the late thirteenth century, a military government set up for business before permanent structures were built for it, with officials living and working in tents. As before it was called *bakufu*, tent government. The name stuck and the Tokugawa regime was always referred to by people who lived under it as *bakufu*, which came to mean simply, "the government."

If any of the people who saw the area around construction of the castle could have been transposed ahead 150 years they would surely have been astounded at what lay around them. They would have found themselves in the middle of one of the largest cities on earth. The castle at its center was actually a walled city within a city. Covering more than twice the area of the present-day Imperial palace, home and work place to a bureaucracy of hundreds of *samurai* who kept detailed records of activities throughout the land. Outside, a city spread beyond the castle for miles, with more than a hundred temples, more than two hundred large estates for the elite, and homes for close to a million Japanese of lesser ranking.

Sankin kotai

What spawned the rapid and extensive urban development was something called in Japanese *sankin kotai*, usually rendered in English as "alternative residence." It was an elaborate hostage system whereby all *daimyo* were forced to construct a residence compound on grounds close to the Tokugawa castle in Edo, and to physically reside in that residence for one-half of each year. During the other six months when a *daimyo* was allowed to return and attend to affairs of his domain (within limits of the may rules and regulations constantly being issued and revised from the *bakufu*), his parents if they were alive, his wife, and his children had to take his place in the Edo mansion. The program did not run on the honor system. Personnel assigned to be at the mansion were verified at intervals by *bakufu* samurai, and checkpoints were established along roads leading to Edo at which every person in a *daimyo* procession going either toward or away from the capital was checked against a list prepared in advance and forwarded to Tokugawa officials manning the checkpoints.

During the first few decades of the seventeenth century there were more than 250 wealthy aristocrats living in the general area of Edo castle. They all needed many things: housing, clothing, artifacts for preparing food, food itself, and they had needs beyond these, things such as domestic help, entertainment, reading material, and all sorts of personal items. An enormous consumer market had been made to spring up out of nowhere. Most peasants were tied to the land and under the control of the *daimyo*. Merchants and craftsmen, on the other hand, were free to locate wherever they liked, and it was clear to large numbers of them that Edo was the place to be. Secular power had shifted firmly to the new capital of Edo, and by 1700 it passed both Kyoto and Osaka becoming the largest city of Japan, and indeed, as stated above, one of the largest in the world.

Sakoku-rei

During the rule of Oda Nobunaga and Hideyoshi, and for the last thirty years or so of the civil wars preceding unification of Japan under Oda, Europeans had begun to have a hand in Japanese power politics. They introduced firearms, which completely changed the character of warfare in Japan, and Christianity was embraced by some *daimyo*, a result of close relations some warlords had with specific groups of Dutch, Portuguese or Spanish. Oda had actually encouraged Christianity in Japan as a way of offsetting the power of large Buddhist groups, some with private military units, headquartered near the capital at Kyoto. Tokugawa Ieyasu apparently considered this incursion of foreigners and a foreign religion to be a threat to the Tokugawa regime's absolute power. Christianity was banned, and all foreigners ordered to leave Japan. The regime then took the radical step of closing Japan off from the outside world. Japanese living abroad were given a few years to return, and then when *sakoku-rei*, literally, "locked country rule," went fully into effect in 1639 (twenty-three years after the death of Ieyasu), no one could leave or enter the country. There were a few exceptions such as Deshima island in Nagasaki harbor which Dutch and Chinese ships were allowed to visit on occasion, and one branch family of the Tokugawa clan was allowed to trade with the Ryukyu islands, then under Chinese control. But for the most part, Japan was sealed off from the world, officially for more than two hundred years.

Edo culture

Although for the bulk of the Japanese population, the peasants, life remained austere and difficult, the Tokugawa period ushered in a highly developed and relatively prosperous urban culture in Edo and other large cities. It is somewhat ironic how this came about, because the driving force behind the explosion of urban culture was the lowest ranked category of Japanese. The regime based its economic policy on controlling land and the products of the land. The entire population was officially frozen into occupation castes based on a type of Japanese interpretation of the theories of Sung Dynasty new-Confucianism. At the top, representing a little less than 10 percent of the population were the warrior elite and court nobility, with the Imperial family at the top of this category and the *samurai* at the bottom. According to theory, the peasants were ranked next in line, but in reality they were the most exploited and abused of all categories. Craftsmen were ranked next in the four-part system, and the bottom of the list were merchants, people seen by the ruling warrior class as parasites who served no real national purpose.

The warrior/noble class held all political power, but a new kind of power was emerging in Japan, the power of money. By bringing lasting peace to the land, the Tokugawa regime created conditions of stability and predictability, which were very favorable to the one rank they held in greatest contempt: merchants. Business thrived in urban Japan, with some members of the merchant class becoming very wealthy creating markets for elaborate material and non-material products. The industrial revolution had passed them by, and in the realm of technology Edo Japan fell behind Europe. However Tokugawa Japan was run with great administrative skill, and (often in spite of the heavy hand of the *samurai* officials) the cultural life of its cities was as vibrant and intricate as any city of its time.

See also: guilds; Meiji restoration

Further reading

Dore, R. (1984) *Education in Tokugawa Japan*, London: Athlone Press.

Lehmann, J.-P. (1982) *The Roots of Modern Japan*, London: Macmillan.

Murayama, M. (1974) *Studies in the Intellectual History of Tokugawa Japan*, Tokyo: University of Tokyo Press.

Totman, C.D. (1967) *Politics in the Tokugawa Bakufu*, Cambridge, MA: Harvard University Press.

Tsukahira, T.G. (1970) *Feudal Control in Tokugawa Japan: The Sankin-Kotai System*, Cambridge, MA: Harvard University Press.

JOHN A. McKINSTRY

Tokyo University

Standing at the top the hierarchy of the Japanese university system is the government-financed and operated Tokyo University. It is more central to the selection of leadership in the governmental and economic life of the nation than that of any university in any other country. Tokyo University graduates dominate top government and business leadership positions. Only the brightest students (or at least, the best test takers) in Japan sit for entrance examinations to Tokyo University, and entrance is a virtual guarantee of career success.

There are more than 500 universities in Japan, second only to the United States in number and *per capita*. About twenty Japanese universities are particularly respected as places where quality graduates are produced and which are recruiting grounds for leadership for important private and government employers. It is widely agreed that within that group of twenty or so, five universities stand out above the rest as elite schools: Tokyo University, the two private universities, **Keio University** and Waseda University (both also in Tokyo), Kyoto University, and Hitotsubashi, also located in Tokyo. Entry into these elite schools is sought after by the brightest of Japan's youth, and to be a graduate of one of these top five universities is an advantage in any career.

Around the world, other famous universities have played a prominent role in providing leadership in countries around the world: Oxford, Harvard, Moscow University, the University of Paris, Chulalongkorn University are examples. It is no exaggeration to state that none of these institutions even comes close to Tokyo University as a place where future leaders are provided for a nation. It is a large institution with about seven thousand undergraduate, and about seven thousand graduate students. The student body of Tokyo University is highly selected; it is extremely difficult to pass the examination for entrance. The faculty is, as one would imagine, quite distinguished. However, some observers have concluded that the quality of scholarship and academic programs is not commensurate with its position in such an advanced society.

Japan is often depicted as a society dominated by three significant power sources, what some have called the "iron triangle:" the elected government, the bureaucracy, and the large corporations. The proportion of people at the top of each of these power sources who have graduated from that one institution provides evidence of the overwhelming importance of Tokyo University in the leadership of Japanese society. More than twenty people have held the office of prime minister since the end of the Second World War; ten of them have been graduates of Tokyo University. That same kind of concentration of graduates can be found in top bureaucratic posts and among top leaders in banking and industry.

To underscore the narrowness of conditioning of Japanese life at the top, all ten of the postwar prime ministers mentioned above graduated from a single department of the university, the Faculty of Law (which, as is the case in all Japanese universities, does not grant law degrees, but administers a rather general undergraduate program). For the various ministries of the national bureaucracy, a more strategic center of power than for similar agencies in the United States or Britain, graduates of the Faculty of Law of Tokyo University are even more in evidence. For important ministries such as the **Ministry of Finance**, **Ministry of International Trade and Industry**, and the Foreign Ministry, graduates of Tokyo University have always made up more than 70 percent of top-level personnel.

While such a narrowly concentrated channeling of leadership identification and conditioning may seem extraordinary, clearly unprecedented in contemporary advanced societies, history reveals a rather simple answer for it: Tokyo University was founded precisely to play such a role, and it has to date never relinquished that role. Leadership in the **Tokugawa period** had been rooted largely in heredity. Young men who conceived of and brought to realization the **Meiji restoration** were quick to grasp that if the new society could hope to compete with Western powers, it was

essential to have a new kind of leadership, based not on heredity, but upon specific skills and training, upon understanding of modern systems of administration, upon knowledge of a wider world.

During the final half-century of the Tokugawa regime, a growing fear of the price of isolation and ignorance of the outside world was openly expressed by people within the government. Several small institutes were established to familiarize a cadre of *samurai* with whatever information was available about foreign societies. A few studied the Dutch language, and there was more knowledge of the outside world circulated within that small group than is generally believed. Meiji leaders consolidated these institutes immediately after taking the reigns of control, and by 1877, nine years into the new regime, they were all merged into an institution copied from European and American models with faculties of agriculture, economics, engineering, law, letters, medicine and science. In 1886 the institution was officially titled Tokyo Imperial University. After the Second World War the name was shortened to the present Tokyo University.

This government institution was not the only center of learning during the early Meiji period. In fact the private school which later came to be known as Keio University actually predated the beginning of Tokyo University, having its beginnings the very first year of Meiji in 1858. Waseda came into existence a little later, in 1882. However, Tokyo University was then, and remains today, the primary training institute for top Japanese leadership.

See also: Men in charge of MOF

Further reading

Cutts, R.L. (1997) *An Empire of Schools: Japan's Universities and the Molding of a National Power Elite*, Armonk, NY: M.E. Sharpe.

Kerbo, H.R. and McKinstry, J.A. (1995) *Who Rules Japan: The Inner Circles of Economic and Political Power*, Westport, CT: Praeger.

Koh, B.C. (1989) *Japan's Administrative Elite*, Berkeley, CA: University of California Press.

JOHN A. McKINSTRY

tonya

In a modern society where the social division of labor prevails, consumer products (commodities) reach the consumers through a successive process of transactions, which is called a **distribution system**. The last stage of transaction that involves consumers, is designated as retail or retail distribution, and relates to the function of distribution *vis-à-vis* consumers, which is assumed by those called "retailers" (*kouri gyousha* or *kouri*). All the other transactions in the distribution process, including purchases by retailers, are known as intermediary distribution, but the term is rather notional and often replaced by the term "wholesaling" (*oroshiuri gyousha* or *oroshi*).

In Japan, the term *tonya* has traditionally been used to designate the wholesalers (individual and collective) that specialize in the intermediary functions in distribution. The term derives from *toi* or *toi maru*, the section of medieval seigniorial domain in charge of storage and transport of impost. As commercial activities grew, this section became independent from landowners and expanded to transport and warehouse businesses. During the Muromachi period (1336–1573), they widened the scope of operations into such areas as transactions of commodities and provision of accommodation and other services for peddlers, the then retailers. These business entities were called *toiya*, and the appellation was transformed to *tonya* after the **Meiji restoration**.

Until the mid-twentieth century, when the capitalistic economy in Japan reached the point of mass consumer society, the *tonya*'s role in regard to producers and retailers was significant. Producers that lacked sales know-how or financial strength to run their business often accorded to a strong *tonya* the exclusive license to sell particular or all items that they produced. In return, producers received some money before the purchase of their product by consumers took place, which was a critical arrangement in the formers' cash flow management. *Tonya* with abundant financial resources thus functioned as *de facto* lenders to producers.

Tonya also assumed the marketing function for producers that relied on the *tonya* to sell their products, by proposing modifications or additions of items. In the pre-Second World War period, Meiji-Ya, a leading food products wholesaler founded in 1885, expanded its business through the acquisition of a sole distributor license from Japan Brewery (presently Kirin Brewery Co., Ltd.), and from the Tsuneyoshi Okura Brewery, a sake maker, for preservative-free sake that Meiji-Ya itself had proposed.

On the other hand, *tonya* also held the position of allocating merchandize of high demand to individual retailers under its networks. As the *tonya* also sold merchandize to retailers on credit spanning a certain period, it acted as a credit institution for both ends of the distribution channel. This financial role provided the *tonya* with an overwhelming power to control the whole distribution process. The *tonya* generally retained this power throughout the periods when producers and retailers were fragmentary and small in scale.

A Japanese saying, still in use, *Souwa ton-ya ga orosanai* (*tonya* does not wholesale), relates to the practical lesson that life never proceeds as one hopes, and derives from the historical fact that the *tonya* exerted very strong influence on the everyday life of the ordinary people and sometimes abused it for profit. The hegemony of *tonya* still persists today in areas where production and distribution structures are fragmentary. Exemplary commodities are the fresh vegetables and fish, and publishing.

After the Second World War, the consumer goods industry grew rapidly throughout the periods of **economic growth**. In the 1960s so-called mass production and mass consumption was heralded. Mass production led to the birth of nationwide producers in a variety of commodities, while mass consumption was spurred and accelerated by mushrooming superstore (supermarket) chains (see **superstores**). As large-scale nationwide operators increasingly dominated both ends of the distribution channel in Japan, the intricate traditional intermediary distribution industry, the *tonya* system, was put under question along with the practices of *tonya* to often impose arbitrary and unilateral terms of transactions.

In the early 1960s, Shuji Hayashi, a professor at the University of Tokyo, called for modernization of the distribution system in line with that of the country's industrial development under the slogan of *Ryuutsuu Kakumei* (revolution in distribution). His proposal was that leading producers and large retailers should deal directly with each other, or that the intermediary distribution should be eliminated altogether in order to have an efficient distribution system.

Contrary to these arguments, however, the number of wholesalers continued to increase until into the 1980s. Three factors were influential. Firstly, the considerable expansion of the consumer market in Japan also made room for the traditional small retailers to increase (but often with new business formats), to which the traditional wholesalers responded by slimming down and diversification in the commodities and service that they provided.

Secondly, organized retail firms such as superstores, needing to control the inventory and timely purchase of an ever-increasing array of items on their shelves, regarded the *tonya* as a means of outsourcing to bear this function. The *tonya* did not only eagerly assume it but also participated in the marketing activities of superstores with suggestions and proposals under the self-designation of "retail support" partners.

Thirdly, the importance of *tonya* for the leading producers of consumer goods did not diminish either. Since the *tonya* controlled a wide range of distribution channels and outlets, a stable relationship with a large *tonya* gave producers a number of advantages in the exchange of rebates and sales promotion fees paid to the former. Firstly, the producers could readily make use of the existing retail networks under the control of the *tonya*. Secondly, they could expect that the *tonya* would purchase the minimum lot of production necessary to cover the initial investment. And thirdly, the *tonya* could, to a certain extent, function as a shield against fluctuations of demand, which allowed producers to dispatch their products in an orderly fashion.

Due to these factors, the *tonya* system retained importance through the 1960s and 1970s, even if not so powerful as in the prewar period when their hegemony was almost absolute. By the end of the 1980s, however, traditional forms of retail business had lost ground within the Japanese **retail industry**. The main arena of competition shifted, from the one between the traditional retailers and the chain operators, to competition among the latter. The application of information and telecommunications technologies made it possible for chain store headquarters to collect sales and inventory data of individual stores on an item-by-item basis using point-of-sale (POS) technology. These data were useful to avoid excessive inventory or opportunity loss, and increasingly were transmitted to producers in order to streamline logistics.

In the late 1980s, the **bubble economy** in Japan, coupled with *endaka*, brought about a series of speculative purchases of foreign real estate. This prompted Japan's trade partners, especially the USA, to demand that Japan open its domestic market to foreign operators. The complex and inefficient structure of the country's intermediary distribution system became one of the heated issues in **trade negotiations**. It was then that the term *tonya* acquired international recognition, and the *tonya* system was thought, not only by foreigners but also at home, to be a major barrier against free entry and one of the principal factors contributing to high retail prices in the country.

In 1991, Toys R Us, an American toy retailer, began deploying a chain network in Japan. The company's strategy was to skip *tonya* or the intermediary distribution stages as extensively as possible, and to make direct purchases in bulk from producers in order to lower the costs. After Toys R Us, a number of foreign retailers began to make inroads with identical strategies.

These changes reactivated the once-rejected argument that the *tonya* system should be eliminated. The fact that the number of wholesalers was in decline and that chain operators controlled a considerable share within each regional market, seems to have further strengthened the views that direct transactions between producers and retailers will dominate.

Around the turn of the twenty-first century, the world's leading retailers have established various systems of procurement and purchase through the Internet. Wal-Mart pioneered this approach with Retailers Market Xchange.com, which prompted its competitors to launch similar B2B (Business to Business) or "marketplace" networks such as WorldWide Retail Exchange and GlobalNetXchange. In line with foreign companies, several leading Japanese retailers have announced their intention to participate in one of these networks, and the purchase volume is gradually increasing.

Surrounded with a rapidly changing environment, many *tonya* are struggling to rediscover some new and proper function in relation to producers and retailers. The additional functions sought include logistical support, assistance to the lineup of merchandises, information management and its maintenance, and finance. However, as the whole economy of Japan tends to be deflationary after the collapse of the bubble economy, the retail industry itself has been experiencing a structural slump. The situation, in turn, makes it inevitable that the *tonya* system will undergo a period of **restructuring** and consolidation.

See also: after-sales pricing; Daiei; deregulation; guilds; Ito-Yokado; marketing in Japan; pricing practices; promissory notes

Further reading

Hayashi, S. (1963) *Ryuutsuu Kakumei* (Revolution in Distribution), Tokyo: Chuuoukouronsha.

SHINTARO MOGI

torishimariyakukai

The official title for executives at the highest level of a Japanese firm is *torishimariyaku*, translated as "director." As a group, these *torishimariyaku* comprise the Japanese firm's formal board of directors, *torishimariyakukai*. The activities of the *torishimariyakukai* differ substantially from its US or Western European counterparts.

Historically, *torishimariyakukai* were based on a Western model of organization in which responsibility at the top was divided into two general categories: shareholder trusteeship and general management. Shareholder trusteeship refers to the responsibility of members of the board of directors to protect the interests of shareholders through oversight of the firm's professional managers. Duties pertaining to the administration of company policies and day-to-day operational activities of the firm fall under the category of "general management" and fall under the purview of the professional managerial cadre, usually a set of senior managers at the top of the organization.

In most US and UK companies, these two responsibilities are differentiated more clearly than in Japan. In US firms, for example, the board of directors meets and reviews the performance of the company and ratifies policy decisions that are likely to have a major influence on the company's performance. Once the board ratifies such policies, professional managers, led by the *shacho* (equivalent to a chief executive officer in Western firms), take responsibility for the general management of the company. It is common in US and Western European firms for the Chief Executive Officer (CEO) and several senior executives to simultaneously hold general manager posts as well as positions on the board in order to accurately represent management's position on various decisions made at the board level. Because of this arrangement, the distinction between the board's responsibility to shareholders and general managers' responsibility for policy development and implementation is clearly demarcated, though some overlap does exist.

In Japan, the distinction between shareholder trusteeship and general management duties is more ambiguous. On average only one director in thirty is an outside director, i.e., one who does not have some area of operational responsibility within the company. In fact, most directors are promoted from posts as department heads, and, though they are promoted to the *torishimariyakukai*, continue to carry out their responsibilities as department heads. Nevertheless, directors with department head duties have a different relationship to the firm than their non-director counterparts. When elected to the board and appointed as directors, the new executive formally retires from the company and collects a retirement bonus. He is then immediately re-hired as a director of the company, with a two-year appointment to the board.

Further comparisons of *torishimariyakukai* with boards in the USA and UK reveal that *torishimariyakukai* appear to be 25 to 30 percent larger. However, such a comparison is misleading. The double duty that a Japanese executive performs implies that, to make a proper comparison with Western firms, both directors and general managers should be included. When general managers are included in the calculation, the size of *torishimariyakukai* is actually smaller.

Torishimariyakukai structure and function

The *torishimariyakukai* includes all directors as well as **kansayaku**, the firm's internal auditors. The formal *torishimariyakukai* is not a sovereign body. No legal powers are granted it under Japanese commercial law, although the law requires that there be one. Generally the *torishimariyakukai* meets less than once a month. Under a Western model of the firm, boards of directors make final decisions on whether or not to approve long-range plans. For example, 35 per cent of boards in the US authorize long-range plans. In the UK that figure approaches 65 per cent. In Japan, by contrast, only 13 per cent of boards surveyed are involved in the authorization of long-range plans.

Though the *torishimariyakukai* is assumed to represent shareholders, this is largely a fiction. Directors are selected by the CEO, summarily approved by the formal board, and then voted on at the general shareholders' meetings once a year. Even at the general shareholders' meeting it is unlikely that shareholders will have much power to influence the choice of directors as votes are usually vested by proxy in the formal board itself and companies may enlist the aid of **sokaiya**, strong arms with ties to the *yakuza*, who intimidate vocal shareholders from asking embarrassing questions. Though legislation in 1983 outlawed *sokaiya*, they are still widely influential. The average annual shareholder's meeting lasts twenty-five minutes.

At the same time that shareholders appear powerless to influence the *torishimariyakukai*, Japanese commercial law grants them broad power to call it to accountability. A shareholder with as few as 3 per cent of a company's stock can request that the civil courts remove a director. Similarly, such a shareholder can demand that a board meeting be held within two weeks of a request for such a meeting. Comparable power does not exist for shareholders with equally small stock positions in US firms. Finally, shareholders in possession of 10 per cent or more of a company's stock can claim access to confidential financial statements relating to a company's performance.

There are a number of reasons why share-holders hold little sway over the *torishimariyakukai*. In prewar days there were numerous outside directors. These outside directors viewed themselves as independents who were charged mainly with carrying out the duties of shareholder trusteeship. With only one in thirty directors originating from outside in Japanese boardrooms today, *torishimariyakukai* are in a position to resist attempts to change their nearly unassailable control over the company. Additionally, as noted above, from the immediate postwar years up to the early 1980s many companies employed *sokaiya* to silence shareholders who might raise uncomfortable questions or challenge the board during the general shareholders' meeting. The final reason shareholders have little influence on directors and the *torishimariyakukai* has to do with the composition of shareholders. In most large corporations, small shareholders account for just over 30 per cent of outstanding shares. Institutional investors are responsible for the lion's share of company stocks. But unlike the USA or UK, where institutional investors consist mainly of pension funds and insurance companies, Japanese institutional investors consist mainly of a company's main bank and affiliated companies. This group of institutional investors does not seek control of the company even though it has ownership.

Members within the *torishimariyakukai* can be divided in two ways, by legal authority and by hierarchical rank. Under Japanese commercial law at least one director must be granted authority to represent the company to third parties and to sign documents for it. This representative authority, **daihyoken**, is usually reserved for CEOs and selected senior officers. The number of executives possessing representative authority varies by company size and by industry. Banks have the largest number of executives vested with such power per *torishimariyakukai* of any industry in Japan.

Torishimariyakukai have a pronounced hierarchy which can range from as few as three different levels to as many as seven. The average number of levels is six. These are, in descending order of rank: chairman, vice-chairman, president, vice-president, senior managing director, managing director, and director. The level most frequently omitted in companies is that of vice-chairman. Additionally, the authority associated with each level is relatively clear for all positions from vice-president on down. However, the relationship between chairman and president is ambiguous and varies by company and by specific occupants of those positions. In some companies the chairman is the supreme authority within the *torishimariyakukai*, while in others the chairman is a figurehead and the president is the true powerholder. Differences in power arrangements at the top of *torishimariyakukai* appear to be based solely on the preferences of the individuals involved and not on any formal or informal policy within companies.

The structure of the *torishimariyakukai* and the manner in which it carries out the dual responsibility of general management and shareholder trusteeship lead to some advantages for the company. First, the combining of top management's responsibilities into one body leads to a smaller operating unit at the top and contributes to a potential for greater flexibility than is usually possible in US and Western European companies where the responsibilities are divided and the number of executives and directors comprising the top echelon of the company is larger. The second advantage is the freedom from pressure for short-term returns that the *torishimariyakukai* has by virtue of both the weak position of the shareholder and the fact that institutional shareholders do not seek to exercise their right to control the firm. This freedom gives it greater latitude in developing long-range policy and strategy for the firm.

There are, a number of disadvantages and weaknesses with the *torishimariyakukai*. First, the smaller size of the operating unit increases the likelihood that power within the group can be seized by just one or two executives in key positions. A second weakness is that the freedom from shareholder pressure can also constitute freedom from accountability. This weakness is further exacerbated by the fact that only directors with managerial assignments within the company have extensive knowledge about the company. In most instances, shareholders do not have access to sufficient information so as to make informed choices at shareholder meeting elections.

Torishimariyakukai do not usually function effectively as decision making bodies. Consequently, there are likely to be other organs operating within it which fulfill the policy formulation role more effectively. Two types of organs which firms have developed to do so are the *jomukai*, executive committee, and *kaigitai*, ad hoc committees. Related to its decision-making weakness is the changing nature of organizational structure in Japanese companies, which is altering decision systems and increasing pressure for line management responsibility to be vested in one individual.

The presence of **habatsu**, factions based on school ties or common background, can create schisms within a *torishimariyakukai* if not kept in check. Traditionally factions are kept in check through the use of crisis management approaches. The large number of baby-boom managers who have reached the age of promotability to director, is increasing the likelihood of greater political behavior within *torishimariyakukai* in the future.

Because *torishimariyakukai* carry out general managerial duties as well as directoral duties, there is no clear distinction between policy makers and policy-implementers. Consequently, the group making policy may tend to become entangled in operational decisions. This can lead to a tendency to focus on departmental problems within the firm rather than on comprehensive, whole-firm issues.

Weaknesses in the ability of *torishimariyakukai* regarding policy and strategy formulation have not gone unnoticed. In response, many companies have established executive committees to take over responsibility for decision making in this area. Executive committees are usually comprised of a CEO and four to six senior officers, usually of managing director rank or higher. In 1984 over 90 per cent of companies listed on the Tokyo Stock Exchange had operating *jomukai*. In most large companies, *jomukai* meet once a week or more often if required, with the planning department acting as its clerical office and support staff.

Further reading

Bird, A. (1988) *Nihon kigyo executive no kenkyu* (Research on Japanese Executives), Tokyo: Sangyo Noritsu Daigaku Shuppansha.

Clark, R. (1979) *The Japanese Company*, New Haven, CT: Yale University Press.

Kono, T. (1984) *Strategy and Structure of Japanese Enterprise*, London: Macmillan.

Mills, G. (1981) *On the Board*, Aldershot: Gower.

Okumura, A. (1982) *Nihon no toppu manejimento* (Japanese Top Management), Tokyo: Daiyamon-dosha.

Shimizu, R. (1986) *Top Management in Japanese Firms*, Tokyo: Chikura Shobo.

ALLAN BIRD

Toshiba

Toshiba Corporation, along with Hitachi and **Mitsubishi**, is one of the three big "integrated" electric and electronics companies in Japan. As the world's eighth largest integrated company in the industry, it has over 198,000 employees and annual sales of over US$40 billion worldwide as of 1999. With its long history since 1875 (1939 as Tokyo Shibaura Electric Co. and 1978 Toshiba Corporation), it developed from a heavy electric company to a "one set" electrical and electronic manufacturer. It is one of the most innovative companies in Japan, manufacturing a large number of Japan's first products such as telegraphs, incandescent lamps, radio receivers, laptop PCs and the world's first 16-megabit NAND type EEPROM.

Toshiba has been a typical conservative and reluctant Japanese multinational enterprise (MNE) in terms of **overseas production** activities, in comparison with active MNE-type consumer electric and electronics companies such as **Matsushita**, Sanyo and **Sony**. Globalization is now its most important initiative, expanding overseas production facilities and extending international strategic alliance with GE, IBM, Siemens, Time-Warner, and so forth. Its manufacturing and development range from medical electronics equipment to highly integrated DRAM, to turbine generators to multi-media systems composed of information and communication systems, including audio-visual, which are led by DVD and media entertainment such as movies, music and publication businesses.

The major reasons for the "conservative" nature of Toshiba's overseas business activities are as follows. Historically, its domestic market, relying on its traditional brand name and based on a reputation of innovative products were more profitable than its overseas markets. It is also a "reluctant" MNE because of its heavy reliance on human-relations, Japanese-style management, and a production system that is deeply influenced by the socio-cultural environment in Japan. Additionally, Japanese-type engineering and manufacturing technologies at most domestic Toshiba plants have been so typical in their worksite-oriented methods such as "all member participation-style" that it is not easy to effectively transfer such methods into different social backgrounds. Therefore, the company has preferred to implement the main part of its strategic R&D and manufacturing activities at its home facilities and to export its products to foreign markets. A good example of this is its semiconductor business. Semiconductor production depends largely on economies of scale, the huge size of plant and equipment and high level of maintenance skills for such machines are carried out at Toshiba's domestic laboratories and plants while its major Japanese competitors such as **NEC** and Fujitsu have been more active in setting up and organizing worldwide networks of semiconductor plants. It was not until the mid-1990s when the "ruleless" appreciation of the yen finally dissuaded the company from relying on a domestic production management approach (see **appreciating yen**). Since then, Toshiba has begun deploying very actively international alliance initiatives in its semiconductor business with western companies.

On the other hand, Toshiba has pursued a merger and acquisition (M&A) strategy to start many of its foreign operations, a distinctive feature of Toshiba relative to other Japanese MNEs. Of the six major production plants for television and semiconductors in developed countries, three (in the USA and UK) were **joint ventures** or acquisitions, though all were bought out and became wholly owned subsidiaries. Toshiba is one of the most innovative electric companies in Japan in the sense that international strategic alliances were employed from the beginning of its founding, and continue to play a major role in developing new products. This may reflect Toshiba's historical experience, especially the long alliance relationship between Toshiba (and its antecedents) and GE through licensing and joint venture agreements since the late 1880s.

It appears that this experience has provided a strong foundation for recent strategic alliances in its global business activities. One evidence of this is the joint-venture semiconductor production contract with IBM in 1995. At its newest large scale plant in the US, Toshiba appears to at last have been able to overcome the limit of scale at Toshiba America Electronic components, which was a reorganization of a small American integrated circuit plant acquired by Toshiba. The alliance relationship with IBM, which will be changed to a wholly owned Toshiba operation from 2001, was one of the critical factors for the success in terms of the scale of investment money and market, and the cooperation for developing process technologies. It is also interesting to note that Toshiba also has joint-venture production contracts with Motorola in Japan and a close joint R&D with Siemens and IBM. The first one will be converted to a wholly owned operation by Motorola with which Toshiba will continue a contract of processing on commission. The outcome of these strategic alliance activities is the rationalization of Toshiba's worldwide R&D and production activities

With this effort complete, Toshiba will initiate a globalization strategy focused in "Six Sigma" methodology, a Westernized TQM (total quality management) system for promoting the transformation of Toshiba's overall management that is expected to advance the "creative destruction." Toshiba is striving to create a new corporate culture worldwide. This is a notable challenge for such a traditional large Japanese company.

Further reading

Abo, T. (ed.) (1994) *Hybrid Factory*, Oxford: Oxford University Press.

—— (1998) "Toshiba's Overseas Production Activities: Seven Large Plants in the USA, Mexico, the UK, Germany and France," in H. Mirza (ed.), (1998) *Global Competitive Strategies in the New World Economy*, Cheltenham: Edward Elgar.

TETSUO ABO

total productive maintenance

Total productive maintenance (*zen-in sanka no seisan hozen*), or TPM, was developed in Japan as a means to support manufacturing firms in seeking superior equipment effectiveness, an essential condition to accomplishing the goals of quality, cost, delivery performance, safety and employee morale. In its narrowest sense, TPM involves the transfer of various maintenance-related duties to the machine operators themselves. TPM has evolved, however, into a broad managerial approach that involves multiple business functions with the aim of strengthening production capabilities and corporate competitiveness. Along with **just-in-time** (JIT) and TQM (see **quality management**), TPM forms the third leg of a triad of approaches adopted by many companies to attain world-class manufacturing excellence.

The initial development of TPM took place in the late 1960s from a productive maintenance program conceived by Denso, a member of the Toyota Group. Denso's purpose was to enable sustainable implementation of the **Toyota production system**/JIT, which depends on highly reliable equipment. However, credit for the further development and diffusion of TPM is given to the Japan Institute of Plant Maintenance (JIPM), a private non-profit organization that offers an array of services concerning plant maintenance management and technology. A former officer of JIPM, Seiichi Nakajima, contributed to the dissemination of the early definition and propositions of TPM. The diffusion of TPM outside Japan gained momentum in 1988 with the English translation of one of Nakajima's books, *Introduction to TPM*. Also during the 1980s, TPM spread from its original base in fabrication and assembly industries, such as automobiles, auto parts and machinery, into process industries, such as chemicals, food, paper and pulp. Today, TPM has been adopted by a myriad of companies in many industries worldwide.

The definition of TPM, as well as its purpose and scope, have undergone numerous refinements over the years, building upon its original base in the production and maintenance functions. Driving these changes was the perception that to improve the efficiency of the production system to the fullest extent, activities confined to the production system were not enough. Over time, TPM came to be implemented with a company-wide scope, prompting

JIPM in 1989 to formulate a broader definition of TPM, stating that it means to:

1 build a corporate constitution that maximises the effectiveness of the production system;
2 organize a practical shop-floor system for preventing all types of losses throughout the entire life cycle of the production system (ensuring zero accidents, zero defects, and zero failures);
3 involve all departments, including production, development, sales and administration;
4 ensure participation of every member, ranging from top management to frontline operators;
5 accomplish zero losses through the activities of overlapping small groups.

TPM is more than a methodology or package of tools. It has become a philosophy and systematized approach for manufacturing management. By emphasizing employee participation, teamwork, development of maintenance skills, and continuous improvement (see **kaizen**), TPM nurtures a culture where operators develop ownership of their equipment and work side by side with managers and engineers to strengthen the effectiveness of operations. One means of employee participation is through TPM overlapping small groups. While these groups share some similarity to **quality control circles** in the sense that groups of employees carry out improvement activities and further develop their skills, some important points of difference are that TPM's groups are built into the permanent, formal organization and involve employees at each level of the organization from top management down to frontline level.

Another major feature of TPM is the productive maintenance (*seisan hozen*) approach which incorporates such disciplines as maintenance prevention design, reliability engineering, and maintainability engineering so as to enhance the economic efficiency of equipment investment over the equipments' life cycle.

The primary equipment evaluation metric adopted by TPM is "overall equipment effectiveness (OEE)," which considers the up-time availability of equipment, actual output compared to standard, and conformance quality of outputs. Typically, OEE in ordinary manufacturers ranges from 40 percent to 60 percent. The goal of TPM is to elevate OEE to 85 percent or more, implying that production output can be doubled through better use of existing resources. Progress toward this goal is made by systematically identifying and then minimizing or eliminating the diverse kinds of losses that hamper production system effectiveness. These losses are typically classified into sixteen major loss categories including failures, set-ups and adjustments, cutting blade changes, start-up, minor stoppages and idling, reduced speed, and defects or rework, as well as other factors related to workers and the production system.

Originally, TPM focused on the immediate production system with the establishment of the following "five pillars": (1) equipment efficiency improvement through project teams (*kobetsu kaizen*); (2) autonomous maintenance (*jishu hozen*); (3) planned maintenance; (4) education and training; and (5) initial phase equipment management. With the enlargement of TPM's scope and purpose over time, the fifth pillar evolved into initial phase management for new products and equipment, and additional guidelines were added in the form of three more pillars: (6) quality maintenance system; (7) effective administrative system; and (8) safety and environmental management system.

While the approaches used to implement JIT or TQM vary by company, JIPM advocates a standard, twelve-step program for implementing TPM. The first five steps are of a preparatory nature: (1) announcing TPM implementation; (2) beginning introductory TPM education; (3) establishing an organization to promote TPM; (4) defining basic TPM policies and goals; and (5) formulating a master plan for TPM implementation. Following these, step (6) is the kickoff of actual TPM implementation. Next, step (7) involves installing the first four pillars of TPM, while steps (8) to (11) involve the implementation of the last four pillars of TPM, respectively. Finally, step (12) is for completing TPM implementation, evaluating its outcomes and setting future goals.

Since 1971, JIPM has conferred TPM Awards to plants excelling in the implementation of TPM. Separate categories are established for small and large applicants. The highest level of recognition is the Award for World Class TPM Achievement, with several other award levels for TPM Achievement, Consistent TPM Commitment, and TPM

Excellence. In recent years, there has been a steady increase in the number of applicants from outside Japan.

Sometimes confused with TPM, **5S campaigns** aim to establish good housekeeping practices for clean and orderly facilities and have become popular in manufacturing and service industries. 5S activities can be implemented independently of TPM, but manufacturers often incorporate them as a foundation for the autonomous maintenance pillar of TPM.

Further reading

Japan Institute of Plant Maintenance Web Site, http://www.jipm.or.jp.

Nakajima, S. (1988) *Introduction to TPM: Total Productive Maintenance*, Cambridge, MA: Productivity Press.

Nakajima, S. *et al.* (eds) (1996) *TPM – Total Productive Maintenance – Encyclopedia*, Tokyo: JIPM.

Shirose, K. (ed.) (1996) *TPM New Implementation Program in Fabrication and Assembly Industries*, Tokyo: JIPM.

Suzuki, T. (ed.) (1994) *TPM in Process Industries*, Portland, OR: Productivity Press.

DARIO IKUO MIYAKE

Toyota

Toyota is the largest firm in the Japanese auto industry, with about 40 percent of the domestic market, and consolidated revenue (fiscal year 2000) of $120 billion and worldwide sales of 5.4 million units. Production began in 1937, driven by the fascination of Toyoda Kiichiro with autos, and drawing upon his family's textile machinery fortune. As late as 1966, however, trucks were its largest product, and virtually all sales were domestic. Today, 60 percent of revenue comes from overseas sales, dominated by North America, and foreign production accounts for one-third of output. However, the rise in the foreign share is not all positive: in part it reflects a drop in domestic production of 1 million units since 1990.

Toyota is a participant in the global consolidation of the auto industry. Domestically, it has absorbed its sales subsidiary, Toyota Motor Sales, and the producers Daihatsu (minicars) and Hino (heavy trucks), adding them to the existing set of six affiliated assemblers (Toyota Auto Body, Kanto Auto Works and others). The firm also has large stakes in parts suppliers, including Denso and Aishin Seiki. However, it has not been active in acquisitions overseas, and in most markets operates through "greenfield" manufacturing facilities. It remains heavily committed to the auto industry; its ventures in housing construction, trade and finance (and more recently telecommunications and the Internet) account for only 14 percent of revenue.

The defining event in Toyota's history was a brush with bankruptcy in 1949, avoided only by a bank bailout. At that time its sales operations were spun off into a separate company, as were several parts operations (including a steel mill and the forerunner of Denso, currently the world's fourth largest automotive parts manufacturer with $12 billion in sales). This meant that while Toyota proper remained focused on core engineering and manufacturing operations, it could not force output onto dealers. In turn Toyota Motor Sales concentrated on developing dealers, but as the sole purchaser of output, it could interject marketing concerns into vehicle design and corporate strategy. Furthermore, the bailout made it clear that it needed to work with parts makers. It responded by bringing in consultants in 1952–3 to help set up guidelines, including a program of ongoing technical and management consulting for its suppliers.

Toyota is known for innovative management. Drawing heavily upon Japan's postwar productivity movement, and with the executive suite dominated by engineers and factory managers, it emphasized a "flow" approach to manufacturing, epitomized in what only later came to be known as JIT (**just-in-time**) production. Implemented on the shop floor by **kanban** tags that authorized the "pull" of parts from upstream operations, it required the ability to change dies rapidly, calling for careful attention to machine maintenance and maintaining a "level" production schedule that minimized the variation in daily output. In addition, this drew upon a labor relations environment and a no-layoff policy that facilitated developing a skilled workforce amenable to operating and maintaining multiple machines, while bearing responsibility for quality control and participating in systematic productivity improvement activities (**quality control circles**, TQC and so on). JIT was only systematically implemented within the firm in the late 1960s, and among suppliers from 1970, with a particular boost from the sales downturn in 1974 following the first oil crisis.

Toyota also is an early adopter of "platform teams" for product development, which kept engineers from becoming compartmentalized within the vehicle design and engineering process. Improved feedback allows otherwise discrete stages of this process to be overlapped – body engineering and die design are initiated before all the details of styling are locked into place – allowing a new vehicle to be developed more quickly. This generates both cost savings and potentially a better fit to the market with the shorter lag between styling choices and the commencement of sales. In addition, coordination between different functional specialties – for example, manufacturing engineers and stylists – facilitates developing cars that are easier to make and have higher intrinsic quality. With many high-volume models, however, Toyota has been conservative in implementing new technology and styling trends, generally waiting until after other firms have proven their acceptance in the marketplace.

Despite its reputation for manufacturing prowess, Toyota was not always successful domestically. It lagged at home in the late 1960s, and again in parts of the 1980s and the latter 1990s. In general, however, it suffered fewer downturns than its rivals, and was able to maintain a stronger and more profitable dealer network; indeed, Toyota's marketing strengths are probably the biggest element in its overall success. One element was a full-line product strategy, made possible by affiliate firms specializing initially in low-volume cars. These firms now make Toyota's light and heavy trucks and its minicars – over 40 percent of Toyota-badged vehicles – while Toyota focuses on regular passenger cars.

Toyota did particularly well as an exporter in the late 1970s and early 1980s, earning the nickname "Toyota Bank" for the profits it accumulated. Nevertheless, it was the last of the major Japanese producers to enter into overseas production (its Georgetown, Kentucky plant began operations in 1988, following the success of the 1984 NUMMI joint venture with General Motors in Fremont, California). It now has ten manufacturing sites in NAFTA, assembling over 1 million units, including full-sized pickups and sport utility vehicles aimed at the domestic NAFTA market. Likewise, within the EU it now has plants in the UK and France, as well as operations in Mercosur and in Southeast and East Asia, with its most recent venture in Tianjin, China. Despite its success in the USA and its strong share in many export markets, the firm still must deal with significant overcapacity within Japan. Its profitability in export markets has also been hurt in recent years by the strong yen and (in the EU) the strong British pound. Finally, given its parochial roots in rural Aichi Prefecture, the firm must develop the long-run ability to manage operations around the world.

MICHAEL SMITKA

Toyota production system

Also known as "lean production," the Toyota production system (TPS) is an integrated approach to achieving the efficiencies of mass production with small production volumes. Developed by **Toyota** Motor Corporation in the 1950s, TPS is based on the elimination of waste throughout the process of design and manufacturing, and relies heavily on **just-in-time** (JIT) production, the building of quality and productivity into production processes, and the continuous and incremental improvement of quality (*kaizen*). This approach to **quality management** is credited with Toyota's remarkable global success in the **automotive industry** during the second half of the twentieth century.

TPS was developed by Taiichi **Ono**, who was Toyota Motor Corporation's chief production engineer in the post-Second World War period, with the support of Eiji Toyoda, the company's managing director. This alternative to mass production was born of necessity. Immediately following the war, Toyota faced considerable capital constraints. Unlike the large Western automobile manufacturers, Toyota's production volumes were small, a few thousand vehicles per year, compared with 7,000 per day at Ford Motor Company's River Rouge plant in Detroit. Toyota had neither the financial backing nor the scale of production to implement the western mass production approaches. Ono recognized the need to develop flexible production processes that were not dependent on huge production volumes of individual vehicle models to be economical. TPS involves great flexibility, in terms of both production equipment and workers. The system focuses on designing processes that create cost reductions through the elimination of waste. This extends far beyond the machines on the factory floor, and includes the management of employees, inventory control, and supply chain management. Both suppliers and customers are expected to cooperate in the common quest for ever-better quality and productivity. Very much in line with the teachings of **Deming**, TPS is an integrated system that has three key aspects: *jidoka* (literally "self-work-change"), JIT (see *kanban*), and standardized work with *kaizen*.

Jidoka refers to self-regulation of the entire process, either automatically or through human intervention. Preferably, machines are designed to detect problems (such as malfunctions, quality problems, or delays) and to stop the production line when problems are encountered. Many such *poka-yoke* (mistake-proofing) devices were developed by **Shingo** during his tenure at Toyota. When such mechanical solutions are unavailable, workers have the authority, and the responsibility, to stop the production line immediately, rather than waiting for supervisory or managerial authorization. *Jidoka* permits the clear identification of trouble spots and prevents poor quality output from being sent to the customer (internal or external), while reducing the need for inspectors. With *jidoka*, quality is constantly being built into production processes.

Consistent application of JIT principles throughout the system permits each customer order to be processed with speed and efficiency, not necessarily in large batches of similar models. Because parts are delivered as needed all through the system, inventory is reduced, which means that quality problems are obvious quickly, and less floor space is required to store work in process. In addition, JIT facilitates the customization of finished product, providing increased customer satisfaction.

The purpose behind standardized work and continuous, incremental improvement of quality is to permit the organization to respond quickly to changing demand patterns, while eliminating waste throughout the system. Adhering to rigidly defined standard operating procedures results in less variation in outcomes, making process outcomes and quality more predictable. This facilitates the arrangement of production activities into a single, continuous flow, which involves careful balancing of production scheduling. Given their direct knowledge regarding the production processes, employees are empowered to assist in making the processes progress more smoothly and quickly.

People

People are crucial to TPS. Implementation of the system requires a workforce that is both highly skilled and very motivated. Labor problems at Toyota in the late 1940s created an environment that facilitated the development of such a workforce, as unions negotiated for **lifetime employment** for their members, as well as pay based on seniority, rather than specific job function, with bonuses based on the company's profitability. In return, workers agreed to accept increased flexibility in their work assignments.

These developments meant that Toyota and its workers had a strong, mutual commitment to each other, which made TPS feasible. The long-term nature of the employment relationship made it logical for the company to expend resources on continuously enhancing workers' skills, as it would benefit from their Toyota-specific knowledge and experience for many years to come. Workers perceived value in initiating process improvements, given their emotional and financial stakes in the company's success. This mutual relationship became a cornerstone of TPS.

Workers face rigid work rules in TPS. Production procedures are tightly choreographed, with workers participating in their development. While adhering strictly to the rules, workers are encouraged to develop ways to revise them, to generate improvements. Both **quality control circles** and **suggestion systems** are used extensively, with workers offered the security that efficiency improvements will not result in job losses. Workers are also encouraged to request help when necessary. The routing of the help request is specific, with one person explicitly responsible for reacting quickly. Production-related information is shared widely in the plant, with *andon* boards which detail daily production targets, cars produced, equipment breakdowns, etc., visible from every workstation. Cross-training is extensive, and managers are expected to be able to do the jobs of all the people they supervise.

Reducing cost by eliminating waste

In TPS, eliminating waste in systems is the primary approach to reducing costs. For example, mass production systems have typically been characterized by considerable worker redundancy, due to narrow job descriptions, high worker absenteeism, and a hierarchical structure. Ono viewed this redundancy as wasteful. In contrast, TPS employs a team structure, in which teams have latitude with respect to how they accomplish their assigned operations. The cross-training of the team members provides flexibility. The team leader performs assembly tasks and fills in for absent workers. Time is allocated for teams to work together to develop process improvements, for *kaizen* and waste reduction.

Another distinction between TPS and mass production systems is the treatment of rework. Western mass production systems have long relied on rework to correct quality problems late in the production process. While this approach is now widely seen as inefficient and ineffective, Ono recognized the waste inherent in rework in the early 1950s, noting that the system allows a process problem to go unnoticed for too long. Instead, he developed TPS such that each worker has the authority to stop the production line immediately if a problem emerges that he or she cannot fix. As a plant becomes mature in its implementation of TPS, this approach results in minimal rework, few line stoppages, lower costs, and higher quality.

Supply chain management

The coordination of the engineering, manufactur-ing, and delivery of the thousands of parts in a vehicle is a monumental task. Toyota's approach to supply chain management, based on long-term, cooperative relationships, recognizes the interde-pendency of suppliers and customers and differs substantially from those of most Western auto-motive firms.

Western firms have traditionally awarded fixed-term contracts to suppliers based on the lowest bid, creating short-term perspectives regarding the customer–supplier relationship. In this system, suppliers are placed in competitive situations against each other and the customer. Western automobile firms have also traditionally done their component design in-house, with minimal input from suppliers regarding manufacturing feasibility or the potential for improvements. Suppliers tend to work only on their own components, with little information regarding the interface of their part with the larger system; such information is considered proprietary to the automotive firm. The competitive nature of this contract system provides incentives for suppliers to warehouse large inventories of product, making quality problems difficult to detect.

Toyota adopted a different approach, emphasiz-ing long-term relationships with their suppliers and cooperation, rather than **competition**. Suppliers are organized in functional tiers. First-tier suppliers have design responsibilities. As part of Toyota's product development team, their engineering work is done in cooperation with that for other vehicle systems being designed by other suppliers. Second-tier suppliers are responsible for manufacturing; their customers are the first-tier suppliers. The suppliers tend to be quite specialized. Because they do not compete against each other, cooperation is facilitated.

There are generally equity cross-holdings be-tween Toyota and the first-tier suppliers, and among the first-tier suppliers. The result of this relationship is not complete vertical integration, as often practiced in the West, but partial integration. Permanent and temporary personnel transfers among Toyota and the suppliers strengthen the long-term relationships.

These structured and long-term customer–supplier relationships serve to reduce variation in both process and product, and fit well with the systems approach to product development that characterizes TPS. Teamwork and coordination at lower levels in the organizational hierarchy permit a faster design process, which leads to increased responsiveness and faster response to changing market conditions.

Risks associated with TPS

The primary risk in TPS is that the unceasing elimination of waste reduces organizational slack. There is little redundancy in the system to provide a safety net. JIT reduces inventory levels (or shifts them down the supply chain), making the system vulnerable to external shocks (e.g., weather, accidents, and natural disasters). JIT thus requires processes that are in control. Ono believed that the lack of a safety net would serve to focus the attention of everyone in the system toward anticipating and addressing problems before they became serious.

The lack of slack can be stressful for workers. The assumption is that the increased intellectual challenge associated with working in a TPS environment creates intrinsic rewards (see **Deming**). Management has the responsibility of ensuring that workers have the training and skills to undertake the additional responsibilities.

Knowledge creation and transferability

One of the most powerful aspects of TPS is its tacit nature, which makes it individual to an organization and, therefore, very difficult for competitors to imitate. Workers are trained to seek the root causes of problems, rather than grabbing at quick solutions. The combination of standardized work with *kaizen* leads workers to use the scientific method to conduct repeated controlled experiments. This continuous experimentation makes possible the type of **organizational learning** and knowledge creation described by **Nonaka**, essentially creating *kaizen* of *kaizen*, continuous improvement of both the process and the approach to improving. This is extremely powerful, and creates solutions that are specific to the organization.

While successful implementation of TPS is context-specific, the system is not unique to Toyota, to Japan, to the automotive industry, or

to the manufacturing sector. TPS was used successfully in **New United Motor Manufacturing Incorporated** (NUMMI), the 1984 joint venture between Toyota and General Motors in Fremont, California that was Toyota's first automotive assembly site in the USA. The other North American Toyota plants (such as Georgetown, Kentucky, established in 1988) use TPS, with some very minor modifications to accommodate cultural differences between US and Japanese workers. The Toyota Supplier Support Center (TSSC), established in Lexington, Kentucky in 1992, provides assistance to companies interested in implementing TPS. This free help is provided to firms in a variety of industries; no affiliation with Toyota is necessary.

TPS is credited with allowing Toyota Motor Corporation to develop from a small, domestic manufacturer in the 1950s to an international power by the 1980s. The combination of *jidoka*, JIT, and *kaizen*, with emphases on people and on the reduction of waste, has produced a flexible system that enables considerable responsiveness to customers.

Further reading

Cusumano, M. (1985) *The Japanese Automobile Industry: Technology and Management at Nissan and Toyota*, Cambridge, MA: Harvard University Press.

Monden, Y. (1983) *The Toyota Production System*, Atlanta, GA: Institute of Industrial Engineers.

Spear, S. and Bowen, H.K (1999) "Decoding the DNA of the Toyota Production System," *Harvard Business Review* (September–October): 96–106.

Womack, J.P., Jones, D.T. and Roos, D. (1991) *The Machine that Changed the World: The Story of Lean Production*, New York: HarperPerennial.

ELIZABETH L. ROSE

trade barriers

From the initial postwar period onward, Japan has been embroiled in a series of trade conflicts. Though some of these have involved foreign market penetration by Japanese firms, the vast majority have focused on the inability of foreign firms to access the Japanese market. Potential exporters to Japan have confronted a host of obstacles. Foreign firms setting up operations in Japan have found themselves equally hampered. Over time, the nature of these barriers to trade and market entry has shifted from formal government controls to a variety of non-governmental and informal constraints and, eventually, to the removal of most barriers. Nonetheless, Japan is still viewed as one of the most difficult markets in the world to penetrate.

Formal barriers to trade were put in place immediately following the Second World. These formal controls included foreign exchange controls, import quotas, high tariffs and restrictions on the type and nature of permissible foreign direct investment. The primary purpose was to allow Japanese firms to rebuild unhindered by foreign competition as well as to allow the government to strategically deploy its limited foreign reserves. Consequently, Japan has developed a reputation for not "playing fair" in trade of invward foreign direct investment. In fact, Japan was kept out of the General Agreement on Tariffs and Trade (GATT) until 1955, eighteen years after the agreement was initially reached, because of its unfair trade practices.

The strong recovery and subsequent rapid growth of the Japanese economy led to increasing liberalization in the late 1960s and early 1970s. This was, in part, a response to external trade friction resulting from Japan's aggressive export of first textiles in the early 1960s followed by steel in the late 1960s. Threat of trade sanctions and demands for reciprocity, particularly by the USA, provided a powerful incentive for removing or reducing the formal barriers. Still, the pace of liberalization has been reluctant and remarkably slow. Exchange controls were not removed until 1980, and other financial controls remained in place through the 1990s. Similarly, import quotas tended to be dropped only in response to external pressure – *gaiatsu* – and only for the specified industry or market. At present, import quotas remain for only a few selected, primarily agricultural products.

In a similar vein, tariffs on Japanese goods have gradually lowered over time. Again, reductions tended to come only on the heels of external criticism or pressure. The current average tariff is less than 3 per cent and the lowest of all OECD countries. Nevertheless, the average can be misleading because there are still products, such as leather goods, for which the tariff remains quite high.

Another formal trade barrier can be found in the technical standards that the government imposes on all manner of products. It has not been unusual for Japan to reject internationally accepted product design and safety standards in favor of its own. Foreign laboratory test data or product certifications were, similarly, not usually recognized by Japan. This often meant that foreign firms had to arrange for products previously tested in their home country to be re-tested in Japanese laboratories. Further exacerbating frustration over inability to access the Japanese market was a routine custom of not informing foreign firms as to why their products did not meet government standards or what could be done to bring them into compliance.

In the case of food, chemical or other substances, the Japanese employed a policy of "positive listing," meaning only substances listed by the government were permitted. Non-listed substances were not permitted, and obtaining permission often involved an elaborate, costly and time-consuming process. Moreover, various regulating agencies were known to share product data with domestic Japanese competitors of importing firms.

As Japan entered the 1980s, there was a feeling that the increasing international profile of its MNCs and concerns over reciprocity would lead to significant easing trade friction and removal of trade barriers. However, the conflict simply moved from formal to informal, or what came to be know as "non-tariff barriers." Non-tariff barriers include a host of government and industry practices which effectively close out foreign competition. For example, during the 1980s the Japanese government lifted nearly all restrictions on foreign participation in government tenders, however, the qualifying conditions, filing deadlines and processing procedures effectively precluded most foreign firms from bidding. The complex, multi-layer, multi-channel **distribution system** was seen as another type of non-tariff barrier. Wholesalers would often resist distributing foreign products because they competed directly with domestic products they were already handling.

From 1980 forward there have been at least eight packages of market opening measures aimed at removing informal barriers to trade. For instance, in 1980 foreign firms were finally allowed to use the Japan Industrial Standard (JIS) mark on their products. This was significant – and also indicative of the type of non-tariff barriers that foreign firms faced – because in numerous cases, industry associations had agreed to limit purchases of parts and materials to only products carrying the JIS mark.

Despite these various packages, Japanese trade surpluses with other countries have remained high. Its surplus with the US was over $50 billion in the early 1990s. In fact, 1993 Japan trade surplus jumped 20 percent to about $60.5 billion. Sixty percent of Japan's trade surplus with the United States was attributable to automobiles and car parts. Because Japan put artificial trade barriers around its auto and the auto parts markets, the US imposed sanctions on Japan. In 1995, Japan agreed to begin to open its automobile and parts markets to American companies.

The current generation of trade barriers constitutes a complex mix of government, industry and consumer group initiatives that often require aggressive, creative and persistent means to overcome. The experience of California rice exporters provides an instructive case study. In 1993, a bad rice harvest in Japan led to a significant price hike in domestic rice. The government tried to prevent rice imports and to encourage Japanese consumers to buy government-subsidized, expensive Japanese rice. However, the Rice Accord under GATT prevented Japan from using import quotas and other previously identified non-tariff barriers. So in 1994, the Japanese enacted a new law requiring that no specific foreign rice could be sold as such. Rather it had to be a mix, specifically 30 percent Japanese, 50 percent California, Chinese and Australian, and 20 percent Thai. The rice from these four sources differ significantly in appearance and taste. Not surprisingly, Japanese consumers found the mixture unappealing. Japanese consumers particularly did not like the Chinese or Thai rice. The Japanese government had hopes the taste and appearance of the foreign mix would lead

consumers to buy the more expensive Japanese rice, but it did not work out that way. Many retailers did not mix the rice, but sold the California rice separately. At the behest of Japanese farmers and agricultural cooperatives, the Japanese government issued new regulations specifically requiring California rice from being sold in its pure form. The new regulations required it to be mixed with rice from other regions of America. In addition, Japan imposed a 580 percent import tariff, thereby removing its price advantage over domestic rice. The Japanese government then used the $2.7 billion rice import tariff revenues to subsidize Japanese rice farmers. Under the GATT minimum-access rule, Japan has been forced to comply by importing more foreign rice each year. The Japan government is currently stockpiling the surplus rice and using the imported rice in processed foods, not in its pure form. In 2000, rice tariffs were a World Trade Organization (WTO) agenda item. Japanese farmers are concerned that more imported rice will mean more competition.

Because of its past history and the continuing large number of trade barriers, including non-tariff barriers and protective regulations that Japan has erected, many developed countries, particularly the USA, do not believe that Japan is committed to the elimination of trade barriers or to the overall cause of free trade. The current US approach is to pressure Japan to set targets. Japan's response is that targets would harm the free trade system and any bilateral deal with the USA would violate GATT.

For years, the United States tried to get Japan to decrease its trade barriers and open its markets through voluntary export restraints, sector-specific talks, and structural adjustment measures. A textile agreement was signed in 1974 where textile exports from Japan were restricted. NTT gave foreign companies fair opportunities to compete in 1980, NTT's procurement of foreign products increased from 3.8 billion yen in 1980 to 152 billion yen in 1995. There were agreements in wood products, steel, telecommunications, transportation, semiconductors, fish products, meat and citrus fruits, copyright protection on sound recordings, paper products, and computers. Between the mid-1970s and mid-1990s, Japan and the United States signed over twenty-two different trade agreements. In 1994, Japan and the US had the Economic Framework Talks. The main sectors covered in these talks had to do with: government procurement, insurance, automobiles and auto parts, export promotion and competitiveness, intellectual property rights, flat glass, financial services, inward direct investment and buyer–supplier relationships, deregulation and competition policy, global challenges, bilateral cooperation on advancing science and technology, and human resources development. For example, the main point of agreement in automobiles and auto parts had to do with the promotion of dealerships, and strengthening of the function of the Fair Trade Commission. As a result, over 42,000 US cars were newly registered in Japan in 1995, up 19 percent from 1994.

Even with many Japan–US agreements signed, many people in the United States believe that little was accomplished. According to the Economic Strategy Institute, US exports to Japan would increase more than $55 billion if Japan eliminated its trade barriers, $44 billion in service exports.

In 1995, Japan worldwide exports were $443 billion up 12 percent from 1994. Imports also increased to $337 billion up 22.3 percent. Therefore, Japan's trade surplus decreased by 11.6 percent to a four-year low of $107 billion. In trade with the US, Japan's surplus seems to peak in 1994 at $67.3 billion and has decreased to $49.2 billion in 1996.

JETRO stated that three changes in Japan's trade structure helped to decrease the surplus. These include: imports and exports to developing countries surpassed developed countries; growth in exports have been difficult because of the economy whereas imports are easier; and ration of current account surplus to Japan's nominal GDP fell. Furthermore, changes in Japan's trade structure are due to moves by Japanese companies to adapt to changing conditions such as shifting manufacturing overseas, globalization, and concentration of production in Southeast Asia.

While Japan has recently removed many import quotas and duties, non-tariff barriers still prevent foreign firms from entering the Japanese markets. These include the Large Retail Store Law; the informal job-bidding systems which goes on behind closed doors; and the common practice of below-cost bidding, all of which eliminate foreign firms from competing. The Japanese government is beginning to put pressure on firms to stop these practices. However, there is still friction over trade imbalance between Japan and the rest of the world. As deficits with Japan remain large, more and more countries are putting pressure on Japan to eliminate its trade barriers. If not, other countries will expand trade barriers against Japanese companies. For example, the United States may put up trade barriers against Japanese autos and car parts that would hurt the Japanese auto industry.

JETRO has also changed its focus. It is now more involved with promotion of imports to Japan. JETRO has organized numerous trade missions for foreign firms to Japan; it has hosted exhibits and fairs to assist foreign importers. Since the mid-1990s, the Japanese have had a working group monitoring the progress of the Deregulation Action Plan. In 1995 the Japanese government drafted a deregulation program, with a first review in 1996. Measures to facilitate competition and fair trade include increasing the personnel working in The Japanese Fair Trade Commission to 200 employees in 1998; and a review was conducted for the sectors for which the application of the Antimonopoly Law has been waived, so that the system was abolished by the end of 1998.

See also: business ethics; economic crisis in Asia; Japanese business in the USA

Further reading

The Japan Times, Japan-US Economic Handbook

TERRI R. LITUCHY

trade negotiations

Japan in the postwar period has engaged in a seemingly constant series of negotiations with its major foreign trading partners, usually led by the United States, that have been designed to curb its export competitiveness and to increase the openness of the Japanese market. The American Chamber of Commerce in Japan counts some forty-five major agreements negotiated between Japan and the United States between 1980 and

1996. Negotiations have covered the entire range of goods and services: agricultural products such as rice, citrus, beef, and tobacco; materials industries including steel, aluminum, chemicals, wood, and paper; manufactures such as footwear, textiles, and automobiles; high technology industries including semiconductors, supercomputers and satellites; and services such as construction, telecommunications, aviation, insurance, and financial services.

Through the mid-1990s the Japanese government was relatively responsive to foreign trade demands, although more reluctantly and more slowly than its trading partners had desired. Since the mid-1990s, however, Japan has shown an increasing willingness to resist bilateral trade pressures, and now strongly prefers to deal with trade problems in a multilateral setting. (Trade negotiations are distinct from other efforts to reduce Japan's trade surplus, such as alterations in the dollar-yen exchange rate, or pressures on the Japanese government to increase domestic demand through monetary or macroeconomic policies.)

Efforts to curb Japanese exports

Trade negotiations with Japan through the 1970s were mainly motivated by the desire to deal with the social and economic costs of Japan's rising exports. Although Japan ran overall trade deficits with the USA until 1965, its export competitiveness in certain industries led to rising social and economic costs in many of its trading partners. Early trade negotiations with Japan were designed to deal with these costs by slowing Japanese exports, particularly in the textile industry. In the early 1950s, for instance, rapidly rising Japanese exports of cotton textiles led to growing calls for protectionism in major markets in the USA and Europe. In 1955 the US government negotiated a bilateral agreement with Japan in which the industry agreed to curtail its exports to the USA. American efforts to curb Japanese exports of synthetic fibers and textiles in the late 1960s also resulted in the Japanese government agreeing to voluntarily reduce its exports of this type of textile. When the Japanese industry refused to abide by these curtailments, the result was a period of intense and acrimonious negotiations with the USA, now known as the Textile Wrangle.

In the late 1970s protectionist pressures in the USA continued to rise, in part due to the rapid increase in Japan's overall surplus as well as growing exports in politically sensitive industries. During the Carter administration, the USA negotiated a long series of bilateral agreements that sought to slow Japanese exports. An oft-used policy tool was the voluntary export restraint, used in industries such as televisions, footwear, steel, and automobiles. Japanese producers were generally not in the position to say no to these demands for export restraint, since failure to do so risked more protectionist measures by the US Congress. In most cases these industries were dependent on exports to the US market; when faced with the choice of having no access to that market or abiding by the VER, most chose the latter. (It also turns out that at least one industry, automobiles, indirectly ended up benefiting from the VER, as it encouraged Japanese firms to export higher-value added automobiles to the USA.)

Opening the Japanese market

In the early 1980s trade negotiations shifted to a focus on gaining greater access to the Japanese market. In the context of rapidly rising Japanese trade surpluses, its foreign trade partners pointed to the closed nature of the economy as the main aspect of Japan's "unfair" or "adversarial" trading practices.

Formal tariffs on imported goods were not the main problem. Although Japan had enjoyed relatively high tariffs in the immediate postwar period, as the Japanese economy recovered and exports began to grow, Japan was gradually forced to lower these barriers to imports. As the condition for joining the international economic organizations, and then during successive rounds of international tariff negotiations, Japan agreed to reduce its formal tariff barriers. Although it faced criticisms for its reluctance to remove tariffs until after the protected industry was competitive, by the 1970s Japan could argue that it maintained the lowest level of tariffs on manufactured goods in the industrialized world. (Japan did maintain some tariffs and quotas in politically sensitive sectors such as rice and leather products.)

Despite the formal openness of the Japanese

market, a growing list of foreign exporters complained that their access to the market was still being impeded by hidden, or non-tariff, barriers. As the Japanese trade surplus continued to grow, Japan's trading partners became convinced that the Japanese market was substantially closed. A popular metaphor compared the Japanese market to an onion: even if one could identify and remove one layer of protection, one would then find another layer of protection underneath, and so on. Furthermore, critics charged that Japan's closed economy gave its firms an unfair advantage, providing them with a safe haven in which they could earn excess profits that could then be used to finance "export offenses" against foreign markets.

Foreign complaints centered on three aspects of the Japanese political economy: government policy, business practices, and economic structure. Foreign critics pointed to many of Japan's industrial policies that served to nurture or protect its domestic industries. Key Japanese industries had enjoyed government regulations that afforded them implicit protection or the ability to "manage competition" – for instance restrictions on entry into an industry, the ability to engage in cartel-like behavior, and implicit and explicit restrictions that made it difficult for foreign firms to invest in Japan. Foreign partners also complained about the collusive nature of business practices in Japan, in which many industries took advantage of a weak antitrust environment to "cooperate" in exclusionary business practices. Foreign governments thus called for the strengthening of Japan's anti-trust rules and enforcement procedures. Finally, foreign partners pointed to a number of structural features of Japan's economy that were seen as impediments to imports, including the *keiretsu* **cross-shareholdings**, and the **distribution system**.

Trade negotiations in the 1980s focused on the identification and removal of specific barriers to trade. In the first half of the decade, these negotiations were mostly carried out on an industry-by-industry basis. The Reagan administration, for instance, initiated the Market-Oriented Sector-Specific, or MOSS, talks, in four general areas: telecommunications, electronics, medical equipment and pharmaceuticals, and forest products. MOSS talks were later extended to include

autos and auto parts. Trade negotiations were also carried out in other sectors, most notably civil aviation, citrus and beef. The US government identified the specific barriers that blocked imports in each particular industry, and applied pressures on the Japanese government to remove them.

A key focus of US–Japan negotiations in this period involved the semiconductor industry. In 1986 the two countries completed the Semiconductor Agreement, in which the Japanese government agreed to stop its firms from "dumping" semiconductors in foreign markets, and (in a confidential side letter to the agreement) to increase foreign sales of semiconductors in the Japanese market. The US government later imposed a total of $300 million in retaliatory tariffs against Japanese exports to the USA when it decided that Japan had not complied with either of these provisions.

The Bush administration continued to seek increased access to the Japanese market through a combination of approaches. As before, the USA pressed for lower tariffs and stronger trade rules through multilateral trade negotiations. On a bilateral basis, the USA and Japan negotiated in a number of sectors, including construction, autos and auto parts, paper, and other sectors. In addition, the Bush administration initiated the Structural Impediments Initiative (SII) in 1989. Rather than dealing with specific trade barriers on a case-by-case basis, the USA now tried to identify more generic barriers to imports in the Japanese economy, including the *keiretsu* system, distribution, and weak anti-trust provisions.

A major shift in the US approach to trade negotiations with Japan occurred early in the Clinton administration: a "results-oriented" approach that sought some form of market share target. The US government stopped short of officially asking for explicit numerical targets, however, which were strongly opposed by the Japanese government. It asked instead for "quantitative indicators" that would be used to measure increases in foreign exports to Japan. This distinction was lost on the Japanese government, which insisted that US demands amounted to "managed trade." After intense negotiations from 1993 through 1995, the USA backed down from these demands.

Trade negotiations after the Framework

Prior to the Framework the Japanese government had usually followed a predictable negotiating style: after a long period of denying or resisting trade demands, Japan would eventually, and often at the last minute, offer some sort of concession that would be enough to placate foreign trade demands. An agreement would invariably be reached, but only after acrimonious negotiations and, quite often, the threat of sanctions by the USA.

During the late 1980s, however, the Japanese government gradually formed a harder line toward US trade demands. During a period in which Japan was growing in power relative to the USA, it was becoming increasingly resentful at what were seen as ever-escalating and "unfair" US trade demands. The 1986 Semiconductor Agreement, and the US sanctions that followed, convinced a number of Japanese government officials, particularly in the **Ministry of International Trade and Industry** (MITI), that Japan should no longer give in to US demands. Japanese officials also resented the 1988 revision of the US Trade Act, which included the so-called Super 301 provision that required the US government to identify and remove foreign "unfair trade practices," a provision that was seen as clearly aimed at Japan. In addition, the strengthening of the multilateral trading system, including the creation of the World Trade Organization, gave Japan a viable alternative to dealing with the USA on a bilateral basis.

The US demands during the Framework talks, which were deemed by Japan to be the equivalent of numerical targets, led to a galvanizing of opinion in the Japanese government. To the surprise of many, Japan stuck to its hard-line position all the way through the 1995 conclusion of the Framework negotiations. For the first time, it was the USA rather than Japan that retreated at the final moment.

Trade negotiations in the last half of the 1990s have been less politicized and controversial, at least compared to the pre-Framework situation. The USA toned down its market access demands on Japan, for a variety of reasons: Japan's growing resistance to bilateral pressures, the recovery in the USA economy as the Japanese economy shifted into recession, and the need to cooperate with Japan on regional security issues. The USA has shifted away from a focus on sectoral trade barriers, and instead has applied more general pressure on **deregulation** in the hopes of increasing competition in the Japanese economy. The USA also continues its efforts to strengthen anti-trust enforcement in Japan.

For its part, the Japanese government has relied more and more on a multilateral approach to trade negotiations with the USA. In 1996 a top MITI official went so far as to declare that "the era of bilateralism is over." Although Japan continued trade negotiations with the USA in this period, it has refused to discuss anything resembling numbers or indicators, or even the removal of specific barriers to trade. Japan has instead demonstrated a clear preference to deal with US trade demands in a multilateral setting. In particular, Japan has sought to use the new dispute settlement mechanisms of the WTO rather than engaging in direct trade negotiations with the USA.

See also: foreign companies in Japan; trade barriers; US investment in Japan

Further reading

American Chamber of Commerce in Japan (1997) *Making Trade Talks Work: Lessons From Recent History*, Tokyo: American Chamber of Commerce in Japan.

Encarnation, D. (1992) *Rivals Beyond Trade: America Versus Japan in Global Competition*, Ithaca, NY: Cornell University Press.

Lincoln, E. (1999) *Troubled Times: U.S.-Japan Trade Relations in the 1990s*, Washington, DC: The Brookings Institution.

Schoppa, L. (1997) *Bargaining With Japan: What American Pressure Can and Cannot Do*, New York: Columbia University Press.

Tyson, L. (1992) *Who's Bashing Whom?: Trade Conflict in High-Technology Industries*, Washington, DC: Institute for International Economics.

ROBERT URIU

Tsukiji market

The Tsukiji market is the largest single wholesale market for seafood products in Japan, probably in the world. The marketplace – officially, Tokyo Chuo Oroshiuri Shijo, Tsukiji Shijo (Tokyo Central Wholesale Market, Tsukiji Market) – is the flagship of Tokyo's wholesale market system, a network of fifteen main and branch markets for fresh and semi-processed seafood, fruits and vegetables, meat, and flowers. In 1998, Tsukiji's seafood auctions had a total annual sales volume of approximately ¥583 billion. The auctions handled 623,000 metric tons of seafood (approximately 2.3 million kilograms per trading day), down about 20 percent from the market's peak year, 1987. Tsukiji's reach is global, and increasingly large percentages of the products sold at Tsukiji's auctions are imported.

Tsukiji is a spot market organized around competitive auctions among licensed participants. The regulated institutional structure carefully defines roles within the auction system in order to limit vertical integration "above" and "below" the auctions. Through informal trading alliances, however, most traders maintain relationships with long-term partners both upstream and downstream. Currently, Tsukiji's auctions are supplied and run by seven large brokerages (*niuke gaisha*, consignees, or *oroshi gyosha*, primary wholesalers) who accept seafood on consignment from producers, regional brokers, and importers, or purchase it directly on their own account. Several of these brokerages are affiliated with parallel auction firms that supply other major urban markets; these *keiretsu* were organized around some of the large fishing companies (for example, Taiyo Gyogyo KK, now known as Maruha Corporation) that dominated Japanese seafood production and distribution until the 1970s. Brokerages sell at auctions six days a week, charging regulated commissions on sales, on terms set by national and municipal regulations. The licensed auctioneers (*serinin*) are employees of these seven firms.

Their customers are independent intermediate wholesalers (*nakaoroshi gyosha*) whose licenses permit them to buy at auction and to operate stalls within the marketplace to resell seafood to retailers, chefs, and processors. There are a total of 1,677 licenses for intermediate wholesalers, currently held by about 900 separate firms. These intermediate wholesalers are divided among a dozen and a half trade specialties (for example, tuna, octopus,

shrimp, live fish, fish paté, etc.), each represented by a *gyokai* (trade association) that negotiates specific terms of trade with the wholesale auction houses. Each trading community forms a semi-autonomous institution within the market, affecting and affected by its economic, political, and social relationships with producers, auctioneers, market administrators, and the particular subset of Tsukiji's clientele that is attracted to the products this specialized group of traders handles. Members of each *gyokai* are further distinguished among themselves according to their highly specialized individual market niches (e.g., suppliers to high-end vs. mass-market sushi chefs; suppliers to supermarkets vs. retail fishmongers).

Since the 1970s, the Japanese fishing industry has undergone major structural changes, in part triggered by the spread of 200-mile fishing limits throughout the world as well as domestic economic realignments and rising labor costs. Domestic production of seafood has declined sharply; in 1975, the Japanese government calculated the ratio of domestic production to consumption of seafood at 100 percent self-sufficiency; in 1997, the ratio was 60 percent. In 1980 gross domestic production of fish, shellfish and seaweed totaled 10.6 million metric tons and 1.7 million metric tons of imports; in 1997, domestic production was 6.9 million and imports were 6.0 million metric tons. Major Japanese fishing corporations have largely withdrawn from direct fishing operations and shifted into food importing, processing, and distribution. Major trading firms have made direct investments in foreign seafood production and have established direct distribution channels with supermarkets and restaurant chains, both sectors that have increased greatly during the last twenty years. As a result of these and other changes in Japanese domestic consumption patterns, the overall percentage of fresh and frozen seafood that passes through Tsukiji and other wholesale seafood markets has shrunk; increasingly large amounts of seafood go directly from producers to retailers (in a distribution pattern known as *jogai ryutsu*, meaning channels that do not pass through regulated wholesale markets). Since the early 1990s, Tsukiji's sales have actually declined in both volume and value; the market has become increasingly specialized on high-end products, a category which has suffered during the prolonged stagnation of the 1990s.

Like many major urban marketplaces through-out the world, Tsukiji is a significant historical and cultural landmark. Tokyo's seafood market has been located at Tsukiji, near the city center along the banks of the Sumida River just a few blocks east of the Ginza, since 1923, when it moved there from Nihonbashi, where the city's major fish market had been located just outside the gates of Edo castle since the early seventeenth century. Until the 1860s the Nihonbashi marketplace operated as a system of feudal guild monopolies; from the 1860s through the 1920s it functioned as a speculative cartel, which engaged in flagrant bribery of government officials. In the 1920s, a new Central Wholesale Market Law established uniform regulations for urban markets for perish-able foods. The Kanto earthquake of 1923 destroyed most of central Tokyo and forced the market's relocation to its present site. Tsukiji officially began operation under the terms of the Central Wholesale Market Law in 1935. During the Second World War, civilian food supplies were severely rationed and Tsukiji suspended ordinary commercial functions. Rationing ended in 1950, and the marketplace was reconstituted along much the same lines it continues to follow at present.

Despite the major transformations in the institutional structure of the marketplace, as well as in conditions of supply and demand, Tsukiji's businesses continue to include many small-scale, family-run shops that can trace long histories of involvement with the marketplace, in some cases stretching back generations to the Nihonbashi marketplace. The market as a whole is steeped in the lore of Japanese cuisine and traditions of mercantile life. In particular, the so-called "outer market" (*jogai shijo*), several square blocks of tiny shops that sell to both a wholesale clientele and ordinary shoppers, located just north of the official market (referred to as the "inner market" (*jonai shijo* or simply *jonai*)), is a popular and colorful shopping area for gourmets and bargain hunters seeking both culinary and cultural tradition.

Tsukiji's future is in doubt, however. Because of changing patterns of distribution, as well as congested transportation and antiquated market facilities, plans are now being drawn up to relocate the official marketplace to another site, possibly in Toyosu, across the mouth of the Sumida River. New facilities would probably not be ready until around 2010. If this move takes place, major changes in the structure of the marketplace are also likely, and the numbers of licensed participants will probably be dramatically reduced.

See also: central wholesale markets

Further reading

Bestor, T.C. (2002) *Tokyo's Marketplace*, Berkeley, CA: University of California Press.

THEODORE BESTOR

U

Ueno, Yoichi

A management consultant, writer and educator, Yoichi Ueno (1883–1957) was a pioneer in the **industrial efficiency movement** and the most prominent advocate of American management techniques in Japan during the interwar period. As Japan's foremost proponent of Frederick Winslow Taylor's theories of scientific management, Ueno authored dozens of works on business administration, industrial psychology and personal development. In addressing the material and spiritual dilemmas of modern society, Ueno sought to develop a holistic vision of economic life that fused Japanese cultural traditions to Taylorite methods and ideals.

A graduate of Tokyo University in psychology, Ueno became interested in industrial management in the 1910s, when Taylor's revolutionary ideas swept through Japanese business circles. Inspired by Taylor's pursuit of the utmost efficiency in the production process, Ueno became a self-taught expert in scientific management, lecturing and writing extensively on the latest American advances. His reputation was made in the early 1920s after he attained remarkable results as one of Japan's first management consultants. Applying the techniques of scientific management – time-and-motion study, job simplification, standardization – Ueno significantly boosted labor productivity in the factories of Lion Toothpowder, Fukusuke Tabi and other manufacturers.

Through the 1920s, Ueno spearheaded efforts to modernize Japanese labor and production management. In 1921, he founded the Industrial Efficiency Institute, a research, consulting and educational organization, and in 1927 established the Japan Efficiency Federation, a national umbrella group of management associations. He also chartered a Japanese branch of the Taylor Society. During the 1930s and the Second World War, Ueno's consulting practice declined and he turned more to writing and teaching: his encyclopedic *Nooritsu handobukku* (Efficiency Handbook) was published in 1939 and he opened a management academy (now SANNO University) in 1942. During the **American occupation**, thanks to his experience with modern administrative techniques, Ueno was appointed one of the three original commissioners of the National Personnel Authority. He continued to lecture on scientific management until his death.

As the premier interpreter of Taylorism in mid-twentieth-century Japan, Ueno had a profound influence on the evolution of Japanese management practices. Although dedicated to the rationalizing principles of scientific management, Ueno was no mere translator or mindless imitator of American managerial trends. Ueno, for example, had deep respect for Confucian morality and Zen doctrine, and he attempted to align Japan's cultural heritage with the demands of modern management. Trained as a psychologist rather than an engineer, Ueno focused on the human element in industry, rejecting the mechanistic, dehumanizing elements of American mass production. He also questioned Taylorism's faith in self-interest (and its consequent emphasis on incentive wages), stressing instead cooperation, mutual understanding and unity of purpose in managing a complex organization. Ueno's conviction that effective management had to combine a systematic, scientific quest for efficiency with a concern for the humanity and well-being of workers would come to characterize Japanese managerial practices in the high-growth years after the Second World War.

Further reading

Tsutsui, W.M. (forthcoming) "The Way of Efficiency: Ueno Yooichi and Scientific Management in Twentieth-Century Japan," *Modern Asian Studies.*

Ueno, Y. (1967) *Ueno Yooichi den* (The Life of Ueno Yoichi), Tokyo: Sangyoo Nooritsu Tanki Daigaku.

WILLIAM M. TSUTSUI

unemployment

Traditionally, Japan is viewed as having a lower unemployment rate than that prevailing in other developed and developing nations. Quoted unemployment in Japan can run from one-half to one-third of the stated rate of the US and European nations. The declared unemployment rate of Japan does not, however, tell the entire employment story. It hides a number of unrecorded factors.

As early as 1980, the **Ministry of Labor** admitted that different criteria were used in the US and Japan, adding that the Japanese rate would rise if US criteria were applied. In 1987, the Ministry of Labor also admitted that the Japanese rate counts military personnel as employed, while the US does not include them in its calculations.

More importantly, in the USA laid-off workers are immediately classified as unemployed. In Japan, if they continue to receive any salary payments (regardless of how small), they are not counted as unemployed. Similarly, in the USA unemployed workers are treated as unemployed until they start work. In Japan, they are considered employed as soon as they accept a job offer, even if the work will not start for up to thirty days. If a job applicant in the USA declines a job offer, he or she is still considered unemployed. In Japan, if they are offered a job through a labor exchange they are considered employed even if they decline the offer.

Another difference is the treatment of stay-at-home parents. In the USA, if a housewife registers at a government employment office, she is considered unemployed. In Japan, she would not be, since she did not previously have a job. Workers with jobs but seeking new jobs are also treated differently. In the USA, if they apply for a new job, they are considered unemployed. In Japan, they are not.

For these reasons, many writers have argued that national employment statistics are only valid for comparisons within the same nation. Reflecting differences in calculations, they point out that they are misleading when compared from one country to another.

Writers who have nevertheless tried to adjust Japanese unemployment statistics to US standards have increased Japanese numbers significantly. For instance, Hachiro Koyama, former chief executive officer of Smith-Kline Beckman Japan, argued that Japan's quoted 2.8 percent unemployment rate, if calculated in accordance with US methods, would be 7.3 percent.

ROBERT BROWN

US investment in Japan

United States foreign direct investment (FDI) in Japan has been strikingly limited throughout the modern period. The first American firms established operations in Japan during the latter half of the nineteenth century, yet these firms performed only limited trade and trade-related operations and were confined to a small number of treaty ports such as Yokohama and Kobe. Roughly a dozen US manufacturing firms, together with a handful of banking and insurance companies, had set up modest facilities in Japan by the early 1930s, yet Japan hosted far less US FDI throughout the pre-Second World War period than did major European economies such as the United Kingdom, Germany and France. Indeed, official US data for the year 1936 suggest that the UK alone was host to more than ten times the quantity of accumulated US FDI in Japan in that year.

Nor did the relative amounts of US FDI in Japan increase substantially during the ensuing decades. In wartime and occupation, of course, virtually no new US direct investment entered the country, and much of the previous investment was literally destroyed. Yet even during Japan's high-growth postwar period the level of US FDI remained extraordinarily limited. By 1965, for example, Mexico and Brazil each hosted greater quantities of accumulated US FDI than did Japan, and by 1980 Japan still lagged considerably behind other major industrialized countries as a host to US FDI.

The amount of US FDI in Japan increased significantly during the latter half of the 1990s, yet in comparative terms still remains quite modest. The US government reported that between the end of 1994 and the end of 1999, the total value of accumulated US FDI in Japan on an historical cost basis grew from roughly $34 billion to almost $48 billion, which represents an increase of some 40 percent. Included in that latter total are such large and high-profile investments as the acquisition of the **Long-Term Credit Bank** of Japan by a US consortium led by Ripplewood and a number of major direct investments by General Electric and other large US firms. Yet even at the end of 1999, Japan – still the world's second largest economy – ranked just sixth among host countries to US FDI, trailing the United Kingdom, Canada, the Netherlands, Switzerland and Germany. Indeed, as Japan entered the new millennium, its huge economy played host to just 4.2 percent of total US FDI abroad.

Why has there been so little US FDI in Japan? Clearly part of the explanation stems from home (or source) country considerations. Some US firms, for example, lacked requisite knowledge of Japanese language, customs and business practices to successfully enter and expand in Japan. Other American companies apparently did not make adequate efforts to break into the market, or chose to limit or withdraw from ongoing operations. And some US multinationals lacked the patience necessary to succeed in a country notorious for the long lead times required before adequate returns are realized on direct investments.

Yet the primary explanation for low levels of US FDI in Japan stems from a series of host (or recipient) country factors. Often backed by domestic firms fearful of foreign competition and for other reasons, the Japanese government prevented or deterred US direct investment in Japan for well more than a century. Host country policies can be divided into a number of more or less distinct phases. The Japanese authorities first permitted US (and certain other foreign) companies to directly invest in Japan in 1859 upon the conclusion of a series of bilateral commercial treaties, but such investments were strictly limited to the treaty ports. Host government policy entered a second phase in 1899, when in exchange for revision of the so-called unequal treaties, Japan permitted US firms to directly invest throughout the nation with relatively few encumbrances.

This second phase came to an end in 1931 when the Japanese government, under the increasing sway of the military, began to institute increasingly strict controls over the operation of US and most other foreign direct investors. The period of war and occupation, during the decade of the 1940s, constitutes yet a third distinct stage in host government treatment of US business. Virtually all US direct investment was expropriated and then turned over to local business interests during the Second World War, but even during the American-led occupation period local officials – often at the behest of the occupiers – prevented US companies from entering or resuming their businesses in Japan.

The Japanese authorities initiated a fourth stage of policy when they passed and then applied a complex set of rules and regulations under the Foreign Investment Law of 1950. This law, which effectively screened out most FDI for more than two decades, was part of Japan's larger strategy during this period to *dis*courage fresh inflows of direct investment from abroad but *en*courage fresh inflows of foreign technology. Powerful domestic companies played key roles in this screening process, and the few large US firms that did manage to enter Japan in these years, such as Coca-Cola, IBM, and Texas Instruments, generally had to satisfy the demands of their domestic competitors before gaining official government approval to invest.

In more recent years, however, the principal barriers to greater US FDI in Japan have originated in the Japanese private sector. Under-developed secondary labor markets, for example, have contributed to the host of challenges US firms must confront in order to hire qualified Japanese employees often frightened of losing their jobs if their foreign employer downsizes or departs and they are left unemployed. The high costs of living, real estate and other aspects of doing business in Japan similarly discourage greater US investment. And, perhaps most importantly, high levels of intra-corporate shareholdings between allied members of the same business groups make US acquisitions of many Japanese companies unusually difficult to accomplish.

What are the prospects for US FDI in Japan? Although numerous factors will continue to deter many American companies from undertaking major new investments, some recent developments point to modestly increasing levels in the foresee-able future.

First, the mobility of the Japanese labor force has been increasing in recent years, and this should stimulate renewed investment interest among American firms as they discover new opportunities to hire quality local employees. Second, the declining cost of Japanese real estate and related cost factors have substantially brought down the cost of office space and residential housing for foreign executives. Third, the gradual unwinding of intra-corporate shareholdings between keiretsu firms and other changing features of Japanese industrial organization and practice spell new opportunities for US firms to enter Japan via merger and acquisition. Finally, in recent years powerful sectors of the Japanese bureaucracy such as the Ministry of Economy, Trade and Industry (or METI, the former MITI) as well as prefectural and municipal government agencies have come to appreciate some of the many benefits foreign companies can bring to Japan. This important change has led to the adoption of new government policies and programs which encourage rather than hinder the entry of US direct investment in Japan.

See also: American occupation; trade barriers

MARK MASON

V

venture capital industry

Estimates on the size of the Japanese venture capital (VC) industry and the invested stock and flow of VC funds face similar problems of precise definition and accurate recording as in other countries. The most acknowledged sources for empirical data on the Japanese VC industry are the semi-annual survey of the Venture Enterprise Center (VEC), a semi-public institution founded by the **Ministry of International Trade and Industry** (MITI) in 1974, and the joint annual survey by the **Nihon Keizai Shimbun** and the Nikkei Research Institute of Industry and Markets, the results of which are compiled in the annual Nikkei Venture Capital Yearbook. The VEC survey distinguishes between direct capital investments by VC firms and investments into partnerships, and subdivides the invested funds into equity-only, equity plus near-equity, and equity plus near-equity plus debt. As of September 1999 it reports a total amount of ¥722 billion equity plus near-equity funds managed by eighty-three VC firms. According to the Nikkei survey, 108 VC firms committed ¥268 billion for new investment in venture firms during 1999. Thus, compared to the over $46 billion raised by 409 VC funds in 1999 in the USA, the domestic Japanese VC industry is still small.

History

The origins of the Japanese VC industry date back to the enactment of the Small and Medium-Sized Business Investment Development Law in 1963.

Following the model of the American Small Business Investment Act of 1958, it intended to foster VC investment into innovative small firms and led to the establishment of three semi-public VC firms called Small Business Investment Companies (SBICs) in Tokyo, Nagoya, and Osaka. In contrast to the US model, these firms are not allowed to provide loans, but are required to invest in equity or equity-linked securities of small, but profitable, dividend-paying enterprises with a nominal capital of less than ¥300 million in one of twenty-eight designated industrial fields. The investment guidelines determine that the SBICs assume substantial risk by taking a share of no less than 15 percent and up to 50 percent of a portfolio company's equity.

The history of Japan's private VC industry is comparatively short and marked by distinct periods. The first wave of private VC investment occurred between 1970 and 1973 and was led by Japanese banks and security firms which were inspired by the take-off of VC in the USA and backed by ample cash reserves piled up during the high growth period. Altogether eight firms were established, starting with the independent Kyoto Enterprise Development (KED), and followed by Nippon Enterprise Development (NED), a joint venture between the **Long-Term Credit Bank of Japan**, the **Daiichi Kangyo Bank** and the ITOCHU general trading company. The establishment of Japan's largest VC firm, the Japan Associated Finance Company (JAFCO), a listed affiliate of **Nomura Securities**, also dates back to this period. The first wave of Japanese VC was short-lived and the majority of the funds ended in high losses which was partially due to the oil shocks of the 1970s, but more so due to inexperience and inflexibility in VC management as well as the enforcement of stricter regulations by the **Ministry of Finance** (MoF) in regard to listing and accounting standards for young growth firms.

The second wave of private VC investment occurred between 1982 and 1986, triggered by the emergence of Silicon Valley and **liberalization of financial markets** in Japan. Improvements in the regulatory environment such as the relaxation of listing requirements for the OTC market and the Tokyo Stock Exchange Second Section, the liberalization in the use of warrants, or the introduction of a rating system created a more favorable environment for VC investment in Japan. In addition to the six firms remaining from the first period, over fifty new VC firms were established and investment grew to a sizeable amount with a focus on high-tech firms in areas like electronics or new materials. Furthermore, the first investment partnership (*toshi jigyo kumiai*) was established by JAFCO in 1982, thereby providing venture capitalists with an option for risk diversification. The rapidly **appreciating yen** after the Plaza Accord followed by a series of large-scale bankruptcies of well-known venture businesses led to a collapse of the second VC wave in 1986. However, despite the decline in domestic VC investment, Japanese investment into USA and European venture funds increased. Most notable are investments by Japanese corporations into high-tech venture firms in the field of computer hardware and software or biotechnology in the California area with the commercial objective to gain access to emerging technologies and to initiate future business partnerships.

From the beginning of the 1990s the Japanese VC industry experienced a significant, though unsteady increase in the level of equity-linked VC investment as second-tier financial institutions like regional banks, mutual loan and savings banks, or cooperative associations, as well as more and more firms independent from financial institutions were established. Since the late 1990s Japan's VC system is becoming more diversified and versatile due to market entry by large-scale funds of well-known foreign VC firms and investment banks, and the rapid rise of internet-related VC firms led by Softbank Corporation.

Characteristics of Japan's VC industry

The Japanese VC industry is highly concentrated and dominated by affiliates of financial institutions and semi-public funds. As of March 31, 1999, the top ten Japanese VC firms managed about two-third of the reported venture investment of ¥806 billion, with Nomura-affiliated JAFCO, Daiwa-affiliated Nippon Investment & Finance Company, and Japan Asia Investment Company alone commanding a 42 percent share. In regard to the stock of managed funds, the semi-public SBICs account for significant investment shares, notably the Tokyo Small and Medium Business Development Fund and the Osaka Small and Medium Business Development Fund. At the same time, smaller funds composed of individual venture capitalists and partnerships as well as, more importantly, pensions funds, are negligible as a source of VC in Japan mainly due to Japan's regulatory framework. Until the passage of the Limited Partnership Act for Venture Capital Investment (*toshi jigyo yugen sekinnin kumiaho*) of November 1998 liabilities of investor partnerships were not limited, thereby increasing the risk for individual venture capitalists. In regard to pension funds investment that nowadays contributes over half of the VC in the US regulatory deficiencies are considered to be a significant barrier to an increase of VC investment by institutional investors in Japan. Japan lacks rules and regulations like the US Employee Retirement Income Security Act (ERISA) that, by means of an amendment to the "prudent man" rule in 1979, permitted investment of pension money into high-risk assets like VC funds and, thereby, contributed largely to the surge in US VC investment.

A second important obstacle for VC investment in Japan relates to regulations for initial public offering (IPO) procedures. Although the relaxation of the listing standards for securities on the OTC market in 1983 resulted in a surge of new listings in the late 1980s and early 1990s, it still requires fifteen to twenty years on average for a company to obtain a listing on the Japanese OTC market, as compared to an average of five years in the USA.

These long time requirements for an IPO, combined with high cultural barriers to MBOs or mergers and acquisitions in Japan constrain the options for a viable exit strategy by the venture capitalist. The establishment of the Mother's Section at the Tokyo Stock Exchange as well as the foundation of NASDAQ Japan, a joint venture between NASDAQ, Softbank Corporation and the Osaka Stock Exchange, in 1999 is a major step to stimulate future growth of VC investment in Japan, as both exchanges explicitly target young growth firms and thereby widen the options for a smooth and speedy exit.

Compared to the USA, Japanese VC firms usually are more risk averse and conservative reflecting their strong affiliation to financial institutions. Investments usually concentrate on later stage companies in their business expansion phase and on bridge/mezzanine finance prior to an IPO, while high risk, early stage investments into seed or start-up firms are rather limited. These patterns reveal substantial differences between Japan and the USA in regard to the underlying philosophy of the VC business. Seed and early stage investment lie at the heart of the US-style VC, because during these phases VC firms are provided with ample opportunities to generate value added for venture firms, while at the same time foundations for high financial returns are created. Japanese VC firms often pursue multiple objectives. Due to their affiliation with banks or security firms, they not only aim for high capital gains, but also for access to profitable underwriting or future lending business.

A further contrast between US and Japanese-style venture capital is the nature of the relationship between the VC firm and the venture company. US VC firms usually maintain a close relationship with their portfolio companies, engage in active monitoring, and provide various value-adding services, management support and expertise in respect to business planning, marketing, organization or personnel. They regularly exchange information and become actively involved in company affairs through board membership. In Japan, VC investment is usually not associated with an active monitoring and governance role. Instead, the relationship between the VC firms and their portfolio companies is, in general, distant and at

arm's length, exchange of information is limited, and board membership of the venture capitalist an exception. In fact, until 1995, the anti-monopoly law prohibited board membership of employees of VC firms in their portfolio companies. In addition, Japanese venture capitalists are said to lack sufficient industry experience and management expertise due to their finance-related career background.

Many of the differences between VC in Japan and the USA or Europe can be explained by structural and regulatory factors. Next to financial regulations in regard to listing requirements or pension management, insufficient incentive schemes for venture capitalists such as stock option plans or tax breaks for "business angels" are often quoted as examples. Regulations are also held responsible for insufficient exchange between academic research and business causing a lack of involvement by university professors and researchers with the VC community. Next to differences in the regulatory framework, it is argued that the state of Japan's VC industry reflects distinct features of Japan's industrial culture. One such feature is the predominant position of large Japanese corporations as a major source for new technologies and innovations. By means of diversification, in-house company ventures, and corporate spin-offs, large companies have repeatedly succeeded in establishing new growth areas, thereby replacing or crowding out VC investment. Furthermore, the predominance of long-term employment practices and the existence of **internal labor markets** are believed to limit labor mobility, to discourage entrepreneurship, and to make recruitment of qualified employees by new enterprises more difficult. Finally, cultural impediments to entrepreneurship are cited as yet another reason for Japan's underdeveloped VC business by pointing to the high risks of entrepreneurial failure within the Japanese cultural context and to the strong social concerns for stability. However, these culture-based arguments are often disputed by referring to the large number of **small and medium-sized firms** and independent, mid-sized companies (*chusho kigyo*), and their important role for Japan's economic development.

Nevertheless, since the beginning of the 1990s the Japanese government has expressed its concern with the faltering corporate start-up rate and has enacted a series of policies and legal changes in order to foster a US-style VC business. Measures include tax incentives, special funds for loans and loan guarantees for young technology firms, the permission of limited liability partnership, as well as changes in the commercial and tax code in regard to stock options and "angel tax deductions." These measures reflect an important shift in the policy towards small and medium-sized enterprises from protection of existing small firms towards fostering of an entrepreneurial culture.

Further reading

Borton, J.W. (ed.) (1992) *Venture Japan: How Growing Companies Worldwide Can Tap Into the Japanese Venture Capital Markets*, London/New York: Woodhead-Faulkner.

Clark, R. (1987) *Venture Capital in Britain, America and Japan*, London/Sydney: Croom Helm.

Hurwitz, S.L. (1999) *The Japanese Venture Capital Industry*, Cambridge, MA: MIT Japan Program 99–04, Center of International Studies, Massachusetts Institute of Technology.

Mizuno, H., Hayashi, A. and Miura, I. (eds) (1998) *Bencha Handobukku* (Venture Handbook), Tokyo: Nikkan Kogyo Shimbunsha.

Nihon Keizai Shimbunsha/Nikkei Sangyo Shohi Kenkyujo (2000) *Nikkei bencha bijinesu nenkan* (Nikkei Venture Business Yearbook), Tokyo: Nihon Keizai Shimbunsha.

JÖRG RAUPACH-SUMIYA

VLSI Research Cooperative

The Very Large-Scale Integrated Circuit Research Cooperative was a government sponsored research effort involving the **Ministry of International Trade and Industry** (MITI) and five major domestic computer companies: Fujitsu, **NEC**, Hitachi, **Toshiba** and **Mitsubishi**. The cooperative held together for five years, from 1975–9, and was touted as the vehicle by which Japan would gain superiority in integrated circuit (IC) manufacture, specifically 256k DRAM and higher. The project is generally considered a success. In 1989,

Dataquest estimated Japan's market share in 256k and 1Mb integrated circuits at 92 percent and 96 percent respectively. Success is also reflected in the fact that when the US government and a consortium of US firms set up Sematech (the Semiconductor Manufacturing Technology Initiative) in 1987, they used the VLSI Cooperative as both a justification and an example.

The cooperative was a clear attempt by MITI to shape the pace and direction of one of Japan's key high-tech industries – integrated circuits – by increasing funding and encouraging the sharing of information. The government provided ¥300 million and the companies as a group contributed another ¥400 million. While not a significant amount when spread over a five-year period, it sent a symbolic signal about the perceived importance of the industry. Probably of more importance was the encouraging of information sharing among the five firms. Fujitsu, Hitachi, Mitsubishi, NEC and Toshiba are fierce competitors across a range of markets. There was deep concern as to whether or not the five would be willing to work together. However, MITI had also concluded that the increasing competitiveness of the US computer industry required Japanese firms to cooperate.

It is unclear to what extent information sharing took place within the cooperative. Over its five-year lifespan, about 100 engineers were involved. They were divided into three project teams: materials development, wafer size and production process equipment. Company representation was not equally distributed across teams, and some companies appear to have dominated particular projects. Whether this was a conscious attempt to control the project or, instead, represented the varying strengths of firms in different technological areas is hard to conclude. Given that the firms were fierce competitors and that the collectivist nature of Japanese organizations discourages horizontal communication among firms, even modest information sharing can be seen as an important accomplishment.

Another school of thought argues against the importance of the VLSI Cooperative Research Project. They note that Oki Electric, the one major computer firm to not join the cooperative, remained competitive in the IC industry (despite taking twice as long as the other five to reach production). It also noteworthy that three new-comers to IC production – **Matsushita**, Sanyo and **Sharp** – were able to enter the DRAM market at this time. Finally, critics of the coopera-tive point out that the most significant firm in the IC industry did not participate in the project, but contributed more to IC production technology between 1974 and 1980 than the cooperative. **Nippon Telegraph and Telephone**, at the time a quasi-public organization under the regulation of the Ministry of Posts and Telecommunications, maintained several laboratories. Though not an equipment maker, it worked closely with supplier firms, often sending its own engineers to supplier firm research centers. The research centers and close relationships with suppliers was justified on the grounds that NTT set specifications for all telecommunications equipment in order to insure quality.

The VLSI Cooperative Research Project took place in a period in which Western concerns about **Japan, Inc**. was widespread. Western observers noted the close relationship between MITI and the private industrial sectors. The cooperative project reinforced the perception that Japanese govern-ment and businesses were competing in global markets as a partnership.

See also: administrative guidance

Further reading

Methé, D. (1991) *Technological Competition in Global Industries*, New York: Quorum.

ALLAN BIRD

wartime legacy

One can only speculate what Japan would be like today had the military not come to dominate foreign policy in the late 1920s. If that had not happened, Japan would never have provoked war in China, never taken over Manchuria, never designed and carried out an invasion in Southeast Asia, and never drawn the United States into the Pacific War. These things of course did happen, and they led to disastrous defeat for Japan in 1945. Results of Japan's wartime experience and behavior continue to be debated, but some of the effects are quite clear and can be interpreted in both positive and negative ways.

For Americans, the Second World War lasted for a little less than four years; for Europeans it was six years or more in duration. For the Japanese it was over a much longer period; the country had been involved in virtually non-stop military struggle since early in 1931. It is true that involvement in war in the early 1930s was not nearly of the intensity and scale that it grew to be from 1942 through 1945, but the outpouring of human and material resources over such an extended area, and over such an extended period of time, was bound to leave its mark on Japanese society.

The Purge

In addition to the international war crimes trials which resulted in a little over four hundred people being hanged and several thousand imprisoned (see **American occupation**), the United States government directed the occupation authorities to remove from an active role in Japanese society all "exponents of militant nationalism and aggression." In Japan, figuring out just who was an exponent of militant nationalism and aggression was not so easy, and there was great disagreement within the occupation government over who should be purged. All officers of the Imperial army and navy were officially purged. Top government bureaucrats were also an easy target, and several thousand were duly removed from their positions. Members of patriotic societies, groups of government, business and military personnel who had conspired to further Japan's interests on the mainland, and some teachers and publishers were dismissed from their posts. The number of people in the above categories was quite large. About 80,000 in all were purged, in addition to 120,000 army officers.

When SCAP turned to the business community, however, there was more controversy than ever. SCAP officials responsible for identifying business leaders to be purged had come to know many of the business leaders during the business restructuring negotiations immediately after the occupation began. There was strong sentiment among SCAP officials that removing the most proven business minds from the scene would seriously hamper Japan's economic recovery, making some sort of radical take-over of the government more likely. After much internal wrangling, about 1,500 business leaders were added to the purge list; deducting voluntary resignations from that number, only about 450 business leaders were actually purged by SCAP.

History will record that on the whole the purge

did not have a serious effect on Japanese recovery, or any other aspect of the society. The great majority of those purged were "unpurged" in 1951; three years later when Japan was again fully sovereign, all restrictions under the occupation purges were nullified. Several of those purged returned to positions of leadership, including Hatoyama Ichiro who became prime minister in 1954, and Kishi Nobusuke, who followed him in 1956.

Anti-war ideology

Although a military government did not officially run Japan during the war years, the military was an extremely powerful and influential focus of authority. For three years the minister of war, a general, served as prime minister, and a huge amount of Japan's wealth was subsumed by Japan's army and navy forces, subsumed for the express purpose of preparing for and executing war. The Japanese people knew where to place the blame for the catastrophic destruction rained upon their nation. War planners in military uniform together with their clients in the industrial cartels had led them to ruin, a set of events which planted a deep core of fear and resentment in the minds of the great majority of the Japanese people toward war and toward anything associated with military institutions.

Most people in Japan today were not alive to see the pain of war when it was brought upon the nation, but the memory is nourished through the media, by the substantial left-leaning faction of Japanese politics, and with the national observance of the nuclear bombing of Hiroshima and Nagasaki each August. When the war ended, the Japanese military was not only discredited, it was virtually removed as an active force in economic and political life. During the first few years of the American occupation, six generals and one civilian were hanged as class A war criminals, and 400 more as class C war criminals. Several hundred other individuals were sentenced to prison for terms ranging from a few years to life. Although these punishments were handed down by an international war crimes tribunal, there was not much expression of sympathy for the defendants from the Japanese population at large.

The Self Defense Force of today, has not, and under current conditions, cannot function with even a shadow of the power and influence of the prewar and wartime Japanese military. On average, the Japanese are as anti-war in outlook as the people of any large society, and while China and other nations fear a rebirth of aggressive militarism in Japan, one legacy of the war is that Japan was transformed from a warlike and aggressor society into one which is not likely to cause trouble to anyone through military means for the foreseeable future.

Postwar reforms

The totality of defeat, together with the obvious benign intentions of the conquerors, created in Japan an openness for change and a willingness to discard the past to a degree quite rarely seen in any society at any time. Some of the enthusiasm for American-inspired change and reform wore off over time; some aspects of the occupation reforms were frankly not appropriate for Japan. On the whole, however, the occupation freed Japan from some of its own confining themes; it was said by many Japanese that defeat and occupation liberated Japan from itself: in land reform, labor relations, with a new and more open educational system, with an economy less tied to a few wealthy families, in many ways. A liberating wind blew through Japan with the occupation, bringing reforms which the Japanese themselves probably could not have instituted. Left to itself, any society has a difficult time wresting power from vested interests in attempting reforms. Defeat in war and temporary authority vested in an objective outside force offered a chance to redesign aspects of Japan's institutional framework. Some of that redesign has had a lasting and positive effect on the culture and society.

End of aristocracy

For hundreds of years, hereditary feudal elite had run Japan. During the Meiji period, on the other hand, education and economic performance came to be more important than connection to an aristocratic past; indeed Japan seemed to make more progress in overcoming a traditional caste-like ranking system than some European societies such as England or Italy. But in spite of the impressive degree to which Japan was able in a very short span of time to throw off the bonds of feudalism, even after modernization it remained a highly stratified society. The new middle class, dynamic as it was, was surrounded on three sides by a large impoverished peasantry, growing working class, not much better off, and a very small privileged elite.

The "privileged elite" included people who lived lives hardly imaginable by ordinary people due to their great wealth, and other privileges as part of the formal nobility. A peerage was put into place during the Meiji period composed of five ranks (see **Meiji restoration**), roughly equivalent to the peerage ranks traditionally used in Europe, with about 900 families making up the official Japanese titled nobility. Some of the families at the center of the largest *zaibatsu* were incorporated into the peerage, and several top industrialists who remained outside the peerage were listed among the wealthiest men in the world. Had Japan not been defeated in war, it is probable that the peerage system would have remained intact, and those wealthy families of commoners would still be in a privileged place, exerting influence at the top of economic and political life.

Reforms discussed above included to a large measure ending hereditary privilege and power in Japan. Indeed it can be argued that, at least for the two and one-half decades following the war, Japan became a model of egalitarian society unparalleled among capitalist nations, significantly more so than its great teacher, the United States. The power of great wealth and advantages associated with social connections began to re-emerge as important factors in Japan during the 1970s and 1980s, and there is evidence that family ties function today in some ways reminiscent of the old aristocracy. In spite of this, however, the top of power and influence in Japanese society will not likely ever again be as closed to those not born to it as it was in the years prior to and during the war.

Relations with Asian nations

One rather powerful wartime legacy has been the way events during the war have been kept alive in the collective memories of other Asians. When Japanese reflect on the war, they are most likely to call to mind the people of Japan as victims of the carpet bombing of their capital and several other cities, victims of the dropping of nuclear bombs on Hiroshima and Nagasaki, victims of the miserable conditions of ordinary people at war's end. For Japan's neighbors, it is quite another matter. People and governments in Korea, China, and several countries of Southeast Asia are more likely to conjure up images of invasion, brutal treatment at the hands of Japanese military personnel, forced labor, imposed foreign currency, images which continue to influence the way Japan is seen and dealt with.

In 1998, South Korea finally lifted some of its ban on Japanese popular culture, but there remains virulent anti-Japanese sentiment in some quarters of the population, in some cases encouraged by the government. A museum on the outskirts of Seoul, isited by thousands of school children each year, exhibits in vivid fashion some of the cruelty of Japanese against Koreans during the colonial period. China has been critical of Japan for not owning up to the brutal behavior of the Japanese Army during its long occupation of China. Chinese government officials monitor political events in Japan, with an eye on right-wing groups, feared by many Chinese as potentially a rebirth of Japanese militarism.

Japan has to a significant degree repaired its reputation in Southeast Asia through trade and economic investment, but there remain unpleasant memories for those who lived through Japanese incursion into their lands, and for some of the older generation, Japan is always looked upon with suspicion.

Further reading

Baerwald, H.H. (1959) *The Purge of Japanese Leaders under the Occupation*, Berkeley, CA: University of California Press.

Gibney, F. (1992) *The Pacific Century: America and Asia in a Changing World*, New York: Scribner's Sons.

Hachiya, M. (1965) *Hiroshima Diary*, ed. and trans. W. Wells, Chapel Hill, NC: University of North Carolina Press.

Jansen, M. (1975) *Japan and China: From War to Peace*, Chicago: Rand McNally.

Kerbo, H.R. and McKinstry, J.A. (1995) *Who Rules Japan: The Inner Circles of Economic and Political Power*, Westport, CT: Praeger.

JOHN A. McKINSTRY

white-collar workers

The term "white-collar worker" refers to salaried male workers in Japanese organizations. The term "**salaryman**" is synonymous in Japan for white-collar worker. "Salaryman" was used in Japan as far back as the **Meiji** period (1868–1912) to refer to salaried workers in desk jobs. Today it refers specifically to white-collar male workers. Salaried female workers are referred to as "career women."

The white-collar worker in Japan designs his life on the expectation of a guarantee of lifetime employment, the promise of increasing wages for the length of his working life (seniority pay), and representation in decision-making within the company (company union). He joins the company upon graduation from college, is educated by it, and remains loyal to the company in spite of low wages while he is young because the seniority system guarantees that his salary will eventually grow and his job will be secure.

However, recent data suggest that Japan's employment system is in transition and perhaps is moving away from the lifetime employment model and shrinking the number of white-collar workers. Mid-career recruitment in large enterprises, even for top executives, is growing. With an aging workforce, less committed young workers, and pressing needs for skilled specialists, employers are adjusting their permanent employment and seniority reward systems. Workers are seeking greater job mobility and not relying on the company for their career development and job security.

In addition, as employment restructuring moves forward, white-collar workers will eventually find themselves being downsized because they are a group having no special qualifications that are valued in the labor market. Most of their skills come from on-the-job training and job rotations within their companies, making their knowledge and skills non-transferable. Advances in technology and computers made the jobs previously held by administrative staff redundant. As more emphasis is placed on specialization and individual skills, white-collar workers are finding that they need to systematically improve their abilities to survive in a competitive labor market.

The Ministry of Labor anticipates an increase in labor movement activity as a result or because of such changes in the working environment. The ministry's goal is to encourage employment stability for the white-collar worker while allowing the labor market to become more dynamic. Training schemes and re-employment programs will be the focus of the Ministry of Labor in its efforts to stabilize the careers of the white-collar worker.

Further reading

Chinone, K. (1996) "Coping With Freedom: Can the Salaryman Change His Spots?" *Tokyo Business Today* 64(1): 28–32.

Hitoshi, C. (1997) "Salaryman Today and Into Tomorrow," *Compensation and Benefits Review* 29(5): 67–75.

Mantsun, M. (1997) "How Permanent Was Permanent Employment?: Patterns of Organizational Mobility in Japan," *Work and Occupations* 24(1).

Toshiaki, O. (1999) "Report on Labor Trends in Japan," Ministry of Labor White Paper, Tokyo.

White, O. (1996) "Japanese Seek Skilled Workers Over Cheap Labor," *World Trade* 9: 66.

MARGARET TAKEDA

women's roles

Women's roles in the post-Second World War era have centered on the dual roles of wife-mother and secondary worker. Women have participated in the labor force at high levels, but the development of economic and social institutions have shaped their roles to complement male breadwinners. Women are expected to support their husband's careers. This usually involves complete devotion to their husband's company, nurturing of the children, and caring for aging parents. The rapid expansion of the new middle class since the mid-1950s gave rise to a new image of the ideal of housewife: a woman that is free from the labor intensive work the previous generation of women endured. The increasing level of educational competition among children since the 1970s intensified women's responsibilities in children's education. Thus, contrary to the popular image of Japanese women who devote themselves to the family, the "traditional" women's roles are not so traditional as one might think. More recent trends show a growing ambivalence on the part of young women in their acceptance of women's dual roles. The direction of change is not yet clear.

Historically high rates of female labor force participation are due to the size of the traditional sector (agriculture, fishing and forestry) and the strong presence of small family-owned enterprises. The traditional sector, absorbing the largest segment of the work force until about 1960, declined to account for less than 10 percent by 1980. The decline in the traditional sector was offset by the expansion of the secondary (manufacturing, construction, and mining) and tertiary (service and trade) sectors. The secondary sector absorbed 20 percent of the work force in 1960 and 27 percent in 1987. The service sector accounted for 37 percent in 1960 and 63 percent in 1987. Continuing industrialization opened new employment opportunities to young women in the factories and modern corporations in urban centers.

Women combined their economic and family roles within the traditional industries that offered flexibility in working schedules. Only those women who could afford not to work stopped working upon marriage or having children. The contraction of traditional industries reduced family enterprise workers. The concomitant growth of the modern economy increased female employment outside the home, accentuating the temporary withdrawal from the labor force for many women. The withdrawal from the labor force during child-bearing years and the re-entry into the work force in middle age was most pronounced in the 1970s and early 1980s, with 55 percent of women aged 25–34 not working. More recent patterns are a reversal to the earlier trend. The dip during the childbearing years has gradually decreased, and in 1990 the labor force participation rates among women aged 25–34 returned to the 50 percent level, but is still lower than the rates among women of the same age group before 1960 (55 percent).

The ideology of the middle-class housewife, which accentuated the division of gender roles was particularly strong in the 1970s and 1980s. For example, an overwhelming majority of women, 76 percent, supported the gender division of work and family in 1982. This number had decreased to 56 percent in 1992. Similarly, women's support for withdrawal from the labor force during middle-age years was 71 percent in 1972, 74 percent in 1983, and 64 percent of women in 1990. Women's support for work careers without disruptions was 12 percent in 1972, 17 percent in 1983, and 14 percent in 1990. Educated women, who are more likely to marry educated men who can provide the economic security of the middle class, were less likely to return to work in their middle-age years than those with only a high school education. The weak correlation between the level of women's education and their employment during the years of middle age is still pronounced today.

The image of middle-class women may obscure the complexities of women's dual roles and the implications for society. Corporate policies related to hiring, training and promotion, as well as socialization at home and the education systems, all contribute to woman's dual roles as wife-mother and secondary worker. Women supply full-time labor when they are young, and they support their husband's career after they are married. Women perform types of jobs that are drastically different from those of men of similar age. When young, women work full-time in auxiliary or dead end jobs, young men are placed in more responsible positions and go through the firm-based internal labor market. Once leaving their jobs upon marriage or having children, middle-aged women who need to supplement their family income re-enter the labor market as part-time or temporary (non-regular full-time) workers. In 1990, within a group of working women aged 34–55, 51 percent held full time positions, 43 percent held part-time or temporary positions, and 6 percent were self-employed.

Until about 1980 men and women showed a striking normative and behavioral consensus on the proper age of marriage. Incorporating this norm and expecting women to leave the company to raise a family, employers have been reluctant to invest heavily in training women. For example, large firms actively recruit male university graduates but seek women who have a high school or two-year college degree. While male workers receive in-house training and are rewarded on the basis of seniority, women are precluded from such investment from the very beginning. Such corporate practices perpetuate a pattern whereby women perform less responsible work until they marry or have children.

Most parents monitor their son's education more carefully than their daughter's education because of the close relationship between education and future occupational success. Japanese women enter college in higher numbers than do men (46 percent vs. 41 percent in 1993), but half of them go to junior colleges rather than four-year universities (whereas more than 90 percent of men go to four-year universities). A four-year university education for daughters is considered a barrier to finding employment and a hindrance to their chances for a good marriage. Thus, parents are hesitant to push their daughters through the "examination hell" demanded for entry into elite universities. Higher education for daughters is viewed more in terms of general educational development in preparation for meeting a man who will bring high social status and economic security. Such socialization leads to a lack of career aspiration and a more family-oriented career among young women.

Working women, especially those who are committed to their work careers, have been aware of the systematic inequalities imposed by the corporate system, and as early as the 1960s they sought legal redress. Clauses stipulating that women must retire at marriage or pregnancy were litigated first. In the 1960s and 1970s, the courts awarded several female workers back wages and an injunction that barred large corporations from using mandatory retirement at marriage clauses in contracts (for example, the 1966 Sumitomo Cement case). Earlier successful litigation cases guaranteed women's rights to work and promotions. However, discriminatory hiring and training practices remained firmly in place, at least until the passage of the Equal Employment Opportunity Law (EEOL) of 1986.

Most observers maintain that the EEOL has not been a success. Even though large firms began to offer a two-track hiring system for women, the general clerical track (*ippanshoku*) and the management track (*sogoshoku*), the number of women who took advantage of the new hiring system did not increase. The management track promises career advancement, but in exchange, women are expected to work like men, emulating "corporate *samurai*" careers. The long commute and working hours, extensive overtime, attendance at social events after work, and transfers are all prerequisites to corporate career advancement. Women are reluctant to seek the managerial track out of concern that the transfers and long working hours will conflict with their family needs. In 1990, less than 15 percent of large private firms assigned relocation to women as part of career development. Lack of maternity leave and child-care facilities are additional barriers to women who are committed to career advancement. Employers do not groom women for future promotion, and women fail to aspire to and to apply for such positions. In 1990 women held only 2.2 percent of managerial positions in large firms.

In contrast to the "hostile" corporate environment in which women hit a "concrete ceiling," the public sector is much more hospitable to women's needs and career development. Gender equality is acknowledged and women are rewarded with equal pay for equal work and their jobs are protected by maternity leave policies. Yet, even in the public sector, women in leadership positions are few, accounting for less than 2 percent of the managerial class.

Women's entry into managerial positions is inversely related to the size of the firm. According to a study by the Women's Bureau of the Ministry of Labor, the probability that a woman holds a *kacho* position (section manager) is ten times greater in the small firms and a *bucho* position (division manager) is thirty times greater. In addition, there are a large number of female owners of small and medium-size firms. Retail women's or children's clothing was the most common business headed by a female president in 1989. Studies show that these women are not necessarily highly educated. They are more likely to be married and have children than their counterparts in large firms. These women appear to come from families that encourage work in small and medium-sized businesses, with their parents (especially fathers) providing the role model. In addition, studies on career progression of female managers suggest that women typically rose to their position by working around the dominant male career pattern, rather than by competing within it.

During the booming economy of the 1980s, Japan experienced a severe nationwide labor shortage and "women power" was one of the biggest catch phrases in corporate job advertisements. The government recognized the need to support working women's needs (child care, flexi time, elder care). Studies report that multinational corporations made a positive impact on working women as they recruited diverse workers based on ability. However, there are also reports that Japanese multinational firms operating in the US hired more Japanese women in managerial positions in their American offices than they did in their home operations. More studies are needed to assess the impact of multinational corporations in women's employment.

Currently, Japan faces an uncertain trend. Since the economic bubble burst in 1989, young women are struggling with a very tight job market, and they are postponing marriage. The average age of marriage for women rose from twenty-five in 1975 to twenty-eight in 1995, and in the Tokyo area, it is thirty-one. Women on average are having 1.39 children, one of the lowest birth rates in the world. Some observers interpret these changes as a "quiet revolution," with women initiating a re-negotiation of gender roles. According to this view, young women are disillusioned with Japanese men and marriages that only constrain them and so have become more selective in their life course options.

Others, however, paint a more pessimistic picture by pointing to the absence of concrete structural and institutional changes that promote long-range employment opportunities for women and a new family division of labor. According to this view, the postponement of marriage and women's reluctance to raise children are far from the advancement of women's new roles.

Further reading

Adler, N.J. (1993) "Competitive Frontiers, Women Managers in the Triad," *International Studies of Management and Organization* 23(2): 3–23.

Awaya, N. and Phillips, D. (1996) "Popular Reading: The Literary World of the Japanese Working Women," in A. Iwamura (ed.), *Re-imaging Japanese Women*, Berkeley, CA: University of California Press, 244–70.

Brington, M.C. (1993) *Women and the Economic Miracle*, Berkeley, CA: University of California Press.

Clammer, J. (1997) *Contemporary Urban Japan*, Oxford: Blackwell.

Department of Labor Women's Bureau (1992) "Women Workers: Outlook to 2005," *Facts on Working Women* 92(1): 1–7.

Inoue, T. and Ehara, Y. (eds) (1995) *Women's Data Book*, Tokyo: Yuhikaku.

Saso, M. (1990) *Women in the Japanese Workplace*, London: Hilary Shipman.

Steinhoff, P.G. and Tanaka, K. (1993) "Women Managers in Japan," *International Studies of Management and Organization* 23(2): 25–48.

Usui, C. (1994) "Do American Models of Female Career Attainment Apply to Japanese?" Center for International Studies, Occasional paper No. 9408, University of Missouri-St. Louis.

CHIKAKO USUI

Yamato Transportation

Yamato is the pioneering company of truck haulage in Japan and the leading firm in the overnight delivery service of small parcels, which it introduced to the country in 1976. As of 1999, Yamato Transport handled 836 million parcels, which represented a 35.6 percent share of the industry. At the end of June, 2000, the company possessed 31,690 vehicles, linking its networks of 2,702 depots, storage points, and transshipment centers throughout the country. It has 87,658 employees nationwide. The total operating revenue for fiscal 1999 was ¥744 billion, with operating profit of ¥32 billion and recurring profit of ¥32 billion.

Yasuomi Ogura laid the company's foundation when he began a charter truck haulage service with four lorries at Kyobashi, Tokyo, in 1919, at a time when there were only 204 lorries in Japan. In early times, Ogura struggled to find customers, since carriage by motor vehicles was considerably more expensive than by horse-drawn ones. In 1923, he signed an exclusive contract of delivery with **Mitsukoshi**, the first department store in Japan, which made his business much more stable.

Four years later, Ogura attended an international conference of road cargo transport companies in London, and visited Carter-Patterson, a British company which operated scheduled long haul transport linking networks for collection and delivery. Inspired by this, he started, between Tokyo and Yokohama, the first scheduled bulk road transport in Japan two years later. This service was extended to the Kanto area by 1935.

After a disruption during the Second World War, the company's activities had resumed fully by 1949, and the scope of operations was extended to overland legs of air and sea cargo, road haulage between railway terminus and ports, and packaging. In the 1950s, the principal mode of cargo transport in Japan began to shift from railway (**Japan National Railways**) to trucking. Yamato was comparatively late in establishing the long haul operation, and it was only in 1960 that the company started the Tokyo-Osaka service. Due to high competition, Yamato suffered from low profitability throughout the 1960s.

Masao Ogura, who succeeded his father in 1971 as president, was inspired by visiting UPS and started, in 1976, overnight delivery service of parcels focusing on individual customers in the Kanto area under the name of *Takkyu-bin* (home express). Contrary to the prevailing belief that the business was not feasible, Yamato's simple and innovative concept of uniform pricing and overnight delivery was a stunning success. In 1986, the company extended its geographical scope to overseas destinations through a cooperative agreement with UPS. The coverage of its parcel collection and delivery service was extended to all of Japan by 1989. Meanwhile, Yamato developed new services such as transporting skiing and golf equipment to site from home, articles of perishable food by temperature-controlled vehicles, delivery at designated times, book delivery, and home moving. In the 1990s, this leader of the overnight delivery service industry began "cash on delivery" service of items marketed by direct mailing companies and Internet retailers.

SHINTARO MOGI

Z

zaibatsu

Literally "financial clique(s)," *zaibatsu* refers to the business groups that dominated the Japanese economy throughout much of the prewar and wartime period. These are typically divided into two categories: the four groups centered around the well-established names of Mitsui, Mitsubishi, Sumitomo, and Yasuda (Fuji), which were widely diversified across finance, industry, and commerce; and a larger number of emerging groups (*shinko*, or new, *zaibatsu*) with substantial economic power in a more limited range of industries. Postwar economic reforms initiated by the Occupation forced out the families that had dominated many of the groups, as well as their top management, but the 1950s saw the reconstitution of the *zaibatsu* as *keiretsu* groupings based around the same nucleus of prewar companies.

The *zaibatsu* is an organizational form of considerable substantive and theoretical significance. Japan's private sector development in key industries like banking, international trade, and new technologies was dominated by *zaibatsu* firms from the late 1800s until Japan's defeat in the Second World War. Even today, *zaibatsu* descendents are disproportionately represented among Japan's financial, trading, and high-tech companies. Moreover, in their early years, the *zaibatsu* were leaders in introducing new management and organization systems into the Japanese economy, including the employment guarantees that later became institutionalized as "**lifetime employment**."

Earlier postwar research (Hadley 1970; Caves and Uekusa 1976) emphasized the economic power of the *zaibatsu* and their central role in executing the industrial plans of Japan's wartime government. But the continued growth in Japan's economy after the war, with the reconstituted *zaibatsu* clearly playing a major role, has led in the past two decades to alternative, efficiency-oriented, explanations. Reinforcing this search for affirmative explanations is evidence that family-based industrial networks have also been central in other fast-growing economies (such as Korea and Taiwan). It has become increasingly clear that business groups are not simply vestigial "**cartels**" of a pre-anti-trust world, but a fundamental feature of many developing economies.

The emergence of *zaibatsu* in Japan is the product of several factors. One of these is the strong role played by the state in early modern Japan. Modern industries like the railroads were owned and managed by the government during the early years of Meiji. Even when these industries were later sold off to private investors, it was to entrepreneurs that maintained close relationships to government and who continued to benefit from government largesse. Political connections were scarce, and those who had them stood to benefit across a range of industries. Meiji entrepreneurs like Yataro **Iwasaki**, founder of Mitsubishi, cultivated close ties to the finance minister, which resulted in direct and indirect subsidies from the government for his shipping line to help beat foreign competition. He then used these ties to expand into warehousing and insurance. Similarly, Eiichi **Shibusawa** (the founder of present-day **Toshiba**) used his political acquaintances to start many other companies, including those in the banking, paper, textile, and brewing industries.

Another consideration was simultaneous developments in the Japanese financial system. Unlike the USA and UK, where independent stock markets developed early as an important source of external capital, corporate financing in Japan came primarily through private, non-market mechanisms – wealthy entrepreneurs, *zaibatsu* families, and commercial banks. Japan's banking system developed rapidly in the 1870s and 1880s, and prior to most other Western industries in Japan. Several decades later, banks with close ties to merchant houses and industrial clients were well positioned to take advantage of a wave of banking consolidation forced by financial crises, creating the concentrated financial centers that continue today. Reinforcing these ties were lax securities regulation and opaque accounting systems that made Japanese securities markets, until the postwar period, the locus of unsavory speculation rather than serious investment.

The primary explanation for *zaibatsu* development, however, must be traced back to the organizational requirements of Japan's catch-up economy, and especially the way in which the *zaibatsu* managed the competing tensions it was facing in a world of rapid industrial change: the need for strategic centralization, on the one hand, and the need for operational decentralization, on the other. Forces pushing toward strategic centralization were reflected in attempts by Japanese groups to reallocate resources among enterprises based on some notion of collective interest. Catch-up required investments in technical, managerial, and organizational learning, as well as institution building along a chain of relations extending from research and development through prototyping to final production and sales. Various stages along the chain were often underdeveloped: key upstream materials or component supplies might be lacking; potential downstream customers had to be convinced to commit to new products of uncertain value and longevity; and basic know-how concerning how to link the various stages was scarce. Making this even more challenging, all of the pieces in the chain had to be accomplished simultaneously and rapidly to compete successfully with Western competitors.

Firms that developed internal capabilities at critical stages in the development of a technology were able to reduce entrepreneurial risks, providing important advantages to large, well-organized producers. It was the leading *zaibatsu* that had the financial wherewithal, the political connections, and the overseas contacts to promote development of Japan's frontier industries: buying foreign technology and product licenses, funding learning missions to and from Japan, investing in supply and distribution infrastructure, and investing in plant and equipment. Three institutions were vital in this: the group bank helped to raise capital that was used in expansion projects; the group trading firm provided international and overseas intelligence and resource support; and the head office coordinated overall resource allocation through a small team of decision makers.

This is not a complete explanation, however, since hierarchical organizations have their own limitations. They may lack internal capital, technical, or managerial resources necessary to control all of the stages along the production process. Worse, they are frequently poorly adapted to handling the process of industrial change itself. Head office employees often had little experience in the technical and market requirements of emerging industries, and were often more adept at managing financial and strategic affairs (monitoring subsidiary accounts, cultivating political relationships, etc.) than they were at handling local operations.

Therefore, while the centralized *zaibatsu* head office managed overall strategic decisions over resource allocation, it often allowed considerable autonomy to managers at the level of the enterprise or line of business over just how those resources would be allocated, especially during Japan's rapid diversification in the 1920s and 1930s. These forces toward operational decentralization were reflected in the process of spinning off new enterprises organizationally segregated from the head office. Where there was rapid expansion into promising new technologies or markets, group executives found, this relative autonomy promoted a more entrepreneurial attitude in its local managers and also provided an independent focus for strategic partnerships.

By segregating activities, the head office was able to accomplish two important objectives. First, it provided greater autonomy for localized decisions and incentives to operate and created a more entrepreneurial environment in the satellite operation. Rather than applying the standardized rules and procedures of the central organization, spin-off companies were granted a higher degree of autonomy to develop new and locally appropriate procedures to follow and were provided strong managerial incentives toward venture growth. A degree of control was no doubt given up by the head office, but the underlying logic was that the agency costs produced by a weakened administrative control structure are oftentimes less important than the organizational flexibility and entrepreneurial initiative that results.

A second major advantage of *zaibatsu*-based growth was its usefulness in building of relations outside of the group. By segregating operations, the *zaibatsu* were able to create a coherent organizational focus for localized strategic alliances with other companies. The partner firm's investments, personnel, and other resource contributions could be directed toward a limited set of activities. This had the advantages of concentrating the partner's efforts while at the same time protecting the core firm from undue external influence by the partner over its own operations. In addition, the resulting operation was freer than the core firm to pursue new markets and customers (especially those involving firms that might, due to strategic conflicts, be reluctant to deal directly with the parent firm).

These dual pressures – one toward integration and the other toward disintegration – operated throughout the prewar period as centripetal and centrifugal forces continually defining and redefining organizational boundaries as groups and their member firms evolve over time. Given the special needs of Japan's enterprises, and the resource limits they faced, it made sense to leverage what resources were available across as broad a set of business opportunities as possible. At the same time, Japanese leaders found it useful to have a stable "core" of enterprise groups that could be counted on to have both the broad capabilities necessary to make complex expansion projects work and to be reliable and trustworthy in carrying them out.

The basic *zaibatsu* model provided a significant legacy on which Japan's postwar economy would build. Important transformations in Japan's corporate systems during the wartime period had already shifted the emphasis away from the traditional capitalist notion of enterprise – as an instrument of profit for shareholder owners – to one in which the company's managers and workers became the dominant stakeholder. Much of what we now think of as central features of the Japanese economy took root then, as the planners in Japan's wartime machine found that stabilizing industrial relations and internalizing capital markets made it easier to control strategic enterprises than was the case under a more market-like system.

This evolution continued after the war, as tense labor–management relations gave way to accommodation based around the idea of long-term employment guarantees, internal promotion, and company-based unions. The **internal labor markets** that developed in large enterprises required careful management of the "core" workforce, leading to heavy reliance on external subcontractors to handle fluctuations in production output. It also required cultivation of stable shareholders willing to overlook short-term performance problems in favor of long-term business growth. While occupation reforms introduced the "rationalization" of some of these financial and corporate governance relations, they did not eliminate the densely connected, inter-company hierarchy that had developed during the war. Indeed, despite the fact that the occupation set out to eliminate the *zaibatsu* from the Japanese economy, economic reforms initiated by the occupation actually helped to institutionalize a tighter, better organized, more *zaibatsu*-like network architecture throughout Japan's business system. Corporate financial policies across Japanese industry saw an increase in bank financing and a continued decline of dividend payouts as companies reinvested profits into plant expansions and new businesses. And a new generation of professional managers took over Japan's largest companies, with managerial pay becoming less and less tied to company performance, while labor markets became increasingly internalized, as they had already become in *zaibatsu* enterprises.

Interestingly, after largely disappearing from the Japanese lexicon, the *zaibatsu* terminology has reappeared in recent years. One reason for this is the revision of the **Commercial Code** in 1997 which lifted the ban on holding companies that had been originally imposed to dissolve the *zaibatsu*. While the primary intentions of the reform were to facilitate the closing or selling of failing businesses, critics pointed to the irony of returning to a prewar form of organization to restructure Japanese industry. Some also worried that lifting the ban would revive conditions that had led to the economic concentration and military expansion of the 1930s.

This terminology has also re-appeared in the context of Japan's emerging information industries. Masayoshi Son, founder of Softbank, is among those who now refer to his emerging empire as a "*zaibatsu*" to tap into historical connections to Japan's earlier era of entrepreneurial capitalism. The key feature of this model is that Softbank seeks to gain implicit control in ventures by taking minority stakes in ventures and then building in synergies through a web of cross-investments in sales and technology, much as the *zaibatsu* did before the war.

Further reading

Caves, R. and Uekusa, M. (1976) *Industrial Organization in Japan*, Washington, DC: The Brookings Institution.

Gerlach, M.L. (1992) *Alliance Capitalism: The Social Organization of Japanese Business*, Berkeley, CA: University of California Press.

Gordon, A. (1985) *The Evolution of Labor Relations in Japan: Heavy Industry, 1853–1955*, Cambridge, MA: Council on East Asian Studies, Harvard University.

Hadley, E. (1970) *Antitrust in Japan*, Princeton, NJ: Princeton University Press.

MICHAEL GERLACH

Index

5S campaign **153–4**, 164
7–11 Japan **399–400**
   7dream.com 317
   distribution system 118
   e-commerce 126
   Ito-Yokado **206**
   konbini 268, 269
7dream.com 317

Abegglen, J.C. **1**
accounting **2–4**
acquisition of technology 152–3
administrative guidance (*gyosei shido*) **4–6**, 40
advertising **6–7**
   creative houses **94–6**
   Dentsu **108**
   motorcycle industry 322
   see also marketing
Africa **224–5**
after-sales pricing (*ato-gime*) **7–9**, 368
aging
   domestic markets 131
   lifetime employment 282
agricultural cooperatives **9–10**
   Central Union of **65–6**
agricultural policy **10–12**
aid, foreign **154–5**
air pollution 142–3
airline industry **12–15**
   see also individual airlines
Ajinomoto **15–16**
Akihabara **16–17**
All Nippon Airways (ANA) 12–14
alliances
   airline industry 13–14
   strategic 421–2, 446–7
   technology acquisition 153

allowances **17–20**
amakudari (descent from heaven) **20–3**
   bid-rigging (*dango*) 104
   Ministry of Construction 305
   Ministry of Finance 308
America *see* United States of America
American occupation **23–6**
   Anti-monopoly Law 63
   dissolution of *toseikai* 173
   Dodge, J.M. **119**
   enterprise unions 141
   post-Second World War recovery 363–5
amino acids 15–16
ANA *see* All Nippon Airways
ancestor worship 183–4
ancestry, *burakumin* 56
antei kabanushi (stable shareholders) 400
Anti-monopoly law
   cross-shareholdings 98
   Fair Trade Commission **150–1**
anti-trust measures
   Depressed Industries Law (1978) 113
   post-Second World War recovery 364
Apple Computers 421
appraisal systems **26–9**
appreciating yen (AY) (high yen) **29–31**
Arabian Oil **31**
aristocracy 472–3
Asahi Bank 70
ASEAN countries 128
Asia
   economic crisis **127–8**
   wartime legacy 473
assembly plants 423–4
assets 2, 3, 52
Association of Corporate Executives **211**
ato-gime see after-sales pricing

auction houses (primary wholesalers) 67–8, **459–61**
audits 4, 73
Australia **225–7**
  just-in-time 226
  kaizen 226
  Mitsui 226
  quality control 226
  Toyota 225
Automobile Manufacturers Association (JAMA) **212–14**
automotive industry **32–5**, 212–14
  Canadian investments 227
  Honda Motor **179–80**
  New United Motor Manufacturing Incorporated **330–1**
  Nissan **337**
  Toyota **449–53**
  United States of America 245–6
autonomous control (*jishu kanri*) 426
AY *see* appreciating yen

bad debt **36–7**, 46
bakufu (tent governments) 437, 438
balance sheets 4
balanced budget principle 307
Bank of Japan (BOJ) **37–9**
  bubble economy 52
  creation 43
  role in banking crises 42
  window guidance (*madoguchi shido*) **286–7**
Bank of Tokyo **39**
banking
  bad debt **36–7**
  corporate finance **89–91**
  corporate governance 92–3
  crises **41–3**
  cross-shareholdings 99–100
  industry **43–6**
  main bank system **288–91**
  Nomura Securities **337–9**
  Norin Chukin Bank **339–40**
  postal savings **366–8**
  regulation 53
  scandals 103
  tan system 302
  window guidance (*madoguchi shido*) **286–7**
Banking Act of 1982 **39–41**
bankruptcies **46–9**

banto **49–50**
barriers to trade **453–6**
Basic Law of Food, Agriculture and Rural Areas 11–12
behavior, *giri* **169–71**
benefits *see* non-salary compensation
bento 268
bid-rigging (*dango*) **103–5**
Big Bang reforms 279
Big Four Pollution Suits 57–8
board of directors (*torishimariyakukai*) **443–6**
BOJ *see* Bank of Japan
bonds
  corporate finance 89, 90
  government 61
  Nomura Securities **337–9**
books, history of imports 146
booms, economic 177, 208–9
bottom-up decision making **50–1**
  nihonteki keiei 333
  organizational learning 346
box lunches *see bento*
brand stores 117
Britain *see* United Kingdom
brokerages, Tsukiji market 460
bubble economy 44, **51–4**
  Asian economic crisis 127
  capital markets 61–2
  corporate finance 91
  corporate governance 93
  cross-shareholdings 99
  Heisei boom **177**
  United States of America 246
Buddhism **54–5**, 183–4
budget, national 307
building *see* construction industry
burakumin **55–7**
bureaucracy
  amakudari **20–3**
  shingikai 403
bushi (warriors) 392
business ethics **57–9**
business negotiation, *naniwa bushi* **325**
buyers as stakeholders 93
buying and selling 75

calculators 138
Canada
  automotive industry investment 227

business **227–8**
  Honda 228
  Toyota 228
Canon **60–1**
capital
  liberalization 310
  Toyota 255
capital markets **61–2**, 157
capitalism
  dual structure theory 122–3
  Japanese version 53, 131–2
  Shibusawa, E. **401–3**
career paths of salarymen 390–1
"carrot and stick" enforcement 5–6
cars *see* automotive industry
cartels **62–5**
  after-sales pricing (*ato-gime*) 8
  automotive industry 34
  Fair Trade Commission 151
  see also dango
castes 392, 436, 472–3
category killer retailers 116, 118–19
celebrities in advertising 7
cell phones *see* mobile phones
Central Union of Agricultural Cooperatives
  (*Zenchu*) **65–6**
central wholesale markets **66–9**
centralization, strategic 480
certification, ISO 9000 204–5
chain stores
  Daiei **101–2**
  discounters **115–16**
  Nakauchi, Isao 324
Chamber of Commerce **215**
chemical industry
  Ajinomoto 15–16
  competition 75–6
  Marubeni 293
children **133–6**
China
  Buddhist influence 54
  business **229**
  relations 473
  Toyota 229
  see also Asia; Southeast Asia
Chubu region 199
Chugen **69–70**
citizenship, corporate 59
city banks 44–5, **70–2**

civil code, contracts 88
civil engineering *see* construction industry
civil servants **20–3**, 304–5
climate 168
cliques *see habatsu*
cohort recruitment 398
Cold War 154, 364–5
Cole, R. **72–3**
collective bargaining 141
Commercial Code **73–4**
  accounting 2, 3–4
  corporate governance 92
  daihyoken 102
common cause variation 107
communication, negotiations **326–9**
companies, foreign **155–8**
compensation (remuneration)
  allowances and non-salary benefits **17–20**
  human relations management 181–2
compensation (restitution) 57–8
competition **74–7**
  after-sales pricing (*ato-gime*) 7–8
  Akihabara electronic products 16
  appraisal systems 28
  deregulation **113–15**
  Fair Trade Commission **150–1**
  financial market liberalization 276–7
  foreign companies in Japan 156–7
  impact on lifetime employment 282–3
  motorcycle industry 321–2
  pharmaceuticals industry 361–2
  technology domain selection 152
  see also excessive competition
computer industry **77–80**, **325–6**
concrete ceilings, women in corporate environment
  476
conflict resolution, negotiations 326–7
consolidated financial statements 4
construction industry **80–3**
Construction, Ministry of **303–6**
consumer credit 393–4
consumer movement **83–6**
consumption tax **86–7**
contract employees **87–8**
contracts **88–9**
control associations (*toseikai*) 173, 199
control methods 259
convenience stores (*konbini*) **268–70**, **399–400**
convoy system 42, 47, 72, 276, 287, 307–8

cooperatives
 agricultural **9–10**
 research **382–3**
 Very Large-Scale Integrated Circuit Research **469–70**
copyright 356–7
Corporate Executives Association **211**
corporate finance **89–91**
corporate governance **92–4**
 bank-centered system 53
 main bank system **288–91**
 takeovers 431–2
Corporate Income Tax Law 2
corporate warriors (salarymen) **390–1**
corporations, business ethics 57–9
Council for Science and Technology (CST) 395
creative houses **94–6**
credit activities, agricultural cooperatives 9–10
Crew Resource Management (CRM) 14–15
crime 414
crises
 Asian economic **127–8**
 banking **41–3**, 44
CRM *see* Crew Resource Management
cross-shareholdings **96–100**
 corporate finance 91
 mochiai **318–19**
CST *see* Council for Science and Technology
culture, group 7
currency, appreciating yen **29–31**
customers, one-to-one marketing **343–4**

DAC *see* Development Assistance Committee
Daiei **101–2**, 115
daihyoken **102**
Daiichi Kangyo Bank (DKB) **102–3**
daimyo 437, 438
Daiwa Bank 70
dango **103–5**
DBJ *see* Development Bank of Japan
death from overwork (*karoshi*) 391
debt
 bad **36–7**
 bankruptcies **46–9**
 corporate finance 89–90
 equity ratios **105–6**
decentralization 480
decision making
 bottom-up **50–1**, 333

human relations management 181
 influence of W.E.Deming 106–7
 nemawashi **329–30**
 ringi seido **388–9**
decline, industrial 110
deference 397
deliberation councils (*shingikai*) **403–4**
Deming Prize 204–5
Deming, W.E. **106–8**
democratization 24–5
demographics
 economic growth 130–1
 foreign workers 158–9
Dentsu **108**
department stores **109–10**
 Ito-Yokado 399
 Mitsukoshi **317–18**
 retail industry 385–7
depressed industries **110–13**
deregulation **113–15**
 agriculture 11
 airline industry 12–13, 15
 Asian economic crisis 127
 banking 42
 consumer movement 84
 financial markets 277–8
 industrial policy 197
 Japanese economy 52–3
 see also regulation
descent from heaven *see amakudari*
designs, patent system 358
developing countries 456
development
 overseas **354–5**
 product **370–2**
Development Assistance Committee (DAC) 154
Development Bank of Japan (DBJ) 216
developmentalism 132
differentials 18
dioxin pollution 144, 145
directors (*daihyoken*) **102**
directors (*torishimariyaku*) **443–6**
discounters **115–16**
discrimination 56, 407
disputes 326–7
distribution **116–19**
 automotive industry 33–4
 foodstuffs 66–9
 konbini 269

Tsukiji market **459–61**
division system, Matsushita Electric 297
DKB *see* Daiichi Kangyo Bank
Dodge, J.M. **119**
Dokoh, T. **119–20**
dollar shock (Nixon) **120–1**
domains, technology 152
Domei 412
domestic market 129
Dore, R. **121**
double-loop learning 345–6
downsizing, white-collar workers **474**
Draft Law on Temporary Measures for Promotion
    of Specified Manufacturing Industries 310–11
dual structure economy 47, **122–3**, 432
Dutch Learning 146, 161
duty, *giri* **169–71**

e-commerce **124–7**
Earth Summit 1992 408
earthquakes 169
ecological issues *see* environmental and ecological
    issues
economic growth 51, 74–5, **128–31**, 187–8
Economic Organizations, Federation **217–18**
economic reforms 363–5
economics
    growth 51, 74–5, **128–31**, 187–8
    ideology **131–2**
    scale 129–30
Edo culture 438–9
    see also Tokugawa period
education **133–6**
    American occupation reforms 26
    overseas **350–1**
    women 475–6
EEOL *see* Equal Employment Opportunity Law
efficiency
    industrial movement **188–90**
    multinational enterprises 251–2
    production 462–3
    total productive maintenance 447–9
Electric Town *see* Akihabara
electrical products 16–17
electronic games 335–6
electronics industry **136–9**
    Matsushita Electric Industrial Corporation
    294–5
    Sharp **401**

Sony **415–16**
    Toshiba 446–7
    United States of America 246
elementary schools 134
employees
    contract **87–8**
    corporate governance 93
    nihonteki keiei 332–4
    office ladies (OL) **341–2**
    outplacement **347–8**
    see also employment; industrial relations;
    labor force
Employers' Associations Federation **218–21**
employment
    airline industry 13
    Asian economic crisis 127–8
    dual structure theory 122–3
    enterprise unions **139–42**
    foreign workers **158–60**
    general trading companies 166
    internal labor markets **202–4**
    labor movement history **177–9**
    lifetime 280–3, 332
    Ministry of Labor **312–15**
    permanent employees **359**
    white-collar workers **474**
    women **341–2**, **474–7**
    see also employees; industrial relations; labor
    force; unemployment
engineers: Ono, T. **344**
enterprise groups 191–3
enterprise unions **139–42**
entrepreneurs 479–80
environmental and ecological issues **142–5**
    ISO 14000 205
    Ministry of International Trade and Industry
    311
Equal Employment Opportunity Law (EEOL) 476
equity financing, corporate finance 90–1
espionage 59, 167
ethics **57–9**, **169–71**
examinations 134–5
excessive competition (*kato kyoso*)
    concept 76
    industrial decline 111
    motorcycle industry 322
exchange of knowledge, *shukko* **404–6**
exchange rates
    appreciating yen **29–31**

dollar (Nixon) shock **120–1**
experience curves, motorcycle industry 321–2
experimental design 431
Export-Import Bank of Japan **148–9**
exports
    technology 147–8
    see also imports

failed banking institutions 41–2
Fair Trade Commission (FTC) **150–1**
family allowance 18–19
family separation (*tanshin funin*) 391
farmers 9–10, 26
FDI *see* foreign direct investment
Federation of Economic Organizations **217–18**
Federation of Employers' Associations **218–21**
feedback, appraisal systems 27, 29
fiefdoms 392
film, photographic 160
FILP *see* Fiscal Investment and Loan Program
finance
    companies 393–4
    corporate **89–91**
    market liberalization **276–80**
    tan system 302
    see also banking
Finance, Ministry of **306–9**
financial cliques (*zaibatsu*) **479–82**
financial *keiretsu* 190–1, 318
financial reporting 3–4
financial services
    Nomura Securities **337–9**
    Norin Chukin Bank **339–40**
    postal savings **366–8**
firm strategies for technology **151–3**
Fiscal Investment and Loan Program (FILP) 307,
    366–8
floating exchange rate system, appreciating yen 30
food
    Ajinomoto 15–16
    consumer movement 83, 85
    self-sufficiency 11, 12
    wholesale markets **66–9**
foreign aid **154–5**
foreign companies in Japan **155–8**, 361
foreign direct investment (FDI) 248, 351–3
    American **463–5**
    appreciating yen 30
foreign relations, Meiji restoration 300–1

foreign trade, banking 45
foreign workers **158–60**
    Germany 231
    Nikkei jin **335**
    research and development 354–5
franchises
    7–11 Japan **399–400**
    automotive industry 33–4
FTC *see* Fair Trade Commission
Fuji Photo Film **160**
Fukuzawa, Y. **160–1**

gaku-batsu (university cliques) 176, 266
games, Nintendo **335–6**
GATT *see* General Agreement on Tariffs and Trade
genba-shugi (shop-floor approach) **162–5**
genchika see localization
General Agreement on Tariffs and Trade (GATT)
    454, 455
General Council of Trade Union (Sohyo) **411–13**
General Motors (GM) **330–1**
general trading companies (*sogo shosha*) **165–8**
    Australia 226
    ITOCHU **206–7**
    Mitsubishi **316–17**
    Mitsui **317**
genkyoku (original bureaus) 309
geography **168–9**
Germany
    business **229–32**
    foreign employees 231
    history 229–30
    labor laws 230–1
    middle managers 231
gifts 69–70, 88
giri **169–71**, 184
global management 250
globalization
    Sony **415–16**
    strategic partnering 421
GM *see* General Motors
goal setting 151–2
goso sendan/goso sendan hoshiki see convoy system
governance, corporate **92–4**
government
    bubble-related changes 53
    see also civil servants; individual Ministries;
    Liberal Democratic Party
group culture

advertising 7
  habatsu **175–6**
  ie **183–6**
group orientated capitalism 402
growth, economic 51, 74–5, **128–31**
guilds (*za*) **171–4**
gundan (army units) 433
gyokai (trade associations) 460
gyosei shido see administrative guidance

habatsu **175–6**, 266
Hatoyama, I. 273
Hayakawa, T. **176–7**
health care 10
Heisei boom **177**
high yen *see* appreciating yen
higher education 135
hirashain see permanent employees
Hitachi 238
Hokkaido Takushoku Bank 71, 72
holidays 19–20
Honda **179–80**
  Canada 228
  Italy 233
  motorcycle industry **320–3**
Honda, S. **180–1**
Hosonomics 127
household units, *ie* **183–6**
housewives 475
housing 19, 82–3
human relations management **181–2**
human resource adjustments **347–8**

i-mode (Internet) 125
IBJ *see* Industrial Bank of Japan
IBM 77, 79
  antitrust investigations 409
  software cloning 408
  strategic partnering 421
ideology
  anti-war 472
  economic **131–2**
  middle-class housewife 475
ie **183–6**
Ikeda, H. **186**, 187, 274
ILMs *see* internal labor markets
image, advertising 6
immigration 159
imports

technology 145–7
  see also exports
Inamori, K. **186**
Income Doubling Plan **187–8**, 274, 395
indirect taxation **86–7**
Industrial Bank of Japan (IBJ) 45
industrial efficiency movement (*nouritsu undou*)
  188–90, **462–3**
industrial groups *see keiretsu*
industrial policy 254
  administrative guidance 5–6
  cartels **62–5**
industrial relations **139–42**, **177–9**, 220, 240
Industrial Standards **247–8**
industrialization
  economic ideology 132
  environmental and ecological issues **142–5**
industries, depressed **110–12**
industry
  airline **12–15**
  associations **199–202**, 247
  automotive **32–5**, 449–53
  banking **43–6**
  chemical 15–16, 293
  computer **77–80**
  construction **80–3**
  dual structure theory **122–3**
  electronics **136–9**, 294–5, 401, 415–16, 446–7
  finance 302, 393–4
    see also banking
  food 15–16
  manufacturing 351–4, 423
  Meiji restoration 300
  motorcycle **320–3**
  petrochemical 75–6
  pharmaceutical 15–16, **360–2**
  policy **193–7**
  primary regions **197–9**
  research and development 396
  retail 16–17, **385–8**, 427–8, **441–3**
  scale economics 129–30
  seafood 459–61
  small and medium-sized enterprises **406–7**
  software **408–11**
  steel 64–5
  subcontracting 422–5
  telecommunications **433–6**
  textile 457
  transport 478

venture capital **466–9**
inflation 365
information exchange 327–8
information gathering
  bottom-up decision making 50
  general trading companies (*sogo shosha*) 167–8
information sharing 469
information technology **124–7**
inheritance customs 184
initial public offering (IPO) 467–8
innovation 153, 296–7
intangible assets 2
intellectual property 58–9, 361
intermediate wholesalers (*nakaoroshi gyosha*) 460
internal labor markets (ILMs) **202–4**
internal supply chains (*kigyouai sapurai chien*) 430
International Organization for Standardization
  (ISO) **204–5**
international trade
  barriers **453–6**
  negotiations **456–9**
International Trade and Industry, Ministry of
  309–12
internationalization 399
Internet
  e-commerce **124–7**
  NEC **325–6**
  slow uptake 435–6
inventories 2, 259
  see also kanban
investment
  accounting 2–3
  American **463–5**
  appreciating yen 31
  Canadian automotive industry 227
  economic growth 129–30
  patterns **248–50**
  shareholder weakness **400–1**
  United Kingdom 243–4
  venture capital industry **466–9**
  World War II 248–9
IPO *see* initial public offering
ippanshoku (general clerical track) 476
Iran 242–3
iron triangle 440
Ishikawa, K. **204**
ISO *see* International Organization for Standardization
Italy

business **232–4**
  Honda 233
  Japan External Trade Organization 232
  Sony 233
Ito, D. 122
Ito-Yokado **206**, 399
ITOCHU **206–7**
Iwasaki, Y. **207–8**
Iwato boom 177
Izanagi boom 177, **208–9**

JAFCO *see* Japan Associated Finance Company
JAL *see* Japan Airlines
JAMA *see* Japan Automobile Manufacturers
  Association
Japan Air System (JAS) 12–14
Japan Airlines (JAL) 12–14, **210–11**
Japan Associated Finance Company (JAFCO)
  466–7
Japan Automobile Manufacturers Association
  (JAMA) **212–14**
Japan Bank for International Cooperation (JBIC)
  149
Japan Chamber of Commerce (JCCI) **215**
Japan Development Bank (JDB) **215–17**
Japan Electronic Computer Company (JECC)
  77–8
Japan External Trade Organization (JETRO) 157,
  217, 232
  Saudi Arabia 242
  United Kingdom 243
  United States of America 245
Japan Fair Trade Commission (JFTC) 63–5
Japan, Inc. **221–2**
Japan Productivity Center for Socio-Economic
  Development (JPC-SED) **223**
Japan Socialist Party (JSP) 411–12
Japan Software Company 409
Japan Standards Association (JSA) 416–17
Japanese Confederation of Labour (Domei) 412
Japanese Industrial Standards (JIS) **247–8**, 416–18,
  455
Japanese management system, *banto* 49–50
Japanese-style management *see nihonteki keiei*
Japanese Trade Union Confederation *see* Rengo
Japanization, British industry 244
JAS *see* Japan Air System
JBIC *see* Japan Bank for International Cooperation
JDB *see* Japan Development Bank

JECC *see* Japan Electronic Computer Company
JETRO *see* Japan External Trade Organization
JFTC *see* Japan Fair Trade Commission
jidoka (self-regulation) 451
jigyosha dantai see trade associations
Jiminto *see* Liberal Democratic Party
JIS *see* Japanese Industrial Standards
jishu kanri (autonomous control) 426
JIT *see* just-in-time approach
Jiyu Minshu To *see* Liberal Democratic Party
Johnson, C. 132, **254**
joint stock corporation (kabushiki kaisha) **255–6**, 263
joint ventures **256–7**
    Latin America 237
    Taiwan 234
    Toyota 256
    United States of America 246
JSA *see* Japan Standards Association
JSP *see* Japan Socialist Party
juku 135
Juran, J.M. **257**
just-in-time (JIT) approach **257–9**
    7–11 Japan 269
    Australia 226
    kaizen 258
    kanban 261
    multinational enterprises 251–2
    operational efficiency 251–2
    quality management 258
    Toyota production system 258
    see also supply chain management

kabushiki kaisha **255–6**, 263
kaizen **260–1**
    airline industry 14
    Australia 226
    just-in-time approach 258
    multinational enterprises 252–3
    quality management 377–8
    Southeast Asia 240
    TPS 453
kanban 258, **261**
Kanebo Company 425–6
Kansai culture **261–3**
Kansai region 198–9
kansayaku **263–4**
Kanto 262
Kao **264**

karoshi (death from overwork) **265**, 391
kato kyoso see excessive competition
Keidanren 220–1
Keio University **266**
keiretsu (industrial groups) **190–3**, 318, 427, 429
kibo kakaku (suggested retail price) 368–9
kigyouai sapurai chien (internal supply chains) 430
kinship 184, 185
Kirin Brewery **266–7**
Kishi, N. 273–4
kizuki system 14
knowledge 107
Kobe earthquake 124
Koike, K. **267**
Komiya, R. **268**
konbini **268–70**
Korea **234–7**
Korean War 365
Kyocera **270**
kyosei 60–1

Labor, Ministry of **312–15**
labor force 314
    contract employees **87–8**
    dual structure theory 122–3
    economic growth 130–1
    foreign workers **158–60**
    mobility 391
    white-collar workers **474**
    women **474–7**
    see also employees; employment; industrial relations
labor laws, Germany 230–1
labor markets
    seniority promotion 397–9
    takeovers **431–2**
labor movement **177–9**
labor negotiations 219–20
labor reforms 364
ladies, office **341**
land reform
    agricultural cooperatives 9
    agricultural policy 10–11
    American occupation 26
    post-Second World War recovery 364
Large Retail Store Law 109–10, **271–3**
Latin America **237**
laws
    accounting 2, 3–4

agriculture 9, 11–12
Banking Act of 1982 **39–41**
bankruptcy 48–9
Commercial Code **73–4**
environmental protection 142–3, **144–5**
Equal Employment Opportunity Law (1986) 476
investment 466
New Bank of Japan 38–9
retail 406
trade 395
see also individual laws
LCA *see* life-cycle assessment
LDP *see* Liberal Democratic Party
leadership 440
lean production 450–3
learning, organizational **344–7**
leaves of absence 20
see also holidays
leverage, debt/equity ratios **105–6**
Liberal Democratic Party (LDP) 218, 219, **273–6**
  leaders 273–5
  Tanaka 433
liberalization
  consumer movement 83, 84–5
  financial markets **276–80**
  trade and capital 310
life-cycle assessment (LCA) 145
lifetime employment (*shushin koyo*) 249, **280–3**
  nihonteki keiei 332
  United States 246
  white-collar workers **474**
limited liability corporations *see yugen gaisha*
loan sharks (*sarakin*) 393–4
loans
  bad debt **36–7**
  corporate finance 89
lobbying 200, 201–2
localization **283–5**
Long-Term Credit Bank of Japan (LTCB) **285**
long-term credit banks 45
LTCB *see* Long-Term Credit Bank of Japan

MacArthur, Douglas 24–5
madogiwa zoku **286**
madoguchi shido (window guidance) **286–7**
mafia (*yakuza*) 393
main bank system **288–91**
  corporate finance 89–90

cross-shareholdings 99
financial *keiretsu* 192
management
  airline industry 13–15
  appraisal systems **26–9**
  automotive industry 32
  banto 49–50
  convenience stores 399
  Deming, W.E. **106–8**
  Korea 235–6
  naniwa bushi **325**
  nihonteki keiei **332–5**
  openness 420
  quality **375–9**
  sacred treasures 397
  Southeast Asia 240–1
  supply chain **429–30**, 452–3
  Taiwan 235–6
  three pillars 332–3
  Ueno, Y. **462–3**
  women 476–7
manufacturing
  automotive industry **32–5**
  overseas production **351–4**
  subcontracting 423
market debt instruments *see* bonds
Market-Orientated Sector-Specific (MOSS) talks 458
market-oriented adjustments 111, 112
marketing **291–2**
  one-to-one **343–4**
marketing information system (MIS) 264
markets
  capital **61–2**
  central wholesale **66–9**
  domestic 129
  internal labor **202–4**
Marubeni **292–3**
maruyu **293–4**
mass media *see* media
Matsushita
  Mexico 238
  televisions 227
Matsushita Electric Industrial Corporation (MEI) **294–5**
Matsushita, K. **295–8**
media
  advertising 7
  creative houses 94–5

Dentsu 108
    Nihon Keizai Shimbun **331**
meetings, industry and trade associations 200
MEI *see* Matsushita Electric Industrial Corporation
Meiji restoration 194, **298–301**
MEMA *see* Motor and Equipment Manufacturers
    Association
merchandising strategies 428
MERCOSUR *see* Southern Common Market
mercury poisoning 57, 142
mergers 220–1
Mexico **238**
    see also Latin America
Middle East **241–3**
middle managers, Germany 231
militant nationalism 471
mimaikin (sympathy payment) 57
mimic strategies 152
Minamata pollution case 57, 142
minimum wage policy 313–14
Ministry of Agriculture, Forestry and Fisheries
    (MAFF) 67
Ministry of Construction (MOC) **303–6**
Ministry of Education (MOE) 133–4
Ministry of Finance (MOF) **306–9**
    administrative guidance 5, 6
    bad debt 37
    Bank of Japan 38–9, 43
    Banking Act of 1982 39–41
    city banks 71–2
    history 255
    mofutan **301–3**
    multinational enterprises 253
Ministry of International Trade and Industry
    (MITI) **309–12**
    cartels 63–4
    depressed industries 111–12
    industrial policy 194–5
    Japan External Trade Organization 217
    Japan, Inc. 221
    multinational enterprises 252
Ministry of Labor (MOL) 219, **312–15**
Minomura, R. **315–16**
MIS *see* marketing information system
MITI *see* Ministry of International Trade and
    Industry
Mitsubishi **316–17**
    origins 207–8
    Shoji, Australia 225, 226

    United Kingdom 244
    United States of America 246
Mitsui **317**
    Australia 226
    Bussan 226
    Minomura, R. **315–16**
    United Kingdom 244
Mitsukoshi **317–18**
Mizuho Financial Group 70
MNEs *see* multinational enterprises
mobile phones 435–6
MOC *see* Ministry of Construction
mochiai **318–19**
modernization, Income Doubling Plan 187
MOF *see* Ministry of Finance
mofutan **301–3**
MOL *see* Ministry of Labor
monetary policy
    Bank of Japan 37–8
    bubble economy 52
monopolies
    American occupation 63
    NTT 433, 434–5
    Sumimoto Corporation **426–7**
morality, *giri* **169–71**
Morita, A. **319–20**
Morita, Y. 320
MOSS *see* Market-Orientated Sector-Specific talks
motivation, Deming, W.E. 107–8
Motor and Equipment Manufacturers Association
    (MEMA) 214
motorcycle industry **320–3**
    Honda Motor **179–80**
    see also automotive industry
multinational enterprises (MNEs) **250–4**
    features 252–3
    profitability 252–3
multinationalization 283–5
mutual aid services 10
mutual (*sogo*) banks 45

Nagoya 199
nakama see trade associations
nakaoroshi gyosha (intermediate wholesalers) 460
Nakauchi, Isao **324**
naniwa bushi **325**
naniwa melodies *see naniwa bushi*
NASDAQ Japan 468

National Income Doubling Plan *see* Income Doubling Plan
National Railways **222–3**
National Research Institutes 394
National Tax Agency 394
NEC 246, **325–6**
negotiations **325**, **326–9**
nemawashi 276, **329–30**
nenko joretsu (seniority promotion) 280, 397–9
neoclassical economic growth 129, 131
New Bank of Japan Law 38–9
New United Motor Manufacturing Incorporated (NUMMI) **330–1**, 450, 453
newspapers, *Nihon Keizai Shimbun* **331**
Nihon Keizai Shimbun **331**
Nihon Rodo Kumiai Sorengokai *see* Rengo
nihonteki keiei **332–5**
Nikkei see Nihon Keizai Shimbun
Nikkei jin **335**
Nintendo **335–6**
Nippon Telegraph and Telephone (NTT) **336–7**, 433–6
Nissan 244, 246, **337**
Nixon shock *see* dollar shock
nobility 473
nokyo see agricultural cooperatives
Nomura Securities **337–9**
non-performing loans *see* bad debt
non-salary compensation **17–20**
non-tariff barriers 454–6
Nonaka, Ikujiro 339
Norin Chukin Bank **339–40**
nouritsu undou see industrial efficiency movement
NTT *see* Nippon Telegraph and Telephone
NUMMI *see* New United Motor Manufacturing Incorporated

obligation, *giri* **169–71**
Occupation of Japan *see* American occupation
ochugen (gifts) 69–70
ODA *see* official development assistance
office ladies (OL) **341–2**
official development assistance (ODA) 154–5
Ohmae, K. **342–3**
oil **31**, 196
    see also petrochemical industry
OJT *see* on-the-job-training
OL *see* office ladies
on-the-job-training (OJT) 267

one-to-one marketing **343–4**
Ono, T. 257, **344**
operating systems (OS) 408–10
operational efficiency 251–2
oral administrative guidance 5
organizations
    bottom-up decision making **50–1**
    Deming, W.E. **106–7**
    habatsu **175–6**
    hierarchical 480
    learning **344–7**
    partnership 469–70
    quality management 378–9
    ringi seido **388–9**
    seniority promotion 397–9
    Shibusawa E. **401–3**
    shukko **404–6**
    sokaiya 419–20
    suggestions **425–6**
    torishimariyakukai **443–6**
    TPM 447–9
    white-collar workers **474**
    zaibatsu **479–82**
    zaikai 402
organized crime (*yakuza*) 414
OS *see* operating systems
Osaka 198–9, 262–3
outplacement **347–8**
overseas
    development **354–5**
    education **350–1**
    motorcycle manufacturing plants 322–3
    production 249, 322–3, **351–4**
    research **354–5**
    small and medium-sized enterprises **348–50**

part-time workers 88
    see also employees
partnerships, strategic **421–2**, 453
Patent Office 394
patents **356–9**, 357–8
peer groups 27
pensions 3
performance appraisal *see* appraisal systems
peripheral employees 280, 281
permanent employees (*hirashain* or *sieshain*) **359**
    see also salarymen
petrochemical industry
    after-sales pricing (*atogime*) 8

Arabian Oil **31**
competition 75–6
pharmaceutical industry **360–2**
Ajinomoto 15–16
plans, economic 187–8
plant species, patent system 358
platform teams 450
poka-yoke (mistake-proofing) 451
policy
agricultural **10–12**
aid 155
banking 43–6
industrial 5–6, **62–5**, 130, **193–7**
minimum wage 313–14
monetary 37–8, 52
science and technology **394–7**
political governance, bubble-related changes 53
politicians, Tanaka **432–3**
politics, depressed industries 111–13
pollution
business ethics 57
environmental and ecological issues **142–5**
population 168, 169
positive listing 454
post-Second World War recovery **363–6**
postal savings 216, **366–8**
power structures 21
prefabricated housing 82–3
presidents' clubs 190–1
pressure groups **83–6**
price **368–9**
after-sales (*ato-gime*) **7–9**, 368
competition 75, 152
pharmaceuticals industry 361
retail price maintenance (*saihanbai kakaku iji koi*) 369
suggested retail (*kibo kakaku*) 368–9
price-fixing (*dango*) **103–5**
Prince Shotoku's Seventeen-Article Constitution **369–70**
privatization, NTT 433, 435
privileged elite 473
product development **370–2**
production
control methods 259
efficiency 447–9, 462
genba-shugi (shop-floor approach) **162–5**
overseas **351–4**
profitability 252–3

promissory notes **372–3**
promotion
nihonteki keiei 332–3
seniority 397–9
protectionism 77
pull system 261
purging, post-war 471–2

quality control circles (QC circles) **374–5**
quality management **375–9**
Deming, W.E. 106–7
genba-shugi 164
Industrial Standards 247
Ishikawa, K. **204**
Juran 257
just-in-time approach 258
Southeast Asia 240
see also kaizen

R & D *see* research and development
radio 136, 137
railways 16–17
ratios, debt/equity **105–6**
recessions 127–8
recruitment 181
recycling 143, 145
reforms
American occupation 25–6
Big Bang 279
economic 363–5
education 26, 133–4
labor, post-Second World War recovery 364
land 9, 10–11, 26, 364
postwar 472
tax 86
regional banks 45
regular employees *see* permanent employees
regulation
administrative guidance **4–6**
banking 42, 53, 302–3
e-commerce 125
trade associations 201
see also deregulation
regulations
accounting 2–4
environmental **144–5**
wholesale markets 67–8
relationship contracting 422
relationships **183–6**, 327

religion
　Buddhism **54–5**
　ie 183–4
　Shintoism 54–5
Rengo (Nihon Rodo Kumiai Sorengokai) 220,
　380–2
reparations, war 154
reporting, financial 3–4
research cooperatives **382–3**
research and development (R & D) 396
　computer industry 78
　construction industry 81
　overseas **354–5**
　pharmaceuticals industry 361–2
　product development processes 370–2
reserves, accounting 3
responsibility
　business ethics 57–8
　decision making 51
restructuring (*risutora*) **383–5**
retail industry **385–8**
　7–11 Japan **399–400**
　Akihabara **16–17**
　Chugen season 69
　Daiei **101–2**
　department stores **109–10**
　discounters **115–16**
　konbini **268–70**
　Large Retail Store Law 109–10, **271–3**
　Mitsukoshi **317–18**
　prices 368–9
　superstores **427–8**
　tonya **441–3**
retirement, *amakudari* **20–3**
rice 11
Rincho (Second Provincial Commission on Admin-
　istrative Reform) 114
ringi-seido (*ringi-sho*) 50, **388–9**
risk, debt/equity ratios **105–6**
risk-avoidance, appraisal systems 28
risutora see restructuring
rules *see* regulations
ruling caste 392

sacred treasures 397, **436**
saihanbai kakaku iji koi (retail price maintenance) 369
sakoku-rei 438
Sakura Bank 70
salaries *see* compensation; wages

salarymen **286**, **390–1**
samurai 390, **391–3**, 438
sankin kotai 438
Sanwa Bank 70–1
sarakin **393–4**
Sato, E. 274
Saudi Arabia
　business 242
　JETRO 242
　unemployment 242
savings
　banking industry 45–6
　maruyu **293–4**
　postal **366–8**
SBICs *see* Small Business Investment Companies
scale economics 129–30
scandals
　banking 103
　business ethics 57, 58
　dango 104
SCAP (Supreme Commander of the Allied Powers)
　24–6
　labor laws 179
　labor legislation 141
　purges 471–2
schools 134–5
science and technology policy **394–7**
scientific management 462
SCM *see* supply chain management
seafood industry **459–61**
Second Provincial Commission on Administrative
　Reform (*Rincho*) 114
secondary schools 134–5
securities
　accounting 2
　Nomura Securities **337–9**
Securities and Exchange Law 2, 3–4
securitization 40
seisaku toshika (strategic investors) 400
seishain see permanent employees
Self Defense Force 472
self-regulation 201, 451
selling *see* buying and selling
semiconductors
　computer industry 78
　electronics industry 137, 138
　patent system 358
seniority promotion (*nenko joretsu*) 280, **397–9**
serial equity 398

serinin (auctioneers) 460
service sector investment, UK 244–5
Seventeen-Article Constitution, Prince Shotoku's **369–70**
shareholder weakness **400–1**
shareholders
  governance 97
  influence 443–5
  meetings 92
  sokaiya **413–14**, 444
  stable 400
  trusteeship 443
shares
  cross-shareholdings **96–100**
  equity financing 90–1
Sharp **176–7**, **401**
Sherman Anti-trust Act 62
Shibusawa, E. **401–3**
shingikai **403–4**
Shingo, S. 259, **404**
shinjinrui 265
Shinohara, M. 122
shinpan (sales finance corporations) 393–4
Shintoism 54–5
shipping 207–8
shitauke (subcontracting system) **422–5**
shoguns, Tokugawa period **436–9**
shop-floor approach *see genba-shugi*
shopping centres 387
  see also retail industry
short-term lending institutions 44–5
Shotoku's Seventeen-Article Constitution, Prince **369–70**
shukko 384, **404–6**
shushin koyo see lifetime employment
Sigma Project 410
single-loop learning 345–6
SM *see* supermarkets
Small Business Investment Companies (SBICs) 466
small and medium-sized enterprises (SMEs) 127–8, **348–50**, **406–7**
social contributions, business ethics 59
social marketing **407–8**
social reform, Shibusawa, E. **401–3**
societal stratification 55–6
Socio-Economic Development Productivity Center **223**
software 78–9, **408–11**
sogo (mutual) banks 45

sogo shosha see general trading companies
sogoshoku (management track) 476
Sohyo **411–13**
sokaiya **413–14**, 420, 444
Sony **415–16**
  Italy 233
  Mexico 238
  origins 319–20
  United Kingdom 244
sougou suupaa 427–8
Southeast Asia
  business **238–41**
  Japanese management styles 240–1
  kaizen 240
  labor relations 240
  management styles 240–1
  quality control 240
  Toyota 240–1
  post World War II recovery 239
Southern Common Market (MERCOSUR) 237
special cause variation 107
Spring labor negotiations 219–20
stable shareholders 400
stakeholders, governance 92–3, 97
standards
  accounting 1–3
  industry associations 247
  ISO issues **204–5**
  setting **416–19**
  technical 152
  trade associations 247
statistics, unemployment **463**
steel 64–5, 147–8
stock exchanges 61
stock market 97
stockholders' general assembly 413–14, **419–20**
stocks, Nomura Securities **337–9**
stores *see* retail industry
strategic centralization 480
strategic management, airline industry 13
strategic partnering **421–2**
strategies, technology development **151–3**
stratification of society 55–6
strikes 179
subcontracting system **422–5**
sudden death syndrome *see karoshi*
suggested retail price (*kibo kakaku*) 368–9
suggestion systems **425–6**
suicide 49

Sumimoto Corporation **426–7**
Sumitomo Bank 71
supermarkets (SM)
   Daiei **101–2**
   discounters 115
   Ito-Yokado **206**
   see also kanban
superstores **427–8**
suppliers
   automotive industry 32–3
   stakeholders 93
   subcontracting 422–5
   tiered 452
supply chain management (SCM) **429–30**, 452–3
supply and demand 7–8
Supreme Commander of the Allied Powers *see*
   SCAP
surveys, Ministry of Labor 313
suupaa (superstores) **427–8**
sympathy payment *see mimaikin*

tacit knowledge 346
Taguchi, G. **431**
Taiwan
   business **234–7**
   joint ventures 234
   management features 235–6
takeovers **431–2**
tan system **301–3**
Tanaka, K. 274–5, **432–3**
tangible assets 2
tanshin funin (family separation) 391
tariffs, international trade 453–6, 457–8
tax, consumption **86–7**
tax evasion, *sarakin* 394
taxation, accounting 3
Taylorism 188–90
teams, *genba-shugi* (shop-floor approach) **162–5**
technology
   acquisition 394–7
   airline industry 14–15
   export and import **145–8**
   firm strategies **151–3**
   see also science and technology policy
telecommunications **433–6**
   deregulation 114
   e-commerce **124–7**
   electronics industry **136–9**

Nippon Telegraph and Telephone Corporation
   336–7
televisions
   electronics industry 136, 137–8
   Matsushita 227
temporary workers 88, 127, 128
   see also employees
tertiary wholesalers (*tonya*) 117–18
textile industry 457
Textile Wrangle 457
"thirty day due" payment arrangements 118
three fundamental labor laws 313
three pillars (sacred treasures) 332–3, **397–9**, **436**
   see also enterprise unions; lifetime employment;
   seniority promotion
tiered suppliers 452
Tokai Bank 71
Tokuanho see depressed industries
Tokugawa Bakufu collapse 402
Tokugawa Ieyasu 436, 438
Tokugawa period 226, 390, 391–3, **436–9**
   ending 298–9
   ie 184, 185
   Osaka 262
   policy 394
   stratification system 55–6
   trade associations (*nakama*) 171, 172–3
tokushu kabunushi 413
Tokyo 198
Tokyo, Bank of **39**
Tokyo-Mitsubishi Bank 39, 70
Tokyo Stock Exchange 61
Tokyo University **439–40**
Tokyo-Yokohama industrial region 197–8
tonya (tertiary wholesalers) 117–18, **441–3**
torishimariyakukai 263–4, 266, **443–6**
toseikai (control associations) 173
Toshiba 421, **446–7**
total productive maintenance (TPM) **447–9**
total quality management, ISO 9000 204–5
Toyota **330–1**, **449–50**
   Australia 225
   Canada 228
   capital 255
   China 229
   joint ventures 256
   just-in-time system **257–9**
   Southeast Asia 240–1
   supply chain management 429

United Kingdom 244
United States of America 246
Toyota production system (TPS) **450–3**
Toys R Us 118–19
TPM *see* total productive maintenance
TPS *see* Toyota production system
trade
    developing countries 456
    general trading companies (*sogo shosha*) **165–8**
    international 453–9
    liberalization 310
    negotiations **456–9**
    see also exports; imports
trade associations
    gyokai 460
    jigyosha dantai **199–202**
    nakama 171–3
    standards 247
trade barriers 82, 225, **453–6**
trade names 359
Trade Organizations *see* Japan External Trade
    Organization
Trade Union Confederation *see* Rengo
trade unions 26, **411–13**
    see also enterprise unions; industrial relations;
    labor movement; unions
trademarks 358–9
training 181
transfers (*shukko*) **404–6**
transistors 137
transnational standards 418–19
transport industry, Yamato **478**
transportation allowance 19
TRON project 408, 410
Tsukiji market **459–61**
Tsukuba Science City 395

Ueno, Y. **462–3**
UK *see* United Kingdom
unemployment **463**
    Ministry of Labor 314–15
    Saudi Arabia 242
    see also employment
unfair trade policies 459
unification, Rengo 380–1
unions
    enterprise **139–42**

history of labor movement **177–9**
nihonteki keiei 333
Sohyo **411–13**
United Arab Emirates 242
United Kingdom (UK)
    business **243–5**
    future 245
    geographical comparison 168–9
    investment 243–4
    Japan External Trade Organization 243
    Japanization of industry 244
    Mitsubishi 244
    Mitsui 244
    Nissan 244
    service sector investment 244–5
    Sony 244
    Toyota 244
United States of America (US)
    anti-trust legislation 62–3
    business **245–7**
    construction industry competition 82
    investment in Japan **463–5**
    Japanese automotive industry 33–5
    Japanese education reform 133
    Motor and Equipment Manufacturers
    Association 214
    Occupation of Japan **23–6**
    trade friction 305–6, 311–12
    see also American occupation
university cliques (*gaku-batsu*) 176
UNIX-based systems 408, 410
US *see* United States of America
utility models, patent system 358

vacations *see* holidays
value-added tax *see* consumption tax
VC *see* venture capital industry
VCRs *see* videocassette recorders
vendors, subcontracting 423–4
venture capital (VC) industry **466–9**
VER *see* voluntary export restraint
Very Large-Scale Integrated Circuit
    (VLSI) Research Cooperative **469–70**
video games, Nintendo **335–6**
videocassette recorders (VCRs) 297
VLSI *see* Very Large-Scale Integrated Circuit
    Research Cooperative

volcanoes 169
voluntary export restraint (VER) 34, 302

wages
  appraisal systems 27–8
  Asian economic crisis 128
  enterprise unions 140
  Ministry of Labor 313–14
  nihonteki keiei 332–3
  see also compensation (remuneration)
war crime punishments 25, 471, 472
warrior caste (*samurai*) 391–3
wartime legacy **471–4**
waste 452
Western civilization 299, 300
Western technology 145–7
white-collar workers **474**
  see also salarymen
wholesale markets **66–9**, **459–61**
wholesalers 117–18, **441–3**
window guidance (*madoguchi shido*) **286–7**
women
  employment 128, 313
  Internet usage 126
  office ladies **341–2**
  roles **474–7**
  small and medium-sized enterprises 407
workgroups 286
World War II 239, 248

see also American occupation
written administrative guidance 5

yakuza (organized crime) 393, 414
Yamaha 320, 322
Yamaichi Crisis (1964) 98
Yamato Transportation **478**
yen
  appreciating **29–31**
  dollar (Nixon) shock 120
  impact on lifetime employment 282
yobiko 135
Yokohama 198
yokowarukyoku (inter-industry bureaus) 309, 310
Yoshida, S. 273–4
yugen gaisha 263

za see guilds
zaibatsu **479–82**
  American occupation reforms 25–6
  cross-shareholdings 98
  Matsushita ruling 297
  reincarnations as financial *keiretsu* 190, 192
  Sumitomo 427
zaikai 402
Zenchu see Central Union of Agricultural
  Cooperatives
Zero Quality Control (ZQC) 404
ZQC *see* Zero Quality Control